PUBLIC PAPERS OF THE PRESIDENTS

OF THE UNITED STATES

PUBLIC PAPERS OF THE PRESIDENTS

OF THE UNITED STATES

Dwight D. Eisenhower

1953

Containing the Public Messages, Speeches, and

Statements of the President

JANUARY 20 TO DECEMBER 31, 1953

PUBLISHED BY THE
OFFICE OF THE FEDERAL REGISTER
NATIONAL ARCHIVES AND RECORDS SERVICE
GENERAL SERVICES ADMINISTRATION

U.S. GOVERNMENT PRINTING OFFICE: 1960

FOREWORD

THERE HAS BEEN a long-felt need for an orderly series of the Public Papers of the Presidents.   A reference work of this type can be most helpful to scholars and officials of government, to reporters of current affairs and the events of history.

The general availability of the official text of Presidential documents and messages will serve a broader purpose.   As part of the expression of democracy, this series can be a vital factor in the maintenance of our individual freedoms and our institutions of self-government.

I wish success to the editors of this project, and I am sure their work through the years will add strength to the ever-growing traditions of the Republic.

Dwight D. Eisenhower

v

PREFACE

IN THIS VOLUME are gathered most of the public messages and statements of the President of the United States that were released by the White House during the year 1953. A similar volume, covering the year 1957, was published early in 1958 as the first of a series. The President's foreword is reprinted from that volume.

Immediate plans for this series call for the publication of annual volumes soon after the close of each new calendar year, and at the same time undertaking the periodic compilation of volumes covering previous years. Volumes covering the years 1953 through 1959 are now available.

This series was begun in response to a recommendation of the National Historical Publications Commission (44 U.S.C. 393). The Commission's recommendation was incorporated in regulations of the Administrative Committee of the Federal Register issued under section 6 of the Federal Register Act (44 U.S.C. 306). The Committee's regulations, establishing the series, are reprinted at page 886 as "Appendix D."

The first extensive compilation of the messages and papers of the Presidents was assembled by James D. Richardson and published under Congressional authority between 1896 and 1899. It included Presidential materials from 1789 to 1897. Since then, there have been various private compilations, but no uniform, systematic publication comparable to the *Congressional Record* or the *United States Supreme Court Reports*.

Preface

For many years Presidential Proclamations have been published in the *United States Statutes at Large.* The Federal Register Act in 1935 required that Proclamations, Executive Orders, and some other official Executive documents be published in the daily *Federal Register;* but the greater part of Presidential writings and utterances still lacked an official medium for either current publication or periodic compilation. Some of them were interspersed through the issues of the *Congressional Record* while others were reported only in the press or were generally available only in mimeographed White House releases. Under these circumstances it was difficult to remember, after a lapse of time, where and in what form even a major pronouncement had been made.

CONTENT AND ARRANGEMENT

The text of this book is based on Presidential materials issued during the calendar year 1953 as White House releases and on transcripts of news conferences. Where available, original source materials have been used to protect against substantive errors in transcription. A list of the White House releases from which final selections were made is published at page 863 as "Appendix A."

The full text of the President's news conferences is here published for the first time. In 1953 direct quotation of the President's replies to queries usually was not authorized by the White House.

Proclamations, Executive Orders, and similar documents, required by law to be published in the *Federal Register* and *Code of Federal Regulations* are not repeated. Instead, they are listed by number and subject under the heading "Appendix B" at page 879.

Preface

The President is required by statute to transmit numerous reports to Congress. Those transmitted during 1953 are listed at page 885 as "Appendix C."

The items published in this volume are presented in chronological order, rather than being grouped in classes. Most needs for a classified arrangement are met by the subject index. For example, a reader interested in veto messages sent to Congress during 1953 will find them listed in the index under "veto messages."

The dates shown at the end of item headings are White House release dates. In instances where the date of the document differs from the release date that fact is shown in brackets immediately following the heading. Other editorial devices, such as text notes, footnotes, and cross references, have been held to a minimum.

Remarks or addresses were delivered in Washington, D.C., unless otherwise indicated. Similarly, statements, messages, and letters were issued from the White House in Washington unless otherwise indicated.

The planning and publication of this series is under the direction of David C. Eberhart of the Office of the Federal Register. The editor of the present volume was Warren R. Reid, assisted by Mildred B. Berry and Robert R. Bolton. Frank H. Mortimer of the Government Printing Office developed the typography and design.

WAYNE C. GROVER
Archivist of the United States

FRANKLIN FLOETE
Administrator of General Services

October 20, 1960

CONTENTS

CONTENTS

LIST OF ITEMS

List of Items

List of Items

xv

List of Items

List of Items

List of Items

List of Items

List of Items

List of Items

List of Items

List of Items

List of Items

List of Items

List of Items

List of Items

List of Items

List of Items

List of Items

XXXVI

List of Items

Dwight D. Eisenhower

1953

1 ¶ Inaugural Address. *January* 20, 1953

[Delivered in person at the Capitol]

MY FRIENDS, before I begin the expression of those thoughts that I deem appropriate to this moment, would you permit me the privilege of uttering a little private prayer of my own. And I ask that you bow your heads:

Almighty God, as we stand here at this moment my future associates in the Executive branch of Government join me in beseeching that Thou will make full and complete our dedication to the service of the people in this throng, and their fellow citizens everywhere.

Give us, we pray, the power to discern clearly right from wrong, and allow all our words and actions to be governed thereby, and by the laws of this land. Especially we pray that our concern shall be for all the people regardless of station, race or calling.

May cooperation be permitted and be the mutual aim of those who, under the concepts of our Constitution, hold to differing political faiths; so that all may work for the good of our beloved country and Thy glory. Amen.

My fellow citizens:

The world and we have passed the midway point of a century of continuing challenge. We sense with all our faculties that forces of good and evil are massed and armed and opposed as rarely before in history.

This fact defines the meaning of this day. We are summoned by this honored and historic ceremony to witness more than the act of one citizen swearing his oath of service, in the presence of God. We are called as a people to give testimony in the sight of the world to our faith that the future shall belong to the free.

Since this century's beginning, a time of tempest has seemed to come upon the continents of the earth. Masses of Asia have awakened to strike off shackles of the past. Great nations of

Europe have fought their bloodiest wars. Thrones have toppled and their vast empires have disappeared. New nations have been born.

For our own country, it has been a time of recurring trial. We have grown in power and in responsibility. We have passed through the anxieties of depression and of war to a summit unmatched in man's history. Seeking to secure peace in the world, we have had to fight through the forests of the Argonne to the shores of Iwo Jima, and to the cold mountains of Korea.

In the swift rush of great events, we find ourselves groping to know the full sense and meaning of these times in which we live. In our quest of understanding, we beseech God's guidance. We summon all our knowledge of the past and we scan all signs of the future. We bring all our wit and all our will to meet the question:

How far have we come in man's long pilgrimage from darkness toward the light? Are we nearing the light—a day of freedom and of peace for all mankind? Or are the shadows of another night closing in upon us?

Great as are the preoccupations absorbing us at home, concerned as we are with matters that deeply affect our livelihood today and our vision of the future, each of these domestic problems is dwarfed by, and often even created by, this question that involves all humankind.

This trial comes at a moment when man's power to achieve good or to inflict evil surpasses the brightest hopes and the sharpest fears of all ages. We can turn rivers in their courses, level mountains to the plains. Oceans and land and sky are avenues for our colossal commerce. Disease diminishes and life lengthens.

Yet the promise of this life is imperiled by the very genius that has made it possible. Nations amass wealth. Labor sweats to create—and turns out devices to level not only mountains but also cities. Science seems ready to confer upon us, as its final gift, the power to erase human life from this planet.

At such a time in history, we who are free must proclaim anew

2

our faith. This faith is the abiding creed of our fathers. It is our faith in the deathless dignity of man, governed by eternal moral and natural laws.

This faith defines our full view of life. It establishes, beyond debate, those gifts of the Creator that are man's inalienable rights, and that make all men equal in His sight.

In the light of this equality, we know that the virtues most cherished by free people—love of truth, pride of work, devotion to country—all are treasures equally precious in the lives of the most humble and of the most exalted. The men who mine coal and fire furnaces, and balance ledgers, and turn lathes, and pick cotton, and heal the sick and plant corn—all serve as proudly and as profitably for America as the statesmen who draft treaties and the legislators who enact laws.

This faith rules our whole way of life. It decrees that we, the people, elect leaders not to rule but to serve. It asserts that we have the right to choice of our own work and to the reward of our own toil. It inspires the initiative that makes our productivity the wonder of the world. And it warns that any man who seeks to deny equality among all his brothers betrays the spirit of the free and invites the mockery of the tyrant.

It is because we, all of us, hold to these principles that the political changes accomplished this day do not imply turbulence, upheaval or disorder. Rather this change expresses a purpose of strengthening our dedication and devotion to the precepts of our founding documents, a conscious renewal of faith in our country and in the watchfulness of a Divine Providence.

The enemies of this faith know no god but force, no devotion but its use. They tutor men in treason. They feed upon the hunger of others. Whatever defies them, they torture, especially the truth.

Here, then, is joined no argument between slightly differing philosophies. This conflict strikes directly at the faith of our fathers and the lives of our sons. No principle or treasure that we hold, from the spiritual knowledge of our free schools and churches to the creative magic of free labor and capital, nothing lies safely beyond the reach of this struggle.

Freedom is pitted against slavery; lightness against the dark.

The faith we hold belongs not to us alone but to the free of all the world. This common bond binds the grower of rice in Burma and the planter of wheat in Iowa, the shepherd in southern Italy and the mountaineer in the Andes. It confers a common dignity upon the French soldier who dies in Indo-China, the British soldier killed in Malaya, the American life given in Korea.

We know, beyond this, that we are linked to all free peoples not merely by a noble idea but by a simple need. No free people can for long cling to any privilege or enjoy any safety in economic solitude. For all our own material might, even we need markets in the world for the surpluses of our farms and our factories. Equally, we need for these same farms and factories vital materials and products of distant lands. This basic law of interdependence, so manifest in the commerce of peace, applies with thousand-fold intensity in the event of war.

So we are persuaded by necessity and by belief that the strength of all free peoples lies in unity; their danger, in discord.

To produce this unity, to meet the challenge of our time, destiny has laid upon our country the responsibility of the free world's leadership.

So it is proper that we assure our friends once again that, in the discharge of this responsibility, we Americans know and we observe the difference between world leadership and imperialism; between firmness and truculence; between a thoughtfully calculated goal and spasmodic reaction to the stimulus of emergencies.

We wish our friends the world over to know this above all: we face the threat—not with dread and confusion—but with confidence and conviction.

We feel this moral strength because we know that we are not helpless prisoners of history. We are free men. We shall remain free, never to be proven guilty of the one capital offense against freedom, a lack of stanch faith.

4

In pleading our just cause before the bar of history and in pressing our labor for world peace, we shall be guided by certain fixed principles. These principles are:

1. Abhorring war as a chosen way to balk the purposes of those who threaten us, we hold it to be the first task of statesmanship to develop the strength that will deter the forces of aggression and promote the conditions of peace. For, as it must be the supreme purpose of all free men, so it must be the dedication of their leaders, to save humanity from preying upon itself.

In the light of this principle, we stand ready to engage with any and all others in joint effort to remove the causes of mutual fear and distrust among nations, so as to make possible drastic reduction of armaments. The sole requisites for undertaking such effort are that—in their purpose—they be aimed logically and honestly toward secure peace for all; and that—in their result—they provide methods by which every participating nation will prove good faith in carrying out its pledge.

2. Realizing that common sense and common decency alike dictate the futility of appeasement, we shall never try to placate an aggressor by the false and wicked bargain of trading honor for security. Americans, indeed, all free men, remember that in the final choice a soldier's pack is not so heavy a burden as a prisoner's chains.

3. Knowing that only a United States that is strong and immensely productive can help defend freedom in our world, we view our Nation's strength and security as a trust upon which rests the hope of free men everywhere. It is the firm duty of each of our free citizens and of every free citizen everywhere to place the cause of his country before the comfort, the convenience of himself.

4. Honoring the identity and the special heritage of each nation in the world, we shall never use our strength to try to impress upon another people our own cherished political and economic institutions.

5. Assessing realistically the needs and capacities of proven

friends of freedom, we shall strive to help them to achieve their own security and well-being. Likewise, we shall count upon them to assume, within the limits of their resources, their full and just burdens in the common defense of freedom.

6. Recognizing economic health as an indispensable basis of military strength and the free world's peace, we shall strive to foster everywhere, and to practice ourselves, policies that encourage productivity and profitable trade. For the impoverishment of any single people in the world means danger to the well-being of all other peoples.

7. Appreciating that economic need, military security and political wisdom combine to suggest regional groupings of free peoples, we hope, within the framework of the United Nations, to help strengthen such special bonds the world over. The nature of these ties must vary with the different problems of different areas.

In the Western Hemisphere, we enthusiastically join with all our neighbors in the work of perfecting a community of fraternal trust and common purpose.

In Europe, we ask that enlightened and inspired leaders of the Western nations strive with renewed vigor to make the unity of their peoples a reality. Only as free Europe unitedly marshals its strength can it effectively safeguard, even with our help, its spiritual and cultural heritage.

8. Conceiving the defense of freedom, like freedom itself, to be one and indivisible, we hold all continents and peoples in equal regard and honor. We reject any insinuation that one race or another, one people or another, is in any sense inferior or expendable.

9. Respecting the United Nations as the living sign of all people's hope for peace, we shall strive to make it not merely an eloquent symbol but an effective force. And in our quest for an honorable peace, we shall neither compromise, nor tire, nor ever cease.

By these rules of conduct, we hope to be known to all peoples.

By their observance, an earth of peace may become not a vision but a fact.

This hope—this supreme aspiration—must rule the way we live.

We must be ready to dare all for our country. For history does not long entrust the care of freedom to the weak or the timid. We must acquire proficiency in defense and display stamina in purpose.

We must be willing, individually and as a Nation, to accept whatever sacrifices may be required of us. A people that values its privileges above its principles soon loses both.

These basic precepts are not lofty abstractions, far removed from matters of daily living. They are laws of spiritual strength that generate and define our material strength. Patriotism means equipped forces and a prepared citizenry. Moral stamina means more energy and more productivity, on the farm and in the factory. Love of liberty means the guarding of every resource that makes freedom possible—from the sanctity of our families and the wealth of our soil to the genius of our scientists.

And so each citizen plays an indispensable role. The productivity of our heads, our hands and our hearts is the source of all the strength we can command, for both the enrichment of our lives and the winning of the peace.

No person, no home, no community can be beyond the reach of this call. We are summoned to act in wisdom and in conscience, to work with industry, to teach with persuasion, to preach with conviction, to weigh our every deed with care and with compassion. For this truth must be clear before us: whatever America hopes to bring to pass in the world must first come to pass in the heart of America.

The peace we seek, then, is nothing less than the practice and fulfillment of our whole faith among ourselves and in our dealings with others. This signifies more than the stilling of guns, easing the sorrow of war. More than escape from death, it is a way of life. More than a haven for the weary, it is a hope for the brave.

This is the hope that beckons us onward in this century of trial.   This is the work that awaits us all, to be done with bravery, with charity, and with prayer to Almighty God.

My citizens—I thank you.

NOTE: This text follows the White House release of the address. The President spoke from a platform erected on the steps of the central east front of the Capitol. Immediately before the address the oath of office was administered by Chief Justice Fred M. Vinson.

2   ¶ Statement by the President on Establishing the President's Committee on International Information Activities.   *January* 26, 1953

IT HAS LONG BEEN my conviction that a unified and dynamic effort in this field is essential to the security of the United States and of the other peoples in the community of free nations. All executive departments and agencies of the Federal Government are authorized and directed, as a matter of common concern, to cooperate with the Committee in its work.

The establishment of this Committee and the scope of its inquiry were discussed at the Cabinet meeting last Friday morning and received full and complete support.

The Committee's final report and recommendations are to be in my hands not later than June 30.

NOTE: The White House release of which this statement was a part announced that the President had appointed the following Committee members: William H. Jackson, Chairman; Robert Cutler, Administrative Assistant to the President; C. D. Jackson, representing the Secretary of State; Sigurd Larmon, representing the Director for Mutual Security; Gordon Gray; Barklie McKee Henry; and John C. Hughes. Abbott Washburn was named Executive Secretary. On February 19, 1953, Roger M. Kyes, Deputy Secretary of Defense, was also appointed.

A summary of the Committee's final report was released by the White House on July 8, 1953. See footnote to news conference of that date, p. 472.

3 ¶ Letter to the President of the American National Red Cross Accepting the Position of Honorary Chairman. *January* 29, 1953

[Released January 29, 1953. Dated January 24, 1953]

Dear Mr. Harriman:

Thank you for your courteous note of January 9th informing me that, under the By-laws of the American Red Cross, and by tradition, the President of the United States, upon his acceptance, becomes Honorary Chairman of the organization.

In all humility and fully conscious of the great importance of the American National Red Cross in our national community, I accept this position. To the extent that my official responsibilities permit, I shall stand ready to assist you, the other officers and members of the Red Cross in carrying on the great work of this important body.

Sincerely,

DWIGHT D. EISENHOWER

Mr. E. Roland Harriman
President
The American National Red Cross
Washington 13, D.C.

4 ¶ Memorandum on the Red Cross Campaign. *January* 29, 1953

To the Heads of Executive Departments, Commissions and Agencies:

The American Red Cross is symbolic of the deep concern of our Nation for human welfare—of the fact that the American way of life places human values above materialism. Because I subscribe so thoroughly to these principles, it is most appropriate that one of my first acts in assuming the great responsibilities of this office is to set in motion machinery for the 1953 Red Cross Fund Campaign.

The work of the Red Cross is well known to all of you. But perhaps you are not aware how the Red Cross continues its vital services to the Armed Forces, veterans and their families through a world-wide network of communication and help, at military installations, with field units, at home through the local chapters and in service and veterans' hospitals. The Red Cross collects blood to meet the urgent needs of the wounded and the many military emergencies in all combat and hospital areas.

In addition, the Red Cross has been asked to enlarge its activities in the coming year in two important areas: First, to provide additional recreation facilities for our troops overseas, and, second, to expand greatly the National Blood Program to obtain plasma for making a serum to protect children against the paralyzing effects of polio. The result is an inevitable enlargement of the Red Cross budget, and higher quotas for its 1953 Fund Campaign.

The success of the Red Cross campaign in the metropolitan area of Washington depends to a great extent on the gifts of those working in the various local, Federal and International agencies. To lead the campaign as Chairman of the Government Unit, I have designated the Honorable William McChesney Martin, Jr., Chairman of the Board of Governors of the Federal Reserve System. I urge every one to pledge to Mr. Martin his unqualified assistance. Will you also kindly request your several field offices to cooperate earnestly in the fund campaign of their respective local Red Cross chapters.

DWIGHT D. EISENHOWER

5 ¶ Remarks Recorded for the American Legion "Back to God" Program. *February* 1, 1953

MY GRATEFUL THANKS go out to each of you for your prayers, because your prayers for divine guidance on my behalf are the greatest gift you could possibly bring to me.

As your prayers come from your hearts, so there comes from mine a very earnest one—that all of us by our combined dedication and devotion may merit the great blessings that The Almighty has brought to this land of ours.

We think often of these blessings in terms of material values— of broad acres, our great factories—all of those things which make a life a more convenient and finer thing in the material sense. But when we think about the matter very deeply, we know that the blessings that we are really thankful for are a different type. They are what our forefathers called our rights— our human rights—the right to worship as we please, to speak and to think, and to earn, and to save. Those are the rights that we must strive so mightily to merit.

One reason that we cherish these rights so sincerely is because they are God-given. They belong to the people who have been created in His image.

Now this means as a very special and second reason for cherishing these rights, that they belong to the lowliest amongst us as well as to the mightiest and the highest. That is the genius of our democracy. It is the very basis of the cause for which so many of our fellow citizens have died.

Today we are especially inspired in our resolution to defend those rights by the memory of the four Chaplains who met death— bravely, quietly, even tranquilly—in the sinking of the *Dorchester*. They gave their lives without complaint, so that their fellow citizens could live.

As we think of their sacrifice, and that of our heroic fellow citizens serving in Korea, we are inspired to take up our own burdens more cheerfully; we are moved to show by greater courage, by patience and mutual understanding—by better citizenship—that we are worthy members of this great American family of free, God-fearing people.

NOTE: The President's remarks were part of an American Legion television program broadcast from New York City at 1:40 p.m.

6 ¶ Annual Message to the Congress on the State of the Union. *February 2, 1953*

[Delivered in person before a joint session]

Mr. President, Mr. Speaker, Members of the Eighty-third Congress:

I welcome the honor of appearing before you to deliver my first message to the Congress.

It is manifestly the joint purpose of the congressional leadership and of this administration to justify the summons to governmental responsibility issued last November by the American people.

The grand labors of this leadership will involve:

Application of America's influence in world affairs with such fortitude and such foresight that it will deter aggression and eventually secure peace;

Establishment of a national administration of such integrity and such efficiency that its honor at home will ensure respect abroad;

Encouragement of those incentives that inspire creative initiative in our economy, so that its productivity may fortify freedom everywhere; and

Dedication to the well-being of all our citizens and to the attainment of equality of opportunity for all, so that our Nation will ever act with the strength of unity in every task to which it is called.

The purpose of this message is to suggest certain lines along which our joint efforts may immediately be directed toward realization of these four ruling purposes.

The time that this administration has been in office has been too brief to permit preparation of a detailed and comprehensive program of recommended action to cover all phases of the responsibilities that devolve upon our country's new leaders. Such a program will be filled out in the weeks ahead as, after appropriate study, I shall submit additional recommendations for your consideration. Today can provide only a sure and substantial beginning.

II.

Our country has come through a painful period of trial and disillusionment since the victory of 1945. We anticipated a world of peace and cooperation. The calculated pressures of aggressive communism have forced us, instead, to live in a world of turmoil.

From this costly experience we have learned one clear lesson. We have learned that the free world cannot indefinitely remain in a posture of paralyzed tension, leaving forever to the aggressor the choice of time and place and means to cause greatest hurt to us at least cost to himself.

This administration has, therefore, begun the definition of a new, positive foreign policy. This policy will be governed by certain fixed ideas. They are these:

(1) Our foreign policy must be clear, consistent, and confident. This means that it must be the product of genuine, continuous cooperation between the executive and the legislative branches of this Government. It must be developed and directed in the spirit of true bipartisanship.

(2) The policy we embrace must be a coherent global policy. The freedom we cherish and defend in Europe and in the Americas is no different from the freedom that is imperiled in Asia.

(3) Our policy, dedicated to making the free world secure, will envision all peaceful methods and devices—except breaking faith with our friends. We shall never acquiesce in the enslavement of any people in order to purchase fancied gain for ourselves. I

shall ask the Congress at a later date to join in an appropriate resolution making clear that this Government recognizes no kind of commitment contained in secret understandings of the past with foreign governments which permit this kind of enslavement.

(4) The policy we pursue will recognize the truth that no single country, even one so powerful as ours, can alone defend the liberty of all nations threatened by Communist aggression from without or subversion within. Mutual security means effective mutual cooperation. For the United States, this means that, as a matter of common sense and national interest, we shall give help to other nations in the measure that they strive earnestly to do their full share of the common task. No wealth of aid could compensate for poverty of spirit. The heart of every free nation must be honestly dedicated to the preserving of its own independence and security.

(5) Our policy will be designed to foster the advent of practical unity in Western Europe. The nations of that region have contributed notably to the effort of sustaining the security of the free world. From the jungles of Indochina and Malaya to the northern shores of Europe, they have vastly improved their defensive strength. Where called upon to do so, they have made costly and bitter sacrifices to hold the line of freedom.

But the problem of security demands closer cooperation among the nations of Europe than has been known to date. Only a more closely integrated economic and political system can provide the greatly increased economic strength needed to maintain both necessary military readiness and respectable living standards.

Europe's enlightened leaders have long been aware of these facts. All the devoted work that has gone into the Schuman plan, the European Army, and the Strasbourg Conference has testified to their vision and determination. These achievements are the more remarkable when we realize that each of them has marked a victory—for France and for Germany alike—over the divisions that in the past have brought such tragedy to these two great nations and to the world.

The needed unity of Western Europe manifestly cannot be manufactured from without; it can only be created from within. But it is right and necessary that we encourage Europe's leaders by informing them of the high value we place upon the earnestness of their efforts toward this goal. Real progress will be conclusive evidence to the American people that our material sacrifices in the cause of collective security are matched by essential political, economic, and military accomplishments in Western Europe.

(6) Our foreign policy will recognize the importance of profitable and equitable world trade.

A substantial beginning can and should be made by our friends themselves. Europe, for example, is now marked by checkered areas of labor surplus and labor shortage, of agricultural areas needing machines and industrial areas needing food. Here and elsewhere we can hope that our friends will take the initiative in creating broader markets and more dependable currencies, to allow greater exchange of goods and services among themselves.

Action along these lines can create an economic environment that will invite vital help from us.

This help includes:

First: Revising our customs regulations to remove procedural obstacles to profitable trade. I further recommend that the Congress take the Reciprocal Trade Agreements Act under immediate study and extend it by appropriate legislation. This objective must not ignore legitimate safeguarding of domestic industries, agriculture, and labor standards. In all executive study and recommendations on this problem labor and management and farmers alike will be earnestly consulted.

Second: Doing whatever Government properly can to encourage the flow of private American investment abroad. This involves, as a serious and explicit purpose of our foreign policy, the encouragement of a hospitable climate for such investment in foreign nations.

Third: Availing ourselves of facilities overseas for the economical production of manufactured articles which are needed for mutual defense and which are not seriously competitive with our own normal peacetime production.

Fourth: Receiving from the rest of the world, in equitable exchange for what we supply, greater amounts of important raw materials which we do not ourselves possess in adequate quantities.

III.

In this general discussion of our foreign policy, I must make special mention of the war in Korea.

This war is, for Americans, the most painful phase of Communist aggression throughout the world. It is clearly a part of the same calculated assault that the aggressor is simultaneously pressing in Indochina and in Malaya, and of the strategic situation that manifestly embraces the island of Formosa and the Chinese Nationalist forces there. The working out of any military solution to the Korean war will inevitably affect all these areas.

The administration is giving immediate increased attention to the development of additional Republic of Korea forces. The citizens of that country have proved their capacity as fighting men and their eagerness to take a greater share in the defense of their homeland. Organization, equipment, and training will allow them to do so. Increased assistance to Korea for this purpose conforms fully to our global policies.

In June 1950, following the aggressive attack on the Republic of Korea, the United States Seventh Fleet was instructed both to prevent attack upon Formosa and also to insure that Formosa should not be used as a base of operations against the Chinese Communist mainland.

This has meant, in effect, that the United States Navy was required to serve as a defensive arm of Communist China. Regardless of the situation in 1950, since the date of that order the Chinese Communists have invaded Korea to attack the United Nations forces there. They have consistently rejected the proposals of the United Nations Command for an armistice. They recently joined with Soviet Russia in rejecting the armistice proposal sponsored in the United Nations by the Government of India. This proposal had been accepted by the United States and 53 other nations.

Consequently there is no longer any logic or sense in a condition that required the United States Navy to assume defensive responsibilities on behalf of the Chinese Communists, thus permitting those Communists, with greater impunity, to kill our soldiers and those of our United Nations allies in Korea.

I am, therefore, issuing instructions that the Seventh Fleet no longer be employed to shield Communist China. This order implies no aggressive intent on our part. But we certainly have no obligation to protect a nation fighting us in Korea.

IV.

Our labor for peace in Korea and in the world imperatively demands the maintenance by the United States of a strong fighting service ready for any contingency.

Our problem is to achieve adequate military strength within the limits of endurable strain upon our economy. To amass military power without regard to our economic capacity would be to defend ourselves against one kind of disaster by inviting another.

Both military and economic objectives demand a single national military policy, proper coordination of our armed services, and effective consolidation of certain logistics activities.

We must eliminate waste and duplication of effort in the armed services.

We must realize clearly that size alone is not sufficient. The biggest force is not necessarily the best—and we want the best.

We must not let traditions or habits of the past stand in the way of developing an efficient military force. All members of our forces must be ever mindful that they serve under a single flag and for a single cause.

We must effectively integrate our armament programs and

plan them in such careful relation to our industrial facilities that we assure the best use of our manpower and our materials.

Because of the complex technical nature of our military organization and because of the security reasons involved, the Secretary of Defense must take the initiative and assume the responsibility for developing plans to give our Nation maximum safety at minimum cost. Accordingly, the new Secretary of Defense and his civilian and military associates will, in the future, recommend such changes in present laws affecting our defense activities as may be necessary to clarify responsibilities and improve the total effectiveness of our defense effort.

This effort must always conform to policies laid down in the National Security Council.

The statutory function of the National Security Council is to assist the President in the formulation and coordination of significant domestic, foreign, and military policies required for the security of the Nation. In these days of tension it is essential that this central body have the vitality to perform effectively its statutory role. I propose to see that it does so.

Careful formulation of policies must be followed by clear understanding of them by all peoples. A related need, therefore, is to make more effective all activities of the Government related to international information.

I have recently appointed a committee of representative and informed citizens to survey this subject and to make recommendations in the near future for legislative, administrative, or other action.

A unified and dynamic effort in this whole field is essential to the security of the United States and of the other peoples in the community of free nations. There is but one sure way to avoid total war—and that is to win the cold war.

While retaliatory power is one strong deterrent to a would-be aggressor, another powerful deterrent is defensive power. No enemy is likely to attempt an attack foredoomed to failure.

Because the building of a completely impenetrable defense

against attack is still not possible, total defensive strength must include civil defense preparedness.　Because we have incontrovertible evidence that Soviet Russia possesses atomic weapons, this kind of protection becomes sheer necessity.

Civil defense responsibilities primarily belong to the State and local governments—recruiting, training, and organizing volunteers to meet any emergency.　The immediate job of the Federal Government is to provide leadership, to supply technical guidance, and to continue to strengthen its civil defense stockpile of medical, engineering, and related supplies and equipment.　This work must go forward without lag.

v.

I have referred to the inescapable need for economic health and strength if we are to maintain adequate military power and exert influential leadership for peace in the world.

Our immediate task is to chart a fiscal and economic policy that can:

(1) Reduce the planned deficits and then balance the budget, which means, among other things, reducing Federal expenditures to the safe minimum;

(2) Meet the huge costs of our defense;

(3) Properly handle the burden of our inheritance of debt and obligations;

(4) Check the menace of inflation;

(5) Work toward the earliest possible reduction of the tax burden;

(6) Make constructive plans to encourage the initiative of our citizens.

It is important that all of us understand that this administration does not and cannot begin its task with a clean slate.　Much already has been written on the record, beyond our power quickly to erase or to amend.　This record includes our inherited burden of indebtedness and obligations and deficits.

The current year's budget, as you know, carries a 5.9 billion dollar deficit; and the budget, which was presented to you before this administration took office, indicates a budgetary deficit of 9.9 billion for the fiscal year ending June 30, 1954. The national debt is now more than 265 billion dollars. In addition, the accumulated obligational authority of the Federal Government for future payment totals over 80 billion dollars. Even this amount is exclusive of large contingent liabilities, so numerous and extensive as to be almost beyond description.

The bills for the payment of nearly all of the 80 billion dollars of obligations will be presented during the next 4 years. These bills, added to the current costs of government we must meet, make a formidable burden.

The present authorized Government-debt limit is 275 billion dollars. The forecast presented by the outgoing administration with the fiscal year 1954 budget indicates that—before the end of the fiscal year and at the peak of demand for payments during the year—the total Government debt may approach and even exceed that limit. Unless budgeted deficits are checked, the momentum of past programs will force an increase of the statutory debt limit.

Permit me this one understatement: to meet and to correct this situation will not be easy.

Permit me this one assurance: every department head and I are determined to do everything we can to resolve it.

The first order of business is the elimination of the annual deficit. This cannot be achieved merely by exhortation. It demands the concerted action of all those in responsible positions in the Government and the earnest cooperation of the Congress.

Already, we have begun an examination of the appropriations and expenditures of all departments in an effort to find significant items that may be decreased or canceled without damage to our essential requirements.

Getting control of the budget requires also that State and local governments and interested groups of citizens restrain themselves in their demands upon the Congress that the Federal Treasury spend more and more money for all types of projects.

A balanced budget is an essential first measure in checking further depreciation in the buying power of the dollar. This is one of the critical steps to be taken to bring an end to planned inflation. Our purpose is to manage the Government's finances so as to help and not hinder each family in balancing its own budget.

Reduction of taxes will be justified only as we show we can succeed in bringing the budget under control. As the budget is balanced and inflation checked, the tax burden that today stifles initiative can and must be eased.

Until we can determine the extent to which expenditures can be reduced, it would not be wise to reduce our revenues.

Meanwhile, the tax structure as a whole demands review. The Secretary of the Treasury is undertaking this study immediately. We must develop a system of taxation which will impose the least possible obstacle to the dynamic growth of the country. This includes particularly real opportunity for the growth of small businesses. Many readjustments in existing taxes will be necessary to serve these objectives and also to remove existing inequities. Clarification and simplification in the tax laws as well as the regulations will be undertaken.

In the entire area of fiscal policy—which must, in its various aspects, be treated in recommendations to the Congress in coming weeks—there can now be stated certain basic facts and principles.

First. It is axiomatic that our economy is a highly complex and sensitive mechanism. Hasty and ill-considered action of any kind could seriously upset the subtle equation that encompasses debts, obligations, expenditures, defense demands, deficits, taxes, and the general economic health of the Nation. Our goals can be clear, our start toward them can be immediate—but action must be gradual.

Second. It is clear that too great a part of the national debt comes due in too short a time. The Department of the Treasury will undertake at suitable times a program of extending part of the debt over longer periods and gradually placing greater amounts in the hands of longer-term investors.

Third. Past differences in policy between the Treasury and the Federal Reserve Board have helped to encourage inflation. Henceforth, I expect that their single purpose shall be to serve the whole Nation by policies designed to stabilize the economy and encourage the free play of our people's genius for individual initiative.

In encouraging this initiative, no single item in our current problems has received more thoughtful consideration by my associates, and by the many individuals called into our counsels, than the matter of price and wage control by law.

The great economic strength of our democracy has developed in an atmosphere of freedom. The character of our people resists artificial and arbitrary controls of any kind. Direct controls, except those on credit, deal not with the real causes of inflation but only with its symptoms. In times of national emergency, this kind of control has a role to play. Our whole system, however, is based upon the assumption that, normally, we should combat wide fluctuations in our price structure by relying largely on the effective use of sound fiscal and monetary policy, and upon the natural workings of economic law.

Moreover, American labor and American business can best resolve their wage problems across the bargaining table. Government should refrain from sitting in with them unless, in extreme cases, the public welfare requires protection.

We are, of course, living in an international situation that is neither an emergency demanding full mobilization, nor is it peace. No one can know how long this condition will persist. Consequently, we are forced to learn many new things as we go along—clinging to what works, discarding what does not.

In all our current discussions on these and related facts, the weight of evidence is clearly against the use of controls in their present forms. They have proved largely unsatisfactory or unworkable. They have not prevented inflation; they have not kept down the cost of living. Dissatisfaction with them is wholly justified. I am convinced that now—as well as in the long run—free and competitive prices will best serve the interests of all the people, and best meet the changing, growing needs of our economy.

Accordingly, I do not intend to ask for a renewal of the present wage and price controls on April 30, 1953, when present legislation expires. In the meantime, steps will be taken to eliminate controls in an orderly manner, and to terminate special agencies no longer needed for this purpose. It is obviously to be expected that the removal of these controls will result in individual price changes—some up, some down. But a maximum of freedom in market prices as well as in collective bargaining is characteristic of a truly free people.

I believe also that material and product controls should be ended, except with respect to defense priorities and scarce and critical items essential for our defense. I shall recommend to the Congress that legislation be enacted to continue authority for such remaining controls of this type as will be necessary after the expiration of the existing statute on June 30, 1953.

I recommend the continuance of the authority for Federal control over rents in those communities in which serious housing shortages exist. These are chiefly the so-called defense areas. In these and all areas the Federal Government should withdraw from the control of rents as soon as practicable. But before they are removed entirely, each legislature should have full opportunity to take over, within its own State, responsibility for this function.

It would be idle to pretend that all our problems in this whole field of prices will solve themselves by mere Federal withdrawal from direct controls.

We shall have to watch trends closely. If the freer functioning of our economic system, as well as the indirect controls which can be appropriately employed, prove insufficient during this period of strain and tension, I shall promptly ask the Congress to enact such legislation as may be required.

In facing all these problems—wages, prices, production, tax

rates, fiscal policy, deficits—everywhere we remain constantly mindful that the time for sacrifice has not ended. But we are concerned with the encouragement of competitive enterprise and individual initiative precisely because we know them to be our Nation's abiding sources of strength.

VI.

Our vast world responsibility accents with urgency our people's elemental right to a government whose clear qualities are loyalty, security, efficiency, economy, and integrity.

The safety of America and the trust of the people alike demand that the personnel of the Federal Government be loyal in their motives and reliable in the discharge of their duties. Only a combination of both loyalty and reliability promises genuine security.

To state this principle is easy; to apply it can be difficult. But this security we must and shall have. By way of example, all principal new appointees to departments and agencies have been investigated at their own request by the Federal Bureau of Investigation.

Confident of your understanding and cooperation, I know that the primary responsibility for keeping out the disloyal and the dangerous rests squarely upon the executive branch. When this branch so conducts itself as to require policing by another branch of the Government, it invites its own disorder and confusion.

I am determined to meet this responsibility of the Executive. The heads of all executive departments and agencies have been instructed to initiate at once effective programs of security with respect to their personnel. The Attorney General will advise and guide the departments and agencies in the shaping of these programs, designed at once to govern the employment of new personnel and to review speedily any derogatory information concerning incumbent personnel.

To carry out these programs, I believe that the powers of the executive branch under existing law are sufficient. If they should prove inadequate, the necessary legislation will be requested.

These programs will be both fair to the rights of the individual and effective for the safety of the Nation. They will, with care and justice, apply the basic principle that public employment is not a right but a privilege.

All these measures have two clear purposes: Their first purpose is to make certain that this Nation's security is not jeopardized by false servants. Their second purpose is to clear the atmosphere of that unreasoned suspicion that accepts rumor and gossip as substitutes for evidence.

Our people, of course, deserve and demand of their Federal Government more than security of personnel. They demand, also, efficient and logical organization, true to constitutional principles.

I have already established a Committee on Government Organization. The Committee is using as its point of departure the reports of the Hoover Commission and subsequent studies by several independent agencies. To achieve the greater efficiency and economy which the Committee analyses show to be possible, I ask the Congress to extend the present Government Reorganization Act for a period of 18 months or 2 years beyond its expiration date of April 1, 1953.

There is more involved here than realining the wheels and smoothing the gears of administrative machinery. The Congress rightfully expects the Executive to take the initiative in discovering and removing outmoded functions and eliminating duplication.

One agency, for example, whose head has promised early and vigorous action to provide greater efficiency is the Post Office. One of the oldest institutions of our Federal Government, its service should be of the best. Its employees should merit and receive the high regard and esteem of the citizens of the Nation. There are today in some areas of the postal service, both waste and incompetence to be corrected. With the cooperation of the Congress, and taking advantage of its accumulated experience in postal affairs, the Postmaster General will institute a program directed at improving service while at the same time reducing costs and decreasing deficits.

In all departments, dedication to these basic precepts of security and efficiency, integrity, and economy can and will produce an administration deserving of the trust the people have placed in it.

Our people have demanded nothing less than good, efficient government. They shall get nothing less.

VII.

Vitally important are the water and minerals, public lands and standing timber, forage and wildlife of this country. A fast-growing population will have vast future needs in these resources. We must more than match the substantial achievements in the half-century since President Theodore Roosevelt awakened the Nation to the problem of conservation.

This calls for a strong Federal program in the field of resource development. Its major projects should be timed, where possible to assist in leveling off peaks and valleys in our economic life. Soundly planned projects already initiated should be carried out. New ones will be planned for the future.

The best natural resources program for America will not result from exclusive dependence on Federal bureaucracy. It will involve a partnership of the States and local communities, private citizens, and the Federal Government, all working together. This combined effort will advance the development of the great river valleys of our Nation and the power that they can generate. Likewise, such a partnership can be effective in the expansion throughout the Nation of upstream storage; the sound use of public lands; the wise conservation of minerals; and the sustained yield of our forests.

There has been much criticism, some of it apparently justified, of the confusion resulting from overlapping Federal activities in the entire field of resource-conservation. This matter is being exhaustively studied and appropriate reorganization plans will be developed.

Most of these particular resource problems pertain to the Department of the Interior. Another of its major concerns is our country's island possessions. Here, one matter deserves attention. The platforms of both political parties promised immediate statehood to Hawaii. The people of that Territory have earned that status. Statehood should be granted promptly with the first election scheduled for 1954.

VIII.

One of the difficult problems which face the new administration is that of the slow, irregular decline of farm prices. This decline, which has been going on for almost 2 years, has occurred at a time when most nonfarm prices and farm costs of production are extraordinarily high.

Present agricultural legislation provides for the mandatory support of the prices of basic farm commodities at 90 percent of parity. The Secretary of Agriculture and his associates will, of course, execute the present act faithfully and thereby seek to mitigate the consequences of the downturn in farm income.

This price-support legislation will expire at the end of 1954.

So we should begin now to consider what farm legislation we should develop for 1955 and beyond. Our aim should be economic stability and full parity of income for American farmers. But we must seek this goal in ways that minimize governmental interference in the farmers' affairs, that permit desirable shifts in production, and that encourage farmers themselves to use initiative in meeting changing economic conditions.

A continuing study reveals nothing more emphatically than the complicated nature of this subject. Among other things, it shows that the prosperity of our agriculture depends directly upon the prosperity of the whole country—upon the purchasing power of American consumers. It depends also upon the opportunity to ship abroad large surpluses of particular commodities, and therefore upon sound economic relationships between the United States and many foreign countries. It involves research and scientific investigation, conducted on an extensive scale. It involves special credit mechanisms and marketing, rural electrification, soil conservation, and other programs.

The whole complex of agricultural programs and policies will be studied by a Special Agricultural Advisory Commission, as I know it will by appropriate committees of the Congress. A nonpartisan group of respected authorities in the field of agriculture has already been appointed as an interim advisory group.

The immediate changes needed in agricultural programs are largely budgetary and administrative in nature. New policies and new programs must await the completion of the far-reaching studies which have already been launched.

IX.

The determination of labor policy must be governed not by the vagaries of political expediency but by the firmest principles and convictions. Slanted partisan appeals to American workers, spoken as if they were a group apart, necessitating a special language and treatment, are an affront to the fullness of their dignity as American citizens.

The truth in matters of labor policy has become obscured in controversy. The very meaning of economic freedom as it affects labor has become confused. This misunderstanding has provided a climate of opinion favoring the growth of governmental paternalism in labor relations. This tendency, if left uncorrected, could end only by producing a bureaucratic despotism. Economic freedom is, in fact, the requisite of greater prosperity for every American who earns his own living.

In the field of labor legislation, only a law that merits the respect and support of both labor and management can help reduce the loss of wages and of production through strikes and stoppages, and thus add to the total economic strength of our Nation.

We have now had 5 years' experience with the Labor Management Act of 1947, commonly known as the Taft-Hartley Act. That experience has shown the need for some corrective action, and we should promptly proceed to amend that act.

I know that the Congress is already proceeding with renewed studies of this subject. Meanwhile, the Department of Labor is at once beginning work to devise further specific recommendations for your consideration.

In the careful working out of legislation, I know you will give thoughtful consideration—as will we in the executive branch—to the views of labor, and of management, and of the general public. In this process, it is only human that each of us should bring forward the arguments of self-interest. But if all conduct their arguments in the overpowering light of national interest—which is enlightened self-interest—we shall get the right answers. I profoundly hope that every citizen of our country will follow with understanding your progress in this work. The welfare of all of us is involved.

Especially must we remember that the institutions of trade unionism and collective bargaining are monuments to the freedom that must prevail in our industrial life. They have a century of honorable achievement behind them. Our faith in them is proven, firm, and final.

Government can do a great deal to aid the settlement of labor disputes without allowing itself to be employed as an ally of either side. Its proper role in industrial strife is to encourage the processes of mediation and conciliation. These processes can successfully be directed only by a government free from the taint of any suspicion that it is partial or punitive.

The administration intends to strengthen and to improve the services which the Department of Labor can render to the worker and to the whole national community. This Department was created—just 40 years ago—to serve the entire Nation. It must aid, for example, employers and employees alike in improving training programs that will develop skilled and competent workers. It must enjoy the confidence and respect of labor and industry in order to play a significant role in the planning of America's economic future. To that end, I am authorizing the Department of Labor to establish promptly a tripartite advisory committee consisting of representatives of employers, labor, and the public.

x.

Our civil and social rights form a central part of the heritage we are striving to defend on all fronts and with all our strength.

I believe with all my heart that our vigilant guarding of these rights is a sacred obligation binding upon every citizen. To be true to one's own freedom is, in essence, to honor and respect the freedom of all others.

A cardinal ideal in this heritage we cherish is the equality of rights of all citizens of every race and color and creed.

We know that discrimination against minorities persists despite our allegiance to this ideal. Such discrimination—confined to no one section of the Nation—is but the outward testimony to the persistence of distrust and of fear in the hearts of men.

This fact makes all the more vital the fighting of these wrongs by each individual, in every station of life, in his every deed.

Much of the answer lies in the power of fact, fully publicized; of persuasion, honestly pressed; and of conscience, justly aroused. These are methods familiar to our way of life, tested and proven wise.

I propose to use whatever authority exists in the office of the President to end segregation in the District of Columbia, including the Federal Government, and any segregation in the Armed Forces.

Here in the District of Columbia, serious attention should be given to the proposal to develop and authorize, through legislation, a system to provide an effective voice in local self-government. While consideration of this proceeds, I recommend an immediate increase of two in the number of District

Commissioners to broaden representation of all elements of our local population. This will be a first step toward insuring that this Capital provide an honored example to all communities of our Nation.

In this manner, and by the leadership of the office of the President exercised through friendly conferences with those in authority in our States and cities, we expect to make true and rapid progress in civil rights and equality of employment opportunity.

There is one sphere in which civil rights are inevitably involved in Federal legislation. This is the sphere of immigration.

It is a manifest right of our Government to limit the number of immigrants our Nation can absorb. It is also a manifest right of our Government to set reasonable requirements on the character and the numbers of the people who come to share our land and our freedom.

It is well for us, however, to remind ourselves occasionally of an equally manifest fact: we are—one and all—immigrants or sons and daughters of immigrants.

Existing legislation contains injustices. It does, in fact, discriminate. I am informed by Members of the Congress that it was realized, at the time of its enactment, that future study of the basis of determining quotas would be necessary.

I am therefore requesting the Congress to review this legislation and to enact a statute that will at one and the same time guard our legitimate national interests and be faithful to our basic ideas of freedom and fairness to all.

In another but related area—that of social rights—we see most clearly the new application of old ideas of freedom.

This administration is profoundly aware of two great needs born of our living in a complex industrial economy. First, the individual citizen must have safeguards against personal disaster inflicted by forces beyond his control; second, the welfare of the people demands effective and economical performance by the Government of certain indispensable social services.

31

In the light of this responsibility, certain general purposes and certain concrete measures are plainly indicated now.

There is urgent need for greater effectiveness in our programs, both public and private, offering safeguards against the privations that too often come with unemployment, old age, illness, and accident. The provisions of the old-age and survivors insurance law should promptly be extended to cover millions of citizens who have been left out of the social-security system. No less important is the encouragement of privately sponsored pension plans. Most important of all, of course, is renewed effort to check the inflation which destroys so much of the value of all social-security payments.

Our school system demands some prompt, effective help. During each of the last 2 years, more than 1½ million children have swelled the elementary and secondary school population of the country. Generally, the school population is proportionately higher in States with low per capita income. This whole situation calls for careful congressional study and action. I am sure that you share my conviction that the firm conditions of Federal aid must be proved need and proved lack of local income.

One phase of the school problem demands special action. The school population of many districts has been greatly increased by the swift growth of defense activities. These activities have added little or nothing to the tax resources of the communities affected. Legislation aiding construction of schools in these districts expires on June 30. This law should be renewed; and, likewise, the partial payments for current operating expenses for these particular school districts should be made, including the deficiency requirement of the current fiscal year.

Public interest similarly demands one prompt specific action in protection of the general consumer. The Food and Drug Administration should be authorized to continue its established and necessary program of factory inspections. The invalidation of these inspections by the Supreme Court of December 8, 1952, was based solely on the fact that the present law contained inconsistent and unclear provisions. These must be promptly corrected.

I am well aware that beyond these few immediate measures there remains much to be done. The health and housing needs of our people call for intelligently planned programs. Involved are the solvency of the whole security system; and its guarding against exploitation by the irresponsible.

To bring clear purpose and orderly procedure into this field, I anticipate a thorough study of the proper relationship among Federal, State, and local programs. I shall shortly send you specific recommendations for establishing such an appropriate commission, together with a reorganization plan defining new administrative status for all Federal activities in health, education, and social security.

I repeat that there are many important subjects of which I make no mention today. Among these is our great and growing body of veterans. America has traditionally been generous in caring for the disabled—and the widow and the orphan of the fallen. These millions remain close to all our hearts. Proper care of our uniformed citizens and appreciation of the past service of our veterans are part of our accepted governmental responsibilities.

XI.

We have surveyed briefly some problems of our people and a portion of the tasks before us.

The hope of freedom itself depends, in real measure, upon our strength, our heart, and our wisdom.

We must be strong in arms. We must be strong in the source of all our armament, our productivity. We all—workers and farmers, foremen and financiers, technicians and builders—all must produce, produce more, and produce yet more.

We must be strong, above all, in the spiritual resources upon which all else depends. We must be devoted with all our heart to the values we defend. We must know that each of these values and virtues applies with equal force at the ends of the earth and in our relations with our neighbor next door. We must know that freedom expresses itself with equal eloquence in the right of workers to strike in the nearby factory, and in the yearnings and sufferings of the peoples of Eastern Europe.

As our heart summons our strength, our wisdom must direct it.

There is, in world affairs, a steady course to be followed between an assertion of strength that is truculent and a confession of helplessness that is cowardly.

There is, in our affairs at home, a middle way between untrammeled freedom of the individual and the demands for the welfare of the whole Nation. This way must avoid government by bureaucracy as carefully as it avoids neglect of the helpless.

In every area of political action, free men must think before they can expect to win.

In this spirit must we live and labor: confident of our strength, compassionate in our heart, clear in our mind.

In this spirit, let us together turn to the great tasks before us.

DWIGHT D. EISENHOWER

NOTE: This is the text of the document which the President signed and transmitted to the Senate and House of Representatives (H. Doc. 75, 83d Cong., 1st sess.). The address as reported from the floor appears in the Congressional Record (vol. 99, p. 748).

7 ¶ Messages to Heads of State on the Storm Disasters in Western Europe. *February 2, 1953*

To Her Majesty Elizabeth, Queen of Great Britain:

My fellow Americans join me in extending to Your Majesty and to the British people heartfelt sympathy for the tragic deaths and sufferings caused by the floods and hurricanes.

DWIGHT D. EISENHOWER

To Her Majesty Juliana, Queen of the Netherlands:

My countrymen and I are deeply shocked at the news of the devastation your people have sustained through the recent storms and floods. They and I wish to extend to Your Majesty our deepest sympathy in these tragic circumstances.

DWIGHT D. EISENHOWER

To His Majesty Baudouin I, King of the Belgians:

The American people join me in extending to Your Majesty heartfelt sympathy for the tragic suffering your people have sustained in the recent violent storms.

DWIGHT D. EISENHOWER

NOTE: Cablegram acknowledgments of the President's messages were released on February 4 and 5. On February 6 it was announced that the President had appointed a committee composed of the Secretary of State, the Secretary of Defense, the Secretary of Agriculture, and the Director for Mutual Security to gather facts on the disaster and to make recommendations as to how the United States could assist the victims.

On February 12 a White House release stated that Secretary Dulles, chairman of the committee, had reported to the President that the immediate relief problem was well in hand, that steps were being taken to prevent further damages by spring tides, and that it would be some time before it would be possible to estimate the total impact of the disaster.

The damage was particularly severe in the Netherlands. On January 15, 1954, the White House released the following message from Queen Juliana, dated January 8:

Mr. President,

Now that the last gap in the dykes has recently been closed, I feel impelled to address myself to you and the American people, moved by a deep sense of gratitude. The floods which ravaged our country in February have brought great distress to hundreds of thousands of my compatriots and caused extensive damage. It has been a great comfort, however, that with a spontaneity to which history furnishes no parallel, sympathy with the victims was shown from all sides while valuable active assistance was given as well.

You sent us aeroplanes, helicopters and amphibious vehicles which have proved to be a tremendous help during the rescue work; goods and clothes were collected from all over the United States and considerable amounts of money were raised. You did even more than that: units of your armed forces rushed up; by their utmost exertions, toiling day and night on the inundated lands at the risk of their own lives under the most unfavourable weather conditions, they saved victims and their cattle and helped in plugging the innumerable breaches in the dykes. All those who did their utmost to help us have earned our deep-felt gratitude because they have proved that human solidarity does not stop at frontiers. On behalf of the victims and all my compatriots I address myself to you and, in doing so, to the American people to express what can hardly be expressed in words: our heart-felt thanks for everything you did when the sea—our faithful friend and eternal enemy—held our country in its crushing grip.

I seize this opportunity to convey to you, Mr. President, my sincere wishes both for the prosperity of the Republic and for your personal well-being.

JULIANA

8 ¶ Remarks at the Dedicatory Prayer Breakfast of the International Christian Leadership. *February* 5, 1953

Mr. Chairman, distinguished guests, ladies and gentlemen:

This has been a wholly enjoyable occasion for me except for the one second when I opened the little blue slip and found that it said there would be an address by the President. I assure you, both for your sakes and for mine, there will not be.

There are a few thoughts, though, that crowd into my mind. With your permission I will attempt to utter them in a very informal and homely way.

First, there is a need we all have in these days and times for some help which comes from outside ourselves as we face the multitude of problems that are part of this confusing situation. I do not mean merely help for your leaders or the people in Congress, in the Cabinet and others in authority, because these problems are part of all of us. They face each one of us because we are a free country. Each of us realizes that he has responsibilities that are equal to his privileges and to his rights.

So, as he approaches them at times, he says: "If we only had the simple, the good old days, how easy all this would be. What a nice life."

Once in a while it might be a good thing for us to turn back to history. Let us study a little bit of what happened at the founding of this Nation.

It is not merely the events that led up to the Revolutionary War. All of the confused problems that we were then called upon to solve were as difficult as those we face now. Did you ever stop to think, for example, that the first year of that war was fought in order that we might establish our right to be free British citizens, not to be independent. From April 1775 until July 4, 1776, there was no struggle for independence. It was a struggle to make people understand that we were free British citizens. So you can understand the confusion of thought that was going on.

So when we came down to the Declaration of Independence, our forefathers had difficulty in meeting their problems which was probably as great for them as we feel our problems today. In the Declaration they acknowledged the need to respect public opinion. They said, "When in the course of human events"— and they went on to say a decent respect for mankind impelled them to declare the decisions which led to the separation. They realized that the good opinion of the whole world was necessary if this venture was to succeed. At least they felt that an understanding of this venture should be abroad in the world.

They went on to try to explain it. What did they say? The very basis of our government is: "We hold that all men are endowed by their Creator" with certain rights.

When we came to that turning point in history, when we intended to establish a government for free men and a Declaration and Constitution to make it last, in order to explain such a system we had to say: "We hold that all men are endowed by their Creator."

In one sentence we established that every free government is imbedded soundly in a deeply-felt religious faith or it makes no sense. Today if we recall those things and if, in that sense, we can back off from our problems and depend upon a power greater than ourselves, I believe that we begin to draw these problems into focus.

As Benjamin Franklin said at one time during the course of the stormy consultation at the Constitutional Convention, because he sensed that the convention was on the point of breaking up: "Gentlemen, I suggest that we have a word of prayer." And strangely enough, after a bit of prayer the problems began to smooth out and the convention moved to the great triumph that we enjoy today—the writing of our Constitution.

Today I think that prayer is just simply a necessity, because by prayer I believe we mean an effort to get in touch with the Infinite. We know that even our prayers are imperfect. Even our supplications are imperfect. Of course they are. We are imperfect human beings. But if we can back off from those problems and make the effort, then there is something that ties us all together. We have begun in our grasp of that basis of understanding, which is that all free government is firmly founded in a deeply-felt religious faith.

As we sympathize with our great friends in Holland and Britain today in this distressing disaster that has overtaken them, it is good to know that the American soldiers, the American Navy, the American airmen, are sharing those disasters and are moving in as units and as individuals to help. I have had messages from both of those countries expressing their great thanks to America for the work they are doing. They, to my mind, are part of this understanding that a government such as ours hopes to produce people who are moved by sympathy, by all of those wonderful qualities that are implicit in a deeply-felt religious faith. They are living up to what we hope for our government, both as units and as individuals.

I think my little message this morning is merely this: I have the profound belief that if we remind ourselves once in a while of this simple basic truth that our forefathers in 1776 understood so well, we can hold up our heads and be certain that we in our time are going to be able to preserve the essentials, to preserve as a free government and pass it on, in our turn, as sound, as strong, as good as ever. That, it seems to me, is the prayer that all of us have today.

It has been very wonderful to meet you. Until I started over I had the picture, which Frank Carlson gave me last summer, of a small Congressional group of Congressmen and Senators who met on a morning each week. I had an idea of coming over to see 20 or 25 or maybe 50 people. I had no idea that our host had such a party as this. I do hope I may speak for all of you in thanking him for such a breakfast, the like of which I have not had in 10 years. As long as you feed me grits and sausage, everything will be all right.

Thank you.

NOTE: The President spoke at the Mayflower Hotel in Washington. His opening words "Mr. Chairman" referred to U.S. Senator Frank Carlson of Kansas.

9 ¶ Message to the Boy Scouts of America on Their 43d Anniversary. *February 7, 1953*

[Released February 7, 1953. Dated February 4, 1953]

To the Boy Scouts of America:

It is with great personal pleasure that I extend to you my warmest congratulations on your Forty-third Anniversary and greet you on the occasion of Boy Scout Week 1953.

Your present crusade "Forward on Liberty's Team" is proving to be most effective. Americans everywhere must be proud to know that the Boy Scouts of America registered its three-millionth active member during the past year. I understand that the present membership has now reached a new high of 3,200,000 Scouts, Explorers, and leaders, and that since 1910 there have been 20,200,000 American boys and men enrolled.

This birthday message is addressed to every Scout and leader in the Boy Scouts of America.   I urge you all to live up to the high ideals for which Scouting stands—your duty as patriotic citizens. If you will follow the Scout oath, America will be better able to meet its full responsibility in cooperation with other nations in maintaining peace on earth.

DWIGHT D. EISENHOWER

10   ¶ Statement by the President After Reviewing the Case of Julius and Ethel Rosenberg. *February* 11, 1953

I HAVE GIVEN earnest consideration to the records in the case of Julius and Ethel Rosenberg and to the appeals for clemency made on their behalf.   These two individuals have been tried and convicted of a most serious crime against the people of the United States.   They have been found guilty of conspiring with intent and reason to believe that it would be to the advantage of a foreign power, to deliver to the agents of that foreign power certain highly secret atomic information relating to the national defense of the United States.

The nature of the crime for which they have been found guilty and sentenced far exceeds that of the taking of the life of another citizen; it involves the deliberate betrayal of the entire nation and could very well result in the death of many, many thousands of innocent citizens.   By their act these two individuals have in fact betrayed the cause of freedom for which free men are fighting and dying at this very hour.

We are a nation under law and our affairs are governed by the just exercise of these laws.   The courts have provided every opportunity for the submission of evidence bearing on this case. In the time-honored tradition of American justice, a freely selected jury of their fellow-citizens considered the evidence in this case and rendered its judgment.   All rights of appeal were exercised and the conviction of the trial court was upheld after full judicial review, including that of the highest court in the land.[1]

I have made a careful examination into this case and am satisfied that the two individuals have been accorded their full measure of justice.

There has been neither new evidence nor have there been mitigating circumstances which would justify altering this decision, and I have determined that it is my duty, in the interest of the people of the United States, not to set aside the verdict of their representatives.

11 ⁋ Letter to Colonel C. M. Boyer, Executive Director, Reserve Officers Association, Concerning National Defense Week. *February* 16, 1953

[Released February 16, 1953. Dated February 15, 1953]

Dear Colonel Boyer:

I am delighted to join with the Reserve Officers Association and patriotic Americans everywhere in the observance of National Defense Week. A more fitting period for such purpose could hardly be chosen, for it embraces the birthdays of our two greatest Presidents—the one who led the founding of the Republic and the other who led its salvation.

National security is everybody's job today; I feel keenly that the Reserve Officers Association is deserving of commendation for its outstanding contribution in bringing public attention to bear on our urgent defense needs. The Association is uniquely equipped to do this, for its membership is at once part of the Armed Forces and part of the civilian community of the nation. The Reserve Officers Association has members in service from Europe to the Korean battlefront, and it has members in every city and town across the broad expanse of America.

[1] 344 U.S. 838, 889.

Please accept my personal gratitude for your continued service to the nation and my best wishes for every success in your program for National Defense Week.

Sincerely,

DWIGHT D. EISENHOWER

12   ¶ The President's News Conference of *February* 17, 1953.

THE PRESIDENT. First of all, ladies and gentlemen, let me assure you that I welcome this opportunity to meet with representatives of the radio and press, many of them old friends of mine, and to continue the kind of relationship that I have had in the past with them.   I look forward to many of these meetings during the ensuing 4 years.

Now, one of the topics that made an interesting subject for speculation during the past few months was a thought that I would develop a great deal of antagonism for the press.   I wouldn't know why.   I feel that no individual has been treated more fairly and squarely over the past many years now, that I have been dealing with them, than I have by the press.   Through the war years and ever since, I have found nothing but a desire to dig at the truth, so far as I was concerned, and be open-handed and forthright about it.   That is the kind of relationship I hope we can continue.

Now, of course, you know we can talk here all day.   There are a lot of things in a big country such as ours, and the kind of world we are living in, that make interesting subjects for conversation.   My next appointment is in my office at 11 o'clock.   This morning I have chosen four subjects that I think are of immediate interest, both in the domestic scene and in the international scene, that can stand a little bit of discussion.   Thereafter, we will use such time as you might want, to ask questions on these subjects, and then if there is a little time left, why we can extend it even wider and see if there are other questions of which you might like to inquire.

The first one that I want to talk about is farm prices. I want to read to you a sentence from the Republican Platform: "A prosperous agriculture, with free and independent farmers, is fundamental to the national interest."

Now, that is a simple generalization that involves a terrific amount of work, a terrific amount of planning and study; and much of it has been going on for the past 20 years or more—a great deal of it on a bipartisan basis. But the point I want to emphasize is this: just simple control of an industry through arbitrary governmental power is easy, but it means control clear across the board. And that is something we neither want in our national life as a system or as a practice, nor will the farmers, the most independent, I think, of all of our citizens, stand it for a minute.

So the programs that we devise must have at their basis—one of their fundamentals—this retention of this right of freedom on the part of the farmer.

Now, we have had, for the past 2 years, falling prices. Manifestly, every problem that I can talk to you about today is an inherited problem. These Republicans have been in office, you will recall, only since January 20, and we have scarcely had time to do more than to begin earnest study of these problems. And they, in a complex society such as ours, go slowly, ordinarily.

We have had falling farm prices for 2 years. In January 1952, that late, beef was $34.22 a hundred pounds, and the peak had been passed a year earlier than that, in February 1951. By November that price had fallen to $31.00, by January 24 of this year, $25.51. It continued to fall down to approximately $24.00—$23.90. But since the removal of controls on the price of beef—something that was earnestly requested by the beef growers, let me assure you—beef has gone up a bit, and started back up the other way.

In addition, this removal of price controls has had one effect that the beef growers thought it would, which was narrowing the gap between the amount that the farmer received on the farm and the amount you were paying at the meat market. The reason for that was because the regulation required a very severe gradation of beef. Those restrictions have been removed, and the gap has been somewhat narrowed, so that while the retail prices are still down at their lowest point, the other prices have started up a little bit.

In addition to this, of course, the second the problem first arose, we urged upon and directed the armed services—the procurement agencies of the armed services—to procure and maintain a maximum supply of beef. They can usually carry a 120-day supply very easily with no danger of spoilage. They have been going up in their reserves, in order to help in the support of this beef price.

Now let me point out that this whole farm program is a serious thing. Beef prices are an immediate and interesting thing, and have occasioned quite a bit of discussion in the press and in governmental circles. But all the way through—today we are buying butter at a million pounds a day, and that butter, of course, in time grows rancid. We have other stocks in storage, altogether I think—of farm products—there is something over a billion dollars' worth of these stocks in storage.

What I am pointing out again is that even those stocks would be vastly increased except for two things: the subsidization we give to exports through this wheat distribution pool—I forget its exact name, but you people will know it, so we won't worry about it.[1] It's a big pool now meeting in which we subsidize our wheat exports to the tune of about 70 cents a bushel. Then, on top of that, the different kinds of aid we give abroad, which provide the dollars so that the wheat can be bought. If it

---

[1] The President referred to the Commodity Credit Corporation Wheat and Flour Export Program which facilitated exports to member nations of the International Wheat Agreement.

weren't for those two features, our surpluses would be very much greater.

I merely show—and I must emphasize here—that it is a very complicated problem. But above all things, let me emphasize this: all through the campaign I stated—and promised—to the farmers of America: we will support the present law which goes, as you know, to December 1954, and in the meantime, we will convene commissions. We have one now—the Advisory Commission, Department of Agriculture, has on it representatives of all branches of agriculture, and we try, of course, to put on people representing the public. So, any plan devised to take effect after the expiration of the current law, will represent the thinking of America—not only of the producers but of the consumers and everybody else—so as to get as broadly based a program as it is possible to get.

Everybody, of course, sympathizes with the farmer's plight, with the special difficulties he has in his industry; and I refer you again to that sentence of the Republican Platform, which I certainly intend to do my best to carry out.

The second point I want to raise, and very briefly, is this thing of secret agreements. By no means do I assume that it is either feasible or desirable that the United States Government should take any action, just saying everything that was agreed to at such and such a place, or such and such a spot, or at such and such a time, is repudiated; by no manner of means.

I do believe this: it is necessary that this Government make clear that never has the heart of America agreed to the enslavement of any people. And in the proper way—the thing is still under study as to the exact, proper, way—we are going to make clear that determination with some kind of pronouncement that can leave no doubt that it means exactly what it says.

Another subject that has occupied some space in the newspapers is price controls. We, of course, are moving in the direction of attempting to unshackle the economy and to allow it to operate so as to keep up standards of living—in the belief that, with many of our peak problems in wartime production already solved, the workings of the economic laws will keep prices in their proper relationship one to the other.[1]

Now, we had a situation that was very difficult to meet, and no one would attempt to minimize the problem that past officials working on these problems had to solve. We went in June 1950 into a situation that did not call for total mobilization, the kind of a situation in which we have come to expect full controls. But neither was it peace. We had a war production problem thrown on our economy that threw things out of balance. It was difficult to get control of such a situation and keep it in balance. And finally, these prices did get pretty badly disarranged.

If what we are now trying to do cannot accommodate the situation, and a bad result is obtained, I have no hesitation in saying I will go right back to Congress and ask for whatever we believe to be necessary.

We do think that the present situation calls for this removal of controls which is going on, as you know, now, gradually; and as a result we believe that the situation will take care of itself very definitely. Some prices will go up. Many will go down. But in any event, people will be free of the threat and continued annoyance of governmental interference in everything that they do.

Of course, such a decision represents something of my faith that American business leaders, American labor leaders, and others will face this problem as I am trying to face it, honestly and fairly, and will remember that it is not well to try to gouge or do anything unreasonable in this situation that would create the kind of economic emergency that would demand a further action by the Congress—further price control system.

Now I realize that when you say that, you are saying quite a

---

[1] On February 6 the White House announced two major actions in the direction of eliminating wage and price controls. These actions included (1) immediate suspension by Executive order of all wage and salary controls, and (2) issuance by the Office of Price Stabilization of orders removing from price control a wide and varied list of consumer goods, including all meat products, all furniture, all apparel, and many other items. The release stated that this was the first of a series of orders under which all prices would be decontrolled.

bit. I am talking by and large about the mass of these people. And I must say I could have no greater disappointment than to be forced to go back to Congress and say: "Well, this just won't work; we have got again to our price controls."

I want to say just a word about this matter of the atom bomb. I am going to read to you a statement that you probably have all read. I want to read this statement again, merely to announce that every bit of evidence leads me to say I agree with this statement, by the Chairman of the Atomic Energy Commission, absolutely.

It starts: "The U.S.S.R. has produced fissionable materials in quantity. With fissionable materials in hand, it is not a difficult technical job to make workable atomic weapons. The U.S.S.R. has exploded three—one in the late summer of 1949, two in 1951. On the basis of the above facts, and other scientific and technical evidence, there is no doubt of the existence of a supply of atomic weapons."

I have been asked that question so often, ladies and gentlemen, I merely want to say that so far as I am concerned, that is absolutely true—word for word.

And now, our last subject: taxes. In spite of some things that I have seen in the papers over the past 8 or 9 months, I personally have never promised a reduction in taxes. Never.

What I have said is, reduction of taxes is a very necessary objective of government—that if our form of economy is to endure, we must not forget private incentives and initiative and the production that comes from it. Therefore, the objective of tax reduction is an absolutely essential one, and must be attained in its proper order.

But I believe, and I think this can be demonstrated as fact by economists, both on the basis of history and on their theoretical and abstract reasoning, that until the deficit is eliminated from our budget, there is no hope of keeping our money stable. It is bound to continue to be cheapened, and if it is cheapened, then the necessary expenses of government each year cost more because the money is worth less. Therefore, there is no end to the inflation; there is finally no end to taxation; and the eventual result would, of course, be catastrophe.

So, whether we are ready to face the job this minute or any other time, the fact is there must be balanced budgets before we are again on a safe and sound system in our economy. That means, to my mind, that we cannot afford to reduce taxes, reduce income, until we have in sight a program of expenditures that shows that the factors of income and of outgo will be balanced. Now that is just to my mind sheer necessity.

I have as much reason as anyone else to deplore high taxes. I certainly am going to work with every bit of energy I have towards their reduction. And I applaud the efforts of the people in Congress that are going in that way. But I merely want to point out that unless we go at it in the proper sequence, I do not believe that taxes will be lowered. We might for the moment lower the "chit" you get for this year, but in the ensuing years, it would be a very different thing.

Now, ladies and gentlemen, I have covered my four subjects, and we will take, first, a period of addressing questions to these. I will see if I can answer any of them. I believe that you are to introduce yourselves to me.

Q. Merriman Smith, United Press: Mr. President, in connection with your farm statement, do you plan to ask Congress for standby control powers?

THE PRESIDENT. On price—did you say price controls?

Q. Mr. Smith: Yes, sir.

THE PRESIDENT. Price controls. On price controls, I do not intend to ask for standby controls. I believe that if any standby control bill is enacted it must be in very general terms. I do not believe that you can, at this moment, foresee the conditions of a future, 3 months or 6 months from now, and write the details of a law that would fit it. Therefore, it would have to be in very general terms, and I will accept that if they do it.

Q. Edward T. Folliard, Washington Post: Mr. President, you are so emphatic in what you said about taxes, that I would gather, sir, that you would veto a tax reduction bill, if one should be passed by Congress?

THE PRESIDENT. Well, you must know, Mr. Folliard, we don't have any item veto authority. In the executive department you have to veto a bill, a total bill—and you never know how a thing like that might come up to you. So I couldn't possibly predict in advance what would be my action. I assure you of this: the simple thoughts I have expressed on the subject this morning will govern me just so far as it is possible to be governed in this line.

Q. Raymond P. Brandt, St. Louis Post-Dispatch: Mr. President, will the administration sponsor a bill to retain the excess profits tax which expires on June 30th?

THE PRESIDENT. I would say this—I can't answer that in exact terms—I shall never agree to the elimination of any tax where reduction in revenue goes along with it. In other words, it would have to be a substitute of some kind in that same area.

Q. Mr. Brandt: Are you thinking along those terms, sir?

THE PRESIDENT. My people are.

Q. Sarah McClendon, Texas papers: Mr. President, are the press conferences in the future to follow along this form?

THE PRESIDENT. Ladies and gentlemen, there are a lot of you that know me, and you know I am rather apt to change a habit at any time. Let's don't take this one as a necessary pattern. If we find some method among us that would be more convenient, an hour, or a day, or anything else, I am certainly open to suggestions; I have never thought I had quite all the answers. So I should say as time goes on we will see what happens, and I would hope that they at least will be friendly. That would be the only basis I would want to retain for certain.

Q. Alan S. Emory, Watertown (N.Y.) Times: Mr. President, this is somewhat allied to the beef problem. There is also a considerable problem in relation to dairy prices these days. I wonder if you would endorse the proposal to keep hearings on problems such as dairy prices, as close to the farmers involved as possible?

THE PRESIDENT. Indeed I do. On that problem, I might tell you that all the representatives of the dairy industry are in the Department of Agriculture this morning, discussing their problem. And I would tell you this: everything that has been said and done in the agricultural field since January 20 has been on the basis of an advisory commission I appointed last December. It has been meeting, and we have brought in different panels on wool, sugar, now dairy, there have been about six different panels, and they cover the industries, so far as I know.

Q. Andrew F. Tully, Jr., Scripps-Howard Newspapers: Mr. President, have you discovered any other secret agreements besides the one signed at Yalta?

THE PRESIDENT. Personally, I have discovered no secret agreements. I use the word "secret" in this respect: when they were made, they were necessarily secret. They remain secret on this basis: they have never been presented to the Senate for their advice and consent, and therefore they never have achieved the standing of public treaties.

So, I am merely talking about those and only those parts of agreements that appeared to help the enslavement of peoples or, you might say, have been twisted by implication to mean that.

Q. Richard Harkness, National Broadcasting Company: Mr. President, we have had in the last 10 days or 2 weeks a welter of statements regarding Korea, statements attributed to Gen. James Van Fleet regarding an offensive, statements attributed to the testimony of Mr. Dulles—supposedly secret testimony, a statement by a Senator that we might use Formosa as an air base to bomb the mainland of China, every conceivable kind of statement. Can you say anything this morning to clarify this situation?

THE PRESIDENT. No, I think I could say very little, except this: let's take General Van Fleet. He will come back—he is my classmate—he will undoubtedly come in to see me. If you people would like to see him, I will ask him, as a favor to me, to have a press conference if you like; because I think the more all of us know about the conditions over there, about how our soldiers are faring, what the situation looks like, the better for all of us. I believe in facts.

Now I don't know about these statements that you talk about, but I have said this publicly time and again: in these matters affecting the broad policy of the United States, and not mere expedients within the proper purview of the responsibilities of a mere Commander in Chief, they will never be undertaken until they are discussed with the proper leaders of the Congress; and if necessary they will have to act on them. I don't believe in doing these things haphazardly and on an individual and arbitrary basis.

Q. Mrs. May Craig, Portland (Maine) Press Herald: If I may go back to the secret agreements a moment, are you aware that many Members of Congress on both sides feel that the agreements were never binding, anyway, because they were not presented to Congress—to the Senate?

THE PRESIDENT. Well, I think there are, in our practice, certain things that are of course binding when the people are acting as proper representatives of the United States—say, in war, as in establishing staffs and commands and that sort of thing. That extends out into some fields that are almost politico-military in nature. I do agree that nothing can have the binding force of a treaty on us until it is submitted to the Senate—that's what I am trying to get at.

Q. Mrs. Craig: Sir, are you aware that many Members of Congress also feel that the President had no right to take us into Korea without consulting Congress, also that he had no right to send troops to Europe without consulting Congress? Now I would like to ask——

THE PRESIDENT [*interposing*]. Mrs. Craig, I want to say this one thing.

Q. Mrs. Craig: Yes sir.

THE PRESIDENT [*continuing*]. That all took place long before

I came to this office. I have a hard time trying to determine my own path and solve my own problems. I am not going back and try to solve those that someone else had.

Q. Mrs. Craig: I wanted to ask you if you had given thought to your relationships with Congress in those fields.

THE PRESIDENT. Mrs. Craig, indeed I have. I don't believe that this Government is set up to be operated by anybody acting alone. I think it is clear what our founding documents mean; and I intend to function, as far as I am concerned, in that way.

Now, we have always demanded that in an emergency where there was no time, not even hours, then someone had to act. In natural disasters—in Corpus Christi, or storms overseas—just this recent storm where our friends suffered such disaster in Holland and other countries—then they expect somebody to do something. But in the normal case, we have our system of consultations laid out, and it will be followed, as far as I am concerned.

Q. Joseph A. Fox, Washington Evening Star: Is it intended eventually, sir, to replace all the Americans in Korea with South Korean troops?

THE PRESIDENT. I don't want to discuss such things in too great detail, but I would say this: I do not believe that as long as the United Nations carries responsibility over there, that they can—as long as there is a dangerous situation—remove themselves completely from the whole area. I do believe this at the same time, which I have stated before publicly: the South Koreans are good soldiers, and they really want the opportunity of defending themselves so far as that is possible—namely, they want to be on the front lines, and it is merely a question of armaments, organization, and the leadership which, of course, is difficult to provide. But as fast as they can go up there, other United Nations troops will be pulled back. The military authority will have to decide how many of those people have to stay in order to make certain of the carrying out of the responsibilities we picked up.

Q. Richard L. Wilson, Cowles Publications: Are you considering recommending an embargo or blockade of any kind against shipments into Red China?

THE PRESIDENT. That has not been discussed with me except in the papers. There has been no study on it that has been brought up yet to me. So personally I am not—the answer is, I have no answer.

Q. Leslie R. Honeycutt, Army Times: Mr. President, does your reorganization plan on the Federal Security Agency contemplate any transfer of VA functions to that department?

THE PRESIDENT. I would be glad to answer you—I think I know it, but I just could be wrong; and I will answer that the next time. I think I know the exact answer, but I don't want to make a mistake.

Q. Laurence H. Burd, Chicago Tribune: Back to taxes, can you say when you hope to have the budget balanced?

THE PRESIDENT. No, because, as you know, the 1954 budget was prepared and submitted to the Congress before the Cabinet officers that I have appointed came in. They are digging into every obligation, every authority asked for, to try to find those places where savings can be made.[1]

---

[1] On February 3, the White House issued the following release relating to the Budget:

"With the approval of the President and following his State of the Union Message to the Congress, Joseph M. Dodge, the Director of the Bureau of the Budget, has established policies, concurred in by the Cabinet, to be applied in arriving at recommendations for revisions of the fiscal year 1954 Budget.

"These policies today are being transmitted by Mr. Dodge to all Department and Agency heads in the Executive Branch.

"*General*. It is clear that the Budget will not be brought under control without action to reduce budgetary obligational authority, reduce the level of expenditures, critically examine existing programs, restrain commitments for new programs, and generally drive for greater efficiency and reduced costs.

"*Personnel*. It is the policy to achieve a progressive reduction of Government personnel. To accomplish this each Department and Agency head shall immediately restrict the hiring of additional personnel. No vacancies shall be filled until it has been determined that the positions represented by vacancies cannot be eliminated; existing employees cannot be shifted to cover the vacancies; and increased efficiency, better utilization of personnel, or changes in standards and policies make the additions unnecessary.

"*Construction*. It is the policy to proceed only with projects which are clearly essential, and on such projects to employ the strictest standards of economy.

"All proposed or authorized construction projects on which work has not yet begun

(*Footnote continued on following page*)

Now, already, as you know, in the fiscal year which is now rapidly drawing to a close, there is a 5.9 [billion dollar] deficit. That can't be closed.   That is just too late, although we are closing some, by cutting down deficiency appropriations.   Then there is a, I think, 9.9 deficit for 1954 contemplated.

That is what we are working on.   When that happens, then I think the United States can heave a sigh of relief and we can begin to look toward tax reduction.

Q. Robert J. Donovan, New York Herald Tribune: Could I ask you, if I understand this right, on the embargo, that the question of an embargo or blockade has not been brought up to you at all?

THE PRESIDENT. It has not been brought up officially to me. Naturally, I discuss these things with a good many people, but there hasn't been a study made in the proper sections of the Government and brought up to me for action and decision.

Q. Mr. Donovan: These are not actively under consideration by you at the present time?

are to be reviewed and construction initiated only on those projects which meet these criteria.

"All going construction projects are to be reviewed according to the same criteria and appropriate action taken, including action to stop the work if this appears advisable.

"*Programs.* It is the policy to operate at a minimum level of costs and expenditures. This requires that the necessity for all work be questioned and action be taken to eliminate unnecessary programs and hold the remainder to minimum levels.

"The January rate of obligation by the Department or Agency shall not be increased except on complete justification and specific approval, unless such increases are clearly necessary to meet requirements fixed by law.

"There will be an immediate review directed toward recommendations for a downward adjustment of program levels and the probable effect of such adjustments.

"*Legislation.* Recommendations pertaining to the 1954 Budget are to include the possibilities of making adjustments in subsequent budgets where it appears advisable that legislation now in effect should be amended or repealed.

"New legislative proposals which affect financial requirements are to be reviewed in the light of these budget policies.

"*Timing.* All proposals for specific revisions of Department and Agency Budgets are expected to be transmitted to the Bureau of the Budget as early as possible in March for the consideration of the President."

(Footnote continued on following page)

THE PRESIDENT. By me? They are under consideration, I suppose in several departments. Not by me.

Q. G. Gould Lincoln, Washington Evening Star: Mr. President, this is a political question. Mr. Stevenson said in New York he fears that your administration might become a "big deal," because of the businessmen you have appointed to office. Do you have any such fear?

THE PRESIDENT. Do you? [*Laughter*]

Look—let me make myself clear, and I don't mean to brush off a question that easily. First of all, I am not going to engage in any semantics that are directed toward gaining fancied political advantage. I haven't time. What I should like to point out is this: I have lived with the American people. I have lived very intimately with those people, these youngsters, that we have sent out to fight our battles. I can't conceive of having to answer the accusation that I am not concerned with 158 million Americans.

Now we have a Defense Department that spends two-thirds of all the money we appropriate. And it seems to me if we are going to make a big savings in that place, we have got to get some businesslike practices there. I deliberately went out to find the men that I thought had made the biggest record for efficiency in business, to get into that department.

Now, in the other departments of the Government, I have tried to find people that I thought fitted, and I haven't paid the slightest attention to whether they were in business or not. I have tried to pick people on character, and I think they have character; I think they are going to do a grand job for the United States of America.

And with that little bit of—as he called it—political speech—with that, ladies and gentlemen, for the morning, goodbye; I will see you again.

NOTE: President Eisenhower's first news conference was held in the Executive Office Building at 10:30 a.m. on Tuesday, February 17, 1953.

13　¶ Letter to James W. Cothran, Commander in Chief, Veterans of Foreign Wars.
February 17, 1953

Dear Mr. Cothran:

I am most sorry that it is impossible for me to be with you this evening. The Annual Dinner Honoring Members of Congress Who Have Served in the Armed Forces is an occasion of real dignity and high purpose, in the honor it pays to those many men in Congress who have responded to their country's need with such distinction.

Quite naturally, I have a feeling of special comradeship with the Veterans of Foreign Wars who will be with you this evening, for so many of the service veterans in the Congress were associated with me in our Crusade in Europe. They have proved themselves to be not only fine soldiers but also statesmen. Their service overseas profoundly strengthened their capacity and understanding to meet the soberest problems of government.

I should like, with this greeting which I beg you to convey, to congratulate and salute them.

Sincerely,

DWIGHT D. EISENHOWER

14　¶ Letter to the President of the Senate and to the Speaker of the House of Representatives Transmitting a Proposed Resolution on Subjugated Peoples.　*February* 20, 1953

Dear ——————:

In my message to Congress of February 2, 1953, I stated that I would ask the Congress at a later date to join in an appropriate resolution, making clear that we would never acquiesce in the enslavement of any people in order to purchase fancied gain for ourselves, and that we would not feel that any past agreements committed us to any such enslavement.

In pursuance of that portion of the message to Congress, I now have the honor to inform you that I am concurrently informing the President of the Senate (the Speaker of the House) that I invite the concurrence of the two branches of the Congress in a declaration, in which I would join as President which would:

(1) Refer to World War II international agreements or understandings concerning other peoples;

(2) Point out that the leaders of the Soviet Communist Party who now control Russia, in violation of the clear intent of these agreements or understandings, subjected whole nations concerned to the domination of a totalitarian imperialism;

(3) Point out that such forceful absorption of free peoples into an aggressive despotism increases the threat against the security of all remaining free peoples, including our own;

(4) State that the people of the United States, true to their tradition and heritage of freedom, have never acquiesced in such enslavement of any peoples;

(5) Point out that it is appropriate that the Congress should join with the President to give expression to the desires and hopes of the American people;

(6) Conclude with a declaration that the Senate and the House join with the President in declaring that the United States rejects any interpretations or applications of any international agreements or understandings, made during the course of World War II, which have been perverted to bring about the subjugation of free peoples, and further join in proclaiming the hope that the peoples, who have been subjected to the captivity of Soviet despotism, shall again enjoy the right of self-determination within a framework which will sustain the peace; that they shall again have the right to choose the form of government under which they will live, and that sovereign rights of self-government shall be restored to them all in accordance with the pledge of the Atlantic Charter.

I am enclosing a form of draft resolution, which, in my opinion, carries out the purposes outlined above, and in which I am prepared to concur.

Sincerely,

DWIGHT D. EISENHOWER

NOTE: This is the text of identical letters addressed to the Honorable Richard M. Nixon, President of the Senate, and to the Honorable Joseph W. Martin, Jr., Speaker of the House of Representatives.

The draft resolution is published in House Document 93 (83d Cong., 1st sess.).

15 ¶ The President's News Conference of *February* 25, 1953.

THE PRESIDENT. Ladies and gentlemen, there is one announcement this morning that I think would be of interest to all of you. It is a conference that is to open tomorrow morning at 10 o'clock. It will be composed of a group of Governors, leaders from both the House and the Senate, and certain individuals of the administration.

The purpose of the conference is to examine into a question that constantly recurs, sometimes in aggravated form. It is the question of the proper division of functions between the State and the Federal Government, and the consequent division of tax fields and tax revenues between these two echelons of government.

It is, as you can see, not a subject that is susceptible to any clean-cut, quick answer. But it is one that must be studied. And this first group will meet to work out ways and means for continuing the study and making effective such conclusions as it may reach.

The President of the Governors' Conference is Governor Shivers. He will be here. The Chairman of the subcommittee set up by the Governors to study the question, I believe, is Governor Driscoll; he will be here, with Governor Kohler. And there is one other—[*confers with Mr. Hagerty*]—oh yes— Governor Byrnes of South Carolina. So that group with, as I say, three of the House leaders and three of the Senate leaders and three Cabinet officers, will start meeting with me at 10 o'clock and stay through lunch—they will be my luncheon guests tomorrow.

Now, there is only one other item that I have—specifically I thought you might take a real interest in. This question of doctors in the United States has been very troublesome, particularly since the Korean war started. The services have demanded so many, because of the needs of the campaign. However, the services have been reviewing their requirements and have reduced them for this last quarter; and the quota of doctors called in will be 1200 instead of 1800.

In order to make this study, they have had the benefit of, I believe it is called, the Medical Advisory Commission; Dr. Rusk, as I remember, is Chairman.[1] They have been advocating that the services get along with somewhat fewer numbers of doctors.

They are going to try it this quarter. They believe they will make it but at least they are going to relieve 600 doctors in this coming last quarter.

Now, I think that's the only two points I had in my own mind that I thought might be of particular interest, so we will start the questions.

Q. Merriman Smith, United Press: Mr. President, would you give us the three Cabinet officers who will participate?

THE PRESIDENT [*to Mr. Hagerty*]. Do you have them?

Mr. Hagerty: Secretary of the Treasury, Director of the Budget, and Federal Security Administrator.

THE PRESIDENT. I shouldn't have called them all Cabinet officers but I refer to them in that way because they all attend Cabinet meetings.

---

[1] The Health Resources Advisory Committee of which Dr. Howard A. Rusk was Chairman was established in the Office of Defense Mobilization to advise and assist the Director on problems of the Nation's health relating to national mobilization.

Q. Robert J. Donovan, New York Herald Tribune: Mr. President, what subjects will this conference consider besides taxes?

THE PRESIDENT. The proper function—particularly in this whole field of security, old age insurance, and all of the social security program—what are the proper functions of a State; what are the proper functions of Federal Government? They will take these related questions up and try to decide——

Q. Mr. Donovan: Resources—would resources enter into it?

THE PRESIDENT. I have no doubt they will touch on everything. There will be certainly no limitations on what they may properly take up.

Q. Edward H. Sims, Columbia (S.C.) State and Record: Mr. President, have you gone into it thoroughly enough to know whether you favor a continuation of the soil conservation payments?

THE PRESIDENT. Well, there is one thing certain: I do believe in soil conservation. And I believe that we must pay far more attention to it, and far more intelligent attention. This morning I met with a group that was, I guess, a third the size of this, who are here on this great task. A volunteer group, they carefully identified themselves as a nonpressure group, interested only in the conservation of soil and water, particularly by the system, you know, of basin development and conservation. And they are meeting today with the Secretary of Agriculture, the Secretary of the Interior, and others. All of us have this problem up—it is a very live one.

I cannot say that I specifically approve at this moment of the continuation of certain payments in a certain line—may be better ways to do it. I do believe the Federal Government must take the lead and follow through on this problem.

Q. Sarah McClendon, Texas papers: I have a question along that same line, sir. Do you favor keeping the building of upstream dams for soil conservation in the Department of Agriculture?

THE PRESIDENT. Well, I'll tell you, I have a very definite personal opinion on the question you asked me. It has not at this moment been studied by my associates who should appropriately take it up and come to advise me, because I could easily be mistaken. I will see whether I can answer that question at the next meeting.

Q. Paul Martin, Gannett papers: Could you tell us your attitude, sir, on the St. Lawrence Seaway and power project?

THE PRESIDENT. No, I cannot.

I don't mean to be evasive. I have had it under study. There are so many controversial factors, and they seem to vary geographically as to their content, that I just think it takes a longer time than I have had to reach a real decision.

Q. [*Speaker unidentified*]: Mr. President, would you care to comment on the statement by Mr. Dodge, the Budget Director, before the Senate Banking and Currency Committee, that it would be very difficult to balance the budget in 1954?

THE PRESIDENT. I don't know who said it, I didn't quite understand you, but I'll tell you this——

Q. It was reported in the press yesterday that Mr. Dodge testified to that effect.

THE PRESIDENT. Of course it is going to be difficult to balance the budget. If it weren't difficult, it would have been done long ago, because no one wants an unbalanced budget, I hope.

It is a most difficult task, because far over and beyond those projects and programs which are contained in the budget, that you have seen in the budget proposals, there are other projects, some of which look to the casual observer to be terrifically important, are not even budgeted for; lying behind all of the things we are doing, and plan to do, are other things that you can easily point up are desirable to do.

So it is a terrifically difficult thing to balance this budget, to get income and outgo balanced, and still do all the things that we need to do; that's the point I am trying to make, because there are so many other things to do, if you had any surplus.

Q. Robert Spivack, New York Post: Mr. President, do you think that Senator McCarthy's investigation of the Voice of

America is helping the fight against communism?

THE PRESIDENT. Well, I don't know exactly what he is aiming to do, but I would say this: it is a question that I will not answer without a bit more preparation on the thing, because I just haven't thought about his particular function—what he can do and what would happen if he didn't do it. So it's a question that I can't answer.

Q. [*Speaker unidentified*], Washington Evening Star: Do you think it would be unwise for Congress to be more specific in changing your resolution on World War II agreements?

THE PRESIDENT. Well, I am certainly not one to say that none of my proposals can be improved by the combined wisdom of a number of others. At the same time, I do believe this very clearly: we want to know exactly what we are doing when we propose anything in the form of a congressional resolution. For example, I personally believe we might be in a very awkward situation with respect to a few spots in this world—Berlin and Vienna—if you would just say we repudiate all agreements we have ever made during the war. I think that what the United States repudiates is the idea that we will agree to the enslavement of any other people.

Our whole tradition is one here of being an asylum for the politically persecuted, and for supporting people that want to be free and rule their own destinies. That is our record.

Take the Philippines, an enormously rich area; as quickly as we thought they were capable of self-government we moved out.

I believe that the United States, by and large, is just as concerned about those people as it is possible to be, and therefore we ought to state so; because without such a statement, I think those people forget. They say "we are forgotten," and I don't think we can afford to let them think that they are forgotten.

Q. Mrs. May Craig, Maine papers: Mr. President, in your letter to the Speaker, you spoke of Russia having violated the clear intent and having perverted. There is a good deal of criticism of your two predecessors having made those agreements. Do you think they could have foreseen this perversion and violation?

THE PRESIDENT. Oh, I think I have made it quite clear, Mrs. Craig, before a number of such press conferences, that I have no interest in going back and raking up the ashes of the dead past. I think there is little to be gained by such things, except as we can find lessons for improving in the future.

Now I think it was perfectly right, in the past years, to try to establish a method of friendship, of working through friendship, of finding this thing that Latin scholars call a "modus vivendi." Of course we should have sought it. But, as it is now, we believe that there has been twisted interpretation—distortion—and we should make ourselves clear, that's all. I am not trying to criticize.

Q. Roscoe Drummond, Christian Science Monitor: Mr. President, Senator Taft remarked this week, in connection with the congressional investigation, that he thought that Communists who might be teachers in the schools should not be automatically fired unless it was demonstrated that they were using their position to influence the thinking of the students on the subject of communism. I would like to ask if you share this view, or would be willing to comment on it?

THE PRESIDENT. Well, Mr. Drummond, there are certain things that are personal, personal in the terms of practicality—feasibility. Now I have no doubt that most—say almost 100 percent of Americans—would like to stamp out all traces of communism in our country; it is methods of approaching it.

Now, for myself—I don't mind telling you, for it's a matter of record—I went to Columbia as its President, and I insisted on one thing, that the facts of all philosophies and doctrines of government should be taught there, including communism; the facts should be taught; but that if we had a known Communist in our faculty and he could not be discharged because of anything else, I was automatically discharged. I personally would not be a party to an organism where there was a known card-carrying Communist in such a responsible position as teaching our young a philosophy, because there it becomes preaching, it is exhortation, it is doctrine as opposed to teaching facts.

Q. Mr. Drummond: One thing more, then.   I think perhaps the Senator was referring to Communists who might be teaching mathematics or calculus or something like that.   His view was——

THE PRESIDENT. Well, again, Mr. Drummond, it is not quite so simple as you think.   I was shown a book, just after the close of World War II; it was a German textbook in arithmetic. Now, instead of having the traditional apples or bushels of wheat, and so on, to deal with in the problems, it was problems couched in this language: "if there are so many Sudeten Germans in Czechoslovakia who actually belong to Mr. Hitler," and so on.   So you can use mathematics to be rather doctrinal.

Q. Barnet Nover, Denver Post: Do you plan to recommend early congressional action on statehood for Alaska?

THE PRESIDENT. I believe the Republican Platform says that Alaska's situation will be studied, to make a determination as to whether or not statehood should be recommended and granted. I think in the case of Hawaii the case has been proved.   It's a large population, it has a broad local industry to support it, a broad tax base; they provided fighting men in the war that made a fine record, and in numbers.   The case has been proved.

To my mind, not yet has the Alaskan case been completely proved.   It is more of a dependency than it is a separate and self-supporting region.   I think the cases are not the same, so I am not yet prepared to make such a recommendation.

Q. Fletcher Knebel, Cowles Publications: Mr. President, at the time of your inauguration, stories were printed that you had told friends you would not run for a second term.   Have you in fact made a decision, or imparted it to anyone?

THE PRESIDENT. Very naturally, I wouldn't make a serious declaration on such a subject at this moment.   I probably have made as many facetious remarks as I thought my friends could bear. I have said nothing seriously on the subject. [*Laughter*]

Q. Raymond P. Brandt, St. Louis Post-Dispatch: Mr. President, have your studies reached the point where you can say anything about the reciprocal trade agreements act, whether you want it extended "as is," or whether you would eliminate the peril points and the escape clauses?

THE PRESIDENT. No—I can't say that, and I don't believe that I have heard anyone say yet that you could just extend it exactly "as is." But on the other hand, I think that some kind of peril point or escape clause must be contained; because to me that represents somewhat the middle way in this thing, and you cannot go wholly one way nor the other.

Q. Mr. Brandt: On that point, would you liberalize it or make it stricter? Now some of the Congressmen would make it very strict, and others would give you greater discretion in considering a broader picture, such as they did in the Swiss watches, garlic, and so forth.

THE PRESIDENT. Well, I really can't answer it in such specific terms this morning. I can only say this: that we must never be in the position of being too wise for the moment, and hurting ourselves for the long pull. And I think, however, that our Congress can see such a point as well as can the administration. I would certainly hope to make them see such a view, but as to exactly how that idea will crystallize into law, I cannot yet foresee.

Q. Merriman Smith, United Press: Mr. President, can you comment on the break in relations between Russia and Israel?

THE PRESIDENT. No, I have no study on it at all.

Q. [*Speaker unidentified*]: Mr. President, going back to Roscoe Drummond's questions, would you comment on what you regard the role of Congress—on what investigating powers, in your judgment, it should have in the field of education, specifically Communists in education?

THE PRESIDENT. I think that it would be extremely dangerous to try to limit the power of Congress to investigate. I think it is one of those things that, in the long run, as we trust the will of the American people to produce the best answer for America, then I think in the long run this power in the hands of Congress—which they must have—must be treated properly and used properly by their long-term self-restraint, let us say, in bringing always into the problem moral values as well as strictly legal and constitutional values. Now I can't answer it more specifically than that, because it's one of those questions not capable of being answered. I can have an idea how they ought to use it at the moment, but I would certainly be the last to attempt to curtail their power.

Q. [*Speaker unidentified*]: Mr. President, in terms of the methods of congressional committee investigations, there have been three speeches from the pulpit, two of them Sunday, and one yesterday by Bishop Oxnam, criticizing the methods and procedures of congressional investigating committees, not—and take the same position that you do, that the power of investigation not be curtailed. Could you be more specific in terms of your opinion of the methods that are being adopted by congressional committees now in the investigative field, and may I add, too, that two congressional resolutions, one by Senator Kefauver and another by Senator Morse, have been introduced recommending improvements in the methods and safeguards for witnesses testifying before such committees. Have you any comment in a specific fashion on the methods?

THE PRESIDENT. I hope that you will allow me to remind you that this is a coordinate branch of Government that you are asking me to comment about. They establish their own rules within their constitutional rights and responsibilities, and they follow them.

Now, frankly, I think it would be completely inappropriate for me to comment specifically on individuals in Congress and their methods, because presumably the Congress approves these, or they wouldn't go on. I don't mind repeating what I have said as often as I have spoken publicly about this subject: I believe there is power in the Federal Government to defend itself against subversion, and against any kind of internal disease, if it wants to put

66

its heart into it. But I believe also that we must never think that we are protecting the United States, at the same time destroying or attacking those values which have made it great. One of those values is the right of the individual to be innocent until proved guilty.

Now, that's all I will say on the subject.

Q. [*Speaker unidentified*], Washington Daily News: Do you plan to name a District Commissioner soon?

THE PRESIDENT. As a matter of fact, I am not certain, and I don't think I should discuss it. Next week, though, I will try to give you an exact answer.

Q. Robert J. Donovan, New York Herald Tribune: Mr. President, on a somewhat lighter vein, you have been in office now for a month. I wonder if you would tell us a little bit about how you like your new job? [*Laughter*] I don't think you have expressed yourself on the subject?

THE PRESIDENT. I should say or remind you, sir, that in the many months, indeed the many years that I talked about such a prospect—even in those days when I thought I had removed it forever by a letter that I wrote—I never said I would like it. It is not a job that I suppose it is intended one should like.

I merely say this: like everything else there are compensations. It is an inspiration to deal with people that believe in America, that want to do right by a country and by a people, rather than merely selfishly seeking their own welfare. I honestly believe that in Government today I find the selfless class really far overwhelming what I would call the strictly selfish group. So to that extent, at least, there is a very great satisfaction. Now the confinement, and all the rest—those of you that have gone with me for years, you know the degree in which I like informality, my own individual freedom to do as I please. Those things are what you pay.

Q. [*Speaker unidentified*]: Mr. President, can you comment on your attitude toward UMT legislation?

THE PRESIDENT. Since the days when I first studied this problem as a postwar thing, it has gone through many changes. Before I came home from Europe in 1945, I could not conceive of this country ever again allowing itself to be caught in the position that we were when we went into war in 1942. None of us here that were war reporters or soldiers in those days, I think, can ever quite forgive ourselves for not making certain that our youth were properly trained before they went into Africa. There are many, many homes today that are bereaved because we did so fail.

Now, as to the exact position today of UMT, while we are having this kind of a draft call to prosecute a fairly major war over in Korea, I am not prepared to say. It is a little confused for me, and I am awaiting final studies. There is a commission, as you know, working on that problem. I think that commission probably differs a little bit. They think it can be done simultaneously; I don't quite see how it can be done, and I am waiting on those studies.

I do say this: never will you find me hesitant in speaking up for the discharge of the responsibility America has to train its own youth in this day and time, until we can reach the happy day when we don't have to fear force, and the threat of force, like we do now.

Q. [*Speaker unidentified*]: Mr. President, going back to the question about reciprocal trade. On domestic policy, you spoke of the natural workings of economic law, I wonder what the application of that philosophy is to our foreign trade laws.

THE PRESIDENT. Of course, Henry Ford's speech the other day wants you to go the full way—each nation making exactly what it can make best; and through the trade of these economically produced articles throughout the world, everybody's living standards will presumably go up.

There is one factor that I should like to call to your attention, and that is this: the terrific importance this business of trade and partial self-sufficiency, at least in the industrial field, has for national security. One of the difficulties in Europe all these many years has been this: each government has found it necessary to produce all the articles that an army or navy might need, and consequently they have been forced into an unnatural economic framework. The pattern has not been good.

Suppose France got into war with some other nation. Now, France, let us say, does not make clothing, does not make certain other things, due to the free operation of economic law. Now, under the laws of neutrality, how can she get clothes for her soldiers, and how can she do anything in this field during the war? So they have been forced to try to achieve self-sufficiency, and that one thing puts a certain limit upon this free working of the economic law in the international field.

Now, there are other factors that come into it, and of course the age-old argument is that it is cheap labor competing with our labor of higher standards. I do believe that we must keep our people on the highest possible standards—certainly standards that compare with the rest of our economy throughout.

Q. Do you believe, then, Mr. President, that considerations of national security are the chief limiting factors on——

THE PRESIDENT. No, I don't say it's the chief limit; I say it's a very obvious one and that therefore when you go full-out into this field, it will have to be in a world in which you have confidence that we are going to have peace.

Q. Robert E. Clark, International News Service: Stalin is quoted a few weeks ago as saying that he would look favorably on a face-to-face meeting with you. Do you think anything could be accomplished by such a meeting at this time? Would you be willing to go out of this country to meet with Stalin?

THE PRESIDENT. Well, you are asking me in advance either to say I think there is a good chance, or isn't a good chance.

I will say this: I would meet anybody, anywhere, where I thought there was the slightest chance of doing any good, as long as it was in keeping with what the American people expect of their Chief Executive. In other words, I wouldn't want to just say, "Yes, I will go anywhere." I would go to any suitable spot, let's say halfway between, and talk with anybody, and with the full knowledge of our allies and friends as to the kind of thing I was talking about, because this business of defending freedom is a big job. It is not just one nation's job.

Q. Andrew F. Tully, Jr., Scripps-Howard Newspapers: Mr. President, would you have any faith in any promises or agreements that Stalin entered into?

THE PRESIDENT. This is what I believe: any worthwhile programs for peace in the future must provide some kind of terms and provisions that make certain it is a self-enforcing treaty; that is, ample provisions for the kind of inspections and the kind of things that leave no doubt as to what will happen.

Q. [*Speaker unidentified*], New York Times: Mr. President, can you give us any idea of when your order on the new loyalty program may be ready for issuance?   That has been held up for some weeks.

THE PRESIDENT. Of course, that is in the hands of somebody else working on it, so I can't give you the exact time.   The only thing I can say is they are working very hard, and I think it ought to be ready quite soon.

[*Speaker unidentified*]: Thank you, Mr. President.

NOTE: President Eisenhower's second news conference was held in the Ex-   ecutive Office Building at 12:15 p.m. on Wednesday, February 25, 1953.

16   ¶ Statement by the President Concerning the Need for a Presidential Commission on Federal-State Relations.   *February 26, 1953*

FOR A LONG TIME I have thought that there must be a clarification of the responsibilities of the State and Federal governments in many fields of public activity. The Federal Government has assumed an increasing variety of functions, many of which originated or are duplicated in State Government.

Another phase of this problem relates to taxation. The existing systems of taxation, both at the Federal and State level, contain many gross inequalities insofar as the tax burden between citizens of different states is concerned. There is often a pyramiding of taxation, State taxes being superimposed upon Federal taxes in the same field.

The development of the Federal Social Security system warrants study. This analysis should encompass not only the distribution of costs between the State and Federal government but also the operation and coverage of the system itself. It is a proper function of government to help build a sturdy floor over the pit of personal disaster, and to this objective we are all committed. However, we are equally committed to carrying out that great program efficiently and with greatest benefit to those whom it is designed to help.

The purpose of the meeting to which you are invited is to discuss with me proposed legislation providing for the creation of the Commission, the manner of its procedure, financial support and other related matters, and the selection of a working staff in order to accomplish the purposes of the study.

NOTE: The White House release of which this statement was a part announced that the President had met on February 26 with representatives of the Congress and the Governors' Conference, and with members of the administration. At the meeting the President proposed the establish-ment of a bipartisan Presidential commission on Federal-State relations. On March 30, in a special message to the Congress the President formally recommended the establishment of such a commission (see Item 39).

17 ¶ Remarks Recorded for the Opening of the Red Cross Campaign. *March 1, 1953*

[Broadcast over national radio and television networks]

My fellow citizens:

The American Red Cross is one of the free institutions which has helped to make this country great.

What people do through the Red Cross, they do in the spirit of free men and women voluntarily giving of themselves to help their neighbors in time of personal tragedy, disaster, or emergency.

There are 3,700 Red Cross chapters making up one American Red Cross—your Red Cross.

I have here at the White House three guests whose personal experiences have given them a vivid understanding of what the Red Cross means.

Here is Captain Bernard Abrams who served in Korea as a company commander in the Third Division. Captain Abrams tells me that Red Cross field directors and Army chaplains always got to his unit when there were personal or family problems to handle for his men. And when he, himself, was critically wounded he received large quantities of plasma and blood.

And I have with me little Susie Giardina of Brooklyn, New York, who suffers from Cooley's anemia. She is 6½ years old. In the past 4 years she has received nearly 150 pints of blood donated through the Red Cross. She is still receiving blood each month.

My third guest is Miss Barbara Hussey who served as a recreation worker in hospitals in Korea during the bitterest of the fighting.

The men and women of the Red Cross give their time and their skill and the hard work of their hands, but only you and I— all the people acting together—can give them the resources they need to carry on the great work.

This year the Red Cross needs $93 million to do its job. It also must collect five million pints of blood—for the Armed Forces, for civil defense, for civilian sick and injured—and for those most precious civilians of all—our children. For now the Red Cross joins in the fight against infantile paralysis by providing gamma globulin which helps to prevent the crippling effects of polio.

This year your Red Cross serves the men and women of a military establishment nearly 3,600,000 strong—many of them still enduring the rigors and dangers of Korean combat.

Your Red Cross will serve in an unknown number of disasters. No one knows where these calamities will take place. But everyone knows that the Red Cross will be there.

My fellow Americans, I know the Red Cross. I have known it in peace and in two world wars. Whatever the time or the need, it is dedicated to strengthening the Nation by helping people to help themselves and their neighbors. It is ready to serve. But only we—the American people—can keep it ready.

I feel that it is one of our American privileges to support the 1953 Fund Appeal of the American Red Cross.

18 ¶ Statement Following Discussions With Prince Faisal, Foreign Minister of Saudi Arabia. *March 2, 1953*

THE PRESIDENT received His Royal Highness Prince Faisal, Foreign Minister of Saudi Arabia, today at the White House. During the meeting matters of mutual interest to Saudi Arabia and the United States were discussed. The President expressed his great pleasure at having the opportunity of receiving so distinguished a representative of a country with which the United States enjoys especially close relations. He expressed his concern over some evidence that there had lately occurred a deterioration in relations between the Arab nations and the United States. He stated that it would be his firm purpose to seek to restore the spirit of confidence and trust which had previously characterized these relations and he hoped that the Arab leaders would be inspired by the same purpose.

The President alluded to the many strong educational and cultural ties which had developed between the Arab world and the United States over a period of many decades and stated that he was confident that this provided a foundation of good will on which to build during the coming years to mutual advantage.

The President also emphasized his great personal interest in the welfare and progress of Saudi Arabia and the other States in the Near East. The President requested Prince Faisal to convey his cordial greetings to His Majesty King Abdul Aziz Ibn Saud.

19 ¶ Citation Accompanying the Distinguished Service Medal Presented to General Van Fleet. *March 3, 1953*

THE PRESIDENT of the United States of America, authorized by Act of Congress July 9, 1918, has awarded the Distinguished Service Medal, Third Oak Leaf Cluster, to

GENERAL JAMES A. VAN FLEET, USA

for exceptionally meritorious service in a duty of great responsibility:

General James A. Van Fleet, United States Army, distinguished himself by exceptionally meritorious service to the United States Government and the United Nations in a position of great trust and grave responsibility during the period 14 April 1951 to 11 February 1953. Commanding the Eighth United States Army in Korea and exercising operational control over the forces of the Republic of Korea and those of sixteen United Nations, General Van Fleet's outstanding services have been instrumental in furthering the United Nations' resistance to the Communist armed aggression against the peace and freedom of the world.

DWIGHT D. EISENHOWER

NOTE: The Distinguished Service Medal, Third Oak Leaf Cluster, was presented by the President to General Van Fleet at the White House.

74

20 ¶ Statement by the President Concerning the Illness of Joseph Stalin. *March 4, 1953*

AT THIS MOMENT in history when multitudes of Russians are anxiously concerned because of the illness of the Soviet ruler the thoughts of America go out to all the peoples of the U.S.S.R.—the men and women, the boys and girls—in the villages, cities, farms and factories of their homeland.

They are the children of the same God who is the Father of all peoples everywhere. And like all peoples, Russia's millions share our longing for a friendly and peaceful world.

Regardless of the identity of government personalities, the prayer of us Americans continues to be that the Almighty will watch over the people of that vast country and bring them, in His wisdom, opportunity to live their lives in a world where all men and women and children dwell in peace and comradeship.

21 ¶ Statement by the President on the Occasion of the Swearing In of Val Peterson as Administrator, Federal Civil Defense Administration. *March 4, 1953*

THE TASK of civil defense is vital to our national life. It demands a preparedness that can do more than limit the damage of a wartime disaster. It means developing a preparedness, a vigilance, so impressive as to deter aggression itself.

Here—as throughout our national policy—we must act from a lesson learned at terrible cost. That lesson is: to serve our reasoned hope for the best, we must be ready steadfastly to meet the worst.

There is no other way to confront the despot, no other language to talk to the aggressor.

This awareness must touch every community, every citizen, of our land. The recruiting, training and organizing of volunteers competent to meet any emergency are tasks largely of our state and local governments.

The responsibility of the Federal Government is to provide leadership. This entails more than the stockpiling of supplies and furnishing of technical guidance. It demands inspiring our whole citizenry to be alert to their collective task.

I am happy that the direction of this vital work of the Federal Government is now entrusted to so able and dedicated a public servant as Governor Val Peterson, our new Federal Defense Administrator.

22   ¶ The President's News Conference of *March* 5, 1953.

THE PRESIDENT. Well, ladies and gentlemen, I have little of my own repertoire that I want to present this morning.

I think that the one subject that is engaging the attention of the world today, more than any other, is the illness of Generalissimo Premier Stalin, and its possible effect upon the struggle that has been going on so long between the free world and the Communist world.

I did issue a statement yesterday, to express the hope—which I believe is that of all America—that no matter what these personalities are, who they may be, that all of us will seriously pursue the goal of peace, to see whether or not we cannot resolve questions so that real progress can be made.

As to the effect this change in Russia will have upon us, upon this whole struggle, I cannot say. Of course, we discuss it—all of us, my most intimate advisers. We take the various possibilities and we end up largely where we started, I imagine just as you folks do.

But in all of the possibilities, we all must—as I see it—cling to the one determination: to make progress in this line.

Two other subjects I have meant to mention briefly: one was reorganization, which you know we have been working very hard on. It is progressing, and I think that next week the first of our plans will be ready to go before the Congress. Not that it has priority of itself, but merely because it is more nearly ready to go than any other. It will involve the Federal Security Agency, and will be presented, I think, next week.

The other item was just to make a comment about the removal of price controls. I have been gratified to see that there has been little discernible evidence that anyone is trying to gouge, or take advantage of the situation. There has been a moderation and a restraint observed that I think have been noticeable and admirable.

The only real price change was one that everybody knew would occur, which was in copper, in which we had a control price of 24½ cents and the world price was considerably higher. There has been a shift upward of 6 or 7 cents a pound, I think, in our own domestic market, or a little less in some cases. But in any event, it inspires, or you might say it certainly confirms, my belief that the American people are ready to be considerate, to be moderate. I am very hopeful that there is going to be a climate established that will involve labor-management relations and all of the other difficult problems here at home, which will minimize the inflationary pressures on our economy.

That is to be done, and can be done, as I see it, only as each of us, all of us, tries to weigh his opportunity for immediate gain against the long-term good of the country—which means the long-term good of all of us. And I hope that the experience, so far, in this removal of price control gives renewed evidence that we are not entirely naive in looking for such a development in all fields.

Now, with those brief comments, we will start the questions.

Q. Merriman Smith, United Press: Mr. President, in view of what seems to be an inevitable change in Russian leadership, do you think that such a change will worsen or improve the anti-Semitic situation which Russia seems responsible for now?

THE PRESIDENT. Well, no, I can't tell, of course; and it would be foolish to give anything that would appear to be an authoritative conclusion. Here is something that has come up that is distressing to all of us. We deplore it. In a way it is heartbreaking, particularly so for one who, like myself, had so much experience with the horror camps of World War II, and saw these remnants of these people of this same faith and blood ground down to nothing but just remnants of humanity.

And to think of that going on again, it is—it is rather depressing; it's worse—it's just heartbreaking, as I said.

Now, as to exactly what effect this change will have on that, Mr. Smith, I am just not prepared to say. But certainly, we can hope for the best. And you are even puzzled as to whether it is wise to say anything, because anything that one in my position might say could be used as an excuse to make these conditions worse. So it comes down to it that it is a part, again, of this whole world effort that we are making, and which is going to be successful only as all America—indeed, all the free world—keeps its heart right into the job.

Q. [*Speaker unidentified*]: Mr. President, will the discussion with Foreign Secretary Eden now be broadened to include eventualities in connection with this illness of Premier Stalin?

THE PRESIDENT. I would scarcely say broadened, and I would scarcely talk about eventualities, for the reason that whatever is going to happen is going to happen inside of the Soviet Union. We would have nothing to do about that. We might, say, discuss some of the results or possible consequences. But as I say, only time can foretell what that can be.

The talks are informative. The British officials have come over here to apprise us of certain developments in the Commonwealth conferences of some months back, and they are not intended to be the basis of an immediate agreement of any kind. So these talks will be informative for us. I think there will be a communique issued—probably a joint one, when they have finished these conferences. That is about all I can say.

Q. [*Speaker unidentified*]: Did you discuss the economic aspects of Anglo-American relations with Mr. Eden yesterday or, specifically, the illness of Premier Stalin?

THE PRESIDENT. Well, all I discussed in the world was old friendships—he brought me greetings from an old friend of mine, the Prime Minister—we had a friendly talk, and then we discussed the world situation as we saw it, the identity of our hopes in many ways, but nothing that was specific enough to make the subject of a talk here at all.

Q. Douglas Cornell of United—Associated Press—[*loud and prolonged laughter*]. Going back to old relations of my own.

I would like to ask you, sir, whether you favor the adherence to the wording of the enslavement resolution as you originally presented it, or whether it is satisfactory to you the way the Senate has now changed it?

THE PRESIDENT. Well, I think I mentioned last week that I had sent a resolution to Congress that I thought was representative of the convictions of the American people in their refusal to recognize the enslavement of any people. I also said at that time, as I recall, that I had no particular authorial pride, and if it was found necessary to change some wording, I had no objection.

Now, on the other hand, there has developed, apparently, a sort of technical difference on the Hill as how best to express a certain thought. I think no one disagrees with the thought that has been put in this amendment. But how they settle it, I say, very definitely is their business. I would certainly hate to see the general meaning and tone of the resolution changed, but so far as I know, there is no such purpose.

Q. Roscoe Drummond, Christian Science Monitor: Mr. President, may I ask whether you feel that it would be wiser to have no resolution than to have one which could only pass by a narrow vote because of partisan differences?

THE PRESIDENT. Well, Mr. Drummond, I don't believe that I want to express a very definite conviction. I would want to see the thing exactly, know all the circumstances. But I do believe this: unless we are successful in showing that here is a thought that expresses the mass opinion of America, then it is no good.

In any dealing in a foreign problem, if America is 50–50 in looking at this, or 51 percent–49 percent, then the person abroad with whom you are dealing, or the individual, or situation, or atmosphere, is not much affected.

Q. Mr. Drummond: May I ask another question, Mr. President? May I ask whether, in view of the news from Moscow, you are considering sending Mr. Bohlen to Moscow somewhat earlier than might otherwise be the case?

THE PRESIDENT. I haven't discussed the thought, this is the first time it has occurred to me. I haven't considered it up to this moment.

Q. James B. Reston, New York Times: I wondered, sir, if you would comment on the Iranian situation, and especially whether you had made any appeal to the Shah or to the Prime Minister there recently?

THE PRESIDENT. I exchanged greetings with the Prime Minister before the inauguration, to assure him of our continued friendly interest in that region. Since this latest difficulty has arisen, I have not personally sent any message, although, of course, our whole Government watches this with the closest attention. It is a very delicate situation, and since it is an internal one, there is little that any outsider can do, even when they intend to be very helpful.

We have a lot of hopes, of course, that this thing will straighten itself out, but it is, to say the least, delicate.

Q. Mr. Reston: Do you regard the activities of the Tudeh

Party—the Communist Party in Iran—as an internal situation?

THE PRESIDENT. We may not. But in any country where a Communist Party is recognized, for them it is an internal situation. We would very greatly resent anyone coming in America from the outside and telling us what we should do about Communists; we think we know, or that would be our attitude. So for them, it is an internal situation, no matter where the inspiration for the Tudeh Party comes from.

Q. Leslie R. Honeycutt, Army Times: There have been reports, sir, that you are planning to name Congressman Kearney of New York to the post of Administrator of Veterans Affairs. Are those reports true?

THE PRESIDENT. This is the first time I have heard the name suggested in this connection.

Q. [*Speaker unidentified*]: Mr. President, you said last week that you would be willing to go halfway to a meeting with Stalin or other world leaders in the cause of peace. Does this hold for any Russian leader who might succeed Stalin?

THE PRESIDENT. So far as I can tell from this moment, yes; I have no feeling about this. If there is any way to promote the cause of peace, there is no personal inconvenience or sacrifice that I wouldn't make that I can think of. Now, the only thing that I would demand is, after all, that things be done in accordance with what America thinks is fitting to do and where there is, as I say, legitimate reason to believe that some advance can be made.

Q. Richard L. Wilson, Cowles Publications: Mr. President, I would like to put this question to you, about the resolution before Congress, a little more directly. Some people have interpreted the amendment which was made by the committee as representing a break between you and Senator Taft. Would you care to comment on that line of comment with regard to the resolution?

THE PRESIDENT. So far as I know, there is not the slightest sign of a rift or break between Senator Taft and me. And if anyone knows of any, I don't.

Q. Mr. Wilson: You are in complete agreement on the resolution?

THE PRESIDENT. I don't say the resolution itself. As to whether or not it was necessary to put in this particular point, I don't know. As I say, it is a technical point that arose. Everybody agrees on the sentiment. It's a technical point rather than one of substance.

Q. Pat Munroe, Albuquerque Journal: Mr. President, they have been getting careless with fire down in our State, and burned some ballots in the recent election—[*laughter*]—the Hurley-Chavez election. I wonder if you have any comment to make on the upcoming contest that General Hurley is making for the seat of Mr. Chavez in the Senate?

THE PRESIDENT. Well, I don't believe that the Executive has a single thing to do with such a contest. Is not a Senate committee completely responsible, a Senate group? I think they are, and it hasn't been brought to my attention.

I didn't know they had the fire. [*Laughter*]

Q. [*Speaker unidentified*], Christian Science Monitor: Do you feel the executive branch of the Government should make the loyalty files available to the legislative branch?

THE PRESIDENT. You bring up a technical question that has been bothering administrations and people for a good many years. I think there are certain types of papers that cannot be exposed to view. Now, whether or not the type of record that you are talking about can be properly turned over, I don't know. The subject has been under study by groups of the administration since we have come in, but no one has made a report to me.

Q. [*Speaker unidentified*], Washington Daily News: You indicated last week that you might have something to say today about the appointment of a District Commissioner. I wonder if you do?

THE PRESIDENT. I should like to. I will tell you this: it has been the subject of study and investigation, and search and research ever since you asked the question. We are not quite ready to make an announcement, I am sorry.

Q. Mrs. May Craig, Maine papers: Mr. President, going back to the enslavement resolution, quite apart from anything else, do you think that imminent change of leadership in Russia makes it more or less desirable to deal with that in Congress now?

THE PRESIDENT. Well, I have the feeling that Russia works out for itself a plan, and follows it. Little changes in the details of the foreign situation from their viewpoint, I believe, make little difference. I believe they follow a studied plan. Consequently, I don't think they would give too much importance over there to the timing of a resolution such as this.

What I really want to do is to put ourselves on record before all the world, including ourselves, that we never agreed to the enslavement of peoples that has occurred, and that as long as that condition persists, we see a danger to freedom and to ourselves in the world. That's all I am trying to do.

Q. [*Speaker unidentified*]: Mr. President, I would like to ask you two questions that are not quite related: first, in regard to the developments in Russia, is your feeling or the feeling of your advisers one of misgiving now, or one of optimism, as a result of the events in the last day or so?

THE PRESIDENT. I think it is a very definite watchfulness; that is the way I would express it.

Q. Now, the second question is on a somewhat different subject: I have been told that the Attorney General has advised you that in the Rosenberg case, that if the Rosenbergs were to discuss in full or tell in full all they know about Russian espionage, that their sentence would be commuted to life. Is that correct?

THE PRESIDENT. Well, I don't know how he could tell me that. I believe that I am the only person that can commute. So I don't know how anybody else could tell me they would do it.

Q. It has not been discussed then?

THE PRESIDENT. On all the evidence I had in front of me, I decided that the courts had done for these people everything possible, given them every right, and I was not going to interfere. If any other different situation arises that makes it look like a question of policy, of state policy, they can bring it back to me. As of now, my decision was made purely on the basis of what the courts had found in all this long discussion.

Q. Sarah McClendon, Beaumont Enterprise: There is some confusion, sir, about the submerged lands and the policy of the administration. Would you say if you still favor restoring full ownership to the States within historic boundaries?

THE PRESIDENT. Within historic boundaries?

Q. Mrs. McClendon: Yes sir.

THE PRESIDENT. Which doesn't mean, of course, that the Federal Government does not perform certain functions in that region. There are all sorts of things—security, smuggling, many other things that fall to the Federal Government to do—that they do in those regions, but up to historic boundaries, as far as I am concerned, that is State property.

Q. Mrs. McClendon: State property. All right, sir. The other question you promised last time you would have for me the answer this time. [*Laughter*] Do you favor retaining control and construction planning of upstream dams by the Soil Conservation Service within the Department of Agriculture?

THE PRESIDENT. In other words, your question is, do I favor keeping it in the Department of Agriculture, not some place else?

Q. Mrs. McClendon: Yes.

THE PRESIDENT. Well, that is the very point that is under study this moment. I have been informed by both Interior and Agriculture that they are not quite ready to report on it. I do say, as a matter of conviction, that I am very hopeful of getting it done in an efficient and effective manner, because I believe in this upstream conservation very much, as an individual. I don't know what either the Interior or Agriculture would say to me about that, but that is my view.

Q. Anthony H. Leviero, New York Times: The Attorney General has suggested some complications on offshore oil, and the one formula he offered before Congress was that the States be given the right to take out oil but not full title——

THE PRESIDENT. But not what?

Q. Mr. Leviero:——not full title to the deposits. Now, does that agree with your concept of it?

THE PRESIDENT. The Attorney General necessarily has to delve into the legal questions involved, but every State has within its historic boundaries certain public lands that belong to that State. Now, that is the way I look upon these lands. And I think I told you last week, or a couple of weeks ago, how my convictions on this thing were formed some years back when I studied the documents that had to do with the Texan admission into the Nation. I believe I can read English, and after I formed my conviction, I have never found anything to change it.

Q. Alan S. Emory, Watertown (N.Y.) Times: Last week you said you did not want to comment on the St. Lawrence Seaway proposition until the study made by certain Government agencies had been made available to you. However, in your Abilene speech of last June, if I remember correctly, you did endorse the St. Lawrence power project. Now, I would like to ask two closely allied questions: first, do you favor the proposition that New York develop the power jointly with the Province of Ontario; and secondly, have you communicated with, or do you intend to communicate to the Federal Power Commission your views on the situation, in view of the fact that the hearing on the power question has now ended?

THE PRESIDENT [*laughing*]. The St. Lawrence Waterway seems to reach into a lot of places. Actually, I have heard no objection to this proposition of power development with New York State, but on the other hand, there has been no finalized type of recommendation placed in front of me. And so I couldn't say that the administration is prepared to give a complete blessing or to abandon it.

As a matter of personal conviction, I still believe what I said in Abilene. I remember distinctly. I also said, at that time, that if the St. Lawrence Waterway was an economic necessity for our country, eventually it would come. It would make little difference what I thought about it; if it does turn out to be an economic necessity, it's bound to come someday.

Q. [*Speaker unidentified*]: Mr. President, I wonder if you would care to comment on the Bell report?

THE PRESIDENT. On the what?

Q. The Bell report on foreign trade, that you received yesterday?

THE PRESIDENT. He brought it in, and we discussed it only very briefly, so briefly that I don't believe it would be fair to comment. I must say this: I was certainly favorably impressed by the process which they had gone through, not only the membership of the commission, but the people to whom they turned it over for review, including among others John Williams, whom I admire greatly. While they had comments to make on it, the general reaction was favorable; so I would think in general it is probably a very, very good report, and worthy of study.[1]

Q. [*Speaker unidentified*], Akron Beacon Journal: Mr. President, this week the RFC sent you its recommendations for selling the Government synthetic rubber plants. Do you favor getting the Government out of the rubber business this year?

THE PRESIDENT. Well, the recommendation hasn't reached me yet; therefore I don't know any of the arguments on either side of the question. As all of you people know, I have reiterated time and again the generalization by which I live; I believe in getting the Federal Government out of everything it can legitimately get out of, but I don't know anything about this particular question.

Q. Merriman Smith, United Press: Mr. President, do you favor extension of the draft to 30 or 36 months, as General Van Fleet favors it?

---

[1] On March 3, the White House announced that Daniel W. Bell, Acting Chairman of the Public Advisory Board for Mutual Security, presented to the President the report of the special survey of United States trade policies. The study was initiated on July 13, 1952. The report is titled "A Trade and Tariff Policy in the National Interest: A Report to the President by the Public Advisory Board for Mutual Security" (Government Printing Office, 1953).

THE PRESIDENT. No.

Q. Glenn Thompson, Cincinnati Enquirer: Mr. President, do you have any information in anywise different from that that has been published about the state of Premier Stalin's health?

THE PRESIDENT. None.

Q. Edward T. Folliard, Washington Post: Mr. President, is there anything you can say about Korea, as a result of General Van Fleet's visit to the White House?

THE PRESIDENT. No. I think that every conclusion and conviction that we have had, formed over the late months, have been expressed publicly. I don't think there is anything new. Nothing that I can think of, anyway.

Q. [*Speaker unidentified*]: Mr. President, on your Federal Security reorganization, does that provide for the creation of a new Cabinet post—a new department of Government?

THE PRESIDENT. I certainly intend to recommend that. Now I am not certain whether it's right in the plan, whether that's the way it will be done or not, but I think so.

Q. If it's in that plan it will be——

THE PRESIDENT. I will certainly recommend it.

Q. Arthur Sylvester, Newark News: Mr. President, do you, by considering Iran an internal problem, relinquish the initiative to the Russian Communists operating through the Tudeh Party?

THE PRESIDENT. Very naturally—we are represented there. We do every single thing we can to protect the interests of the United States everywhere on the globe, including Iran. What I meant was, that it is not proper for me here to comment on things that are internal and which could be properly resented. But make no mistake: the reason we have representatives around the world is to protect American interests wherever they may be endangered or in difficulties.

Q. Mr. Sylvester: May I ask one other question? Do you consider that a field for your psychological warfare man, Mr. Jackson or whoever it may be?

THE PRESIDENT. I rather dislike the term "psychological warfare," although no one really has invented a better one. The United States is trying to present certain salient facts to the world, facts, for example, as to what our purpose is, our intent, what we are doing and what we are prepared to do to further those purposes. And they are not understood. All of you are familiar with stories of where we have tried to be helpful and have earned nothing but vituperation and criticism. What we are trying to do is to find some way of making effective all of the things we do in one concerted plan, of showing the world what this purpose, what these methods, what they are specifically—that we are not imperialistic, we are simply trying to help create a world in which free men can live decently.

Q. [*Speaker unidentified*]: Mr. President, do you think that Senator McCarthy's investigations into the Voice of America are furthering the purpose about which you just spoke?

THE PRESIDENT. I think last week I declined to speak about that point. I have always supported and insisted upon the right of the Congress to conduct such investigations as it sees fit. I think it is inherent in its powers and its responsibilities. Now, when it gets into fields in which I think some misunderstanding or damage or difficulty can arise, why, I have to watch it—do my best to show them my convictions. But I don't believe it is really a proper thing for me to be discussing publicly a coordinate branch of Government. If ever I find that necessary, it will be through some change of views. I try to avoid it.

Q. [*Speaker unidentified*], Washington Star: In connection with this—your reorganization of Federal Security—is the administration giving any—has it any plans concerning change of functions of any kind from the Veterans Administration to the FSA?

THE PRESIDENT. No—oh, as a matter of fact, there may be some tiny included thing; but in general, no.

Q. Health and education programs——

THE PRESIDENT. Not so far as I know.

[*Speaker unidentified*]: Thank you, Mr. President.

NOTE: President Eisenhower's third
news conference was held in the Executive Office Building at 10:30 a.m.
on Thursday, March 5, 1953.

23 ¶ Remarks to the American Retail Federation.
March 5, 1953

Ladies and gentlemen:

As I walked in, your president thanked me for taking the time
out of what I rightfully described as a busy day, to come over
here. I felt that I should thank him for doing just that, and
getting me out of the maelstrom I was glad to leave behind for
a bit.

Besides, I had a chore—a sort of obligation, a duty—that I
thought I might discharge here.

As you all know, my education in politics has been very short
but intense. I have been learning something of the functions of
the different sectors of our economy and of our Government.
And I learned that you people have been doing something for
the Government without getting paid for it: that you have been
collecting taxes for us. So I thought it would be no less than my
duty to come over and thank you most gratefully for those contributions, because I assure you they are needed these days, as far
as I can see.

I am not going to pretend to a wisdom in retailing and marketing that would justify my taking your time. I hope your meeting
here is profitable, and I hope also that you are having an enjoyable convention. But I am willing to call attention to one responsibility you people have, that I doubt that anyone else has
spoken about.

It is in the realm of memory. I see some of you here—I hate
to be insulting—who I could call contemporaries of mine. Now,
particularly if you came from the smaller towns and villages—
farming areas of our country—you have memories that are priceless. They so often centered around the retail store, the open

cracker barrel, the prune barrel, the pickle jug or keg. Places where things were sold and people gathered because they needed them. They were the social centers of our time.

And our memories today—since we know that man does not live by bread alone those memories are valuable. They center around that time, that place, those connections, those contacts.

This is what I want to know from the retailers of today: what are you doing to give the kids that are 6 years old to 12 similar memories when they are our age? Memories that will live with them?

Now, I think this important. I know that during Christmas time you get out the finest and biggest Santa Clauses with more pillows and more beards than they ever had in my time. As a matter of fact I don't think we had them then. But that is not quite enough. They have got to have something that so far as possible makes up for what we had. They have their television, but that they will have with them always. Those won't be their valuable memories. Something that brings about homely contacts with other Americans, where they learn something—something they carry with them—some proverb—even an aphorism.

I hope that the American retailers will not forget to sell memories. I don't think there's a lot of philosophy in this thought of mine, yet it is something that has some value.

Now, frankly, I came over to bid you welcome as representatives of a great portion of our economy and of our American life—a very necessary part; to come here and say how glad the administration is to see you here, to wish you a very enjoyable and fine time, to hope you will come again, that the sun will shine and everything will be wonderful while you are here. I came for nothing else, then I just got to talking, as I so often do. Thank you very much, and goodbye.

NOTE: The President spoke at the Statler Hotel in Washington at 1:00 p.m. In his opening words he re- ferred to Rowland Jones, Jr., president of the federation.

24 ¶ Message Conveying the Government's Official Condolences on the Death of Joseph Stalin.
March 5, 1953

THE GOVERNMENT of the United States tenders its official condolences to the Government of the U.S.S.R. on the death of Generalissimo Joseph Stalin, Prime Minister of the Soviet Union.

NOTE: This message, sent by the Secretary of State at the request of the President, was transmitted through the American Embassy to the Soviet Foreign Office.

25 ¶ Letter to Horace M. Albright Concerning a Mid-Century Conference on Resources.
March 6, 1953

[Released March 6, 1953. Dated March 2, 1953]

Dear Mr. Albright:

I have been most interested to learn from time to time that your arrangements for a mid-century Conference on Resources have been taking shape, and that you will hold early this spring a national meeting of sponsors to review plans and set the conference date.

As you know from our previous discussions, I believe the full and economical development of natural resources is essential to economic growth and national security. I hope the conservation movement, begun under President Theodore Roosevelt, will continue to prosper and grow in influence. This letter will assure you that you and your associates have my sincere wishes for a successful conference.

The demands placed upon our resource base of land, forests, minerals, fuels and water have been exceedingly great during recent years of war and defense preparation. The prospect for large continued requirements for resources and raw materials means we shall have to rely increasingly upon new sources, new technology and more rigorous conservation. Clearly, the Government, as well as private groups—including industry, agriculture, labor, conservation, education—has a considerable responsibility for the better management of resources. Accordingly, I am asking the Secretary of Agriculture, the Secretary of the Interior, and other Federal officials concerned with resources to render appropriate staff assistance in preparing for the conference.

I believe that private organizations, such as Resources for the Future, Inc., should be encouraged to undertake studies and promote discussion of national issues on a competent and nonpartisan basis, and I am sure that both the Executive Branch and the Congress will review with interest the conclusions reached.

I have been told that you contemplate extending to me an invitation to attend the conference. Barring some presently unforeseen circumstances, I think the chances are good of my being able to accept an invitation to express a word of welcome and appreciation.

Sincerely,

Dwight D. Eisenhower

NOTE: A letter from Mr. Albright, dated February 21, 1953, was released with the President's reply.

Mr. Albright served as President, Resources for the Future, Inc.

26 ¶ Statement by the President Following Meeting With Elliott Newcomb, Secretary General of the World Veterans Federation. *March 7,* 1953

I HAVE been greatly encouraged to learn from Mr. Newcomb of the progress made among these millions of veterans in support of the United Nations and its stand in Korea, as well as its support of European Unity and collective security against aggression. No one can deny the right of those who have fought in the defense of freedom to unite in its defense today. The participation of several of our American veterans' organizations in this international federation of millions of ex-servicemen from many nations is gratifying proof that veterans of our nation are aware of the necessity of mutual understanding and common effort among men of good will from many lands.

27 ¶ Citation Accompanying the Medal of Honor Presented to Corporal Duane E. Dewey. *March* 12, 1953

THE PRESIDENT of the United States in the name of The Congress takes pleasure in presenting the Medal of Honor to

CORPORAL DUANE E. DEWEY
UNITED STATES MARINE CORPS RESERVE,

for service as set forth in the following

CITATION:

For conspicuous gallantry and intrepidity at the risk of his life above and beyond the call of duty while serving as a Gunner in a Machine-Gun Platoon of Company E, Second Battalion, Fifth Marines, First Marine Division (Reinforced), in action against enemy aggressor forces near Panmunjom, Korea, on 16 April 1952. When an enemy grenade landed close to his position while he and his assistant gunner were receiving medical attention for their wounds during a fierce night attack by numerically superior hostile forces, Corporal Dewey, although suffering intense pain, immediately pulled the corpsman to the ground and, shouting a warning to the other Marines around him, bravely smothered the deadly missile with his body, personally absorbing the full force of the explosion to save his comrades from possible injury or death. His indomitable courage, outstanding initiative and valiant efforts in behalf of others in the face of almost certain death reflect the highest credit upon Corporal Dewey and enhance the finest traditions of the United States Naval Service.

DWIGHT D. EISENHOWER

NOTE: The medal was presented by the President in his office.

28 ¶ Special Message to the Congress Transmitting Reorganization Plan 1 of 1953 Creating the Department of Health, Education, and Welfare.   *March* 12, 1953

To the Congress of the United States:

I transmit herewith Reorganization Plan No. 1 of 1953, prepared in accordance with the provisions of the Reorganization Act of 1949, as amended.

In my message of February 2, 1953, I stated that I would send to the Congress a reorganization plan defining a new administrative status for Federal activities in health, education, and social security. This plan carries out that intention by creating a Department of Health, Education, and Welfare as one of the executive departments of the Government and by transferring to it the various units of the Federal Security Agency. The Department will be headed by a Secretary of Health, Education, and Welfare, who will be assisted by an Under Secretary and two Assistant Secretaries.

The purpose of this plan is to improve the administration of the vital health, education, and social security functions now being carried on in the Federal Security Agency by giving them departmental rank. Such action is demanded by the importance and magnitude of these functions, which affect the well-being of millions of our citizens. The programs carried on by the Public Health Service include, for example, the conduct and promotion of research into the prevention and cure of such dangerous ailments as cancer and heart disease. The Public Health Service also administers payments to the States for the support of their health services and for urgently needed hospital construction. The Office of Education collects, analyzes and distributes to school administrators throughout the country information relating to the organization and management of educational systems. Among its other functions is the provision of financial help to school districts burdened by activities of the United States Government. State assistance to the aged, the blind, the totally disabled, and dependent children is heavily supported by grants-in-aid administered through the Social Security Administration. The old age and survivors insurance system and child development and welfare programs are additional responsibilities of that Administration. Other offices of the Federal Security Agency are responsible for the conduct of Federal vocational rehabilitation programs and for the enforcement of food and drug laws.

There should be an unremitting effort to improve those health, education, and social security programs which have proved their value. I have already recommended the expansion of the social security system to cover persons not now protected, the continuation of assistance to school districts whose population has been greatly increased by the expansion of defense activities, and the strengthening of our food and drug laws.

But good intent and high purpose are not enough; all such programs depend for their success upon efficient, responsible administration. I have recently taken action to assure that the Federal Security Administrator's views are given proper consideration in executive councils by inviting her to attend meetings of the Cabinet. Now the establishment of the new Department provided for in Reorganization Plan No. 1 of 1953 will give the needed additional assurance that these matters will receive the full consideration they deserve in the whole operation of the Government.

This need has long been recognized. In 1923, President Harding proposed a Department of Education and Welfare, which was also to include health functions. In 1924, the Joint Committee on Reorganization recommended a new department similar to that suggested by President Harding. In 1932, one of President Hoover's reorganization proposals called for the concentration of health, education and recreational activities in a single executive department. The President's Committee on Administrative Management in 1937 recommended the placing of health, education and social security functions in a Department of Social Welfare. This recommendation was partially implemented in 1939 by the creation of the Federal Security Agency—by which action the Congress indicated its approval of the grouping of these functions in a single agency. A new department could not be proposed at that time because the Reorganization Act of 1939 prohibited the creation of additional executive departments. In 1949, the Commission on Organization of the Executive Branch of the Government proposed the creation of a department for social security and education.

The present plan will make it possible to give the officials directing the Department titles indicative of their responsibilities and salaries comparable to those received by their counterparts in other executive departments. As the Under Secretary of an executive department, the Secretary's principal assistant will be better equipped to give leadership in the Department's organization and management activities, for which he will be primarily responsible. The plan opens the way to further administrative improvement by authorizing the Secretary to centralize services and activities common to the several agencies of the Department. It also establishes a uniform method of appointment for the heads of the three major constituent agencies. At present, the Surgeon General and the Commissioner of Education are appointed by the President and confirmed by the Senate, while the Commissioner for Social Security is appointed by the Federal

Security Administrator. Hereafter, all three will be Presidential appointees subject to Senate confirmation.

I believe, and this plan reflects my conviction, that these several fields of Federal activity should continue within the framework of a single department. The plan at the same time assures that the Office of Education and the Public Health Service retain the professional and substantive responsibilities vested by law in those agencies or in their heads. The Surgeon General, the Commissioner of Education and the Commissioner of Social Security will all have direct access to the Secretary.

There should be in the Department an Advisory Committee on Education, made up of persons chosen by the Secretary from outside the Federal Government, which would advise the Secretary with respect to the educational programs of the Department. I recommend the enactment of legislation authorizing the defrayal of the expenses of this Committee. The creation of such a Committee as an advisory body to the Secretary will help ensure the maintenance of responsibility for the public educational system in State and local governments while preserving the national interest in education through appropriate Federal action.

After investigation I have found and hereby declare that each reorganization included in Reorganization Plan No. 1 of 1953 is necessary to accomplish one or more of the purposes set forth in section 2(a) of the Reorganization Act of 1949, as amended. I have also found and hereby declare that by reason of these reorganizations, it is necessary to include in the reorganization plan provisions for the appointment and compensation of the new officers specified in sections 1, 2, 3, and 4 of the reorganization plan. The rates of compensation fixed for these officers are, respectively, those which I have found to prevail in respect of comparable officers in the executive branch of the Government.

Although the effecting of the reorganizations provided for in the reorganization plan will not in itself result in immediate savings, the improvement achieved in administration will in the future allow the performance of necessary services at greater savings than present operations would permit. An itemization of these savings in advance of actual experience is not practicable.

DWIGHT D. EISENHOWER

NOTE: Reorganization Plan 1 of 1953 is published in the U.S. Statutes at Large (67 Stat. 631) and in the 1949–1953 Compilation of title 3 of the Code of Federal Regulations (p. 1022). Public Law 13, 83d Congress (67 Stat. 18), advanced the effective date to April 11, 1953.

29 ¶ Remarks to the Members of the House of Delegates of the American Medical Association. *March* 14, 1953

Dr. Bauer, distinguished guests, ladies and gentlemen:

Sometimes an individual finds himself in a position that he would like to explain, even to himself. I certainly have no prescriptions to offer for anything that you people might be thinking about. So my appearance here is confined mainly to exercising my privilege of welcoming you here, on behalf of the administration, in your deliberations in this city, and to express our great belief that the decisions you reach in the administrative field, particularly as they touch upon the functions of government, will represent your views of what is best for the United States of America, and not from any other viewpoint.

I have found, in the past few years, that I have certain philosophical bonds with doctors. I don't like the word "compulsory." I am against the word "socialized." Everything about such words seems to me to be a step toward the thing that we are spending so many billions to prevent; that is, the overwhelming of this country by any force, power, or idea that leads us to foresake our traditional system of free enterprise.

Now, that is the doctrine of the administration. It is most certainly the doctrine of the Republican Party and those Republican leaders in Congress. They are here to speak for themselves, but I am sure they will allow me that one word. We live by it, and we intend to practice it.

Now, we thoroughly understand, also, the importance of your functions in our society. We also understand and are determined to meet the requirements of our population in the services that only you can provide. But we do have faith that Americans want to do the right thing, and the medical profession will provide the kind of services our country needs better, with the cooperation and the friendship of the administration, rather than its direction or any attempt on its part to be the big "poobah" in this particular field.

That is what I came to repeat. In many sections of the country, in every area, I have said these things before—and to some of you that are here today. I repeat them, and I tell you it is going to be the philosophy of this administration for the next 4 years, or as long as the good Lord allows me—all or part of it— to spend those 4 years.

That is our pledge, and again I express the confidence that you people will be helpful, according to your judgment of what is good for the United States of America.

And now let me repeat, on the part of the administration, a most hearty welcome.

Actually, right now, I have got something I can consult with you about. I have got a sore wrist, and the problem is whether I can play golf or not this afternoon. But I am going to try it, I assure you.

Goodbye, and good luck.

NOTE: The President spoke in the Presidential Room at the Statler Hotel in Washington at 10:35 a.m. His opening words referred to Dr. Louis H. Bauer, President of the American Medical Association.

30 ¶ Remarks to the Business Advisory Council of the Department of Commerce.   *March* 18, 1953

FIRST, I must thank you for the honor of this invitation, and secondly, for the rather unusual compliment that is paid me in the reversal of the normal order of business here between speeches and eating.

When I first went to England some years ago, I was a very heavy smoker.   In those days because of the struggle that was going on, it was the rule always to toast the King, and I seemed to cause them great embarrassment.   I didn't know why until one day, right after the soup, the host jumped up and said "Gentlemen, the King," and then turned to me and said, "Now you may smoke."

I have a very great privilege today of bearing witness to the significant service that this body has performed over the past years.   I have known something about it.   I met with you at least once before and I met with different groups of you, at different times.   The value of your service, particularly as it served as a balance wheel, has been most greatly appreciated, at least by the successors to the prior administrations.   And when we look at some of the balance sheets, such as those we look at this morning, we could have wished that you might have been a little bit tougher to move at times.

This brings us right square up to the subject of balancing the budget, the balancing of your estimated outgo and income.   It is a terrific problem, complicated by the fact, that I think you are all well aware of, that we carry over from past administrations in terms of obligated money, appropriations approved, something like $80 billion more than we will have to appropriate to carry on the business of government.   In other words, we have got that $80 billion to find—maybe most of it in the next 4 years, because all of those expenses that we incur will naturally be carried over.

That gives you one—just one—part of the difficulty of the problem of balancing the budget.

Now, we claim that unless we balance the budget, there will never be any lowering of taxes, because we thoroughly believe that an unbalanced budget is the greatest possible spur to a continued cheapening of our money. If the money continues to cheapen, our idea is that we will never catch up with the indebtedness, never have a balanced budget; therefore, there will never be a lowering of taxes in the long run.

So we think there is no choice as to the order in which these things must be accomplished. We must have a balanced budget in sight, a proved capability, before we can begin to lower revenue—which doesn't mean you may not reform taxes, but you must never lower revenues.

And then, when you measure a thing like that against the prospects in the world, what we have accomplished over these past years—take a drain like the Korean war. It has never been a budget drain. It has been conducted largely over hopes and borrowings from other commitments. That is, the hope has always been it would be over in another 3 months, and therefore there has never been any money in our budget for the carrying on of the Korean war. The result is that you have to make up for it from other places. So when you begin to examine programs that have been offered—NATO, the Middle East, other places where we find our interests are involved—we find ourselves in a position that allows no slackening up.

There has been some opportunity to apply other tenets of our doctrine of free enterprise and progress toward decontrolling of prices. I think the business community, by and large, ought to have a special word of commendation for the fact that there has been such obvious restraint displayed throughout the country. A few prices have gone up. And I do hope that this coffee thing that I hear about in this country is caused by our Brazilian friends and not by our own importers, jobbers and retailers.

The beef people reported to me that the consumption of beef

in our country is going up tremendously; in this city alone, increased almost 100 percent. They reported that, far from feeling discouragement, they are on the up-and-up.

So, possibly, just the plain workings of economic law will reestablish itself as a sound system for a country such as ours. Certainly that is our plan and our hope.

Now, in looking into the future we are quite sure that some things are going to arise where there will be a great deal of complaint back and forth; it will cause friction. For example, as some of these prices get somewhat out of line and begin to hit the cost of living index, there will be trouble. But we must have the faith and courage to stand by our guns all the way through the Capital and in the Nation.

This brings me up to another subject I think would interest you people. I will go back and tell you a little bit of a story.

Over the past 7 years, there have been frequent references made to me about a political career—and they have been made on both sides of the fence. One of the arguments made by Democratic friends that came to me in the past was that there was no possibility of the Executive working with a number of the Republican personalities on the Hill, particularly anyone who held the beliefs I do—which I think can be fairly classed as middle-of-the-road. Well, there were very cogent reasons, at least in my mind, that completely outweighed all such reasons. I believed I had to be a Republican for very definite reasons of my own.

Nevertheless, I want to say to you gentlemen that, by and large, those scoffers and those prophets of doom in that respect were completely wrong. Since January twentieth the growth of cooperation between the Hill and the executive department is a noticeable day-by-day increase. And I know that it is felt on the Hill as well as it is felt in the department which I head because I have letters, I have people coming into my office. I had a letter only last evening that, had I thought about it, I would have brought it along to read to you. One of the leaders on the Hill this morning, just before I went through one of the busiest mornings I have had, dropped in because he had heard something he was proposing was causing me some embarrassment. He called on his own to see whether he couldn't work this thing out. Now that is, to me, quite an occurrence.

What it means to you is this: that Government can work together, can find out, first, what are the real functions that Government should be performing today; then determine what we know and see what we must do. Then when we have determined upon that, how to do it efficiently, how to meet our obligations, we will go ahead. But we will not try to get in and tell each one of you gentlemen how to run your business.

On the other hand, I think it properly fair to just call you or ask you to help us how to do our business. We are merely your agents, trying to do your work, to stay out of those things we should stay out of, and do those things we ought to do.

So, much as I appreciate the work that you are doing, let me tell you frankly that I think it is also your duty to be right here. Every department of Government, so far as I know, is organizing something of the same character, not always of the same size, nor with the same objectives. But the success of this body over the years, has given the lead. I think that so far as I know now, every department of the Government is organizing these bodies on a more or less formal basis, so that we may keep in touch with the daily thinking of American professions, American business, American labor—everything that makes this country tick.

And so you will furnish us a balance wheel. Let's not get too far to one side or the other.

For all this, for what you have done, what you are now doing, by being here and doing what is expected of you, my grateful thanks—thanks that I will hope to repeat from time to time, when I can stay and sample your lunch. But I happen to be giving one of my own today.

Thank you very much.

NOTE: The President spoke at the Mayflower Hotel in Washington at 12:45 p.m.

31 ¶ The President's News Conference of *March* 19, 1953.

THE PRESIDENT. This morning, ladies and gentlemen, I should say that one subject occupying the attention of the world is still speculation as to the meaning and possible significance of the changeover in the Kremlin, what it means to us, and whether there is any significance to the attacks we have had on our planes in different sections of the world—whether that has any connection with this changeover.

I can only say to you that as far as we are concerned, and as seriously as we view these attacks on the planes of the West, that we see no pattern, no different intention written into these incidents. Watchful and as analytical as we may be, we don't see anything different than has been the attitude in the past.

As for the changeover in the Kremlin itself, as you know, there has been an expression of an intent to seek peace, from the Kremlin. I can only say that that is just as welcome as it is sincere.

There is a very direct relationship between the satisfaction of such a thing and the sincerity in which it is meant. They will never be met less than halfway, that I assure you; because the purpose of this administration will forever be to seek peace by every honorable and decent means, and we will do anything that will be promising towards that direction.

One of the things that I continually talked about during the campaign was a desire, a purpose, and a hope of reducing expenditures, so that we would approach a balanced budget.

Well, as all of us know, it is never easy. Everybody wants to cut revenues in Government before they cut expenditures; and of course, I want to do it in the opposite order.

There has been a very encouraging sign. I notice in the Secretary of Commerce's report yesterday to the Congress, he is recommending a cut in his 1954 budget that amounts to about 15 percent.

But I don't expect any such general overall success in our budget. I must say that that is very hopeful, so far as I am concerned, and it is certainly indication of the earnestness with which the Secretary of Commerce and his staff are going about the thing.

All the rest of them are studying it the same way, but I don't anticipate that all of them will have that same degree of success.

I think those are the two points I had on my mind as I walked over here this morning, ladies and gentlemen, and I think we might as well go to the questions.

Q. Harry W. Frantz, United Press: All of your predecessors since President Coolidge, I believe, have made good will visits to one or more of the Latin American countries during their terms. Have you given any thought to such a journey in the near or remote future?

THE PRESIDENT. I have thought a great deal about good will tours, and certainly as far as South America is concerned, I have stated many, many times, how terrifically interested I am in that region. I believe we can much improve our relationships with them; but whether or not the President of the United States can find time these days to make one of these trips, with their physical drain and the other features that go with them, I am not so sure. You might make a short one, but I think possibly it would be better to find real emissaries that could go down and spend more time than would be possible for the President.

Q. Robert W. Richards, Copley Press: Mr. President, I have been told that the administration has reached some conclusions about the St. Lawrence Seaway. Would you care to comment at this time about it?

THE PRESIDENT. Well, we have reached some tentative conclusions for the moment, but I must admit you caught me to this one extent—I have forgotten whether we have agreed to keep those confidential until we could examine them a little bit more among ourselves. I am not certain. I will say this: I personally have held for a long time several things about this.

First, I should personally be distressed to see Canada go ahead completely independent of the United States so that in the future we might have reason to regret our lack of participation and cooperation in such a project.

Secondly, I believe that the power project there near the Niagara region is properly an object for negotiation between New York State and Ontario.

And thirdly, I believe this: if the St. Lawrence Seaway is really an economic necessity for the United States, eventually it is going to be built, and there is just nothing that my attitude for the moment could do to prevent it. You might delay it, you might make it a little more difficult; but in the long run, if it's an economic necessity, it is going to come about.

We have gone, I don't mind admitting, a little bit further than that in our own thinking; but I am giving you my personal thoughts that I have been expressing for a long time.

Q. [*Speaker unidentified*]: Could you comment on Senator Knowland's speech in the Senate the other day, in which he urged this Government to attempt to have the United Nations brand Russia as an aggressor in Korea, and adopt a little more aggressive policy in Korea?

THE PRESIDENT. I am not going to comment in terms either of agreement or criticism. My own feeling is this: every time that any opponent, in a situation such as we now find ourselves, is ready to say "Let's try to wipe the slate clean and take a look at the present and the future," you will find me ready to do it. I wouldn't want to do anything unnecessarily provocative at the moment. On the other hand, I will not, by any manner of means, countenance anything that I think is an infringement on our rights, our position, or our opportunity for a future peaceful agreement. So I don't want to comment more specifically than that on this statement.

Q. David P. Sentner, Hearst Newspapers: On the previous question of good will, do you anticipate any visit from Marshal Tito to Washington?

THE PRESIDENT. I haven't at the moment. As a matter of fact, someone mentioned on the way over here that I might have that question. I haven't heard it even discussed up to this point, and so I couldn't comment.

Q. Merriman Smith, United Press: Mr. President, there have been several reports in recent days that you have before you under consideration some large study of heavily expanded expenditures for civil defense and our air defense, stemming from the MIT survey for the Air Force? Would you discuss that for us, please?

THE PRESIDENT. There was a committee appointed by the past administration that submitted a report, and it has been under consideration by different sections of the staff. It has some very serious implications in it. I have not, in person, yet studied that in detail, and there have certainly been no general conclusions reached in the National Security Council, the Cabinet, or elsewhere, as to the extent to which it should be taken as a guide.

Now, I have forgotten the exact name of that commission, but Mr. Hagerty can give it to you after this meeting.

Q. Felix Belair, New York Times: Mr. President, would you tell us something of the new job you have reportedly turned over to Lew Douglas in the field of foreign economic policy?

THE PRESIDENT. Well, there is really no assignment except in this way. I believe thoroughly in the practice of the various sections of Government departments keeping in touch with the normal economic and business activities of this country through every possible means. There is just not the time on the part of a busy governmental official to make policy decisions, often, without such aid, because he is given so little time, really, to think, to reflect, to study it, and to do his research.

Now, what these committees do—the one that Lew Douglas is heading up does exactly the same thing, takes a look at our foreign trade position, what it means both in strictly money and what it means in our commodities, the raw materials we have to get, the markets we need in order to make certain that our surpluses are absorbed, and all that sort of thing. It is a broad study, in which he is simply the head individual, that is all.

Q. Mr. Belair: Mr. President, would that be a continuing body, or merely to report and then drop it?

THE PRESIDENT. If I can make it so, it shall be a continuing one, because these factors change every month of our lives. Our trade relationship of 20 years ago has no relationship to what it is now. It continues to change.

I don't mean to say the identity of the individuals has to remain the same, the function is still important.

Q. Alice A. Dunnigan, Associated Negro Press: Mr. President, the Department of the Army is now operating several schools on military posts in Virginia, Oklahoma, and Texas, which eliminate colored children. And in line with your announced policy to eliminate segregation in the Army, I wonder if anything has been done to correct that situation?

THE PRESIDENT. All I can say is, I will look it up. I haven't heard it; I will look it up—[*to Mr. Hagerty*]: will you make a point of it?

I will say this—I repeat it, I have said it again and again: wherever Federal funds are expended for anything, I do not see how any American can justify—legally, or logically, or morally— a discrimination in the expenditure of those funds as among our citizens. All are taxed to provide those funds. If there is any benefit to be derived from them, I think they must all share, regardless of such inconsequential factors as race and religion.

Q. Mrs. May Craig, Maine papers: Mr. President, yesterday in your speech to the Business Advisory Council, you referred twice to the "Korean war." Was that a manner of speaking, or do you differ from Mr. Truman, who always called it "police action"?

THE PRESIDENT. Of course, Mrs. Craig, it could be my upbringing, but when you see American soldiers called out under a draft, serving on that kind of a front, and suffering casualties in the numbers they have, so far as I am concerned it must be called a war.

Now I admit that this is not a war in the sense that you have a particular, clean objective and you go out for the destruction of all of the armed forces wherever they may be, and use every kind of political, economic, and military device to gain a major and positive victory. But I would refer you to Clausewitz. He knew even 150 years ago that there were various kinds of wars, and some partake of little more than police action, others get to be great conflagrations. So far as I am concerned, it is a war. It is a particular kind—but it is a war.

Q. Marvin L. Arrowsmith, Associated Press: Mr. President, before the Foreign Relations Committee vote yesterday, Senator McCarthy had said that he thought it was a serious mistake for you not to withdraw the Bohlen nomination. Do you care to comment on that?

THE PRESIDENT. I had a full report, so far as we have it, from the Secretary of State. I have considered Mr. Bohlen a man to be thoroughly trained in State Department functions and practices, familiar with Russia—at least, so far as we have anyone familiar with Russia; and he seemed to me to be a very fine appointment.

Certainly, even if we were wrong, there is one thing about it: it was based strictly upon merit, as we saw the merits of the case. Now, that's all I can say.

Q. Sarah McClendon, San Antonio Light: Mr. President, the question of an Air Academy has long been kicked around. Do you think we ought to have it, or not?

THE PRESIDENT. I think we ought to have an Air Academy. I was on a board some years ago, and I thought it was all settled that we were to have an Air Academy. I think we should.

Q. Laurence H. Burd, Chicago Tribune: Do you favor Senator Bricker's proposed constitutional amendment that he discussed with you yesterday—on treaties?

THE PRESIDENT. Well, of course, it is one of the most argumentative matters that I have heard discussed so far, even in front of my own people, I must assure you. I have to remember the old adage that a man has two ears and one tongue, and I therefore have tried to keep twice as still as I would in other places. It is a highly argumentative point.

I think that people that are arguing for a constitutional amendment are not trying really to amend the Constitution. What they are trying to say is, "we are going to make it impossible in the Constitution to break it." Now that seems to me to have a little bit of an anomaly, right in that kind of reasoning: you amend it in order to show that it is going to remain the same. However, it is one of those things where the President does not have to take a decision. If a constitutional amendment is enacted, as you know, it's two-thirds of each House and three-fourths of the States—and ignore the President in that.

Q. Lucian C. Warren, Buffalo Courier-Express: I wonder if we could clarify the St. Lawrence matter, the second point where you talk about discussion between Ontario and New York. You mention, in that connection, a project near the Niagara. Were you referring to the Niagara project, or the St. Lawrence?

THE PRESIDENT. There are two of them right there together.

Q. Mr. Warren: There is one on the St. Lawrence and one on the Niagara. They are separate, and the discussions with Ontario are the ones on the St. Lawrence. I would be interested very much in your comment on the Niagara, as to whether you favor one of the three plans envisaged there, the private or the State or the Federal construction of it? Have you made up your mind on that?

THE PRESIDENT. I will say this: if it is possible to keep the Federal Government out of it, and insure fairness, I would give you a negative decision to that extent. I just don't believe the Federal Government should be in these things except where it is clearly necessary for it to come in, and then it ought to come in as a partner and not as a dictator.

Now, for the other two, I haven't seen the details of the plan. We discussed it really in philosophy.

Q. Joseph A. Fox, Washington Evening Star: Could you tell us anything about that Commissioner situation here yet, sir?

THE PRESIDENT. I can say this: it is a subject of discussion every single morning; beyond that I can't, really, further.

Q. Mr. Fox: If I might press that, just to get one thing straightened out, sir. There has been some suggestion that the administration really would like to appoint two Commissioners. Is that correct, sir?

THE PRESIDENT. I understand they are appointed according to terms, and that they serve until their terms expire, as laid down by the law; so that being the law, I shall not comment on it.

Q. Martin Agronsky, American Broadcasting Company: Mr. President, are you in favor of the Federal Government, through the Congress of the United States, investigating communism in churches?

THE PRESIDENT. I really don't know how to comment on that in the larger sense. Now, I believe that if our churches—which certainly should be the greatest possible opponents to communism—need investigation, then we had better take a new look and go far beyond investigation in our country, in our combating of this what we consider a disease. Because the church, with its testimony of the existence of an Almighty God is the last thing that it seems to me would be preaching, teaching, or tolerating communism. So therefore I can see no possible good to be accomplished by questioning the loyalty of our churches in that regard.

Q. [*Speaker unidentified*]: Mr. President, Federal employees generally have been pretty jittery about their jobs. I wonder if you would comment on how far the administration plans to go in removing jobs from civil service?

THE PRESIDENT. I have said time and again, several things. First, I am a very strong supporter of civil service. And one of the reasons for certain of the moves I am trying to make is to protect the civil service so that that great body of our governmental servants that attain their positions through proper examination, that advance through the grades through service and competency, shall be protected. I know of no reason why any great number of these people should have the slightest concern about their jobs, because the only thing we have talked about, so far, is policy-making jobs, which must necessarily be subject to appointment by the people that the United States holds responsible for policy.

You can't possibly put policy in the hands of a body that cannot be removed, if necessary, by the electorate. That is the way I see it. So there is no excuse whatsoever for the great body of people to believe that their jobs are in jeopardy.[1]

---

[1] On March 3 the White House released the following statement in answer to questions concerning the administration's attitude toward the career Civil Service:

"During the campaign the President assured the people that he would do everything possible to strengthen the Civil Service System. That is and will continue to be the policy of this administration.

"From the beginning of the Civil Service System in 1883 it has been recognized that there are certain types of positions that do not belong in the Civil Service System. Such exempt positions have traditionally been placed in what is referred to as "Schedule A" of the Civil Service Rules. It is clear from the history of the Civil Service System that the following types of positions were intended to be put in Schedule A:

"1. Those positions where the incumbents should receive, in the interest of sound administration, a delegation of authority from the head of the agency which enables them to shape the policies of the Government in specific areas of activity.

"2. Those positions where the duties are such that there must be a close personal and confidential relationship between the incumbent of the position and the head of the agency.

"Some positions that do not belong in the Civil Service System have been placed in that system by taking them out of Schedule A. Executive orders were issued in 1947 and in 1948, (Order 9830(f) sec. 6.1 of February 24, 1947 and Order 9973 of June 28, 1948) providing the incumbents of many Schedule A positions with the same procedural safeguards in connection with removals that govern those that are legitimately in career Civil Service positions. Such actions undermine the foundations on which a genuine career service should be built. A Civil Service System is not an end in itself. It is a method for obtaining more efficient administration. Whenever it is permitted to drift to the point where it may hamper rather than assist our top administrators, immediate action should be taken if the Nation is to retain confidence in the entire system.

"The President has directed, therefore, that an Executive order be drafted immediately which will repeal parts of the 1947 and 1948 orders so as to provide the heads of agencies with greater freedom in determining who is to occupy Schedule A positions, subject, of course, to the provisions of the Veterans Preference Act of 1944.

"In addition, the President is directing the Civil Service Commission to immediately undertake a review of all positions that are in Schedule A to see whether or not they should properly remain in that classification. He is also asking the heads of all de-

Q. Anthony H. Leviero, New York Times: Mr. President, have you any comment on the atomic bomb test out in Nevada, especially in view of your calling back Val Peterson?

THE PRESIDENT. Of course, all these tests had been approved before I came to Washington. This one, as you know, had a very large body of spectators. The only comment on this one that I would have is that there ought to be a wider understanding in our country of the power of this weapon, its limitations, everything about it, than there was before. I have no other comment to make on it.

Q. Robert J. Donovan, New York Herald Tribune: Mr. President, coming back to that question about the MIT studies, so far as you can see do you anticipate in the near future a radical increase in the amount of money we will have to spend for air defense? It was a gigantic increase.

THE PRESIDENT. The one they were talking about was not merely air defense, it was also civil defense. Now, as I have tried to point out several times, it is my conviction that civil defense by its very nature must necessarily be primarily a local matter. The training, the understanding, the knowledge, and indeed the self-imposed discipline of our local populations is far more important than a mere digging of shelters. I would put shelters possibly in the last, final, category of work that you would undertake. The training of the civilian, the location and placing of new facilities both residential-wise and production-wise that you have, all of those things are important; passive and active measures for air defense, both locally, and then of course on a wider scale—your radar, your warnings, your interceptors—

partments and agencies to review their existing positions to determine whether there are some which are not in Schedule A which should be placed in that classification. The President is asking them to submit the results of their review to the Civil Service Commission and asking that body to report to him on the actions taken as a result of these submissions.

"These actions will not involve more than several hundred positions."

Executive Order 10440 of March 31, 1953, amending Civil Service Rule VI, is published in the Code of Federal Regulations (3 CFR, 1949–1953 Comp., p. 932).

which become exclusively Federal; and finally the leadership, the coordination through the State and through the Government, become important.

But this is what I would say: if you would carry forward the static defense of any country to what it could be, you have a most expensive thing—terribly expensive thing; but that expense would not certainly be all Federal. I would say a greater portion would be local in the aggregate than it would be Federal.

Q. [*Speaker unidentified*], Washington Post: In speaking of reaching a budget balance before approval of a tax cut, are you thinking, sir, of the conventional budget or cash budget, which is somewhat easier to reach?

THE PRESIDENT. As a matter of fact, the cash budget is one that is a little bit out of your control, because frequently one of the big factors in it is obligations that were made 2 or 3 years ago. Contracts were let; and now, as time comes for payment, you have no control over certain of those things. I think that before we can talk year by year of a balanced cash budget, we must reach a budgetary balance.

I do not even mean to say that I am not in favor of certain tax reforms. There may be certain tax revisions. What I do say is, we should not think primarily of just reducing the amount of revenue until we have reduced expenditures, and that means a budgetary expenditure.

Q. Sir, if I may press that point, the reason I asked you that was you have stressed the inflationary aspects of the unbalanced budget——

THE PRESIDENT. That's right.

Q. ——and the paper budget, so-called conventional budget, includes a lot of intergovernmental exchanges which don't have that effect; whereas the cash budget, as I understand it, refers to the money that is actually paid out of the Treasury, and into it.

THE PRESIDENT. That's right. And that money being paid out of the Treasury; you have to have the money and not just the power to, say, induce banks to take up more of your bonds. That is where more money comes from—more inflation, more cheapening of the money that you have in your pocket.

Now, both these budgets—both these balances—are as important, one as the other. I merely pointed out on the one, you haven't the same control as you have on the other, because the obligation is already there and yet you must run the Government this year. You have got 80 billion dollars of these obligations now floating around, and must be paid sometime. Suppose 20 billions of it comes due in one year; well, you have got—I mean a particular, big portion—cash payments you must make that year out of the Treasury, regardless of the present cost of Government. You see? That is what I am talking about.

Q. Raymond P. Brandt, St. Louis Post-Dispatch: Has the administration reached the point where it is going to take affirmative action so that there will be no reduction of revenue?

THE PRESIDENT. You mean, absolutely no reduction? No, I wouldn't hold out for any such.

Q. Mr. Brandt: You have a plan—apparently have to take some sort of action?

THE PRESIDENT. That's right, and I would be perfectly glad to see substitutes for certain of the taxes.

Q. Mr. Brandt: You have the excess profits tax which expires June 30th. You would like to have a substitute for that?

THE PRESIDENT. If they don't continue it, then I want a substitute.

Q. Mr. Brandt: Now, what about the personal income tax reduction in the Reed bill, which is Mr. Daniel Reed's?

THE PRESIDENT. I want the revenue. [*Laughter*] As a matter of fact, ladies and gentlemen, I think we must have it. Certainly, ladies and gentlemen, I am not trying to take an arbitrary position on this. I merely say that as long as you have got almost an incentive to cheapen and cheapen your money, then next year taxes will be higher and higher. Finally, you cannot catch yourself as you chase your tail around the tree.   And that is just exactly what I am trying to prevent, that thing just going in a spiral until it is hopeless.

Now, I recognize that this means pretty tough going for a little while.   But once we are on that sound basis, when we can believe that prices are stable so far as the value of our money is concerned, we will be far better off, the taxes could come down with a certainty and a confidence that I think will be very necessary.

Q. Frank Bourgholtzer, National Broadcasting Company: Mr. President, in your speech yesterday, you said that it might take 4 years to get through this 80-billion-dollar obligation hanging over.   Would you think it would be 4 years before you get to a balance that would permit tax reduction?

THE PRESIDENT. Oh, no.   Look, I should make this clear. Some of this 80 billion dollars is inescapable.   If you buy an airplane or a battleship, or build a dam, or anything else, you appropriate certain money for it.   It takes time to expend it. At the end of 4 years, there will be a certain amount that will bear some relationship to this 80 billion dollars that will be passed on.   We hope it won't be too great.   But, you see, it must be passed on at the end of this quarter, so it doesn't take necessarily 4 years to reach the balancing of the budget.   You have to allow, though, for the amount of money that you have to pay out each year from past obligations.

Q. Richard L. Wilson, Cowles Publications: Mr. President, Senator Symington who, as you know, was formerly Air Secretary, said in a speech last week, that he did not think either the form or the size of the defense program was adequate to protect us from a prospective attack from Russia.   Let me ask you a whole series of really military questions.   Are you familiar with that speech?

THE PRESIDENT. Well, they brought to me a summation of it.

Q. Mr. Wilson: Would you have any comment on it?

THE PRESIDENT. No, except this one thing: ladies and gentlemen, there is no amount of military force that can possibly give you real security, because you wouldn't have that amount unless you felt that there was almost a similar amount that could threaten you somewhere in the world.

Now, you finally have to make certain very tough decisions. I know of no better way to express it than George Washington did, many years ago. He said this country must always be careful to have a reasonable posture of defense. And I just don't believe that it is possible to depend too far on that.

Q. Mr. Wilson: I wondered, sir, if that might not have a bearing on the whole question of cutting the budget? You said earlier that the Commerce Department had cut out 15 percent, but even if some of the civilian departments do that, that is pretty small.

THE PRESIDENT. I will put it this way: in the total amount of combat strength that is being provided, I do not think that we could afford, at this time, to cut. I wouldn't want to recommend any major cut.

Q. Mr. Wilson: May I pursue that with one more question? There has been some talk at the Capitol that contrary to a cut, that there might be an increase in both military strength and in the dollars spent. Can you comment on that?

THE PRESIDENT. Well, I will comment on it, to this extent: I am dedicated to one idea, which is to get less money spent for overhead and what I believe still to be certain duplications and unnecessary expenses, and to get out of that same money more combat strength. Now, when you have the level of combat strength, then it is time to begin to reduce.

Q. Robert G. Spivack, New York Post: Mr. President, in each press conference, I think, since the beginning, the subject of relations with Russia has come up and you have made a friendly gesture in each case. Have you had any direct or indirect response from Soviet officials or Iron Curtain officials or are there any negotiations going on now that give you hope?

THE PRESIDENT. I have had only what you have seen in the papers. And I said, in reply to a statement of the Generalissimo's, or reported statement, of last December, that there are open the proper channels for any presentations that they wanted to make, and that when this administration went into office, we would view them very sympathetically and seriously. That is all I have had.

Q. Merriman Smith, United Press: Mr. President, then there have been no presentations through the proper channels?

THE PRESIDENT. No. No definite presentations to me—at least none that have reached me, I assure you.

Q. Edward J. Milne, Providence Journal-Bulletin: Mr. President, in connection with Mr. Wilson's question, are you in a position yet to know whether your budget for 1953–1954 will be about the same as, or substantially lower than the Truman budget, so far?

THE PRESIDENT. Well, I don't have any budget. There is a budget put in, and all my people can possibly do is to go down and, through re-examination of it, state: "We believe we can do with a little less of it there," or "you ought to take part of that and put it here." But we hope, in our complete re-examination, to find ways and means to reduce it. The amount remains to be seen, but we are certainly working at that.

But we are not putting in a budget of our own, as you know.

[*Speaker unidentified*]: Thank you, Mr. President.

NOTE: President Eisenhower's fourth news conference was held in the Ex- ecutive Office Building at 10:30 a.m. on Thursday, March 19, 1953.

32 ¶ Statement by the President on the Occasion of the Swearing In of Philip Young as a Member of the Civil Service Commission and His Designation as Chairman. *March* 23, 1953

THIS IS an important occasion for everyone in the employ of the Federal Government.

The appointment of Mr. Philip Young brings to the office of

Chairman of the Civil Service Commission a man of the stature and capacity demanded by that office. Serving in that capacity, he is to be my chief representative and overseer on all civilian personnel matters for which the President is responsible. As such, his task is of an importance comparable to that of the Director of the Budget, and he will sit with the Cabinet in any discussion of major personnel problems and policies.

It is important the employees of the Federal Government know this. For I most earnestly want them to understand the high regard and appreciation I hold for their public service.

One of the firm purposes of this Administration is to strengthen the career service, so that it may command the esteem of the whole nation. It is essential, in the highest public interest, that the privileges accorded conscientious civil servants be guarded by a strong merit system. I intend to see that they are guarded zealously.

To improve a system, in any fair and wise way—as I believe our Civil Service system can be improved—is not to endanger legitimate rights of the past. No merit system should be a haven for the few who are incompetent, dishonest, or disloyal. I intend to see the Government rid of all such persons precisely because that is the only way to make the merit system itself work.

There is no other way to win for the vast majority of competent and devoted public servants the public honor that is due them. I have known and worked with them for many years. I respect them. I want all our people to share that respect.

The public interest is the decisive, over-riding concern of us all. I expect all public servants to share—deeply—this simple, essential ideal. It is my intention—and that of Mr. Young—to ensure that the Federal Government be a truly progressive and just employer, coherent in policy and dedicated to service.

33   ¶ White House Statement Concerning Steps Taken To Strengthen and Improve the Operations of the National Security Council. *March* 23, 1953

THE PRESIDENT has been giving attention to strengthening and improving the operations of the National Security Council. On several occasions he has stressed the importance which he places upon the effective functioning of the Council. He feels that in these critical times the Council can afford the greatest possible assistance to the President in deciding policy issues affecting the national security.

The President has decided that he expects to have in regular attendance at Council meetings, in addition to himself and the Vice President, the following: the Secretary of State, the Secretary of Defense, the Secretary of the Treasury, the Director for Mutual Security, and (when appointed) the Director of Defense Mobilization.

Beside the above Council members, those regularly attending Council meetings as advisers will be the Chairman of the Joint Chiefs of Staff, the Director of Central Intelligence, and the Special Assistant to the President for Cold War Planning (C. D. Jackson). For executive and staff functions at Council meetings, there will be in attendance Robert Cutler, Administrative Assistant to the President, and the Council's Executive Secretary and Deputy Executive Secretary.

The President has named Mr. Cutler as Special Assistant to the President for National Security Affairs. Mr. Cutler will be the principal executive officer of the National Security Council and serve as Chairman of its newly established Planning Board.

To bring to Council deliberations a fresh point of view, not burdened with departmental responsibilities, the President plans from time to time to call upon qualified civilians to act as informal consultants to the Council. At present, seven prominent citizens are spending a good part of the month of March in Washington as Civilian Consultants. The President believes that this procedure will prove useful to him and to the other Council members.

In order to provide continuous assistance to the Council in its planning operations, the President has established an NSC Planning Board to take the place of the former NSC Senior Staff. This Board will be composed of qualified members and advisers from the departments and agencies represented at the Council table. Each person selected for the Planning Board is appointed by the President, on nomination of the chief of the department or agency concerned, and for this purpose will become a Special Assistant for National Security Affairs. To date the President has appointed the following:

Chairman: Robert Cutler, Special Assistant to the President for National Security Affairs.

Treasury Member: Andrew N. Overby, Assistant Secretary of the Treasury.

Defense Member: Frank C. Nash, Assistant Secretary of Defense.

Mutual Security Member: Frank N. Roberts, Military Adviser, Director for Mutual Security.

ODM Member: William Y. Elliott, Office of Director of Defense Mobilization.

Joint Chiefs of Staff Adviser: Major General John K. Gerhart, Office, Joint Chiefs of Staff.

Central Intelligence Agency Adviser: Robert Amory, Jr., Assistant Deputy Director for Intelligence.

Psychological Strategy Board Adviser: George A. Morgan, Acting Director, Psychological Strategy Board.

A member from the Department of State will be named during the next few days.

The President has authorized additional technical staff assistance for the Council. He also has reappointed James S. Lay, Jr., and S. Everett Gleason as Executive Secretary and Deputy Executive Secretary, respectively. They will continue to head the permanent staff of the Council.

NOTE: On March 11 the White House announced the names of the seven consultants referred to in the foregoing statement, as follows: Dillon Anderson, Houston, Tex.; James B. Black, San Francisco, Calif.; John

Cowles, Minneapolis, Minn.; Eugene Holman, New York, N.Y.; Deane W. Malott, Ithaca, N.Y.; David B. Robertson, Cleveland, Ohio; Charles A. Thomas, St. Louis, Mo. The release stated that they would serve as individual consultants rather than as a committee "because, as the President said, 'What is desired is the individual view of each person on a particular problem or problems, rather than the collective view of the group.' "

34 ¶ Message for Queen Elizabeth II on the Death of Queen Mother Mary. *March 24, 1953*

PLEASE EXTEND to Her Majesty and to all the members and peoples of the British Commonwealth my deep personal sympathy on the passing of Queen Mary. The hearts of all Americans go out to Her Majesty tonight as our prayers are extended to her, Princess Margaret and the members of the Royal Family for the great personal loss they have sustained. Queen Mary was a good and great Queen. Free peoples the world over will mourn her loss.

DWIGHT D. EISENHOWER

NOTE: The President's message was sent through Winthrop Aldrich, United States Ambassador to the Court of St. James.

35 ¶ Special Message to the Congress Transmitting Reorganization Plan 2 of 1953 Concerning the Department of Agriculture. *March 25, 1953*

To the Congress of the United States:

I transmit herewith Reorganization Plan No. 2 of 1953, prepared in accordance with the Reorganization Act of 1949, as amended, and providing for reorganizations in the Department of Agriculture.

Reorganization Plan No. 2 of 1953 is designed to make it possible for the Secretary of Agriculture to simplify and improve the internal organization of the Department of Agriculture. It is substantially in accord with the recommendations made in 1949 by the Commission on Organization of the Executive Branch of the Government.

With certain exceptions, Reorganization Plan No. 2 of 1953 transfers to the Secretary of Agriculture the functions now vested by law in other officers, and in the agencies and employees, of the Department. It allows the Secretary to authorize any other officer, agency, or employee of the Department to perform any function vested in the Secretary. He is directed to utilize this delegation authority in such a way as to further certain objectives set forth in the reorganization plan. Those objectives are to simplify and make effective the operation of the Department of Agriculture, to place the administration of farm programs close to the State and local levels, and to adapt the administration of the programs of the Department to regional, State, and local conditions. Further, to the extent deemed practicable by the Secretary, he is required to give appropriate advance public notice and to afford appropriate opportunity for interested persons and groups to present to the Department of Agriculture their views on such proposed delegations of the Secretary as involve assignments of major functions or major groups of functions to major constituent organizational units of the Department or their officers.

Reorganization Plan No. 2 of 1953 will permit the establishment of a clearer line of responsibility and authority from the President through the Secretary of Agriculture down to the lowest level of operations in the Department. It will make the Secretary responsible under law for activities within his Department for which he is now in fact held accountable by the President, the Congress, and the public. Also, it will enable the Secretary, from time to time, to adjust the organization of the Department in order to achieve continuous improvement in operations to meet changing conditions.

The Congress has in the past repeatedly followed the sound policy of vesting functions directly in department heads so that they can be held accountable for the performance of their agencies. In acting upon recommendations of the Commission on Organization of the Executive Branch of the Government, the Congress approved, in 1949 and 1950, a series of statutes and reorganization plans which applied that policy to all the executive departments except the Department of Defense and the Department of Agriculture. While some laws vest important functions directly in the Secretary of Agriculture, others place major functions in subordinate officers and agencies of the Department. By transferring to the Secretary the latter functions, with certain exceptions, the reorganization plan corrects the present patchwork assignment of statutory functions in the Department.

The functions excepted from transfer to the Secretary are the functions of hearing examiners under the Administrative Procedure Act; of the corporations of the Department, including their boards of directors and officers; of the Advisory Board of the Commodity Credit Corporation; and of the Farm Credit Administration and the banks, corporations, and associations supervised by it.

The exception of the hearing examiners is in accordance with the intent of the Administrative Procedure Act, and is consistent with the status of hearing examiners in other departments and agencies.

The corporations of the Department, together with their boards of directors and officers, are excepted because they have a different legal status than other constituent agencies of the Department. Bodies corporate have independent legal personalities and act in their own name rather than in the name of the Department of Agriculture or of the United States.

The same reasons which prompt the exception of the corporations of the Department make desirable the exception of the entities supervised by the Farm Credit Administration. The Farm Credit Administration itself is also excepted, since it is anticipated that general legislation covering this field will be recommended to the Congress.

The Department of Agriculture now has only one Assistant Secretary. Reorganization Plan No. 2 of 1953 provides the Secretary with two more Assistant Secretaries and an Administrative Assistant Secretary to aid him in supervising the Department. The Assistant Secretaries will be appointed by the President, by and with the advice and consent of the Senate. The Administrative Assistant Secretary will be appointed under the classified civil service by the Secretary, with the approval of the President. These methods of appointment are similar to those prevailing in other executive departments.

The Secretary will prescribe the functions to be performed by these new assistants. It is his intention to have the new Assistant Secretaries aid him in providing closer policy and program supervision over the Department of Agriculture, and to have the new Administrative Assistant Secretary perform substantially the same role as that performed by the Administrative Assistant Secretaries in other departments. Thus, the new officers will assist the Secretary in giving continuous attention to matters which are essential for the most efficient and economical operation of the Department.

The Secretary of Agriculture has advised me that the two new offices of Assistant Secretary of Agriculture, and the one new office of Administrative Assistant Secretary of Agriculture, provided for in the Reorganization Plan, will merely replace existing positions in the Department, and that hence the creation of these offices will not result in any net increase in the personnel in the Department of Agriculture. He has further advised me that both the number of officers and employees in the Office of the Secretary and the aggregate of their salaries will be less than those existing prior to January 1, 1953.

The Secretary of Agriculture, aided by the Interim Agricultural Advisory Committee, has been studying the organization and functions of the Department of Agriculture. Recently the

Secretary rearranged the organizational units of the Department so as to form (in addition to the Office of the Solicitor and a reorganized Foreign Agricultural Service) four major groups of agencies, each with a supervising head to whom the agencies within the group report. By so doing, the Secretary sought both to reduce the number of separate officials reporting to him and to improve coordination within the Department. Reorganization Plan No. 2 of 1953 will make it possible for the Secretary to make further internal adjustments within the Department as study and experience identify opportunities for improvement. It will thus further the better management of the affairs of the Department of Agriculture.

After investigation I have found and hereby declare that each reorganization included in Reorganization Plan No. 2 of 1953 is necessary to accomplish one or more of the purposes set forth in section 2(a) of the Reorganization Act of 1949, as amended.

I have found and hereby declare that it is necessary to include in the accompanying reorganization plan, by reason of reorganizations made thereby, provisions for the appointment and compensation of two Assistant Secretaries of Agriculture and an Administrative Assistant Secretary of Agriculture. The rates of compensation fixed for these officers are those which I have found to prevail in respect of comparable officers in the executive branch of the Government.

Reductions in expenditures will result from reorganizations of the Department of Agriculture made possible by the taking effect of Reorganization Plan No. 2 of 1953, but such reductions cannot be itemized at this time.

I recommend that the Congress allow the accompanying reorganization plan to become effective.

DWIGHT D. EISENHOWER

NOTE: Reorganization Plan 2 of 1953 is published in the U.S. Statutes at Large (67 Stat. 633) and in the 1949–1953 Compilation of title 3 of the Code of Federal Regulations (p. 1024). It became effective on June 4, 1953.

36 ¶ Memorandum Concerning Segregation in Schools on Army Posts. *March* 25, 1953

Memorandum for the Secretary of Defense
Subject: Segregation in Schools on Army Posts

At my request, following last week's news conference a memorandum addressed to my Press Secretary was received from the Secretary of the Army relative to the above subject.

(1) It states that by the opening of the school term next Fall all schools operated by the Army under provisions of Section 6 of Public Law 874 will be on a completely integrated basis. Consequently, the process of integration is almost completed, but in any event will be concluded prior to the opening of the schools next September.

(2) The memorandum likewise discusses the operation of schools by state authorities on Federally-owned property under the provisions of Section 3 of Public Law 874. Since these schools are operated with State funds but on Federal property and in Federally-owned buildings, complicating factors are present.

The Secretary of the Army's memorandum indicates that the Army commanders are in the process of making a survey relative to this question designed to bring about agreement with local authorities for integrating the schools. If such integration is not achieved, other arrangements in these instances will be considered.

DWIGHT D. EISENHOWER

37 ¶ The President's News Conference of *March* 26, 1953.

THE PRESIDENT. For a long time, many people—including myself—have been concerned about this subject of the proper division of functions between Federal government, State governments, municipal governments, and even private enterprise.

Some time ago we began to take this subject up seriously, and I had an informal conference here, at which there were Governors and Members of the Cabinet, Members of the Senate and House, attending. We decided that an official commission ought to be appointed to study this thing. It reaches into the whole subject of grants-in-aid, of security and welfare programs, all sorts of things, including even sources of taxation that are properly available to the several echelons of government.

So we are just about ready, and will in the course of a day or so—or certainly very quickly—send to the Senate and the House recommendations on the establishment of such a commission to study this whole question, and to bring into some kind of correlation and coordination this whole vastly complex subject.

That is one point that I have been studying on lately, where action has just about come up for accomplishment.

I mention that at the beginning of this press conference. The rest of it will be yours.

Q. Merriman Smith, United Press: Mr. President, how does this plan fit in or is there any conflict with the work of your reorganization commission?

THE PRESIDENT. No conflict whatsoever. This is to deal with this whole special subject. The reorganization committee that is working with the several departments of Government, and working with the Congress in any way that they find most fitting, has a function completely outside of this business of determining the relationship between the various echelons of government—vertically, you might say. What the reorganization committee is concerned in is how best to organize the Federal Government itself for the performance of the functions that properly fall to it.

Q. Marvin L. Arrowsmith, Associated Press: Mr. President, would that recommendation call for the creation of a Presidential commission?

THE PRESIDENT. Yes. My idea would be that the resolution itself specify the membership of the commission in general terms, but the—I assume it would be called a Presidential commission and the President would have the responsibility of appointing certain of the members. I should think probably some of the members would be appointed properly by the leaders in the House and the Senate.

Q. George H. Hall, St. Louis Post-Dispatch: Mr. President, this question has to do particularly with the nomination of Albert Cole to be Housing Administrator, and Edward Howrey to the Federal Trade Commission, but I have a general question in mind. Could you identify the group, or persons, in the White House or the administration who give final clearance to nominations such as that, before you send them to the Senate?

THE PRESIDENT. *I* do.

Q. Mr. Hall: Who recommends them to you?

THE PRESIDENT. The recommendations come from numerous sources. All recommendations are gathered together; they go over them. But before I appoint anybody to any important position, I call him in and ask him about his philosophy, whether he is biased so distinctly in favor of some doctrinal idea that he can't operate according to the facts, whether he cannot possibly execute laws that are written by Congress and approved by the President. I try to get a man who is logical, who is devoted to the service, and who in general conforms to what I call—as you so often have heard me say—the middle-of-the-road philosophy.

I don't like extremists of any kind, particularly when they make up their minds before they know their facts; so I always take these people and bring them in and talk to them myself.

Q. Mr. Hall: Before they get to you, who screens them? You can't see everybody——

THE PRESIDENT. Many people. If they belong in a department, then they are screened thoroughly by the department head before they are brought to me. If they don't belong in that, if they come for some other purpose—commissions—they are always screened by Governor Adams, and then he brings them in personally to me.

Q. Vance Johnson, San Francisco Chronicle: Mr. President, Senators McCarran and McCarthy in the Senate this week have questioned whether Mr. Bohlen is your personal choice for Ambassador to Moscow; and one of them yesterday—I have forgotten which one—suggested that some of Mr. Acheson's leftover lieutenants slipped in by you, in someway. I wonder if——

THE PRESIDENT. Well, of course, I suppose that if they are talking about a shell game, why they can have their own conclusions, and I couldn't say they are wrong, because I have guessed wrong myself as to which shell the pea was under.

I would say this: in this particular case it was one of the appointments in which I was very deeply and personally concerned, not because the Ambassador in the Soviet Union has the same leeway, the same opportunity for, you might say, broad service that an Ambassador would have in this country; but I am particularly concerned to find a man that understands something of those people and, so far as I could find out, whose record of service showed a dedication to the United States.

Now, I have known Mr. Bohlen for some years. I was once, at least, a guest in his home, and with his very charming family. I have played golf with him, I have listened to his philosophy. So far as I can see, he is the best qualified man for that post that I could find. That is the reason his name was sent to the Senate and the reason it stays there, because I believe, still, that he is the best qualified man we could find today.

If anyone put him over on me, well, they must have found a blind side that I don't know about myself.

Q. Alan S. Emory, Watertown (N.Y.) Times: Mr. President, at the conclusion of yesterday's debate, Senator Lehman of New York said all his life he had urged young people to go into the service of their government; but he said, "I am beginning to doubt whether I any longer have the right to encourage men to go into public service, when all that they can expect to receive is calumny and accusation of treason if their honest opinions sometime later prove to have been incorrect." I wonder if you would care to comment on that?

THE PRESIDENT. I can only say this: in my brief but rather intensive career in the civil service of government, I have encouraged young men to go into it. I believe in them. I think they should go into it, and I believe if we are going to have fine, splendid operation of our form of government here, we have to get young men into it.

Now, we are going to have, in a government such as ours, often the kind of thing that Senator Lehman seemed to be criticising. People have to "take it" and go on and do the best they can for the United States of America. That is the way I see it.

Q. Mrs. May Craig, Maine papers: Mr. President, Senator Bridges yesterday enunciated the doctrine which would certainly apply not only to Mr. Bohlen but to others, that the American people in the election rejected the Truman-Acheson foreign policy in the Far East, that Mr. Bohlen was identified with it and therefore could not serve you well in your foreign policy, which seemed to apply to all others who had worked with the Truman-Acheson policy in the Far East. And I wonder if that were your theory?

THE PRESIDENT. As usual, I will not comment on anyone else's theories, but I would like to point this out: I served a long time in the uniformed services of the United States. I was compelled, during all that time, to give loyalty to the properly constituted civil authorities set over me. I gave my oath to do so. Had I failed to do so, I should have resigned; and I would have been, in my own opinion, treasonous if I did not resign and still tried to defy those civil authorities.

Consequently, if we are going to have worth-while career services in our government, whether they be civil or in the uniformed services, and we find a man who cannot give loyal service to his superiors, then he has one recourse only: to resign. Otherwise, he is not doing his duty.

Consequently, I should say, in the State Department, they must loyally carry out the policy that they are given by their superiors. If they cannot loyally carry them out—and that doesn't mean, necessarily, that they will agree with them—then they must resign. That is the only recourse they have.

Q. Neal A. Stanford, Christian Science Monitor: Mr. President, I would like to follow up last week on the Bricker amendment. As that proposal deals specifically with treaty-making power, in which you have a constitutional obligation, do you feel this Bricker amendment would restrict your conduct of foreign affairs?

THE PRESIDENT. The Bricker amendment, as analyzed for me by the Secretary of State, would, as I understand it, in certain ways restrict the authority that the President must have, if he is to conduct the foreign affairs of this Nation effectively.

Now, I do not mean to say that that is the intent of the amendment. I am perfectly certain that the men that have written the amendment, that are supporting it, are convinced that it would work only to the good of the United States and protect the individual rights of citizens of the United States inside our own country.

I do believe that there are certain features that would work to the disadvantage of our country, particularly in making it impossible for the President to work with the flexibility that he needs in this highly complicated and difficult situation.

Q. David P. Sentner, Hearst Newspapers: Mr. President, can you comment on the present status of the ammunition problem in Korea as well as the general situation there?

THE PRESIDENT. I know of only this: I did have time to check up the military service and ask the question about this late struggle on Baldy Ridge, where the papers said that two companies of the 7th Division had given it up. I asked whether that had any relationship to the ammunition shortage. I was told it most emphatically did not, that in fact a recent ship out-loaded with ammunition for Korea found that the reserves in Japan were sufficiently high, at least in the particular brand of ammunition that was on this ship, that they did not want—did not accept it.

So I was told emphatically that the present situation in ammunition was perfectly sound compared to the kind of operations now going ahead.

Q. Mr. Sentner: Does that apply to all types of ammunition, or just artillery?

THE PRESIDENT. I didn't ask for all of them, but the items we know—we have been short in three items, which have been brought out, but they told me the situation in those was improving constantly. I do know this: Secretary Wilson gives attention to it every day; that I *know*. And I am sure that everything possible is being done on that phase.

Q. Nat S. Finney, Buffalo Evening News: Mr. President, Mr. Wilson, in his press conference late last week, said that the budget for the Korean war, which previously has been unbudgeted, would be a separate budget. I am curious to know as to whether that budget would go over to the Hill separate from the general defense budget, or whether it would be a segment of the budget, or can you throw any light on how it might be handled?

THE PRESIDENT. No. I know only about the first part of the statement you make—in other words, your premise, which is that up to this moment the cost of the Korean war has never been really budgeted. There has merely been an expression of hope that it would be over soon. Now, just exactly how the Defense Department and the Bureau of the Budget expect to come up with a plan for correcting that, I am not sure, so I couldn't comment.

Q. Marvin L. Arrowsmith, Associated Press: When you said that you found the ammunition situation perfectly sound in Korea, are you referring just to the Old Baldy situation, or to the overall picture?

THE PRESIDENT. Well, I said perfectly sound only in comparison with present operations. I didn't say that in every respect the commander in the field wouldn't have some possibility of criticism. I have never known one that didn't. I did myself, and I must tell you this: some of you know that in the beachhead we rationed our principal guns down to 17 rounds a day, in order to accumulate the reserves needed for the breakout; and at times certain of our guns, as I remember, down to 2 or 3 rounds a day. So no commander ever has all he wants.

But what I am merely trying to say: the situation in ammunition now, including the reserves in Japan and elsewhere, seems to be satisfactory for meeting the present scale of operations. I would assume that if anything else were contemplated, it would have to be a different level.

I have not, by any manner of means, investigated every last caliber of these myself. Of course, I can't.

Q. Edward T. Folliard, Washington Post: Mr. President, at your last news conference, you told us that there would be no reduction in the total combat strength of our armed forces. I read this morning that Mr. Wilson is proposing a 10 percent reduction now in our armed forces, skeletonizing our divisions at home. Is there any conflict between what you told us and what Mr. Wilson appears to have in mind?

THE PRESIDENT. Not so far as I know. He and I meet—well, we meet several times a week. We talk over these things. Quite naturally, we are trying to get the expenditures of the United States within manageable proportions. It is quite clear that a continuation of deficit spending has a very bad effect on our whole economy. We are working desperately on that side. Now, if he has found some place where he thinks there might be some element of military force disappear, without hurting our immediate combat position in the world—I mean, in Korea particularly—he would be justified in making a recommendation. But he hasn't spoken to me definitely on that one point.

Q. Arthur T. Hadley, Newsweek: Could you give us any indication, sir, of what you intend to talk to Mr. Rene Mayer about while he is here?

THE PRESIDENT. Well, I haven't had my first meeting—it starts this morning—but I know certain things will be discussed, of course. We are going to discuss the relative position of NATO, as to what we expect it to be at this time. We are going to talk about the French problem in Indochina and its relationship to its capabilities in Europe. We are going to talk about many things that affect the French ability to do everything that the size of its population would indicate at first glance that it should be able to do.

France, let us not forget, was bled white in World War I, had a long and difficult political and economic re-adjustment, and then was plunged into World War II and was overrun, its pride was trampled in the dust. It was a long time coming back. France has had a very hard time. I still think, though, that America has not forgotten the very great sentimental ties that bind us to a nation which even as far back as 1776 and 1777 was coming and helping us out.

Q. Merriman Smith, Associated Press: Mr. President, we haven't had an opportunity to ask what you think of the payment of more than $700,000 in accumulated leave to outgoing members of the past administration?

THE PRESIDENT. I am sorry that I have not talked on that subject specifically with my Cabinet, but I will tell you this: I don't see how a high-ranking officer of Government can possibly accumulate leave, or accumulate a claim against the United States for leave.

The way I see such responsible jobs—and I am expressing now a personal philosophy—I do not see how a man can go on leave. If I go away from the city for a few days recreation, I cannot conceive that I am laying down my responsibilities. I don't think any Cabinet officer can lay down his responsibilities either. Certainly, every instant of that time he is responsible to me for the operations of his department. Therefore, since I don't see how he can go on leave, I don't see how he can accumulate leave. And therefore, I for my part would never acquiesce in accumulation of obligations, so-called obligations, against the Government based upon leave in these high-ranking offices.

I do believe that we must provide for proper leave for all of our great body of civil servants; they not only earn it and deserve it, but they have to have it, if they are going to remain efficient. And if one should be discharged without ever having gotten that leave, I should think that for whatever the law allows him to accumulate, he should be paid. But that doesn't mean that I could hire him back the next day.

Q. [*Speaker unidentified*]: Mr. President, I don't believe a political question has come up this morning. Is there any change in your mind on the status of Wes Roberts, Chairman of the National Committee?

THE PRESIDENT. No one could be more earnestly hopeful than I that every important post in government, and even in such quasi-governmental bodies as political parties, that every important post will be occupied by a man whose integrity and straightforwardness are almost a byword in our Nation.

Now, Mr. Roberts, a man whom I have known for a short time, but for whom I have conceived a great admiration, has been accused of something. There are not available to me—as a matter of fact, I have no authority with respect to that, but I do have a great influence, of course, because of my position—there are not available the Federal agencies that you would normally use if you were thinking of putting someone in the Federal Government.

But I do have great faith in the Kansas legislature and the Kansas courts. I think we ought to find out what the answers are, and then I will make up my mind what to do.

I have tried all my life to resist finding, in my own mind, a man guilty of something merely because there is an unsubstantiated charge. But if he does become guilty of something that renders him unfit for office, then I certainly don't intend to be defending anybody in his holding of office.

Q. Sarah McClendon, Beaumont Enterprise: Mr. President, do you expect to send to Congress this year a plan for reorganizing the water control agencies—I mean, the Army Engineers, and Bureau of Reclamation?

THE PRESIDENT. I know this: the reorganization committee is working, and they will come up one of these days with a plan. I think it is going to take longer than some of the just internal organization things—I mean internal with respect to a simple department—because it is complicated. The Engineers have a long record of efficient service, but on the other hand, of course, it does look rather odd that we have got two great organizations competing in this field. And so I should say it will probably be some time before they finally reach conclusions in long and exhaustive hearings.

Q. Robert G. Spivack, New York Post: Mr. President, following up the question about Mr. Roberts, have you ever formed any judgment on the Senate subcommittee discussion of findings on Senator McCarthy's finances?

THE PRESIDENT. No.

Q. Mrs. May Craig, Maine papers: Sir, is there any difficulty in budgeting separately for a Korean war which has never been declared by Congress? Is there any difficulty about that?

THE PRESIDENT. Well now, you say something that I don't know. I know that there was no war declared in the first instance, but certainly Congress has recognized the war with many commissions and committees that have gone out there. And I would see no difficulty about the budgeting because we have a *de facto* recognition, whether or not it has been legally done.

Q. Edward J. Milne, Providence Journal: During the campaign, sir, you drew sharp distinction between Senator McCarthy's methods and objectives. I wonder if you would tell us what you think his objectives have been in the Bohlen case, as affecting your appointment?

THE PRESIDENT. I am not going to talk about Senator McCarthy. I will talk about this: I believe that—I told you before—the Senate and the House have a right to make any investigation that they see fit, to make certain that there is no influence creeping into this Government that is subversive, that is inimical to its interests.

I believe that you can carry investigations in method to the point that you are damaging from within what you are trying to protect from without. And I believe that it takes statesmanship and real wisdom to distinguish between these points and not let enthusiasm for any one thing carry us too far at any one time.

Q. Mr. Milne: I wonder if you think that point has been reached in this case?

THE PRESIDENT. I think that that is one point I will allow you people to speculate on, instead of giving you my idea. And I don't mean to be facetious, but these are things that, if you are going to give a public opinion, you have to have time to sit and ponder and look at all sides of the case. I have to take my own judgments on things as they come up to me, and I pass them along. I try to avoid criticism of somebody else, as long as there is any possible chance of believing that he is acting in the public service—if he thinks he is acting in the public service, I should have said. Now go ahead.

Q. Robert W. Richards, Copley Press: The Democrats are reported to be enjoying this little scrap within your party in the Senate very much. Would you say it might be reminiscent of some that they have had with such people as Huey Long and "the man Bilbo," and so forth?

THE PRESIDENT. I would put it this way: I am trying to be President of all the United States. Arguments are going to come up—these partisan arguments; when they come within the membership of your own party, they are of course saddening, because it looks like someone is doubting your efforts to be President of all the United States. But I am still trying, so I am not going to comment on that particular point.

Merriman Smith, United Press: Thank you, Mr. President.

NOTE: President Eisenhower's fifth news conference was held in the Ex-　ecutive Office Building at 10:30 a.m. on Thursday, March 26, 1953.

38 ¶ Statement by the President on the Resignation of C. Wesley Roberts, Chairman, Republican National Committee.
March 27, 1953

I HAVE just received a letter from C. Wesley Roberts informing me that he is submitting to the Republican National Committee his resignation as National Chairman. He was selected for that post in January by the Republican National Committee, with my concurrence, because of our confidence in his abilities, integrity and character.

A situation involving him has arisen and I have read the forthright public statement concerning it that he has released.

Resignation was decided upon by Mr. Roberts on his own initiative. I believe his decision a wise one. Nevertheless, I should like to express appreciation of the valuable and tireless efforts he has devoted to the Republican Party both during the campaign, and, since January, as Chairman.

39 ¶ Special Message to the Congress Recommending the Establishment of a Commission To Study Federal, State, and Local Relations.
March 30, 1953

To the Congress of the United States:

In the State of the Union Message, I expressed my deep concern for the well-being of all of our citizens and the attainment of equality of opportunity for all. I further stated that our social rights are a most important part of our heritage and must be guarded and defended with all of our strength. I firmly believe that the primary way of accomplishing this is to recommend the creation of a commission to study the means of achieving a sounder relationship between federal, state and local governments.

The way has now been prepared for appropriate action. Shortly after stating my original intention, I called an exploratory meeting of interested officials, including members of Congress and a group of governors representing the Council of State Governments, to confer with me on such a study. This conference produced general agreement on the importance of the problem and an offer of cooperation in the proposed study. Within a few days representatives of several leading organizations of local governmental officials will meet at the White House with several of my associates to give their considered and needed counsel.

The present division of activities between Federal and state governments, including their local subdivisions, is the product of more than a century and a half of piecemeal and often haphazard growth. This growth in recent decades has proceeded at a speed defying order and efficiency. One program after another has been launched to meet emergencies and expanding public needs. Time has rarely been taken for thoughtful attention to the effects of these actions on the basic structure of our Federal-state system of Government.

Now there is need to review and assess, with prudence and foresight, the proper roles of the Federal, state and local governments. In many cases, especially within the past twenty years, the Federal Government has entered fields which, under our Constitution, are the primary responsibilities of state and local governments. This has tended to blur the responsibilities of local government. It has led to duplication and waste. It is time to relieve the people of the need to pay taxes on taxes.

A major mark of this development has been the multiplication of Federal grants-in-aid for specific types of activities. There are now more than thirty such grant programs. In the aggregate, they involve Federal expenditures of well over $2 billion a year. They make up approximately one-fifth of state revenues.

While by far the greater part of these expenditures are in the fields of social security, health, and education, they also spread into many other areas. In some cases, the Federal Government apportions fixed amounts among the States; in others, it matches State expenditures; and in a few, it finances the entire State expenditure. The impact of all these grants on State governments has been profound. While they have greatly stimulated the development of certain State activities, they have complicated State finances and administration; and they have often made it difficult for States to provide the funds for other important services.

The maintenance of strong, well-ordered state and local governments is essential to our Federal system of government. Lines of authority must be clean and clear, the right areas of action for Federal and state government plainly defined. This is imperative for the efficient administration of governmental programs in the fields of health, education, social security, and other grant-in-aid areas.

The manner in which best to accomplish these objectives, and to eliminate friction, duplication, and waste from Federal-state relations, is therefore a major national problem. To reallocate certain of these activities between federal and state governments, including their local subdivisions, is in no sense to lessen our concern for the objectives of these programs. On the contrary: these programs can be made more effective instruments serving the security and welfare of our citizens.

To achieve these purposes, I recommend the enactment of legislation to establish a commission on governmental functions and fiscal resources to make a thorough study of grants-in-aid activities and the problems of finance and federal-state relations which attend them. The commission should study and investigate all the activities in which federal aid is extended to state and local governments, whether there is justification for federal aid in all these fields, whether there is need for such aid in other fields. The whole question of federal control of activities to which the federal government contributes must be thoroughly examined.

The matter of the adequacy of fiscal resources available to the various levels of government to discharge their proper functions must be carefully explored.

The commission should be of such size and composition as to permit appropriate representation of the various governmental levels and of outstanding members of the general public. It should be provided with an excellent staff, able to draw on the great amount of work which has already been done in this field.

In order that the commission may complete its report in time for consideration by the next session of the Congress, I urge prompt action on this matter.

DWIGHT D. EISENHOWER

NOTE: Public Law 109, 83d Congress, establishing a Commission on Intergovernmental Relations, was approved on July 10, 1953 (67 Stat. 145).

40 ¶ Special Message to the Congress Transmitting Reorganization Plan 3 of 1953 Concerning the Organization of the Executive Office of the President. *April 2, 1953*

To the Congress of the United States:

I transmit herewith Reorganization Plan No. 3 of 1953, prepared in accordance with the provisions of the Reorganization Act of 1949, as amended.

The reorganization plan is designed to achieve two primary objectives. The first is to improve the organization of the Executive Office of the President. The second is to enable one Executive Office agency to exercise strong leadership in our national mobilization effort, including both current defense activities and readiness for any future national emergency.

The National Security Resources Board was established by the National Security Act of 1947 to advise the President concerning various aspects of future military, industrial, and civilian mobilization. The areas of responsibility assigned to the Board included the use of national and industrial resources for military and civilian needs; the sufficiency of productive facilities; the strategic relocation of industries; the mobilization and maximum utilization of manpower; and the maintenance and stabilization of the civilian economy.

The vigorous and efficient discharge of these vital functions is not well served by the simultaneous existence in the Executive Office of the President of the National Security Resources Board (charged with planning for the future) and the present Office of Defense Mobilization (charged with programs of the present). The progress of the current mobilization effort has made plain how artificial is the present separation of these functions.

Both functions should now be combined into one defense mobilization agency. Accordingly, the reorganization plan would create in the Executive Office of the President a new agency, to be known as the Office of Defense Mobilization. It would transfer to the new Office the functions of the Chairman of the National Security Resources Board and abolish that Board, including the offices of chairman and vice chairman.

The reorganization plan also transfers to the new agency the statutory functions of the present Office of Defense Mobilization. These are of a minor nature, the major functions of the present Office of Defense Mobilization having been delegated to it by the President, principally under the Defense Production Act of 1950, as amended. It is my intention to transfer the latter functions to the new agency by executive order, and to abolish the Office of Defense Mobilization established by Executive Order No. 10193. There will thus result a new agency which combines the activities of the National Security Resources Board and both the statutory and delegated functions of the heretofore existing Office of Defense Mobilization.

The proposed plan would also reorganize various activities relating to the stockpiling of strategic and critical materials. Those activities are principally provided for in the Strategic and Critical Material Stock Piling Act, as amended. It has become increasingly apparent that the policy and program aspects of stockpiling are an integral part of mobilization planning. They should not be administered separately from plant expansion, conservation of materials, and materials procurement under the Defense Production Act of 1950, or from the duties placed in the National Security Resources Board by the National Security Act of 1947. Therefore, the reorganization plan would transfer to the Director of the new Office of Defense Mobilization responsibility for major stockpiling actions, including the determination of the nature and quantities of materials to be stockpiled. In the main, these functions are transferred from the Secretaries of the Army, Navy, and Air Force (acting jointly through the agency of the Munitions Board) and the Secretary of the Interior. The duties of the Administrator of General Services regarding the purchase of strategic and critical materials and the management of stockpiles are not affected by the reorganization plan, except that he will receive his directions, under the plan, from the Director of the Office of Defense Mobilization instead of from the Department of Defense.

This transfer of stockpiling functions will correct the present undesirable confusion of responsibilities. The functions of the heads of the military departments of the Department of Defense and the Secretary of the Interior under the Strategic and Critical Materials Stock Piling Act, as amended, are at present in considerable measure subject to other authority of delegates of the President springing from the Defense Production Act of 1950, as amended. The allocation and distribution of scarce materials among essential civilian and military activities and the continued maintenance of adequate stockpiles of strategic and critical materials are of major current importance. The reorganization plan will make possible more effective coordination and close control over the Government's whole stockpile program. It will speed decisions. It can result in significant economies.

The Department of Defense will, of course, continue to be responsible for presenting the needs of the military services. That Department and the Department of the Interior are specifically designated in the plan as additional agencies which shall appoint representatives to cooperate with the Director of the Office of Defense Mobilization in determining which materials are strategic and critical and how much of them is to be purchased. Final authority with regard to such determination will, however, be in the Director of the Office of Defense Mobilization.

Section 5(a) of the reorganization plan withholds from transfer to the Director and abolishes the functions of the Chairman of the National Security Resources Board with regard to being consulted by and furnishing advice to the President concerning the placing of orders of mandatory precedence for articles or materials for the use of the armed forces of the United States or for the use of the Atomic Energy Commission, and with regard to determining that a plant, mine or other facility can be readily converted to the production or furnishing of such articles or materials. These abolished functions were vested in the National Security Resources Board by section 18 of the Selective Service Act of 1948 (later renamed as the Universal Military Training and Service Act) and were transferred to the Chairman of that Board by Reorganization Plan No. 25 of 1950. The practical effect of this abolition is to obviate a statutory mandate that the President consult and advise with another officer of the executive branch of the Government.

Section 5(b) of the reorganization plan abolishes the direction, authority, and control of the Secretary of Defense over functions transferred from the Department of Defense by the reorganization plan. The Secretary's functions in this regard are provided for in section 202(b) of the National Security Act of 1947, as amended (5 U.S.C. 171a(b)).

Section 5(c) of the reorganization plan abolishes any functions which were vested in the Army and Navy Munitions Board or which are vested in the Munitions Board with respect to serving as the agent through which the Secretaries of the Army, Navy, Air Force, and the Interior jointly act in determining which materials are strategic and critical under the provisions of the Strategic and Critical Materials Stock Piling Act, as amended, and the quality and quantities of such materials to be stockpiled. These abolished functions are provided for in section 2(a) of the Strategic and Critical Materials Stock Piling Act, as amended.

After investigation I have found and hereby declare that each reorganization included in Reorganization Plan No. 3 of 1953 is necessary to accomplish one or more of the purposes set forth in section 2(a) of the Reorganization Act of 1949, as amended. I have also found and hereby declare that by reason of these reorganizations it is necessary to include in the reorganization plan provisions for the appointment and compensation of a Director and a Deputy Director of the Office of Defense Mobilization. The rates of compensation fixed for these officers are, respectively, those which I have found to prevail in respect of comparable officers of the executive branch of the Government.

The reorganization plan will permit better organization and management of the Federal programs relating to materials and requirements and will thus help to achieve the maximum degree of mobilization readiness at the least possible cost. It is not practicable, however, to itemize, in advance of actual experience, the reductions of expenditures to be brought about by the taking effect of the reorganizations included in Reorganization Plan No. 3 of 1953.

I urge that the Congress allow the proposed reorganization plan to become effective.

DWIGHT D. EISENHOWER

NOTE: Reorganization Plan 3 of 1953 is published in the U.S. Statutes at Large (67 Stat. 634) and in the 1949–1953 Compilation of title 3 of the Code of Federal Regulations (p. 1025). It became effective on June 12, 1953.

41 ¶ The President's News Conference of
April 2, 1953.

THE PRESIDENT. Please sit down. We don't have our friends
[the photographers] with us today.

This morning there went to the Congress the third reorganization plan for the Government. It involves the Office of Defense Mobilization, the National Security Resources Board, and
the old War Production Administration—all three consolidated
into one office, which will now be called the Office of Defense
Mobilization.

Of course, we expect this not only to result in a considerable
increase in efficiency by centralizing these functions where they
should be centralized, including the direction of our efforts at
stockpiling, but it will be a much more streamlined organization
than the three overlapping ones were in the past.

I was looking for some little announcement to make of my own.
That was it. Ladies and gentlemen, we will go right to the
questions.

Q. Merriman Smith, United Press: Mr. President, what is
your estimation or analysis of the recent peace overtures from
Russia and Communist China?

THE PRESIDENT. Well, Mr. Smith, it is very difficult to say that
any speculation on this affair should be dignified with the term
"analysis." You really are doing some pretty definite guessing.
But I think in this whole business of the peace approach, in which
the hearts of America are so deeply involved, that we should take
at face value every offer that is made to us, until it is proved not
to be worthy of being so taken. By that I do not mean that we
ignore the history of the past and some of the frustrating experiences we have had in trying to promote peaceful arrangements
with some of the people with whom we would now have to deal.
But I do say, here is something that, when the proffer comes
along, we should go right at it like it is meant exactly as it is said.

Now, in the proposal made by the Chinese commanders in Korea, which was in response to a request made by General Clark in February, and in line with the recommendations that the United Nations side of the negotiators have repeated over and over again, it was stated that it was believed that the exchange of sick and wounded prisoners during hostilities would do much to promote negotiations for an armistice.

We have, therefore, the hope that this exchange of sick and wounded prisoners will be quickly accomplished. Certainly, to my mind, that would be clear indication that deeds, rather than words and more frustrating conversations, are now to come into fashion—something that certainly every right-thinking person would welcome very heartily.

Therefore, without speculating further as to the motivation lying behind this, I should just say this Government is prepared to meet every honest advance, and in this instance, for example, has been trying to arrange this for a long, long time.

Q. Anthony H. Leviero, New York Times: Mr. President, you have commented on the Bricker resolution, which attempts to restrict your treaty-making powers. Now we have an instance of a Senator who negotiates an agreement that bears on foreign policy. I just want to ask you if you would comment, insofar as it bears on the prerogatives of the Presidency?

THE PRESIDENT. Every Senator or Member of Congress, every committee, subcommittee, has a right in their investigative and other processes to give advice to individuals, to indicate the judgment of the speaker as to what he believes our country might do under a given set of circumstances. But the power to negotiate, the responsibility for negotiating with others, rests absolutely and completely in the Executive. And this fact, of course, being so obvious, has universal recognition, including recognition by every Senator that I know. That excludes no one, and so stated the Senator to Mr. Dulles himself, yesterday.

So there is no effort here, at least so far as reported through the communications we have, to take over the power of negotiating on behalf of our Government.

Q. Richard L. Wilson, Cowles Publications: Mr. President, would you agree that Senator McCarthy's actions on the Greek ship matter had undermined administration policy?

THE PRESIDENT. You have asked a question, of course, that is one of opinion; many people can have different kinds of answers.

I think not, because I think there is sufficient power in the Secretary of State, and in the Presidency, to remind all peoples—others, and including our own—that the exclusive power of negotiating such arrangements, anything that is legal, belongs to the Executive, and comes into being when two-thirds of the Senate ratify.

So I doubt that an action—even, let us say, that we would agree it was misguided; if that were so, I doubt that act can undermine the prestige and the power that resides in the Government and in its various parts as viewed by the Constitution.

Q. David P. Sentner, Hearst Newspapers: Mr. President, have you discussed, or will you discuss with Ambassador Bohlen, the possibility of a meeting between yourself and Premier Malenkov?

THE PRESIDENT. I do not expect to see the Ambassador again before he leaves. As a matter of fact, I saw him this afternoon. We did not discuss that particular point because as I see it, there is no basis, at the moment, for discussing it.

Q. [*Speaker unidentified*]: Mr. President, there seems to be considerable unhappiness among some Congressmen, and some editors, over a charge that Secretary Weeks has dismissed the Director of the Bureau of Standards without hearing his side of all charges which appear to reflect basically on his good character and integrity. I wonder if you would comment on that, sir?

THE PRESIDENT. Well, I can't, for the simple reason that no such report has reached my ears. This is the first time I have heard it, so I can't possibly comment.

Mr. Weeks forwarded to me an application for resignation,

and I accepted it. Now, if there is any such thing as this behind it, I know nothing about it at this moment. But I do have faith that Secretary Weeks will be the last person to be arbitrary and unjust in such circumstances.

Q. [*Speaker unidentified*], United Press: Mr. President, would you accept an invitation for the United States to participate in the Anglo-Soviet air safety talks in Berlin, or has such an invitation come to you?

THE PRESIDENT. No such invitation has come to me, and of course, any invitation would have to be examined on exactly what it says; but if it were one that looked like there would be useful discussions, why I would think the Secretary of State would recommend its acceptance.

Q. Lloyd M. Schwartz, Fairchild Papers: Mr. President, I wonder if you could tell us your view of the Simpson bill for extending the reciprocal trade agreements act, which is being represented by some as a high tariff bill, and whether the administration will have a bill of its own?

THE PRESIDENT. I have forgotten now—[*confers with Mr. Hagerty*]—as a matter of fact, I have to check my memory, not as to what has been done but as to whether it has been done at a time that I am free to talk. I am merely trying to be as helpful as I can to any legitimate question.

I just want to say this: the matter has been under earnest study for a long time. Long before I came down to Washington, I convened people to look at this thing. We are going to try to decide it on the overall good, and I hope that there will be no necessity for yielding to any narrow consideration in the whole business.

Now, I am informed by Mr. Hagerty that these negotiations have not yet gotten to the point that I am free to talk about them.

Q. Paul R. Leach, Chicago Daily News: Mr. President, in December 1951, President Truman issued an Executive order permitting all the departments of Government—all the heads of departments—to classify information, which was regarded by a good many newspaper editors as restricting the flow of news to the press. There have been some reports that that was to be rescinded or amended. Is that contemplated, or has it been done?

THE PRESIDENT. It is one of the things, of course, that has been mentioned from time to time. I have not yet personally gotten into it. But I did have this to say about the thing within my own family: that if any press man has a specific instance where this rule or Executive order has been applied to what he believes to be the detriment of the proper functions of the newspaper world, I wish he would give the specific instance to my Press Secretary and let me take a look.

I do believe, by and large, as you people well know, in the principle of decentralization. I do not believe that there should be an attempt, as there frequently is in some governments, to centralize power too much in the hands of one person, particularly administrative power. It tends to slow up and it tends to make impossible the work that you people would largely do otherwise.

So I would like to see those people responsible for their own actions. But if that action becomes what experience would show to be inadvisable, or it tends toward unjust choking off and strangling of news, I would like to know about it before I proceed to—towards action.

I do assure you it is not forgotten. It has just been something that we have not gotten to in the analysis and study.

Q. [*Speaker unidentified*]: Mr. President, you were represented today by Speaker Martin as favoring straight 1-year extension of the reciprocal trade agreements act, presumably pending further study that you have mentioned. Could you say whether you favor such an interim extension now?

THE PRESIDENT. Yes I do. If he announced that—that is perfectly clear, that's exactly my position. I do not believe that it is possible to settle these questions specifically on the various aspects of the welfare of the United States, except with a more profound study than has been possible to make.

Consequently, if he has already stated that—and I am taking your report that he has—why, I stand by it.

Q. G. Gould Lincoln, Washington Evening Star: Mr. President, has there been a crystallization on selection of a Republican National Chairman, and is former Representative Leonard Hall a likely choice?

THE PRESIDENT. So far as I know, there has been none. Now, as you well know, that is not my prerogative, to select a National Chairman. As I told you when it was mentioned before, I assume that my wishes and desires would have a very considerable influence, so I am not trying to divest myself of responsibility; but I think it will be a job that the National Committee, in collaboration with all of the leaders of the party everywhere, will have to undertake with the utmost seriousness.

And the only thing I can say: I am going to try to find a man who commands the highest respect from every way that I can find, as far as my own choice of person is to be considered.

As for Mr. Hall, I have heard his name along with a dozen others mentioned, but I haven't heard any drive on the part of anybody. I don't know whether anyone really wants the job.

Q. [*Speaker unidentified*]: Mr. President, I understood before leaving office, President Truman sent you a report of the Contract Compliance Committee, which was set up to eliminate discrimination in plants with Government contracts. That Committee doesn't have a chairman now, and many of the members are resigning. What steps have been taken to vitalize that group by appointing a chairman for the Committee, and public officers—public members, that is?

THE PRESIDENT. Again, I am sorry; you have asked me a question that I will have to answer next week. That has not been reported to me—that we are lacking a chairman in it. We will look it up, and I will try to give you an answer.

Q. [*Speaker unidentified*], Baltimore Sun: Mr. President, I would like to go back to this other question. I wonder if you would consider it in the national interest for a congressional committee to undertake negotiations—conduct negotiations with foreign ship owners, to get an embargo on trading with Communist countries?

THE PRESIDENT. Personally, I don't believe they can possibly have the facts that would make such negotiations really profitable, unless the fact in some matter were so obvious that there was universal, unquestioned agreement, and they might have some personal contact that might work out for the good of the United States. I wouldn't say.

You know, there is an aphorism "There is no never." Well, I am not going to say there never could be any good come out of such things. I should say, on the average, now, I would doubt it.

Q. James B. Reston, New York Times: Mr. President, on Monday, Harold Stassen told Senator McCarthy's committee that he thought the Senator's actions in the Greek ship deal did undermine the efforts that his Agency was making to try to block off East-West trade. In your reply earlier this afternoon, you indicated that those acts did not undermine the prestige of Government, and I thought that that statement was open to the interpretation that you disagreed with Mr. Stassen's position?

THE PRESIDENT. Well, I disagree this much, possibly, Mr. Reston. As I understand it, this discussion came up on the word negotiation, which you will remember I used this afternoon very distinctly and emphatically. He said the attempt to negotiate agreements was an infringement—I think he probably meant infringement more than he did undermining—and I was also trying to make clear that to undermine required a lot more doing than merely making an error, no matter how badly I might consider the error to be.

So that I think in Senator McCarthy's later statements, as I understand them and the Secretary does, he had no idea he was negotiating anything; and as long as he is not, he is probably in his proper function. He can discuss, suggest, advise—and that's all right; but negotiating is something else.   I tried to make that clear.

Q. Mr. Reston: Mr. President, I wonder if your attention has been called to his Saturday announcement, which was handed to us in writing, which says that as a result of negotiations undertaken by representatives of this subcommittee with the Greek owners of 242 merchant ships, they have agreed to break off all trade with North Korea, Communist China, and the far eastern ports of Soviet Russia?

THE PRESIDENT. Well, I would say, how do you negotiate when there is nothing that you can commit?   Now, I don't see how any of us here can hold the idea that a group of legislators or an individual can commit the United States to any action; so I would not understand what "negotiations" means.   They might obtain promises, they might obtain some kind of expression of opinion or intention from these people, and he could announce it; that, I would say, is all right.   If that represents his conviction on what he should do, there would be no criticism.   But that, in my mind, is not negotiation.

Q. Merriman Smith, United Press: Mr. President, I am a little confused.   Are we to understand, then, that it is your opinion that Senator McCarthy changed his position from the time of his original announcement when he used the word "negotiate," until the time he met with Secretary Dulles yesterday?

THE PRESIDENT. I am certain of this: negotiation in the way I am talking about it now is something that he could not have done because he had no power to do it—the negotiating which commits our Government to some form of action, subject always in our form of government, if it gets on the treaty basis, to approval by the Senate.

Q. Murrey Marder, Washington Post: Mr. President, do you feel that this in any way interfered or impeded the efforts to conduct other negotiations, as Mr. Stassen indicated?

THE PRESIDENT. I haven't discussed this point that you raise, in detail, with either Secretary Dulles or Mr. Stassen. Governor Stassen, as you know, has been out of town—just got back, at least to my knowledge, today; and Secretary Dulles has been pretty busy. So I wouldn't have a real opinion on the point.

Q. Robert G. Spivack, New York Post: Mr. President, just to recapitulate all this, are you unhappy with what Mr. Stassen said the other day, or with what Senator McCarthy——

THE PRESIDENT. I am not in the slightest bit unhappy. I think that I know where we are trying to go. I think, by and large, we are developing and getting better cooperation with the Senate and House every day. The mere fact that some little incident arises is not going to disturb me. I have been scared by experts, in war and in peace, and I am not frightened about this.

Q. Mrs. May Craig, Maine papers: Mr. President, if I could get away from high politics to butter, do you think there is anything that you can do in the long term, so that people can get butter at reasonable prices, and not have it stored away at taxpayers expense to spoil? It is a long term problem, I know, but it's a symbolic thing.

THE PRESIDENT. Well, of course, you are talking about something where you could far better go to the Secretary of Agriculture and get a really definitive answer to such a question. As a matter of fact, under the provisions of law, we are buying butter at 67⅔ cents a pound, I believe. Currently, I believe—although I may be wrong a few hundred thousand pounds—we are buying about 2 million pounds a day. At the same time we are buying at that price, the finest oleomargarine, I am told, is sold at half that price. What you come down to is that butter is pricing itself out of the market. And yet if you can tell the difference sufficiently that you insist on having butter, why, I guess that all you want is there at 67⅔ cents a pound.

Until there is some change in the program, or a change in the rate of production of these things in our country, I don't know what should be done.

Q. Mrs. Craig: But, sir, the reason we have so many million—nearly half a billion—pounds in storage, is because the taxpayers' money is taken to buy, put it there.

THE PRESIDENT. I think you are exaggerating the figures somewhat, but still it's too large, in my opinion.

And I think there is this very great danger which adds to the problem, that since we don't have deep-freeze facilities all over the United States, some of this can enter the spoilage danger zone very soon.

I would hope this: as long as we have to have such surpluses, if we believe that to be to the best interests of our country—remember these programs have been developing and evolving over almost three decades—if that is true, then I should certainly hope that Congress would place upon the President the responsibility of finding outlets for anything that is in danger of spoiling. I think it would be a crime today against civilization, and against ourselves, to allow anything to spoil that could be used by anybody, even if those surpluses have to be disposed of at almost zero value; because I couldn't conceive of anything worse than to have openly to destroy it, when people are hungry and need such things.

Q. Mrs. Craig: Well, sir, if you did not—this administration did not price support it, couldn't you find an outlet in the ordinary people buying it—the housewives—at prices they could pay?

THE PRESIDENT. I would say, Mrs. Craig, that you cannot possibly be guilty of lack of good faith with your own people. This thing was done by law, long before we came along. And when we saw the extent to which it had gone, we had to prolong the thing until some kind of arrangements or some kind of new philosophy, at least, could be brought out. That is what they are working at now, through these commissions and committees that work with the Department of Agriculture, representing every part of our agriculture and the public. What are we going to do about these things to have reasonable, proper policies? It is a very difficult and intricate one.

Of course, it will arouse a lot of emotion, because certain people will be affected right square in the pocketbook, while others say we are looking at the, by and large, good of the Nation.

Q. Alan S. Emory, Watertown (N.Y.) Times: Early this week, sir, Mr. John A. Ulinsky, who is the United States Commissioner for the International Boundary Commission, United States, Canada, and Alaska, was dismissed from his post and replaced by, I believe, Mr. Samuel L. Golan of Chicago, Illinois.

Now, the treaty with Canada which set up the Commission specifies that the United States Commissioner can be removed only through death, disability, or retirement, none of which applied to Mr. Ulinsky, and that his successor—again in the treaty—should be a qualified geographer or surveyor. Mr. Golan, the successor, is a lawyer.

I wonder if you thought this complied, either—first—with the spirit of the treaty; or, second, with your campaign pledge to get the best brains for the best jobs in Government?

THE PRESIDENT. Well, you have stated a case—[*laughter*]—that sounds terrible. And if the facts as you state them, now, are really facts—and I assume they certainly are as you understand them—someone is going to be questioned as to why I was not informed of those facts before. Of that I am sure.

Q. [*Speaker unidentified*]: Mr. President, did you convince Dan Reed he should balance the budget before he cut taxes?

THE PRESIDENT. The question did not come up—not the subject of our luncheon conversation.

Q. Fred W. Perkins, Scripps-Howard Newspapers: Mr. President, I have two related questions: (a) would you care to comment on your opinion of the prospects of the Washington baseball team this year [*laughter*]; (b) would you throw out the ball at the opening game?

THE PRESIDENT. Well, first, I am most certainly not a baseball prophet. The only thing I have in such things is sentiment. I know who I am for. As long as I am living in Washington, I am for the Senators from the beginning, and I will be there on the last day of the game.

Now, I am going to the game of April 23d. I am not going to be there the 13th. I think I told you people before, that week of April 13th is one I am desperately fighting to save. I have lost 1 day—I have to come back to meet your friends the editors on the 16th; but aside from that, I am fighting to keep that week as 5 or 6 days of my own. So I won't be able to make it on the 13th, but I hope to be there on the 23d. There's a day game, the first series home.

Q. Anthony H. Leviero, New York Times: Senator Taft and Congressman Simpson said you had taken a long look to the 1954 elections, and how you might win it. Could you give us some insight into your thinking?

THE PRESIDENT. I think it is just as simple as looking at the palm of your hand. If the Republican Party can show as its record over the next 2 years a progressive, sane program of accomplishment, one that is in keeping with the constitutional processes of this country, which takes care of the welfare, the interest, of all our people and doesn't give itself away to any section or any group, any class— and that program, that accomplishment, is properly advertised, we will be back with a very greatly enhanced majority.

Q. Merriman Smith, United Press: Mr. President, last week you said you were not aware of a plan by Mr. Wilson to cut the size of combat strength. You said you left it up to him to decide. Well, since last week a plan has become somewhat apparent from the Pentagon, that they are studying a plan to reduce combat strength. We wondered during the week if you thought maybe we have reached a point where it is safe to reduce the total size of our armed forces?

THE PRESIDENT. I don't think I said exactly what you say I said, Mr. Smith. I never said that I would leave to anyone else the final decision as to what should be the level of combat strength. I said that I was waiting on detailed recommendations. Moreover, as I urge the streamlining of organization, of getting rid of duplications and what I still believe to be unnecessary expense in that Department, we are studying, all of us, every day, I assure you, what is the level of strength in being that, in our judgment would conform to what I always go back to—Washington's old precept of the respectable posture of military defense. But by no means would that be a responsibility that I could delegate.

Q. John M. Hightower, Associated Press: Could you tell us anything about your meeting with Ambassador Bohlen, sir, particularly whether you are sending any sort of personal message to Premier Malenkov?

THE PRESIDENT. Well, I will give you this much on the question: in conformity with the practice every newly appointed Ambassador observes, Ambassador Bohlen came in to call on me this afternoon. He is leaving immediately, I believe, either this evening or tomorrow, for Europe—soon hopes to be in Moscow. We discussed only, as far as any general subject is concerned, the situation there of the American Ambassador, the hope that he could be helpful in anything that came up, the general nature of the problems that we could possibly anticipate. As far as anything further is concerned, I would have nothing to say.

Q. John D. Morris, New York Times: Mr. President, I take it from what you said, that your conference with Mr. Reed and Mr. Simpson might have been on reciprocal trade. Could you give us any idea as to any decisions that might have been made?

THE PRESIDENT. There were no decisions made. We just were exchanging ideas. Actually, among other things, we talked about the question which you brought up a minute ago, which was the congressional elections of 1954. As you know, Mr. Reed is the chairman of the congressional committee, and he wanted to know——

Q. Mr. Morris [*interjecting*]: Mr. Simpson.

THE PRESIDENT. Mr. Simpson, I mean, is chairman of the congressional committee. He wanted to know whether I would be cheering for him; and I certainly had no difficulty in assuring him that I would.

Q. Marvin L. Arrowsmith, Associated Press: Mr. President,

did I understand you to say that you favor extension of reciprocal trade as is, without any changes, for 1 year?

THE PRESIDENT. I can't say that there shouldn't be any change. The way I feel is, it should be extended for 1 year; because when you start changing—and I want that to be done on the basis of study—such changes necessary should be the product of mature deliberation and representation of all viewpoints, and not giving way to any one special interest.

Q. Anthony H. Leviero, New York Times: Mr. President, is there any light you can throw on the statement by General Van Fleet that he was prohibited from carrying out an amphibious landing by General Ridgway behind the enemy lines?

THE PRESIDENT. That I haven't heard. I haven't heard a word about it.

Q. Mr. Leviero: He made that statement before a subcommittee.

THE PRESIDENT. Just recently?

Q. Mr. Leviero: Yesterday.

THE PRESIDENT. Oh. I don't know. It could have been there wasn't amphibious equipment there; I don't know. I couldn't comment. I have talked to General Van Fleet several times, and we have gone over past events, but that easily could have been omitted just inadvertently. He never mentioned such an occurrence to me.

[*Speaker unidentified*]: Thank you, Mr. President.

NOTE: President Eisenhower's sixth news conference was held in the Executive Office Building at 3:30 p.m. on April 2, 1953.

42 ¶ Statement by the President on the Fourth Anniversary of the Signing of the North Atlantic Treaty. *April 4,* 1953

JUST FOUR YEARS ago today the representatives of twelve free nations met in Washington to sign their names to a document which free men will long remember. That document was the North Atlantic Treaty.

In the years since that date other nations have signed their names and pledged their strength—to make NATO the central source of strength for defense of the western world.

This year it happens that we commemorate the anniversary of NATO at Easter time. To peoples of all faiths the spiritual idea of the Prince of Peace carries meaning. And NATO is an instrument of peace. It endangers none who will respect freedom. It serves all who love freedom—and wish to enjoy it in peace.

We have learned from bitter and conclusive experience that peace cannot be defended by the weak. It demands strength—strength of our armies, strength of our economies and, above all, strength of our spirit.

This strength can be born only of unity. NATO signifies the resolve of the free nations of the North Atlantic community to be united against any aggression. The North Atlantic Treaty served notice that an attack upon any of the NATO countries would be resisted by all. It did yet more: It called upon all participating nations to develop that strength which could not only win war but more importantly could prevent war.

The two hundred million people of the NATO nations of Europe are in the deepest sense bound together by a unity more profound than any pact. They are skilled in work, courageous in spirit, and tenacious in their love of freedom. They—their spirit and strength and resources—are indispensable to the defense of freedom everywhere. If they and their resources ever were captured and exploited by an aggressor, there would be no corner of safety anywhere in the world. But so long as these people and these resources are joined with those of the United States in our common cause, no aggressor can be blind to the folly of attack.

The work of NATO is far from complete. This anniversary, then, should be the signal for all NATO nations to dedicate themselves with renewed vigor to the work that remains to be done. So doing, each and all must know that they are serving—not the wishes or needs of some big alien power, nor even a lofty abstract ideal—but simply their own salvation and survival in freedom.

Each and all must remind themselves that the faint of heart and the slow of deed are the first and the surest to invite the torment of aggression.

Each and all of us must summon to mind the words of Him whom we honor this Easter time: "When a strong man, armed, keepeth his palace, his goods are in peace."

43 ¶ Message to the Members of the United Nations Commission on Human Rights.
April 7, 1953

I AM ASKING Mrs. Oswald B. Lord, the new Representative of the United States on the United Nations Commission on Human Rights, to express to the Commission my deep personal interest in its work. In these days of international tension and strain, it is encouraging to know that the members of the Commission on Human Rights are working to develop effective programs to promote human rights and fundamental freedoms for all people and all nations throughout the world.

The United Nations Charter states the human rights goals which the United States and the other Members of the United Nations have pledged themselves to achieve in cooperation with the United Nations—the promotion of universal respect for human rights and fundamental freedoms for all without distinction as to race, sex, language, or religion.

For the people of the United States as well as for people everywhere, the United Nations Universal Declaration of Human Rights is a significant beacon in the steady march toward achieving human rights and fundamental freedoms for all.

People everywhere are seeking freedom—freedom to live, freedom from arbitrary restraint, freedom to think and speak as they wish, freedom to seek and find the truth. We must press ahead to broaden the areas of freedom. The United States is convinced that freedom is an indispensable condition to the achievement of a stable peace.

Unfortunately, in too many areas of the world today there is subjugation of peoples by totalitarian governments which have no respect for the dignity of the human person. This denial of the freedom of peoples, the continued disregard of human rights, is a basic cause of instability and discontent in the world today.

For these reasons, the work of the Commission on Human Rights assumes greater importance and meaning. For these reasons also, there is need for a new approach to the development of a human rights conscience in all areas of the world. I have accordingly asked Mrs. Lord to present positive UN action programs to the Commission which we feel will contribute to that recognition of human rights and fundamental freedoms which people are seeking throughout the world.

NOTE: The United Nations Commission on Human Rights convened in Geneva on April 7. A statement by Mrs. Lord before the Commission on April 8, outlining the new approach mentioned in the President's message, is published in the Department of State Bulletin (vol. 28, p. 581).

44 ¶ Special Message to the Congress Recommending the Renewal of the Reciprocal Trade Agreements Act. *April 7,* 1953

To the Congress of the United States:

In my State of the Union Message I recommended that "the Congress take the Reciprocal Trade Agreements Act under immediate study and extend it by appropriate legislation."

I now recommend that the present Act be renewed for the period of one year.

I propose this action as an interim measure. As such, it will allow for the temporary continuation of our present trade program pending completion of a thorough and comprehensive re-examination of the economic foreign policy of the United States.

I believe that such a reexamination is imperative in order to develop more effective solutions to the international economic problems today confronting the United States and its partners in the community of free nations. It is my intention that the Executive Branch shall consult with the Congress in developing recommendations based upon the studies that will be made.

Our trade policy is only one part, although a vital part, of a larger problem. This problem embraces the need to develop, through cooperative action among the free nations, a strong and self-supporting economic system capable of providing both the military strength to deter aggression and the rising productivity that can improve living standards.

No feature of American policy is more important in this respect than the course which we set in our economic relations with other nations. The long term economic stability of the whole free world and the overriding question of world peace will be heavily influenced by the wisdom of our decisions. As for the United States itself, its security is fully as dependent upon the economic health and stability of the other free nations as upon their adequate military strength.

The problem is far from simple. It is a complex of many features of our foreign and domestic programs. Our domestic economic policies cast their shadows upon nations far beyond our borders. Conversely, our foreign economic policy has a direct impact upon our domestic economy. We must make a careful study of these intricate relationships in order that we may chart a sound course for the nation.

The building of a productive and strong economic system within the free world—one in which each country may better sustain itself through its own efforts—will require action by other governments, as well as by the United States, over a wide range of economic activities. These must include: adoption of sound internal policies, creation of conditions fostering international investment, assistance to underdeveloped areas, progress towards freedom of international payments and convertibility of currencies, and trade arrangements aimed at the widest possible multilateral trade.

In working toward these goals, our own trade policy as well as that of other countries should contribute to the highest possible level of trade on a basis that is profitable and equitable for all. The world must achieve an expanding trade, balanced at high levels, which will permit each nation to make its full contribution to the progress of the free world's economy and to share fully the benefits of this progress.

The solution of the free world's economic problems is a cooperative task. It is not one which the United States, however strong its leadership and however firm its dedication to these objectives, can effectively attack alone. But two truths are clear: the United States' share in this undertaking is so large as to be crucially important to its success—and its success is crucially important to the United States. This last truth applies with particular force to many of our domestic industries and especially to agriculture with its great and expanding output.

I am confident that the governments of other countries are prepared to do their part in working with us toward these common goals, and we shall from time to time be consulting with them. The extension for one year of the present Reciprocal Trade Agreements Act will provide us the time necessary to study and define a foreign economic policy which will be comprehensive, constructive and consistent with the needs both of the American economy and of American foreign policy.

DWIGHT D. EISENHOWER

45 ¶ Remarks at a Meeting of the United Defense Fund Organization. *April 7, 1953*

Mr. Ryerson and ladies and gentlemen:

I consider it indeed an honor to be here with you this morning. I consider it a greater honor that you have selected me as your Honorary Chairman and so designated.

I did not come over this morning in the role of a professor to give you a lecture. I did not come to tell you things that you know as well as I. Certainly I did not come in any effort to inspire. Your presence here, and the work that you are now doing as a service to your country, is evidence enough of the inspiration that you carry, each of you, within your own heart.

I did come, though, to try to express with all my past and present experience, something of the appreciation I feel for what you are doing. I know of what it means to a soldier in a lonely land—in a strange land—to have around him something that means home, something in the way of entertainment, something in the way of a hot dog or a Coca Cola, or whatever, that brings him back closer to those surroundings and those people with whom he has lived—where his heart is.

The U.S.O. in war was one of the great agencies for sustaining morale. Time and again I had occasion officially to express to the U.S.O.—and of course now, to the United Defense Fund—my thanks for the work it had been doing.

We still have war going on, and a war that is conducted under bleak surroundings. There is little in Korea that is entertaining for a soldier, except for those few who have the privilege, maybe, to go off on half a day's duck shooting when they get to the rear— something of that kind. There is just nothing to do. Consequently, your services are more important than ever.

Now, every person—every right-thinking individual, I think, in the world, utters a prayer to his God each night that there may come peace, and particularly peace in Korea.

If that peace does come—for which we so devoutly hope—there is still equal need for the services you people are now providing; possibly in a way, greater. Because, as you well know, in such a complicated procedure as developing armistices and peace, there must be developed also a confidence that it is permanent; our men and those of our Allies will have to stay in that region for quite a while. It will be a trying period, as those of you who went through World War I and World War II well know.

Once inaction sets in, and the impatience of the American can begin to manifest itself, it is really tough to keep before him just the conception of stern duties, and expect him to forget his grouses and his gripes and his disappointment in being so far from home.

Then is when the U.S.O. can be of even added value. So, much as you know of what it is doing now and your own sense of the worth of your work, I assure you that if this armistice can come, don't let anyone tell you that the need for your services will be lessened.

And I feel, in addition, to give you this one conclusion about that contingency, that I have rather a special right to thank you for your work. I had the very great honor, in my time, of commanding the greatest number of Americans who were ever given to any one man. I feel that I should attempt to be their spokesman in return for what they did, when it comes to talking about their needs and their expectations, for them and for their successors.

I do not come here to plead with you for them, because I know that you already understand that. But if my words or my conclusions on this can be of any help to you in presenting this picture to the world, then you are certainly at liberty to quote me freely. For the soldier of America doing his duty on the battleground, or in any far and foreign fields, I feel he never demands more than is reasonable. We should always be ready to give—to promise and to give that much.

That is what I think the American soldier deserves, and what you are trying to give him.

I repeat—if my ideas on this subject will help you as you go about the business of raising the funds and getting the support for your work, then for once you may quote me, as widely and as freely as you please.

Again, let me thank Mr. Ryerson and your Executive Committee, and indeed each of you, for doing me the honor of asking me to come in front of you. It is a cause in which I am proud to serve, even in only the rather vicarious way that I can give of my support.

To each of you my thanks, and my thanks also to everybody that helps you in this great task.

Thank you again.

NOTE: The President spoke at the Statler Hotel in Washington at 10:53 a.m. In his remarks he referred to Edward L. Ryerson, Chairman of the United Defense Fund.

46　¶ Special Message to the Senate Transmitting Agreements With Germany Relating to the Settlement of Certain Debts and Claims. *April* 10, 1953

To the Senate of the United States:

I transmit herewith for the consideration of the Senate a copy of each of the following Agreements:

1. Agreement on German External Debts, signed at London on February 27, 1953 by the Federal Republic of Germany, and by the United States and seventeen other creditor countries.

2. Agreement between the United States and the Federal Republic of Germany regarding the Settlement of the Claims of the United States for Postwar Economic Assistance (other than Sur-

plus Property) to Germany, signed at London on February 27, 1953.

3. Agreement between the United States and the Federal Republic of Germany relating to the Indebtedness of Germany for Awards made by the Mixed Claims Commission, United States and Germany, signed at London on February 27, 1953.

4. Agreement between the United States and the Federal Republic of Germany concerning the Validation of German Dollar Bonds, signed at Bonn on April 1, 1953.

I request the advice and consent of the Senate to the ratification of these four Agreements.

In addition, I transmit for the information of the Senate two related Agreements between the Federal Republic of Germany and the United States and a report made to me by the Secretary of State covering all six of these Agreements. One of the Agreements is concerned with the settlement of the obligation of the Federal Republic of Germany to the United States for surplus property furnished to Germany. This Agreement was signed at London on February 27, 1953, and was concluded under the authority of the Federal Property and Administrative Services Act of 1949 (P.L. 152–81st Congress). The other Agreement, signed at Bonn on February 27, 1953, is an executive agreement relating to the establishment of procedures for the validation of dollar bonds of German issue.

The arrangements set forth in these several Agreements provide for the orderly settlement of German external debts, including the pre-war debts due mainly to private persons and the claims of the United States Government arising from post-war economic assistance to Germany. On the former of these categories, the effect will be to end the state of default which has existed for about twenty years. The consideration of reparation and other governmental claims arising from World Wars I and II is deferred under the terms of the agreement.

The complex documents transmitted herewith are the result of negotiations, extending over more than two years, in which all of the interests concerned have been represented. In particular, it is to be noted that the settlement terms and procedures for debts due to private creditors were worked out by negotiations between representatives of private creditor interests and of the debtors. In the light of all of the circumstances, it is the view of the Executive Branch of the United States Government that the settlement arrangements, embodied in the Agreement on German External Debts and in the various bilateral agreements, are reasonable, satisfactory and equitable to the interests concerned.

With regard to debts due to private creditors, maturity dates have been extended and the creditors are called upon to accept a reduction in interest arrears and interest rates, but the principal of the debts is unchanged. With regard to the claims for economic assistance given to Germany in the post-war period, for which the United States Government is by far the largest claimant, the settlement is comparable to the terms which other countries have received for similar assistance. On both categories of debt, the German Federal Republic has undertaken to make very considerable payments, but these payments may reasonably be considered within the Federal Republic's capacity to pay. Should the German Federal Republic, however, get into payment difficulties, consultative machinery to deal with the situation is provided for.

The elimination of the German state of default will contribute substantially and directly to the development of normal commercial relationships between the German Federal Republic and the rest of the free world. It will open up the possibilities of new credit, for both short-term trade financing and long-term investment.

These Agreements should be considered by the Senate not only in the light of the direct financial benefits to the United States, but also in relation to the contribution they will make to the achievement of the principal objective of United States policy toward Germany, that of restoring Germany to the position of a responsible nation in the community of free nations.

I recommend, therefore, that the Senate give early and favorable consideration to the Agreement on German External Debts and to the three bilateral agreements between the United States and the Federal Republic of Germany relating, respectively, to the settlement of claims for postwar economic assistance to Germany, to the indebtedness of Germany for the Mixed Claims Commission awards, and to the validation of German dollar bonds, and give its advice and consent to their ratification, in order that the debt settlement arrangements may be made effective as promptly as possible.

DWIGHT D. EISENHOWER

NOTE: The agreements and related papers are printed in Senate Executive D, E, F, and G (83d Cong., 1st sess.). The four agreements were favorably considered by the Senate on July 13, 1953, and after ratification entered into force September 16, 1953 (4 UST 443 et seq.).

47 ¶ Letter to the Governors of the States Inviting Them to a Conference at the White House. *April* 11, 1953

[Released April 11, 1953. Dated April 9, 1953]

Dear —————:

It is with great pleasure that I extend to you and the Governors of the other States of the nation a most cordial invitation to attend a conference here in the White House on May fourth and fifth, for the purpose of participating in confidential discussions relating to problems facing America and the free world in these most difficult times.

It is my earnest conviction that you will find this conference a worthwhile occasion. The program will give consideration, among other matters of national concern, to current developments in the field of international relations, the American defense effort, the problems of national security, and an analysis of our fiscal policies as related thereto. The presentation by Cabinet members and officials charged with the responsibility of administering these affairs will be designed to give you a first-hand picture of the present state of the world and the role of the United States in it.

In these critical times an occasion which offers the prospect of America's leaders, State and national, working side by side to give the United States enlightened leadership warrants vigorous support. I am firmly convinced that this conference will produce a better understanding of the need which I feel for the full co-operation of each of you in dealing with the variety of problems which confront the nation.

I hope very much you will be able to join with me at ten o'clock on May fourth in Room 474 of the Executive Office Building, Pennsylvania and West Executive Avenues. I shall call upon my associates in the Executive Branch to lead subsequent discussions, but I do look forward to greeting you at the opening session, and I would very much like you to have luncheon with me at the White House at one o'clock on that day. After luncheon the discussions will resume that afternoon and the following morning until noon.

I trust you can be with us on these days.

Sincerely,

DWIGHT D. EISENHOWER

48 ¶ Address Before the Council of the Organization of American States. *April* 12, 1953

Mr. Chairman, members of the Council, ladies and gentlemen:

My pride and pleasure in participating in the ceremonies today have a simple source. They spring from the pride which the whole citizenry of the United States feels in the Pan American Union and the ideals for which it stands.

The code that governs our union is founded upon the most deeply held moral convictions. And this fact makes especially appropriate our meeting on this, our Sabbath Day.

Ours is an historic and meaningful unity. It has been—for our whole continent—an honest and productive unity. It can be—for other areas of the world—a prophetic and inspiring unity. For it is triumphant testimony, before all the world, that peace and trust and fellowship can rule the conduct of all nations, large and small, who will respect the life and dignity of each other.

In this deepest sense, then, we nations of America do more than enjoy a political system constructed for ourselves. We are custodians of a way of life that can be instructive for all mankind.

The history of the Americas over the span of the 63 years since the founding of our regional organization has not been spotlessly perfect. Like all peoples, our nations—every one of them, the United States included—have at times been guilty of selfish and thoughtless actions. In all dealings with our neighbors we have not always bravely resisted the temptations of expediency.

But the special merit of the Pan American achievement is to have triumphed as well as we have over the temptations of heedless nationalism. We have seen and we have acted on the need to work cooperatively together to achieve common purposes. So doing, we have forged a true community of equal nations.

I am profoundly dedicated personally to doing all that I can to perfect the understanding and trust upon which this community must rest.

The vitality of this unity springs, first of all, from our common acceptance of basic moral and juridical principles. But it is inspired no less by our recognition of the rights of each of our nations, under these principles, to perfect its own individual life and culture. Ours is no compulsory unity of institutions. Ours is a unity that welcomes the diversity, the initiative and the imagination that make our common association progressive and alive. This is the true way of the Americas—the free way—by which people are bound together for the common good.

I know that these facts, these simple ideals, are not new. But they are given a new, a sharp meaning, by the nature of the tension tormenting our whole world. For it is not possible for this hemisphere to seek security or salvation in any kind of splendid isolation.

The forces threatening this continent strike at the very ideals by which our peoples live. These forces seek to bind nations not by trust but by fear. They seek to promote, among those of us who remain free and unafraid, the deadliest divisions—class against class, people against people, nation against nation. They seek not to eradicate poverty and its causes—but to exploit it and those who suffer it.

Against these forces the widest oceans offer no sure defense. The seeds of hate and of distrust can be born on winds that heed no frontier or shore.

Our defense, our only defense, is in our own spirit and our own will. We who are all young nations, in whom the pioneering spirit is still vitally alive, need neither to fear the future nor be satisfied with the present. In our spiritual, cultural and material life, in all that concerns our daily bread and our daily learning, we do and should seek an ever better world.

We know that this economic and social betterment will not be achieved by engaging in experiments alien to our very souls, or listening to prophets seeking to destroy our very lives.

We know that it can come to pass only by faithfully applying the rules of national conduct we know to have been tested and proven wise: a mutual trust that makes us honorable and understanding neighbors, and a self-reliance that summons each nation to work to the full for its own welfare.

I do not think it unjust to claim for the government and the people of the United States a readiness, rarely matched in history, to help other nations improve their living standards and guard their security. Despite unprecedented burdens of national debt and world wide responsibility, our people have continued to demonstrate this readiness.

Private investment has been the major stimulus for economic development throughout this hemisphere. Beyond this, the United States government is today engaged with our sister republics in important efforts to increase agricultural productivity, improve health conditions, encourage new industries, extend transportation facilities, and develop new sources of power.

The pursuit of each of these goals in any one nation of the Americas serves the good of all the Americas. Knowing this, I am anxious that the government of the United States be fully informed of the economic and social conditions now prevailing throughout our continent and of all the efforts being pressed to bring a better life to all our peoples. Such an assessment can properly be made only through direct personal understanding of the facts. Because my current duties make impossible my making personal visits of courtesy to the countries of Latin America, as I wish I could do, I have asked my brother, Dr. Milton Eisenhower, President of Pennsylvania State College, to visit shortly a number of these great republics. He will carry to each of the governments he visits the most sincere and warm greetings of this Administration. He will report to me, to Secretary of State Dulles and to Assistant Secretary Cabot, on ways to be recommended for strengthening the bonds of friendship between us and all our neighbors in this Pan American Union.

Today, Mr. Chairman, I think it appropriate to conclude with this one thought: However real and just be our concern with constructive material development, we must never forget that the strength of America continues ever to be the spirit of America.

We are Christian nations, deeply conscious that the foundation of all liberty is religious faith.

Upon all our peoples and nations there rests, with equal weight, a responsibility to serve worthily the faith we hold and the freedom we cherish—to combat demagoguery with truth, to destroy prejudice with understanding and, above all, to thwart our common enemies by our fervent dedication to our common cause.

So dedicated, our republics, united in spirit, can look forward to a future of happy and productive peace.

Mr. Chairman, for the great honor you have done me in inviting me to this platform, I am grateful. To you, to the other members of the Council, and to each member of this audience, thank you very much.

NOTE: The President spoke at 12:30 p.m. at the Pan American Union. His opening words "Mr. Chairman" referred to Ambassador Rene Lepervanche Parparcen, Representative of Venezuela.

On June 22 the White House released a statement by Dr. Milton S. Eisenhower on the eve of his departure to visit the 10 Republics of South America. In a later statement, released July 29, Dr. Eisenhower reported briefly on his 36-day tour, during which he and his associates held extended discussions with Presidents, Cabinet ministers, and leaders in the fields of labor, educa-

tion, agriculture, and finance. He stated that he returned with a deep conviction that sound, friendly relations with the Republics of South America are tremendously important to the United States—economically, militarily, and culturally—and critically important in the worldwide struggle for the winning of men's minds and allegiances.

On November 19 the President made public a summary of Dr. Eisenhower's final report, based on the good-will tour and on several months of further study and consultation. The report, dated November 18, 1953, was made available by the State Department.

49 ¶ Special Message to the Congress Recommending Legislation for the Disposal of Government-Owned Synthetic Rubber Facilities. *April* 14, 1953

To the Congress of the United States:

The Rubber Act of 1948, as amended, requires my legislative recommendations with respect to the disposal to private industry of the government-owned synthetic rubber facilities. When at the onset of World War II the United States was denied access to its normal supplies of natural rubber, a huge government-owned synthetic rubber industry was created at a cost of some $700 million. There remain in government ownership facilities which cost approximately $550 million and which now supply nearly all of the nation's requirements of synthetic rubber, which, in 1952, amounted to 806,500 long tons out of a total consumption of 1,260,000 long tons of new rubber. Pursuant to the Rubber Act, these facilities are operated for the government's account by a number of rubber, petroleum and chemical companies.

The policy of the United States with respect to rubber is stated in Section 2 of the Rubber Act, which provides as follows:

"It is the policy of the United States that there shall be maintained at all times in the interest of the national security and common defense, in addition to stock piles of natural rubber which are to be acquired, rotated, and retained pursuant to the Strategic and Critical Materials Stockpiling Act, a technologically advanced and rapidly expandible rubber-producing industry in the United States of sufficient productive capacity to assure the availability in times of national emergency of adequate supplies of synthetic rubber to meet the essential civilian, military, and naval needs of the country. It is further declared to be the policy of the Congress that the security interests of the United States can and will best be served by the development within the United States of a free, competitive synthetic-rubber industry. In order to strengthen national security through a sound industry, it is essential that Government ownership of production facilities, Government production of synthetic rubber, regulations requiring mandatory use of synthetic rubber, and patent pooling be ended and terminated whenever consistent with national security, as provided in this Act."

In accordance with Section 9(a) of the Rubber Act, the Reconstruction Finance Corporation on March 1, 1953 rendered a report to me and to the Congress concerning plant disposal.

Having considered that report, and after consultation with the National Security Resources Board, I recommend the prompt enactment of disposal legislation.

I am in hearty accord with the policy determination of the Congress that the security interests of the nation will best be served by the development within the United States of a free competitive synthetic rubber industry, and I believe that now is the time to undertake plant disposal. The program recommended in the report of the Reconstruction Finance Corporation appears to provide the basic outline of a satisfactory method to achieve this result.

The nation's security in its rubber supply is, of course, of paramount importance in any consideration of the disposal of these facilities. For such security, two things are essential, namely, an adequate stock pile of natural rubber and a healthy, progressive synthetic rubber industry. Our stockpiling objectives are adequate and have been virtually achieved and, from the economic and technological data available to me, I am confident that if the government-owned synthetic rubber facilities are sold as recommended, competitive private industry will amply, efficiently and economically supply our synthetic rubber requirements.

Disposal of the government-owned facilities must be consistent with three objectives. In the first place the government should realize their full fair value; secondly, disposal should be effected in such a way as to ensure to the consuming public, and to large and small rubber fabricators the benefits of fair competition; and finally, to ensure against the hazards of unforeseeable contingencies the facilities must be sold on such terms as will guarantee their ready availability for the production of synthetic rubber in time of emergency. Disposal pursuant to these criteria will best serve the public interest.

The program proposed by the Reconstruction Finance Corporation is designed to achieve these objectives. Accordingly, I recommend the enactment of legislation which would permit the prompt implementation of such a program, recognizing at the same time that upon examination in detail, modifications of that program may appear necessary or desirable.

I have not prepared the text of legislative proposals to implement the recommendations of the Reconstruction Finance Corporation. It is my belief that such legislation would most appropriately result from the joint efforts of representatives of the interested executive agencies and those committees of the Congress having this matter under consideration.

DWIGHT D. EISENHOWER

NOTE: The report of the Reconstruction Finance Corporation entitled "Program for Disposal to Private Industry of Government-Owned Rubber-Producing Facilities" and dated March 1, 1953, was published by the Government Printing Office (61 pp., 1953).

On August 7, 1953, the President approved an act authorizing the disposal of Government-owned rubber-producing facilities (67 Stat. 408).

50 ¶ Address "The Chance for Peace" Delivered Before the American Society of Newspaper Editors. *April* 16, 1953

IN THIS SPRING of 1953 the free world weighs one question above all others: the chance for a just peace for all peoples.

To weigh this chance is to summon instantly to mind another recent moment of great decision. It came with that yet more hopeful spring of 1945, bright with the promise of victory and of freedom. The hope of all just men in that moment too was a just and lasting peace.

The 8 years that have passed have seen that hope waver, grow dim, and almost die. And the shadow of fear again has darkly lengthened across the world.

Today the hope of free men remains stubborn and brave, but it is sternly disciplined by experience. It shuns not only all crude counsel of despair but also the self-deceit of easy illusion. It weighs the chance for peace with sure, clear knowledge of what happened to the vain hope of 1945.

In that spring of victory the soldiers of the Western Allies met the soldiers of Russia in the center of Europe. They were triumphant comrades in arms. Their peoples shared the joyous prospect of building, in honor of their dead, the only fitting monument—an age of just peace. All these war-weary peoples shared too this concrete, decent purpose: to guard vigilantly against the domination ever again of any part of the world by a single, unbridled aggressive power.

This common purpose lasted an instant and perished. The nations of the world divided to follow two distinct roads.

The United States and our valued friends, the other free nations, chose one road.

The leaders of the Soviet Union chose another.

The way chosen by the United States was plainly marked by a few clear precepts, which govern its conduct in world affairs.

First: No people on earth can be held, as a people, to be an enemy, for all humanity shares the common hunger for peace and fellowship and justice.

Second: No nation's security and well-being can be lastingly achieved in isolation but only in effective cooperation with fellow-nations.

Third: Any nation's right to a form of government and an economic system of its own choosing is *inalienable*.

Fourth: Any nation's attempt to dictate to other nations their form of government is *indefensible*.

And fifth: A nation's hope of lasting peace cannot be firmly based upon any race in armaments but rather upon just relations and honest understanding with all other nations.

In the light of these principles the citizens of the United States defined the way they proposed to follow, through the aftermath of war, toward true peace.

This way was faithful to the spirit that inspired the United Nations: to prohibit strife, to relieve tensions, to banish fears. This way was to control and to reduce armaments. This way was to allow all nations to devote their energies and resources to the great and good tasks of healing the war's wounds, of clothing and feeding and housing the needy, of perfecting a just political life, of enjoying the fruits of their own free toil.

The Soviet government held a vastly different vision of the future.

In the world of its design, security was to be found, not in mutual trust and mutual aid but in *force:* huge armies, subversion, rule of neighbor nations. The goal was power superiority at all cost. Security was to be sought by denying it to all others.

The result has been tragic for the world and, for the Soviet Union, it has also been ironic.

The amassing of Soviet power alerted free nations to a new danger of aggression. It compelled them in self-defense to spend unprecedented money and energy for armaments. It forced them to develop weapons of war now capable of inflicting instant and terrible punishment upon any aggressor.

It instilled in the free nations—and let none doubt this—the unshakable conviction that, as long as there persists a threat to freedom, they must, at any cost, remain armed, strong, and ready for the risk of war.

It inspired them—and let none doubt this—to attain a unity of purpose and will beyond the power of propaganda or pressure to break, now or ever.

There remained, however, one thing essentially unchanged and unaffected by Soviet conduct: the readiness of the free nations to welcome sincerely any genuine evidence of peaceful purpose enabling all peoples again to resume their common quest of just peace.

The free nations, most solemnly and repeatedly, have assured the Soviet Union that their firm association has never had any aggressive purpose whatsoever. Soviet leaders, however, have seemed to persuade themselves, or tried to persuade their people, otherwise.

And so it has come to pass that the Soviet Union itself has shared and suffered the very fears it has fostered in the rest of the world.

This has been the way of life forged by 8 years of fear and force.

What can the world, or any nation in it, hope for if no turning is found on this dread road?

The worst to be feared and the best to be expected can be simply stated.

The *worst* is atomic war.

The *best* would be this: a life of perpetual fear and tension; a burden of arms draining the wealth and the labor of all peoples; a wasting of strength that defies the American system or the Soviet system or any system to achieve true abundance and happiness for the peoples of this earth.

Every gun that is made, every warship launched, every rocket fired signifies, in the final sense, a theft from those who hunger and are not fed, those who are cold and are not clothed.

This world in arms is not spending money alone.

It is spending the sweat of its laborers, the genius of its scientists, the hopes of its children.

The cost of one modern heavy bomber is this: a modern brick school in more than 30 cities.

It is two electric power plants, each serving a town of 60,000 population.

It is two fine, fully equipped hospitals.

It is some 50 miles of concrete highway.

We pay for a single fighter plane with a half million bushels of wheat.

We pay for a single destroyer with new homes that could have housed more than 8,000 people.

This, I repeat, is the best way of life to be found on the road the world has been taking.

This is not a way of life at all, in any true sense. Under the cloud of threatening war, it is humanity hanging from a cross of iron.

These plain and cruel truths define the peril and point the hope that come with this spring of 1953.

This is one of those times in the affairs of nations when the gravest choices must be made, if there is to be a turning toward a just and lasting peace.

It is a moment that calls upon the governments of the world to speak their intentions with simplicity and with honesty.

It calls upon them to answer the question that stirs the hearts of all sane men: *is there no other way the world may live?*

The world knows that an era ended with the death of Joseph Stalin. The extraordinary 30-year span of his rule saw the Soviet Empire expand to reach from the Baltic Sea to the Sea of Japan, finally to dominate 800 million souls.

The Soviet system shaped by Stalin and his predecessors was born of one World War. It survived with stubborn and often amazing courage a second World War. It has lived to threaten a third.

Now a new leadership has assumed power in the Soviet Union. Its links to the past, however strong, cannot bind it completely. Its future is, in great part, its own to make.

This new leadership confronts a free world aroused, as rarely in its history, by the will to stay free.

This free world knows, out of the bitter wisdom of experience, that vigilance and sacrifice are the price of liberty.

It knows that the defense of Western Europe imperatively demands the unity of purpose and action made possible by the North Atlantic Treaty Organization, embracing a European Defense Community.

It knows that Western Germany deserves to be a free and equal partner in this community and that this, for Germany, is the only safe way to full, final unity.

It knows that aggression in Korea and in southeast Asia are threats to the whole free community to be met by united action.

This is the kind of free world which the new Soviet leadership confronts. It is a world that demands and expects the fullest respect of its rights and interests. It is a world that will always accord the same respect to all others.

So the new Soviet leadership now has a precious opportunity to awaken, with the rest of the world, to the point of peril reached and to help turn the tide of history.

Will it do this?

We do not yet know. Recent statements and gestures of Soviet leaders give some evidence that they may recognize this critical moment.

We welcome every honest act of peace.

We care nothing for mere rhetoric.

We are only for sincerity of peaceful purpose attested by deeds. The opportunities for such deeds are many. The performance of a great number of them waits upon no complex protocol but upon the simple will to do them. Even a few such clear and specific acts, such as the Soviet Union's signature upon an Austrian treaty or its release of thousands of prisoners still held from World War II, would be impressive signs of sincere intent. They would carry a power of persuasion not to be matched by any amount of oratory.

This we do know: a world that begins to witness the rebirth of trust among nations *can* find its way to a peace that is neither partial nor punitive.

With all who will work in good faith toward such a peace, we are ready, with renewed resolve, to strive to redeem the near-lost hopes of our day.

The first great step along this way must be the conclusion of an honorable armistice in Korea.

This means the immediate cessation of hostilities and the prompt initiation of political discussions leading to the holding of free elections in a united Korea.

It should mean, no less importantly, an end to the direct and indirect attacks upon the security of Indochina and Malaya. For any armistice in Korea that merely released aggressive armies to attack elsewhere would be a fraud.

We seek, throughout Asia as throughout the world, a peace that is true and total.

Out of this can grow a still wider task—the achieving of just political settlements for the other serious and specific issues between the free world and the Soviet Union.

None of these issues, great or small, is insoluble—given only the will to respect the rights of all nations.

Again we say: the United States is ready to assume its just part.

We have already done all within our power to speed conclusion of a treaty with Austria, which will free that country from economic exploitation and from occupation by foreign troops.

We are ready not only to press forward with the present plans for closer unity of the nations of Western Europe but also, upon that foundation, to strive to foster a broader European community, conducive to the free movement of persons, of trade, and of ideas.

This community would include a free and united Germany, with a government based upon free and secret elections.

This free community and the full independence of the East European nations could mean the end of the present unnatural division of Europe.

As progress in all these areas strengthens world trust, we could proceed concurrently with the next great work—the reduction of the burden of armaments now weighing upon the world. To this end we would welcome and enter into the most solemn agreements. These could properly include:

1. The limitation, by absolute numbers or by an agreed international ratio, of the sizes of the military and security forces of all nations.

2. A commitment by all nations to set an agreed limit upon that proportion of total production of certain strategic materials to be devoted to military purposes.

3. International control of atomic energy to promote its use for peaceful purposes only and to insure the prohibition of atomic weapons.

4. A limitation or prohibition of other categories of weapons of great destructiveness.

5. The enforcement of all these agreed limitations and prohibitions by adequate safeguards, including a practical system of inspection under the United Nations.

The details of such disarmament programs are manifestly critical and complex. Neither the United States nor any other nation can properly claim to possess a perfect, immutable formula. But the formula matters less than the faith—the good faith without which no formula can work justly and effectively.

The fruit of success in all these tasks would present the world with the greatest task, and the greatest opportunity, of all. It is this: the dedication of the energies, the resources, and the imaginations of all peaceful nations to a new kind of war. This would be a declared total war, not upon any human enemy but upon the brute forces of poverty and need.

The peace we seek, founded upon decent trust and cooperative effort among nations, can be fortified, not by weapons of war but by wheat and by cotton, by milk and by wool, by meat and by timber and by rice. These are words that translate into every language on earth. These are needs that challenge this world in arms.

This idea of a just and peaceful world is not new or strange to us. It inspired the people of the United States to initiate the European Recovery Program in 1947. That program was prepared to treat, with like and equal concern, the needs of Eastern and Western Europe.

We are prepared to reaffirm, with the most concrete evidence, our readiness to help build a world in which all peoples can be productive and prosperous.

This Government is ready to ask its people to join with all nations in devoting a substantial percentage of the savings achieved by disarmament to a fund for world aid and reconstruction. The purposes of this great work would be to help other peoples to develop the undeveloped areas of the world, to stimulate profitable and fair world trade, to assist all peoples to know the blessings of productive freedom.

The monuments to this new kind of war would be these: roads and schools, hospitals and homes, food and health.

We are ready, in short, to dedicate our strength to serving the *needs,* rather than the *fears,* of the world.

We are ready, by these and all such actions, to make of the United Nations an institution that can effectively guard the peace and security of all peoples.

I know of nothing I can add to make plainer the sincere purpose of the United States.

I know of no course, other than that marked by these and similar actions, that can be called the highway of peace.

I know of only one question upon which progress waits. It is this:

What is the Soviet Union ready to do?

Whatever the answer be, let it be plainly spoken.

Again we say: the hunger for peace is too great, the hour in history too late, for any government to mock men's hopes with mere words and promises and gestures.

The test of truth is simple. There can be no persuasion but by deeds.

Is the new leadership of the Soviet Union prepared to use its decisive influence in the Communist world, including control of the flow of arms, to bring not merely an expedient truce in Korea but genuine peace in Asia?

Is it prepared to allow other nations, including those of Eastern Europe, the free choice of their own forms of government?

Is it prepared to act in concert with others upon serious disarmament proposals to be made firmly effective by stringent U.N. control and inspection?

If not, where then is the concrete evidence of the Soviet Union's concern for peace?

The test is clear.

There is, before all peoples, a precious chance to turn the black tide of events.   If we failed to strive to seize this chance, the judgment of future ages would be harsh and just.

If we strive but fail and the world remains armed against itself, it at least need be divided no longer in its clear knowledge of who has condemned humankind to this fate.

The purpose of the United States, in stating these proposals, is simple and clear.

These proposals spring, without ulterior purpose or political passion, from our calm conviction that the hunger for peace is in the hearts of all peoples—those of Russia and of China no less than of our own country.

They conform to our firm faith that God created men to enjoy, not destroy, the fruits of the earth and of their own toil.

They aspire to this: the lifting, from the backs and from the hearts of men, of their burden of arms and of fears, so that they may find before them a golden age of freedom and of peace.

NOTE: The President's address was broadcast over television and radio from the Statler Hotel in Washington.

51   ¶ Special Message to the Congress Transmitting Reorganization Plan 4 of 1953 Concerning the Department of Justice. *April 20, 1953*

To the Congress of the United States:

I transmit herewith Reorganization Plan No. 4 of 1953 prepared in accordance with the Reorganization Act of 1949, as amended, and providing for reorganizations in the Department of Justice.

Under present law, the Solicitor General is required to exercise the duties of the Attorney General in case of the absence or disability of the latter, or in case of a vacancy in the office of Attorney

General. This arrangement originated in 1870. The Solicitor General is no longer the appropriate officer of the Department of Justice to be first in the line of succession of officers to be Acting Attorney General. His basic and primary function is to represent the United States before the Supreme Court. He is not concerned with the day-to-day administrative direction of the affairs of the Department of Justice. Thus, he is not likely to be the officer of the Department whose regular duties best prepare him to assume the occasional responsibility of guiding the affairs of the entire Department in the capacity of Acting Attorney General.

The Department of Justice now has a Deputy Attorney General, provision for that title having been made in Reorganization Plan No. 2 of 1950. The duties of this officer include supervision over all major units of the Department of Justice and over United States Attorneys and Marshals. He is the chief liaison officer of the Department of Justice with the Congress and with other departments and agencies. He is, both by title and by the nature of his functions, the officer best situated to act as the administrative head of the Department of Justice when the Attorney General is absent or disabled or the office of Attorney General is vacant.

Accordingly, the reorganization plan would transfer from the Solicitor General to the Deputy Attorney General the functions conferred by statute upon the former with respect to acting as Attorney General. The reorganization plan makes further provision for Acting Attorney General in circumstances where both the Attorney General and Deputy Attorney General are unavailable. The plan would authorize the Attorney General to prescribe the order of succession in which the Assistant Attorneys General and the Solicitor General shall, in such circumstances, act as Attorney General.

There are in the Department of Justice eight offices of Assistant Attorney General. Each incumbent of seven of these offices has the sole statutory function of assisting the Attorney General in the performance of his duties. However, the statute prescribes that the eighth Assistant Attorney General (along with certain assistants) shall have charge of the interests of the Government in all matters of reappraisement and classification of imported goods. This officer is known as the Assistant Attorney General in charge of customs matters.

By Reorganization Plan No. 2 of 1950 all functions of all subordinate officers, and of all agencies, of the Department of Justice were transferred to the Attorney General. Accordingly, the Assistant Attorney General in charge of customs matters would now perform only such functions as may be delegated to him by the Attorney General. However, the effect of the present statute may well be to require the appointment of the Assistant Attorney General in charge of customs matters, whereas this official should be appointed simply as an Assistant Attorney General, as are other Assistant Attorneys General. All doubt in this regard should be resolved.

To accomplish this end, the accompanying reorganization plan would abolish the now-existing office of Assistant Attorney General in charge of customs matters and establish in lieu thereof a new office of Assistant Attorney General. Appointment thereto would be by the President, by and with the advice and consent of the Senate.

After investigation I have found and hereby declare that each reorganization included in Reorganization Plan No. 4 of 1953 is necessary to accomplish one or more of the purposes set forth in section 2(a) of the Reorganization Act of 1949, as amended. I have also found and hereby declare that it is necessary to include in the accompanying reorganization plan, by reason of reorganization made thereby, provisions for the appointment and compensation of an Assistant Attorney General. The rate of compensation fixed for this officer is that which I have found to prevail in respect of comparable officers in the executive branch of the Government.

Reorganization Plan No. 4 of 1953 neither increases nor decreases the number of officials or employees, or the functions, of the Department of Justice.   Accordingly, it is not probable that reductions in expenditures will be brought about by the taking effect of the reorganizations included in the reorganization plan.   I am persuaded, however, that the reorganization plan will promote the best utilization of the top officers of the Department of Justice and the most effective conduct of the affairs of the Department.

DWIGHT D. EISENHOWER

NOTE: Reorganization Plan 4 of 1953 is published in the U.S. Statutes at Large (67 Stat. 636) and in the 1949–1953 Compilation of title 3 of the Code of Federal Regulations (p. 1026).   It became effective on June 20, 1953.

52   ¶ Letter to the President of the Senate and to the Speaker of the House of Representatives Recommending Emergency Legislation for the Admission of Refugees.   *April* 22, 1953

Dear Mr. ―――――:

We are all aware of the tragic developments of the past several years which have left countless thousands of individuals homeless refugees in the heart of Europe.   In recent months, the number of refugees has been increased by the steady flow of escapees who have braved death to escape from behind the Iron Curtain. These refugees and escapees searching desperately for freedom look to the free world for haven.

In addition, the problem of population pressures continues to be a source of urgent concern in several friendly countries in Europe.

It is imperative that we join with the other nations in helping to find a solution to these grave questions.   These refugees, escapees, and distressed peoples now constitute an economic and political threat of constantly growing magnitude.   They look to traditional American humanitarian concern for the oppressed. International political considerations are also factors which are involved. We should take reasonable steps to help these people to the extent that we share the obligation of the free world.

Therefore, after consideration of all the points of view which have been presented, I recommend, within the framework of the immigration laws, the enactment of emergency immigration legislation for the special admission of 120,000 immigrants per year for the next two years.

In order to help resolve this current immigration and refugee problem in the tradition of our American policy, I urge that the Congress give this recommendation its earliest consideration.

Sincerely,

DWIGHT D. EISENHOWER

NOTE: This is the text of identical letters addressed to the Honorable Richard M. Nixon, President of the Senate, and to the Honorable Joseph W. Martin, Jr., Speaker of the House of Representatives.

53 ¶ Exchange of Letters Between the President and Queen Juliana of the Netherlands Concerning Refugees. *April 23, 1953*

[Released April 23, 1953. Dated April 4, 1953]

My dear Queen Juliana:

Prince Bernhard has given me your letter of March 18, 1953 and an accompanying memorandum concerning the plight of refugees throughout the world. Your preoccupation with the challenge which refugees present to the free world at a time when your own country and people are facing so nobly the burdens of over-crowding and the disastrous effects of the recent floods, demonstrates again the compassion which Your Majesty has always shown for those in distress beyond her own borders. I share this concern with you. The United States Government stands ready at any time to consider constructive international measures to alleviate the problems presented so sympathetically in your letter and memorandum.

The refugees in Germany constitute a substantial proportion of the German population. The United States Government, in planning economic measures of assistance with the authorities of the German Federal Republic, has always taken the refugees into account. Along with the indigenous population, they have in large part contributed to and benefited from the rising level of the German economy. The achievement of economic balance and the expansion of employment opportunities in Germany have been primary objectives of United States measures of assistance to the German economy. The United States Government will persist in these efforts in collaboration with the German Federal authorities. This collaboration has been particularly close and continuous in recent months since the flow of refugees into Berlin has increased.

Your letter points out that emigration may also play a role in relieving population pressures in Germany and other countries whose governments also provide asylum for refugees. To provide opportunities for decent livelihood in countries of immigration for migrants and refugees, the United States Government has given active support to the Intergovernmental Committee for European Migration. At its forthcoming session in Geneva, the Migration Committee will give further attention to ways and means of expanding opportunities for emigration overseas.

The United States Government, under its Escapee Program, is also providing assistance in assimilation and resettlement for those who are currently fleeing from Eastern European countries into Germany, Trieste, Austria, Turkey, Italy and Greece. This assistance is supplementary to that provided by these countries of first asylum and the voluntary agencies which provide the essential human touch in their services to refugees.

Present efforts to re-establish refugees either through integration in their present countries of residence or emigration, should

56616—60——16

be intensified. I am confident that the free world will respond to meet the challenge which the refugees present not only because they are human beings whose dignity and self-respect are at stake, but because they desire with us to play their part in achieving peace and order in the world.

With expressions of great respect and warm personal esteem,
Sincerely,

DWIGHT D. EISENHOWER

NOTE: Queen Juliana's letter of March 18 follows:

My dear Mr. President,

The people of the United States have magnificently shown their warmhearted sympathy for those in our country who through the flood lost their homes and are in great distress. American help came pouring into our stricken land. Help came indeed, from all over the world, to relieve us in our dire need. With profound gratitude in our hearts we see the problem of our homeless solved on a world basis by one spontaneous move of generosity from peoples and governments alike. This generous support has been of great material, and also of immeasurable moral help to us.

Sympathy for the victims of distress is well known to be a great American tradition. I feel justified, therefore, to ask for your warm attention to the problem of those who became homeless by persecution: the refugees of the entire world.

I appeal to you for personally taking the lead in solving this ever increasing world problem on a world basis. I strongly feel that this problem is one of the most dangerous and tragic elements in an uncertain future.

I am aware that in the past year, through international effort generously supported by the United States Government, a great many refugees have found a new home, but the problem is still far from solved. Thousands of new refugees, mostly in circumstances of great distress and often in a state of mental despair are in need of our help.

There are still over 400,000 refugees living in camps in Europe. Tens of thousands of refugees are fleeing from the Eastern Zone of Germany into West Berlin. There are still many thousands of refugees elsewhere in the world. A concerted international action is therefore indicated.

The problem of the refugees can only be solved if they are given opportunities to resettle in new countries, or if they are assimilated in their countries of present residence.

Mass resettlement schemes, however, are seriously hampered at the present time, because in various countries of immigration refugees are not given enough economic opportunities. Moreover, in certain European countries, like my own, the pressure of surplus population leaves little room for absorbing them.

Unless legislation in the countries of immigration specifically permits the entry of refugees and their families, including those in destitute circumstances, it is to be feared only very small numbers of refugees will get a chance to emigrate.

A new approach is necessary, therefore, which opens large opportunities for immigration and also creates the necessary economic conditions permitting the assimilation of refugees in the countries of their present residence.

Efforts to stimulate this assimilation are at the present time being made in several countries, in particular through the operation of an important grant from an American foundation, in close cooperation between the Governments concerned and the Voluntary Agencies working on behalf of the refugees. However, private agencies do not dispose of the necessary resources. Governmental action will be necessary to open credit facilities for all those refugees who are only too willing to support and house themselves if they are given the initial opportunity to regain their independence.

These aspects should receive due attention whenever plans are made to promote the economic development and stability of the world. Neglecting them means that tens of thousands of refugees are condemned to live in camps without any hope for the future for many more years. Such a tragedy, if it were to occur, would destroy the faith in the privileges of freedom not only of the refugees themselves, but also of their kinsmen whom they have left behind.

Discontentment, frustration and even despair is felt by millions of uprooted people, dislocated all over the world. The free world cannot tolerate so much suffering in its midst without having to suffer itself.

To preserve their human dignity and restore their self respect, the right psychological and spiritual approach is of overriding importance. How could refugees ever trust free society if it shows interest only for trained muscles or brains, but lacks respect for the higher values of life; if it looks at refugees only as labor potential, and refuses those who cannot work; if it separates them from their families?

It is my conviction that the refugee problem should be tackled in the shortest possible time in its entirety.

The Netherlands will be glad to cooperate in any planning and, within the practical limits of its capacities, in any constructive effort to arrive at results.

Although I fully understand the multitude and magnitude of the problems confronting you, I had to lay this matter of ever-growing importance before you, conscious of the responsibility of all for all, a responsibility which in the plight of the Netherlands the entire world has accepted and lived up to in such an impressive way. In all humility we saw the lesson of loving one's neighbor being observed in a world otherwise so deeply disturbed by international strife.

I am confident you will find the right approach to this problem. May it be given you to solve it. Thus world peace will gain.

Yours sincerely,
JULIANA

54   ¶ The President's News Conference of *April 23, 1953.*

THE PRESIDENT. It has been a little time since we have met, and a number of things have happened. One or two things that occur to my mind involve, first, further plans for reorganization. We have been going over very intensively, lately, plans for reorganization in both State Department and in Defense. They are not quite ready for publication, but are coming along, and will be sent down to the Congress very soon.

Another question has been the St. Lawrence Seaway. I remember that several times there have been individual questions asked in this meeting about it. Of course, there are no easy answers, because it is very controversial.

But the National Security Council has advised me that in the opinion of the members there is an advantage to the Nation's security if the Seaway should be constructed. They believe it would be desirable for the United States to participate in someway in that construction, if it is to go ahead; although the extent and the limitations upon such participation by the United States are still undergoing study, and we are not prepared to express our opinion on that in exact detail.

However, as I have, I think, said before in front of this body, we are in favor of permitting the State of New York to participate in the power development and have made no change in our attitude toward that one.

I think those are two items that were fresh in my mind, and I believe there is no use of using up the time speculating on my own, so we will start the questions.

Q. Merriman Smith, United Press: Mr. President, now that we are beginning to see some details from North Korea and how our prisoners were treated over there, some of the stories of brutality and atrocities, I wonder what your feeling is about the prisoner exchange and how our men have been treated?

THE PRESIDENT. Well, Mr. Smith, I have as yet no complete and full report on this matter so that I can separate actual fact from, let us say, just isolated instances.

Everything that we have heard does make us, of course, happier that we are getting even some of our prisoners back, because it is quite obvious that there has been something wrong.

I am not prepared, at this moment, to express any sweeping conclusions as to what has been going on. But we are studying it, trying to examine—analyze—as rapidly as we can.

Q. Chalmers M. Roberts, Washington Post: Would you care to state, sir, about the reciprocal trade program, is it your desire to have a 1-year extension of the present law without any amendments, or are you willing to accept some type of amendments?

THE PRESIDENT. I wouldn't say, by any manner of means, that I am not ready to accept any amendment whatsoever. As I recall, in my message, when I sent it down, I merely asked—as the simplest thing that I thought could be done pending a combined executive-legislative study of this thing—an extension for 1 year of the existing reciprocal trade act.

Now, if there are some logical and necessary minor amendments to it, I don't know; I haven't seen them, so I couldn't give you an unequivocal answer to your question.

Q. Mr. Roberts: Might I ask further, sir, the Simpson bill, which is the one on which the hearings actually will be heard next week, would you reject that bill?

THE PRESIDENT. Well, from what I have heard of it, there are certain items in it that I couldn't possibly accept. But I am not certain, because I have not studied it in detail myself, nor have any detailed reports been made to me about it. As it stands now, I stand merely on my recommendation for the extension by 1 year.

Q. Mr. Roberts: Could I ask a third related question, sir? Very recently, the Secretary of Defense has rejected a British bid on some machinery, which was more than a million dollars lower than any American bid. I wonder if you are familiar with that and would care to comment?

THE PRESIDENT. Yes, that point was brought up in detail. The decision was made, and I think very properly, by the Secretary of Defense, that those bids would be rejected and reopened, because there was nothing in the specifications to show that there was equivalent quality in the two items upon which the bids were submitted. Now the specifications are being rewritten and put out, and I assure you there is nothing in them that would tend to exclude the British bids.

We do want to make certain, though, in the face of certain technical advice that we were given, that we are getting items of equal quality and equal suitability to the purpose, that's all.

Q. Joseph R. Slevin, New York Journal of Commerce: Mr. President, all other things being equal, in a case such as this English bid, if the British firm was low bidder, would it be administration policy then to award the contract to the low bidder?

THE PRESIDENT. I think there probably would be some differential made. I have not tried to carry this decision forward into any specific case and into complete detail. Generally speaking, if that bid is a substantially favorable one for us, why that would be the one accepted.

Q. Robert E. Clark, International News Service: Mr. President, have you gotten any reaction from the Russians to your peace program?

THE PRESIDENT. I have had no direct reply of any kind.

Q. Martin S. Hayden, Detroit News: Mr. President, in relation to the St. Lawrence Seaway question, would you anticipate, sir, that the studies that are being made would be finished in time for you to make a recommendation to Congress for or against the Wiley bill, which is now pending?

THE PRESIDENT. Well, I think, yes. As a matter of fact, we will be in a position to make such a recommendation at a suitable time.

Q. [*Speaker unidentified*], Colorado papers: Mr. President, I want to ask you, what have you done or what are you going to do to develop atomic energy as the source of industrial power?

THE PRESIDENT. Wasn't there a statement issued on that subject just a short time ago? [*Confers with Mr. Hagerty*]

I thought there was a statement issued by the Atomic Energy Commission, but I assure you that it is a subject that is challenging the attention of the Atomic Energy Commission, and a good many other people in the Government. While I think that certain modifications or revisions of law will be necessary, there is no question whatsoever as to the hope of doing something in that line, and the expectation to do something.

Q. Lucian C. Warren, Buffalo Courier-Express: Mr. President, Dr. Earl McGrath sent you his letter of resignation yesterday from the United States Commissioner of Education office, in which he complained that he was not getting a fair deal on budget matters for the Office of Education. Have you any comment on that?

THE PRESIDENT. Well, not on the specific case, because I have not received his letter. I have appointed certain Cabinet people, and people of equivalent rank. They are held responsible for the operations of their organization, and they are expected to find the right kind of people to do it.

Now, just exactly what is going on in this case, I don't know, but if someone wants to resign because administration policy is not acceptable to them, why that is of course, their privilege.

Q. Nat S. Finney, Buffalo Evening News: Mr. President, have you received, since you took office, the resignations of officials in the Government who customarily would offer their resignations at the beginning of a new administration? I mean, by immemorial political custom?

THE PRESIDENT. I can't say that I have gotten them all; I don't believe there has been any report made to me. I have gotten a very vast number, and some of them have asked merely to be relieved upon qualification of their successor. Some have fixed certain dates. Generally speaking, they have been accepted under the terms specified by the individual submitting the resignation.

Q. Arthur T. Hadley, Newsweek: A rather serious situation seems to be developing in Indochina, sir, and I wonder if you have any comment on what this Government might do, either singly or in concert with some of our United Nations allies, to deal with that situation?

THE PRESIDENT. You mean with respect to Laos?

Q. Mr. Hadley: Yes, sir.

THE PRESIDENT. No, I wouldn't be in a position to comment, at this moment, on what would happen. I will say only this: it is being carefully watched; it is something that is discussed every day.

Q. Mrs. May Craig, Portland (Maine) papers: Mr. President, Price Daniel, Senator from Texas, who supported your nomination, has sent to you about a week ago a letter asking you to consider revoking the Truman order for nonmilitary censorship in some of the civil departments—executive departments. Have you considered his letter yet, or replied?

THE PRESIDENT. Well, I haven't seen Senator Daniel's personal letter. It is apparently going through staff processes. What I did tell this group, I believe, a few weeks ago, was that if anyone knew of any obstruction to what they considered the proper flow of news, due to that order, please to let me know. And as I was walking over this morning, Mr. Hagerty told me there had been, involving the Defense Department, one instance. That is the only one reported, and that instance was straightened out. But because of that question that came up several weeks ago,

I did put this matter into the hands of the Justice Department, telling them please to study it and let me know whether there were any obstructions contemplated in this order. The Justice Department has not yet reported to me.

Q. Mrs. Craig: Well, Mr. President, have you considered that we do not know what news is hidden from us, and so we can't complain to you about it?

THE PRESIDENT. Well, I have never seen you backward in reporting on your suspicions. [*Laughter*]

Q. Frederick Kuh, Chicago Sun-Times: Mr. President, I would like to ask whether it is your intention and wish that at the conference which would follow an armistice in Korea, broad problems of a Far Eastern settlement should be discussed, and that such a conference should not be confined exclusively to Korean questions?

THE PRESIDENT. Well, just exactly where these things will be done, you are getting into questions of procedure and method, which I purposely in my speech left very flexible. I am ready to do anything and to confer anywhere, as I say, within the limitations I have already expressed to you people, to bring about peace. Now, whether the thing is done there or not, I don't know. But I did in that speech, you will recall, flatly state that there can be no real peace in Korea that ignores the other and broader problems in Asia.

Q. Louis R. Lautier, National Negro Press: Mr. President, would you care to comment on the filibuster against the tidelands oil bill now going on?

THE PRESIDENT. Well, I see by the papers that they claim it is not a filibuster.

My position with respect to the tidelands has been stated time and again in front of bodies similar to this, and other places. I believe, simply, what I think is justice is a fact. So I have nothing further to state about it except that I do think that after 4 weeks, they ought to be getting pretty well educated about the facts, even as they are seen by someone who opposes my viewpoint very diametrically.

Q. David P. Sentner, Hearst Newspapers: Mr. President, are there any steps being taken for a four-power meeting, as reported this week?

THE PRESIDENT. No, I couldn't say that anything definite is being undertaken. There are no negotiations—I assume you mean preliminary negotiations—going on to set up a meeting place or an agenda.

Q. Mr. Sentner: Even diplomatic feelers, you might say?

THE PRESIDENT. None that I know of.

Q. Mr. Sentner: You said before, sir, that there was no direct response to your speech. Were there any indirect responses you could discuss?

THE PRESIDENT. Only what I see by the papers. When I say "direct," I was not trying to confuse anybody. I meant that no diplomatic correspondence has come to my attention through channels. I have seen in the papers this kind of thing, and that kind of thing. No communication directed to me.

Q. Eleanor Hamilton, Winston-Salem Journal and Sentinel: A great many cotton and tobacco organizations think that repeal of the Buy-American Act would help our declining farm price situation. A bill has been introduced to repeal that act. How do you feel about this, the Buy-American Act?

THE PRESIDENT. Well, I don't think I could give you a categorical answer at this moment. Every one of these questions brings into the scope of the answer a number of others.

I personally have always felt that there should not be a rigid Buy-American Act, or anything of that nature. I believe that in every case the best interests of the United States should be determined, and they should be followed. If the best interests of the United States require or seem to indicate a broader or better trade with someone else, then we should do that. And when the best interests of the United States demand some other action, we should follow that.

I doubt whether you can solve these problems ordinarily just by fixed policies, prohibitions, or limitations of that kind.

Q. John Madigan, Hearst Newspapers: Mr. President, there seems to be some question as to where you and the administration stand on public housing, in view of the appropriations action in the House in recent days—holding in suspension. Some Democrats have charged that you, during the campaign, had pledged public housing to continue. Would you care to comment on it?

THE PRESIDENT. I don't know, and I do not recall—although I sometimes don't like to be too positive when I depend completely on memory—I do not recall that I ever said I was in favor of the continuation of Federal public housing. But I did say this: that I was quite concerned that the Federal Government perform the functions that are proper for it, for the welfare of our people, as well as for its position in the world, and all of the other functions that naturally fall to the Federal Government.

Consequently, I think that at one of our earliest press conferences, I pointed out to you people that I proposed, among other things, to ask for the establishment of an official commission which, made up of people representing the public, the executive departments and the Legislature, and so on, would determine the proper division of functions between the Federal Government and the State governments. I am not certain in my own mind where that dividing line always falls; but I have also said that pending the meeting of such a commission, pending its finding of responsibilities and establishment of division of function and authority, that I thought we should go ahead with the programs now in existence—and in effect, marking time. My own idea of marking time was to take the number of housing units that was in the current bill and let them go ahead. But there has been no positive argument on the point, because the matter of principle was not involved.

All of us have agreed, as I understand it, that we are going to depend upon this commission to tell us how much the Federal

Government belongs in this, and how much of this should be taken up by the State governments themselves.

Q. Mr. Madigan: Would you say your position as stated there is in variance in any way with the fact that no money has now been appropriated for continuation at this time?

THE PRESIDENT. The bill is not out of Congress.

Q. Mr. Madigan: Do you think it may be changed?

THE PRESIDENT. I don't know.

Q. Richard L. Wilson, Cowles Publications: There is a point of view, Mr. President, that the resignations of some of the heads of established agencies of the Government, like the Bureau of Standards and the Fish and Wildlife Service, is kicking out of Government people who rightfully belong there, who have been part of the career service, and it is a bad thing. Would you care to discuss that development?

THE PRESIDENT. I will say this: the people that I have put in charge of these great departments and responsibilities are the finest people I thought I could find. I made it a matter of my own responsibility to pick people that are Secretaries of these departments, and they know that I have no desire of any kind to get rid of a person merely for change's sake, particularly of career people where they are properly career people. But I do expect of these Secretaries of these departments that they will get assistants that will support the policies that are agreed upon in the Cabinet and the Security Council and so on; and if people cannot support those policies, those positions, then they have no other recourse except to resign, as I see it.

Now, none of these cases has been brought to me as a special case for determination by me. I am not sure, in certain of them that you mention, what my own answer would have been. But I do hold these people at the heads responsible, and I expect them to be fair, and just, and decent, and not to be merely conducting a vendetta for any reasons whatsoever—partisan or otherwise.

Q. Mr. Wilson: I was going to ask that final point. That applies also to perhaps the desire of the member of the Cabinet to make patronage available for members of the party. Should that be a controlling factor, or should it be minimized?

THE PRESIDENT. None whatsoever. In my own opinion, there is this: there is a natural desire, as each of you people certainly understand, for a man to have around him in responsible positions people that he likes and trusts and believes in. Now, if someone has lost his confidence, and I don't care what his job is, you can well understand that he is uneasy with him around. But so far as any discharge having taken place in this Government for patronage reasons, if they have occurred, I am—I tell you flatly—completely unaware of it. That has no appeal to me whatsoever.

Q. Alice A. Dunnigan, Associated Negro Press: Mr. President, would you tell us whether any steps have been taken, since your last press conference, to revive the work of the Contract Compliance Committee, by appointing a chairman to that Committee?

THE PRESIDENT. I don't know about appointing a chairman. I did have the matter looked up, and they told me they were looking into the whole matter to see where there was noncompliance, if any, and to do their best on the thing. I haven't heard about it—[*confers with Mr. Hagerty*]—no chairman. There will be some announcement on it, the secretary tells me, very soon.[1]

Q. [*Speaker unidentified*], Christian Science Monitor: Mr. President, may I go back to the housing matter just a minute? Do you approve of the action of the House yesterday in rejecting the money for housing?

THE PRESIDENT. It did not agree with my own personal belief of what would be the wise thing and the convenient way of keeping this matter in the status quo, until it could be decided on an objective basis. Now, it does not mean, though, that I have asked these people, as a matter of responsible party leadership, to support my position. I made no attempt to do that, and there-

---

[1] On August 13, 1953, the President signed Executive Order 10479 establishing the Government Contract Committee. Vice President Nixon was appointed Chairman of the Committee.

fore I do not sense that they have in any way defied me. I certainly don't intend to get up and criticise them. I assume they are all voting their conscience.

Q. Merriman Smith, United Press: Mr. President, when we were discussing the prisoner situation, you said quite obviously there had been something wrong. Were you referring to the exchange itself or the treatment?

THE PRESIDENT. No, I was referring to the almost universality of the stories coming back, that there had been a lot of difficulty.

Q. Mr. Smith: Treatment?

THE PRESIDENT. Treatment. And I must say, knowing something about the things that occur, a thing like that weighs very heavily on your heart. And if you know anything about it at all— I feel badly when I read those stories, and I hope therefore that we can exchange just as many prisoners as we possibly can, as rapidly as we can.

Q. Joseph R. Slevin, New York Journal of Commerce: Mr. President, in answering an earlier question on reciprocal trade, you referred to an executive-legislative commission that would study the question. Could you tell us something about your plans for this commission, the scope of operations?

THE PRESIDENT. No. We merely agreed that we are studying the thing thoroughly. We agreed that it would take a long time to do it, and so we are taking—we hope to take about—well, we don't hope to use the whole year, but that is the reason for asking for the year's extension as it now stands.

Q. Mr. Slevin: You agreed with the Congress?

THE PRESIDENT. I agreed with the congressional leaders, yes.

Q. Robert J. Donovan, New York Herald Tribune: Mr. President, in view of the National Security Council's finding on the St. Lawrence, do I understand, sir, that you now favor the building of the St. Lawrence Seaway eventually? I wasn't sure what your policy now——

THE PRESIDENT. I said this: that they believe that it would have an advantage from the standpoint of national security, and that whether or not this program went ahead with Canada alone, or with our participation, we must remove any obstacles to its progress. And finally, they also believed it desirable that we participate in some degree, but the limitations upon that participation and exactly how far we would go, they were not yet ready to announce their opinion. Now that is exactly what they said, and exactly what I have approved.

Q. Mr. Donovan: Your extent, so far as you are concerned, sir—you favor at least participation to some extent?

THE PRESIDENT. That is correct. That is correct.

Q. Sarah McClendon, Texas papers: Sir, you speak of having a bipartisan commission for studying reciprocal trade. Then, I believe, you mentioned——

THE PRESIDENT. I don't know whether I said "bipartisan" on the question of trade or not. I have forgotten. If I did, I probably used the word inadvertently. What I did say was in respect to this State-Federal division of functions. There I am getting Governors to participate, bipartisan people, people representing the public. In the other one, I am not sure. I said the legislative-executive study; if I used the word "bipartisan," I may have done it in error, because I don't recall that we intended that to be bipartisan.

Q. Mrs. McClendon: Well, I am confused on that. I am just wondering, isn't that what we have in the House Ways and Means Committee? We have a bipartisan group studying this matter. Are you going to set up another commission to study trade, in addition to the studies that are being undertaken by the committee in Congress?

THE PRESIDENT. That is correct.

Q. Marvin L. Arrowsmith, Associated Press: Mr. President, have you reached any conclusion yet on defense spending, whether you are going to be able to cut it?

THE PRESIDENT. Well, I think expenditures will be cut some, yes. I am not ready to predict the amount or the order of that cut, but I think there will be savings effected in that department.

Q. Frederic W. Collins, Providence Journal: Mr. President, again in the field of international trade policy, do you feel that you were fully informed of the views of former Representative Talbot at the time of his appointment as a member of the Tariff Commission?

THE PRESIDENT. Well, no, I couldn't be. I couldn't, certainly, be informed of all of the ideas and feelings. I tried to get in each of these individuals and determine, on the basis of all the reports that are made to me, that I have got hold of an honorable man that can look facts in the face and judge according to the facts as to what he should do. I can't go back into each of these men's minds and try to figure out every prejudice or slant or leaning that they may have. Not at all.

Q. [*Speaker unidentified*]: I wanted to ask, sir, about the mobilization base matter. The Secretary of Defense has, I believe, already canceled some Air Force contracts, or the Pentagon has, in order to concentrate them for purposes of saving money. Then there has been some question as to whether this really represents a change in the policy of spreading the mobilization base as a precautionary matter in case of all-out war. Would you care to comment on that?

THE PRESIDENT. You are obviously asking a question you ought to take to the Department of Defense. You are getting into some details of which I wouldn't know anything.

Q. [*Speaker unidentified*]: There has been no discussion at the White House?

THE PRESIDENT. Not on that particular point that you raise.

Q. Edward T. Folliard, Washington Post: Mr. President, in connection with the NATO conference in Paris, there are reports that this country and Britain have agreed on—I think the word is "stretch-out"—to spread this build-up over quite a number of years. Does that represent a change in policy from the time that you were in command of the North Atlantic Treaty forces?

THE PRESIDENT. Eddie, you start off with a premise that I

don't know to be correct, and therefore I couldn't answer the question.

Q. Mr. Folliard: Yes, sir.   I said reports.

THE PRESIDENT. We go into these conferences; the reason for holding them is to have a new review of the facts—where do we stand?

No one, in my opinion, can stand even where I stood in January of 1951, and looking at Europe and living with Europe, can say Europe can do so much and should do so much in such and such a period, divided 3 months, 6 months, or a year—whatever. There must be constant review.   And what can you do?

Now, the first thing that any nation, any locality, any region, must do, before they can really defend themselves is to be able to make a living.   That is the thing you are constantly trying to cor-relate in this job of security that depends upon force.   How do you make a living and bear this expense?   Now, if you can't make a living in the long run, your people are ground down, and you have a new form of government.

So, I look upon the NATO conference as another honest at-tempt on the part of all of us to review what we are doing, where we are going, and what we hope to accomplish, and how soon.

Q. Richard Harkness, National Broadcasting Company: Mr. President, my question is connected with Mr. Folliard's.   More than a few of us have been told here, Mr. President, that as against a target date for Western European defense, say 1953, 1954, that the policy now will be one of a slower, long-range 10-year build-up?

THE PRESIDENT. Well, I would object to 10 years just as much as I object to '54.   From the time I went into this, one thing that I have insisted on is that for anybody that is in the defensive posi-tion—strategically or tactically, or anything—who bases his de-fense on his ability to predict the day and the hour of attack, is crazy.   There is just no sense to it.   If you are going on the defen-sive, you have got to get a level of preparation you can sustain over the years.   And I don't know—whether it's 1 year, 10 years,

20 years, or what; but if you try to build up all of a sudden to have an attack in '54, and it doesn't come, what do you do? Now, it just doesn't make sense.

So I don't say that the attack is coming in 10 years or that we should build us up in 5 years. I say we have got to devise and develop a defensive program we can carry forward in company with our allies. And until we have got a better solution to these terrible tensions in the world, that is our answer—and not to build up to a maximum in '54 and then look around, and say: What happens to us now?

Q. Mr. Harkness: But, sir, before this, have you looked forward on this long-range basis that you have just described?

THE PRESIDENT. I have never looked at it in any other way, and I have raised my voice in inner circles arguing for it forever. You cannot build a defense, where it has to last for years, reach a peak in '54 and then start to deteriorate. To my mind it makes no sense. And I have never changed my mind one instant about that.

Q. Jean Davidson, France Presse: Would you tell us, sir, how you feel now about the chances for a prompt truce in Korea?

THE PRESIDENT. No; like you, I am waiting.

Q. Robert G. Spivack, New York Post: Mr. President, in the letter that you sent to Congress today, regarding changes in the immigration laws, have you had any indication from the congressional leaders about their attitude; and secondly, does this meet the objections you raised last fall to the McCarran-Walter immigration law?

THE PRESIDENT. They are two separate questions. One, I have had communications with the leaders of the subcommittee, and I have listed for these people those directions in which complaints have come to me about the operation of the law. The other, the emergency question, is entirely different. On that, I asked for special legislation because I believed it to be necessary.

[*Speaker unidentified*]: Thank you, Mr. President.

NOTE: President Eisenhower's seventh news conference was held in the Executive Office Building at 11 a.m. on Thursday, April 23, 1953.

55 ¶ Memorandum on Payment for Unused Leave to Persons Appointed by the President. *April* 23, 1953

To the Heads of Executive Departments and Agencies:

Pending consideration by the Congress of legislation amending the coverage of existing leave laws, I request that no person appointed by the President shall, upon leaving the Government, receive payment for unused annual leave except upon a clear showing of entitlement.

To that end, it will be the general practice to maintain formal leave records for Presidential appointees wherever practicable. Where the nature of the position is such that the keeping of formal leave records is impracticable, the individual concerned will be expected to maintain an accurate personal record of his leave status.

In any case where there is the slightest doubt as to the sufficiency of a leave record to support a lump-sum payment for accrued leave upon separation from the Government service, the head of the agency will either request an advance decision from the Comptroller General of the United States as to the propriety of the payment, or submit the matter to the General Accounting Office for settlement as a claim.

Until further notice, the Bureau of the Budget is to be informed of all terminal leave payments to Presidential appointees.

DWIGHT D. EISENHOWER

NOTE: An act to provide for the exemption from the Annual and Sick Leave Act of 1951 of certain officers in the executive branch of the Government (Public Law 102, 83d Cong.) was approved on July 2, 1953 (67 Stat. 136).

56 ¶ Letter to the Chairman, Senate Committee on Foreign Relations, Concerning the St. Lawrence Seaway. *April 24, 1953*

[Released April 24, 1953. Dated April 23, 1953]

Dear Senator Wiley:

At my request, the National Security Council has considered the national security interests in the Saint Lawrence-Great Lakes Seaway Project. The Council has advised me:

1. Early initiation and completion of the Saint Lawrence-Great Lakes Seaway is in the interest of national security.

2. The United States should promptly take whatever action may be appropriate to clear the way for commencement of the project, whether by Canada alone, or, now or as may be later developed, by Canada and the United States jointly.

3. It is desirable that the United States participate in the construction of the Seaway; the extent of and limitations upon such participation to be the subject of separate determination by authority other than the Council.

The Council's findings and recommendations have my approval; and I propose now to discuss with the Cabinet the extent of and limitations upon United States participation in the project.

I am forwarding a copy of this letter to the Chairman of the Federal Power Commission for his information and such action as he may deem appropriate.

Sincerely,

DWIGHT D. EISENHOWER

The Honorable Alexander Wiley
Chairman, Committee on Foreign Relations
United States Senate
Washington, D.C.

57 ¶ Remarks at the Luncheon of the Republican Women's Spring Conference. *April* 24, 1953

THIS IS INDEED a very great, although somewhat terrifying, honor. The last time I can remember seeing this many women in one place was in St. Louis during the last campaign. I well remember the inspiration I got that night when suddenly the gathering displayed American flags. It was indeed a memorable sight.

There is, of course, another and very distinct reason for the feeling of honor and pride in addressing such a group. It has been proven, I think, that the average of intelligence among women—and their understanding—is a trifle higher than among men. And I can understand it, because there was a greater percentage of women who voted Republican last fall than there were men!

You will recall that three of the issues raised in that campaign were those that had some distinct, even special, appeal for women.

The first was the cost of government and its attendant inflation imposed upon every housewife in the land—the constantly increasing burden in bringing home a reasonable market basket to her family.

And so one of the promises made was that with a change in administration, there would be a trend toward the cutting of expenditures, particularly every unnecessary expenditure. We would eliminate waste, sheer waste, or a function for which the money demanded was merely desirable and not necessary.

The security of our Nation was promised over and over again, but because security ranked at the head of the list of all our requirements, the promise was also made that other expenditures would be brought within the proper relationship to that demanding one.

The second issue was the general subject of inefficiency, corruption, and subversion in government—things that had come about by reason of a long tenure of office of one political party, and then existing without proper measures being taken for their eradication. And the promise was made to go after that particular objective.

Third, there was raised the question of our foreign relations: the matter of pursuing peace in the world from a position of strength, security and unity in the free world, of trying to reason with potential enemies, and of bringing peace out of misunderstanding and chaos, if that were possible in any degree.

Now, I think it is only fitting, in front of such a body as this, to attempt some little bit of review of what has been accomplished.

Let us take, first, this area of costs.

From the day that the new administration came into position of responsibility and authority, every single proposed expenditure of government, indeed some of those already in progress, have been under constant examination by men who are experts in the business—by business men. These are men who believe that the soundness of your money is absolutely essential to our form of government. These are men who believe that unless you have a sound and stable value to your money, then there is no point in your taking out an insurance policy, or investing in a savings bond, or doing any of those other things which in the American way means putting aside some money for a rainy day, or against the time of danger. If that money deteriorates while it is in your bank, or in your bonds, or in your pocket, the incentive for saving is removed.

And so this very great issue has been tackled from every single standpoint. First of all, the new administration is trying to cut costs in the effort to get rid of recurring deficits in our national budget—in spite of the necessary and staggering costs of providing for security in this modern world.

Now, if we can work toward eliminating that deficit, one of the most terrific incentives for the cheapening of your money will have been removed. No one will pretend that the recurring deficits are the only reason for inflation, but they are an important one. It is not too much to say that with recurring deficits, you must have inflation, because the only way to meet the debt is to secure more money, which means cheaper money—printing press money.

I assure you that in every single direction that does not endanger the security and position of the United States in the world, that objective is being pursued.

This does not mean, of course, that any social gains of the past are being neglected; nor, indeed, does it mean that Republicans have forgotten their promise that the advantages of social security coverages will be extended to others that have been excluded in the past without any real reason.

The whole objective of bringing costs and income in balance is so that we may look forward with future savings to real reduction in taxes. That work is going ahead every day.

Second: inefficiency, corruption, and subversion in government. Since January 20th, these have been subjects that have never been absent from the discussions of any Cabinet meeting or the meetings of any other body of governmental officials—legislative and executive. They are constantly on the minds and hearts of everybody. And we are pursuing them, by trying to put into every important position men and women who know their job, and who are devoted to the public welfare.

I would be the last to maintain that no mistakes have been made. So long as we are human, of course there have been and there will be mistakes. But I do assure you that all of those in high position in the present administration have their hearts in the right place. They are searched for honesty and integrity, probity and devotion to the United States of America.

We believe that it is absolutely possible, and mandatory, that subversion shall be removed under methods by which every right-thinking American will approve.

We believe the same thing with respect to even pecuniary matters.

We believe inefficiency must be eliminated, and in its stead we must have a government by people who not only are intending to do right by our 158 million people, but who have the capacity to do so.

In the field of foreign affairs, I made a talk a week ago yesterday—I think you were listening. As I recall, I was standing in this same spot. I want to point out this: that that talk was not an isolated incident, merely thought of out of a sudden inspiration and brought out as words, as phrases, and its meaning exposed to the public as sometimes my lawyer friends say "de novo," which means "for the first time."

What I am getting at is this: from last January twentieth, we have consulted together every day—the Secretary of State, the Secretary of Defense, the Secretary of the Treasury, the Director of the Budget Bureau, the head of the new Department, Mrs. Hobby. All of us have sat together and tried to work out what is the position from which America should approach the rest of the world—both our friends, those who are not so friendly. How do we want to express ourselves, to ourselves; and how do we want to express ourselves to others. That has been the preoccupation of all of us.

Possibly it has been the most important subject that has been discussed day by day, and on which each of us has tried to contribute his bit. No matter what we are thinking about doing with our government, no matter what we are thinking in the ways of reducing expenditures and costs, of reducing taxes eventually, all of those problems are overshadowed by, and indeed greatly influenced by, our position in the world.

Moreover, in that subject is such an immediate and critical problem as the Korean war, a war bringing sorrow still, in this day and time, to thousands of American homes. Quite naturally, therefore, it is essential that we have a whole program of standing before the world—an America strong and unafraid, but nevertheless conciliatory and friendly, and firm in this one belief: that all people want peace.

This is opposed only by misguided governments, governments

that believe that only when they are surrounded by enemies may they keep their positions of power, or governments who because of their lack of understanding believe that every other government shares their own thirst for power.

What we are trying to do is to show that America wants nothing from anyone else except the decency, the respect, the consideration that America herself is ready to accord to every other nation in full measure.

The one thing to say about all these problems is that no miraculous overnight accomplishment can be expected. These things affect not only all of our 158 million people; they affect the whole world—two and a half billions. Consequently, what happens is that trends must be set up, doctrines must be officially instilled, truth must be held up patiently before the world, until all of us understand that decency and justice are words that are still important to all humans and that greed and power, military strength, are after all only transitory, and cannot prevail over the spirit of man.

It is in these terms, ladies, and in this kind of incessant, endless work that your administration—the one that you sent here—is trying to discharge its responsibilities and to fulfill the promises made not only to you but to all the American people of all political parties.

Thank you very much.

NOTE: The President spoke at the Statler Hotel in Washington.

58 ¶ Letter to Senator Anderson Concerning the Submerged Lands Bill. *April* 24, 1953

My dear Senator Anderson:

I have received the letter signed by yourself and other Senators relative to S.J. Res. 13.

The Republican Platform clearly stated, "We favor restoration to the States of their rights to all lands and resources beneath navigable inland and offshore waters within their historic boundaries."

During the past campaign on October 13th I made the following statement:

"So, let me be clear in my position on the tidelands and all submerged lands and resources beneath inland offshore waters which lie within historic state boundaries. As I have said before, my views are in line with my party's platform. I favor the recognition of clear legal title to these lands in each of the forty-eight states.

"This has been my position since 1948, long before I was persuaded to go into politics. . . .

"The Supreme Court has declared in very recent years that there are certain paramount Federal rights in these areas. But the court expressly recognized the right of Congress to deal with the matters of ownership and title.

"Twice by substantial majorities, both Houses of Congress have voted to recognize the traditional concept of state ownership of these submerged areas. Twice these Acts of Congress have been vetoed by the President.

"I would approve such Acts of Congress."

The next day, October 14th, I made specific reference to the State of Texas:

"Just a hundred and seven years ago, the United States Senate decided that the public lands of Texas were not worth ten million dollars . . . . So the United States said to Texas: 'Keep your debts—and keep your lands. We don't want either.' And so the State of Texas paid off the ten million dollar debt of the Republic. It kept its two hundred million acres of lands—including the submerged area extending three marine leagues seaward into the Gulf of Mexico."

My position is the same today. It was further amplified by the Administration representatives in the hearings before the Senate and your committees considering the legislation.

I favor the prompt passage by the Senate of S.J. Res. 13 with any amendments the Senate may approve, not inimical to the principles which I have expressed. It has never been my belief that the several states should have any title to lands beyond their historical boundaries on the continental shelf.

I hesitate to express an opinion on legislative procedure, but I am deeply concerned with the delay of the entire Administration program in the Senate of the United States.

However, let me make it clear that I am not criticizing the Senators who have views on this subject different from mine. I respect their sincerity and their right to vote as they think best.

Sincerely,

DWIGHT D. EISENHOWER

59 ¶ Memorandom Convening the President's Conference on Administrative Procedure.

April 29, 1953

[Released April 29, 1953. Dated April 28, 1953]

To All Executive Departments and Administrative Agencies:

I am in receipt of a communication from the Chief Justice of the United States, in his capacity as Chairman of the Judicial Conference of the United States, concerning unnecessary delay, expense and volume of records in some adjudicatory and rule-making proceedings in the Executive Departments and Administrative Agencies. I attach a copy of that letter.

The suggestion there transmitted has the endorsement of the Attorney General. It affords opportunity for a public service of benefit to both citizens and Government. Accordingly, I am happy to call a conference of representatives of the departments and agencies, and of the judiciary and the bar, for the purpose of studying the problems thus described.

It is not contemplated that the conference will attempt to impose rules or procedures upon the departments, the agencies, or litigants. The purpose is to exchange information, experience and suggestions and so to evolve by cooperative effort principles which may be applied and steps which may be taken severally by the departments and agencies toward the end that the administrative process may be improved to the benefit of all.

I request the Attorney General to cause a list to be prepared of those departments and administrative agencies which have these functions, and to transmit to each of those listed a copy of this call. I also request him to designate, in addition to a delegate, a representative of his Department to act as Secretary of the conference.

I request each department and agency receiving this call from the Attorney General to designate a representative to meet with other such representatives as delegates in a conference for the purposes I have designated. I request that in designating representatives for these purposes care be taken to name persons who will undertake to devote to the work the considerable time which probably will be required.

With the agreement of the Chief Justice, I have invited Circuit Judge E. Barrett Prettyman of the United States Court of Appeals for the District of Columbia, Judge Morris A. Soper of the United States Court of Appeals for the Fourth Circuit, Baltimore, and Associate Judge Walter M. Bastian of the District Court of the United States for the District of Columbia, to participate in the conference, and have requested Judge Prettyman to act as Chairman.

I am requesting J. Earl Cox, Jay D. Bond, and William F. Scharnikow, all of Washington, D.C., who are federal trial examiners of experience, to attend and participate as members of the conference.

I am also inviting the following lawyers, experienced in the field of administrative law, to attend and participate as members of the conference:

Hon. John A. Danaher, Washington, D.C.

Richard S. Doyle, Esq., Washington, D.C.

Edmund L. Jones, Esq., Washington, D.C.

H. Cecil Kilpatrick, Esq., Washington, D.C.

Wilbur R. Lester, Esq., Washington, D.C.

Breck P. McAllister, Esq., New York, N.Y.

George M. Morris, Esq., Washington, D.C.

Prof. Charles B. Nutting, Pittsburgh, Pennsylvania

Garnet L. Patterson, Esq., Akron, Ohio

John R. Turney, Esq., Washington, D.C.

J. Albert Woll, Esq., Washington, D.C.

Joseph W. Wyatt, Esq., Washington, D.C.

The secretary of the conference will announce the time and place for the initial meeting of the conference. Thereafter, the conference will organize and fix its program and procedure. After the program which seems initially possible has been completed, provisions may be made by the conference for further meetings from time to time. Should a member of the conference be unable to continue in attendance, the vacancy may be filled by the authority which originally designated the retiring member.

I shall be happy to receive from time to time reports from the conference as to its work.

DWIGHT D. EISENHOWER

NOTE: Chief Justice Fred M. Vinson's letter, dated March 24, 1953, follows:

My dear Mr. President:

Some time ago, the Judicial Conference of the United States undertook to examine into the causes of long delay, great expense, and voluminous records in certain classes of cases, including some which reach the courts from the executive departments and administrative agencies.

A committee of judges and an advisory committee composed of representatives of the agencies and of the bar presented a report to the Conference at its September 1951 session, and that report was approved. The findings were that, while the number of such cases is not large, those in which unnecessary delay, expense and volume of record occur create a serious problem in the administration of justice, that the problem should be considered by the departments and agencies, and that a cooperative approach to it affords the best promise for remedy.

Pursuant to a resolution of the Judicial Conference, I have the honor to transmit a suggestion that you call a conference of representatives of the executive departments and administrative agencies having adjudicatory functions, for the purpose of studying cooperatively possible steps to remedy the conditions which were the subject of the report. It is further suggested that representatives of the bar and members of the judiciary, in such numbers and in such capacity as you may deem appropriate, might well be included in such a conference.

I venture to add my own view that the suggested conference appears to be a practical step toward remedying a condition which impedes the economical and efficient determination of serious controversies between citizens and the Government. The excessive time consumed, of course, diminishes the court hours for all other cases and necessarily impedes their determination. I, therefore, personally endorse it.

Copies of the report to the Judicial Conference are available for your information.

Sincerely,

FRED M. VINSON

60 ¶ Special Message to the Congress Transmitting Reorganization Plan 5 of 1953 Concerning the Export-Import Bank of Washington. *April 30, 1953*

To the Congress of the United States:

I transmit herewith Reorganization Plan No. 5 of 1953, prepared in accordance with the provisions of the Reorganization Act of 1949, as amended.

The purpose of the reorganization plan is to simplify the organization and strengthen the administration of the Export-Import Bank of Washington by providing for a single Managing Director at the head of the Bank. The management of the Bank is now vested in a Board of Directors consisting of four full-time members and the Secretary of State, ex officio. The functions performed by the Board are essentially of an executive nature and are comparable to those vested in the heads of other executive agencies. Experience has demonstrated that the most effective performance of executive functions is more likely to be obtained under a single administrator than under a board.

The plan concentrates authority and responsibility for Bank operations in the Managing Director. Safeguards are provided in the plan and in existing law, however, to assure that the Bank follows sound lending and financial policies and that its activities are coordinated with those of other Government agencies having international responsibilities. Under the plan, the National Advisory Council on International Monetary and Financial Problems is authorized to establish the general lending and other financial policies which shall govern the operations of the Bank. The Council is composed of the Secretary of the Treasury, as chairman, the Secretary of State, the Secretary of Commerce, the Chairman of the Board of Governors of the Federal Reserve System, and the Director for Mutual Security.

At present, the Board of Directors is not only subject to policy guidance by the National Advisory Council, under the provisions of the Bretton Woods Agreements Act, but is also required to consult with the Advisory Board for the Export-Import Bank, created by the Export-Import Bank Act, on major questions of policy and to receive recommendations from that Board. The composition of the Advisory Board largely parallels that of the Council. The differences are that only the latter includes the Director for Mutual Security as a member and that the Chairman of the Board of Directors of the Export-Import Bank is the chairman of the Advisory Board whereas the Secretary of the Treasury serves as the chairman of the Council. Because of the similarity of the composition of the Advisory Board and Council, and of their functions as respects the Bank, the reorganization plan abolishes the Advisory Board. It also abolishes the functions of the Advisory Board (conferred by section 3(d) of the Export-Import Bank Act of 1945).

The reorganization plan also provides for the abolition of the functions of the Chairman of the Board of Directors of the Export-Import Bank of Washington with respect to his membership on the National Advisory Council on International Monetary and Financial Problems. The function of membership is conferred upon the Chairman by section 4 of the Bretton Woods Agreements Act, as amended. I contemplate that the Managing Director of the Export-Import Bank of Washington will participate as a non-voting member of the National Advisory Council in relation to matters of concern to the Bank. I believe there is merit in reducing the size of the Council and also believe that the interests of the Bank can be properly placed before the Council without conferring full Council membership on the Managing Director of the Bank.

Under the reorganization plan the Export-Import Bank of Washington will continue in its status of a corporate entity, and independent agency, in the executive branch of the Government. The President will retain authority to terminate or modify any delegation or assignment of function made by the President to the Bank or to any of its agencies or officers.

After investigation I have found and hereby declare that each reorganization included in Reorganization Plan No. 5 of 1953 is necessary to accomplish one or more of the purposes set forth in section 2(a) of the Reorganization Act of 1949, as amended. I also have found and hereby declare that by reason of these reorganizations it is necessary to include in the reorganization plan provision for the appointment and compensation of the new officers specified in sections 1, 2, and 3 of the reorganization plan. The rates of compensation fixed for these officers are, respectively, those which I have found to prevail in respect of comparable officers in the executive branch of the Government.

The taking effect of Reorganization Plan No. 5 of 1953 will accomplish a small immediate reduction of expenditures, since it will substitute one Managing Director, together with a deputy and assistant, for a Board which includes four full-time members. Other reductions in expenditures will probably be brought about also, through increased economy and efficiency in the performance of necessary services of the Bank resulting from the simplification of its organization, but such reductions cannot be itemized in advance of actual experience.

DWIGHT D. EISENHOWER

NOTE: Reorganization Plan 5 of 1953 is published in the U.S. Statutes at Large (67 Stat. 637) and in the 1949–1953 Compilation of title 3 of the Code of Federal Regulations (p. 1027). It became effective on June 30, 1953.

61 ¶ Special Message to the Congress Transmitting Reorganization Plan 6 of 1953 Concerning the Department of Defense. *April 30, 1953*

To the Congress of the United States:

I address the Congress on a subject which has been of primary interest to me throughout all the years of my adult life—the defense of our country.

As a former soldier who has experienced modern war at first hand, and now, as President and Commander in Chief of the armed forces of the United States, I believe that our defense establishment is in need of immediate improvement. In this message, I indicate actions which we are taking, and must yet take, to assure the greater safety of America.

Through the years, our Nation has warded off all enemies. We have defended ourselves successfully against those who have waged war against us. We enjoy, as a people, a proud tradition of triumph in battle.

We are not, however, a warlike people. Our historic goal is peace. It shall ever be peace—peace to enjoy the freedom we cherish and the fruits of our labors. We maintain strong military forces in support of this supreme purpose, for we believe that in today's world only properly organized strength may altogether avert war.

Because we are not a military-minded people, we have some-times failed to give proper thought to the problems of the organi-zation and adequacy of our armed forces. Past periods of inter-national stress and the actual outbreaks of wars have found us poorly prepared. On such occasions, we have had to commit to battle insufficient and improperly organized military forces to hold the foe until our citizenry could be more fully mobilized and our resources marshalled. We know that we cannot permit a repetition of those conditions.

Today we live in a perilous period of international affairs. Soviet Russia and her allies have it within their power to join with us in the establishment of a true peace or to plunge the world into global war. To date, they have chosen to conduct them-selves in such a way that these are years neither of total war nor total peace.

We in the United States have, therefore, recently embarked upon the definition of a new, positive foreign policy. One of our basic aims is to gain again for the free world the initiative in shaping the international conditions under which freedom can thrive. Essential to this endeavor is the assurance of an alert, efficient, ever-prepared defense establishment.

Today our international undertakings are shared by the free peoples of other nations. We find ourselves in an unparalleled role of leadership of free men everywhere. With this leadership have come new responsibilities. With the basic purpose of assur-ing our own security and economic viability, we are helping our friends to protect their lives and liberties. And one major help that we may give them is reliance upon our own military estab-lishment.

Today also witnesses one of history's times of swiftest advance in scientific achievements. These developments can accomplish wonders in providing a healthier and happier life for us all. But—converted to military uses—they threaten new, more dev-astating terrors in war. These simple, inescapable facts make imperative the maintenance of a defense organization commanding the most modern technological instruments in our arsenal of weapons.

In providing the kind of military security that our country needs, we must keep our people free and our economy solvent. We must not endanger the very things we seek to defend. We must not create a nation mighty in arms that is lacking in liberty and bankrupt in resources. Our armed strength must continue to rise from the vigor of a free people and a prosperous economy.

Recognizing all these national and international demands upon our military establishment, we must remain ever mindful of three great objectives in organizing our defense.

First: Our military establishment must be founded upon our basic constitutional principles and traditions. There must be a clear and unchallenged civilian responsibility in the defense establishment. This is essential not only to maintain democratic institutions, but also to protect the integrity of the military profession. Basic decisions relating to the military forces must be made by politically accountable civilian officials. Conversely, professional military leaders must not be thrust into the political arena to become the prey of partisan politics. To guard these principles, we must recognize and respect the clear lines of responsibility and authority which run from the President, through the Secretary of Defense and the Secretaries of the military departments, over the operations of all branches of the Department of Defense.

Second: Effectiveness with economy must be made the watchwords of our defense effort. To maintain an adequate national defense for the indefinite future, we have found it necessary to devote a larger share of our national resources than any of us have heretofore anticipated. To protect our economy, maximum effectiveness at minimum cost is essential.

Third: We must develop the best possible military plans. These plans must be sound guides to action in case of war. They must incorporate the most competent and considered thinking from every point of view—military, scientific, industrial, and economic.

To strengthen civilian control by establishing clear lines of accountability, to further effectiveness with economy, and to provide adequate planning for military purposes—these were primary objectives of the Congress in enacting the National Security Act of 1947 and strengthening it in 1949.

Now much has happened which makes it appropriate to review the workings of those basic statutes. Valuable lessons have been learned through six years of trial by experience. Our top military structure has been observed under changing conditions. The military action in Korea, the buildup of our forces everywhere, the provision of military aid to other friendly nations, and the participation of United States armed forces in regional collective security arrangements, such as those under the North Atlantic Treaty Organization—all these have supplied sharp tests of our military organization. Today, in making my specific recommendations, I have also had the benefit of the report prepared by the Committee on Department of Defense Organization established by the Secretary of Defense three months ago.

The time is here, then, to work to perfect our military establishment without delay.

I.

The first objective—toward which immediate actions already are being directed—is clarification of lines of authority within the Department of Defense so as to strengthen civilian responsibility.

I am convinced that the fundamental structure of our Department of Defense and its various component agencies as provided by the National Security Act, as amended, is sound. None of the changes I am proposing affects that basic structure, and this first objective can and will be attained without any legislative change.

With my full support, the Secretary of Defense must exercise over the Department of Defense the direction, authority, and control which are vested in him by the National Security Act. He should do so through the basic channels of responsibility and authority prescribed in that act—through the three civilian Secretaries of the Army, the Navy, and the Air Force, who are responsible to him for all aspects of the respective military departments (except for the legal responsibility of the Joint Chiefs of Staff to advise the President in military matters). No function in any part of the Department of Defense, or in any of its component agencies, should be performed independent of the direction, authority, and control of the Secretary of Defense. The Secretary is the accountable civilian head of the Department of Defense, and under the law, my principal assistant in all matters relating to the Department. I want all to know that he has my full backing in that role.

To clarify a point which has led to considerable confusion in the past, the Secretary of Defense, with my approval, will shortly issue a revision of that portion of the 1948 memorandum commonly known as the Key West Agreement which provides for a system of designating executive agents for unified commands. Basic decisions with respect to the establishment and direction of unified commands are made by the President and the Secretary of Defense, upon the recommendation of the Joint Chiefs of Staff in their military planning and advisory role. But the provision of the Key West Agreement, under which the Joint Chiefs of Staff designate one of their members as an executive agent for each unified command, has led to considerable confusion and misunderstanding with respect to the relationship of the Joint Chiefs of Staff to the Secretary of Defense, and the relationship of the military chief of each service to the civilian Secretary of his military department.

Hence, the Secretary of Defense, with my approval, is revising the Key West Agreement to provide that the Secretary of Defense shall designate in each case a military department to serve as the executive agent for a unified command. Under this new arrangement, the channel of responsibility and authority to a commander of a unified command will unmistakably be from the President to the Secretary of Defense to the designated civilian Secretary of a military department. This arrangement will fix responsibility along a definite channel of accountable civilian officials as intended by the National Security Act.

It will be understood, however, that, for the strategic direction and operational control of forces, and for the conduct of combat operations, the military chief of the designated military department will be authorized by the Secretary of Defense to receive and transmit reports and orders and to act for that department in its executive agency capacity. This arrangement will make it always possible to deal promptly with emergency or wartime situations. The military chief will clearly be acting in the name and by the direction of the Secretary of Defense. Promulgated orders will directly state that fact.

By taking this action to provide clearer lines of responsibility and authority for the exercise of civilian control, I believe we will make significant progress toward increasing proper accountability in the top levels of the Department of Defense.

II.

Our second major objective is effectiveness with economy. Although the American people, throughout their history, have hoped to avoid supporting large military forces, today we must obviously maintain a strong military force to ward off attack, at a moment's notice, by enemies equipped with the most devastating weapons known to modern science. This need for immediate preparedness makes it all the more imperative to see that the Nation maintains effective military forces in the manner imposing the minimum burden on the national economy.

In an organization the size of the Department of Defense, true effectiveness with economy can be attained only by decentralization of operations, under flexible and effective direction and control from the center. I am impressed with the determination of the Secretary of Defense to administer the Department on this basis and to look to the Secretaries of the three military departments as his principal agents for the management and direction of the entire defense enterprise.

Such a system of decentralized operations, however, requires, for sound management, flexible machinery at the top. Unfortunately, this is not wholly possible in the Department of Defense as now established by law. Two principal fields of activity are rigidly assigned by law to unwieldy boards which—no matter how much authority may be centralized in their respective chairmen—provide organizational arrangements too slow and too clumsy to serve as effective management tools for the Secretary. In addition, other staff agencies have been set up in the Office of the Secretary of Defense and their functions prescribed by law, thus making it difficult for the Secretary to adjust his staff arrangements to deal with new problems as they arise, or to provide for flexible cooperation among the several staff agencies.

Accordingly, I am transmitting today to the Congress a reorganization plan which is designed to provide the Secretary of Defense with a more efficient staff organization. The plan calls for the abolition of the Munitions Board, the Research and Development Board, the Defense Supply Management Agency, and the office of Director of Installations and vests their functions in the Secretary of Defense. At the same time, the plan authorizes the appointment of new Assistant Secretaries of Defense to whom the Secretary of Defense intends to assign the functions now vested in the agencies to be abolished and certain other functions now assigned to other officials. Specifically, the reorganization plan provides for six additional assistant secretaries—three to whom the Secretary will assign the duties now performed by the two Boards (based on a redistribution of staff functions), two who will be utilized to replace individual officials who presently hold other titles, and one to be assigned to a position formerly but no longer filled by an assistant secretary. The new assistant secretary positions are required in order to make it possible to bring executives of the highest type to the Government service and to permit them to operate effectively and with less personnel than at present. In addition, the plan also provides that in view of the importance of authoritative legal opinions and interpretations the office of General Counsel be raised to a statutory position with rank substantially equivalent to that of an assistant secretary.

The abolition of the present statutory staff agencies and the provision of the new assistant secretaries to aid the Secretary of Defense will be the key to the attainment of increased effectiveness at low cost in the Department of Defense. These steps will permit the Secretary to make a thorough reorganization of the non-military staff agencies in his office. He will be able to establish truly effective and vigorous staff units under the leadership of the assistant secretaries. Each assistant secretary will function as a staff head within an assigned field of responsibility.

Without imposing themselves in the direct lines of responsibility and authority between the Secretary of Defense and the Secretaries of the three military departments, the Assistant Secretaries of Defense will provide the Secretary with a continuing review of the programs of the defense establishment and help him institute major improvements in their execution. They will be charged with establishing systems, within their assigned fields, for obtaining complete and accurate information to support recommendations to the Secretary. The assistant secretaries will make frequent inspection visits to our far-flung installations and check for the Secretary the effectiveness and efficiency of operations in their assigned fields.

Other improvements are badly needed in the Departments of the Army, the Navy, and the Air Force. Accordingly, the Secretary of Defense is initiating studies by the three Secretaries of the military departments of the internal organization of their departments with a view toward making those Secretaries truly responsible administrators, thereby obtaining greater effectiveness and attaining economies wherever possible. These studies will apply to the organization of the military departments some of the same principles of clearer lines of accountability which we are applying to the Department of Defense as a whole.

Immediate attention will also be given to studying improvements of those parts of the military departments directly concerned with the procurement and distribution of munitions and supplies and the inventory and accounting systems within each military department. We must take every step toward seeing that our armed forces are adequately supplied at all times with the materials essential for them to carry on their operations in the field. Necessary to this effort is a reorganization of supply machinery in the military departments. These studies of the organization of the military departments have my full support.

One other area for improved effectiveness is civilian and military personnel management. In this area certain specialized studies and actions are desirable. Accordingly, I have directed the Secretary of Defense to organize a study of the problems of attracting and holding competent career personnel—civilian and military—in the Department of Defense. As a part of this study, an examination of the Officer Personnel Act of 1947 and its practical administration will be undertaken to see if any changes are needed. I am directing that this study also include a review of statutes governing the retirement of military officers aimed at eliminating those undesirable provisions which force the early retirement of unusually capable officers who are willing to continue on active service.

The Secretary of Defense, with my approval, is issuing revised orders relating to the preparing and signing of efficiency reports for military personnel who serve full time in the Office of the Secretary, and new instructions to the military departments to guide selection boards in their operations. These actions are aimed at giving full credit to military officers serving in the Office of the Secretary of Defense for their work for the Department of Defense as a whole. Henceforth, civilian officials who have military officers detailed to their offices on a full-time basis will be responsible for filling out and signing the formal efficiency reports for such officers for the period of such service. In the case of officers serving in the Office of the Secretary of Defense, no other efficiency reports for such service will be maintained. The Secretary of each military department is being instructed to direct the boards convened in his department for the selection of military officers for promotion, to give the same weight to service in the Office of the Secretary of Defense and the efficiency reports from that Office as to service in the military department staff and to efficiency reports of departmental officers. These actions are desirable in order to reward military officers equally for service on behalf of the Department of Defense and service on the staff of a military department.

These actions and others which will be undertaken are aimed at a more effective and efficient Department of Defense; indeed, actions toward this objective will be continuous.

The impact of all these measures will be felt through the whole structure of the Department of Defense, its utilization of millions of personnel and billions of dollars. A simple token testimony to this is this fact: in the Office of the Secretary of Defense alone a staff reduction of approximately 500 persons will be effected.

III.

Our third broad objective is to improve our machinery for strategic planning for national security. Certain actions toward this end may be taken administratively to improve the organization and procedures within the Department of Defense. Other changes are incorporated in the reorganization plan transmitted to the Congress today.

The Joint Chiefs of Staff, as provided in the National Security Act of 1947, are not a command body but are the principal military advisors to the President, the National Security Council, and the Secretary of Defense. They are responsible for formulating the strategic plans by which the United States will cope with the challenge of any enemy. The three members of the Joint Chiefs of Staff who are the military chiefs of their respective services are responsible to their Secretaries for the efficiency of their services and their readiness for war.

These officers are clearly overworked, and steps must be devised to relieve them of time-consuming details of minor importance.

They must be encouraged to delegate lesser duties to reliable subordinate individuals and agencies in both the Joint Chiefs of Staff structure and in their military department staffs. One of our aims in making more effective our strategic planning machinery, therefore, is to improve the organization and procedures of the supporting staff of the Joint Chiefs of Staff so that the Chiefs, acting as a body, will be better able to perform their roles as strategic planners and military advisors.

Our military plans are based primarily on military factors, but they must also take into account a wider range of policy and economic factors, as well as the latest developments of modern science. Therefore, our second aim in assuring the very best strategic planning is to broaden the degree of active participation of other persons and units at the staff level in the consideration of matters before the Joint Chiefs of Staff and to bring to bear more diversified and expert skills.

The reorganization plan transmitted to the Congress today is designed—without detracting from the military advisory functions of the Joint Chiefs of Staff as a group—to place upon the Chairman of the Joint Chiefs of Staff greater responsibility for organizing and directing the subordinate structure of the Joint Chiefs of Staff in such a way as to help the Secretary of Defense and the Joint Chiefs of Staff discharge their total responsibilities.

Specifically, the reorganization plan makes the Chairman of the Joint Chiefs of Staff responsible for managing the work of the Joint Staff and its Director. The Joint Staff is, of course, a study-and-reporting body serving the Joint Chiefs of Staff. The plan makes the service of the Director of the Joint Staff subject to the approval of the Secretary of Defense. It also makes the service of officers on the Joint Staff subject to the approval of the Chairman of the Joint Chiefs of Staff. These new responsibilities of the Chairman are in consonance with his present functions of serving as the presiding officer of the Joint Chiefs of Staff, providing agenda for meetings, assisting the Joint Chiefs of Staff to perform their duties as promptly as practicable, and keeping the Secretary of Defense and the President informed of issues before the Joint Chiefs of Staff. In addition, the proposed changes will relieve the Joint Chiefs of Staff, as a body, of a large amount of administrative detail involved in the management of its subordinate committee and staff structure.

In support of our second aim—broadened participation in strategic planning—the Secretary of Defense will direct the Chairman of the Joint Chiefs of Staff to arrange for the fullest cooperation of the Joint Staff and the subcommittees of the Joint Chiefs of Staff with other parts of the Office of the Secretary of Defense in the early stages of staff work on any major problem. If necessary, to aid in this additional burden, an Assistant or Deputy Director of the Joint Staff will be designated to give particular attention to this staff collaboration. Thus, at the developmental stages of important staff studies by the subordinate elements of the Joint Chiefs of Staff, there will be a proper integration of the views and special skills of the other staff agencies of the Department, such as those responsible for budget, manpower, supply, research, and engineering. This action will assure the presentation of improved staff products to the Joint Chiefs of Staff for their consideration.

Also, special attention will be given to providing for the participation of competent civilian scientists and engineers within the substructure of the Joint Chiefs of Staff. Such participants will be able to contribute a wide range of scientific information and knowledge to our strategic planning.

Only by including outstanding civilian experts in the process of strategic planning can our military services bring new weapons rapidly into their established weapons systems, make recommendations with respect to the use of new systems of weapons in the future war plans, and see that the whole range of scientific information and knowledge of fundamental cost factors are taken into account in strategic planning.

Taken together, the changes included in the reorganization plan and the several administrative actions should go a long way toward improving the strategic planning machinery of the Joint Chiefs of Staff, and lead to the development of plans based on the broadest conception of the over-all national interest rather than the particular desires of the individual services.

I transmit herewith Reorganization Plan No. 6 of 1953, prepared in accordance with the Reorganization Act of 1949, as amended, and providing for reorganizations in the Department of Defense.

After investigation I have found and hereby declare that each reorganization included in Reorganization Plan No. 6 of 1953 is necessary to accomplish one or more of the purposes set forth in section 2(a) of the Reorganization Act of 1949, as amended.

I have found and hereby declare that it is necessary to include in the accompanying reorganization plan, by reason of reorganizations made thereby, provisions for the appointment and compensation of six additional Assistant Secretaries of Defense and a General Counsel of the Department of Defense. The rates of compensation fixed for these officers are those which I have found to prevail in respect of comparable officers in the executive branch of the Government.

The statutory authority for the exercise of the function of guidance to the Munitions Board in connection with strategic and logistic plans, abolished by section 2(d) of the reorganization plan, is section 213(c) of the National Security Act of 1947, as amended.

The taking effect of the reorganizations included in Reorganization Plan No. 6 of 1953 is expected to result in a more effective, efficient, and economical performance of functions in the Department of Defense. It is impracticable to specify or itemize at this time the reduction of expenditures which it is probable will be brought about by such taking effect.

The Congress is a full partner in actions to strengthen our military establishment. Jointly we must carry forward a sound program to keep America strong. The Congress and the President, acting in their proper spheres, must perform their duties to the American people in support of our highest traditions. Should, for any reason, the national military policy become a subject of partisan politics, the only loser would be the American people.

We owe it to all the people to maintain the best military establishment that we know how to devise. There are none, however, to whom we owe it more than the soldiers, the sailors, the marines, and the airmen in uniform whose lives are pledged to the defense of our freedom.

Dwight D. Eisenhower

NOTE: Reorganization Plan 6 of 1953 is published in the U.S. Statutes at Large (67 Stat. 638) and in the 1949–1953 Compilation of title 3 of the Code of Federal Regulations (p. 1027). It became effective on June 30, 1953.

62 ¶ The President's News Conference of *April* 30, 1953.

THE PRESIDENT. For several reasons, I shall want to take some of the time available to us today, actually to read to you a statement. Now, Mr. Hagerty tells me that a mimeograph of it is being made and is going to be over here before the conference is ended. If that is true, I suggest there is no need for your making notes during the time I am dealing with this paper.

The paper deals with an approach to the security problem, and there are three reasons that I should like to take it up today.

First, I have sent down today to the Congress a reorganizational plan for the Defense Department. It is not radical in most ways, certainly, but it does attempt to point up that organization so as to secure a greater effectiveness, economy, speed in action, and more rapid production of materiel that has been appropriated for.

Another reason is that there is just back, as you know, from Europe, a team which the administration sent over there: the

Secretary of State, the Secretary of the Treasury, Secretary of Defense, and the Director of Mutual Security. They have all returned, or at least all have returned except Secretary Wilson; and we have been having conferences on this same global problem.

And finally, I met this morning with some of the legislative leaders, and we had this problem up for a long and exhaustive discussion. So I want to give you really the approach that we are now making toward this problem.

[*Reading*] I would like to present to you in a general way, and with fairly broad strokes, what I consider the sensible framework within which the United States and its allies can present in hard military fact an ever more effective posture of defense. A true posture of defense is composed of three factors—spiritual, military, and economic. Today I shall talk only about the last two.

We Americans have frequently called for unity of basic purpose among our allies. I feel quite strongly that the least we can do is to display a similar continuity and unity in American purpose.

This policy of ours, therefore, will not be tied to any magic, critical year which then has to be "stretched out" because of economic or production problems, but will be based on the sounder theory that a very real danger not only exists this year, but may continue to exist for years to come; that our strength, which is already very real, must now be made stronger, not by inefficient and expensive starts and stops, but by steady continuous improvements.

I have always firmly believed that there is a great logic in the conduct of military affairs. There is an equally great logic in economic affairs. If these two logical disciplines can be wedded, it is then possible to create a situation of maximum military strength within economic capacities.

If, on the other hand, these two are allowed to proceed in disregard one for the other, you then create a situation either of doubtful military strength, or of such precarious economic strength that your military position is in constant jeopardy.

It has been the purpose of this administration ever since it took office, finding itself confronted with a crazy quilt of promises, commitments, and contracts, to bring American military logic and American economic logic into joint strong harness.

No more glaring illustration of the lack of balance between the military logic and the economic logic could possibly be found than the situation that existed when we took office. On the one hand, we found our allies deploring our unfulfilled defense promises. On the other hand, we found there was a total carryover of $81 billion in appropriated funds, largely committed, for which cash must be provided from revenues in future fiscal years, over and above the normal annual cost of government. It's just as if the late administration had gone to the store and ordered 81 billion dollars worth of goods, which we've got to pay for as they're delivered, in addition to paying the regular household running expenses.

The fiscal situation represented by these two extremes absolutely has to be brought into some kind of realistic focus, and the only way to do it is to have a completely new, fresh look without any misleading labels.

As you know, over the past years I have been involved in the European end of defense, and therefore I think I know all about paper divisions and cardboard wings. For the last 3 months, I have been heavily involved in the American end of defense, and day after day have had to struggle with the basic equation that links the military safety of this country and of the free world with the ability of the world to pay its bills and earn a living.

This morning I told the legislative leaders that already we can see our way clear to ask the Congress to appropriate at least 8½ billion less in new money for the fiscal year 1954 than had been asked for by the previous administration. This is a preliminary figure based on 3 months' hard work. The great bulk of it, of course, relates to security programs. More definite figures will become available as appropriation requests are presented to the Congress during the next few weeks.

You will note that I have been talking about the new appropriations for fiscal 1954. Actual cash savings for 1954 will be determined only as Congress acts on the appropriation requests.

These savings will not reduce the effective military strength we will deliver to ourselves and our allies during fiscal 1954. [*Interrupts reading*] Those deliveries are already appropriated for. They are already on the books and in contracts. [*Continues reading*]: Deliveries actually will be speeded up through the reduction of lead time, and concentration on producing those items which make the most military sense for the immediate future.

Establishing the most effective relationship between defense requirements and economic capability in these days is probably the most complex and ramified problem to be faced by any government. Practically everyone concerned with the problem can with some justification be a special pleader.

But I am sure that what the overwhelming majority of Americans want to believe is that their Government is working with diligence and intelligence to bring about as rapidly as possible a condition of true military strength. I also believe that the overwhelming majority of the people of the free world appreciate the fact that a healthy American economy and a functioning economy in their own home country are inseparable from true defense.

Furthermore, I have a deep conviction that all these people possess a fundamental common sense which permits them to grasp the difference between a quiet, steady, long-term improvement in their defense position and the tempests stirred up by public arguments over the artificial arithmetic which is so easy to produce in the defense field.

The program we are presenting is a long-term program, calling for a steady and adequate flow of men and materials to present a position of genuine strength to any would-be aggressor.

The basic elements of our strategic problem have not materially changed in recent years, and certainly not in recent days. The areas and peoples vital to our Nation's welfare are the same as they have been for a long time. What we are doing is to adopt a new policy for the solution of the problem.

This change in policy is radical and cannot be effected overnight. There exists what is, in effect, a straitjacket, comprising prior authorizations, appropriations, and contracts.

The essence of the change is this. We reject the idea that we must build up to a maximum attainable strength for some specific date theoretically fixed for a specified time in the future. Defense is not a matter of maximum strength for a single date. It is a matter of adequate protection to be projected as far into the future as the actions and apparent purposes of others may compel us.

It is a policy that can, if necessary, be lived with over a period of years.

Finally, I would like to remind you of what I have said many times before, and will probably say many times again.

Security based upon heavy armaments is a way of life that has been forced upon us and on our allies. We don't like it; in fact, we hate it. But so long as such an unmistakable, self-confirmed threat to our freedom exists, we will carry these burdens with dedication and determination.

Our hope and our prayer is that this dedication and determination will bring about a world condition when we can once again return to the arts of peace, which we have always and will always cherish above all other arts.

That is the end of my statement. I read it because I wanted to make it exactly as I have been thinking over it in these recent days. Now gentlemen, the rest of the time is yours.

Q. Edward T. Folliard, Washington Post: Mr. President, can you tell us of any specific field in which there will be a reduction, say, in the size of forces, or what effect this might have, say, on the Air Force, its plans to build up to—I think it's 143 groups?

THE PRESIDENT. As to long-term objectives that may have been specified, I can't tell you exactly what will be the effect. But I can tell you this: there will be more buildup in 1954 than was possible under the operations and the activities as they were proceeding in January of this year. This is due to the shortening up of lead times, and the concentration on critical areas and items.

Q. Mr. Folliard: May I put it this way, Mr. President? As a result of these cuts, will we have fewer people in the armed services in the days ahead?

THE PRESIDENT. If you look far enough ahead, Mr. Folliard, that is possibly true. We cannot tell yet, because we have been here only 90 days. There is a tremendous job of inspecting and analyzing of forces, personnel, activities throughout the world. It stretches all the way around the world, this activity of which we are speaking. It is impossible to find the utmost of efficiency, businesslike methods, starting right back at the production line, until you get to the end. So until we know what those examinations, analyses, and corrections will yield, we cannot say what the final result will be.

Q. Anthony Leviero, New York Times: Mr. President, this increased buildup in 1954, will that be in all three of the armed forces?

THE PRESIDENT. I should think so.

Q. Mr. Leviero: In general?

THE PRESIDENT. Again I say I should think so; and I say this advisedly: we have been going over these things—you do get a little bit confused in trying to remember exact detail.

But the fact is that in this coming year, there is nothing deducted in the way of money, and there is added the idea of shortening up of lead times, and getting these things proper.

Q. Richard Harkness, National Broadcasting Company: If you attain this preliminary figure of an $8½ billion decrease, sir, will that not mean a balanced Federal budget in the coming fiscal year?

THE PRESIDENT. No, it does not, because I particularly specified *new* money, money that you are requesting in new authorizations. To be exact, the budget now before the Congress asked for 72.9 billion. This is an 8.4—at least in that order, 8½—reduction in that, that we now believe we can do after this 90 days. And I am giving you that, as I say, as a tentative figure. But that is not the deficit. The deficit comes about from the amount of the appropriated money of this year that will be spent, added to the amount of carried-over money that will be spent, and deduct from that your anticipated revenues. Incidentally, anticipated revenues will probably be a bit lower. Now, that is the deficit. Therefore the 9.9 which you probably had in your mind will not be reduced by 8.5. No, it will not.

Q. Edwin Dayton Moore, United Press: I want to get straightened out, is this 8.5 just in defense and military aid, or is it the overall?

THE PRESIDENT. Overall, and I said, the great bulk of which, of course, is in security programs.

Q. Mr. Moore: Will you give us some figures on military and foreign aid?

THE PRESIDENT. No.

Q. Jack L. Bell, Associated Press: At least one Member of Congress has said your 8.5 savings in appropriations will be translated into a 4.4 savings in expenditures. Do you have such a figure? In other words, actual spending?

THE PRESIDENT. We have, of course, dealt with all kinds of figures, and the reason I told you that—actual figures or estimates are not going to be available until we go before Congress, because there is no sense in creating confusion. We are not certain of those figures, and there will be changes, both in the expenditure figures and in the new appropriations figures. I am giving you simply the order of the savings that we expect to accomplish in the new appropriations.

Q. Mr. Bell: You are not prepared at this time to give any figure?

THE PRESIDENT. That is correct.

Q. James R. Shepley, Time Magazine: Some of us are under the impression, sir, that this year of maximum exposure that you now discourage, came about because the Joint Chiefs of Staff thought that in 1954 the Soviets could deliver an atomic attack on the United States. Is there something now that is available to you and the Joint Chiefs of Staff which indicates that will not be a possibility?

THE PRESIDENT. I am not going to quarrel with their estimate on when they will have atomic bombs. But I do not admit that anyone can predict when, if ever, another government would want to launch global war. I just don't believe there is a necessary relationship between those two concepts.

Q. [*Speaker unidentified*], United Press: Is it true, sir, that considering the carryover funds and other money available, that there will be about as much money for our allies in the new year as in the present?

THE PRESIDENT. You mean as much money spent in 1954? I have forgotten the exact figure.

Q. About how much?

THE PRESIDENT. As a matter of fact, I must tell you, I definitely determined not to talk in more exact figures than I have already given you today because I was so certain that some of them would become confused. I have dealt with nothing but figures for weeks. I will say this: the expenditure program for 1954, of course, is very largely fixed. As I said, it is in something of a straitjacket, so that the changes that will be made will be gradual. But I will not be more exact on the expenditure program for foreign aid in 1954 than that.

Q. Joseph R. Slevin, New York Journal of Commerce: Mr. President, could you explain in a little more detail how your long-range concept of a long-range program differs from the previous administration's military program, which called for reaching a peak of strength sometime in 1955, and then maintaining that strength over the long pull?

THE PRESIDENT. Well, let me ask you this: if you have a maximum production program, to reach maximum strength by July 1st, 1954—1955—or any other figure, how do you then suddenly level off and maintain it? It is simply not possible. You cannot

suddenly reach with all your production lines up and say everything is shut off and becomes zero. You have a job of leveling
this thing out, and it means it has to be approached really, literally, many, many months ahead. So it's a change—instead of
going to a maximum in the belief you can predict at a certain
point—to do this thing in as orderly a fashion, making always the
economic factor the secondary, but the important support to your
strictly defense factor.

Now, it is really no more susceptible of exact statement than
that, but you cannot go full blast with all productive capacity to
a single point and then suddenly just level off. You can't do it.

Q. Frank O'Brien, Jr., Associated Press: Since presumably not
all of the 8.5 reduction in appropriations will be reduction in
spending during fiscal 1954, is it now definite that there will not
be a balanced budget for fiscal 1954?

THE PRESIDENT. Well, I think it would be safe to say that you
can't achieve—I don't see how you can achieve complete balance
in your expenditure program. I don't believe it could be done.

Q. Sarah McClendon, Texas papers: Mr. President, last fall,
Congressman Mahon, who was then the chairman of the Military Appropriations Subcommittee, said that the House Appropriations Committee would cut the budget by 10 billion. Now,
if they cut it below your 8.4 billion, would they seriously hamper
the defense program, do you feel?

THE PRESIDENT. Well, if they cut very far, it would require very
definite changes in policy, yes.

Actually, these people that I am talking about—the professional people, the civilians, everybody else—have been working
very hard to find that money that you can find in a hurried or,
you might say, an intensive but quick examination of this thing.
There will finally be great or, at least, other savings accomplished.

When you get into the field of logistics, of procurement, storage, issue, evacuation, care of sick and wounded, there are lots
of places; but I would say that those cuts cannot be made

suddenly and in great amount without causing a great deal of embarrassment.

Q. Marvin Arrowsmith, Associated Press: Can you tell us, on the basis of the outline you have given us, what the possibilities seem to you to be for a tax cut now? Any change in that?

THE PRESIDENT. No, I am not going to speculate on that one just now, Mr. Arrowsmith.

Q. Richard L. Wilson, Cowles Publications: Do your figures, Mr. President, include an expenditure for the Korean war?

THE PRESIDENT. Yes. They include certain items that have never been included before; for example, budgeting for ammunition.

Q. Mr. Wilson: Does that anticipate a reduction in the cost of the Korean war over last year?

THE PRESIDENT. Well, I don't believe I have got the exact comparison of it, Mr. Wilson. I don't believe I have.

Q. Mr. Wilson: I would like to ask you one final question. Does your new policy indicate that there will be a new kind of a defense establishment? The point I am getting at——

THE PRESIDENT. Not radical, not radical. We do want to concentrate more on the latest weapons, and in this buildup that I am talking about—orderly buildup—constantly getting the latest and best to prevent the factor of obsolescence from overtaking us too quickly. That is one factor for which we take a little bit of credit.

Q. Mr. Wilson: Are those the critical items of which you speak?

THE PRESIDENT. Yes, indeed.

Q. Mr. Wilson: Mr. President, do these figures in your program mean that there will be a new team on your Joint Chiefs of Staff after their terms expire?

THE PRESIDENT. I am afraid that is something you will have to talk to the Secretary of Defense about. That is his responsibility.

Q. Paul R. Leach, Chicago Daily News: Mr. President, this question was asked a little while ago, but I did not get the answer clearly. You were asked if you regarded, with this reduction in cash spending, a reduction also in income, whether it is definite that there will not be a balanced budget for 1954 fiscal?

THE PRESIDENT. I said I thought it was safe to predict that complete balance in the expenditure program probably would not be achieved. I don't know; I don't see how the full amount can be met. However, I will tell you this: there is progress made in that direction every day.

Q. Mrs. May Craig, Maine papers: Mr. President, if you open up the Key West agreement, will you open up also the roles and missions assignments made there?

THE PRESIDENT. Well, I must tell you, Mrs. Craig, I am not going back into some of those things. I have got other things that occupy my time, and I have got people to go into them. Now finally it will——

Q. Mrs. Craig: I thought the message to Congress would mention this.

THE PRESIDENT. ——it will be—there are certain philosophies of control, particularly emphasizing civilian control, that are contained in the plan that went to Congress today, and I assume that will be made public in a day or so.

Q. Merriman Smith, United Press: Mr. President, do you plan to spend some time in Colorado this summer?

THE PRESIDENT. I hope so. [*Laughter*]

Q. Mr. Smith: Could you give us a little run down on when we go? [*Laughter*]

THE PRESIDENT. Well, I will be perfectly frank with you. I think that whatever Congress does would determine something of my own moves. And I will promise this group this, if it is of any interest to you: as quickly as I get any real information on it, then I will let you know, and let you know what I expect to do; because I realize that you people, after all, go on vacations, too. I would like to go, and I am planning on doing it, if the situation here in Washington will allow me.

Q. Sterling F. Green, Associated Press: I wanted to ask whether there remains in your request a $½ billion item for production equipment to provide mobilization base?

THE PRESIDENT. I don't remember the size of that item. I don't remember the size of it.

Q. Mr. Green: Does it remain an identifiable item?

THE PRESIDENT. I don't see how you can take it out completely.

Q. Laurence H. Burd, Chicago Tribune: Can you say, sir, in what year you do expect a balanced budget? Do your studies go that far?

THE PRESIDENT. Well, I would have to put it relatively. I must say that a great deal of my waking moments are given over to that problem. And we are going to do it. Now, that's all I can say.

Q. [*Speaker unidentified*], Journal of Commerce: Mr. President, since you expect to shorten lead time on military items, will the defense expenditures be greater over the next several months?

THE PRESIDENT. Well, that is probably true. I haven't asked for the exact schedule of output of money, but that would sound to me like it were true, yes. And it would mean also, of course, a very reduced carryover of money that is appropriated and has not yet been raised at the end of the fiscal year 1954. If you use up some of that carryover now, and then don't ask for as much new money as you have in the past, then you reduce that carryover from an $81 billion figure down to something else.

Q. Joseph A. Fox, Washington Evening Star: Mr. President, do we have an estimate of income for 1954 yet?

THE PRESIDENT. Yes, we do; but as a matter of fact, I am not going to give it today, because this morning the question was raised as to its authenticity.

There is one in the budget now before Congress. You know that; I think it is—68.7 isn't it?—that is close to it. But there is some question raised about it.

Q. John O'Donnell, New York News: Mr. President, in regard to the Nelson committee study of the Defense departments, their recommendations which I imagine will be released very shortly——

56616—60——19

THE PRESIDENT. Nelson?

Q. Mr. O'Donnell: Nelson Rockefeller. Oh, I beg your pardon. It is my mistake, sir.

THE PRESIDENT. Go ahead. Now I am on the track.

Q. Mr. O'Donnell: I wanted to ask on what lines their views went toward reorganization of the Defense Department with this idea in mind, that over the years there had been two schools of thought, fundamentally: one that wanted to have a loose federation of the services, each one sovereign in its own right; and the other school of thought that wanted strong central control. I wanted to ask which, could you tell me—to which school of thought do you subscribe to—and the Nelson Rockefeller——

THE PRESIDENT. Well, first of all, I am not certain how the Nelson Rockefeller committee met that problem because, you see, they have been my committee for reorganizing in other departments of Government. And when it came to the Defense Department, because of the size of it, I loaned them to Mr. Wilson, who appointed a committee of his own, and they were incorporated into it. Now, just exactly what that committee felt about the points you raise, I don't know.

I do feel this: that all of us agree that each of these departments should be separately administered, that it is inconsistent, I should say, with good management that we don't have real central direction so far as there are any fields in which duplication or waste can occur. The business of war, and preparing for war, has just got so unconscionably expensive that we cannot waste one single dollar uselessly.

Now, the purpose of putting a strong business organization—which you devoutly hope will stay out of details that are none of its business; but after all, people are human, we understand that—their purpose is to save money through effective management for the United States of America. Now, that's what it is.

And what they have to do: I don't believe that any of us are smart enough—and I put in 40 years in that business, as you know—I don't believe any of us are smart enough to lay out a blueprint for a perfect organization. I believe you have to try something and correct it a little, and try something else and correct it a little. Sometimes you never really get done—we finally go to war, many things affect organization. So I think here, I hope we never get so rigid and solidified that we can't change when we need to.

Q. Thomas O'Neill, Baltimore Sun: Day before yesterday the Army announced they were taking the 5th Division out of service.

THE PRESIDENT. It did what?

Q. Mr. O'Neill: It was taking the 5th Division out of service—deactivating it—a training division. Was that done after consultation with you?

THE PRESIDENT. No, that would not have to come to me, and I haven't heard of it before.

Q. Mr. O'Neill: Will the budget reductions you are contemplating bring about a balanced cash budget in fiscal 1954, sir?

THE PRESIDENT. That is the third time that question has been asked, and I will answer it again. I don't think that it possibly can, because the expenditures for 1954 are already fixed by contracts, by commitments that we cannot get out of. It can't be done. That new money has nothing to do, really, with the cash budget for 1954.

Q. Mr. O'Neill: I was speaking of the—of the cash income and cash outgo, not the——

THE PRESIDENT. The income is fixed by tax law, isn't it? Not fixed by this budget that we are asking for at all. It is fixed by tax law. The outgo is fixed by plans that are already in existence, by appropriations that have already been made. Now, largely that is true. You have certain detailed differences.

But there is nothing much you can do about that particular item that you raise.

Q. Sarah McClendon, Texas papers: Sir, are you planning a conference Saturday with the Governor of Texas and the Governor of Colorado on the question of oil imports?

THE PRESIDENT. I haven't heard of it. I am having all the

Governors here very quickly; but the only thing I heard, I have been challenged to a golf game by one of the Governors. [*Laughter*]

Q. Mrs. McClendon: Which one?

THE PRESIDENT. I think it was Texas. I am afraid he's too good.

Q. [*Speaker unidentified*], Akron Beacon Journal: Mr. President, can you comment on Representative Ayres' of Ohio request to you to hold up a Veterans Administration order legalizing discounts on GI housing loans?

THE PRESIDENT. No, I haven't heard it.

[*Speaker unidentified*]: Thank you, Mr. President.

NOTE: President Eisenhower's eighth news conference was held in the Executive Office Building at 3 p.m. on Thursday, April 30, 1953.

63 ¶ Letter to the President of the Senate and to the Speaker of the House of Representatives Recommending Establishment of a Commission on Foreign Economic Policy. *May* 2, 1953

[Released May 2, 1953. Dated May 1, 1953]

Dear ————:

In the Message which I sent to the Congress on April seventh requesting a one-year extension of the present Reciprocal Trade Agreements Act, I referred to the need for a thorough reexamination of our whole foreign economic policy.

I now recommend that a commission be established to make this review. The review should provide the basis for action during the next session of the Congress.

It is my belief that the proposed commission should be made up of members of the Congress appointed by the Vice President and the Speaker of the House, and members appointed by myself from outside the Congress. It should be representative of both major parties. This is appropriate since commercial policy is an integral part of our total foreign policy for which broad national support is vital.

This commission naturally should work within the framework of our foreign policy and our global defense plans. Close liaison should be maintained with the group set up under the auspices of the State Department to follow up the economic and financial talks held earlier this spring between the United States and various European countries.

The commission should study all existing legislation and the regulations and administrative procedures stemming from it which bear directly on our foreign economic relations. This review should seek to determine how these laws can be modified or improved so as to achieve the highest possible levels of international trade without subjecting parts of our economy to sudden or serious strains.

An inquiry of this nature is imperative. The economic policy of this nation exercises such a profound influence on the entire free world that we must consider carefully each step we take. Changes in foreign economic policy—even those which at first have relatively slight consequences within this country—may either strengthen our allies or plunge them into a downward spiral of trade and payment restrictions, lower production, and declining living standards.

Our foreign economic policy also has important implications here at home. Declining imports will necessarily mean falling exports, resulting in a serious loss of markets for our agriculture and other industries. Expanded imports may require some adjustments in our country. We must make sure that changes in foreign economic policy consonant with our position as the world's greatest creditor nation do not benefit particular groups at the expense of the national welfare, but we must also make sure that such changes do not place unequal burdens on particular groups.

As I indicated in my previous Message, the achievement of a strong and self-supporting economic system in the free world, capable of providing adequate defense against aggression and of achieving rising standards of living, must be a cooperative effort. Through increasing two-way international trade and stimulating in every practical way the flow of private investment abroad we can strengthen the free world, including ourselves, in natural and healthy ways. By so doing, we can lessen and ultimately eliminate the heavy burden of foreign aid which we now bear. Both we and our friends abroad earnestly desire to see regular trade and investment replace grant assistance.

In launching a broad-gauge study into the question of what our foreign economic policy should be, I think we can prepare the way for a fuller utilization of the economic strength of the free world in the cause of peace and prosperity.

Sincerely,

DWIGHT D. EISENHOWER

NOTE: This is the text of identical letters addressed to the Honorable Richard M. Nixon, President of the Senate, and to the Honorable Joseph W. Martin, Jr., Speaker of the House of Representatives.

64 ¶ Excerpts From the President's Remarks Opening the White House Conference of Governors. *May 4,* 1953

AS CHIEF EXECUTIVES of the States and of the Nation, you and I have a tremendous responsibility for the security and welfare of our people. It is fitting, it seems to me, that we should consult on the overriding question of the peace and security of our country.

The conduct of foreign affairs and the business of war and peace are under our Constitution the responsibility of the Federal Government. But in times like ours the danger to our country involves the civilian population in the cities and towns and on the farms of our States. The responsibility of all local governments is immense.

Quite beyond the matter of responsibility is the matter of counsel and judgment. All political wisdom does not reside in the White House, nor in the Executive Branch, nor in Washington itself. It comes from the minds and hearts of sincere and devoted men, wherever their field of action—whether in Federal, State and local government or in private life.

The purpose of these sessions is to share with you some of the information we have and some of the plans we are making in the area of national security.

It is our firm belief that in that way we can take a long step toward the goal of a united people determined to defend its way of life, to prove worthy of the leadership of the free world.

NOTE: The complete text of the President's remarks was not released.

65 ¶ Statement by the President on the Fund-Raising Campaign of the American-Korean Foundation. *May* 5, 1953

I STRONGLY ENDORSE this opening campaign of the American-Korean Foundation to be held June 7th to 14th.

Our own fighting men in Korea have been contributing to the cause of Korean assistance much more than have we who have remained at home. Our forces, having seen the great and cruel needs of the Korean people, have responded in typical American fashion. Now those needs will be further increased by the return of sick and injured South Korean troops.

By contributing to this cause we can support the personal efforts of our own troops. We will help sustain the power of the Korean military effort. Moreover, we will demonstrate to our Korean allies our sincere desire to develop ties of mutual understanding and appreciation between America and the people of Korea.

NOTE: The White House release of which the foregoing was a part stated that the American-Korean Foundation, headed by Dr. Milton S. Eisenhower, President of Pennsylvania State College, was organized to provide a mutual bridge of aid and an exchange of culture between the American and Korean people. Representatives of the Foundation met with the President on the date of the release.

66 ¶ Special Message to the Congress on the Mutual Security Program. *May* 5, 1953

To the Congress of the United States:

I recommend to the Congress the passage of legislation extending the Mutual Security Program in order to enable the United States to carry out its responsibilities of leadership in building up the security of the free world and the prospects for peace both for ourselves and our allies.

The basic purpose of this Program is simply the long-term security of the United States living in the shadow of the Soviet threat.

The program being submitted to you includes approximately $5 billion 250 million for military weapons and support directly to the defense efforts of our friends and allies. It also includes approximately $550 million for technical, economic, and developmental purposes designed to promote more effective use of the resources of the free nations and thus to further the freedom and security of all of us. This total represents a reduction of about 1.8 billion from the previous Administration's 1954 budget.

The devotion of so large a portion of this request to military purposes is a measure of the peril in which free nations continue to live. The blunt, sober truth is that we cannot afford to relax our defenses until we have seen clear, unmistakable evidence of genuinely peaceful purpose on the part of the Soviet Union. As I strived to make clear to all peoples in my recent appeal for real peace and trust among nations, we continue earnestly to hope for such evidence, so that the world may turn its energies and resources to serving the needs, rather than the fears, of mankind.

Until Soviet good faith is proven by deeds, the free nations must rely on their own strength for the preservation of peace. To fail to continue vigorously to strengthen our military forces would be to risk wasting all our efforts for the past five years in defense of our liberties.

Since the initiation of our major bi-partisan foreign aid program in 1947, the accomplishments of the free world have been very great. In Greece, the onrush of communist imperialism has been halted and forced to recede. Out of the ruins left by that aggression, a proud, self-reliant nation has re-established itself. Threatened economic and political collapse in Western Europe was averted through the intensive efforts of the great peoples of that continent aided by American resources. Revitalized economies in Europe today are producing more than ever before and are in a far better position to defend themselves from external or internal aggression. In the Near East and Far East, American aid is helping many new nations on their way to a better life for their citizens. And the free nations everywhere—realistically facing the threat of Soviet aggression—have in addition sought to create, with American assistance, the military strength essential to guard their security.

The Mutual Security Program for 1954 has been developed by the new administration after the most careful study and deliberation. All elements of the Program have been reviewed in great detail, all proposals subjected to thorough scrutiny.

From this study I have come to certain clear conclusions.

First: The United States and our partners throughout the world must stand ready, for many years if necessary, to build and maintain adequate defenses.

Second: To accomplish this objective we must avoid so rapid a military buildup that we seriously dislocate our economies. Military strength is most effective—indeed it can be maintained—only if it rests on a solid economic base.

Third: We must help the free nations to help themselves in eradicating conditions which corrode and destroy the will for freedom and democracy from within.

Fourth: It is necessary to do more in the Far East. We are proposing to make substantial additional resources available to assist the French and the Associated States in their military efforts to defeat the Communist Viet Minh aggression.

Fifth: Since it is impossible to forecast precisely the year and moment when the point of maximum military danger may occur, the only prudent course calls for a steady military buildup, with our partners throughout the world, sustained and planned so as to use our joint capabilities with maximum efficiency and minimum strain.

We must and shall keep steadfastly on the course we have set. We must—so long as the present peril lasts—keep constantly growing in a military strength which we can support indefinitely. These basic principles were agreed upon and applied in the successful meeting of the North Atlantic Treaty Council just concluded in Paris.

While the amounts requested for technical, economic and developmental purposes are small as compared with the military support, these programs are nonetheless of the most vital importance. They will be applied chiefly in South and Southeast Asia, the Middle East, Latin America, and Africa. Through these programs, the United States is proving its interest in helping the peoples of these areas to work toward better and more hopeful conditions of life, to strengthen the foundations of opportunity and freedom. To guard against the external military threat is not enough: we must also move against those conditions exploited by subversive forces from within.

I present this whole Program to you with confidence and conviction. It has been carefully developed by the responsible members of this administration in order to achieve—at least possible cost—the maximum results in terms of our security and the security of our friends and allies. In my judgment, it represents a careful determination of our essential needs in pursuing the policy of collective security in a world not yet freed of the threat of totalitarian conquest.

Unequivocally I can state that this amount of money judiciously spent abroad will add much more to our Nation's ultimate security in the world than would an even greater amount spent merely to increase the size of our own military forces in being.

Were the United States to fail to carry out these purposes, the free world could become disunited at a moment of great peril when peace and war hang precariously in balance.

This is the way best to defend successfully ourselves and the cause of freedom.

Dwight D. Eisenhower

NOTE: The program to which the President refers is published in a Committee Print entitled "The Mutual Security Program for Fiscal Year 1954; Basic Data Supplied by the Executive Branch" (83d Cong., 1st sess.).

The Mutual Security Act of 1953 was approved by the President on July 16, 1953 (67 Stat. 152).

67 ¶ Excerpts From the President's Remarks Closing the White House Conference of Governors. *May* 5, 1953

WE ARE very greatly obligated to you, because in coming here you demonstrate a conviction that we feel every day: that there has been too long neglected the proper relations between the Federal government and the State governments in the solving of our problems.

Yesterday I referred to the fact that there had been at least partial precedent for this particular meeting. I can't believe that any of them was ever as successful as this one, especially from the standpoint of the national administration. Everyone who has been before you, everyone who has come to report to me on this meeting, has stated that from our viewpoint it has been a tremendous success.

Consequently, we are going to look forward to a time, sometime in the future, when you can spare the time and we can be together again.

We are deadly serious about this business of trying to find a logical division between the proper functions and responsibilities of the State and Federal government. We are—all of us here— deeply concerned that the Commission, for which we have asked legislative authority, will soon be organized; that it will soon go to work and will really go into the whole problem of the proper division of tax fields. We hope it will be able to straighten out our complicated tax system, checking up on those functions where the Federal government has gotten into them too deeply.

I know—and I have the promise of your Chairman and your executive committee—that the Governors are going to cooperate. As a matter of fact, you have a special committee in certain of these fields to cooperate with us during this long and exhaustive study. And I certainly hope that by the time we next meet, we will have some kind of report that can enlist your support, so that we can stand before the nation as a logical, decent organization of function, responsibility and authority, as between Federal and State government.

I would be remiss if I didn't attempt to thank each one of you personally for coming. As I told you yesterday, never has there been a meeting of Governors called by any Federal authority where the percentage of attendance was so high. I believe there are all but four of the States, and all of the Territorial Governors here. So to each of you, my personal thanks. May I assure you that you have helped us, and on the even more personal side, my great satisfaction that I have got again to see so many old friends among you, and to form what I hope are new friendships.   And this goes, I must assure you, for those of both political parties.

Thank you very much.

NOTE: The complete text of the President's remarks was not released.

68   ¶ Address at the New York Republican State Committee Dinner, Astor Hotel, New York City. *May 7,* 1953

Governor Dewey, Mr. Chairman, ladies and gentlemen:

I suppose that you all know this is a very new experience for me; and I showed, I think, my respect for the organization of a one-hundred-dollar-a-plate political dinner by having mine on the train.   I should assure you I am now just a bureaucrat.

It is a very great pleasure to come here, a distinct honor to meet with you people who—as your Governor said—by your presence have shown your dedication to the cause of good government.

And first, I should like to pay my own tribute to the government that has been given to this State by Governor Dewey.   I think that he and the Party he has led have proved and shown again to us one simple thing, what we can have through the dedication, the integrity, the unremitting devotion of honest men and women in American government.

I should like, of course, additionally to single out a few of his political associates to whom I would like to make reference. Senator Ives, a tremendous ally and associate in Washington. Len Hall, after long experience as one of your Congressmen from this State, and as a surrogate, with a great personality, he comes to a new position in leadership in the Republican Party; and may I say that already he has done a lot for me.   I personally think that the Republican National Committee has chosen a real leader for victory in 1954.

261

I could not fail, of course, to mention Mr. Pfeiffer, your State Chairman, and his Vice Chairman, Miss Todd; and of course, the National Committeemen Russel Sprague and Judy Weis.

Now, my purpose this evening is to give you a very brief account of what has been going on in Washington, what has been done by the people that you have sent there to be your representatives in running this complex business of the Federal government.

First of all, if I could really bring you an accurate picture of what goes on, it would be done in this way: if I could take each American—each voter—in this country and take you down, one day, to a Cabinet meeting, and allow you to sit there while there came before that body some problem involving the welfare of the United States of America, and for you to see the honest, devoted, studious way in which that problem is pulled to pieces in all its elements. There is discussed every factor that can seemingly affect this country, and from one broad general viewpoint: what is good for the whole country.

Let me submit that as long as that philosophy can govern these public servants, then your administration—your governmental representatives—can be the champions of every class, they can be the champions of the farmer, of labor, of the capitalist, of the business man, and the professional man, the educator, the white-collar worker—and everybody else. Because, if they have the overriding philosophy of what is good for America, then they recognize, as indeed each of us must recognize, that his rights are limited only by the equal rights of others. A realization and practice of that elemental fact is, in my opinion, the secret for the successful operation of representative free government.

If each of us realizes that any invasion of the rights of others is the invasion of his own rights, we eliminate a lot of the troubles that plague us today.

Now, the great objective, stated in slightly different terms in this administration of the men and women of whom I speak, in the Cabinet, and the heads of the great Departments, and their subordinates, or the devoted men and women on the Hill, has been this: a government whose honor at home commands respect abroad. It is as simple as that, because both these qualities are essential in the defense of freedom. Because, you see, today, there is no problem that is simply foreign or domestic. Every major domestic problem has a direct and definite effect upon each of our foreign problems. Vice versa is also true. Every principal domestic problem that we have affects our foreign relations. Prosperity at home means better living conditions for our friends abroad—with those with whom we trade. The security of our personnel here at home—and by security, I mean the loyalty, devotion and dedication of those men to serve us—that affects everything we do.

Only as late as 1949, American scientists were predicting that it would be at least five years before anyone else had solved the secret of nuclear fission. But they did not know that insecure personnel had robbed their predictions of any validity whatsoever.

So this problem of ours, to find the right kind of people to serve in your Federal government, affects everything we do in the foreign field.

The welfare of our whole agricultural society depends upon our foreign trade. The great surpluses we have in certain of our products cannot be absorbed in the long run unless there is capacity abroad to purchase them.

An expanding, liberal trade—properly regulated trade—is the secret to success in many of our own industrial and agricultural activities. And we must never forget it.

Labor peace here at home is essential to a position of sturdy strength abroad, so that we may appear in the councils of the world as men and women who are speaking from a position of strength, not truculent strength, just confident strength, so that words of peace may have weight.

And so as we strive and are determined to have a government of integrity and efficiency at home, we are also struggling abroad for a peace that is true and total.

As I have said, no peace can be a peace if it is either partial or punitive. So these men and women of whom I speak are always conscious that in every effort to regulate affairs here at home, to influence them, whether the problem be of taxes, or income, or balancing the budget, or the farm program—everything they do affects our standing abroad. And they are men and women of the caliber and character to take those complex understandings into their own hearts and minds, and come up at least with an answer that is characterized, we hope, by common sense, and we know by honesty.

They know that in Korea there must be a peace that is fair to the Korean people. It likewise must be fair to those people lately our enemies—at least fighting in the ranks of our enemies—but who, having been taken by the Allies are now seeking political asylum. It must be fair to those people.

Now, working for this kind of peace, we must have a foreign policy that is dedicated to promoting at home and in the world those conditions of life in which freedom can survive, and thrive.

As we help other nations to be prosperous, to trade with us, we are not doing this purely from a standpoint of altruism. This is not a case of passing some man with a tin cup and dropping a few pennies or coppers into his can. Not at all. We are working from the position of enlightened self-interest, well knowing that we—the greatest industrial, the mightiest power on earth—cannot exist unless we have trade with foreign nations.

There are many products, as you well know, that we do not possess—we do not produce. These we must have. They will be obtained only through trade. And therefore, we must have these countries not only producing the things we need, and trading with us, but there must be in those areas a kind of government that wants to trade with us. Once we would allow all these areas to fall into the hands of people who would be delighted to see our trade cut off, then indeed we would be in a sorry situation.

Now, of course, in this exchange of goods we want to see it grow wider and bigger to the benefit of all. There are always, in all such generalities—such truisms—a limiting factor. We know well that we cannot in all cases permit a complete and unregulated flow of goods into this country. But the job that you have given your servants in Washington is so to regulate that trade as to help to the greatest possible extent our political position—our strength in the world, as well as our economic position at home. And again, I say, the two things are definitely and directly related.

Now, this American foreign policy must have three marks: it must be total, it must neglect no area in the world, it must be clear so that all of us can understand it, and it must be consistent. It cannot merely be a succession of reactions to someone else's action. We must have a policy that is pursued vigorously, by intelligent, straight-forward men and women, who believe thoroughly in the moral standards by which that policy has been devised, and who are using only honorable means in extending it throughout the world. That does not mean a complete and total dependence upon military strength, although of course we must have military strength. It covers the entire gamut of spiritual, intellectual, cultural, economic, industrial and military life.

I stress again that no foreign policy really deserves the name, if it is merely the reflex action from someone else's initiative. That is the one thing that must be avoided, if we are to win through to peace, in the situation in which the world now finds itself so often very unhappily involved.

So we must remain strong to stay free. We must stand ever ready to work with all nations in good faith in order to lift the burden of arms from the backs of men, fears from the hearts of men, the fears of isolation and desertion in any country which seeks our friendship and wants to work with us.

It is in all these directions that I have so hastily covered, that these men and women in Washington are working to serve you. We believe that they are producing a government at home of which you will be proud. One that will be characterized by common sense, by integrity, by the probity of action of the individuals composing it, and which will, therefore, be respected abroad.

It has regard for your pocketbook. It strives to lower your

taxes, but it knows also that unless your Nation's bills are paid, any prior attempt to lower taxes is likely to prove only an illusory promise, because if your money continues to cheapen, then the following year expenses will be greater. Likewise, it is equally alert to the dangers of going too far in the direction that could be called deflationary.

The problem of government in its home operations is to retain that balance on the line dictated by common sense—that retains the value of our money for people who invest in long-term savings, insurance policies, and all other kinds of savings of that kind, and at the same time never go so far in that direction as to cause, again, unemployment.

And I want to close by saying to you that this government has already organized informally, and is moving rapidly to put on a more formal basis, a topflight organization that will have no other activity, and no other responsibility, except to keep watching the economy of this country, in order to retain that kind of stability, that kind of industrial level that will give everybody confidence; that will encourage investment, encourage savings. In short, to encourage again the private initiative of 158 million Americans.

Ladies and gentlemen, for the very great honor you have done me this evening in asking me here and listening to me so courteously, I thank you—not only for that, but again in the words of Governor Dewey, for what you have done in the past.

Thank you very much.

NOTE: The President in his opening words referred to Leonard W. Hall, Chairman of the Republican National Committee. He later referred to William L. Pfeiffer and Miss Jane Todd, Chairman and Vice-Chairman of the New York Republican State Committee, and to J. Russel Sprague and Mrs. Charles Weis, Jr., members of the Republican National Committee.

69 ¶ Address at the New York Republican State
Committee Dinner, Waldorf-Astoria Hotel, New
York City. *May* 7, 1953

Governor Dewey, distinguished guests, ladies and gentlemen:

It is indeed a great honor to be with you this evening. And
for me, this evening has several unusual or most unique occurrences. In the first place, I wonder if you could imagine how I
am impressed by a hundred-dollar-a-plate dinner. Since I was
invited to two, I made a very good compromise and had my
dinner on the train. And I think it is only those of you who have
attained some years on the order of mine, who can remember
when it was the fashion to pitch a double-header on the same day.
Seemingly, they are bringing back the custom, because that is
what I am doing tonight.

I should like to start off in making my simple report to you this
evening, by first paying my tribute to your Governor, and to the
government that he has established and given you for the past
eleven years in this State. He has shown what honesty and efficiency and concern for all humans can do in government, so that
your State stands as a leader—as a matter of fact, as an example
for others in many lines of true and proper State endeavor. He
has shown, in short, what can be accomplished by people—as he
expresses it—great groups of people dedicated to the cause of
serving the people, or as we might express it, working for the
people and not just "working them."

I should like, also, to pay a special and personal tribute to others
of his associates—helpers—in this State. To Senator Ives, who
has been such a tower of strength and assistance in Washington
during these momentous days. To an old representative of yours,
Len Hall, a man who by his experience and personality I feel is
pre-eminently qualified to lead the Party to the victory they must
have in 1954.

Of course, before such a gathering, I could not fail to mention your Chairman, Mr. Pfeiffer, and his Vice Chairman, Miss Todd. Likewise, your Committeemen Russel Sprague and of course Judy Weis.

Now I shall attempt to tell you something, in rather broad and general strokes, of what your government—the people you sent to Washington last November—has been trying to do in your service.

First of all, let us not get too complicated an idea in our heads of what government is. Government is men and women. It is men and women assigned to jobs in your service—jobs sometimes designed and prescribed by the Constitution, sometimes by the laws of the land, and other times not even that formally, but they are there, all working together, to perform those functions that are necessary to the welfare of the United States.

Which brings me to the first governing policy, or ideal, of the men and women that are now serving you in Washington. I refer not only to those in high appointive positions of government, those serving under them, those serving on the legislative Hill— everybody that is grouped together to put over the program that is so necessary now for this country.

Their guiding policy is: the welfare of 158 million Americans. Now that is a simple generalization to make, but it does a very definite thing for a public servant, if he lives by it. He can and should be the champion of the farmers, of the laborers, of the bankers, of the businessmen and the professional men, the educator, the white-collar worker. No matter who, he can be the champion of each, because his over-all and governing policy is what is good for all the people. The rights of each group, just like the rights of each individual are limited by one factor only: similar rights of others.

And might I point out that this is probably the most obvious and possibly also the most neglected truth of all representative or free government; each of us to realize that our rights to be maintained must be limited by equal rights for others; and wherever and whenever we unjustly attack those rights of others, we are by that same action attacking our own rights, and they will inevitably fall, unless we preserve that attitude of respect for the rights of others.

And I assure you, ladies and gentlemen, if there is one ruling passion among this group of men, with whom it is my high privilege to serve—men and women—it is that they will observe the rights of all, and in so doing be able to work justly and fairly for the rights of everyone.

Stated in another way, the ideal of that group is this: a government whose honor at home commands respect abroad. Both are essential in the defense of freedom. Unless there is a government of honor at home, it will not be supported by all our people, it will not have that universal strength—that universal support which is the true strength of democracy. It will not command respect abroad, and if it does not command respect abroad, then our interests cannot be maintained, because our voices and counsel will be ignored, there will be no true, spiritual and moral base to support the protestations for peace that we make before all the world. So, a government of honor at home that deserves respect, and commands respect, abroad.

Another point to make in this connection, ladies and gentlemen, is this: that there is no true division, no true and simple segregation of problems into foreign and domestic. The major and overwhelming foreign problem of our time colors, accentuates and emphasizes every problem we have at home. The relationship between our Budget, our tax burden, our men in Korea, is easily established with the difficulty that we are having today in a world where the peace and dignity of man is threatened. The very prosperity of this country is inextricably tied up with the prosperity of those countries with whom we must trade in the world. There are countries from which we must get materials which are absolutely vital to our economy.

We are, of course, the great exponents of what we might call the steel age. Yet I am sure that all of you are aware that we make scarcely a ton of steel in this country without vastly impor-

tant imports—manganese and the alloys that go into our finest
steel.   Without them we would be practically helpless.

The security in the personnel that you have in your government service is of tremendous importance to us in our foreign
relationships.   As late as early 1949 certain eminent scientists,
well-informed scientists, were predicting that it would be some
years yet, possibly five, before any other country solved the secret
of the atomic bomb.   They did not know that their predictions
were rendered completely invalid by the disloyalty of certain
people serving in our own government.

All of these problems have a relationship, one to the other.
The farmer—today there would be no possible prosperity for the
farm population of our country except that we have a prosperous
foreign trade.   We have certain surpluses that have no outlet
except in this foreign trade.   They must be capable of buying our
goods—these other countries.   And consequently the prospect of
keeping up, increasing, the flow of mutually profitable trade with
all of these countries—these free countries in the world, whose
economic health and military strength is so important to us—is
one of the prime and necessary objectives of the men and women
attempting to serve you in Washington.   We strive for a government of integrity and efficiency at home, while abroad we strive
simultaneously for a peace that is true and total.

As I have tried to explain, a peace cannot be a real peace if it
is either merely partial, or if it is punitive.   Peace cannot be
something with which to punish, or it is no peace.   It cannot be
partial because if it were only partial, it would either neglect
areas—important areas of the world, or it would neglect certain
functions.   If it were a peace which we attempted to base strictly
on military strength, it would not be peace.   There must be the
great strength that comes from moral rightness, from knowing
that we are just and fair with all peoples.   There must be the
intellectual strength that comes from knowing that people consider
us just and fair by our actions.   There must be economic strength
so we might make a living and keep up such military strength

as is possible and necessary. There must be, of course, military strength. We must cover, then, peace in its entirety, in its impact upon human beings, not only here but in every corner of the world, if it is to be peace.

Now, along with this, if it is to be durable, we must create conditions in which freedom can survive, and thrive. If we allow any section of the world that is vital to us, because of what it provides us, through trade—say, manganese, or uranium, or cobalt—anything that we need—if we allow any of those areas either to become so impoverished it cannot produce the things we need, or if we allow it to fall to a form of government inimical to us, that wants to see freedom abolished from the earth, then we have trouble indeed.

It is on such simple facts as these, ladies and gentlemen, that your foreign policy is founded and established and maintained. There is nothing mysterious about it. All of this springs from the enlightened self-interest of the United States of America. But it does, fortunately for us, lead us into fields in which our whole moral cells approve of the actions that we take for collective security, strength and health. And so we have the satisfaction of approval of our own conscience, as we proceed along this direction.

And so this body of men and women, as they struggle with all of the intelligence that they have, with their combined experience—and may I say to you, in great humility and in devout attitude—as they struggle to find the right answers, they know that we must create and maintain conditions that promote profitable and increasing trade between us and other vital areas of the world—areas vital to us—occupied by our friends.

Now, working for this kind of peace, of course, demands a policy that is dedicated to promoting at home and in the world, a policy that respects the rights of everybody, not only our friends but as, for example, in Korea, no less those people who have been only lately fighting in the ranks of our enemies. People that have become our prisoners, cannot by any manner of means be denied the right on which this country was founded—and which indeed has been responsible for the presence here of most of the people, or at least great numbers of the people in the United States today—the right of political asylum against the kind of political persecution that they fear and do not like. Consequently, to force those people to go back to a life of terror and persecution is something that would violate every moral standard by which America lives. Therefore, it would be unacceptable in the American code, and it cannot be done.

But, within these limits of moral rectitude and rightness, there is no one that will ever find America's hand of friendship hidden. It will always be extended. It will be ready to meet anyone half-way, as long as deeds and not mere rhetoric and words are there to substantiate the sincerity of their purpose. Particularly, this kind of policy invites all right-minded peoples to work and speak and think for freedom, conceived in the kind of terms that do respect the dignity of man and the moral rightness of his existence.

Unless we have this kind of moral background for a policy, I say again, it is inimical, it is antagonistic to America's basic precepts, and therefore unacceptable.

Which brings me to say that this group of men and women working for you are acutely aware of one basic fact. It is this: free government is founded primarily in a deeply-felt religious faith. I think that is not hard to prove in the case of America. Our own founders, you will recall, in their Declaration, thought it necessary to explain to the world the reason for this new form of government, on what it was based, its nature, its character. They said, you will remember, a decent respect for the opinions of mankind impels them to declare the reasons which led to the separation. And then, they said, "We hold that all men are endowed by their Creator." They did not try to say that these rights came about because people had moved to the shores of America. They said "are endowed by their Creator," because they knew no other simple, direct and positive way to explain this new form of government.

So, these men and women working for you are acutely aware of that relationship, which in their opinion, really, is the beginning of wisdom, in the business of attempting to conduct the government for a free, self-governing people.

Now, foreign policy must be total. It must be clear, and it must be consistent. By total, I mean that it must ignore no area or no people of the world. If it is to be truly permanent, it must be all-inclusive. It does not rely, as I said before, on military might alone. It takes in every kind of factor that touches upon human right. It must be clear, so that it may be understood. And again, I repeat, the foreign policy that America is trying to follow, based upon decency and justice, is clear to all—unless they deliberately shut their eyes to its meaning, its purpose.

Now, it must be consistent because it must not be merely reflex action from the action of others. It must be a policy that is pursued because it is understood and supported at home, and understood and respected abroad. It must be pursued through all kinds of crises. It must not be truculent, but it must be firm and strong.

These are the directions in which our policy must go, if it is going to bring to us, in our time, peace and security. We must be ready, always, to work with all nations in good faith. We work with these nations in order to lift the material burdens of the expense of armaments from the backs of men, to avoid the diversion from productive purposes of the sweat of our laborers, the genius of our management, our material resources, in this country. Others have like burdens and are less able to bear them. So we struggle to lift from the backs of men that kind of burden, and from their hearts, the burden of fear. We are trying to bring to all men and women everywhere the right to go to sleep and sleep peacefully, secure in that trust that they can place in their fellow men, and not believing or fearing that before morning, before next month, or before next year, an atomic bomb may come screaming out of the air to cast destruction in its wake.

Now, these are the directions in which we strive to give our people government that is honored at home and respected in the world.

I should say, or should like to add, as an observation about the more definitely domestic and local problems, that the people of whom I speak are quite well aware of the burden of taxes. You could scarcely expect taxes to be forgotten by a man who is threatened with the possibility, according to the experts, that he may have to borrow 25 thousand dollars a year to carry on his job. In any event, they are acutely aware of the burdens that this country is bearing. They likewise know that there is no burden that a united American people will not bear, if they know it is necessary to preserve freedom in the world. They know what has come to pass through the cheapening of our money. They are trying to preserve policies that will defend and protect the long-term investor, in life insurance, in savings accounts, in bonds, to preserve that cornerstone of a capitalistic system: the incentive to invest in America.

In doing so, they are also aware of the very great danger of making it difficult to save money, either through too high taxes, or making money too dear or too scarce, so that it becomes sort of a tightrope to walk between what you might call inflationary and deflationary forces. All with the aim of keeping stability and strength in this country, and doing justice to 158 million people.

These men and women, with whom I serve, think of these things and a thousand related problems, every day. I know of none of them that is not dedicated to your service, to the service of all you know, to the service of the entire country; and their outlook toward all the rest of the world is: what is good for the world is certainly good for 158 million Americans who are such an important part of this great latter-day civilization.

Ladies and gentlemen, my thanks to each of you, not only for the support evidenced by your presence here this evening, for a group that is working to provide the kind of government I have so haltingly attempted to describe. I thank you for what you have done in the past, by the confidence you have exhibited in these people, and in me, to give an opportunity to this country to have this kind of government, and make sure that it will work. And so, for the honor you do me this evening in coming here, thank you a lot.

NOTE: During his address the President referred to Leonard W. Hall, Chairman of the Republican National Committee; William L. Pfeiffer and Miss Jane Todd, Chairman and Vice-Chairman of the New York Republican State Committee; and J. Russel Sprague and Mrs. Charles Weis, Jr., members of the Republican National Committee.

70 ¶ Joint Statement Following Discussions With Prime Minister St. Laurent of Canada. *May 8, 1953*

THE PRESIDENT of the United States, the Secretary of State, and other members of the Cabinet have held discussions during the last two days with the Canadian Prime Minister, Mr. Louis S. St. Laurent, and the Secretary of State for External Affairs, Mr. L. B. Pearson. The meeting continued a long standing practice of visits exchanged across the border between Prime Ministers of Canada and Presidents of the United States. The conversations consisted of a full and frank exchange of views on the world situation in general and on United States–Canadian relations in particular. They were conducted in that spirit of friendship and cooperation which has long been characteristic of official discussions between the two Governments and they revealed a far-reaching identity of objectives.

In a survey of the world situation today, the President and the Prime Minister gave particular emphasis to recent developments in the USSR and the Soviet orbit and their effects upon the free nations of the world. It was agreed that while every effort should be made to bring about a relaxation of current tensions, the free nations could not afford to diminish their efforts toward the achievement of united strength and ability to meet aggression. Acts, not words, would be proof of Communist intentions. Though recent developments in Korea where Canadian and United States troops are fighting side by side have seemed more hopeful, nevertheless, in Laos a new act of aggression has been committed which might have serious consequences for Thailand and the whole of Southeast Asia. These developments in Southeast Asia must cast doubt on Communist intentions.

In the discussions on the European area, emphasis was placed on the necessity of maintaining the momentum of vigorous support for NATO. The achievements of the recent NATO Ministerial meeting were noted with satisfaction. It was agreed that both countries must continue to do their full share to further NATO objectives.

Views were exchanged concerning progress made toward the expansion of world trade. It was recalled that trade between the United States and Canada is greater than that between any other two countries. The Prime Minister stressed the great importance attached by Canada to the liberation and expansion of world trade and expressed the hope that the United States would play a role of leadership in this field. The President stated that, as an interim step, the Administration has recommended to the Congress the one-year renewal of the Reciprocal Trade Act and intends to submit to the Congress shortly its proposals regarding Customs Simplification. The President also pointed out that he has recommended to the Congress the establishment of a Commission to study all aspects of United States economic foreign policy so that future policies will be comprehensive, constructive and consistent.

The Prime Minister emphasized the importance to Canada of an early start on the St. Lawrence project and the especial urgency to Canada of the power development. The President assured the Prime Minister that the United States is fully aware of Canada's urgent need for St. Lawrence power. He said that he favored the development of the United States share of St. Lawrence power under the authority of New York State and that he hoped for an early favorable decision by the Federal Power Commission in this matter. The President in this connection referred to the decision of the Cabinet on this subject announced today. The Prime Minister said that the Canadian Government was still prepared to discuss United States participation in the international section, provided that arrangements for power construction are completed and provided the whole seaway would not be delayed. He stressed again Canada's readiness to proceed at once with the work under the Canadian St. Lawrence legislation of 1951.

Recognizing the importance to the free world of the adequate defense of the North American continent, the President and the Prime Minister emphasized the desirability and effectiveness of cooperation on the basis of the Ogdensburg Declaration of 1940, which established the Permanent Joint Board on Defense between Canada and the United States. Post-war arrangements for continental defense have continued in this framework. It was recognized by the Prime Minister and the President that joint defense facilities erected in Canada under these arrangements strengthen the defense and the security of both Canada and the United States. The President assured the Prime Minister that the United States, for its part, in such joint actions will continue scrupulously to respect Canadian sovereignty.

The Prime Minister and the President reaffirmed the importance of continuing the wholehearted cooperation between the two countries in the field of continental defense, and in the wider field of international action designed to preserve and strengthen peace.

NOTE: The decision taken in Cabinet on United States participation in the St. Lawrence Seaway Project, referred to by the President, is published in the Department of State Bulletin (vol. 28, p. 753).

71   ¶ Letter to General Ridgway, Supreme
Allied Commander, Europe, Regarding His
Nomination as Chief of Staff of the Army.
May 12, 1953

[Released May 12, 1953. Dated May 9, 1953]

Dear General Ridgway:

I am today forwarding the attached letter to the Chairman of
the Permanent Council requesting that appropriate action be
taken at an early date to secure your release from assignment as
Supreme Allied Commander, Europe, in order that your services
may be available to fill the position of Chief of Staff, U.S. Army.
I desire that you occupy that post as a matter of great interest to
the United States and therefore feel fully justified in making this
request.

If the Permanent Council requests the U.S. to furnish your
successor, I am prepared, with the full agreement of my advisers,
to nominate General Gruenther for that appointment.

By this communication I request that you, as SACEUR, agree
to the early release of Admiral Carney from his appointment as
Commander-in-Chief, South.   I desire to inform the Permanent
Council that it is my intention to appoint Admiral Carney as
Chief of Naval Operations and therefore am withdrawing his
services to N.A.T.O. with the agreement of the proper N.A.T.O.
military authorities.

The question of the successor to the positions of Commander-
in-Chief, South, and Chief of Staff, SHAPE, should be settled at a
later date upon receipt of recommendations by SACEUR.

As to procedure on these changes, the Secretaries of State and
Defense have recommended that previous procedures should be
generally adhered to.   I am sending Brigadier General Beebe to

Paris to work with you and Ambassador Draper on fulfilling these
matters.

Sincerely,

DWIGHT D. EISENHOWER

NOTE: The letter referred to by the   Items 71–76 were part of a single
President is printed as Item 72.   White House release.

72   ¶ Letter to the Chairman, North Atlantic Council, Requesting the Release of General Ridgway as Supreme Allied Commander, Europe. *May* 12, 1953

[Released May 12, 1953. Dated May 9, 1953]

Dear Lord Ismay:

I am addressing you as Chairman of the Permanent Council
with the request that appropriate action be taken at an early date
to secure the release of General Matthew B. Ridgway from assignment as Supreme Allied Commander, Europe, in order that his
services may be available to the United States to fill the position
of Chief of Staff, U.S. Army.   In making this request through
you to the member nations who appointed him, I ask that they
give favorable consideration to his release.

The United States regards the position of SACEUR as of the
highest importance and has solemnly accepted the responsibilities
inherent in the appointment to that position of a United States
officer, General Ridgway.   I have carefully weighed this factor
against our own need to select the next leader of the U.S. Army.

By tradition we, as in other countries, fill that post by a selection from among our most able officers.   General Ridgway's
experience in his present command will contribute immeasurably
of itself to the experience needed in guiding a major portion of
the U.S. defense effort to further achievements.

The Council will, I am confident, provide the selection of an able officer to fill the post left vacant. Certainly no nation, if called upon, could do other than to assign its most eligible officer that is available. The trust extended to General Ridgway by all nations conveys a strong confidence in the future under another commander.

In meeting the needs for military leadership of U.S. Armed Forces, it is necessary to provide also for the appointment of a succeeding Chief of Naval Operations. I desire to place Admiral Robert B. Carney in that position and therefore feel it necessary to withdraw the availability of his services to N.A.T.O. as Commander-in-Chief, South. I assume that the Council is prepared to accept the appointment of a successor on nomination by SACEUR.

Sincerely,

DWIGHT D. EISENHOWER

The Honorable, The Lord Ismay
Secretary General, North Atlantic Treaty Organization
Palais de Chaillot, Paris, France

73 ¶ Letter to General Ridgway on His Service as Supreme Allied Commander, Europe. *May* 12, 1953

[Released May 12, 1953. Dated May 9, 1953]

Dear General Ridgway:

Please accept my personal congratulations on the magnificent performance you have made as SACEUR. The matter of your relief will be a disappointment to our European allies, but I trust they will appreciate the equal importance of your new task.

I am seeking an early resolution to the problem of your relief in order that ample time will be available in the necessary transfer of functions.

You have my confidence as the newly appointed Chief of Staff, U.S. Army.   You will bring to that service the fine traditions and leadership you possess.   The difficult task ahead rests in good hands.

Sincerely,

DWIGHT D. EISENHOWER

General Matthew B. Ridgway
Supreme Allied Commander, Europe
Paris, France

74 ¶ Message to the Chairman, North Atlantic Council, Nominating General Gruenther as Supreme Allied Commander, Europe. *May* 12, 1953

[Released May 12, 1953. Dated May 9, 1953]

The Honorable, The Lord Ismay
Secretary General, North Atlantic Treaty Organization
Palais de Chaillot, Paris, France

Pursuant to the request of the North Atlantic Council that I nominate an officer of the Armed Forces of the United States for appointment by the Council as SACEUR to succeed General Matthew B. Ridgway, I hereby nominate General Alfred M. Gruenther.   I feel that General Gruenther is peculiarly well qualified to perform the duties of Supreme Commander.   Since the beginning of the N.A.T.O. he has given unselfishly of his services in the cause of providing an adequate defense of the N.A.T.O. area.   It is my belief that the confidence expressed by the member nations in his appointment as Chief of Staff, SHAPE, make him an outstanding officer.

As Supreme Allied Commander, Europe, I feel the fine traditions and worthy objectives sought by all the nations will be upheld and carried forward through the leadership of General Gruenther.

DWIGHT D. EISENHOWER

75 ¶ Letter to General Gruenther Regarding His Nomination as Supreme Allied Commander, Europe.   *May* 12, 1953

[Released May 12, 1953. Dated May 9, 1953]

Dear General Gruenther:

By the action in the attached letters I am making you available for appointment as SACEUR to succeed General Ridgway.

I anticipate unanimous desire for this action because of the outstanding importance you bring in continuing the effectiveness and solidarity of N.A.T.O. You have served not only myself and General Ridgway with loyalty and splendid distinction, but have placed these same qualities unselfishly before N.A.T.O. As Supreme Allied Commander, Europe, I know the fine traditions and worthy objectives sought by all the nations will be upheld and carried forward through your leadership.

Let me give you assurance of my personal satisfaction in this matter. The appointment will be well deserved in all aspects.

Sincerely,
DWIGHT D. EISENHOWER

NOTE: This letter to Gen. Alfred M. Gruenther, Chief of Staff, Headquarters, Allied Powers, Europe, was part of a White House release containing Items 71–76.

76 ¶ Letter to Admiral Carney Regarding His Nomination as Chief of Naval Operations. *May* 12, 1953

[Released May 12, 1953. Dated May 9, 1953]

Dear Admiral Carney:

By the attached papers I seek your relief from the position of Commander-in-Chief, South, to permit your appointment at my direction as the succeeding Chief of Naval Operations.

The selection for this appointment is based on the finest traditions of the Naval Service which you have eminently displayed throughout your career. I know that you will regret leaving your present assignment. However, it is in the best interest of the United States that you should bring your long experience in naval matters, and most importantly, your N.A.T.O. experience to the Joint Chiefs of Staff and the Department of the Navy.

I am seeking early resolution of this matter of your relief from N.A.T.O. in order that you may have adequate time to prepare for your transfer of functions.

Let me give you every assurance of my personal satisfaction in making this appointment.

Sincerely,

DWIGHT D. EISENHOWER

NOTE: This letter to Adm. Robert B. Carney, USN, Commander of the Allied Forces, Southern Europe, was part of a White House release containing Items 71–76.

77 ¶ The President's News Conference of
May 14, 1953.

THE PRESIDENT. Ladies and gentlemen, I have one or two points this morning in which you may have some interest.

On Tuesday evening I shall make a radio talk. On that morning I am going to have a conference with the legislative leaders, sort of a final one, in talking about security, budget, and expenditure programs. And that will be mainly the subject of my talk that night, to explain exactly what we are trying to get at in this whole field, the relationships of security, our economy, budgets, and deficits.

Then, a week or so later, I shall probably go on a television program, in an effort to make a report to the Nation on what has taken place up until that moment.

Those are the only items of announcement that I have, and we will go right to the questions.

Q. Merriman Smith, United Press: Mr. President, what do you think of Prime Minister Churchill's proposal for a top-level international conference?

THE PRESIDENT. Of course the State Department, yesterday, released a statement with my approval. All of these things are manifestations of the free world's great longing for some kind of peaceful composition of our difficulties in the world, and all of us share them.

Now, the question comes finally: when can the heads of states, that are very busy men, when can they meet and discuss these things with some promise of progress?

There have been many conferences in the past of foreign ministers, and Secretaries, and other types. I repeat: I am personally ready to do anything, and the only thing that I believe that the dignity and the self-respect of the United States demands is that we have some reasonable indication that progress can be made.

I don't insist upon full progress, or any great blueprint to come out of such a conference for the peace of the world, just something that can be called progress by all of us.

So I have no objection whatsoever to Sir Winston's proposal; but I would like, before I would commit this Government to participation, something that would be an earnest of good faith all around.

Q. Andrew F. Tully, Jr., Scripps-Howard: Mr. President, would you be in favor of calling a conference before a truce in Korea?

THE PRESIDENT. I wouldn't even go so far as to state a series of things, something that had to be done, or something that would not be done. What I would like to say is this: I believe that the common sense of the world can make its own judgments as to acts or deeds that would give a real earnest of good faith. Now, if such an act comes along, I am perfectly ready to engage myself in any kind of an effort, at any time. But I cannot prescribe exactly what would be an earnest of good faith and what would not.

I have, in my speech of April 16, listed two or three that I thought would be definitely indicative of such intent. There could be others, but I do not want to say that unless this is done I won't do so and so; I don't believe that. I am ready to take most any kind of a chance to promote peace in this world.

Q. Nat S. Finney, Buffalo News: Mr. President, do we correctly infer, then, that you have not had the evidence of intent that you would like to have, that these deeds have not occurred?

THE PRESIDENT. That is correct. I see nothing that you could really point to as definite evidence of good faith.

Q. Mrs. May Craig, Portland (Maine) papers: Mr. President, do you believe that the personal method of conferences is better than the impersonal, through subordinate diplomats?

THE PRESIDENT. I suppose there are times when the highest authorities, taking great questions of policy, might do better by meeting, establishing personal contacts, maybe personal confidence, mutual confidence. But, by and large, I think that these things must be done through the Foreign Offices and State Department, because they are so complicated, and so much in the way of procedure, and all that sort of thing, comes into it. It would be unwise to depend entirely on just meeting of the heads of state, and that kind of person.

Q. Alan S. Emory, Watertown (N.Y.) Times: Mr. President, I would like to ask you two allied questions on a single topic. First of all, you endorsed the New York State and Province of Ontario development of the water power in the St. Lawrence River.

THE PRESIDENT. That is correct.

Q. Mr. Emory: Do you also feel that way about the development proposed in the Niagara River at Niagara Falls?

THE PRESIDENT. I think that, from our side of the case, it is primarily a New York State responsibility; and I should be glad to see that authority given New York State to then handle the thing as they saw best.

Q. Mr. Emory: That more or less answers my second question, sir, which was that Secretary McKay, who followed your lead on the St. Lawrence question, has said that he thought the Niagara development should be a matter for settlement on the State level in New York without reflection of White House views.

THE PRESIDENT. That's right. That's right.

Q. Raymond P. Brandt, St. Louis Post-Dispatch: Mr. President, are you personally in favor of the Hells Canyon project, or the Idaho Power Company plan for the Snake River development?

THE PRESIDENT. I doubt that my own opinion on that should be even governing, except as, I suppose, eventually I have to decide between presentations.

I must say that so far as I have seen, so far, the weight of evidence presented is on the side of letting this thing be decided locally. Again, I believe in the local decision. But what the exact, ultimate decision will be, I am not prepared to say this morning.

Q. Mr. Brandt: What are you going to do about the multiple-purpose dams?

THE PRESIDENT. You mean all multiple-purpose?

Q. Mr. Brandt: No—well, yes. What is the policy on multiple-purpose against purely hydroelectrical development?

THE PRESIDENT. I should say in each case it depends upon what is indicated is necessary, and what is the profitable thing in that area. Not always are multiple-purpose dams indicated as necessary; sometimes they are.

Q. Mr. Brandt: Would they be Government problems, then? I know of no private companies developing multiple projects.

THE PRESIDENT. As I have said time and time again, I really believe that no one should attempt to take exclusive jurisdiction over these things. I believe the Federal Government normally has some job that it has to do in connection with these great projects; but what we want to do is to keep the maximum local influence, authority, and direction in the thing. If the local people want also, let us say, to sell power at bus bar, and all that sort of thing, in order to get local interest, local competition, I think it is their right. Now, I don't believe there is any one single answer for any of these problems.

Q. Mr. Brandt: In the Snake River area, is the local support greater for the Idaho Power than for the Federal Government plans?

THE PRESIDENT. Within Idaho, definitely. As a matter of fact, long before I was elected President of the United States I was visited by many, many people. They insisted—not because they were officials—they were mayors, they were people like that—they insisted that they do not believe in this big dam.

Q. Robert J. Donovan, New York Herald Tribune: Mr. President, do you plan any special shipboard conferences this week, sir?

THE PRESIDENT. Well, I hope to have one or two come down. I am taking along the draft of the talk I hope to give Tuesday night—by radio, that is; that is not a television show—I am going to take that along, and I hope no later than Saturday morning to have come down two or three people to confer with me, and at least listen to what I have to say.

Q. Mr. Donovan: Do you expect to have any conferences with naval people in Norfolk when you are down there?

THE PRESIDENT. I expect, of course, to see Admiral McCormick and discuss with him some of his particular problems.

Q. Paul R. Leach, Chicago Daily News: Recently, David McDonald of the CIO-United Steel Workers, proposed that the President of the United States work and use his influence for obtaining a guaranteed annual wage for labor. Do you think that is—have you given any thought to that, is it something that the Government can do, or is it inimical to bargaining—collective bargaining?

THE PRESIDENT. I am not ready to discuss this subject in terms of final conclusions. I do repeat that I believe the White House has no real function in interfering in normal labor-management discussion and argument.

Now, you are bringing up something that can go way beyond that, you can talk about national policy on a very broad scale. I wouldn't, on that point, express an opinion until I have had the most exhaustive kind of analyses and studies made.

Q. Robert E. Clark, International News Service: Mr. President, what do you think of Clement Attlee's statement that he believes there are some people in this country who do not really want peace?

THE PRESIDENT. Again, I do want to say this: I do not criticize individuals as such, or their opinions, and therefore set myself up as an allwise judge that knows the motives that led someone into a particular line of thought, a particular line of statement.

I say this: I have met no one in the United States that doesn't want peace. I must say that there is a wide variety of opinion as to how we will obtain peace. Some believe it can be obtained only if we have almost an overwhelming amount of military power from which to talk in almost dictatorial tones. Others believe that we should start from almost the opposite end of the scale. But if anyone knows of these people—and I believe the statement said both in Britain and America—who do not want peace, I must say I haven't met them.

Q. Alice Johnson, Seattle Times: Mr. President, are you still opposed to the inclusion of Alaska in the Hawaiian statehood bill?

THE PRESIDENT. I am personally of the belief that the Hawaiian bill should be handled by itself on its merits. I have said time and again, and this is entirely aside from what the Republican platform said on it, my own conviction is this: in Hawaii you have an economy that is self-supporting, it has a large population, and on top of that they delivered a record in World War II that to my mind clearly entitles them to the privileges of statehood. I would like to see that case handled directly and specifically on its merits, without complicating it with any other question, any other matter.

Q. Mrs. Johnson: One more question, please, sir. Are you giving any consideration to going to the Governors' Conference this summer?

THE PRESIDENT. Indeed I am. I don't know whether I am going to make the grade; I don't know where Congress will be by that time.

Q. [*Speaker unidentified*]: Mr. President, may we put in direct quotes your statement "I have met no one in the United States who does not want peace"?

THE PRESIDENT. Yes.

Q. Andrew F. Tully, Jr., Scripps-Howard: Mr. President, do you think Senators and Congressmen should get a raise in pay?

THE PRESIDENT. Yes.

Q. Mr. Tully: Would you like to expand on it, sir? Why?

THE PRESIDENT. Because I think this: we are rapidly approaching the time when we are likely to be deprived of the best men we can get in these jobs. With the kind of taxes we have, we are very likely to get to the state where only someone who is fortunately placed in the economic field—financial field—can come to Washington. I believe we should make certain that we can have the very best man, whether he has got a nickel or a lot of money.

Q. Milburn Petty, Oil Daily: Last week Governor Thornton told us that he had suggested to you a proposed voluntary program to cut back oil imports. Would you tell us the status of that now, please?

THE PRESIDENT. He did not describe it to me. He told me that was his plan and he was going over to discuss it with other people in Government. As a matter of fact, Senator Thornton was very kind and realized that I didn't have time to study this problem singly and alone, without help, so he took it directly to the other people. I haven't heard anything further on it; it has not reached me.

Q. John Herling, Register and Tribune Syndicate: As you know, there is considerable restlessness among the labor groups about the staffing in the Department of Labor. Do you plan to send up names of the secretaries which the Department now lacks, in the near future?

THE PRESIDENT. I will send them as rapidly as the Secretary recommends them, and the people recommended meet all the qualifications that are demanded in this Government before going up.

Q. Mr. Herling: Secretary's office?

THE PRESIDENT. I can't say that it is entirely the Secretary's office, because we do make all sorts of investigations, some of which demand quite a bit of time. I can't say at this moment. I would be glad to look it up, and have Mr. Hagerty tell you further on the point.

Q. Edward J. Milne, Providence Journal: Will your fiscal program next week include recommendations for new taxes?

THE PRESIDENT. The program will discuss the whole tax problem and what our general approach to it will be. I can't give you any more details at this moment.

Q. Anthony Leviero, New York Times: I have a question about the Presidential income. I know it can't be raised or lowered while you are in office. In your recent speech in New York you said that the experts said that you might go in the hole. I wonder if you have observed enough to tell us about how much?

THE PRESIDENT. As a matter of fact, I must assure you that I used that sort of facetious allusion merely to show that I was not insensible to the tax problem.

It matters very little to me what happens. I believe that any man who undertakes a job such as I have undertaken would be very foolish to talk about what his tax problem is. And so I am perfectly ready to meet it. I haven't a word of criticism or complaint to make. Whatever it is, I will do my best.

Q. Doris Fleeson, Bell Syndicate: Mr. President, I understood you to refer to Governor Thornton of Colorado as Senator Thornton. Does that suggest that he will run next year against Senator Johnson? [*Laughter*]

THE PRESIDENT. I think your question merely illustrates the speed with which anyone is ready to pick up a slip. If I did that, I am sorry. I meant Governor and nothing further.

Q. Sarah McClendon, Texas papers: Mr. President, was this separate Continental Shelf bill that was introduced in the House this week, was it introduced at your request and with your previous knowledge?

THE PRESIDENT. The separate one?

Q. Mrs. McClendon: Yes, sir.

THE PRESIDENT. I merely say this: I have expressed always the same attitude on this whole question, from 1948 onward. I believe that—outside of the historic boundaries—the State has no possible claim on the areas outside those boundaries. Inside them, I believe they do.

Q. Mrs. McClendon: Back to my question, did you have previous knowledge and was it at your request that this particular separate bill was introduced at this time and in the manner in which it was?

THE PRESIDENT. The technique of introducing those bills I always leave to the people who have that job. The bills do express my general philosophy; that's all I ask of them.

Q. Edward T. Folliard, Washington Post: Mr. President, I ask this question by request. What is your opinion of UNESCO? That is the Educational, Scientific and Cultural Organization of the United Nations.

THE PRESIDENT. There never was an organization started with a finer announced purpose. Because manifestly, if we are going to have peace and understanding in the world, we have got to know about each other's culture, there has got to be greater information disseminated throughout the world—each of the other.

Now, in our own country, there has been a lot of suspicion aroused about this Organization. I think possibly some of the discussions within the body have given rise to this suspicion. But I do know, as of now, there are very good people on our particular section of this Organization; and they are people that I believe are interested in the welfare of the United States of America.

I have not looked up to see on my own, or there has been no report made to me, whether there is any real justification of this suspicion. I do know it exists. It is something I want to get around to, when I can. That's all I can say at the moment.

Q. Mr. Folliard: Senator Flanders of Vermont has a peace plan; I think he flew to Denver and discussed it with you last fall. He has been at the White House twice, recently, within the past 2 weeks. Would you care to comment on it?

THE PRESIDENT. No. Senator Flanders has given me certain suggestions, and I think on a confidential basis; I certainly thought that that is the way I received them. Generally I say this: I find nothing that is different in them from what most of us are working toward, and there is nothing sensational about them.

I always welcome any such suggestions; and I would be very poorly advised, I think, to discuss them in detail, because I would soon be cutting off some of the advice that I do get.

Q. Arthur Sylvester, Newark News: Mr. President, do you expect your new Joint Chiefs of Staff to come up with different strategical concepts and different estimates of the power we should have?

THE PRESIDENT. Well, I should say this: let us remember that the great facts that affect a so-called strategic situation and plan do not change rapidly. It takes no great wisdom to see how important to the general safety of the free world, and of the United States in particular, are certain vital areas of the world.

Take Western Europe: there is no great struggle there to see the relationship between West Europe's freedom and strength and health, and ours. There are other areas from which we get vital materials. There are other areas that are vital to the commerce of the world—lines of communication, or like the Mideast, the storage place of such tremendous amounts of oil.

So, no strategic plan suitable to the United States can be greatly different from any other, as long as it is based upon these facts. Now, you do get into differences of the methods and means by which the safety of these things will be brought about. For example, one extremist believes that merely in the fear of retaliation is safety. I doubt that many believe in that extreme view. Others believe you have just got to put the man on the spot with his bayonet fixed, almost, defending him. I doubt that for the United States many believe that is a sound policy.

There is in all of these things a need for achieving the balance between nationalistic aspirations, the union that must be established between countries in order that their economies and standards of living may go up.

Finally, the basic problem of how do you preserve an independent life at the same time that some of the measures that you are forced to adopt would tend to lead you toward a garrison state? We don't want to become a garrison state. We want to remain free. Our plans, our programs, therefore, must conform to the practices of a free people, which means essentially a free economy.

That is the problem that, frankly, this administration meets on, discusses, works on, every day of its life. There is no easy problem.

Now, the new people coming in: let me, with your indulgence, take a little time out here to discuss something that is very close to my heart. All of the men who have been on these Joint Chiefs of Staff; they are my old friends, they are my old associates. Through years of experience with them, sometimes experiences that were a bit soul-racking, I have found them to be loyal and dedicated men. I have no criticism of anyone that is going out.

We do have a new approach. We feel that the United States has a right to think that there is a new approach, a study that is made without any real chains fastening to the past.

The Secretary of Defense felt he should have an entirely new team, and I agreed with him. But I must assure you this: there is nothing that I can say, from my viewpoint as an old soldier, having served with these men, that would be too high praise for every single man on that Chiefs of Staff as I have seen him operate.

Now, I would hope that those words would be taken just as sincerely and earnestly as I feel them and believe them.

Q. Chalmers M. Roberts, Washington Post: There has been some interpretation of the selection of the new Chiefs as a shift in emphasis from Europe to Asia. I wonder if you would care to comment on that?

THE PRESIDENT. I have insisted, time and time again, that I see nothing in this argument of Europe versus Asia. The world happens to be round, and it has no end. I don't see how you can discuss the great basic problems of today, which are so largely philosophical in character, without thinking in global terms. I think that there may be times when, tactically, your interest is shifted in one direction, at times in another. But in the actual thinking and considering of this whole problem you must think globally, or you are bound to go wrong. And so this shift, so far as I am concerned, means nothing, except that I believe Mr.

Wilson has selected a very able group of people to come in and help him.

Q. Robert J. Donovan, New York Herald Tribune: Mr. President, in your television talk, will that be a straight speech by you, or are you thinking in terms of some new format of panel discussion?

THE PRESIDENT. Thinking in terms of what?

Q. Mr. Donovan: Some new format of panel discussion, or will that be a talk by you?

THE PRESIDENT. Of course now, you are talking about techniques; and these techniques, seemingly, are going through development. I personally would hope to be able to talk very informally on the television. I think when you have to be exact and talk formally, I would rather be on the radio. In any event, however we do the thing on the television, it will attempt to be an accurate report to the American people of what has happened to date, the purposes that have led us, and the accomplishments up to that moment.

Q. Merriman Smith, United Press: Mr. President, you said that you saw nothing that you could really point to as definite evidence of good faith.

THE PRESIDENT. I remember.

Q. Mr. Smith: I know this is redundant, but I just want to be sure we understand you correctly; you are speaking of the need of evidence of good faith from the Russians?

THE PRESIDENT. That is correct, that is correct.

Q. Robert G. Spivack, New York Post: In that connection, do you feel that the Communists' very quick rejection yesterday of General Clark's peace proposals in Korea means that they are stalling again—to drag this out over the summer, or to prevent our bringing the war to a military conclusion?

THE PRESIDENT. I haven't had a definite report from General Clark as to the details of that meeting. But I would say this: it was indicative of a sort of fixed attitude, that they could reject anything so quickly. That's all I would say. I could be mistaken. I would hope I were mistaken, but that is the way it would look.

Q. [*Speaker unidentified*]: Mr. President, to get back to the Attlee and Churchill comments, what is your opinion of their recommendation that Communist China be admitted to the United Nations Security Council should an armistice be signed?

THE PRESIDENT. I do think that you must remember that different nations have different interpretations on what recognition of a nation means. I think, ever since Wilson's time, in this country, we have more or less gone on the theory that recognition means also tacit approval. Now, at one time, as you well know, recognition meant just the recognition of the fact that there was a de facto ruler of an important segment of the world. And I think in certain other countries, that viewpoint still holds. With us, because there has been a different meaning developed in our country of this word recognition of another, we have to view the case differently. And I do not consider it as big a rift, let us say, between British and American policy, as it might appear on the surface, that we don't reach the same conclusion on it.

Certainly I would not say at this moment that I believe that admittance should follow an armistice.

Q. Joseph A. Fox, Washington Evening Star: Mr. President, what is the hour of that speech next Tuesday night?

THE PRESIDENT. I think it is 10 o'clock, but—[*confers with Mr. Hagerty*].

The final hour isn't fixed.

[*Speaker unidentified*]: Thank you, Mr. President.

NOTE: President Eisenhower's ninth news conference was held in the Executive Office Building at 10:30 a.m. on Thursday, May 14, 1953.

78 ¶ Remarks at the House of Burgesses, Williamsburg, Virginia. *May* 15, 1953

Ladies and gentlemen:

I think no American could stand in these halls and on this spot without feeling a very great and deep sense of the debt we owe to the courage, the stamina and the faith of our forefathers.

One hundred and seventy-seven years in some countries, in some histories, is only a moment. With us it is still a very measurable length of time. And 177 years ago Virginians, seeing that it was hopeless to gain through conflict their rights as British citizens, decided the time had come to declare their independence. And in the later version of that Declaration, you will recall that Jefferson wrote: "We hold that all men are endowed by their Creator with certain inalienable rights," thus establishing once and for all that our civilization and our form of government is deeply imbedded in a religious faith.

Indeed, those men felt that unless we recognized that relationship between our form of government and religious faith, that form of government made no sense. Because, remember, they were trying to explain this form of government to mankind, because they started out that Declaration by saying, "When in the course of human events it becomes necessary for one people to dissolve the political bands which have connected them with another, and to assume among the powers of the earth the separate and equal station to which the laws of nature and of nature's God entitle them, a decent respect to the opinions of mankind requires that they should declare the causes which impel them to the separation."

And those reasons were that all men are endowed by their Creator with certain rights. I wish—I wish sincerely that every single man, woman and child that has the proud privilege of calling himself an American, could stand here on this spot and could roam through this building to see the picture of Washington just across the hall, and re-live again their moments, the problems they met in their own time, and thus regain faith to solve the problems of our day.

To each of you here, my very great thanks for the honor that you have done Mrs. Eisenhower and me by being here. We have been privileged to come here with your two Senators—your two United States Senators—Senators Robertson and Byrd. Your Governor met us at the dock. We feel, truly, that we have been highly honored today by Virginia, the State of my mother's birth and girlhood.

NOTE: The President spoke at 9:45 a.m. His visit to Williamsburg and Annapolis (see also Items 79 and 80) occurred during a weekend cruise to Norfolk aboard the U.S.S. Williamsburg.

79 ¶ Address at the Inauguration of the 22d President of the College of William and Mary at Williamsburg. *May* 15, 1953

Mr. Rector, Governor Battle, President Chandler, President of the Student Body, distinguished guests, and ladies and gentlemen:

It would ill behoove me to attempt here a recitation of the glories of this college and of its alumni. If there be any among you who has not a better knowledge than I of the details of this great record, I commend you to a little home study. Because, let us not forget that man takes pride in a brilliant past. There is inspiration in attempting to live up to the records established by those who have gone before us—in the family, and in institutions.

Rather, it is my simple duty today, together with my invaluable, indispensable but publicly inarticulate life-long partner, Mamie Doud Eisenhower, to bring you greetings from your Nation's capital and your national administration.

I think it is appropriate for me to take a minute or two of your time to tell you why we are so pleased and delighted with this opportunity. Quite naturally, it is a great pleasure for me each time I return to the native State of my maternal ancestors. My mother lived in this State until she was of age. Again, it is a great privilege to be admitted into the honorary doctorate of this great institution, and I want to take the opportunity to express my very deep appreciation and thanks to the faculty and the governors of this great institution that they have deemed me worthy of this signal honor.

I want to pay a tribute to President Chandler, a man who, forsaking a life-long and honorable record in the armed services, has shown by his acceptance of this new responsibility that he well recognizes that there is no security for a free nation in the sword alone, that security must spring from the hearts and minds of free men. And he has shown, in his acceptance of this responsibility and this opportunity, that he appreciates that fact.

Again, I am delighted to come here because of my deep respect for the institutions of higher learning of the United States. And it seemed to me particularly fitting that on this 177th anniversary of the signing of the Virginia Declaration, that I could come here to this second oldest college in the United States to pay a word of tribute to these institutions.

Which brings up a thought I should like to discuss, and I assure you it will be very briefly: what is an institution of higher learning? All of us have heard many definitions of colleges. We know they are not merely campuses, they are not merely the stones and mortar of the buildings, they are something deeper and more profound.

And the particular definition that seems to mean the most to me is this: a college, a university, is a place where young minds are exposed to great minds.

And the reason I like that definition is this: if we accept its validity in any small portion, every man, every woman who takes a position in the faculty as instructor, assistant instructor, professor, dean or president—he has not merely a job, and he cannot console himself that he is merely doing his work and earning a daily living. He must achieve, or attempt to strive to achieve, greatness in his dealings with our young.

And this, it seems to me, is the crux of the college of our time, because it is not enough that we can produce doctors who may prolong our lives, unless at the same time we produce social leaders who will tell us how we will handle the greater population that we thus have.

It is not enough that we have iceboxes, and long and luxurious cars, and country homes, because there can be unhappiness in the midst of the greatest of luxury. Again you must know it here, because in the State from which came the man who could say, "As for me, give me liberty or give me death," you know there are values that are not to be measured by any material index. And great minds, therefore, will teach these young leaders not to say, "Of course I like liberty, and if you don't charge me more than fifteen percent of my income, I would like to keep it." The only thing that such people want to know is: is this sacrifice necessary? And it is through your contacts with great men and great minds that you will sort out the proper relationships of government to yourself, of higher government to state government, to local government, of his place in this whole scheme of things; and you will begin to understand whether your sacrifices are properly used by your government—and your sacrifices are ordinarily expressed in terms of taxes, of course.

But there is much more. There is what you are ready to do in the giving of your heart and your mind, not only on the faculty, but every single individual that has ever had the privilege of mingling with that faculty.

Why this Nation; except to preserve those great values recited for us in our founding documents.

If we understand, then we won't have communism. It may be necessary today, and it is necessary, that we earnestly seek out and uproot any traces of communism at any place where it can affect our national life. But the true way to uproot communism in this country is to understand what freedom means, and thus develop such an impregnable wall, that no thought of communism can enter.

In other words, if I may state it in an utterly simple way, I believe this: the true purpose of education is to prepare young men and women for effective citizenship in a free form of government.

If we can do that, we will have accomplished and included all of the techniques and the sciences, disciplines, because they will all be necessary in our security and in our advancement.

But above all, in that way only, I believe, can we permanently aspire to remain a free, independent and powerful people, living humbly under our God.

Thank you.

NOTE: The President spoke at 12:48 p.m. In his opening remarks he referred to James M. Robertson, Rector of the Board of Visitors of the College, Governor John Stewart Battle of Virginia, Alvin Duke Chandler, the new President of the College, and John N. Dalton, President of the Student Body.

80 ¶ Remarks to the Midshipmen at the Naval Academy in Annapolis. *May 17, 1953*

Gentlemen of the United States Navy:

I must first attempt to tell you how deeply honored I feel in the visit I have been privileged to make here at the Academy this morning.   For the friendliness I have seen on your faces, for the warmth of your welcome, both Mrs. Eisenhower and I extend to you our very profound and deepest thanks.

Now, the satisfaction of this visit was just slightly marred, because I was told about this particular part of it, and I must say that my imagination was not quite up to the task of deciding what I could bring to you on a Sunday that was worth taking your time for.   I could understand that if I had taken you from a mathematics or an engineering class, there might have been a little different aspect to the case.   But today, when it is chow and then what you want to do, probably including your "drags," why it seems a different story.

However, the highest authorities here made sure of one point, that there would at least be a few who would mark my visit and my passing with some satisfaction. And I didn't know that there were that many minor offenders in the United States Naval Academy.

If I could bring to you a message this morning that has any worth to it whatsoever, I think it would be in terms of a sense of values. Possibly, after all these years in the service, years of very great pride in that service, I could bring to you a few thoughts that might be worth considering.

They would be these: the young man facing life equipped as you men are being equipped, is puzzled, sometimes, as to the exact direction, lines, in which he would like to shape his career. He may even decide the service is not for him; he would be happier elsewhere. If that is his decision in the long run, of course, he must go out.

I want to express a few thoughts about a sense of values in these terms: material things pass. Most of us went to chapel this morning where we heard a minister express certain thoughts that I for one carried away with me in a very thoughtful mood. The values that last are of man's spirit.

And, with respect to the satisfaction of a service career, let me give you one fact out of my life that I think is significant.

For a long time I have been associating with what is called the service brats: the son and the daughter of a man that has put in his life in the service of his country. I have yet, in all these years, to have one of those children refer to his father's career in terms of disparagement. I have never heard one of them say, "Oh, my father was just a Captain in the Navy—or a Colonel in the Marines—or in the other services." He has pushed out his chest and he has said it proudly, far more proudly, it has struck me, than has the man who has said, "My father is a merchant"—a very honorable, a very necessary calling in our country. But there is something special about dedicating your lives to the United States of America that lives with you, and what is more important, in my opinion, with your children as long as they shall live.

And so, if in this little homely sort of observation you can find something that will help you straighten out your own planning, based upon a sense of values that means something to you, then I should say my trip here is worth while.

I promised not to take much of your time, and I intend to keep that promise, but I must attempt once more to say how very, very glad I am to be here.

I want to make special reference to the First Class, because on my most recent visit to the Academy, they were Plebes. I want to apologize to them for again appearing here to harangue them. I hope that they will take it in the spirit that I mean: one of tremendous admiration for this body as a whole, for the individuals that make it up.

And my final thought: I congratulate every single man here upon the opportunity lying ahead. They are troublous times. They are difficult times, which makes more important the job of conquering them—doing our part well. There is no great glory in conquering a high school team, but when you beat West Point, you have done something.

Thank you.

NOTE: The President spoke at 12:45 p.m. in the Mess Hall.

81 ¶ Remarks at the United Negro College Fund Luncheon. *May* 19, 1953

Mr. Chairman, Doctor Patterson, Mr. Rockefeller, distinguished guests, and friends:

From time to time I find that it is one of my pleasant duties to meet with groups who are convening here in the National Capital for some public-spirited service. It has been my privilege to extend to them a welcome on the part of the Administration and

the National Government.   In none of these cases have I felt
greater satisfaction than I do this afternoon.

By his or her presence here, each person attending this meeting
shows their support for several things in which I passionately
believe.   One of them is support for the Constitution of the United
States which, written in the recognition that all people are the
children of God, made no distinction among them by reason of
inconsequential factors over which they themselves had no control.

I believe those of us who preach so loudly about constitutional
government advance our cause as we meticulously observe that
particular factor or foundation of that great Document.

Another thing I have preached, as have many others, is against
the theory that there can be any second-class citizen.   I believe
as long as we allow conditions to exist that make for second-class
citizens, we are making of ourselves less than first-class citizens.

In other words, I believe the only way to protect my own rights
is to protect the rights of others.

Everything that the Constitution accords to me, I must defend
for others—or else finally there will be nobody left to defend me.

And now I want to tell you a little bit of a story that just
happened the day before yesterday.   I was down at Annapolis,
and I inspected a Marine Guard.   As I went around, I noticed
there were several Negroes occupying different positions in this
Guard.   One of them had on the chevrons of a non-commissioned
officer.   I talked with the commanding officer of this group.   I
said, "Now here occurs one of those things that was always advanced as an argument when we were working for the cause of
eliminating segregation in the armed services—it was said that
white men would not willingly serve under a Negro superior."
And here I noticed that it was evidently not true.   The officer
smiled, and he said: "I must tell you that this man, when it came
to the making of non-commissioned officers, could not pass the
rigid mental examination we gave.   But his personality was so
fine, his qualities of leadership so evident, his character and reputation in the company so great that we had to make special

arrangements so that it was unnecessary for him to pass completely the mental examination."

As I see it, you people today who are supporting the Negro College Fund are not only supporting the idea that men are equal, but you are making it unnecessary for a man to appear in a competitive place in our country, whether it be in governmental service or anywhere else, and have less opportunity than has his brothers for the mental training that would have given him exactly the same opportunities in that company as any other. It spoke to me very eloquently of this lad's very exceptional qualifications.

And so, really, I came only to say I am delighted you are here, I applaud the work you are doing, and particularly to join with you in expressing my own very deep sense of obligation to the Rockefeller family—a family that has seen this type of need and has done something within the terms of private enterprise, private initiative, and spontaneous cooperation, not waiting on some kind of law to get a thing done that they saw needed to be done.

Now that the moment for saying "This is going to be only a brief word" is too late for saying it, I will say it! Thank you for the privilege of allowing me to come here, Mr. Chairman and Dr. Patterson. My very best wishes go with all of you in this great work, and success to you.

NOTE: The President spoke at the National Press Club in Washington at 1:10 p.m. In his opening words he referred to C. D. Jackson, Chairman of the 1953 United Negro College Fund Campaign; Dr. F. D. Patterson, President of Tuskegee Institute and of the United Negro College Fund; and John D. Rockefeller 3d.

82 ¶ Radio Address to the American People on the National Security and Its Costs. *May* 19, 1953

My fellow Americans:

Tonight, as you sit in your homes all across this broad land, I want to talk with you about an issue affecting all our lives. It is the defense of our country, and its cost.

If we ponder this a moment, we all know that this really means the defense of those spiritual values and moral ideals cherished by generations of Americans—the true treasure of our people. This treasure of the spirit must be defended, above all, with weapons of the spirit: our patriotism, our devotion, our readiness to sacrifice.

If we think further, we also know that this defense of America demands still other weapons. We must, of course, want to be free. But this is not enough. To be free and to stay free, we must be strong—and we must stay strong.

Our national security is affected by almost everything that your government does—things far removed from the building of planes or the training of troops. National security involves, for example, the plain honesty and competence of government itself, for no nation is secure whose government does not command respect at home and honor abroad.

Our strength demands, also, healthy two-way trade with our allies and friends—for this nation could not for long enjoy either freedom or prosperity alone in a hostile world. Indeed, our own security demands that we never forget or neglect the military and economic health of these indispensable allies.

And, national security requires an industrious and productive America, for here is the vital source of all our military strength.

We all know something of the long record of deliberately planned Communist aggression. There has been, to this moment, no reason to believe that Soviet policy has changed its frequently announced hope and purpose—the destruction of freedom everywhere.

There is, therefore, no reason for the free nations to alter their course: to hope and work for the best, to arm and be ready for the worst.

We must see, clearly and steadily, just exactly what is the danger before us. It is more than merely a military threat.

It has been coldly calculated by the Soviet leaders, for by their military threat they have hoped to force upon America and the free world an unbearable security burden leading to economic disaster. They have plainly said that free people cannot preserve their way of life and at the same time provide enormous military establishments. Communist guns, in this sense, have been aiming at an economic target no less than a military target.

I believe firmly—and I think the Soviets realize—that the United States, if forced to total mobilization today, could meet and win any military challenge.

I believe no less firmly that we must see and meet the full nature of the present and future danger before us. For the nature of this danger dictates the nature of the defense we summon.

This defense must, first of all, be one which we can bear for a long and indefinite period of time. It cannot consist of sudden, blind responses to a series of fire-alarm emergencies. Even we cannot always be mobilizing forces and materiel with a speed that is heedless of cost, order and efficiency. It cannot be based solely on the theory that we can point to a D-day of desperate danger, somewhere in the near future, to which all plans can be geared.

The truth is that our danger cannot be fixed or confined to one specific instant. We live in an age of peril.

We must think and plan and provide so as to live through this age in freedom—in ways that do not undermine our freedom even as we strive to defend it.

To watch vigilantly on the military front must never mean to be blind on the domestic front. In our present world—in this kind of prolonged tension and struggle—a crippled industry or a demoralized working force could be the equivalent of a lost battle. Prolonged inflation could be as destructive of a truly free economy as could a chemical attack against an army in the field. If, in today's continuing danger, we were to strain our capacity until rigid governmental controls, indefinitely or permanently continued, became mandatory—where then would be the freedom we defend?

Our defense—I repeat—must be carefully planned and steadfastly sustained.

Such planning brings us to another subject, to that bewildering realm of budgets and expenditures and appropriations and deficits and taxes. This, as we all know, is no easy area to explore or to explain. But these rude facts-and-figures of our national economy are, to our body-politic, as vital as pulse-rates or blood-counts.

As you all know, government deficits of past years have been a main cause of the cheapening of our dollar by half its value.

The budget inherited by this Administration, for the year beginning this July 1, called for expenditures of 78.6 billion dollars, and signified another red-ink entry in our national books of 9.9 billion dollars—on top of other big deficits for last year and this year.

Beyond this, when this Administration took office, we faced two stubborn financial facts. The first fact was this: under the former Administration expenditures for the future were so scheduled as to reach their peak during 1954 and 1955. The second fact was this: these are precisely the years when, under existing laws, federal revenues from taxes, under scheduled reductions, will fall sharply downward.

If we do nothing about this, the results of these facts could only be: bigger deficits, greater government borrowing, ever increasing cost of living, depreciated savings, higher and higher cost of the nation's security.

These figures are but a small part of the story. Let me give you a few more facts:

First: The past Administration over-estimated tax collections for the next fiscal year by some 1.2 billion dollars. Obviously, even the most conscientious of men must be allowed some leeway in forecasting tax receipts more than a year ahead. Nevertheless it is unfortunately true that this over-estimate of income would bring the red-ink entry for the coming year up to more than 11 billion dollars.

Second: The military budget proposed by the previous Administration for the fiscal year 1954 did not fully plan for one item that could scarcely be called obscure. That item was the Korean War. No specific budgetary provision was made for continuance of this conflict. No provision was made for the building up of Republic of Korea divisions beyond those currently in being. Our task, then, is not only one of dealing with the planned deficit, but also one of providing for the costs of the Korean War so long as it may continue.

Third: Largely aside from the budget and deficit, there will be, as of June 30 of this year, 81 billion dollars of authorizations to spend money for which cash must be found in the tax revenues of the next several years. Since a large part of this enormous sum is already under contract, mostly for defense purposes, there is little room in which to turn around to make any immediate economies in this area.

This whole matter is rather like buying C.O.D. When you order goods C.O.D., you do not need any money until the items you ordered come to your front doors—and then it is Cash on Delivery. This Administration faces payment on just such an 81 billion dollars C.O.D. over the next several years.

I come now to the critical question: how can we make more bearable, for every family in our land, the burden of this inheritance and at the same time make our nation's security more sound and sure?

To begin with the military front: there must be—far from any slackening of effort—a speeding, a sharpening, a concentration that will extract the last cent of value from every dollar spent.

Our defense establishment has yet to reach the level of performance we want. Until it has, we shall not rest.

I want here to state a few critical facts plainly. They are critical. They are facts. And they should be beyond the reach of any partisan debate.

It is fact that there is no such thing as maximum military security short of total mobilization of all our national resources. Such security would compel us to imitate the methods of the dictator. It would compel us to put every able-bodied man in uniform—to regiment the worker, the farmer, the businessman—to allocate materials and to control prices and wages—in short, to devote our whole nation to the grim purposes of the garrison state.

This, I firmly believe, is not the way to defend America.

It is also a fact that when we seek anything less than this vision of military perfection—total mobilization—we are debating in a realm of speculation—sometimes informed, more often uninformed.

Words like "essential" and "indispensable" and "absolute minimum" become the common coin of this realm—and they are spent with wild abandon. One man will argue hotly for a given number of aircraft as the "absolute minimum." Another, even from the same military service, will answer just as passionately that a smaller number of aircraft but of a different kind is "imperative." And others will earnestly advocate the "indispensable" needs for ships or tanks or rockets or guided missiles or artillery—all totalled in numbers that are always called "minimum." All such views are argued with vigor and tenacity, and I believe honestly. But obviously all cannot be right.

I most deeply believe that it is foolish and dangerous for any of us to be hypnotized by magic numbers in this type of analysis. There is no given number of ships—no specific number of divisions—no magic number of air wings in the Air Force, Navy, and Marine Corps—no special number of billions of dollars—that will automatically guarantee security.

My associates and I have given to this phase of our national planning careful, personal study and analysis. I have, as you know, lived with it for many years. We have also sought, of course, advice from numbers of competent people.

Let me tell you how we approached this analysis. We did not set any fixed sum of money to which our defense plans had to be fitted. We first estimated what is truly vital to our security. We next planned ways to eliminate every useless expenditure and duplication. And we finally decided upon the amount of money needed to meet this program.

Such an analysis rejects the extreme arguments of enthusiasts and of all groups of special pleaders both in and out of the military services.

But this I assure you: what has been so carefully evolved is a sound program. It contemplates in each of the armed forces calculated risks which have been prudently reasoned. And it represents, in our combined judgment, what is best for our nation's permanent security.

There is, I believe, only one honest, workable formula. It is not magical, but it is the best that competent men can define. It is this: a defense strong enough both to discourage aggression and beyond this to protect the nation—in the event of any aggression—as it moves swiftly to full mobilization.

The more swiftly and smoothly we can mobilize, the less our dependence upon costly standing armies, navies and air forces.

The more vigorously we eliminate the non-essential, the more effectively we can concentrate on what is vital.

With all this in mind, we are putting major emphasis on air power, which daily becomes a more important factor in war. Our revised budget will provide the Air Force with more than 40% of all defense funds for 1954. As of this June 30, the Air Force will have available a sum of more than 40 billion dollars. Buttressing this strength are those additional funds allocated to naval air power for 1954—totalling more than half of the Navy budget. This means that almost 60 cents out of every dollar to be available for the entire national defense in the next year will be devoted to air power and air defense.

These investments in air power represent and will continue to represent the heaviest single annual outlay of our government. It is my conviction that our developing program—under constant review and study—will result in a steady growth in the size and efficiency of the air defense, until we have attained an adequate level of security.

I repeat: this security cannot arbitrarily be defined as the simple equivalent of a specific number of aircraft or air wings. For example: today three aircraft with modern weapons can practically duplicate the destructive power of all the 2700 planes we unleashed in the great break-out attack from the Normandy beachhead. Clearly every technological advance profoundly affects this problem of air power—including the development of missiles now in production. Similar advances in civil defense will help shape the nature and size of our Air Forces.

The plain truth is that security is planned, not blindly bought. It is the product of thought, and work, and our ability and readiness to bear our military burden for however long the threat to freedom persists.

The course we must set for ourselves is a difficult one. It must avoid, on the one hand, the indefinite continuance of a needlessly high rate of Federal spending in excess of Federal income. It must avoid, on the other hand, any penny-wise, pound-foolish policy that could, through lack of needed strength, cripple the cause of freedom everywhere.

This middle way may lack drama and sensation. But it has sense and strength.

It may not scream with shrill crisis and emergency. But it speaks with conviction and realism.

Because of the necessary costs of the national security, your government is not just preaching economy but practicing it. Every department of this government has already cut its requests for funds for the next fiscal year. As a result, we have been able to reduce the previous Administration's request for appropriations of new money by some 8½ billion dollars. This prodigious sum means more than $50 for every man, woman, and child in our country. This is the first step in cutting expenditures. And next year we shall spend at least 4.5 billion dollars less than was previously planned.

Here let me add this word. Government cannot do this job—any more than any other job—utterly alone. You and your fellow-citizens who want your government to spend less must yourselves practice self-restraint in the demands you make upon government. You as citizens cannot help the common cause by merely favoring economy for every group except the one to which you belong.

All that we have done and saved to date is an encouraging start. But it is no more than a start. During every day of the coming year we must and shall continue striving to find, in every department of the government, new ways to achieve effectiveness with economy. I need scarcely remind you that the saving of 4.5 billion dollars is less than half the deficit planned by the previous Administration for the next fiscal year.

It is in the light of these facts that all of us must honestly face the matter of taxes. It must be apparent that to accept a great revenue loss at this time would be to ensure longer life to bigger Federal deficits and greater eventual danger to our country.

The convictions of this Administration on these grave subjects are clear and simple.

We believe that for the long term present taxes are too high. We think they are becoming a real threat to individual initiative.

We believe, at the same time, that no citizen—once satisfied that his government is operating with honesty and economy, and planning with foresight—wants any tax saving at the price of essential national security.

We believe, finally, that our truly urgent need is to make our nation secure, our economy strong, and our dollar sound.

For every American, this matter of the sound dollar is crucial.

Without a sound dollar, every American family would face a renewal of inflation, an ever increasing cost of living, the withering away of savings and life insurance policies. An immediate tax reduction, and bigger deficits, which would in turn inflate the dollar still more would cheat every family in America. It would strike most cruelly at the poorest among us.

The balancing of the budget is, therefore, vital—not merely as some abstract, statistical feat to be performed by government accountants but to help give each citizen the kind of dollar with which each family in the nation can begin balancing its own budget.

With this in mind, I am recommending the following measures to the Congress for tax legislation.

First. The excess profits tax on corporations as now drawn should be extended for six months beyond its present expiration date of June 30—an extension that will produce a gain of revenue of 800 million dollars.

Second. The 5% reduction in the regular income tax on corporations, now scheduled to go into effect April 1, 1954, should be repealed. The continuation of this additional 5% will bring in approximately 2 billion dollars a year.

Third. The reduction in excise taxes, which would take place next April 1 under present law, should not be put into effect pending the development of a sounder system of excise taxation, for which I shall make specific recommendations to the Congress next January.

Fourth. There is now scheduled an increase in the old-age security tax from 1½% to 2% on both employees and employers, to go into effect next January 1. It can and should be postponed, for the old-age and survivors trust fund has now reached 18 billion dollars and receipts at present tax rates are in excess of current expenditures. This will be a worthwhile saving to wage-earners and, in my judgment, is simple justice to them.

Finally: Another relief for the taxpayers will be in the reduction in personal income taxes that will go into effect next January 1.

While this is in accordance with the letter of existing laws, it would not have been possible but for the economies in government that have been and are being made by this Administration. At the same time, I do not believe that the American people think that earlier reduction would be prudent. Your communications to me show that—first of all—you want our nation secure and our dollar sound. This Administration agrees. To advance six months the date of this scheduled reduction would take away 1.5 billion dollars and, to that extent, would risk both of the objectives we seek.

I repeat, no effort will be spared in the coming months to achieve additional vital economies. To do this in significant amounts will depend on some gradual improvement in the world situation. If we should be disappointed in this, I shall, of course, be compelled to make recommendations for alternative sources of revenue. But if these efforts prove successful, a balanced budget will come within sight.

Next January, I shall recommend to the Congress a completely revised program of taxation. Already appropriate studies are under way in the House Ways and Means Committee and in the Treasury Department. Our system of taxation must not only provide our government with the resources to be strong for freedom's sake, but also enable our people to apply their initiative and industry fruitfully. This means taxes so adjusted as to fall where payment is least harmful, and so planned as to create jobs and expand the income of the mass of our people.

I have spoken to you tonight not only as your President but as one whose life has been devoted to the military defense of our country.

I have outlined my convictions as to the way to defend America.

This is the way to work for national security—in the full, true sense.

It is with the greatest confidence that I say to you:

We possess, as a people, all the qualities, all the talents, and all the resources necessary to resolve the problems inherited from the past or inherent in the present.

We live, as I have said, not in an instant of danger but in an age of danger.

We will meet it, as Americans, boldly, vigorously, and successfully.

We will make of it an age of productive freedom, unmatched in all man's history.

This is what I ask all of you to help to do.

NOTE: The President spoke from the White House at 10:30 p.m.

83 ¶ Recorded Summary of Address to the American People on the National Security and Its Costs. *May* 19, 1953

I HAVE JUST finished talking, ladies and gentlemen, to the American people on two of the important problems that beset us all today. They involve the budget—our fiscal problems on the one hand—and on the other hand the problems of national security.

Now, when we take these two problems together we get into the question that involves the deepest kind of concern on the part of your Government and should indeed on the part of all of us because on the one hand we have the great burden of taxes that plague us, getting dangerously close to the point where they stifle the initiative and the enterprise of the American worker and businessman, and on the other hand, we have national security with its great and tremendous costs on the Government and on this nation.

Now, I should like first to tell you of the spirit—the attitude—

in which I approach this problem of national security. I believe the American people are proud of and worthy of the traditions they have inherited from their founding fathers. Among those traditions is their memory of one great patriot, Patrick Henry. Do you remember what he said?—"I know not what others may do, but as for me—Give me Liberty or give me Death."

Now, I think that a people who still revere a man that could talk that way are going to throw completely out all of those croakers who now say, "Oh, yes, we like liberty. Give us liberty if it doesn't cost us more than fifteen percent of our income." I think the American people will have nothing to do with that kind of talk but because they are ready to make the sacrifices that mean security for this country of ours they are entitled to the confidence that their Government is spending their money with the greatest concern for its drain upon the pocketbook—the tax drain upon their pocketbook. So—what we are trying to do to-day is to find a program of security that costs the least and then through the most earnest kind of care to abolish duplication and luxury from expenditures to minimize your cost to you.

In my talk I expressed a bit of what we might call the Administration's philosophy of defense. In the first place, we all understand that democracy does not prepare for aggressive war. It has no intention of going to war if that can possibly be helped and still preserve our liberties. Consequently we don't look toward a possible emergency as just some moment of greatest danger. We realize that we are living in an age of danger and we must so conduct our affairs that we can live through that age of danger.

Now, part of our philosophy is this: We do not intend to become a garrison state. We do not intend to impose rigid controls over everything that the American people do—their production, their going into uniform, their living, their thinking, their talking—not at all. We expect to live as a free state, which means that we must develop a program that can, under the general practice of a free economy, carry the security burden for a long, long time if that is necessary, and we will do it without complaining because we prize our freedoms that highly.

Now, in making all of the economies that are possible it is necessary that we concentrate on that which is vitally necessary and tend to put into second place, and even to eliminate where we can, those things which are merely desirable. This, in view, we are concentrating largely on air power—air power not only in the American Air Force but in the Navy arm which absorbs more than half of the appropriations made for the Navy. Indeed, for all of the great costs for national security we find that we put more than sixty cents out of every dollar into air power. That is the measure in which we are concentrating on air power in the defense of this country.

NOTE: The President's summary of his address was recorded for radio, television, and newsreels.

84 ¶ Special Message to the Congress Recommending Tax Legislation. *May* 20, 1953

To the Congress of the United States:

When this Administration took office four months ago, it inherited a critically unsound state of financial affairs. The federal budget was unbalanced by 4 billion dollars in the fiscal year 1952; the estimates of the outgoing Administration indicated a further deficit of 5.9 billion dollars in the current fiscal year, and a still larger deficit of 9.9 billion dollars in the fiscal year 1954. Moreover, the estimate of the former Administration left on hand for the end of this fiscal year 81 billion dollars of unspent appropriations; in effect 81 billion dollars of bills which would fall due and have to be paid by the new Administration.

In addition, revenues appear to have been over-estimated by the former Administration to the extent of at least 1.5 billion dollars in the fiscal year 1953 and about 1.2 billion dollars in the fiscal year 1954. These over-estimates will have the effect of increasing the deficits already indicated for both of these years.

In addition to that, the present tax laws contain certain provisions which will soon begin sharply to reduce Government revenues. These tax reductions will reduce annual revenues by an estimated 8 billion dollars. Only 2.1 billion dollars of this loss falls in the fiscal year 1954. But the full effect falls in 1955— the latter being the first year for which the budget will be prepared by the incoming Administration. The fact is that in 1954 and 1955 we reach the peak of expenditures caused by earlier appropriations and programmed and contracted for expenditure at the same time Government revenues are sharply reduced. These simple facts highlight the problems we have faced in trying to bring prudence and foresight into our budgetary planning.

Despite these problems we have made real progress in attempting to straighten out our financial affairs. Our first effort was a prompt review of the outgoing Administration's budget recommendations for the fiscal year 1954. We have thus far succeeded in reducing those recommended requests for new appropriations by about 8½ billion dollars, an amount equivalent to over fifty dollars for each man, woman and child in the Nation.

Expenditures in the fiscal year 1954 cannot immediately be reduced by the full amount of this 8½ billion dollars, because a large part of the 1954 expenditures will be for the payment of obligations incurred by the Government in previous years. However, the reductions made in requested appropriations will eventually lead to a saving of the full amount. Some of this saving will be reflected in lower expenditures in 1955 and later years as well as in 1954.

Expenditures by the previous Administration in 1954 were estimated at 78.6 billion dollars. They now are estimated at 74.1 billion dollars, 4.5 billion dollars less than had been planned. We intend to continue our efforts to reduce Government spending and to put the Nation's financial affairs on a sound basis. These objectives will be pursued in our everyday operations and will chart our course in every budget this Administration transmits to the Congress.

Almost 73 percent of our spending in 1954 will be for national security purposes, mostly for our own military services, international programs, and atomic energy. Another 15 percent will be for interest and veterans' programs, largely fixed costs brought about by past wars. The remaining 12 percent has already been substantially trimmed, and further reductions are under study.

To reduce expenditures enough to balance the 1954 budget would require more drastic curtailment of our national security programs than we can safely afford in today's troubled world. These programs will be continually reviewed in light of the world situation, our international commitments, and the need for economy and prudence in all Government operations. Substantial reductions have been made already. We are working hard to increase them within the framework of the Administration program.

Against the foregoing revised expenditure estimate of 74.1 billion dollars, net revenues for the next fiscal year are now estimated at 67.5 billion dollars, if all of the reductions in taxes authorized under present laws take place. This would leave a deficit of 6.6 billion dollars.

Receipts for the current fiscal year ending on June 30 will be at an all-time high level. Nevertheless, they will probably fall short of the estimate made in the January budget message of the prior Administration by 1.5 billion dollars, perhaps even more. With the large collections at the end of June, a margin of error of several hundred million dollars must be allowed for even at this late date, but it is clear now that the earlier estimate was too high.

In view of recent experience with collections, the estimate of receipts for the next fiscal year, made early last January by the past Administration, is now revised downward by 1.2 billion dollars. The new estimate is made on the assumption that employment and business will continue at a high level, but in the interest of prudence some relaxation of the extremely high rates of activity now existing is allowed for.

Because of the reduced estimates of receipts, the deficit for the next fiscal year, which the past Administration projected at 9.9 billion dollars, would rise to 11.1 billion dollars if expenditures were not curtailed. With the economies in expenditures which I have recommended, the projected deficit would be brought down to 6.6 billion dollars in the conventional or administrative budget. The deficit on a cash basis, that is, after adjusting for the retirement reserves and other special accounts, would then be 3.3 billion dollars.

The above estimates are based on the assumption that the reductions in tax rates will take effect as now scheduled under the law. Those reductions would involve a loss in revenue of 2.1 billion dollars in the fiscal year 1954, as follows:

ESTIMATED REVENUE LOSS FROM SCHEDULED TAX REDUCTIONS

[In billions of dollars]

	Effective date of reduction	Fiscal year 1954	Full year loss
Corporation:			
Excess profits tax	7/1/53	.8	2.0
Income tax	4/1/54	. . . .	2.0
Individual income tax	1/1/54	1.1	3.0
Excise taxes	4/1/54	.2	1.0
Total	. . . .	2.1	8.0

The discrepancies between the immediate fiscal-year and eventual full-year effects are explained by the date of the scheduled reductions and by lags in collections.

If no reductions were made in present tax rates, estimated receipts would be 69.6 billion dollars in the next fiscal year, which would exceed those of the current year by 2.4 billion dollars. Even if the scheduled reductions in tax rates go into effect, total receipts are estimated to reach an all-time high, exceeding those of the current year by 300 million dollars.

Nevertheless, tax receipts will apparently fall considerably short of our necessary expenditures during the next fiscal year. In view of this fact I have come to the conclusion that no reductions in tax rates should become effective during this calendar year. I regret this conclusion because I share the widespread feeling that our taxes are generally too high and that some of our tax laws are inherently defective. But facts are facts and I propose that we face them. It seems to me that under the conditions stated here and regardless of the origination of the tax reductions now written in the law, no Administration could acquiesce in their taking place as scheduled unless it was willing to take vigorous action to reduce expenditures sufficiently to bring outlays within available revenues.

The problem of fiscal readjustment is one of timing. Under present conditions of high business activity, coupled with a budget deficit, a tax reduction would not be consistent with attaining the vital financial objective of a sound dollar. I want to see a tax reduction carried out; I want it very much. But I want even more to stop the deterioration of the currency which has been going on for so many years under the unsound fiscal and monetary policies of the past Administration.

As a matter of basic long-term policy, we must look forward to reducing tax revenues as Government expenditures are curtailed. But it is also wise under existing conditions not to reduce receipts any faster than we can cut back on expenditures.

Since an immediate tax reduction would be financially unsound, I submit the following six recommendations for tax legislation by the Congress:

(1) The excess profits tax should be extended as now drawn for six months beyond its present expiration date of June 30. This action seems necessary in spite of the fact that this is an undesirable way of taxing corporate profits.

Though the name suggests that only excessive profits are taxed, the tax actually penalizes thrift and efficiency and hampers business expansion. Its impact is especially hard on successful small businesses which must depend on retained earnings for growth. These disadvantages of the tax are now widely recognized. I would not advocate its extension for more than a matter of months. However, under existing circumstances the extension of the present law is preferable to the increased deficit caused by its immediate expiration or to any short-term substitute tax.

The scheduled expiration of the tax in June would be misleading in its consequences. It would simply mean that the tax would be applied at half the full rate, 15 percent, to all of this year's business income. Therefore its bad effects in penalizing efficiency and encouraging waste will continue through this year in any event. The extension of the tax through December 1953 would maintain the full 30 percent rate for the entire year and would produce a gain in revenue of 800 million dollars in the fiscal year 1954.

(2) The reduction in the regular corporate tax rate from 52 percent to 47 percent, now scheduled to go into effect on April 1, 1954, should be rescinded. A continuation of these extra five percentage points on the corporate tax will bring in about 2 billion dollars a year, about the same amount as will be lost annually by the expiration of the excess profits tax at the end of this calendar year.

Though a 52 percent corporate tax rate is too high for the long run, the budget will not now permit a reduction in both individual and regular corporate tax rates. A reduction in individual taxes must come first, for the benefit of the entire economy.

(3) The increase in the old-age insurance tax from 1½ to 2 percent on both employees and employers, now scheduled to go into effect next January 1, should be postponed until January 1, 1955.

The old-age and survivors trust fund has now reached almost 18 billion dollars. Receipts at present tax rates are currently well in excess of expenditures. The further addition to the fund which would flow from the projected tax increase is not required.

From now on, the old-age tax and trust accounts, while maintaining the contributory principle, should be handled more nearly on a pay-as-you-go basis.

The postponement of the tax increase will reduce the impending tax burden on every covered employee and employer. It will not influence the administrative budget, but it will involve an increase in the cash deficit.

(4) The wide variety of existing excise rates makes little economic sense and leads to improper discrimination between industries and among consumers. Specific proposals for a modified system of excise taxation will be included in the recommendations for tax revisions that will be submitted to the Congress next January.

The reductions in excise taxes, which would take place next April 1 under present law, should be rescinded pending the development of a better system of excise taxation.

(5) I believe that a reduction in personal income taxes can and should be made effective next January 1. This reduction will amount to about 10 percent on the lower and middle incomes, graduating down to between one and two percent on the highest brackets. While this reduction is in accordance with existing law, it would have been impossible to accomplish on the basis of the previous Administration's budget without additional deficit financing with its resultant inflationary pressures. A reduction will be justified next January only because of reductions in proposed expenditures which the present Administration has already been able to make and because of additional economies we expect to achieve in the future.

While this Administration will spare no effort to effect further economies, large-scale success in that effort will depend on some easing of the tension that besets the world today. Should this improvement fail to come about and thereby prevent significant further economies, I shall find it necessary to make recommendations for alternative sources of revenue. However, if we are able to follow without interruption the course we have marked out, a balanced budget will be in sight and the much-needed tax relief will be a sound financial measure.

(6) As you know, the Ways and Means Committee of the House of Representatives is currently engaged in a comprehensive re-examination of the existing tax structure. To help achieve this objective, I have asked the Secretary of the Treasury to present by the end of the year recommendations to remove existing inequities of our tax structure, simplify the needless complications which have developed over the years in tax laws, and generally secure a better balance of tax revenues. The analysis in the Treasury is being made in close cooperation with the appropriate Committees of the Congress and their staffs.

The Treasury must be assured of adequate revenues to finance necessary expenditures for national security and other essential purposes. At the same time, we must develop a system of taxation which, to the greatest extent possible, will not discourage work, savings and investment, but will permit and encourage initiative and the sound growth of our free economy.

A recapitulation of the budget position for the next fiscal year is given below, showing the effects of the revisions and recommendations which I have made in this message:

BUDGET OUTLOOK FISCAL YEAR 1954

[In billions of dollars]

	Budget expenditures	Budget receipts	Deficit administrative	Deficit cash
January budget, past Administration......	78. 6	68. 7	9. 9	6. 6
Revisions in estimates.................	−4. 5	−1. 2	−3. 3	−3. 3
Revised budget, with scheduled tax reductions........................	74. 1	67. 5	6. 6	3. 3
Effect of recommended changes in taxes from rates now scheduled to become effective........................	....	1. 0	−1. 0	[1] −. 5
Revised budget........................	74. 1	68. 5	5. 6	2. 8

[1] Difference between effects on administrative and cash budgets is explained by a reduction of 500 million dollars in old-age insurance tax receipts.

The Administration has begun the heavy task of putting the federal government's fiscal house in order. It is moving vigorously to reduce expenditures with due regard for the needs of national security. I am making the above tax recommendations in the conviction that they are prudent and sound. I commend them to the earnest attention of the Congress.

DWIGHT D. EISENHOWER

85 ¶ Statement by the President on the Forthcoming Meeting of the Heads of Government of the United States, Great Britain, and France. *May* 21, 1953

THE GOVERNMENTS of the United States, Great Britain and France have been in consultation with the view of holding an informal high level meeting. We have agreed that such a meeting is desirable at a date convenient to all of us. A primary purpose will be further to develop common viewpoints with these friends on the many problems that must be solved cooperatively so that the cause of world peace may be advanced.

86 ¶ Statement by the President Upon Signing the Submerged Lands Act. *May* 22, 1953

I AM PLEASED to sign this measure into law recognizing the ancient rights of the States in the submerged lands within their historic boundaries. As I have said many times I deplore and I will always resist federal encroachment upon rights and affairs of the States. Recognizing the States' claim to these lands is in keeping with basic principles of honesty and fair play.

This measure also recognizes the interests of the Federal Government in the submerged lands outside of the historic boundaries of the States. Such lands should be administered by the Federal Government and income therefrom should go into the Federal Treasury.

NOTE: As enacted, the Submerged Lands Act is Public Law 31, 83d Congress (67 Stat. 29).

87　¶ Statement by the President on the Armistice Negotiations at Panmunjom.　*May* 26, 1953

THE ATTENTION of the free world is focused upon the armistice negotiations at Panmunjom. There, on May 25, the United Nations Command renewed its efforts to bring an honorable peace to Korea and a fair and humane settlement of the POW issue. To speed these negotiations the United Nations Command requested executive, in other words confidential, sessions. We are continuing to observe the executive nature of those sessions.

There are, however, certain principles inherent in the United Nations Command position which are basic and not subject to change. No prisoners will be repatriated by force. No prisoners will be coerced or intimidated in any way. And there must be a definite limit to the period of their captivity. The procedures used in handling the prisoners must reflect these principles.

In all this, our allies are in full accord. These principles accord also with the prevailing view of a representative bipartisan group of Senators and Congressmen who have been consulted.

Finally: These principles on which we stand are the same as those which were formally approved by fifty-four members of the United Nations.

88 ¶ The President's News Conference of *May 28, 1953.*

THE PRESIDENT. There is one piece of spot news which, of course, I assume all of you people know about.

This morning there was picked up in the monitoring processes a message from Moscow which is apparently an order to the Russian commissioner—the Soviet commissioner—in Germany to disband and dissolve the Soviet control section, and to relieve the commander and the troops of all responsibility in control of what was called, I believe, the Free German Republic.

I bring it up merely to say that there is no use asking any questions on it, because I was informed about it only a little while ago. What the meaning, or the import, or the purpose of the order is, we don't know. So there is just really no use asking questions about it, because what the meaning can be we haven't yet tried to decide.

Now, there has just been too much happening for me to attempt to give you a summary of my own, and I think we might as well start on the questions.

Q. Merriman Smith, United Press: Mr. President, do you share Senator Taft's view that we should forget the United Nations as far as the Korean war is concerned?

THE PRESIDENT. No. I think that you will understand that if you attempt to talk about this whole business of foreign relations, one is apt to get into a lecture that runs a little long. But at the risk of being just a bit verbose, let me explain one or two things.

I have had a very great deal of experience in dealing with coalitions, in filling positions of responsibility under them. It's always difficult. And I am quite certain that there arise occasions when if any one nation or any one authority were acting singly, possibly the decision in that point would be better than to subject it to all of the trimmings and the compromises that come out of the effort to achieve some kind of unanimity of opinion.

But you can't have cooperative action in these great developments and processes in just the spots of the globe, or in just the particular problems, that you would like to select.

If you are going to go it alone one place, you of course in the long run have to go it alone everywhere. If you are going to try to develop a coalition of understanding based upon decency, upon your ideas of justice, common concepts of governments established by the will of free men, then you have got to make compromises. You have got to find that way in between certain conflicting local considerations that will serve the best good of all.

Now, that is what we are up against today. Our whole policy is based on this theory: no single free nation can live alone in the world. We have got to have friends. Those friends have got to be tied to you, in some form or another. But we have to have that unity in basic purposes that comes from a recognition of common interests. That is what we are up against.

Now, not being a particularly patient man, I share the irritations and the sense of frustration that comes to everybody who, working along in what he believes to be a decent purpose, finds himself balked by what he thinks is sometimes the ignorance, or the errors of someone who is otherwise his friend.

I understand those things, but I'll tell you: only patience, only determination, only optimism, and only a very deep faith can carry America forward.

Here at home we have our differences on these opinions because we are 160 million people. But I earnestly believe we cannot desert the great purpose for which we are working.

I apologize for the length of my answer, but I think that the subject deserves that much explanation.

Q. David P. Sentner, Hearst Newspapers: Mr. President, would you care to comment on whether the United States should take every possible step to prevent the entry of Communist China into the United Nations?

THE PRESIDENT. Well, as of this moment, I say this: there has never been proposed to me, seriously, by anybody in Government, that we should allow them in the United Nations. I assume that you mean under the conditions and the circumstances of the world as they now exist, in what we call Red Communist China, believing as we do it is subservient to Moscow, whether it should be in it. I believe it should not.

Q. Roscoe Drummond, Christian Science Monitor: Mr. President, on the same question, do you think that the United States should serve advance notice that if the United Nations should include Red China, that we would withdraw financial support from the United Nations?

THE PRESIDENT. Mr. Drummond, I really don't like answering questions, particularly hypothetical questions, before they arise. No one ever knows exactly the circumstances of proposals. You people used to ask me whether I would ever accept a nomination under such and such and such conditions, and I did not believe those conditions were going to arise. Now, right this moment, I don't believe the condition is going to arise on the question which you talk about.

Q. Mr. Drummond: I would like to say that I didn't think it was a theoretical question, because a Senate appropriations committee yesterday approved such an action.

THE PRESIDENT. Well, I haven't read the papers this morning, I guess, as thoroughly as I should have. Then it is not theoretical, no, because it is at least obvious that someone in a responsible position is thinking in that direction.

I would say this: they propose a very, very drastic sort of cure for something which I would consider a very grave error—now make no mistake there. But I don't know whether I could go along with that answer. I hope you would give me time to think that one over. That is getting pretty drastic, I think.

Q. Robert J. Donovan, New York Herald Tribune: Some commentators—very sympathetic commentators—have taken the opinion that you are confronted with a strong tide of isolationism in this country. Do you feel that, sir? Do you believe that to be the case?

THE PRESIDENT. I don't know how much weight a man in my position should give to the sentiments expressed in the vast amount of mail that we get. Our mail, incidentally, I think has been averaging from three to five times above world's records! It is quite heavy. There is nothing in that mail that would indicate there is any growth of isolationism. I should say, to the contrary; the mass of opinion that I obtain is that our people have come to a very clear realization that there is no safety for any free country alone, that we must have friends.

As I say, I never like to challenge the motives of anybody, because I myself can well understand almost the resentment, the anger that comes at times, when we are trying to do right and we get literally slapped in the face. But I believe that this is something that the world position of America has brought to us as one of the things we must solve—the kind of leadership that lessens these bitter occurrences, and brings forward each day, by a little bit, greater assurance of peace and security.

Q. Marvin L. Arrowsmith, Associated Press: Mr. President, both Prime Minister Churchill and Rene Mayer, before his government fell, have said that they look for the forthcoming Bermuda conference to lead to a Big Four conference, with Russia included. Do you share that objective?

THE PRESIDENT. Not in those terms. I believe that a meeting among the three powers of which we are speaking is important just for itself.

Again, I hope you will allow me to refer to my past experience. When I was in charge of SHAEF, I constantly urged frequent meetings among the commanders on the military side, and among the political leaders and their representatives on the other side, simply for the good that flows out of these contacts through developing understanding.

Let me point out that our Constitution does not require Congress to meet only when there is an emergency to declare, or some other terrible problem is facing the United States; they meet to consult over the business of the United States—the people of the

United States. Now, I don't mean to say these bodies of which we are speaking in the international field are governing bodies in the sense that the Congress is a governing body. But if you are going to get understandings among people, promote the feeling of friendliness and create the atmosphere in which they can work effectively, then occasionally you ought to meet—and, I think, at least very occasionally, among the very highest officials of those governments.

So I feel this: the meeting would be beneficial in itself. If it leads to a meeting of the four, or a later meeting, it would be because of some development that would seem to justify it. But I don't think that it is necessarily going to lead to such a meeting.

Q. Richard L. Wilson, Cowles Publications: As I read Senator Taft's speech, he had refined down the general question on international cooperation to about this: that if the present truce negotiations fail, that then we should go it alone—not prior to that time; but that if they fail, we should then go ahead and finish the war, alone if necessary. That is a little different——

THE PRESIDENT. Well now, I am not going to put words in Senator Taft's mouth, because I did not read the speech in that detail. But I do believe this: when he says go it alone, he must mean that we insist on following our own beliefs and convictions in the situation. He certainly doesn't mean that we just would throw everybody out.

Q. Mr. Wilson: No, sir. But after the truce negotiations have failed, if I read his speech correctly—in fact, that is what he said exactly, that if the truce negotiations break down, then we should go it alone.

THE PRESIDENT. Well, but suppose these negotiations break down because of something that the Chinese won't agree to? Isn't that it?

Q. Mr. Wilson: Yes, sir, but they might also be something that the United States would not advocate, were it not for the position of Great Britain.

THE PRESIDENT. There is something confusing here. I don't

believe I had better try to answer it. I don't understand what could be meant by such a thing. Look—suppose all of us here are friends, and we are trying to get somebody out on the street to agree to something and he disagrees, does that mean we all suddenly here become enemies and break up? I don't understand that.

Q. Mr. Wilson: Would you permit me to read the whole paragraph?

THE PRESIDENT. Yes.

Q. Mr. Wilson: He said: "I believe we might as well forget the United Nations as far as the Korean war is concerned. I think we should do our best now to negotiate this truce, and if we fail, then let England and our other allies know that we are withdrawing from all further peace negotiations in Korea."

THE PRESIDENT. Well, from further peace negotiations; he doesn't say withdrawal from the allies and Britain. They might agree with you, that there is no further use to conduct peace negotiations.

Q. Mr. Wilson: That is correct.

THE PRESIDENT. As I say, there is some idea there that I am not grasping, and I don't think it is fair to ask me to try to comment on it when I don't.

Q. Anthony H. Leviero, New York Times: Mr. President, your opening statement on this question is a pretty important one at this time. I wonder if you would consider letting us quote you directly on it—your answer to Mr. Smith's question, opening statement on whether we go it alone or not?

THE PRESIDENT. I think you had better take the usual rule, because I don't know whether I used even grammatical language. [*Laughter*]

Q. Mr. Leviero: The grammar is incidental, we will be willing to forego that. [*Laughter*]

THE PRESIDENT. I will say this: I don't know what the practices are, but if you find something there that you think is worthy of quoting, you bring it to Mr. Hagerty. If he says, "Yes, that's what the General said," it's okay by me.   I don't care.[1]

Q. Edward F. Creagh, Associated Press: Sir, in your opening statement, you said something about if we go it alone in one place—I missed the last part of that—it's a rather important part.

THE PRESIDENT. I meant merely this: you can't pick and choose the places where you will have partners and friends, and then in other places in the world say, "We pay no attention to you here—we do as we please," when they think that their interests are also involved.   What I am trying to say is that this kind of thing—maybe I shouldn't liken it to a marriage, but let us say to a long-term partnership—you have got to take the ups and downs, you have got to go along with your associates.   You can't say, in North Africa we all agree, in South Africa we all go it alone. It just won't work.   This is an effort to produce a unity that, as I have said so many times, is based on appreciation of common values, common sense of values.

Now, you must remember that Woodrow Wilson once, in using very literary words in this regard, said that the highest form of efficiency is the spontaneous cooperation of a free people.

What we are really trying to do is, in a practical way, translate in the international world the thought that there is greater efficiency in real cooperation among people who are dedicated to fine ideals than there is in a forced unity, brought about by the power of arms.   Now that is really what we are trying to do. It is tough, and it isn't going to be easily accomplished.   It isn't going to be accomplished quickly; this is a long-term thing.

Q. William H. Lawrence, New York Times: Has your attention been directed to the effort by an official of the Rumanian Legation to subvert an American citizen by offering to trade his two children who were held hostage?

THE PRESIDENT. Actually, I have gotten no official report, but

---

[1] Mr. Smith's opening question and the President's reply were released for direct quotation later that day.

I did get the report from the papers, and I believe on a television thing I saw it.

So, I have no official thing on it.

Q. James B. Reston, New York Times: Mr. President, I wondered if you would clarify one point on the discussions on the truce talks in the Far East. There seems to be an assumption in what you have said this morning, that somehow the allies were forcing us to do something in the truce negotiations out there other than what we wanted them to?

THE PRESIDENT. You said I said that?

Q. Mr. Reston: No, sir, but there seems to be in the discussions some assumption that they are forcing us, or asking us to do something——

THE PRESIDENT. There have been, of course, differences of opinion on procedures, one person or one government believing so and so would be persuasive, another believing such and such would best serve our interests. But on the basic factor that there shall be no forced repatriation of prisoners, I have seen no wavering anywhere. As a matter of fact, I think publicly the governments in Europe and elsewhere have supported our position.

There have been, of course, within our own government, some people who want to be much tougher, lay down particularly specific rules and procedures. But the basic thing has been, as explained in my talk of April 16—I tried to do it just as clearly as I could—there has never been any wavering on the idea of no forced repatriation. None that I know of.

Q. Carleton Kent, Chicago Sun-Times: Mr. President, are you satisfied with the explanation that the security people in the State Department have given for their failure to clear Mrs. Mildred McAfee Horton for that United Nations job?

THE PRESIDENT. I really have very little more to say about it than I see Under Secretary Smith has said, where he admitted there was some apparently unwarranted delay in the State Department, and he believed that he had cleared it up for the future.

But I must say this: you people have probably read in the papers some of the impatience that extremists feel because of what they call the slow way in which we are changing the face of government.   But when you change a vast organism, such as the Federal Government has come to be, the job of conducting the necessary investigations is stupendous.   There is one place—the FBI—where is done all of a certain kind of this work.   Their work is detailed, it is laborious, and it really takes time.   So I think that the explanation given has a very great degree of logic in it, although I understand that General Smith also said certain delays occurred within the State Department itself.   It is a terrific job.

Q. Raymond P. Brandt, St. Louis Post-Dispatch: Mr. President, there has been some confusion as to whether the Joint Chiefs of Staff approved the Defense budget cuts, both in appropriations and expenditures?

THE PRESIDENT. Well, I must say that, of course, much as my heart and background is tied up in that work, you must know that I can't be present at every meeting.   I would assume that not always do you get 100 percent agreement on every proposal made.   But I also assume that these men, working together—these Joint Chiefs of Staff and their civilian superiors—come out with what they believe to be the best overall solution they can get to a problem.

You know, if there was only one side to these problems, they wouldn't be problems; you put down the equal sign in a difficult equation only when there are two sides.   So the answers are rarely those that meet the convictions and opinions of very honest men but often men that are extremists or attach greater value to particular factors than the group does.

What I am assured is that the group, as a whole, believes these are the best answers that we can derive at this particular moment, as they see the problem.   And that is the best that I can hope for.

Q. Mr. Brandt: There is indication that the Joint Chiefs individually have said they made recommendations which they thought were necessary for the security of the country, and that those recommendations were cut down.

THE PRESIDENT. I have no doubt about that. I will tell you this: all my life I did it, starting as a major. I used to have to prepare the reports that went before the Appropriations Committee. All my life I have pointed out where there were great dangers—and I believe there were great dangers. No one can assume that any amount of actual military strength is a guarantee against risk; there is no such thing.

Q. Mr. Brandt: Who makes the final decision? You, or——

THE PRESIDENT. They make them. If it is not made in the Defense Department, and they consider a question that is of such broad policy, basic policy, then it comes to me and I make it.

Q. Mr. Brandt: Did you make this one, sir?

THE PRESIDENT. I think that is all I will say about that particular question.

Q. Martin S. Hayden, Detroit News: Mr. President, there seems to be a desire among some of the Republican Members of the Senate to have you give your personal assurance, from your military experience, that the cuts in the Air Force will not jeopardize our defense. Would you be willing to do that, sir?

THE PRESIDENT. I would certainly do this: I would say that, as of this moment and as I see the situation now, they do not jeopardize it beyond that point that I have often spoken to this group, I am sure, about—the reasonable posture of defense.

I do not say that we have got everything ready as I demanded it would be ready before I went across the Channel in 1944. We are not in the same kind of a situation. We picked the day. We knew when we wanted our maximum force. We knew the buildup we wanted. We knew exactly what we were up against, within a matter of a division or two. We knew the exact force. We knew exactly what the enemy's reactions would be.

We don't know those things. We have got to estimate and to live with estimates. I want to point out to you ladies and gentlemen, again and again, you are dealing in equations now where every single factor is an unknown—all of it. Now you have to take those unknowns and through your experience, through the best things you can get together, get reasonable answers, do the best you can.

Now, my own deep conviction is that what we are now doing is going to give us the greatest ultimate and bearable strength over the years that I see ahead, that we have got to maintain it.

I am, of course, as you know, dedicated to the idea that we will produce better conditions in the world, and these burdens can finally be lightened. For the moment, though, we are preparing on the basis of going up to whatever the circumstances of the moment dictate to be a reasonable posture, and to maintain it.

Q. Chalmers M. Roberts, Washington Post: One of the points of difference between ourselves and our allies, and of considerable discussion in Congress, has been the question of East-West trade, both in Europe and in the Far East. There has been a considerable dispute as to what actually is the administration's point of view, the Defense and State Departments apparently being in conflict. Would you give us your concept?

THE PRESIDENT. Well, I don't think they are in very deep conflict, as I understand the presentations they have made to me.

Moreover, I should say that there is no permanent philosophy of action or course of action that has been dictated, so far. But I do know this: there have been pointed out, on both sides of the fence, instances over the past 2 or 3 years where the Communists have been helped by certain kinds of trade. But it has been equally pointed out that we would be foolish just to say that we can win the position we are seeking in the world by just refusing to trade with everybody except people that we happen to like at the moment. All sorts of factors enter into this business of trade, one of them being that it is a great influence in the hands of the diplomat. If you make it completely impossible for a country you are trying to win over, to trade with you, it has got to go somewhere else. And if it goes completely into the arms of someone hostile to you and to your form of life, then you haven't been very intelligent.

Now, I have heard these things discussed by both sides. My own opinion, which I don't expect to express here this morning—it is a personal one—I am perfectly clear in what I think we should do, but I do hope that all my own associates and advisers come to a somewhat similar opinion on their own.

Q. Mrs. May Craig, Portland (Maine) papers: Mr. President, if I may go back to Mr. Reston's question, whether we are being pushed by our allies into terms in Korea of which we do not fully approve, do you think we should accept an agreement which is opposed by the South Korean Government?

THE PRESIDENT. I would say this: we certainly should never adopt a solution that at least our own conscience tells us is unfair to South Korea. I do believe this, though: these things we are talking about, these great objectives, are not attained in one great sudden agreement that everybody sits down and signs and then the world is lovely; you have to go ahead step by step. I believe that if we could, at this moment, get an agreement on the order of the kind that they are now seeking—as you know, it is an executive session; the only thing I have said about these things is the great principle of nonrepatriation we stick to—I believe that then we are in a better position to go ahead with what we think is just in Korea than we are now.

Q. Alice A. Dunnigan, Associated Negro Press: I wondered when we can expect a statement on the Contract Compliance Committee?

THE PRESIDENT. I couldn't hear you.

Q. Mrs. Dunnigan: I said that—could you give us any idea when we might expect the statement on the Contract Compliance Committee?

THE PRESIDENT. They have not reported to me yet; but I will have Mr. Hagerty call them up and give you a report on it.

Q. Merriman Smith, United Press: Mr. President, how is the

delay in forming a new French government affecting the timing on the Bermuda conference? Is there a possibility of delay?

THE PRESIDENT. I suppose it could be delayed. Very naturally, if I would meet there on the basis I am talking about, to promote friendship and a better atmosphere, well, I should like these three friends, that went through so much together in World War II, all there.

Q. Mr. Smith: Would you tell us, please, sir, how you arranged the meeting with Mr. Churchill; and secondly, whether you intend to take to Bermuda representatives of the Congress?

THE PRESIDENT. Ladies and gentlemen, the thing has really gone very little further than I have explained to you this morning. Now, I have been very anxious that it be a small and not a great, full-dress, so-called, meeting. I have even suggested that we could meet without an agenda, and I think that was a little, possibly, surprising to some.

But what I would want to do is to sit down, with the kind of question we have been talking over here this morning, and actually explore someone's mind and to be frank with him.

Now I did suggest when this thing first came up, let us keep our delegations small—very small. I don't know, as a matter of fact, what the accommodations are in Bermuda. Originally, I might tell you, I suggested going into one of our northeastern sections, because in talking to the Prime Minister I felt that I ought to be able to say there is a place we could meet, mutually convenient. He suggested Bermuda; and I was glad, of course, to accept. So I don't even know what the accommodations are.

Now, as far as taking anyone along that would like to know what is going on day by day, I would be delighted. Actually, whether we can do it until we have talked to the others and what they are going to do, if we are thinking of having them right in meetings, where these two other men and I are talking, then I don't know because I haven't explored that far.

Q. Sarah McClendon, Texas papers: Mr. President, there seems to be some contradiction between Mr. Smith's first question on the Taft speech and your answer, and Mr. Wilson's question and his clarification of the speech; you said, you had not read it in detail.

THE PRESIDENT. That's right.

Q. Mrs. McClendon: Would it be asking too much, sir, since there is such a confusion over this and it is so important, would it be asking too much if you were to read it in detail today, and give us a statement of your views?

THE PRESIDENT. No. Sorry—I won't—I can't do that. Besides, to tell you the truth—[*laughing*]—if I had to read all the speeches that are in the papers in detail, I would be pretty badly off.

Now, I have admitted Senator Taft's right to his own convictions and opinions. What I have done is explained my attitude toward this whole business, my philosophy, and what I am going to attempt, to lead this Government and these people in the direction I am going to lead them. I believe in it with all my heart, and I don't believe that discouragement and frustration, and even resentment, have a right to turn us from a course which we believe to be just and good. Now that is my comment on it.

Q. Alan S. Emory, Watertown (N.Y.) Times: Sir, a couple of weeks ago, you said in response to a question, I believe, that you considered the Niagara River power redevelopment primarily a matter of New York State responsibility. Since that time, there has been a little confusion on the Hill as to what exactly you meant by New York State responsibility. Did that mean New York State administration's wishes?

THE PRESIDENT. The New York what?

Q. Mr. Emory: Did you mean by New York State responsibility, sir, the desire of the New York State administration?

THE PRESIDENT. I don't know exactly what their desires are. I have studied this thing only as it was presented to me. New York State has never presented anything to me.

Merriman Smith, United Press: Thank you, Mr. President.

NOTE: President Eisenhower's tenth news conference was held in the Executive Office Building at 10:30 a.m. on Thursday, May 28, 1953.

89   ¶ Special Message to the Congress on the
Organization of the Executive Branch for the
Conduct of Foreign Affairs.   *June* 1, 1953

To the Congress of the United States:

The history of recent decades has brought a profound and
irrevocable change in the role of our Nation in world affairs.
We have assumed a position of leadership among the free nations
of the world in our united quest of a just and lasting peace.   No
national ambition, no selfish desire, but the sheer force of circumstance—the compelling need of freedom's cause—has
brought us to this position and this responsibility.

To meet this responsibility, our Nation today is dedicated to
international action in concert with other nations—through the
United Nations and in regional arrangements with other nations
for collective security, for economic and social cooperation, designed to foster a community of world law.   We have come to
know that national security entails mutual security with other
free nations.   And we have come to know that their freedom, in
turn, depends heavily upon our strength and the wisdom with
which we use it.

To meet the challenge of this responsibility effectively—to convert earnest intent into constructive fact—we must achieve the
most efficient and cohesive possible organization for the conduct
of our foreign affairs.   Slackness, confusion, blurred authority
and clouded responsibility—any of these can defeat the noblest
purposes of any foreign policy.

Our organization for the conduct of foreign affairs has been
built upon a patchwork of statutes which needs careful restudy
as a basis for new legislation.   The development of new legislation will take time.   By early next year we will be prepared, with
appropriate consultation with the Congress, to recommend such
legislation.   In the meantime we must improve the present
arrangements within the framework of existing legislation.

To date, the organization of the executive branch for foreign affairs has been deficient in two major respects. First: there has been no clear assignment of central responsibility for foreign policy below the President. Second: a number of programs which implement our foreign policy have been scattered within the executive branch rather than being grouped together for the most efficient and economical administration.

We must correct these deficiencies. The measures proposed are directed toward that objective. The consideration of new legislation will open up further reorganization possibilities.

First. We are taking the necessary steps to confirm the historic responsibility of the Department of State as the agency responsible under the President for the development and control of foreign policy and all relations with foreign governments. Not only must the Department of State be given clear authority to provide guidance on our foreign policies to all other agencies of the Federal Government; it is equally important that each Chief of Diplomatic Mission in each foreign country provide effective coordination of, and foreign policy direction with respect to, all United States Government activities in the country.

Second. We must bring together in a single organization foreign assistance and related economic operations now dispersed among several agencies of the executive branch.

Third. We must provide a new, separate organization for the international information programs now administered by the Department of State and the Mutual Security Agency.

To achieve the organization I have outlined requires a series of related actions. Accordingly, I am transmitting to the Congress today, by the required statutory message in each instance, Reorganization Plans Nos. 7 and 8 of 1953, under the Reorganization Act of 1949, as amended. Those plans take many of the necessary steps. I am making other changes by executive order. I am, in addition, setting forth in a letter addressed to department and agency heads, the arrangements which will govern relationships among executive branch officials in the conduct of our international responsibilities.

Reorganization Plan No. 7 has as its major purpose the realignment of our foreign assistance and related economic operations. It establishes a new Foreign Operations Administration and abolishes the present Mutual Security Agency and certain offices. It centers in the head of the new Administration the functions vested in the Mutual Security Agency and the Director for Mutual Security, including the Director's functions under the Mutual Defense Assistance Control Act.

To centralize further the foreign assistance and related economic responsibilities in the head of the new Foreign Operations Administration, I am taking certain administrative actions. These include the transfer from the Secretary of State to the Director of the Foreign Operations Administration four responsibilities: the administration of the Act for International Development; assistance to private foreign relief organizations; programs for aiding persons who have escaped from Communist areas; and operating functions with respect to United States participation in the United Nations Technical Assistance Program, the United Nations International Children's Emergency Fund, the United Nations Korean Reconstruction Agency, and the Intergovernmental Committee for European Migration. These administrative actions also include the delegation by the President to the Director of the Foreign Operations Administration of appropriate responsibilities respecting the Palestine refugee program.

The new Foreign Operations Administration will have as its direct responsibility two major related assistance programs which previously have been separately administered. Both the Technical Cooperation Administration in the Department of State and the Mutual Security Agency have administered technical assistance programs. At the very least, this has meant some duplication in the performance of certain common functions, including the recruitment of technicians and the formulation of general policies. It has made difficult the achievement of a balanced programming of technical assistance on a world-wide basis.

The transfer of the Technical Cooperation Administration is not intended to modify the character of the United States technical cooperation program as a long-range effort to cooperate with the governments and peoples of other countries in developing their economies and raising their standards of living. The technical cooperation program will be carried out solely in furtherance of the purposes of the Act for International Development. The transfer of the functions vested in the President by the Act for International Development includes the programs under that act administered by the Institute of Inter-American Affairs.

The new Director of the Foreign Operations Administration will have the same responsibilities as his predecessor for continuous supervision, general direction and coordination of all foreign assistance programs, including the military assistance responsibilities vested in the Secretary of Defense.

Reorganization Plan No. 7 of 1953 provides for abolishing the offices of Special Representative in Europe and Deputy Special Representative in Europe, as authorized by section 504 of the Mutual Security Act of 1951, as amended. I am establishing a new United States mission to the North Atlantic Treaty Organization and European regional organizations. The chief of the mission will report to and receive instructions from the Secretary of State. The mission will include representatives of the Secretary of Defense, the Secretary of the Treasury and the Director of the Foreign Operations Administration.

Reorganization Plan No. 8 establishes a new agency—the United States Information Agency—for the conduct of our information programs. These include, with certain limited exceptions, four programs: the information activities now administered by the International Information Administration of the Department of State; the information programs financed in connection with government in occupied areas; the information program of the Mutual Security Agency; and the Technical Cooperation

56616—60——25

Administration information program. The first three of these programs would be shifted by Reorganization Plan No. 8, while the last would be reassigned by executive order.

Various arrangements have been provided in the past for the coordination of these programs, but the placing of them in a single agency seems the one sound way to provide real unity and greater efficiency. This action, moreover, brings under single management all the funds to be expended on these foreign information activities.

These information activities must, of course, be subject to special guidance and control in view of their direct relation to the conduct of foreign affairs and national security policy. Therefore, Reorganization Plan No. 8 specifies that the Secretary of State shall provide to the Director of the new agency on a current basis full guidance concerning the foreign policy of the United States. The plan also specifies, and I have amplified this in my letter to the department and agency heads, that the Secretary of State shall control the content of a program setting forth official United States' positions for use abroad. The program will be clearly identified as such by an exclusive descriptive label. I have likewise instructed that the new United States Information Agency shall report to the President through the National Security Council or as the President may otherwise direct.

In administering the information program in the Department of State, the Secretary of State has relied on various general statutes authorizing and controlling administrative matters. To insure that adequate authority may be vested in the new Director, Reorganization Plan No. 8 provides that he may, in carrying out his functions, exercise such administrative authorities of the Secretary of State and of certain other officers as the President may specify.

This is necessary because the legislation dealing with the information programs does not contain administrative provisions. For example: the Director of the new United States Information

Agency will need personnel authority. I, therefore, plan to authorize an independent personnel system for this agency's foreign operations under authority of the last subsection of section 2 of Plan No. 8. This system will be based on the provisions of the Foreign Service Act of 1946. It will give authority to the Director to appoint personnel and take such other personnel actions as are necessary, thereby relieving the Secretary of State of responsibility with respect to personnel actions. Such personnel would receive compensation, allowances, and other benefits applicable to Foreign Service Reserve, Staff, and alien personnel. It is not planned to extend to the new agency any authority with respect to the appointment of Foreign Service Officers.

While these arrangements will enable the new agency to function with reasonable effectiveness from the outset, I do not consider them permanently suitable. There is need for a critical analysis of the various systems of employment and compensation for United States Government overseas civilian personnel. I am directing that this entire matter be studied with a view toward recommending appropriate legislation.

While divesting the Department of State of the foreign information programs, the reorganization plan does not transfer the responsibility of that Department for the educational exchange programs authorized by various acts of the Congress. Close coordination of our information and educational exchange programs will, of course, be effected by the Secretary of State and the Director of the United States Information Agency.

The Constitution of the United States places the duty upon the President for the conduct of our foreign affairs. Reorganization Plans Nos. 7 and 8 and the related Presidential actions are designed to protect and strengthen the role of the Secretary of State as the principal officer, under the President, in the field of foreign affairs. In the last analysis, however, the ability of the Secretary of State to discharge his responsibilities depends upon the backing accorded to him by the President, including consultation with the Secretary on the appointment and maintenance in office of the directors created by these reorganization plans. I shall continue to exercise my powers of appointment so that these offices are occupied only by men who support and enjoy the full confidence of the Secretary of State.

I urge the Congress to give its full support to these reorganizations.

Dwight D. Eisenhower

NOTE: This message was released together with the messages transmitting Reorganization Plans 7 and 8 (Items 90 and 91, below), the text of Executive Order 10458 "Providing for the Administration of Certain Foreign Aid Programs and Related Activities" (3 CFR, 1949–1953 Comp., p. 944), and a memorandum on the organization of the Government for the conduct of foreign affairs (Item 92).

90 ¶ Special Message to the Congress Transmitting Reorganization Plan 7 of 1953 Relating to the Establishment of the Foreign Operations Administration. *June 1, 1953*

To the Congress of the United States:

I transmit herewith Reorganization Plan No. 7 of 1953, prepared in accordance with the Reorganization Act of 1949, as amended, and providing for the reorganization of various foreign aid functions and agencies. My reasons for proposing the plan are stated in another message transmitted to the Congress today.

After investigation, I have found and hereby declare that each reorganization included in Reorganization Plan No. 7 of 1953 is necessary to accomplish one or more of the purposes set forth in section 2(a) of the Reorganization Act of 1949, as amended. I have also found and hereby declare that it is necessary to include in the accompanying reorganization plan, by reason of reorganizations made thereby, provisions for the appointment and compensation of officers specified in section 1 of the plan. The rates of compensation fixed for these officers are, respectively, those which I have found to prevail in respect of comparable officers in the executive branch of the Government.

The statutory authority for the exercise of the functions abolished by section 8(a)(5) of the reorganization plan is section 413(a) of the Act for International Development, as amended. The vesting of the functions of planning, implementing, and managing the programs authorized by that Act, as amended, in an officer other than the President is incongruous with the pattern of the Act as a whole, whereby other functions are vested in the President, with power of delegation. In the interest of having the most flexible arrangements for the administration of the Act, the functions in question could be either abolished or transferred to the President. I have concluded that they overlap the authority of the President under the Act generally, are thus dispensable, and should be abolished.

I expect that the improved organizational arrangement provided for in Reorganization Plan No. 7 of 1953 will lead to substantial economies and significantly improved effectiveness of administration. It is not practicable, however, to itemize at this time the reductions in expenditures which will probably be brought about by the taking effect of the reorganizations included in the reorganization plan.

DWIGHT D. EISENHOWER

NOTE: Reorganization Plan 7 of 1953 is published in the U.S. Statutes at Large (67 Stat. 639) and in the 1949–1953 Compilation of title 3 of the Code of Federal Regulations (p. 1028). It became effective on August 1, 1953.

91 ¶ Special Message to the Congress Transmitting Reorganization Plan 8 of 1953 Relating to the Establishment of the U.S. Information Agency. *June 1, 1953*

To the Congress of the United States:

I transmit herewith Reorganization Plan No. 8 of 1953, prepared in accordance with the Reorganization Act of 1949, as amended, and providing for the reorganization of foreign information functions. My reasons for proposing this plan are stated in another message transmitted to the Congress today.

After investigation, I have found and hereby declare that each reorganization included in Reorganization Plan No. 8 of 1953 is necessary to accomplish one or more of the purposes set forth in section 2(a) of the Reorganization Act of 1949, as amended. I have also found and hereby declare that it is necessary to include in the accompanying reorganization plan, by reason of reorganizations made thereby, provisions for the appointment and compensation of officers specified in section 1 of the plan. The rates of compensation fixed for these officers are, respectively, those which I have found to prevail in respect of comparable officers in the executive branch of the Government.

I expect that the improved organizational arrangement provided for in Reorganization Plan No. 8 of 1953 will lead to substantial economies and significantly improved effectiveness of administration. It is not practicable, however, to itemize at this time the reductions in expenditures which will probably be brought about by the taking effect of the reorganizations included in the reorganization plan.

DWIGHT D. EISENHOWER

NOTE: Reorganization Plan 8 of 1953 is published in the U.S. Statutes at Large (67 Stat. 642) and in the 1949–1953 Compilation of title 3 of the Code of Federal Regulations (p. 1030). It became effective on August 1, 1953.

92 ¶ Memorandum on the Organization of the Executive Branch for the Conduct of Foreign Affairs. *June 1, 1953*

To: *The Heads of All Executive Departments*
   The Director for Mutual Security

I have today transmitted two reorganization plans to the Congress and taken other actions by Executive order providing for a significant reorganization of the executive branch for the conduct of foreign affairs. This letter further defines relationships which will govern executive branch officials in the conduct of our international responsibilities.

The over-all foreign affairs reorganization which I desire to achieve is designed to emphasize the primary position of the Secretary of State within the executive branch in matters of foreign policy. I personally wish to emphasize that I shall regard the Secretary of State as the Cabinet officer responsible for advising and assisting me in the formulation and control of foreign policy. It will be my practice to employ the Secretary of State as my channel of authority within the executive branch on foreign policy. Other officials of the executive branch will work with and through the Secretary of State on matters of foreign policy. I shall also look to the Secretary of Defense as the Cabinet officer responsible, within the framework of foreign policy, for advising and assisting me in the formulation and control of military policy. Similarly, the Secretary of the Treasury, within the framework of foreign policy, shall continue to be the Cabinet officer responsible for advising and assisting me in the formulation and control of monetary and financial policy.

The Secretary of State, the Secretary of Defense, and the Secretary of the Treasury, as appropriate, shall review plans and policies relative to military and economic assistance programs, foreign information programs, and legislative proposals of the Foreign Operations Administration and the United States In-

351

formation Agency, to assure that in their conception and execution, such plans, policies and proposals are consistent with and further the attainment of foreign policy, military policy and financial and monetary policy objectives. The Director of the Foreign Operations Administration and the Director of the United States Information Agency will assure the concurrence or participation of the appropriate Secretary before taking up with me any policy matters of concern to that Secretary.

The heads of these new agencies should furnish information to the Secretaries of State, Defense, and Treasury in such manner and form as may be agreed between the head of the agency and the Secretary concerned to insure that the program of the agencies and the implementation of such programs conform with foreign policy, military policy, and financial and monetary policy objectives.

To the maximum feasible extent consistent with efficiency and economy, the internal organization of the new agencies should be designed to permit ready coordination with subordinate levels of the Department of State. This would suggest parallel areas of responsibility for constituent units of the State Department and of the two new operating agencies wherever feasible. The two operating agencies should also enter into appropriate arrangements to insure the necessary coordination with each other. Overseas regional staffs should ordinarily be established for the operating agencies only where there is a regional organization or multi-lateral activity of sufficient importance to warrant the establishment of a diplomatic mission. The Chief of the United States diplomatic mission in each foreign country must provide effective coordination of, and foreign policy direction with respect to, all United States Government activities in the country. To the maximum practicable extent, there should be integrated supervision of personnel performing related economic or information activities in each foreign country. Appointments of all chief representatives abroad of the two new agencies, and of the chiefs of military assistance advisory groups abroad, should be cleared with the Secretary of State.

The Director of the Foreign Operations Administration should take full advantage of the advice and assistance available in other agencies. He should coordinate his operations with related operations in other agencies. At the same time, I expect the Director of the Foreign Operations Administration to maintain full control and direction over all foreign economic and technical assistance programs rather than turn this responsibility over to other agencies. We must have an integrated direction of technical assistance and other foreign assistance activities.

Since I am assigning to the Mutual Security Agency responsibility for paying ocean freight on voluntary relief shipments, I wish to make a corresponding change respecting the Advisory Committee on Voluntary Foreign Aid. This Committee, which was created pursuant to the President's letter to the Secretary of State, dated May 14, 1946, operates under the guidance of the Department of State, and coordinates public and private programs for foreign relief. The Committee should hereafter operate under the guidance of the Director for Mutual Security or the Director of the Foreign Operations Administration, as the case may be, and the State Department staff now assisting the Committee should be transferred to the Mutual Security Agency and thereafter to the Foreign Operations Administration.

The reorganization plan which creates the United States Information Agency also assigns exclusive responsibility to the Secretary of State for the control of the content of a program designed to assure accurate statements of United States official positions on important issues and current developments. It is my desire that this program be so administered as to keep these official United States positions before the governments and peoples of other countries. No material which is not a statement of official United States views, regardless of its nature, or origin, or the medium used for its dissemination, should be identified by the exclusive label which is provided.

The United States Information Agency will be the normal outlet for this program, but the Secretary of State may use other channels for disseminating this program abroad when in his judgment the use of such channels is required. The Director of the United States Information Agency should give full cooperation in providing the services and facilities necessary for the preparation, translation, transmission, and distribution of materials for this program.

The Director of the United States Information Agency shall report to and receive instructions from me through the National Security Council or as I may otherwise direct. I am directing that the necessary changes be made in existing arrangements for Government-wide coordination of foreign information activities to enable the Director of the United States Information Agency to serve as Chairman of the Psychological Operations Coordinating Committee.

The Secretary of State has an obligation to develop means of providing foreign policy guidance fully and promptly. The Foreign Operations Administration and the United States Information Agency must seek such guidance and establish appropriate means of assuring that its programs at all times conform to such foreign policy guidance.

The instructions in this letter supplement the actions which I have taken by Executive order and the reorganization plans. They will in turn be supplemented as necessary by other orders and by interagency arrangements. I am confident that the members of the executive branch, under the clear assignments of responsibility which I have provided, will continue to work together even more effectively as a team. Such teamwork is essential to our success in the conduct of foreign affairs and to the achievement thereby of a greater measure of peace, well-being, and freedom throughout the world.

Dwight D. Eisenhower

93 ¶ Special Message to the Congress Transmitting Reorganization Plan 9 of 1953 Concerning the Council of Economic Advisers. *June* 1, 1953

To the Congress of the United States:

I transmit herewith Reorganization Plan No. 9 of 1953, prepared in accordance with the Reorganization Act of 1949, as amended, and providing reorganizations in the Council of Economic Advisers in the Executive Office of the President.

The legislative history of the Employment Act of 1946 makes it clear that it is the determination of the Congress to help develop a strong economy in the United States. A strong economy is necessary to preserve the peace, to build our defenses and those of the free world, to raise the living standards of our people, and to stimulate trade and industry in friendly countries throughout the world.

A strong economy means a free economy—with full opportunities for the exercise of initiative and enterprise on the part of all individuals.

It means a stable economy—so that satisfying jobs are as numerous as the men and women seeking work, and the production of goods is abundant to meet our needs.

It means an expanding economy—in which workers, managers, and farmers, using more and better tools, constantly increase the output of useful products and services and receive steadily rising incomes in a dollar of stable value.

It means a humane economy—to the end that the aged, infirm, and those suffering hardships receive every needed help.

The achievement and preservation of a strong economy—an economy that is progressive as well as competitive, an economy that remains free from the distortions of inflation and the ravages of depression, an economy that forms the solid foundation for the flourishing of our democratic social and political institutions—is everybody's job. Workers, businessmen, bankers, farmers, housewives—all have an important role to play. The Federal Government, too, shares in this vital task. For example, the duties of the President require that he be fully informed of major economic trends and activities in order to recommend proper measures for the consideration of the Congress, and to take into account economic realities in seeing that the laws be faithfully executed.

It is well that the Congress has declared in the Employment Act of 1946 the continuing policy and responsibility of the Federal Government to coordinate and utilize all its plans, functions, and resources for the purpose of creating and maintaining, consistently with free competitive enterprise and the general welfare, employment opportunities for all. That act dedicates the Federal Government to the promotion of maximum employment, production, and purchasing power.

To assist in carrying out those purposes, the Congress provided for the establishment of the Council of Economic Advisers in the Executive Office of the President to make appropriate recommendations to the President and to assist in the preparation of his annual Economic Report to the Congress.

I believe in the basic principles of the Employment Act, and it is my purpose to take the appropriate actions to reinvigorate and make more effective the operations of the Council of Economic Advisers. Our needs for proper advice on economic matters are equaled only by our needs to have the very best advice and planning on matters of national security.

In taking these actions, I have the benefit of the study and work of the Economic Adviser to the President recently provided by the Congress. The Economic Adviser has reviewed the past operations of the Council of Economic Advisers and has recommended to me a series of actions aimed at making it more fully effective in performing its statutory duties.

Accordingly, I intend to appoint a full membership of three members to the Council of Economic Advisers and to recommend to the Congress that adequate funds be appropriated to operate the Council as a fully going unit capable of providing the kind of economic staff work required.

The accompanying reorganization plan provides changes which strengthen the internal administration of the Council and clarify its relationships with the President.

To achieve the first objective—strengthened internal administration—the reorganization plan will make the Chairman of the Council, rather than the whole Council, responsible for certain administrative functions of the Council. Because the Council is essentially an advisory body, these administrative functions relate principally to managing the staff employed to assist the Council. Placing the Chairman in a position to perform these functions will obtain the benefits of single management of the staff. To make possible such an arrangement, the accompanying reorganization plan transfers to the Chairman the functions vested in the Council of Economic Advisers by section 4(b) of the Employment Act, which relate to employing the staff and other necessary specialists and consultants to work for the Council.

To further the other objective—a clearer relationship with the President—the reorganization plan transfers to the Chairman the function of reporting to the President on the activities of the Council. This change will improve and simplify the relationship of the Council to the President and enable the President to deal with the Council more directly through the Chairman.

The increased responsibilities placed upon the Chairman by this plan would, in my judgment, make it appropriate for the Congress to take action to increase the compensation of the Chairman.

The reorganization plan provides for the elimination of the vice chairman of the Council of Economic Advisers, whose designation is provided for in the last sentence of section 4(a) of the Employment Act of 1946. The objective of this step is to place the members of the Council, other than the Chairman, in an equal status. I shall make provision for one of the members of the Council, other than the Chairman, to act as chairman of the Council on such occasions as necessity may arise therefor.

In order to make the work of the Council of Economic Advisers more effective at the top policy level of the executive branch, I am also asking the heads of several departments and agencies, or the representatives they may designate, to serve as an Advisory Board on Economic Growth and Stability, under the chairmanship of the Chairman of the Council of Economic Advisers. At all times, close liaison must be maintained by the Council with all departments and agencies, and with interdepartmental committees, especially the National Advisory Council on International Monetary and Financial Problems.

It is contemplated that the Advisory Board on Economic Growth and Stability, supported by the existing staffs of the various departments and agencies, will meet frequently, and through its Chairman will keep me closely informed about the state of the national economy and the various measures necessary to aid in maintaining a stable prosperity.

Because of the complexity of our economy and the variety of views regarding its problems, I shall expect the new Council of Economic Advisers to seek advice energetically, not only from the departments and agencies of the Federal Government, but also from representatives of industry, agriculture, labor, consumers, and other groups concerned with economic matters, from representatives of State and local governments, and from universities. I want the best economic thinking in the country to be canvassed by the Council. Through advisory groups, through the employment of expert consultants, and through informal relationships with informed citizens, the Council will make use of economic talent wherever it may be.

I deem it especially significant that the Congress has provided in the Employment Act for the Joint Committee on the Economic Report, composed of members of both Houses of the Congress, to study matters relating to the Economic Report and to make recommedations to the two Houses for legislation. I expect to impress upon the Council of Economic Advisers the importance which I attach to the fullest cooperation of the Council with the Joint Committee to assist the Joint Committee in its important tasks.

After investigation I have found and hereby declare that each reorganization included in the accompanying reorganization plan is necessary to accomplish one or more of the purposes set forth in section 2(a) of the Reorganization Act of 1949, as amended.

The taking effect of the reorganizations included in the accompanying reorganization plan is expected to result in a more effective performance of the statutory functions of the Council of Economic Advisers and to provide the President with better advice upon economic matters. It is impracticable to specify or itemize at this time any reduction of expenditures which it is probable will be brought about by the taking effect of this reorganization plan.

The reorganization plan will make the Federal Government better able to carry out its responsibilities to the American people to foster a strong, free, and prosperous economy so that we may all enjoy an ever-rising standard of living. I urge the Congress to permit the reorganization plan to become effective.

DWIGHT D. EISENHOWER

NOTE: Reorganization Plan 9 of 1953 is published in the U.S. Statutes at Large (67 Stat. 644) and in the 1949–1953 Compilation of title 3 of the Code of Federal Regulations (p. 1032). It became effective on August 1, 1953.

94   ¶ Special Message to the Congress
Transmitting Reorganization Plan 10 of 1953
Concerning Payments to Air Carriers.
June 1, 1953

To the Congress of the United States:

I transmit herewith Reorganization Plan No. 10 of 1953, prepared in accordance with the provisions of the Reorganization
Act of 1949, as amended.

The reorganization plan provides for the separate payment
of airline subsidies, which now are merged with payments for the
transportation of airmail.   The purposes of the plan are to place
responsibility for subsidy payment in the agency which determines
the subsidies and to enable the Congress and the President to
maintain effective review of the subsidy program.   The plan
accomplishes these objectives by transferring from the Postmaster
General to the Civil Aeronautics Board that portion of the present
airmail payment functions which relates to subsidy assistance.

The reorganization plan will not alter the basic national policy
of promoting the sound development of air transportation through
Federal aid.   Nor will the plan in itself change the aggregate
amount of revenue for which any airline is eligible.   The policy
of providing financial aid for airline development was adopted
in the Civil Aeronautics Act of 1938, and reflects the broad
national interest in securing a system of air transport services
adequate to the needs of defense, commerce, and the postal
service.   Federal aid provided under that act has contributed
greatly to the rapid development of commercial air transportation
during the past fifteen years.   Continued subsidy support will
be required for some time to enable certain segments of the
industry to achieve the full measure of growth required by the
public interest.

At present, airline subsidies are provided by means of mail

transportation rates established by the Civil Aeronautics Board and paid by the Post Office Department. In essence, the Civil Aeronautics Act provides that such mail rates may be set at a level sufficiently high to overcome deficits incurred by the airlines on their total operations, including passenger and freight traffic. Total mail payments by the Post Office Department thus include, not only a reasonable compensation for the service of transporting the mail, but also a subsidy element where required to support the general program of airline development. This method of furnishing subsidy restricts the opportunity for congressional and public review, and substantially inflates the reported cost of the postal service.

Under the reorganization plan, the Civil Aeronautics Board will continue to determine the over-all level of payments to be made to the airlines, and will do so in accordance with the existing policy standards of the Civil Aeronautics Act. However, the Post Office Department will pay only that portion which represents compensation for carrying the mail on the basis of fair and reasonable rates determined by the Board without regard to the need for Federal aid. The plan will transfer to the Board the responsibility for paying any amounts in excess of such compensation, this excess being the subsidy element of the aggregate Federal payment.

In the interest of prompt effectuation, the plan contains an interim provision which authorizes the Board to establish without prior notice or hearing the initial rates to be paid by the Post Office Department, subject however to the right of the Board or any affected party to initiate a proceeding at any time for a hearing and a determination of a new rate. The Board has already made studies estimating the subsidy element contained in airmail payments, and for some time has been setting forth in connection with its mail-rate decisions a breakdown between the subsidy and compensatory elements of the over-all rate. The plan will permit the Board to base the initial rates payable by the Post Office Department on the compensatory rates contained in these studies and decisions.

By providing for a complete and formal separation of subsidy from compensation for the transportation of mail, the reorganization plan will clearly fix the fiscal responsibility for the subsidy program in the appropriate agency. It will assure the Congress and the public of continuing information on the cost of this program. It will give the Congress an opportunity to review and take any appropriate action with respect to the level of subsidy aid in the course of the regular appropriation process. It will also result in a more accurate presentation of the cost of the postal service, by removing from the budget of the Post Office Department a nonpostal expenditure currently estimated at nearly $80 million a year.

The basic principle of airline subsidy separation was recommended in 1949 by the Commission on Organization of the Executive Branch of the Government. Legislation to accomplish separation has been under discussion for several years. Such legislation has generally gone beyond a simple transfer of the subsidy function, and has included provisions which would change existing substantive law. Some of these proposed substantive changes have been the subject of controversy, and have been responsible for the past delays in enacting legislation on this matter. The present reorganization plan provides an opportunity to accomplish immediately the important objective of transferring subsidy payment responsibility, within the framework of existing statutory policy. In view of the general agreement on the principle of subsidy separation, I trust that this plan will have widespread support.

At the same time, the immediate transfer of subsidy payment under this reorganization plan should not preclude the consideration by the Congress of legislation to effect refinements and modifications in the basic law in this field. One such change, for example, would be an amendment of the Civil Aeronautics Act to provide specifically that compensatory rates for mail transportation should be based upon the cost of rendering mail service, plus a fair return. I understand that the Civil Aeronautics Board has been following this general policy in those cases where it has established compensatory mail rates. The reorganization plan will not affect its right to continue applying such a policy in the future. However, I believe it would be appropriate to establish the cost principle as a matter of definite legislative policy.

After investigation, I have found and hereby declare that each reorganization included in the accompanying reorganization plan is necessary to accomplish one or more of the purposes set forth in section 2(a) of the Reorganization Act of 1949, as amended.

The reorganization plan, by providing a sounder basis for the administration and congressional review of the affected functions, should in the long run promote increased economy and effectiveness of the Federal expenditures concerned. It is not practicable, however, to itemize in advance of actual experience the reductions of expenditures to be brought about by the taking effect of the reorganizations included in the reorganization plan.

DWIGHT D. EISENHOWER

NOTE: Reorganization Plan 10 of 1953 is published in the U.S. Statutes at Large (67 Stat. 644) and in the 1949–1953 Compilation of title 3 of the Code of Federal Regulations (p. 1032). It became effective on October 1, 1953.

95 ¶ Television Report to the American People by the President and Members of the Cabinet. *June* 3, 1953

[Broadcast at 9:30 p.m. from the Conference Room at the White House]

THE PRESIDENT. Good evening, everybody.

This evening some of the Cabinet members have gathered here with me to discuss points of interest—points of interest to your Government and to you.

Now, of course, everybody's first interest is the family, its security and its happiness. Now the security and the happiness of
any family depends upon a number of things—the income, to see
that the family is well fed and well clothed; that your loved ones
are safe no matter where they may be; that the roof is not leaking,
and the children are getting educated and that fences on the farm
are mended. In short, what you are concerned about is that the
house is in good order.

Now, everybody helps to do that—everybody in the family.
The Government is no different. Everybody that's in the Government is here to help keep your governmental house in good
order, so that you may live the kind of life that you want in this
country.

Now, we are concerned, therefore, with the security of the Nation—externally and internally—its welfare. Now that security,
remember, is not just military. It involves the prosperity of our
farmers and the education of our children; it involves spending
not more than we take in—live within our means like a family
should.

It involves proper protection. Then when you have all of those
things you have the Government house in order.

Now, in previous talks I have told you something about this
job of protecting the national house from threats abroad—from
the threat of communism, what it costs to protect; how we get the
money; how we spend it—all of that sort of thing.

I'm going to refer to that no more except to say there is going
to be no new Munich and at the same time there is going to be no
risk of a general war because a modern war would be too horrible
to contemplate.

We are going to keep our temper; we are going to build our
strength. I am going over to Bermuda to meet with some of our
friends and talk over these things.

But remember in these vast problems that affect every one of
our lives, there is no thought that you can cut the knot, you must
untie it, slowly and laboriously.

Now, tonight, the group that has gathered here to talk with me about this keeping of your Government house in order are four Cabinet members.

The first one is heading the newest department of Government. It has to do with the welfare and the education and the health of our people. And so as you would imagine it is headed by a woman because that's the woman's job in the home. This is a lady from Texas—Mrs. Hobby.

Next, we have a man whose job it is to keep the finances straightened out—and of course that's a real job. We have for that George Humphrey of Ohio.

Now the next thing we have is a farm problem—and for the Secretary of Agriculture we have a farmer. He is Ezra Benson of Utah.

Finally, we have here this evening to discuss with you some of our problems of internal security, keeping the internal house secure against the boring of subversives and that sort of thing—the head of the Justice Department, the Attorney General, Herbert Brownell. He is a Nebraska-born, New York lawyer. And that ought to make a good combination for that particular job.

Now, in order that we discuss what we know you are interested in, I will show you how we get our ideas.

Over here, in this corner, you see a basket of mail. This is a portion of one day's mail at the White House. We have been averaging over 3,000 letters a day in an average week—heavy weeks it's more. Now from this whole mass, I am going to read to you just parts of one letter, to show you what one citizen in our country is thinking about, and it's sort of a challenging letter.

"Dear Mr. President," this lady from Pawtucket, R.I., writes, "I am writing you to ask some questions that have me deeply worried. I am a housewife with four children, and though I don't know much about the budget you and your people have to worry about, I do know something about running my own family budget. That is why I have so many questions, when I read about all the money you have to spend for guns and planes, and all the problems that you must have when you try to balance our country's budget.

"The sums are so huge I really find it almost impossible to grasp them." And I might tell the lady, so do I. "I wonder how you even know where to begin. Won't you please explain to me, in words I can understand, just how you are going to have our money keep its value, and at the same time make our country strong and secure."

I chose that letter because it brings up this great problem of security, and the money that it costs. Now, it's a good starting point and I want to tell you, before Mr. Humphrey takes over to discuss something about finances, we must remember this: during 17 of the past 20 years we have gone in debt. Borrowing cheapens money. That's like water in your coffee—it just doesn't go very far and isn't worth much. Now higher prices mean your savings are worthless. So I have asked Mr. Humphrey and our Director of the Budget, Mr. Dodge, to get after this thing in order to keep spending under the amount we take in so that your dollar will still buy what it should buy. That's his job, and now he is going to tell you about it.

Mr. Humphrey: Mr. President, I think the woman from Rhode Island was right. I think it is a lot harder, a lot tougher job to balance the national budget than it is your own home budget, because we owe so much money nationally, and we are spending so much money every single year.

Let me just take this chart that I have here and show you where all that money goes to. Seventy-three percent of the total money we spend goes for defense; 15 percent goes for fixed charges—that is, things like interest, and all sorts of things that the Congress has voted that we pay, like State aid and all that sort of thing. It only leaves 12 percent for the ordinary running of the Government.

Now then, our job is to balance this budget. Our job is to get our income even with our outgo. That can be done in two ways, either by raising more taxes or by cutting expenses. Well, of course we don't want to raise taxes—we want to reduce taxes—so the way left is to cut expenses.

And that involves two serious problems. The first problem is that we can't so cut our expenses that we interfere with security. As you have said we have got to maintain the security of this country. The second big problem is this—over the last year or two a great many materials, war materials and other materials, have been bought c.o.d. They are delivered now; as the deliveries come we have to pay for them in cash.

I would just like to show you another chart, here, that will illustrate to you the way in which our spending and our income are growing apart as planned for the next few years—the program that we found when we came. Here you will see this line going way up here is spending, and here you will see this line way down here is income.

In between the two is a widening difference, a widening spread which is a deficit. Now that deficit has got to be stopped. Unless it's stopped, we are going to be right back on the old merry-go-round of inflation.

THE PRESIDENT. Well, now, of course, George, we know we are going to stop it. But as an ex-soldier I have promised the American people two things: they are going to be secure, and, next, these expensive military establishments are going to be maintained in the most economical way possible. You are going to get one dollar's worth for every dollar we spend. And I am going to keep that promise.

Mr. Humphrey: That's just right, Mr. President. What we are going to do is to cut these expenses slowly. We are going to study every month what can be done. We have made a good start already, but we are going to continue every month as we go along and make further reductions in those expenses.

By that sort of process I think we will be well balanced out by June in 1954, provided we do not have a much worse condition in the world develop. Of course, something could happen in Russia that would upset our plans.

To accomplish that purpose we have set up a new tax bill. Now in that new tax bill, we ask for an extension of the excess profits tax for an additional 6 months to carry it from July, when it would expire, to the first of January. The reason we do that is because we believe that it is grossly unfair to relieve just a few— the relatively few corporations—who pay an excess profits tax and give them tax relief before we give relief to all the other corporations and to all of the people.

If the Congress will pass the bill that we have before them, the bill that we are recommending to them, with the savings that we have already made, with the savings that we are going to make in the next 14 months and with this tax money—this excess profits tax money that we can use to reduce the deficit—it will justify a reduction on the first day of January for taxes for all the people of the country—individual tax reductions.

That will mean that everyone will get a tax reduction at the same time. There will be no favorite few. It will help to balance the budget. It will help to stop inflation. It will help to keep sound money. It will help to keep business active, and more jobs, and it will provide better living for all.

THE PRESIDENT. Mr. Secretary, I endorse every single word you say. And you could have added that all of us despise this excess profits tax. It's inequitable, it's unjust, it's clumsy, and it's awkward. But, as you say, it must not be taken off until we can reduce the individual income taxes as we should, as quickly as we can get at it.

Now, we know from the mail that we get here, that people are for a decent tax program, to get expenses and outgo in balance; and in those letters we are getting an 8 to 1 vote of confidence for that entire program.

Now, the next person that is going to talk to you is going to talk to the people, particularly, that are key men in our agriculture—the farmers. One out of nine of our wage-earners is a farmer, and when he is in trouble all the Nation is in trouble.

We are going to get a firsthand picture from Mr. Benson, who, as I told you before, is a farmer himself.

Mr. Benson: Thank you, Mr. President. When you called me to this very tough and difficult job back in December, you asked me if I would be willing to try and serve the American people by being a champion of the farmers. Your administration had already pledged itself to greater stability in agriculture, increasing the national income and the proportion that goes to farmers, and building a sound program in which the farmers would take part.

Now, I have traveled from one end of the Nation to the other in years past and since December, as this little chart will indicate; I have been into most of the agricultural areas, and we have held meetings with farmers; I have addressed them and conversed with them, learned of their problems and listened to their comments and their hopes, and their desires; and in order to get a broad picture of the situation in agriculture today we need to go back to 1947. In that year farmers were receiving good prices, and the relationship between their prices and the prices they had to pay for the things they purchased was favorable.

But since that time there has been a rather rapid decline in farm prices. For the last 2 years, as this chart will indicate, the trend of prices received by farmers has been downward, while their costs, represented here, have remained relatively high. That means that, as every farmer knows, he has been caught in a squeeze.

However, during the last few months prices have tended to stabilize, as you can see, and the costs have come down somewhat, reducing that squeeze. But during this 2-year period—1951 to 1952—farm prices declined 16 percent.

THE PRESIDENT. Well, one fellow that's been caught in that squeeze very badly is the cattle raiser, as you and I well know, and we have had many conferences with them.

Now, we must remove that squeeze. We are going to have stability in farm income, and we are going to do it with no farmer being taken over by the Government. We are not going to regiment the farmer.

Mr. Benson: There is another phase of this problem that pertains to our decline in exports, Mr. President. Normally, farmers export about 10 percent of their total production. That's a very important part. However, there has been a decline in exports in the last 2 or 3 years.

Two years ago, for example, we exported about half of our total wheat production. This last year alone there has been a decline of 15 percent in our exports abroad.

In order for agriculture to be prosperous, it must not only have good markets at home but big markets abroad. And of course this is a two-way road, this foreign trade, so if we sell abroad we must also permit them to sell here. That's why farmers are in favor of the extension of the reciprocal trade program.

Now, usually we think of businessmen and manufacturers as being primarily interested in foreign trade. But I presume the individual who is most deeply concerned with this matter of foreign trade is this man we call the American farmer.

THE PRESIDENT. Now, I think, Mr. Secretary, you should talk just a little bit about our surpluses. We hear a lot about them, and remember, from our viewpoint, it's not just dollars that's here involved—it's the moral values that are involved also.

Mr. Benson: That's very true, Mr. President. At the present time, and for some months, we have been purchasing, as you know, large quantities of products. These have been going into storage. They have been part of the present farm program. Of course, it's a very serious thing when we have large accumulations of burdensome surpluses of farm products.

And so we are beginning, now, to build programs from the grassroots that will prevent unreasonable supplies of these commodities which may result in spoilage and some products becoming rancid. We hope that we can prevent these surpluses and the high cost to the taxpayer resulting therefrom.

We can all remember a few years ago when we had the large

surplus of potatoes, which were dyed blue in order to make them unsalable. The answer is not moving products into storage, but into stomachs.

THE PRESIDENT. Well, of course, Mr. Secretary, we do know this: we do need some surpluses. We need surpluses to carry us over from one crop season to another. And we are talking only when these get too large. And here again, the most important part is not the money involved, but I refer again to this business of the moral value.

It's unthinkable, unconscionable, as I see it, that the United States should have wheat molding and crops spoiling, and people—friends of ours—should be starving in the world.

Right now, for example, Pakistan has had a 2-year drought, a drought that has been very, very serious. They need a million tons of wheat. And I have already sent to the Congress a measure recommending that we give it to them. And I hope it will be passed soon.

Mr. Benson: In building these farm programs from the grassroots, Mr. President, there are six important basic concepts that should be kept in mind.

In the first place, these programs should build markets and move products into use at fair prices to the farmers.

Secondly, they should permit adjustments in production and give the farmer some freedom in his operations.

Third, programs should not price our products out of the world or domestic markets.

And fourth, they should not hold an umbrella over synthetics and competing products.

And fifth, basic to the whole program is this matter of research and speedy application of it.

And of course, encouragement of a self-help program for the farmers.

THE PRESIDENT. And the only thing that you did not mention that I want to say just a word about, is the research program in agriculture. It is very important. I visited Beltsville the other day, and I saw wonders in research that I wish every one of you could see. It will show you how the farmer is really getting new outlets for his crops.

Thank you very much, Mr. Benson.

Now, we are going to come to the department that deals with health, welfare, and education. It's the newest department of Government. You see we have had nine for a long time—nine departments. Now we have got a new one. This is one that Mrs. Hobby heads. I am going to ask her to tell you something about it now. Mrs. Hobby.

Mrs. Hobby: Well, Mr. President, there are so many different activities in our department that touch people, young and old, in public health, in education, pure food and drugs, Social Security, and Children's Bureau, and vocational rehabilitation, that it's difficult, sometimes, to say which problems are the most urgent.

But, in line with your suggestions, we have recently sent three pieces of legislation to the Congress. Two deal with the school situation in the United States. The other piece of legislation deals with the restoration of the right of factory inspection to the pure food and drug.

Shortly we shall send to the Congress a piece of legislation which will extend the coverage of old-age and survivors insurance benefits to millions not now covered. We have had a group of twelve experts studying this problem, and together with Treasury we are developing a simplified plan of tax collection. Our plan would extend coverage to farmers, certain State and local government employes, the self-employed, professional people, domestic workers, farm laborers, and others.

Now, we have two laws—or two bills—which relate to the Office of Education. Of course, education is primarily the responsibility of the State and local communities. But there are certain communities in which the Federal Government has created a problem. This occurs in several different ways. One, by removing land from the school tax rolls, and two, by adding student population to the school rolls without taxable property.

This occurs when the parents either live on or work on Federal property.   There are notable examples of this situation in Limestone, Maine; in Derby, Kansas; in Piketon, Ohio.   Now, the Federal Government recognizes its responsibility and shortly the Congress will start hearings on two bills which will aid these overcrowded school districts—one for construction and the other for maintenance and operation.

THE PRESIDENT. Well, now, Mrs. Hobby, tell us something of that trouble we are having with the Food and Drug Act, will you please?

Mrs. Hobby: Well, Mr. President, that concerns me very much. We have sent to the Congress an amendment to the Pure Food and Drug law.   We believe it is vital to the protection of the American people.

If it is adopted by the Congress, it will restore the right of the Pure Food and Drug to inspect the factories which produce and process food and drugs.   Last fall, the Supreme Court held that the factory inspection language was contradictory, and that the inspectors could enter only when given consent.   Fortunately, the great majority of the processors and producers of food and drugs gave consent.   But we need the law for those who refuse consent, and refuse to let our inspectors observe their operations and their sanitary conditions.

THE PRESIDENT. Well, I think, Mrs. Hobby, that everybody will agree that you have about as complicated a task as there is in government.   You run the biggest insurance business and you run a medical research center, and everything between.   But there is one thing that must give you great satisfaction.   You have the department that sort of epitomizes or symbolizes the warm feeling of government for all of our citizens.

And now, my friends, we come to this business of security inside our borders.   It's a complicated job because, as we search out those people that are unfit to serve you, we must protect the innocent.   That is what we are doing every day.   We go after the weeds of disloyalty, but we don't want to uproot a single good plant. The man at the head of that, as I told you before, is Herbert Brownell. And he is going to tell you about it now, and what he is trying to do in this field.

Mr. Brownell: In the Department of Justice, Mr. President, we seek to protect the security of our homes—our internal security, through the use of four laws, or programs.

First, we prosecute and jail the leaders of the Communist Party in this country, and all those who seek to overthrow our Government by force and violence. We can do that largely because of the fine investigative work of the FBI arm of the Department of Justice under Director J. Edgar Hoover, and we are making good progress on that.

Then, second, we seek to enforce the law which requires agents of foreign governments who are in this country to register and to disclose their finances, and to label their propaganda that they send around to the American people. We are meeting resistance on this, but we intend to pursue it vigorously.

Then, third, under the immigration laws, we are making fine progress on the program of denaturalizing and deporting racketeers and subversives who violated the hospitality of our country, or who got here, in the first place, by false affidavits.

And then, finally, our fourth special tool to protect our internal security, is the employee security program that you spoke about as being a matter of good housekeeping, of weeding out from the Federal payrolls themselves persons who are not good security risks. It went into effect just a few days ago, to replace the old loyalty program which was ineffective.

And it's based on two ideas—one is, that working for the Federal Government is a privilege and not an absolute right, so that the Government is entitled to maintain high standards of trustworthiness in its employees. And the other idea is that there is a great difference between disloyalty and being a security risk; for many of the employees could be a security risk and still not be disloyal or have any traitorous thoughts, but it may be that their personal habits are such that they might be subject to blackmail by people who seek to destroy the safety of our country.

Or they may associate themselves with known subversives. Now you and I, in our private affairs, certainly would not trust our secrets to people that we could not confide in. And the same thing with the National Government. We believe that the tremendously important secrets of our national security should be entrusted only to employees who can guard those secrets in the best interests of the country.

Now, as I say, this program has just gone into effect. But we believe that without fanfare and steadily over the course of the next few months, we will be able to weed out from the Federal payroll every security risk.

THE PRESIDENT. There is one other phase of this thing I wish you would speak about for just a minute, Herb. It is this business of governmental action in this field going on behind closed doors—what we are doing to bring things out in the open, so that people will know what is going on.

Mr. Brownell: Well, that is an important function there in the Department of Justice. We have abolished the closed-door policy that we found there. For example, first in the matter of tax settlements. We now disclose those to the public the minute that they are made so that there will be no temptation for skulduggery or behind-the-closed-doors attitude on the part of the lawyers there in the department.

And second, when it comes to these fraud cases, where people used to come into the department and claim that they were too sick to face the music—that was done behind closed doors. But now we take them into court, and let the judges appoint an impartial doctor to see whether or not they should stand trial for these frauds.

And finally, in the matter of Presidential pardons, we also have abolished the closed-door policy. And when a Presidential pardon is granted to anybody who has violated our laws and is incarcerated in our Federal penitentiaries, we disclose that, make it a matter of public record along with the list of sponsors for that pardon.

Now I know you have said to us, and we thoroughly believe there in the department, that one of the most important responsibilities of your administration is the impartial administration of justice without favoritism. And so we are making that a keystone of the department.

THE PRESIDENT. And I hope, my friends, that you agree that our internal security is in very good hands. And let me make one observation about that before we go further. And it is this: the great mass of your Federal employees are a wonderful, dedicated group of men and women, and whose jobs are going to be protected. He was talking only about those few that damage them.

Now, I know we have not answered your problems this evening, ladies and gentlemen, but I hope you see some of the factors in those problems, and how we are approaching their solution. I hope you will realize that since government is just people, you have seen the kind of people that are trying to solve these things for you.

We have done something, and are doing things to repair the holes in the roof, and keep the fences mended, and keep the industries flourishing, employment high, and the farms productive.

Now, on the defense program, just a word: it is very large, but it is logical. We are not going to cripple this Nation, and we are going specifically to keep up its air power. Right now, sixty cents of every dollar that goes into the defense business is in some form of air power or air defense.

Now, we are going to keep reviewing these plans. We are going to report to you from time to time with these, or with other people with me, so that you know what is going on. Because our effort is to secure peace, and prosperity in peace.

My friends, thank you for being with us. Good night. God bless you.

96   ¶ Letter to President Syngman Rhee of Korea, Concerning Acceptance of the Panmunjom Armistice.   *June 7, 1953*

[Released June 7, 1953. Dated June 6, 1953]

Dear Mr. President:

I received on June 2 the cabled text of your communication dated May 30. I have given it the careful and sympathetic consideration it deserves.

The Republic of Korea has engaged all of its resources, human and material, in a struggle which will go down in history as one of the epic struggles of all time. You have dedicated your all without reservation to the principle that human liberty and national liberty must survive against communist aggression which tramples upon human dignity and which replaces national sovereignty with a humiliating satellite status. The principles for which your nation has fought and for which so many of your youth have died are principles which defend free men and free nations everywhere.

The United States has stood with you, and with you we have fought for those principles, as part of the United Nations Command. The blood of your youth and our youth has been poured out on the altar of common sacrifice. Thereby we have demonstrated not only our dedication to the cause of human freedom and political liberty, but also our dedication to an equally important principle which is that there cannot be independence without interdependence, and there cannot be human liberty except as men recognize that they are bound together by ties of common destiny.

The moment has now come when we must decide whether to carry on by warfare a struggle for the unification of Korea or whether to pursue this goal by political and other methods.

The enemy has proposed an armistice which involves a clear abandonment of the fruits of aggression. The armistice would leave the Republic of Korea in undisputed possession of substantially the territory which the Republic administered prior to the aggression, indeed this territory will be somewhat enlarged.

The proposed armistice, true to the principle of political asylum, assures that the thousands of North Koreans and Communist Chinese prisoners in our hands, who have seen liberty and who wish to share it, will have the opportunity to do so and will not be forcibly sent back into communist areas. The principle of political asylum is one which we could not honorably surrender even though we thereby put an earlier end to our own human and material losses. We have suffered together many thousands of casualties in support of this principle.

It is my profound conviction that under these circumstances acceptance of the armistice is required of the United Nations and the Republic of Korea. We would not be justified in prolonging the war with all the misery that it involves in the hope of achieving, by force, the unification of Korea.

The unification of Korea is an end to which the United States is committed, not once but many times, through its World War II declarations and through its acceptance of the principles enunciated in reference to Korea by the United Nations. Korea is unhappily not the only country which remains divided after World War II. We remain determined to play our part in achieving the political union of all countries so divided. But we do not intend to employ war as an instrument to accomplish the world-wide political settlements to which we are dedicated and which we believe to be just. It was indeed a crime that those who attacked from the North invoked violence to unite Korea under their rule. Not only as your official friend but as a personal friend I urge that your country not embark upon a similar course.

There are three major points I would like to make to you:

1. The United States will not renounce its efforts by all peaceful means to effect the unification of Korea. Also as a member of the United Nations we shall seek to assure that the United Nations continues steadfast in its determination in this respect. In

the political conference which will follow an armistice that will be our central objective. The United States intends to consult with your Government both before and during such a conference and expects the full participation of your Government in that conference.

2. You speak of a mutual defense pact. I am prepared promptly after the conclusion and acceptance of an armistice to negotiate with you a mutual defense treaty along the lines of the treaties heretofore made between the United States and the Republic of the Philippines, and the United States and Australia and New Zealand. You may recall that both of these treaties speak of "the development of a more comprehensive system of regional security in the Pacific area." A security pact between the United States and the Republic of Korea would be a further step in that direction. It would cover the territory now or hereafter brought peacefully under the administration of the ROK. Of course you realize that under our constitutional system, any such treaty would be made only with the advice and consent of the Senate. However, the action which the United States has heretofore taken, and the great investment of blood and treasure which has already been made for the independence of Korea are certainly clear indications of American temper and intentions not to tolerate a repetition of unprovoked aggression.

3. The United States Government, subject to requisite congressional appropriations, will be prepared to continue economic aid to the Republic of Korea which will permit in peace a restoration of its devastated land. Homes must be rebuilt. Industries must be reestablished. Agriculture must be made vigorously productive.

The preamble of the Constitution of the United States states the goals of our people, which I believe are equally the goals of the brave people of Korea, namely "to form a more perfect union, establish justice, insure domestic tranquility, provide for the common defense, promote the general welfare, and secure the blessings of liberty." Manifestly, not all of these conditions now prevail in

Korea. Moreover, in existing circumstances they cannot be achieved either by prolongation of the present conflict or by reckless adventure with a new one. Only by peaceful means can these things be achieved.

With the conclusion of an armistice the United States is prepared to join with the Republic of Korea to seek for Korea these ends. We believe that in Korea there should be a more perfect union and, as I say, we shall seek to achieve that union by all peaceful methods. We believe that there should be domestic tranquility and that can come from the end of fighting. There should be provision for the defense of Korea. That will come from the mutual security treaty which we are prepared to make. The general welfare should be advanced and that will come from your own peacetime efforts and from economic assistance to your war-torn land. Finally, a peaceful settlement will afford the best opportunity to bring to your people the blessings of liberty.

I assure you, Mr. President, that so far as the United States is concerned, it is our desire to go forward in fellowship with the Republic of Korea. Even the thought of a separation at this critical hour would be a tragedy. We must remain united.

Sincerely,

DWIGHT D. EISENHOWER

NOTE: President Rhee's communication of May 30 was not released with the President's reply.

97 ¶ Special Message to the Congress Requesting Authority To Make Wheat Available for Famine Victims in Pakistan. *June 10, 1953*

To the Congress of the United States:

The people of Pakistan are faced with famine, and they have asked our help in meeting disaster.

We are fortunate to be in a position to offer help at this time, for we have an abundance of wheat. I strongly believe that we should do so. Accordingly I urge the Congress to make possible the shipment to Pakistan of up to one million long tons of United States wheat.

The specter of famine confronts the people of Pakistan at a crucial time in their growth as a young free nation. Unchecked, it could undermine the very democratic principles and institutions to which Pakistan is dedicated.

The crisis is largely a result of a calamity of nature. Pakistan was self-sufficient in food until severe drought, in two successive years, struck the wheat producing area of West Pakistan.

The wheat consumption of the people of West Pakistan averages less than 12 ounces per day in a diet consisting very largely of this grain. Today Government wheat reserves have fallen to the vanishing point.

The immediate need of Pakistan is to obtain abroad up to 1.5 million long tons of wheat both for consumption and for a small working reserve during the next 11 months. Of this total, the Government of Pakistan expects to be able to obtain about 400,-000 tons of wheat with its own and other aid resources. Canada and Australia have both made generous grants for wheat to Pakistan. There is no important source in the free world other than the United States able to furnish additional help.

Pakistan has, therefore, appealed to the United States for one million tons of wheat. Its approach has been one of dignity—as one sovereign democracy to another—stating a real and urgent need. Between the people of Pakistan and the people of the United States, there exists a strong bond of friendship. I am sure that the people of the United States desire their Government to respond rapidly and effectively to Pakistan's request.

Pakistan has endeavored to keep its request for United States aid to a minimum. The Secretary of State and the Director for Mutual Security sent a special mission, headed by Dr. Harry Reed, Dean of the College of Agriculture of Purdue University, to study at first hand the food situation in Pakistan. Mr. Dulles and Governor Stassen have also visited Pakistan within the last two weeks. With the help of their observations, careful consideration has been given the Reed Mission's recommendations.

One critical fact is that the Government of Pakistan is suffering grave financial difficulties. It has already taken rigorous steps to remedy both the food outlook and its general economic disabilities, and these efforts give some hope for future self-sufficiency. But Pakistan's gold and foreign exchange holdings are barely enough to meet its legal requirements for currency backing and essential working capital. Moreover, Pakistan has little prospect of an exportable wheat surplus which would permit repayment of a loan in kind. Its export earnings and all its prospective financial resources are needed to meet the demand of economic development essential to prevent future food and financial crises. A dollar loan would make it impossible for Pakistan to obtain further necessary development loans from international lending institutions.

These considerations make certain conclusions evident. Pakistan needs a grant of up to 700,000 tons of United States wheat for relief purposes according to the best available estimates. The urgency of the need is underscored by the Reed Mission's recommendation for delivery of 100,000 tons of United States aid wheat in Karachi by August 15 of this year.

This grant would serve a double purpose. It would meet Pakistan's immediate and pressing need for food and at the same time provide local currency for economic development programs. The rupee receipts from the sale of wheat would be placed in a counterpart fund under joint Pakistan-United States administration. This fund will be used for development purposes with emphasis placed on increased food production in Pakistan to lessen the danger of future shortages.

In addition to the 700,000 tons, Pakistan may also need up to 300,000 tons as a necessary working reserve of wheat. The exact amount needed for this purpose can only be determined later;

and only then can we determine whether the remainder of our aid should be supplied as a grant or a loan.

Fortunately, we do have the capacity to help at the present time. Our large wheat reserves have created a grave storage problem, demanding unusual and sometimes costly storage measures.

I propose, therefore, that the Congress authorize me to make available to Pakistan up to one million tons of wheat out of stocks held by the Commodity Credit Corporation. This wheat already is owned by the Commodity Credit Corporation, having been obtained under the price support program. To make it available to Pakistan will create no additional Government expenditure at this time other than the cost of transportation. In order that the operations of the Commodity Credit Corporation will not be impaired, I am recommending that the legislation include authority for the Commodity Credit Corporation to recover its costs, including interest, through an appropriation when the costs of the programs have been ascertained.

The United States Government proposes to designate, with the concurrence of the Government of Pakistan, a group to observe the receipt and distribution of wheat in Pakistan. The group's reports will be available to the Congress.

To provide sufficient United States aid in time, it is imperative that the grain begin to move from United States ports by the end of this month.

I strongly urge that the Congress make such prompt action possible.

DWIGHT D. EISENHOWER

NOTE: See Item 119.

98   ¶ Address at the Annual Convention of the National Junior Chamber of Commerce, Minneapolis, Minnesota.   *June 10, 1953*

President Henderson, Governor Anderson, and Members of this great Chamber:

I thank you sincerely for the warmth of your welcome, and for the honor of your invitation to be with you today.   That invitation had many values for me.   It was brought to me by the distinguished Congressman from this District, my old and dear friend—and valued friend—Congressman Walter Judd.

And yours is an organization with a proud record.   First, each of you is a young and responsible person, already the possessor of a record of achievement, but more than this, collectively you have a most enviable record of achievement.   You have sought nothing for yourselves.   You have sought ways to serve the United States of America and freedom everywhere.   I come here in real humble pride—that I assure you.

I have been fortunate that my own life has been spent with America's young people.   The grave decisions that I have been compelled to make, at least before this calendar year, have been vindicated by the skill, the sense of responsibility, and the sacrifice of America's young men.   My faith in them is as my unbounded faith in America itself.

Now, because you are both young and responsible, you know what is your greatest responsibility of all—it is tomorrow—it is the whole future of freedom.

In the minds of all of you, as in my own mind, is a long list of critical subjects confronting our people today—indeed, confronting all peoples.   I wish I could discuss all of them with you: the problems of healthy foreign trade; the regulation of Government expenditures; the achieving of a more just tax structure; the development of sound agricultural programs; the great work to be done in the fields of education, health, and welfare; the great problem of spiritual rejuvenation of our own people, and of free people throughout the world—all of these people. I should like to discuss with you and have your convictions and conclusions on them.

But there is, however, one matter that overshadows all of these. It is the constant, controlling consideration in our national life today. It is—our Nation's security.

Quickly we can see how this one issue effectively rules all others. It alone comes close to fixing the level of our national budget—when two of every three dollars spent by our Federal Government go to defense purposes. It thereby almost automatically sets the requirements for Federal taxes. It directly affects the welfare of our farms, so dependent upon wide opportunities for export. And it is intimately bound up with foreign trade—for our own imports of such critical products as nickel and cobalt and mica are essential to our national security.

It is no wonder that our national security is so vast a matter— for the struggle in which freedom today is engaged is quite literally a total and universal struggle. It engages every aspect of our lives. It is waged in every arena in which a challenged civilization must fight to live.

It is a military struggle—on the battlefields of Indochina, and still in Korea.

It is an economic struggle—in which the equivalent of a lost battle can be suffered in a ruined rice crop in Burma, or in the lagging of a critical production line in America.

It is a political struggle—speaking at the conference tables of the United Nations, in the daily diplomatic exchanges that flood the cable wires and telephone lines of the whole world.

It is a scientific struggle—in which atomic energy plants and colossal research projects can produce terrible wonders matching in fateful effect the inventions of the wheel or of gunpowder.

It is an intellectual struggle—for the press and the radio, every spoken and printed word, can either inspire or weaken men's faith in freedom.

It is a spiritual struggle—for one of communism's basic assumptions about the nature of men is that they are incapable of ruling themselves, incapable, the Communists say, of attaining the spiritual standards and strength to solve national problems when these require voluntary personal sacrifice for the common good. That is the Communist's justification for regimentation—for dictatorship, called in his language, the dictatorship of the proletariat. All this we deny. And we must seek in our churches, our schools, our homes and our daily lives the clearness of mind and strongness of heart to guard the chance to live in freedom.

For this whole struggle, in the deepest sense, is waged neither for land nor for food nor for power—but for the soul of man himself.

Now, my young friends, these are real, tough facts, not mere poetic fancies. They are facts as true and compelling as any airplane production schedules, or the firepower of our guns, or the armor of our tanks, or the speed of our jets.

I cannot presume today to speak of all the aspects of so vast, so all-embracing, so total a struggle—nor of all the truths that must, I believe, guide us steadfastly.

I wish to speak simply of two of these truths.

The first is this: our military strength and our economic strength are truly one—neither can sensibly be purchased at the price of destroying the other.

And the second is this: this Nation and all nations defending freedom, everywhere in the world, are one in their common need and their common cause—and none can sanely seek security alone.

The first of these two truths concerns our military posture of defense.

The second concerns our whole concept and conduct of world affairs.

Let us consider each of them briefly, for the mere assertion of a general truth proves nothing and convinces no one.

Now the central problem of our military defense is not merely to become strong, but to stay strong. The reason is obvious; we cannot count upon any enemy striking us at a given, ascertainable moment. We live, as I have said before, not in an instant of peril but in an age of peril—a time of tension and of watchfulness.

The defense against this peril, then, must be carefully planned and steadfastly maintained. It cannot be a mere repetition of today's reflex to yesterday's crisis. It cannot be a thing of frenzies and alarms. It must be a thing of thought and of order and of efficiency.

Precisely such a defense is now being built for our country. I believe it does several things. It soberly promises more efficient military production. It realistically assesses our long-term economic capacity. It demands the elimination of luxury, waste, and duplication in all military activity. And it allocates funds as justly and as wisely as possible among the three armed services. It recognizes the great importance of air power.

Concretely: these defense plans allocate 60 cents out of every defense dollar for air power. With the enactment of pending legislation, our Air Force will have available for its expenditure more than $40 billion. By mid-1954 its strength will total 114 wings. At the same time the air arm of the Navy will command a full half of all the funds available to the entire Naval establishment. The Navy and Marine air arms will alone total almost 10,000 planes. All this, I believe, promises both powerful air defense and a no less powerful deterrent to any would-be aggressor.

Greater efficiency in production will give us less costly production schedules—and something even more vital: fewer planes "on order," more in the air. Today typical production schedules require 26 to 34 months for important bombing types. Our civilian leadership in the Department of Defense believes that such schedules can be reduced to something like 18 months. I repeat: that will mean fewer planes in theory, more in fact—more swiftly and less expensively.

Now, let's look at something very clearly. How many planes, how many divisions, how great a Navy should we have? Such questions are, these days, earnestly and fervently debated by advocates of different theories, as well as a fair number of self-appointed experts.

Now all this is healthy and proper enough, provided we do not lose sight of certain elemental facts.

First: we must remember always that reasonable defense posture is not won by juggling magic numbers—even with an air of great authority. There is no wonderfully sure number of planes or ships or divisions, or billions of dollars, that can automatically guarantee security. Could I pause long enough to say, in all of this I hope you will not forget the security of the United States is found first in the heart—in the heart of youth. Not only the heart of the man who has been or can be called to put on the uniform, in the heart of the grandmother, and of the child, that dedication and devotion to those great human rights for which our country and other free countries have stood.

If we never lose sight of those great values, nor our devotion and dedication to them, we have achieved the first problem of national security.

Now, the most uncompromising advocates of these magic numbers have themselves changed their calculations almost from year to year. Such changes are reasonable, as technological advance requires. But the insistence that the latest change is final, definitive, sacred—that is not reasonable.

Second: we must remember that all our plans must realistically take account—not just this year but every year—of colossal and continuing technological change. We are living in a time of revolutionary military science. Today 25 aircraft equipped with modern weapons can in a single attack visit upon an enemy as much explosive violence as was hurled at Germany by our entire air effort throughout 4 years of World War II. And those of you here who belonged to the Eighth and the Ninth and the Twelfth and the Fifteenth know what that was.

And a third serious truth about our defense is this: there is no such thing as maximum military security short of total mobilization. Now, this total mobilization would mean regimentation of the worker, the farmer, the businessman—allocation of materials—control of wages and prices—drafting of every able-bodied citizen. It would mean, in short, all the grim paraphernalia of the garrison state.

This would do more damage than merely to strain the economic fabric of America.

It would, if long sustained, imperil the very liberties we are striving to defend.

And it would ignore the most fundamental truth of all, one to which I have already alluded—the fact that this total struggle cannot be won by guns alone.

I do not believe, in a word, that we can wisely subscribe to what I would call the "all-out" military theory of defense—ignoring the other defenses of the heart and mind, and of our economy, that we must build and hold.

There is another theory of defense, another oversimplified concept, which I believe equally misleading and dangerous. It is what we might call the "fortress" theory of defense.

Advocates of this theory ask: "Why cannot the strongest nation in the world—our country—stand by itself? What does the United Nations matter? And particularly in Asia, where so many of our sons have died in freedom's name, why cannot we make our own decisions, fight and stand as only we ourselves may choose?"

There are many answers, of which I will give you a few.

A total struggle—let us never forget it—calls for total defense. As there is no weapon too small, no arena too remote, to be ignored, there is no free nation too humble to be forgotten. All of us have learned—first from the onslaught of Nazi aggression, then from Communist aggression—that all free nations must stand together or they shall fall separately. Again and again we must remind ourselves that this is a matter not only of political principle but of economic necessity. It involves our need for markets for our agricultural and industrial products, our need to receive in return from the rest of the world such essentials as manganese and cobalt, tin and tungsten, without which our economy cannot function.

This essential, indispensable unity means working together— always within a clearly defined, clearly understood framework of principle. We know the need of working together, in harmony with basic principles, within our own Nation. It is the essence of the democratic process. We should not be surprised that it applies just as vitally among nations—in the wide community of the world's free peoples.

How, where, can there be retreat from this unity? Surrender Asia? That would mean leaving a vast portion of the population of the entire world to be mobilized by the forces of aggression. Surrender Europe? That would mean more than doubling the industrial power of those same forces.

Who is there who thinks that the strength of America is so great, its burdens so easy, its future so secure, that it could make so generous a gift to those challenging our very lives?

And very important, there is no such thing as partial unity. That is a contradiction in terms.

We cannot select those areas of the globe in which our policies or wishes may differ from our allies—build political fences around these areas—and then say to our allies: "We shall do what we want here—and where you do what we want, there and only there shall we favor unity." That is not unity. It is an attempted dictation. And it is not the way free men associate.

We all hear, in this connection, a good deal of unhappy murmuring about the United Nations. It is easy to understand this dismay. None of us is above irritation and frustration over the seemingly vain and tedious processes of political discourse, particularly in times of great crisis.

But none of us can rightly forget that neither the world—nor the United Nations—is or can be made in a single image of one nation's will or ideas. The fact is that from its foundation the United Nations has seemed to be two distinct things to the two worlds divided by the iron curtain. To the Communist world it has been a convenient sounding board for their propaganda, a weapon to be exploited in spreading disunity and confusion. To the free world it has seemed that it should be a constructive forum for free discussion of the world's problems, an effective agency for helping to solve those problems peacefully.

But the truth is that even if the United Nations were to conform to the concept held by the free nations, it would still be bound to show infinite variety of opinion, sharp clashes of debate, slow movement to decision. For all this is little more than a reflection of the state of the world itself. An image of perfect symmetry would be a distorted image—the false creation of some nation's or some bloc's power-politics. And perhaps one of the greatest values of the United Nations is this: it holds up a mirror in which the world can see its true self. And what should we want to see in such a mirror but the whole truth at such a time of total struggle?

There are, as you see, certain common denominators to all that I have said, certain constant thoughts I believe to be consistently relevant in facing tomorrow.

We must see clearly that all the problems before us—from farm exports to balanced budgets, from taxes to the vital resources for our industry—all are dependent on our Nation's security. And in this real way freedom's great struggle touches all of us alike—farmer and businessman, worker and student, pastor and teacher.

We know this to be true because we know that there is but one struggle for freedom—in the market place and in the university, on the battlefield and beside the assembly line.

We know that strength means being strong in all these ways and in all these places.

We know that unity means comradeship, patience, and compromise among all free nations.

And we know that only with strength and with unity—is the future of freedom assured. And freedom, now and for the future, is our goal!

And now, my friends, before I leave you, I should like to give to you an announcement that came to me just as I left my airplane.

There was a telegram came from the East, that said that Senator Taft had announced that his physical condition has become so serious that he has had to give up his active duties as the leader of the Republican Party in the Senate.

I am sure that you would allow me to speak for you—indeed, I have already ventured to do so, I think, in a telegram I just sent, saying that as he well knew, that we could not spare such patriotic and devoted service as his, and sent him our prayers for his early recovery.

Thank you very much indeed.

NOTE: The President spoke at the Minneapolis Auditorium at 2:30 p.m. In his opening words he referred to Horace Henderson, President of the National Junior Chamber of Commerce, and Governor C. Elmer Anderson of Minnesota.

99 ¶ Remarks at the Ebenezer Home for the Aged in Minneapolis. *June* 10, 1953

I AM GRATEFUL, both to the Republican State Central Committee and to the members of the Ebenezer Home, for allowing me to stop here and say a brief word of greeting to so many fellow Americans.

I have gone through this town today, and I am very proud and very humble in the realization that I have received a welcome far beyond my deserts.

I can only say here, in the hope that you will carry it to all of your neighbors, that I am grateful for every smile I have seen, and I say thanks to everybody who has yelled "Hi, Ike," or "Hello, there."

I have been in many countries of the world. Some of them have chosen me, as a representative of our people, to receive their very highest awards to bring home to you. But no honor I have ever received has yet equaled in my own heart, in my own mind, just that warm feeling you get from a whole crowd of my fellow citizens looking at me as if to say, "Well, we are sort of glad you came around."

I want to say to you, I am sort of glad I came around to see *you*.

100   ¶ Address at the Closure Ceremonies at Garrison Dam, North Dakota.   *June* 11, 1953

Mr. Chairman, Governor Brunsdale, General Sturgis, distinguished guests, my fellow Americans:

It is a great honor to be here with you at this significant ceremony in the development of the Garrison Dam—the closure ceremonies of the dam.

I hope as I start expressing to you a few of the facts that cross my mind on this significant occasion you will allow me first to reminisce a bit.

I was raised on one of the major tributaries of the Missouri River—in the Kaw Valley in Kansas.   There was a great flood in 1903—50 years ago this year—almost 50 years ago this day.   It was a terrific thing and it covered that whole valley.

I was in the midst of it.   I've tried to cast my mind back today to the thoughts of that time.   Certainly the last thing that would have occurred to us living in the midst of that flood was that man would ever have the temerity to try to harness the Big Muddy.

I might say also that the furthest thing from my mind was that I personally would ever be present at a ceremony where we were celebrating or commemorating such a successful effort.   Who would have thought then of a loudspeaker, or of a radio that carries voices today all over this Nation even as we sit here on this pleasant sunny countryside?

Now, when we think of how far man has come in those 50 years it is almost frightening to project our minds 50 years in advance. And so, I want to address myself first to those doubters who say, "What can be the use of this enormous structure with its 23,-000,000 acre-feet of water stored behind it, with all of the dreams that people have had who designed it, or for its use in flood control, irrigation, regulating navigation further downriver and for the uses of the power?"

And even already, I am told, there have been more requests for power than they contemplate producing in this mighty dam. But beyond all of the immediate uses, think of what it's going to mean to the people who in some similar occasion and some other spot stand 50 years from now to celebrate some other significant development of this kind.

The improvement in our cultivation, the improvement in control of floods that are now so destructive will then probably become commonplace. They will accept them as a part of their lives. They will no longer question the usefulness of these great dams.

Now, I believe that every part of our Government and of our people have a role to play in the development of this kind of conservation effort. The Federal Government, with its great reserves of credit and of money, must participate because out of these things comes a direct and great benefit to the Federal Government.

First, we must recall that our population is increasing now at the rate of about 3,000,000 a year. Certainly before long the rate of increase will be in excess of that number.

Now we talk about our surpluses. Within a matter of a couple of decades the problem will be—where is our wheat, our meat, our grain, our fibers? Where are they coming from? We will have to develop all of these lands so far as the available water will permit so as to bring production to a maximum rate rather than what we sometimes now call a controlled rate.

Everywhere there will be need for the power, for the controls of flood waters, for the irrigation water and for the navigation that will travel our streams.

Now, possibly it would be appropriate for me to express here just a bit of my own philosophy as to the kind of partnership that would develop these great works. As I said, I believe that the Federal Government has a major role to play. But we must not forget that our Founding Fathers found and believed it necessary that in diffusing and dispersing power—the control over our lives in this country—it wasn't enough to disperse it and diffuse it functionally in the executive branch, the legislative branch and the judicial. They felt it also necessary to diffuse it geographically.

In other words, the State has not only a traditional but a very necessary function to perform in our country if we are to be assured of remaining the kind of people under the kind of governmental system that we now enjoy and which has brought us to this point.

And so I believe that in a great work, a great development such as this, the State has a very distinct function and it must be performed. Else too much power will be concentrated in Washington and all people will have to look to that far off place to say, "What may I do and what may I not do," whether you be an industrialist in the city or a farmer tilling the soil.

And in the same way the community, the municipality has a function. And finally there is always a place in our country for private enterprise. Indeed, when that function disappears then we will be under some other alien form of government and one that we would not recognize now.

I wonder if you would allow me for a moment to read an observation from one of the greatest Presidents our country has produced—Abraham Lincoln. He said once, "The legitimate object of Government is to do for a community of people whatever they need to have done but cannot do at all or cannot do so well. In all that the people can individually do so well for themselves Government ought not to interfere."

So far as I'm concerned, I am going to make no attempt to improve on Mr. Lincoln's philosophy.

But obviously Garrison Dam is something that the community—the people here—could not do for themselves. And I am proud, indeed, to be here to symbolize today in a small way the Federal Government's part in this great development. But the dam was built with people's money. Its benefits shall go to the people.

One of the functions that this dam will perform is providing power for this great area. Already there are in this area facilities by which that power is distributed. There are facilities that belong to municipalities; there are REA co-op facilities; there are private power companies. All should be utilized. What man has produced we don't destroy; we don't throw it away. They are here to serve these communities. We could use them all because all have proved their usefulness.

Now, in using the things that already have been produced for the benefit of all people, we will conserve tax dollars at a time when the security of this great Nation—the security that permits this kind of development—is demanding 2 out of every 3 tax dollars we pay.

It is no time to be spending money uselessly. It is time to be doing those things which the needs of today—and even more so the needs of the next 10 years—demand that we do in order that we may stay prosperous and do our work economically and in timely fashion so that the urgency of an immediate need will not drive us into extra cost.

Now, this brings us up to another aspect of this kind of work. It is not something to be conceived of all alone. It is part of a great conservation work that all parts of our Nation must benefit from and must participate in, in order that we must get these things when we need them.

Because; let us take one of these great dams. In itself it possibly is not directly concerned in soil conservation. But if we do not have soil conservation practices up above these great dams they will certainly fill up more rapidly than if we do act intelligently in this fashion and keep these dams for the purposes for which they were intended.

Already some of the earlier dams, constructed as early as 1903 and 1904, in the early part of the century, I am told are showing the results of filling up. So there must be coordination between this kind of work and the other practices that we have in soil, water, timber, wildlife conservation. Happily, this dam is going to serve all of these functions.

Now, my friends, in these days and times we know how necessary it is that we don't forget the spiritual strength of America. We know how necessary it is that we inform ourselves of the facts of the world situation and how we rededicate ourselves to the status of our country in order that we may stand fearless, unafraid, and secure in this troublous time, when we are threatened both from without and from within.

Many men have seen their need for a spiritual renaissance—a rekindling of the kind of spirit that made Patrick Henry say "Give me liberty or give me death." That is one side of the rededication to America that we must never forget, and certainly it is the most important in the sense that all improvements in this world that man now enjoys have come from the heart and the soul of man. Unless he wanted something—unless he demanded something—it did not come about to satisfy his material, his intellectual or his spiritual needs.

At this same time we are here engaged in something else just as important—the material strength of America. Man is both a spiritual being and a material being. He needs and requires his daily bread; he requires his clothing, his shelter and other things that come from the material resources of America and of the world.

We must conserve; we must dedicate ourselves to keeping America—America's soil, America's water—at its very highest level of efficiency. We must improve it where it is possible be-

397

cause the Nation, like each of us, is both a material thing and it is a spiritual thing.

It is spiritual in that it represents for all the world hope—hope of living and freedom, hope of living peacefully, justly, to be spared the great burdens of wars, turmoils, and destruction. But it is also something whose major economic, industrial and material strength must support this purpose throughout the world.

I mean it in this way: if the United States is going to remain free other great areas of this world must remain free. To remain free they must be both spiritually and materially strong just as must we. Since we today are the most powerful nation in the world—the leaders of the world—we must support those who, like us, are determined to observe the dignity of man to make him and respect him rather as made in the image of his God—the equal with all other people.

If we are going to do that we must be materially strong; we must be spiritually strong. I firmly believe that the kind of thing we see today is one of the major efforts that we are making now and we will continue to make in increasing number to keep our material strength great. That is what will keep our spirit and our strength able to say to all others, "Do not attack us except at your peril because we are going to live under God as a free, secure, and peaceful people."

I should like, before I say goodby, to assure you again of the great honor I feel in the invitation to come out here today to be with you to celebrate this significant milestone in the development of this Nation's material strength.

Goodby and good luck.

NOTE: In his opening words the President referred to Governor Norman Brunsdale of North Dakota and Maj. Gen. Samuel D. Sturgis, Jr., Chief of Engineers, U.S. Army. Lt. Gov. C. P. Dahl introduced the guests and R. Fay Brown served as master of ceremonies.

101   ¶ Address at the Annual Convention of the
National Young Republican Organization, Mount
Rushmore National Monument, South Dakota.
June 11, 1953

*Mrs. Chairman, Governor Anderson, distinguished guests and
ladies and gentlemen:*

I have been signally honored in the invitation from this organization to come to this beautiful spot today.   I have been privileged
to come with the two distinguished United States Senators from
this state, Senator Mundt and Senator Case, and with them
Congressman Berry and Congressman Lovre.

We are further complimented today by the presence here of a
group of young Republicans now serving you and all of us in
Congress.   So all in all it makes it an occasion that will live long
in my memory.

Now one of the many responsibilities I acquired last year was
that of becoming leader of the Republican Party.   I am very
proud—and I may add that I am kept intensely aware—of this
special responsibility.

Most Americans would agree with me that it is not appropriate for the President of the United States to indulge incessantly in
partisan political activities—every day on every possible occasion.
Many of the most critical problems before our country are in no
sense partisan issues.   They involve all Americans; and in meeting
them the President must strive to serve all our citizens.   For these
problems threaten freedom itself.   They summon and demand
unadulterated patriotism.

Yet all Americans also have the deep conviction that representative government requires a healthy two-party system.   In this
sense, the responsibility of the President as party leader is recognized as an inescapable duty, essential to democracy itself.

Having been all my life a member of a militant organization, it would be strange indeed if I should lack satisfaction in a meeting with militant Republicans—and the young Republicans have certainly earned that title. I assure you that your zeal, your courage, your energy in serving our country through the GOP excite my admiration and command my deepest respect; likewise my affection.

I therefore welcome this opportunity to meet with a Republican group, and particularly to speak to you young men and women who tomorrow will be leading this party and, let me add with confidence, leading this Nation.

Now some members of the opposition party will, of course, contest this in every way they can. With vast volumes of anguished oratory, they will proclaim their grief over all we do.

We must be philosophic and patient about all this. For this sound-and-fury also is a characteristic element in our two-party system. And we must keep our sense of humor always, for since time immemorial man has heard no cry more agonized than that of the deposed bureaucrat or the demoted politician.

Now understanding all this, let us nevertheless remind ourselves that no party's tenure of office is assured by merely wishing it so. Our tenure will depend, first of all, upon Republican performance—upon the wisdom and the unity we prove in advancing a program that will serve the interests and needs of all our citizens. It will depend, beyond this, upon the efficiency of the Republican organization in bringing to every citizen in the land clear knowledge of our problems and our progress toward their solution.

We Republicans, in short, though identified as a partisan political party, can know and serve our own interests only as we know and serve those of all our people—of all parties and races and creeds. Hence, as we join in a partisan meeting with great satisfaction, we gather in a spirit not so much partisan as American.

Now your individual and collective interest in our party is especially vital, for its whole future belongs to you. You are interested, as are your elders, in the present. You share its burdens—you must provide your share of the required leadership.

But obviously, your youth makes you the possessors of the future—and makes the Republican party yours to commend or to correct, to strengthen in wisdom and in will.

For this reason, you have a special right to ask of me: What is this party of ours achieving in Washington: what are its methods today and its hopes for tomorrow? And, above all, what beliefs are ruling its growth and its future?

Now let me try to answer these questions as briefly and clearly as I can.

To summarize something of what the Republican party has done—in just 5 months—I cite 10 quite specific achievements. These are 10 areas in which deeds, not promises, testify to the work done.

First, in the field of foreign affairs: we have dedicated our party resolutely to a policy seeking to strengthen and secure friendship and cooperation among all nations loving freedom and resisting tyranny. We have recognized that the power to stay free demands spiritual strength, economic strength, military strength; and the fostering of all of these is essential to true collective security.

We have worked not only to improve our defense against threatened Communist aggression—not only to eliminate in the non-Communist world those conditions that invite the propaganda of the Communists, but also to encourage strains and stresses within the ranks of the 800 millions in the Soviet world now denied the hopes and the rewards of a free life.

We have—in the 5 months we have been in office—been striving both to perfect this policy and to make it clearly understood by our friends throughout the world. Our special emissaries have gone, or shortly will be going, to almost every section of the globe, to make plain our single, simple purpose: peace and security for ourselves and for our friends everywhere.

It has been in this spirit, for example, that an American Secretary of State has made, for the first time in our history, a pilgrimage to an area of utmost importance to us all—the Near and Middle East and South Asia. And in the same purpose of good will, in that same spirit, my brother, the president of Pennsylvania State College, will soon start on an extended visit on my behalf to South America.

Signs of such good will must be matched by the evidence of good deeds.

Firm and lasting collective security cannot be built of promises and gestures alone. For this reason, our foreign aid program as now conceived and administered—realistically and economically—is indispensable to all our security arrangements. All the plans we have made, including many of the savings in our security department, are conceivable and practicable only when geared to this essential foreign aid. For only this aid enables our friends in the world to assume their proper roles in the common defense of freedom.

I know that you especially appreciate this truth. For I have found everywhere in our country that young men and women are conspicuously and keenly aware of the meaning and the demands of collective security—without which there is no true security for any one.

Next, we have reviewed and revised military defense plans to meet realistically the needs of our times. These plans are designed to avoid the need for "crash" operations meeting sudden unforeseen crises. They are projected ahead for a continuing, not an intermittent, time of crisis. We must be ready to meet not merely some sudden, lightning like attack but the enduring responsibilities, both military and economic, that fall upon us as the leaders of freedom's forces.

The programs we have devised are calculated primarily to make and keep us militarily secure during such an age. They are conceived—with care and logic—in the hope that even the Soviets can be persuaded to see the utter folly of counting upon the success of aggression or, indeed, of depending solely upon armaments for security. Whenever that day truly dawns, then the burden of arms now so grievously slowing the social progress of mankind can be lifted from the world—and the pursuit of human happiness be gloriously speeded.

Next, we have freed our economy of needless stifling controls and at the same time taken effective steps to assure the well-being of all our people. Throughout our economy, the power of American initiative is being encouraged again to prove itself.

Without resort to emergency measures, for example, we have seen cattle prices show signs of stabilizing, after the drastic drop begun many, many months ago. A new international wheat agreement has been negotiated which, once ratified, will assure for our farmers of an export outlet for large quantities of wheat at a price 25 cents above the previous agreement.

We are revitalizing the foreign agricultural service to promote foreign trade. Legal price supports have been maintained, while spoilage has been reduced and storage costs have been cut. Agriculture, caught today in a harsh squeeze because of high operating costs, needs the prospect of a good, stable income.

We are now busily engaged in consulting farmers from all parts of the United States, to help us work out a program designed to achieve this goal, without regimenting the farm families of America. I am confident we can do it.

Next, and I assure you, most important, we have instituted what amounts almost to a revolution in Federal Government as we have seen it operating in our generation. We have set about making it smaller rather than bigger—we have been finding things it can stop doing rather than new things for it to do. Recommended expenditures for the next year have been cut by $4.5 billion, and requests of the Congress for new money have been reduced by more than $8.5 billion. The Federal payroll is already smaller by more than 50 thousand individuals—which means a saving of no less than $180 million per year. And every single department of the Government has reduced its requests for money for the next year.

Next, we have set about making Government not only more

economical but more efficient in its operations, by speeding reorganizations of whole departments. These have included the Department of Agriculture, the Department of Defense, the State Department, the Government Information Program, the Department of Justice, the Mutual Security Agency.

This has meant that refining and coordination of Government functions ranging all the way from the welfare of the farms of South Dakota to the construction of air bases in North Africa.

Next, we have created a new Cabinet office—the Department of Health, Education, and Welfare. For the first time the problems of the needy and the sick, the aged and the helpless are in charge of a major department of the Federal Government.

Next, we are helping to foster the revitalization of local and State government. We have instituted a complete review of Federal-State relations, with the purpose of clearing lines of authority, eliminating wasteful duplication, and insuring to State and local governments the responsibility for all functions properly theirs.

We have called the Governors of all the States to a conference in Washington, to review with them the whole matter of national security, and this healthy practice is to be repeated regularly in the years ahead. Respecting the rights and responsibilities of the States, we have determined the disposition of the tidelands oil with action that, in my deep conviction, recognizes fairly the Constitutional rights of both Federal and State Governments.

Next, we have attacked the problem of internal security with a vigor long overdue. We have set up security regulations in the Federal Government which, while strictly respecting the just rights of every civil servant, at the same time recognize this basic principle: Government employment itself is not a right but a privilege.

This privilege is at last being categorically denied anyone not worthy of the American people's trust—whether in any department of Government, or in the delegation of the United Nations, or in any Embassy abroad. This assuring of proper security, as I said in the State of the Union Message, is the direct responsibility of the executive branch of the Government. This responsibility is now being met.

And I assure you again it is being met, as it must be met, without resort to un-American methods; the rights of the innocent and the reputation of the devoted public servant must be militantly defended. Should we fail in this, we would have none but failures and wasters left to serve the Federal Government.

And here let me repeat once again: the vast bulk of your Federal employees comprise dedicated and able citizens. I respect and I honor them.

Next, we have, through a healthy and thoroughly renovated Department of Justice, begun effectively to attack crime and corruption. This attack cares more for the substance of the results it achieves than for the size of the television audiences it commands. A completely overhauled Department of Justice staff is directing these operations—from major anti-trust actions to the exposure of vicious crime rings that have long ruled the docks of our major ports.

Next and finally, we have taken substantial steps toward ensuring equal civil rights to all our citizens regardless of race or creed or color.

Again: these actions have been designed to remove terrible injustices rather than to capture headlines. They are being taken, quietly and determinedly, wherever the authority of the Federal Government extends.

Action has been taken in Army camps and schools. And in the District of Columbia, before the bar of the Supreme Court, the Attorney General has successfully appealed for the upholding of laws barring segregation in all public places in our National Capital.

This list, then, suggests some of our forward movement in 10 critical areas of Government. It would be foolish to pretend that these achievements are more than a beginning. But I sincerely believe they are a good beginning.

There is something to be added here that is scarcely less important for our future. It is this: these results have been achieved by ways and means that, while not new in our history, have been too long out of fashion in our Government.

First, one fact I think is particularly meaningful to you: this administration is profoundly young in spirit. Perhaps in this, more than anything else, I can say to you: there has been a change in Washington.

The men directing the work of this administration are uncompromised by years of political promises and campaign oratory. They are not prisoners of their own past mistakes or their own stale habits of handling public affairs. They are busily—freshly—youthfully—at work.

Secondly, another new quality in the working of this administration is reflected in the role of the Cabinet. The Cabinet can be whatever kind of body the administration wants. It can, on the one hand, be a score of heads that do nothing but nod, in neat array—a kind of agreeable approval of everything proposed by the President. It can be, in the other extreme, a babel of discordant voices in which the prize of decision belongs to the loudest voice.

The present Cabinet, I assure you, belongs to neither of these futile extremes. It is a group of capable and purposeful individuals. They give advice candidly and thoughtfully, speaking their several minds freely and lucidly to but one purpose—to offer the best, the wisest programs within their power for all our 160 million citizens. And this applies to the Republican leaders of the Senate and the House as well as the officers of the Cabinet.

In this same spirit of constructive purpose have been shaped the relations between the executive and legislative branches of the Government. I have had the pleasure of meeting at the White House with every Senator and almost every Congressman of both parties—a number of whom, though veterans in Government, had never before entered the President's house.

These meetings have reflected a major purpose of this administration. It is this: to do all that it reasonably can do to encourage cooperation and harmony between the legislative and executive branches. For only such harmony can advance coherent, consistent policies at a time when all the world must be made aware of America's steady direction and aims. This effort has been shared by our party's legislative leaders.

We believe that an essential part of last year's electoral decision was the people's serious summons to restore balance and order and sense and continuity to our national policies. In this, the Chief Executive and his Cabinet heads have special responsibilities of leadership. But they can achieve needed results only by patient persuasion, sound argument, friendly contact.

Government must not allow its policies to be caught in the fatal crossfire of a Congress and an Executive warring upon one another. Such a condition is not going to prevail if it is within the power of this administration to prevent it. My young friends, I don't think anything could be more important to our Government than this particular point. Our very form of Government is in peril unless each branch willingly accepts and discharges its own clear responsibilities—and respects the rights and responsibilities of the others.

There is no compromise in principle involved in seeking to adhere to effective—and let me say constitutional—methods in Government. To every idea, to every specific measure, that this administration has ever endorsed—or to which I subscribed last summer and fall—we continue and shall continue to give our unswerving support.

Under this form of Government, a special duty of the Executive is to devise and present to the Congress broad programs affecting the welfare of America and her citizens both at home and abroad. So long as the Republicans are in power, these programs must conform to certain basic beliefs that distinguish us as a party.

I suggest that these beliefs define this party of ours, its character and its purposes—not in terms merely of the next election, but of the fateful decades stretching out before us.

What are some of these beliefs?

We believe, of course, in the dignity and the freedom of the individual. And we believe that, in determining his own daily welfare, each citizen, however humble, has greater wisdom than any Government, however great.

We believe that every citizen—of every race and creed—deserves to enjoy equal civil rights and liberties, for there can be no such citizen in a democracy as a half-free citizen.

We believe that the just and proper concern of Government is not exclusively the laborer nor the businessman nor the farmer nor the veteran, but all of these, all citizens and families and communities—none with special privileges, but all with special needs of equal concern to truly representative Government.

We believe that, in this age of peril to freedom everywhere, plain patriotism compels us to see that our own Nation's freedom and security depend upon the fate of the entire community of free nations.

We believe that the best way to defend these precious ideals of individual freedom is that middle way which avoids extremes in purpose and in action.

This middle way means—in world affairs—a national policy that is firm without being truculent, specific without being timid.

This means—in domestic affairs—a national policy that heeds both the inalienable liberties of the individual and his need for security against poverty and unforeseen disaster. This middle way means guarding against those enemies who would claim the privilege of freedom in order to destroy freedom itself.

It means guarding, no less, against any who would pretend to defend this freedom with weapons from the arsenal of the tyrant. For to defend freedom in ways that themselves destroy freedom is suicide—perhaps slow, but certainly sure.

And I suggest one thing more: a party truly confident of its devotion to the good of all the people need fear neither partisan criticism nor self-criticism. To be truly good servants, we need not pretend perfection. We do make mistakes. We shall continue to make them. But to see them and to acknowledge them is half to atone for them.

Let us always, in this spirit, strive to scrutinize ourselves no less carefully than our opponents. Let us remember that the middle way, which we are following in confidence, compels us to leave to others the rolling of loud drums and the shouting of empty slogans.

Let us remember always to be fearless and uncompromising in speaking the truth to the people, whether this truth concerns the perils of world affairs, deficits in our budgets, disappointments in our own programs.

Let us remember, in the affairs of the market place, how vast is the difference between a healthy, rugged individualism and a heartless, ruthless selfishness.

Let us remember—at every instant—that no interest of party can ever come before the interest of the Nation.

Let us remember that our Government—however grand its philosophy, however majestic its processes—is simply as good and as wise and as just as the thousands of people serving it, staffing the offices, filling the halls of Congress, advising the President. And this call to work, to serve, reaches to all of you, in every community in our land—each to do his part in helping us to stay free.

And let us always, even as we rightly revere the past and its heritage of freedom, never fear or doubt the future. For this— the future—is the hope and the home of all who are young and are free, if only they are brave.

The simple words that must ever guide us are those I have repeated so often today. We believe. We have faith. For the very foundation of our Government is this: we trust in the merciful providence of God, whose image, within every man, is the source and substance of each man's dignity and freedom.

My young friends, my pride in the Republican Party and my special loyalty to its young standard-bearers springs from my deep conviction that you are faithfully dedicated to the respect of that dignity, to the defense of that freedom, for all our people.

Thank you very much, indeed.

NOTE: In his opening words the President referred to Mrs. Carol R. Arth and Governor Sigurd Anderson of South Dakota.

102   ¶ Exchange of Messages Between the President and Prime Minister Nehru of India on the Prisoner of War Agreement Reached at Panmunjom.   *June* 12, 1953

[Released June 12, 1953. Dated June 11, 1953]

My dear Mr. Prime Minister:

I thank you for your message received June 9 regarding the prisoner of war agreement reached at Panmunjom. I greatly appreciate your words regarding the part which the United States has played in this matter. It is my earnest hope that this agreement will speedily lead to an armistice and just peace in Korea, and to a relaxing of world tensions. India's participation in the work of the Repatriation Commission will mark a further significant contribution toward these ends.

Sincerely yours,

DWIGHT D. EISENHOWER

NOTE: Mr. Nehru's message, transmitted by the Indian Ambassador, follows:

Please convey to President Eisenhower my congratulations on the signing of the P.O.W. Agreement at Panmunjom. The United States under the leadership of the President has played a wise and generous part in these negotiations which have resulted in an Agreement and I should like to offer my respectful congratulations to President Eisenhower for his leadership at this critical moment. I earnestly trust that this Agreement will lead to peace not only in the Far East but elsewhere.

JAWAHARLAL NEHRU

The messages were released at the Game Lodge, Custer State Park, South Dakota.

103 ¶ Remarks at the Dedication of the Ellsworth Air Force Base, Rapid City, South Dakota. *June* 13, 1953

Mrs. Ellsworth, Governor Anderson, distinguished guests, members and friends of the United States Air Force:

We are met here in tribute to a gallant and patriotic American, a man whose name will always be an inspiration to the members of his family and his loved ones, his friends, to the members of his garrison, to all the Armed Services, and to Americans everywhere.

It is now my very great honor to dedicate this great base in memory of Brigadier General Richard Ellsworth.

104 ¶ Remarks at the Dartmouth College Commencement Exercises, Hanover, New Hampshire. *June* 14, 1953

President Dickey, Secretary Pearson, members of Dartmouth's family and their friends:

Your president possesses a brash bravery approaching fool-hardiness when he gives to me this platform in front of such an audience, with no other admonition except to speak informally, and giving me no limits of any other kind.

He has forgotten, I think, that old soldiers love to reminisce, and that they are, in addition, notoriously garrulous. But I have certain limitations of my own I learned throughout these many years, and I think they will serve to keep me from offending too deeply. But even if I do offend, I beg, in advance, the pardon of those families and friends, sweethearts that are waiting to greet these new graduates with a chaste handshake of congratulations, and assure you that any overstaying of my time was unintentional and just merely a product of my past upbringing.

First, I could not pass this occasion without the traditional congratulations to this Class, the completion of 4 years of arduous work at a college of such standing as Dartmouth, and of which there is no higher.

Next, I think I may be pardoned if I congratulate you on the quality of the addresses you have heard today up to this moment. I think that your commencement address and the two valedictory addresses established a standard that could well be one to be emulated even here in the future.

Now, with your permission, I want to talk about two points— two qualities—today that are purely personal. I am not going to be an exhorter, as Secretary Pearson has said. I want to talk about these two things and merely suggest to you certain ideas concerning them.

I am going to talk about fun—joy—happiness, just fun in life. I am going to talk a little about courage.

Now, as to fun: to get myself straight at once, for fear that in my garrulous way I might stray from my point, I shall say this: unless each day can be looked back upon by an individual as one in which he has had some fun, some joy, some real satisfaction, that day is a loss. It is un-Christian and wicked, in my opinion, to allow such a thing to occur.

Now, there are many, many different things and thoughts and ideas that will contribute—any acts of your own—that will contribute to the fun you have out of life. You can go along the bank of a stream in the tropics, and there is a crocodile lying in the sun. He looks the picture of contentment. They tell me that often they live to be a great age—a hundred years or more— and still lying in the sun and that is all they do.

Now, by going to Dartmouth, by coming this far along the road, you have achieved certain standards. One of those standards is: it is no longer so easy for you to have fun, and you can't be like a crocodile and sleep away your life and be satisfied. You must do something, and normally it must involve others, something you do for them. The satisfaction—it's trite but it's true— the satisfaction of a clear conscience, no matter what happens.

You can get a lot of fun out of shooting a good game of golf. But you wouldn't have the slightest fun out of it if you knew to achieve that first 79—you broke 80 today—if you did it by teeing up in the rough or taking the slightest advantage anywhere, and no one else in the world but you knew it. That game would never be a 79 to you, and so it was not worth while because you had no fun doing it.

Whatever you do—a little help to someone along the road— something you have achieved because you worked hard for it, like your graduation diploma today, those things have become worth while, and in your own estimation will contribute to your happiness. They will measure up to your standards because your standards have become those that only you know, but they have become very high. And if you do those things, they are the kind of things that will satisfy you and make life something that is joyous, that will cause your face to spread out a little, instead of going this way [*indicating a long face*]. There's too much of that in the world, anyway.

You are leaders. You are bound to be leaders because you have had advantages that make you leader to someone, whether you know it or not. There will be tough problems to solve. You have heard about them. You can't solve them with long faces— they don't solve problems, not when they deal with humans. Humans have to have confidence. You have got to help give it to them.

This brings me up to my second little topic, which is courage. I forget the author, but one many years ago, you know, uttered that famous saying, "The coward dies a thousand deaths, but the brave man dies but once." In other words, you can live happily if you have courage, because you are not fearing something that you can't help.

You must have courage to look at all about you with honest

eyes—above all, yourself. And we go back to our standards. Have you actually measured up? If you have, it is that courage to look at yourself and say, well, I failed miserably there, I hurt someone's feelings needlessly, I lost my temper—which you must never do except deliberately. You did not measure up to your own standards.

Now, if you have the courage to look at yourself, soon you begin to achieve a code or a pattern that is closer to your own standards. By the same token, look at all that is dear to you: your own family. Of course, your children are going to be the greatest, the most extraordinary that ever lived. But, also, look at them as they are, occasionally.

Look at your country. Here is a country of which we are proud, as you are proud of Dartmouth and all about you, and the families to which you belong. But this country is a long way from perfection—a long way. We have the disgrace of racial discrimination, or we have prejudice against people because of their religion. We have crime on the docks. We have not had the courage to uproot these things, although we know they are wrong. And we with our standards, the standards given us at places like Dartmouth, we know they are wrong.

Now, that courage is not going to be satisfied—your sense of satisfaction is not going to be satisfied, if you haven't the courage to look at these things and do your best to help correct them, because that is the contribution you shall make to this beloved country in your time. Each of us, as he passes along, should strive to add something.

It is not enough merely to say I love America, and to salute the flag and take off your hat as it goes by, and to help sing the Star Spangled Banner. Wonderful! We love to do them, and our hearts swell with pride, because those who went before you worked to give to us today, standing here, this pride.

And this is a pride in an institution that we think has brought great happiness, and we know has brought great contentment and freedom of soul to many people. But it is not yet done. You must add to it.

Don't join the book burners. Don't think you are going to conceal faults by concealing evidence that they ever existed. Don't be afraid to go in your library and read every book, as long as that document does not offend our own ideas of decency. That should be the only censorship.

How will we defeat communism unless we know what it is, and what it teaches, and why does it have such an appeal for men, why are so many people swearing allegiance to it? It is almost a religion, albeit one of the nether regions.

And we have got to fight it with something better, not try to conceal the thinking of our own people. They are part of America. And even if they think ideas that are contrary to ours, their right to say them, their right to record them, and their right to have them at places where they are accessible to others is unquestioned, or it isn't America.

I fear I have already violated my promise not to stay too long and not to exhort. I could not, though, go back to that chair without saying that my sense of distinction in Dartmouth's honorary doctorate, in the overgenerous—extravagantly overgenerous remarks of your president in awarding me that doctorate, in the present of the cane from the young men of the graduating class—all of these things are very precious to me.

I have been fortunate in that my life has been spent with America's young men, probably one of the finest things that has happened to me in a very long life.

I thank you again for this.

NOTE: The President spoke at 12:22 p.m. In his opening words he referred to John Dickey, President of Dartmouth College, and Lester B. Pearson, Secretary of State for External Affairs of Canada.

105   ¶ Remarks at the Dedication of the
Theodore Roosevelt Home at Sagamore Hill, Oyster
Bay, New York, as a National Shrine.
June 14, 1953

*Mr. Chairman, President Hoover, Governor Dewey, members of
the Roosevelt family, and friends and admirers of Theodore
Roosevelt:*

My first act in the tribute that I hope to pay to our ex-President today is an official one. It is a Proclamation that I have to sign, and as I sign it, I shall read it to you.

It is headed [*reading*] "Theodore Roosevelt Week. By the President of the United States of America, A Proclamation.

"Whereas Theodore Roosevelt holds an honored place in the annals of our country as a spirited soldier, a farsighted statesman, an intrepid explorer, and a forceful writer; and

"Whereas the dedication of Theodore Roosevelt's home at Sagamore Hill, Oyster Bay, New York, as a national shrine is to take place during the week of June 14, 1953; and

"Whereas the Congress, by a joint resolution approved on June 13, 1953, has designated the week beginning June 14, 1953, as Theodore Roosevelt Week, in honor of our former President, and has requested the President to issue a proclamation calling upon the people of the United States to observe that week by paying tribute to the achievements and memory of Theodore Roosevelt:

"Now, therefore, I, Dwight D. Eisenhower, President of the United States of America, do hereby call upon the people of the United States to observe the week beginning June 14, 1953, as Theodore Roosevelt Week by paying tribute to the achievements and memory of that great American, and I urge interested individuals and organizations to take part in appropriate ceremonies commemorative of the inspiring role of Theodore Roosevelt in our national heritage.

"In witness whereof, I have hereunto set my hand and Seal." [*The President then signed the Proclamation*] Which I trust makes this ceremony the beginning of a week of spontaneous tribute to one of the greatest Americans that we have produced.

I want to refer, for a second, to the Army and some of its practices. In its schools and in its educational systems, we are required to study the processes, the acts and decisions of leaders of the past. Now, contrary to popular notion, these studies are not confined to the decisions of military commanders. We look up and study the actions of leaders, to see what were the problems facing them; how did they analyze them; how did they reach their decisions; what did they do.

One of the men who was a favorite for study in my generation was Theodore Roosevelt. Now, there is one thing that I should like to speak about that I learned during that study. We are apt, I think, when we cast our minds back to dramatic figures of the past, to overdramatize them. For he seems, Teddy Roosevelt, a rough rider. We like to think of him, in his relationships with the Congress, that he galloped down Pennsylvania Avenue on a spirited charger, with sabre drawn, and rushed into the House and Senate, demanded what he wanted, and rode out with everybody cowed.

And that, in more or less similarity, is paralleled in every picture we have in our minds of what he did. But the fact is that he was a wise leader. He was not a swashbuckler and he was not a bull in a china shop.

Governor Dewey has spoken about the illustrious predecessor he had up in Albany. And when he went up there, he found that a great branch of his party, headed by Mr. Platt, was horrified at some of the programs for which Teddy Roosevelt stood. And did he get a ball-bat and pound him over the head? Did he take the stump and curse this man? He did not. His biographers say that he set out to win this man, and they said he resorted to cajolery. He used every form of polite advance that there was open to him including, the biographer says, many breakfasts.

I want to point out that leaders do become different things in our minds. Often when they have been possessed of certain dramatic mannerisms, they are quite apt to get lopsided in our minds. Here was a man who was rounded. He not only was the great moral leader that Governor Dewey spoke about, possessed of great moral courage, a great soldier in his regiment. He was a great leader and a great student and a great writer. His "Winning of the West" is today a classic. He was a man who understood his fellow human beings. He understood those things for which they yearned and which they deserved under the principles in which he believed.

And he set out by patient work. Nothing was too mean for him to do. Nothing was too difficult for him to tackle. There was no one of whom he was frightened as he started to do them. And he had the stamina, the courage, the persistence to carry through.

I remember as a young officer in World War I, I saw in the paper that he had volunteered his services to command a division if his Government wanted him. And I remember so well, in the regiment in which I was then serving in Texas, at least half a dozen young officers went up to the Adjutant to put down our names to say could we go to the division commanded by Theodore Roosevelt.

That, I think, explains what he meant to us as young men. In these later years, as we look back and study his career, and get more perspective, it grows only more brilliant with time. I believe it will continue to do so. I think that along with the dedication of this house today, if each of us could dedicate himself to attempt to emulate Theodore Roosevelt in his consideration for what we so futilely call "the common man"—for want of a better word—that if we could emulate the devotion of that American citizen to all citizens, if we could have his courage in carrying through, his wisdom in seeing what was right and adhering to the right, then I am quite certain that not only will Sagamore Hill and this house stand as a great monument, but each of us in his own way will build a little monument to America.

And that is what, after all, he did. He built a monument to America.

My friends, thank you very much.

NOTE: The President spoke at 5:12 p.m. His opening words "Mr. Chairman" referred to Leonard W. Hall, Chairman of the Republican National Committee, who was also the chairman of the dedication ceremonies.

106 ¶ Statement by the President on the Death of Douglas Southall Freeman. *June* 15, 1953

I AM profoundly distressed at the news of the sudden passing of Douglas Southall Freeman.

America has lost one of her most distinguished citizens—a fine historian and an outstanding American. He was a true and valued personal friend whom I shall miss greatly.

Mrs. Eisenhower and I extend our deep sympathy to Mrs. Freeman and the members of her family.

107 ¶ Veto of Bill Concerning the Claim of J. Don Alexander. *June* 15, 1953

To the United States Senate:

I return herewith, without my approval, the enrolled bill (S. 484) "Conferring jurisdiction upon the United States District Court for the District of Colorado to hear, determine, and render judgment upon the claim of J. Don Alexander against the United States."

The bill confers jurisdiction on the United States District Court for the District of Colorado to hear, determine, and render judgment on the claim of J. Don Alexander, of Colorado Springs, Colorado, against the United States for recovery of income tax paid by him for the year 1929, which covered the capital net gain for the sale of 9,000 shares of stock in the Alexander Industries, Incorporated, which stock was later held by the United States Circuit Court of Appeals to be the property of Alexander Industries, Incorporated, and not of J. Don Alexander (69 F. 2d. 610 (1934)). Section 2 of the bill provides that such suit may be instituted within one year after date of enactment of the Act; that proceedings for the determination of the claim and review thereof and payment of any judgment thereon, shall be as in other cases under 28 U.S.C. 1346(a)(1); that nothing contained in the Act shall be construed as an inference of liability on the part of the United States.

The Congress, in changing this bill from its original form to that of a jurisdictional bill, apparently believed that its action would provide a greater degree of protection to the interests of the United States. A review of the facts and of the decision of the Circuit Court of Appeals convinces me that this action of the Congress has had quite the opposite effect from what was intended.

The opinion of the Court in the case of *Alexander* v. *Theleman* referred to in the bill discusses in some detail (1) the relationship of Mr. Alexander to the Corporation, in which he owned a considerable portion of stock, and (2) the question of the ownership of the 9,000 shares, the sale of which Mr. Alexander had assumed, in paying his income tax in 1930, gave rise to a capital net gain to him. Although the opinion raises some doubt whether equitable considerations are presented so as to justify a refund of the principal amount of the tax payment of $16,720.41, the bill, in conferring jurisdiction upon the United States District Court for the District of Colorado, provides for the payment of any judgment recovered in accordance with the provisions of law applicable to tax cases of which the court has jurisdiction. Accordingly, the bill might permit Mr. Alexander to recover, not only the amount paid by him, but also interest at the rate of 6% per annum for the period from 1930 to date of payment. Thus, in effect, Mr. Alexander might recover over $23,000 in interest alone.

The requirement that the United States pay interest on a refund is entirely proper where the Government has retained a taxpayer's money, notwithstanding the fact that by means of a timely refund claim the officials of the Treasury were put on notice and had an opportunity to examine the merits of the claim. Such circumstances do not exist in this case. No reason appears why the Government should pay in interest a sum far in excess of the original amount claimed by Mr. Alexander.

If the Congress should decide again to review Mr. Alexander's original claim and should resolve the equities in this case in favor of the claimant, I would be willing to give the case further consideration.

Dwight D. Eisenhower

108 ¶ Veto of Bill for the Relief of Helmuth Wolf Gruhl. *June* 15, 1953

To the House of Representatives:

I return herewith, without my approval, H.R. 1334, "For the relief of Helmuth Wolf Gruhl."

The bill would provide for the retroactive payment of a child's insurance benefit under the Federal old-age and survivors insurance program of the Social Security Act to Helen Mann Gruhl for the use and benefit of Helmuth Wolf Gruhl on the wage record of Werner Gruhl for the period December 1942 to February 1947, amounting to $868.53.

The facts in the case are as follows: It appears that in 1931 Helen Gruhl married Werner Gruhl. In April 1932 a son, Helmuth Wolf Gruhl, was born of this marriage, and in 1935 Mrs. Gruhl separated from her husband and took her son from their home in Elizabeth, New Jersey, to Chicago, Illinois, and ultimately to Madison, Wisconsin. In June 1941 she obtained an absolute divorce from Werner Gruhl.

Werner Gruhl entered into another marriage. He died in November 1942, in Middlebury, Vermont. Helen Gruhl, the mother of Helmuth Wolf Gruhl, stated that she had no knowledge of the death of her former husband until April 1947, but that she would have learned of the death and would have filed a claim for the child's insurance benefits as early as November 1942, if the widow of Werner Gruhl had not, in her petition for administration of his estate, erroneously made the statement that she was his sole heir. Mrs. Helen Gruhl made application on behalf of her minor son for child's insurance benefits under title II of the Social Security Act in June 1947, and such benefits were awarded retroactive to March 1947 in the amount of $17.03 a month. Such benefits were paid until the child reached the age of eighteen. Had she been informed, in 1942, of the death of her husband, and had timely application been made for the benefits, payment for the 51 months from December 1942 through February 1947 would have accrued to the benefit of the child, which would have amounted to $868.53. The Bureau of Old-Age and Survivors Insurance held that the provisions of the Social Security Act then in effect prevented the payment of retroactive benefits for the period covered by this bill. The action of the Bureau was upheld on appeal by a Referee and by the Appeals Council of the Federal Security Agency.

The Social Security Act does provide for the payment of retroactive benefits for a limited period when the filing of an application is delayed after the individual is first eligible for payments. Under the law in effect before September 1950, which was applied in this case, this period was three months. (The 1950 Social Security Act Amendments have since increased the period to six months—effective with regard to months after August 1950.)

The legislative history of the Social Security Act indicates that, in providing for retroactive benefits for only a limited period, the

Congress took into account the fact that persons otherwise eligible for benefits might "not know of their right to benefits or . . . for some other reason, have delayed filing their applications." (H. Rept. No. 728, p. 40; S. Rept. No. 734, p. 47, 76th Cong.) The courts have ruled that the fact that a claimant is unaware of his rights under the Social Security Act does not extend rights beyond the statutory period of grace when no application for benefits has been filed as required by statute.

I appreciate the fact that the limitation on retroactive benefits in the Social Security Act may seem like an unjust penalty to those who, as the child and the mother in this case, had no timely knowledge of the wage earner's death. However, provision against retroactive benefits in the law—except for a reasonable period to allow for normal delays—was not intended as a penalty or forfeiture, but to carry out the purpose of this insurance program. Old-age and survivors insurance benefits are primarily intended to provide a regular, though small, income to beneficiaries to help meet their current living needs. That purpose would not be served by lump-sum payments to individuals to cover previous months for which provision had already been made in other ways, as the present case illustrates. The child has passed the age of eighteen at which social insurance benefits for minors are cut off. Moreover, the facts that the father was not supporting the child and that the death of the father was not known to the mother and child for so long indicate that there was no continuing relationship between the father and the child and that the child was not dependent economically upon the father.

Special legislation permitting one individual to receive social insurance benefits under conditions identical with those in which benefits are denied to another is undesirable and contrary to sound principles of equity and justice. If any modification of a provision in the Social Security Act is needed, I believe that the Congress should make such changes in the basic law so they will be available to all persons equally. The Congress, on two separate occasions—in 1939 and 1950—has considered the question of retroactive benefits and has decided that the period should be definitely limited.

For these reasons, I feel compelled to return the bill without my approval.

Dwight D. Eisenhower

109 ¶ The President's News Conference of *June* 17, 1953.

THE PRESIDENT. This morning, ladies and gentlemen, I have one or two announcements I think may be of some interest.

The first is about this so-called security order that was issued a year or more ago—I forget just how long—and about which I have been questioned here several times. We have been working on that for a long time, and the Attorney General has given me an analysis of what we have been doing, and what we have not. He has given me in his letter certain recommendations; along with it, we have drawn up a new order.

This order is not yet approved, but it is being put out now for simultaneous comment, both from the press of this land and from the Cabinet departments who have not yet had their final say on it. This is in conformity with the frequently announced methods I tried to use, that where people are affected by a proposed order of Government, to give them a chance to talk about it in advance. So in this case, the press and the other media of publicity will have a chance to give their opinions.

Now, this is what we think our new order does: first—we know this—it withdraws original authority to classify information from 29 of the existing agencies of Government. They will not have the right to classify anything as secret or in any other fashion that keeps it away from the public.

It limits the authority to classify in 16 additional departments exclusively to the head of the department, and nobody under that authority can do so.

Then, the information may be classified only if required in the interests of the defense of the United States.

One of these categories, which has been a great catchall, is abolished, and that is "restricted." So that no longer has any effect. The three remaining categories are very explicitly defined so as to prevent indiscriminate use of the power to classify.

By the way, you don't need to copy too much. I should have said you will get copies of the letter from the Attorney General, and you will get the copies of the proposed regulations, so you can do all you please in the way of reading; but I do want to emphasize what we think we are doing. I am sorry if I caused you needless work.

Positive provisions are included for reviewing classified material for the purpose of removing classifications or downgrading it when the interests of national defense no longer require the protection of classification.

Finally, procedures have been revised to make them more definite and certain, so that employees that are required to handle classified information will be alert to the dangers of unauthorized disclosure.

As I say, those documents are out there. Any comments that are submitted on their contents will be considered. I don't by any manner of means promise that your detailed ideas are going to be accepted, but they will certainly be considered, as will those, of course, of the Cabinet departments.

There is a document coming out at 4 o'clock—it will go out through Mr. Hagerty—in which, I think, you will have some interest. It is on the Coal and Steel Community, our relationships with it, the Coal and Steel Community of Europe under Jean Monnet. There will be official documents that will be released showing what the hoped-for relationships will be.

The final thing, a subject that I want to open up personally before we go to the questions, is merely the Korean question.

I wrote a letter to Mr. Rhee in which I earnestly tried to express what is my understanding and, I believe, the American understanding of how we got into that war, what we were trying to achieve, where we are now, and what we are trying to do. In no case have we weakened, as I see it, by the slightest degree on what we attempted to accomplish; and we accept no armistice except within that general framework of objective and purpose. Consequently, I think the fears so often expressed that there has been a complete weakening, or even sellout, are completely groundless. Certainly they are from my understanding of why we went into that war in the first place, and where we are coming out if this armistice is signed.

There is one other point: the possibility of these latest attacks of the Communists delaying or interfering with the signing of an armistice. Frankly, ladies and gentlemen, I am not exactly certain what that effect will be, but I would like to call your attention to this one thing. Let us assume that the North Koreans and the Chinese Communists are definitely sincere in their desire for an armistice. Then, I believe, we cannot escape this implication of these attacks: their complete indifference to human life and to the individual, because what would be the purpose of these attacks if they are definitely sincere in wanting an armistice, attacks obviously designed for taking a hill here or a little portion of a position there, and willing to waste the human lives that are involved in such attacks? Those defensive lines are strong, and even little portions of them are taken only at terrific cost in lives.

I think that comprises the things I had personally in mind, and so we will start the questions.

Q. Merriman Smith, United Press: Mr. President, your speech this last Sunday at Dartmouth was interpreted or accepted by a great many people as being critical of a school of thought represented by Senator McCarthy; is that right or wrong?

THE PRESIDENT. Now, Merriman, you have been around me long enough to know I never talk personalities. I think that we will get along faster in most of these conferences if we remember that I do not talk personalities; I refuse to do so.

My speech, I think, should stand by itself, but I will amplify to this extent: by no means am I talking, when I talk about books or the right of dissemination of knowledge, am I talking about any document or any other kind of thing that attempts to persuade or propagandize America into communism. Indeed, our courts found 11 Communists guilty of practically traitorous action; they pointed out that these men were dedicated to the destruction of the United States form of government by force, and that they took orders from a foreign government. So, manifestly, I am not talking about that kind of thing when I talk about free access to knowledge.

I believe the United States is strong enough to expose to the world its differing viewpoints—from those of what we call, almost, the man who has Socialist leanings to the man who is so far to the extreme right that it takes a telescope to find him. But that is America, and let's don't be afraid to show it to the world. Because we believe that form of government, those facts, that kind of thinking, that kind of combination of things, has produced the greatest system of government that the world has produced. That is what we believe; that is what I am talking about. And let no one try to think that I am attempting to propagate Communist beliefs by using governmental money to do it.

Excluding that kind of thing, I am against "book burning" of course—which is, as you well know, an expression to mean suppression of ideas. I just do not believe in suppressing ideas. I believe in dragging them out in the open and taking a look at them. That is what I meant, and I do not intend to be talking personally and in personalities with respect to anyone.

Q. Raymond P. Brandt, St. Louis Post-Dispatch: Mr. President, are you taking any steps to change the directives that have gone to our foreign missions on our libraries abroad?

THE PRESIDENT. Other than to ask Secretary Dulles to come in and talk to me about it, I have done nothing.

Q. Mr. Brandt: Because we have not been able to find the texts of the directives or to find out what they meant, and I could well understand why the foreign missions heads could not understand it.

THE PRESIDENT. Well, I don't mean to say that I have dropped this; I just mean to say I don't know any more about that possibly than you do.

Q. D. Harold Oliver, Associated Press: Mr. President, George Meany 2 weeks ago complained of the delay in getting revision of the Taft-Hartley Act this session, and asked, among other things, "Is President Eisenhower going to keep his pledge to labor?" He complained, among other things, that the President was not following up his pledge to get revision by specific proposals at this session.

THE PRESIDENT. Again, I am not answering Mr. Meany nor am I discussing it, but I promised several things: one, that I would, above all things, try to be a friend of every portion of our population. That definitely and specifically included labor. Now, that is a personal attitude, and I think I am keeping that pledge.

Next, I promised that there would be a revision of the law, if I could bring it about, that would eliminate that one provision that can be used for union busting—you know, it is the kind that prevented men on strike from voting as to their representatives. I promised that, and certainly we are going to do our best to bring it about.

There was another thing, the Communist oath. I said that I didn't believe that labor leaders should be required to sign any such thing because I found no evidence that they required manufacturers to sign it; and I still believe in it.

Now, so far as progress in this field is concerned, I don't know why everybody gets so worried that we have not made great visible progress to lay out in the field in 5 months, when people have been trying for a good many years now to do something about it.

I personally believe we are making progress. Certainly we are not going to stop until we have got an agreed position of the administration which will contain, at least, these minimum things and, unquestionably, certain other recommendations, and lay them out as our position on this labor thing. I cannot promise the exact time that is going to take place, but it is going ahead.

Q. Marvin L. Arrowsmith, Associated Press: Mr. President, in your opening remarks about the Communist offensive, is it correct to interpret what you said as feeling that the Communists are not sincere because of these attacks that have been going on?

THE PRESIDENT. No, I don't think it is; I don't think it is, Mr. Arrowsmith. I don't pretend to any secret way of interpreting their intentions that is infallibly correct. I believe they see in it some value that I don't.

I merely point out that, assuming them to be sincere, we do have some evidence again of how little they value the individual citizen as compared to the state.

Q. Martin Agronsky, American Broadcasting Company: Following up Mr. Brandt's question, Senator Hennings of Missouri remarked that if you were against "book burning," since the State Department came under the executive branch of the Government, you could demonstrate your distaste for "book burning" by rescinding the State Department order which permits books to be removed from our foreign libraries because of their authorship. Could you address yourself to that comment of Senator Hennings?

THE PRESIDENT. Well, I am not going to try to answer Senator Hennings because, again, I don't know the background from which he is talking, and I don't know the details of the order of which he is speaking.

I would say this: if the State Department is burning a book which is an open appeal to everybody in those foreign countries to be a Communist, then I would say that falls outside of the limits in which I was speaking; and they can do as they please to get rid of them, because I see no reason for the Federal Government of the United States to be supporting something that advocates its own destruction. That seems to me to be about the acme of silliness.

I do say, within the limits of decency and within the limits of—

inside—something that our courts could possibly call treasonous or traitorous, then let's don't be afraid of the kind of thinking that goes on in the United States, the kind of writing, the kind of argument. Let's put it out. Because if we go too far— suppose we go a little further and we try to establish more flexible limits for getting rid of these books—we are not advertising America, because we don't take those things out of American libraries. So I don't think we are honest then in advertising America abroad.

Now, I have not seen that order. As I said before, I have asked them to bring it in and discuss it with me, because I have not seen it. In fact, I didn't know they had issued one in the form that you now apparently intimate that it has. I didn't know there was a definite prescription, that we had a list of books.

Q. Mr. Agronsky: There is such a list, sir, only you cannot get hold of it. I know a number of us have tried.

THE PRESIDENT. Well, I will take a look.

Q. Douglas B. Cornell, Associated Press: Regarding your new information order, the proposed one, do you believe that the effect of that will be to promote a freer flow of information from the Government to the people?

THE PRESIDENT. That is certainly its purpose.

Q. Mr. Cornell: May I ask another question along that line? Has the Truman order, as such, been canceled at this point?

THE PRESIDENT. Well, it will as quickly as this one is approved and ready for issue.

Q. Mr. Cornell: It will stay in effect, then, until this new one is effective?

THE PRESIDENT. I should say so, yes.

Q. Roland Sawyer, Christian Science Monitor: Would it be your policy, sir, to advise the American people when the Russians explode more atomic bombs?

THE PRESIDENT. Would it be my policy to do so?

Q. Mr. Sawyer: Yes; when you have solid evidence of that fact.

THE PRESIDENT. You asked me a question I would not want to answer right off, just shooting from the hip, because I don't know. I will say this: in the past 5 months no such solid evidence has been brought to me. I will give you that negative answer. The other one, I will have to decide when it comes up; I had not thought of that.

Q. Robert J. Donovan, New York Herald Tribune: Sir, this is just one more clarifying question on the book issue. Is it your thought, sir, that, leaving out Communist books entirely, if a controversial book can be on our bookshelves in this country, is it all right that it can be on the bookshelf of one of our libraries abroad?

THE PRESIDENT. I should think so, speaking generally.

Q. Mr. Donovan: Leaving out Communist?

THE PRESIDENT. After all, I have never known any generalization that did not need some modification when it came to applying it to a specific case.

Generally speaking, my idea is that censorship and hiding solves nothing; that is exactly what I believe. But I do say I don't have to be a party to encouraging my own self-destruction. That is the limit; and the other limit I draw is decency. We have certain books we bar from the mails and all that sort of thing; I think that is perfectly proper, and I would do it now.

I don't believe that standards of essential human dignity ought to be violated in these things, and human decency; also, as I say, this Communist propaganda.

Now, on the other hand, let me point out something to you gentlemen. After we got in World War II, and so many of us were astonished at what was taking place, do you remember the self-criticism in which we indulged—in newspapers, in broadcasts, and everything else—because we had failed to read *Mein Kampf* seriously? We said, "There they laid it out, and we didn't read it."

Why shouldn't we, today, know what is going on? How many of you have read Stalin's *Problems of Leninism*? How many of

431

you have really studied Karl Marx and looked at the evolution of the Marxian theory down to the present application?

Now, gentlemen, what I am talking about is let's educate ourselves if we are going to run a free government, and let's don't be afraid of its weaknesses as well as its strength. From our viewpoint, its strength so far outweighs its weaknesses that we can afford to be generous in this thing.

I think I am as implacable a foe of the communistic theory as there is in this world; but I am certain in my own mind that the methods of just trying to pretend communism does not exist, or trying to pretend that it does not have a great appeal for people in certain areas and under certain conditions, is silly. We must combat it with something more constructive.

Q. Arthur T. Hadley, Newsweek: Mr. President, during the past few weeks, there have been certain subtle indications around town that your administration has reached a climax in thermonuclear weapons. Within the very proper limits of national security, could you indicate what the position of your administration is in this field and any advances that may have been made?

THE PRESIDENT. You have raised a subject that, with due respect, I must say I will not talk about. This is a very serious and sensitive field, and I just feel that at this moment, at least, I can't talk about it.

Q. Chalmers M. Roberts, Washington Post: Mr. President, the Secretary of State said the other day that this Government was considering, assuming a truce in Korea, allowing the subsequent political conference to cover not only Korean problems, but Far East problems in general. Could you spell that out and tell us if, sir, that means that there might be an effort to get a general Far East settlement before, say, a Big Four meeting on world problems?

THE PRESIDENT. I can't talk about it very definitively, for this reason: he was absolutely correct when he said "we are considering." He was obviously taking you into his confidence, to show that these things are very weighty questions. As I said—I think it was probably in the talk I made to Congress early in this administration or it may have been in the April 16th talk—there is no such thing, as we see it, of a real Korean armistice that merely frees Chinese forces to do something else equally inimical to our interests. So you can't separate these things entirely. But how they will be expressed and where they will be handled is still a moot question, in my own mind.

Q. John Herling, Register and Tribune Syndicate: In your trip out West, you referred in one of your speeches, I believe, to your intention to turn back creeping socialism of the past 20 years. That has caused some confusion in some minds, and I wonder whether you could give us some concrete examples of that creeping socialism.

THE PRESIDENT. Well, I will give you specific examples. Not long ago I had this appeal made to me in behalf of the expansion of Federal expenditures in the TVA region, and it was this: that since the Federal Government had seized and was practicing a monopoly in power down there, it was impossible for that locality now to expand unless the Federal Government spends more money down there. They quoted as one of their needs for more power that a number of industries from other sections of the country—New England and other places—want to come down there seeking cheap power. So we get to this curious thing in the socialistic theory: that we, all of us, provide such cheap power for one region—apparently it is subsidized by taxes from all of us all over the country—but then it can appeal and take away the industries from the other sections of the country. It seems to me that we have got to have some kind of reevaluation of all these things.

Now, please understand me. I have stated a thousand times, I am not out to destroy TVA. It is one experiment. I have also said that in other areas, when we repeat that thing, I want the local people to have a greater interest and a greater voice in it.

Now, that is what I say—getting on a middle-of-the-road trend and not merely go to the socialistic idea that the central government is the controlling factor in every one of these great economic things.

Q. Mr. Herling: Would that affect your intention to do anything about diminishing the impact of social security legislation?

THE PRESIDENT. We have promised, as a matter of fact, in social security, to expand its benefits in certain directions. There again, you go to the middle of the road for this reason. A strict application, let us say, of economic theory, at least as taught by Adam Smith, would be, "Let these people take care of themselves; during their active life they are supposed to save enough to take care of themselves."

In this modern industry, dependent as we are upon mass production, and so on, we create conditions where that is no longer possible for anybody. So the active part of the population has to take care of all the population, and if they haven't been able during the course of their active life to save up enough money, we have these systems.

There are many ways of implementing this idea. So far as you can, I am always delighted to see local and State people participating so that again the whole power does not get into the Federal Government.

What I am trying to say is that we find a middle-of-the-road basis here, and that is what I call stopping. I don't mean to say turn back the clock; and I hope you understand it.

Q. Roscoe Drummond, Christian Science Monitor: Mr. President, some Republican Members of Congress have stated that they think that unless taxes are reduced at this session on both individual incomes and corporations, it will be a violation of the Republican campaign commitments and the Republican platform. Would you express your view on that?

THE PRESIDENT. I think I have several times, Mr. Drummond, but I will try again. Everybody, of course, is convinced that taxes are too high to stay where they are, particularly over a long-term period, and still have that great incentive that we think is inherent in the opportunity of a man to earn and save for himself and his family. I agree, and everybody else has agreed.

Now, I personally know of not a single man during the last campaign that promised immediate tax reduction. Certainly I didn't. I did say, "Here is an objective, and here is the way we've got to do it."

I think I could bring out talks where I said you are not going to have any real tax reduction until we find a system in the world, some kind of peace and security arrangement in which we have confidence, where there is going to be great and deep tax reduction.

I think that through an easing off of the situation and better administration, we can accomplish some. As a matter of fact—as expressed, I think, by the Secretary of the Treasury several times—we are now counting on definite tax reductions next January 1st. But we are certainly doing our best to get our house in order.

Here is what I believe to be a sound argument. If we don't close the gap in our deficits, in the long run there is no tax reduction; because the constant cheapening of your money, as a result of that, finally brings you to the point that your prices go up and everything goes up on you faster than you can catch it. Inflation has a way of galloping away from you. Consequently, unless we close the gap in our budget, I don't believe that tax reduction in the long term is possible.

Now, that is what I believe. However, don't let anyone quote me as saying I don't believe in tax reduction. I am talking about timing.

Q. Anthony H. Leviero, New York Times: Mr. President, I would like to ask two questions, if I may, one on the books, and one on the security order.

Now, in mentioning a couple of particular books, Marx and Stalin, I believe you are getting back to the old maxim about, "Know your enemy." Certainly, we had that plastered on the walls of G–2 in the war.

THE PRESIDENT. Yes.

Q. Mr. Leviero: But these books are being kept under lock and key in a lot of American libraries. I wondered if you thought that was proper. These are basic documents about the enemy. Should students and others have free access to these books? I wonder what your opinion is on that.

THE PRESIDENT. With your permission, I will quote myself. On October 12, 1948, I made an inaugural address as President of Columbia, and I insisted that communism, the facts of communism, were going to be taught at Columbia. I insisted likewise that if there were any teacher there who was persuaded of communism and who was trying to induce students to follow communism, I wouldn't stay there if we couldn't get rid of that person. I think the distinction is not difficult.

The facts of communism are one thing. Lay it out in front of us. Do you cure cancer by pretending it does not exist? To my mind, this thing has got to be understood. What is its appeal for man? It does no good for me just to get up and shout, "I am against communism." What is it? To some people that actually believe in it, it is practically a religion—although it calls religion in our sense an opiate of the masses, an opiate of the people.

So, these things that expose to us right from the original source what is communism, I don't believe we should hide them. We should attempt to show our students the way in which they should approach them. We shouldn't give that text to a Communist teacher and say, "Now, take your students off, and try to lead them astray," any more than you would give them, let us say, Al Capone's book on how to be a crook. I think this is just as bad. But there is a very great distinction in teaching facts and exhorting, teaching doctrine.

Q. Mr. Leviero: Pardon me, I did reserve another question.

THE PRESIDENT. I will have to consult your governing board. But go on.

Q. Mr. Leviero: About the security order, I know that it has been put to us for discussion. But for some understanding in advance, I believe you said there were 29 departments——

THE PRESIDENT. Agencies.

Q. Mr. Leviero: ——agencies, which would no longer have the authority. Suppose one of them did get involved in a national defense project. I wonder where they would get their guidance for classification.

THE PRESIDENT. They would immediately appeal to the Security Council. They would say, "We have a subject here that we just think, if we let it go, it would be bad."

But they have no right in themselves to classify things. And, of course, one of the great kicks you people have made is that anyone right down the line, right down to, you said, pretty low down, could classify something and stamp it secret, and then you were helpless.

Q. Mr. Leviero: By delegating authority?

THE PRESIDENT. Yes.

Q. Robert E. Clark, International News Service: Mr. President, I am still not clear in my mind on one point. Would you remove books by Marx and Lenin from our State Department libraries overseas?

THE PRESIDENT. Now, listen; I would be the last to pretend that I have read all of their books. I would say this: in our libraries overseas, it would seem to me that they have plenty of access to the documents that are definitely communistic. But the question that I was answering was in our own libraries, here, that they brought up.

Overseas, I see no reason for bringing these things up unless it were some area where we believed that we had a particular group where we had to show them exactly what communism was out of the mouths of the Communist leaders themselves.

I've said, "Don't let me be the apostle of the doctrine that all generalizations are always true"; on the contrary, I hold with the old Frenchman that said, "All generalizations are false, including this one."

437

Now, I believe that. I believe that men have got to be wise enough and strong enough to take a look at the problem they have in deciding it. And I just don't believe in making these sweeping "always and invariably true."

Q. Joseph A. Fox, Washington Evening Star: Mr. President, on that story, to carry it a bit further, sir, you feel, then, I take it, that people in foreign countries know enough about communism without being briefed further on it; is that, generally speaking, true?

THE PRESIDENT. Generally, I think that is true. I think the uprisings in Berlin this morning ought to be a good lesson for most of us.

Q. Charles S. von Fremd, CBS Television: Mr. President, prior to the coronation, there appeared to be a slight rift between the British and the United States. Do you think that the coronation with its apparent good effect since then has brought that rift closer together? Do you think our two countries are now more friendly?

THE PRESIDENT. It is unfortunately true in this world that often the best of friends seem to have the greatest right to criticize each other in public. I don't know why this is, but it seems to be true.

I honestly believe that basically the American people respect and admire the British record, and therefore the British people. Of course, we do have exceptions; I am not trying to say that we all agree, but I think basically we do. I am sure that is basically true also in Britain.

Now, when something comes along about the coronation and we are reminded of some of the history of the past, the type of law that we inherited from those people, when we think of our heritage from them of the Magna Carta and other great documents and traditions, I think it is a good thing, and I think it was a good thing to show it to as many people of America as possible.

So far as I can see, only good resulted from it. From the reports I have had from people coming back, they were greatly impressed.[1] The British, of course, are masters of this solemnity and ceremony. I have gone through some of them and practically shuddered, almost, at the requirements of the thing. But I think it was, in all, a good thing.

However, I disagree with the contention that we are constantly at each other's throats down deep.

Q. Mrs. May Craig, Portland (Maine) Press Herald: Mr. President, the Agriculture Department is considering selling off our surplus butter at 10 cents a pound. Republicans advocated free enterprise in their platform. Do you think the continued accumulation of unsalable surpluses is free enterprise?

THE PRESIDENT. Well, Mrs. Craig, you have opened up a whole philosophy that we could talk about for hours.

I don't know that they are contemplating selling butter at 10 cents, but I do know this: the price of butter has gotten to the point that it is sort of pricing itself out of the market.

Now, if we look at the total surpluses we have, just in money value, you say, "Well, now, if by that kind of purchases we have provided a reasonably stable economy, then we haven't invested too much, because we still have these things we can use."

For example, I hope and I believe that the Congress will approve a million-ton grant to Pakistan. If we didn't have that in a surplus somewhere, it wouldn't be possible, would it?

I don't think that we should get too excited about these surpluses, until we approach that place of unusability, deterioration, and spoilage. Then it gets serious, because I believe now that we have a moral value involved. I just don't think it is right for the sweat and toil and resources of the United States to be thrown out in the middle of the ocean when someone else is starving.

---

[1] The White House announced on March 6 that the President had designated the following as his representatives at the coronation of Queen Elizabeth II: George Catlett Marshall as the President's Special Representative; Governor Earl Warren of California and Mrs. Gardner Cowles as Assistant Representatives; and General Omar N. Bradley, Chairman, Joint Chiefs of Staff, to represent the three United States Services.

Now, you say "all right, if it is not socialistic, it is based on a purely humanitarian thing"—and I believe George Kennan argues that humanitarian and moralistic values have no place in foreign relations. But after all, we do believe that we are a product and a representative of the Judaic-Christian civilization, and it does teach some concern for your brother. And I believe in that.

So I am not too concerned about these surpluses yet. If the thing keeps building up on us, then we've got a problem we've got to meet, and it is going to be tough. I haven't got the answers yet. But I do say, if we would make a complete practice of buying up butter at 67⅔ cents and selling it at 10 cents, we would finally be in an awful mess, and I couldn't go with that.

There will be one more question. I am sorry. [*To Merriman Smith*] You haven't done your duty. [*Laughter*]

Q. Joseph A. Fox, Washington Evening Star: Is there anything that you would care to say about that uprising in East Germany?

THE PRESIDENT. I can't say much about it, except this: in the face of the propaganda of the happiness and the concern for people's governments that we have heard has been the general feeling just behind the Iron Curtain, this is a significant thing. I know nothing more about it. Frankly, my dispatches are a little behind the papers this morning, and that is all I know about it.

Merriman Smith, United Press: Thank you, Mr. President.

NOTE: President Eisenhower's eleventh news conference was held in the Executive Office Building from 10:30 to 11:08 o'clock on Wednesday morning, June 17, 1953.

110　¶ Statement by the President on a Proposed Executive Order Entitled "Safeguarding Official Information in the Interest of the Defense of the United States." *June* 17, 1953

I HAVE TODAY arranged to distribute to all interested agencies a proposed Executive Order entitled "Safeguarding Official Information in the Interest of the Defense of the United States". This order revokes Executive Order No. 10290 of September 24, 1951, and provides more effective controls on classification and protection of that official information which must be safeguarded for national defense purposes. At the same time this order through its severe limitation on the authority to classify, through its elimination of one of the categories of classified material, and through its provisions for continuing review of classified information for downgrading and declassification, will open the door for citizens to obtain more information about their government.

I request that the authority of original classification of defense information or material in certain agencies be eliminated, and in other agencies be limited to the Head of the agency, without further delegation of said authority. The term "original classification" refers only to information or material originating in the department or agency which first classifies it. It does not include the classification of documents which must be classified merely because they incorporate information which has been received from another agency and which has already been classified by the agency having primary responsibility therefor.

Under the proposed order the following departments and agencies of the Executive Branch and their constituent agencies, shall be subject to the limitations contained in Section 2 of this order commencing with the effective date thereof, as follows:

A. *Original Classification Authority Eliminated:* American Battle Monuments Commission, Arlington Memorial Amphitheater Commission, Commission of Fine Arts, Committee on Purchases of Blind-Made Products, Committee For Reciprocity Information, Commodity Exchange Commission, Economic Stabilization Agency, Export-Import Bank of Washington, Federal Deposit Insurance Corporation, Federal Mediation and Conciliation Service, Federal Reserve System, Federal Trade Commission, Housing and Home Finance Agency, Indian Claims Commission, Interstate Commerce Commission, Missouri Basin Survey Commission, National Capital Housing Authority, National Capital Park and Planning Commission, National Forest Reservation Commission, National Labor Relations Board, National Mediation Board, Railroad Retirement Board, Securities and Exchange Commission, Selective Service System, Smithsonian Institution, United States Tariff Commission, Veterans Administration, Veterans Education Appeals Board, War Claims Commission.

B. *Original Classification Authority Limited to Head of Agency:* Civil Aeronautics Board, Defense Transport Administration, Department of Agriculture, Department of Health, Education and Welfare, Department of Interior, Department of Labor, Federal Communications Commission, Federal Power Commission, National Science Foundation, National Security Training Commission, Panama Canal Company, Post Office Department, Reconstruction Finance Corporation, Renegotiation Board, Subversive Activities Control Board, Tennessee Valley Authority.

Heads of departments and agencies not named herein shall limit the classification authority in accordance with Subsection 2(c) of this order.

If, because of operational responsibilities, the Head of any agency listed herein determines that these limitations will endanger the national defense, he shall submit a written request to the President for an exception including a full justification for such a request based on national defense considerations.

I have asked the heads of all agencies and departments to review the proposed order and submit any comments to the Attorney General.

DWIGHT D. EISENHOWER

NOTE: A letter from the Attorney General, dated June 15, 1953, concerning the need for a revised order, was released with the President's statement, together with a draft of the proposed order. In its final form the order was approved by the President on November 5, 1953 (E.O. 10501, 3 CFR, 1949–1953 Comp., p. 979).

111 ¶ Letter to Chairmen of Senate Foreign Relations and House Foreign Affairs Committees Concerning the European Coal and Steel Community. *June 17, 1953*

[Released June 17, 1953. Dated June 15, 1953]

My dear ————:

While in Europe, I watched with keen interest the efforts to work out the first steps toward European federation. My experience there convinced me that the uniting of Europe is a necessity for the peace and prosperity of Europeans and of the world.

The recent visit to Washington by the members of the High Authority of the European Coal and Steel Community has given me the opportunity to review with them the work and plans of the Community. This Community seems to me to be the most hopeful and constructive development so far toward the economic and political integration of Europe. As such, this European initiative meets the often expressed hopes of the Congress of the United States.

M. Monnet, President of the High Authority, has described the general program of the Community for the development of its coal and steel resources which will require extensive investment for increasing production and improving productivity. The new

Community does not wish to obtain grants for these purposes, but requires loan capital. The proceeds from the taxes now being levied and collected by the Community would appear to provide security for substantial borrowing.

In due time the Community will probably seek loans for these purposes from United States and European sources public and private. It appears to me that a portion of the financing of this development program by the United States Government or one of its agencies, out of moneys available for such purposes and under conditions insuring proper use and ultimate repayment, would foster European integration in a tangible and useful way.

Today the Common Assembly of the Community convenes to receive the first Annual Report from the High Authority regarding the activities of the Community. Your Committee might consider this an appropriate occasion to express its approval of the progress to date and its keen interest in the success of this and future steps toward European integration.

Sincerely yours,

DWIGHT D. EISENHOWER

NOTE: This is the text of identical letters sent to the Honorable Alexander Wiley, Chairman of the Senate Foreign Relations Committee, and to the Honorable Robert B. Chiperfield, Chairman of the House Foreign Affairs Committee. Their replies, dated June 16, were released with the President's letter and are published in the Department of State Bulletin (vol. 28, p. 928).

On June 3 the White House announced that at the President's invitation, Jean Monnet, President of the High Authority of the European Coal and Steel Community, Franz Etzel, Vice President, and Dirk Spierenburg, one of its members, were making an official visit to the United States; and that on that date the President, Secretary of State Dulles, William Rand, Deputy Director for Mutual Security, and David K. E. Bruce, U.S. Representative to the European Coal and Steel Community, met with these members of the Community.

112 ¶ Statement by the President on the Prevention of Forest Fires. *June* 18, 1953

OUR NATURAL RESOURCES are an integral part of this Nation's strength and security. Today, more than ever before, we need to protect, rebuild and maintain our renewable resources to insure a plentiful supply of their products for the welfare of all people. The protection and wise use of our forest, range and watershed lands are a part of the Nation's responsibility to its citizens.

I am greatly concerned over the continuing heavy loss of our natural resources by forest fires, and over the fact that nine out of every ten of these fires are caused by human carelessness or thoughtlessness. It is squarely up to every American to realize that he has a definite personal responsibility in the protection of these resources.

This is the time of the year when most people, including myself, are making hopeful plans to visit our forests and mountains to enjoy the many forms of healthful outdoor recreation which they afford and which we all need for spiritual and physical well-being. If every man, woman and child will join in the nation-wide drive to prevent forest fires—if each one of us will use extra care this year—we can surely cut down on the unnecessary destruction of vital resources by wildfire.

113 ¶ Statement by the President Regarding a Grant of Additional Aid to West Berlin. *June* 18, 1953

IT GIVES ME particular satisfaction at this time to announce that, following discussions with the authorities of West Berlin and the Federal Republic of Germany, the United States is granting an additional $50 million aid for West Berlin. This grant of Mutual Security Program funds will be used further to strengthen West Berlin's economy and enable the people to withstand the great pressures to which they are constantly exposed.

About one-third of this sum will be used in the city's industrial investment program. This aid will help provide jobs for Berlin's unemployed and will assist the city in paying its own way.

The balance will contribute to the fulfillment of the "stockpiling" program bolstering the West Berliners' security by providing stores of food, fuel, raw materials and other essentials.

No material contribution such as this, however, can adequately express the admiration of the American people for the courageous stand of the people of Berlin in the face of existing hazards and economic difficulties.

114 ¶ Statement by the President Declining To Intervene on Behalf of Julius and Ethel Rosenberg. *June* 19, 1953

SINCE ITS original review of the proceedings in the Rosenberg case by the Supreme Court of the United States, the Courts have considered numerous further proceedings challenging the Rosenbergs' conviction and the sentence imposed. Within the last two days, the Supreme Court, convened in a special session, has again reviewed a further point which one of the Justices felt the Rosenbergs should have an opportunity to present. This morning the Supreme Court ruled that there was no substance to this point.[1]

I am convinced that the only conclusion to be drawn from the history of this case is that the Rosenbergs have received the benefit of every safeguard which American justice can provide. There is no question in my mind that their original trial and the long series of appeals constitute the fullest measure of justice and due

---

[1] 346 U.S. 273, 322, 324.

process of law. Throughout the innumerable complications and technicalities of this case, no judge has ever expressed any doubt that they committed most serious acts of espionage.

Accordingly, only most extraordinary circumstances would warrant executive intervention in the case.

I am not unmindful of the fact that this case has aroused grave concern both here and abroad in the minds of serious people, aside from the considerations of law. In this connection, I can only say that, by immeasurably increasing the chances of atomic war the Rosenbergs may have condemned to death tens of millions of innocent people all over the world. The execution of two human beings is a grave matter. But even graver is the thought of the millions of dead whose deaths may be directly attributable to what these spies have done.

When democracy's enemies have been judged guilty of a crime as horrible as that of which the Rosenbergs were convicted;— when the legal processes of democracy have been marshalled to their maximum strength to protect the lives of convicted spies;— when in their most solemn judgment the tribunals of the United States have adjudged them guilty and the sentence just, I will not intervene in this matter.

115 ¶ Memorandum on the Community Chest and United Fund Campaigns. *June* 22, 1953

To the Heads of Executive Departments and Agencies:

Community Chests and United Funds all over the country will conduct their annual campaigns this fall under the designation, "United Community Campaigns." In addition to some 18,500 health, welfare and recreation organizations, these appeals will provide financial support for the United Defense Fund whose job it is to furnish USO services to the armed forces, help to communities disrupted by defense activities and relief to Korea. The goals of these campaigns will aggregate over $280,000,000. By virtue of their size and the range of their services, these campaigns are clearly of great importance.

I have assured the leaders of United Community Campaigns of the cooperation of the Federal government in their endeavors. To that end I am confident that you will extend the full cooperation of your department in each community throughout the United States and its territories and possessions where it conducts its operations. Such cooperation would logically include the assumption of equitable unit goals, the effective solicitation of all employees and the setting up of an adequate collection method for the convenience of those who wish to make contributions on an installment basis.

It is my hope that all employees will give generously keeping in mind the fact that their gifts will be used to support a number of different organizations for a full year.

DWIGHT D. EISENHOWER

116 ¶ Statement by the President Upon Signing Bill Providing for the Treatment of Narcotics Users in the District of Columbia. *June 24,* 1953

I HAVE TODAY signed H.R. 3307, "To provide for the treatment of users of narcotics in the District of Columbia."

This measure makes available for the first time a civil procedure under which the United States District Court for the District of Columbia may order compulsory commitment of narcotic drug users to approved hospitals for treatment and rehabilitation. I believe that the enactment of this legislation is a forward step in meeting the problem of drug addiction.

The law does not take effect for a period of six months. In that time I am confident that the Board of Commissioners of the District of Columbia will be able to develop a program under which adequate care for narcotics patients can be provided in hospitals under the jurisdiction of the District Government.

I am concerned, however, that in the course of consideration of this measure attention was given to other bills now pending in the Congress which would authorize the care and treatment at facilities of the United States Public Health Service of narcotics addicts committed by state courts and the United States District Court for the District of Columbia.

I wish to make it clear that inauguration of the program authorized by H.R. 3307 is not and cannot be contingent upon additional legislation authorizing the use of the United States Public Health Service hospitals. The existing capacity of appropriately equipped hospitals is not great enough to enable the United States to assume responsibility for a large volume of commitments from the District and from state courts.

The implications of the legislation which would authorize such commitments, aside from limitations of Federal hospital capacity, need to be thoroughly studied from the state as well as from the Federal point of view. I therefore express the hope that the Congress will defer action on the pending proposals until such a study can be conducted by the commission on Federal-State relationships which will soon be established under legislation now in the final stages of Congressional consideration.

NOTE: As enacted, H.R. 3307 is Public Law 76, 83d Congress (67 Stat. 77).

117 ¶ Remarks at the American Red Cross Convention. *June* 24, 1953

Mr. Harriman, and members and friends of the Red Cross:

Late this evening, I was shown a copy of a program for this evening's meeting, and on it I found—I suppose you did, if you saw this same document—"Greetings from the President of the United States."

449

Now, I talked to some of my associates on the way over, and I said: "What do you say when you have the subject of greetings? Now they know I am glad to see them or I wouldn't be there." Well, one of them mentioned you might say it rather loudly. But, still pursuing this question, I asked your president, who gave me rather a roguish look and said, "You are on your own."

Now, ladies and gentlemen, with that kind of a liberal, unrestricted directive, as I get up here, I am about as interested as you are in finding where I am coming out.

I noticed one thing on the part of your president. As he opened the proceedings this evening, he mentioned that the Red Cross and its officials rarely mention names. I agree with him that it is wise to avoid personalities. It is rather unprofitable business. But he immediately proceeded to break his own rule and introduce to us certain distinguished people we were all very happy to meet. So I think I may be pardoned for breaking my rule.

My first observation would be to assure Mr. Melton that if this audience could have any influence with the board of the Metropolitan, we are sure he would get his raise. And speaking for myself, at least, I should like to thank his 7-year-old daughter for her suggestions as to songs.

And a word about Mr. Harriman, who came to my office shortly after I moved into my new address over here on Pennsylvania Avenue. He told me his term was up, and he indicated with a smile on his face, he was going somewhere. I said, "If it is that easy to quit, Roland, let's both go fishing." He got the point and said, "I will go right back to work." And as long as I am there, as far as I am concerned, he will be here.

But, my friends, I had a very real reason for coming over here that has nothing to do with just saying I am glad to see you, which I most emphatically am. In a way, it is a continuation of a record of frustration that I have.

For 11 long years, at least, I have been trying to make the American Red Cross understand how deeply grateful I am for their work that I have seen, that I have experienced, and indeed the kind of work for which I have felt personally responsible. Because any commander in the field is responsible for the morale of his men. That is his business. He lives with it. No morale factor in wars that America has had to wage is more important than the American Red Cross.

For that, and many other things, I have been trying to say thank you. And I have said it. But I have the frustrating feeling that I have never really been able to convey the depth of the sentiments in my heart on this particular subject.

And so I have usually resorted to attempting to tell something of what I saw, some little feeble description of what I experienced. It struck me, almost 11 years ago today, I think. I went to my first Red Cross meeting in London, in 1942. We dedicated a club. And the thing that struck me that day was this: everybody in the Red Cross had discovered one great truth of life and is practicing it: there is no satisfaction in life except as it is experienced through people. People constitute the one great important factor in all human existence, and it is our relationships to those people that make satisfactions for ourselves.

Consider a picture. Any picture would pall on any one of us finally, no matter what its artistry, no matter how much we appreciated it, unless we could at the very least have the satisfaction of describing it to someone in whom we were interested, or bring them with us to view it, and to share the joy of that picture. Or of a poem. Indeed, of your favorite restaurant. Anything in this life would pall if an individual had to experience it all alone.

And so, by membership in the Red Cross, caring for the needs, the spiritual and intellectual and material needs of others, you not only express by that act the greatest truth of all life, but I venture to say that you are making a very great investment yourselves that will yield you, some day, the greatest of dividends— if you have not already experienced it.

Each of us must, one day, withdraw a little more from the

activities, particularly the physical activities of life, than he undergoes as he passes through his most vigorous years. And when he does, the self-satisfaction that comes from service performed, I am quite certain, will be the nearest to Heaven we will ever get on this earth: to feel that you have served others—which you are doing.

I do not mean to attempt to be a philosopher here, ladies and gentlemen. That is far beyond me. I am merely trying to say that you have been doing something that to me is so worth while, not only for this reason.

When I saw you, or the people you sent, in England, in Algiers, in Tunis, in Sicily, in Italy, on the beaches, all the way to the center of Germany, caring for and cheering up the wounded, and establishing what they always called "homes away from home," when every other individual except themselves was important and they were selfless and unimportant in their own estimation, my admiration went out to them.

So what I am trying to say is: that example has meant much to me, and I am moved to say congratulations to every single individual that belongs to such a body.

Now, as we come down through the years, of course, fortunately not all our experiences are war. But we have other disasters. Every time we have one, the Red Cross has a record of moving in and expressing this same spirit, this same understanding of the importance of humans—of people.

So I was lucky, this evening, as I started over here. I got two telegrams. With your permission, I shall read them, because they help to express what I am trying so inadequately to say.

The first one is from the Mayor of Worcester, Massachusetts, and it is addressed to me, and it says:

"The true American spirit of people helping people through the Red Cross, is being demonstrated here in the Worcester tornado area. As you address the Red Cross Convention tonight, please express to the delegates our sincere thanks for their timely aid, not only during our emergency but also in the rehabilitation period which is now in the process." That is signed Andrew Holstrom, Mayor of the City of Worcester.

And then, here is one from the Governor of the great Commonwealth, who says: "Understand that you are addressing the National Convention of the American Red Cross tonight, including delegates from Massachusetts. Wish to advise you that the Red Cross has done an outstanding job in this State during the recent Central Massachusetts tornado disaster. Christian Herter, Governor of Massachusetts."

I am, of course, grateful to those people for helping me attempt to give you the message I should so like for each of you to have from me and to understand. But I want to call attention also: those are merely two telegrams from areas in which we have dramatic instances of disaster.

We find the Red Cross on duty everywhere. Not merely where the incident that occasioned the help gets in the headlines, but in the humblest of homes. The Red Cross is always true to the belief that people, and only people, matter.

And so again, as I have done so often through these many years since I first encountered the Red Cross, thank you, each one of you.

NOTE: The President spoke in Constitution Hall at 9:13 p.m. In his opening words he referred to E. Roland Harriman, President of the American National Red Cross; he later referred to James Melton of the Metropolitan Opera Association of New York.

118 ¶ Remarks to Veterans Making the Last Trip on the U.S.S. Williamsburg. *June 25, 1953*

I APOLOGIZE for being a bit late, but it was not intentional, I assure you.

I haven't been able, before, to come down and greet the guests of Commander Burke on the Williamsburg that makes these trips down the Potomac. I have wanted to. I couldn't.

Since this is the final trip before she is deactivated, I wanted to come down and assure you that all of us—the Red Cross, and the Navy, and I—have all looked on it as a real privilege, to see if we couldn't do something to let you spend a nice afternoon up and down this historic river, on a fine ship, and through the services of the Navy.

If you have a bit of fun, more power to you. That is what it is for. We hope you will enjoy every single bit of it, and remember it kindly.

Through you, we would like to let all the others know how welcome they have been.

Now, the trip is the thing, and you didn't come down here to listen to a lot of words from me—I realize that.

I hope you will allow me to come around—particularly these lads in front of me—to say "Hello" before I go.

NOTE: The President spoke at the U.S. Naval Gun Factory in Washington at 12:40 p.m. During his remarks he referred to Commander Julian T. Burke, Captain of the former Presidential yacht U.S.S. Williamsburg.

119   ¶ Statement by the President Upon Signing the Pakistan Wheat Aid Act. *June* 25, 1953

I AM DEEPLY GRATIFIED to sign this Act which makes it possible to send up to one million tons of wheat to help avert famine among the people of Pakistan. We are fortunate in being able to help them by sharing some of the fruits of our labor and soil.

Americans have a strong feeling of friendship for the people of Pakistan. We have great admiration for this young country which is engaged in a valiant and determined effort to overcome problems of tremendous magnitude. Their efforts remind us of the turmoil and struggle of our own early days—and the struggle which confronts us on a broader scale today.

We are proud to have such staunch friends as the people of

Pakistan, who are dedicated to the democratic way of life. We are happy to be able to respond to their need with this aid.

The swift action by the Congress in making possible this aid, within two weeks after my message requesting such assistance, reflects the sympathy and concern of the people of the United States for the people of Pakistan.

Our sincere hopes for peace and prosperity go with this grain.

NOTE: The Pakistan Wheat Aid Act is Public Law 77, 83d Congress (67 Stat. 80).

120 ¶ Letter on Intellectual Freedom to the President of the American Library Association. *June* 26, 1953

[Released June 26, 1953. Dated June 24, 1953]

Dear Dr. Downs:

Thank you for your letter of June fifteenth. I am glad to know of the annual conference of the American Library Association convening this week, and of the spirit of conscientious citizenship ruling its deliberations.

Our librarians serve the precious liberties of our nation: freedom of inquiry, freedom of the spoken and the written word, freedom of exchange of ideas.

Upon these clear principles, democracy depends for its very life, for they are the great sources of knowledge and enlightenment. And knowledge—full, unfettered knowledge of its own heritage, of freedom's enemies, of the whole world of men and ideas—this knowledge is a free people's surest strength.

The converse is just as surely true. A democracy smugly disdainful of new ideas would be a sick democracy. A democracy chronically fearful of new ideas would be a dying democracy.

For all these reasons, we must in these times be intelligently alert not only to the fanatic cunning of Communist conspiracy—

but also to the grave dangers in meeting fanaticism with ignorance. For, in order to fight totalitarians who exploit the ways of freedom to serve their own ends, there are some zealots who—with more wrath than wisdom—would adopt a strangely unintelligent course. They would try to defend freedom by denying freedom's friends the opportunity of studying Communism in its entirety—its plausibilities, its falsities, its weaknesses.

But we know that freedom cannot be served by the devices of the tyrant. As it is an ancient truth that freedom cannot be legislated into existence, so it is no less obvious that freedom cannot be censored into existence. And any who act as if freedom's defenses are to be found in suppression and suspicion and fear confess a doctrine that is alien to America.

The libraries of America are and must ever remain the homes of free, inquiring minds. To them, our citizens—of all ages and races, of all creeds and political persuasions—must ever be able to turn with clear confidence that there they can freely seek the whole truth, unwarped by fashion and uncompromised by expediency. For in such whole and healthy knowledge alone are to be found and understood those majestic truths of man's nature and destiny that prove, to each succeeding generation, the validity of freedom.

Sincerely,

Dwight D. Eisenhower

NOTE: The President's letter was read by Dr. R. B. Downs, President of the American Library Association, on June 26 at the 72d Annual Conference of the Association in Los Angeles.

121   ¶ Exchange of Messages Between the
President and Chancellor Adenauer Concerning the
Uprisings in East Berlin and East Germany.
June 26, 1953

[Released June 26, 1953. Dated June 25, 1953]

I HAVE RECEIVED with deep interest and sympathy your
message of June 21st. The latest events in East Berlin and Eastern Germany have stirred the hearts and hopes of people everywhere. This inspiring show of courage has reaffirmed our belief
that years of oppression and attempted indoctrination cannot
extinguish the spirit of freedom behind the Iron Curtain. It
seems clear that the repercussions of these events will be felt
throughout the Soviet satellite empire.

The United States Government is convinced that a way can
and must be found to satisfy the justified aspirations of the German people for freedom and unity, and for the restoration of
fundamental human rights in all parts of Germany. It is for
the attainment of these purposes that the government you head
and the United States Government have been earnestly striving
together. Although the Communists may be forced, as a result
of these powerful demonstrations in East Germany to moderate
their current policies, it seems clear that the safety and future
of the people of Eastern Germany can only be assured when that
region is unified with Western Germany on the basis of free
elections, as we urged the Soviets to agree to in the notes of
September 23, 1952 dispatched by the American, British and
French Governments. It is still our conviction that this represents the only realistic road to German unity, and I assure you
that my Government will continue to strive for this goal.

In their hours of trial and sacrifice, I trust that the people of

Eastern Germany will know that their call for freedom has been heard around the world.

DWIGHT D. EISENHOWER

NOTE: Chancellor Adenauer's message of June 21 follows:

Mr. President:

The people of the East sector of Berlin and of the East zone have despite the use of Soviet troops and tanks risen up unarmed against the regime of terror and force and demanded their rights of freedom. Many have had to pay for their bravery and courage with their lives. Nothing shows more clearly than the outcry of these tormented people how intolerable the conditions in this area

of Central Europe are. I should like to appeal to you urgently, Mr. President, in accordance with a resolution of June 10 of the German Bundestag, of which the American Government was notified, to do everything in your power in order that these conditions may be done away with, the human rights which have been violated may be restored and the entire German people may be given back the unity and freedom which alone guarantee a lasting peaceful development in Europe.

ADENAUER

122 ¶ Citation Accompanying the Medal of Honor Presented to Sergeant David B. Bleak, USA. *June* 26, 1953

THE PRESIDENT of the United States of America, authorized by Act of Congress March 3, 1863 has awarded in the name of The Congress the Medal of Honor to

SERGEANT DAVID B. BLEAK, USA

for conspicuous gallantry and intrepidity at the risk of his life above and beyond the call of duty in action with the enemy:

Sergeant Bleak, Army Medical Service, United States Army, a member of the Medical Company, 223d Infantry Regiment, 40th Infantry Division, distinguished himself by conspicuous gallantry and indomitable courage above and beyond the call of duty in action against the enemy in the vicinity of Minari-gol, Korea, on 14 June 1952. As a medical aidman, he volunteered to accompany a reconnaissance patrol committed to engage the enemy and capture a prisoner for interrogation. Forging up the rugged slope of the key terrain, the group was subjected to intense automatic weapons and small arms fire and suffered several casualties. After administering to the wounded, he continued to advance with the patrol. Nearing the military crest of the hill, while attempting to cross the fireswept area to attend the wounded, he came under hostile fire from a small group of the enemy concealed in a trench. Entering the trench, he closed with the enemy, killed two with bare hands and a third with his trench knife. Moving from the emplacement, he saw a concussion grenade fall in front of a companion and, quickly shifting his position, shielded the man from the impact of the blast. Later, while ministering to the wounded, he was struck by a hostile bullet but, despite the wound, he undertook to evacuate a wounded comrade. As he moved down the hill with his heavy burden, he was attacked by two enemy soldiers with fixed bayonets. Closing with the aggressors, he grabbed them and smashed their heads together, then carried his helpless comrade down the hill to safety. Sergeant Bleak's dauntless courage and intrepid actions reflect utmost credit upon himself and are in keeping with the honored traditions of the military service.

DWIGHT D. EISENHOWER

NOTE: See also Item 229.

123 ¶ Message to Prime Minister Churchill of Great Britain Concerning Postponement of the Bermuda Conversations. *June* 27, 1953

[Released June 27, 1953. Dated June 26, 1953]

Dear Winston:

I am deeply distressed to learn that your physicians have advised you to lighten your duties at this time and that consequently you will be unable to come to Bermuda for our talks.

I look upon this only as a temporary deferment of our meeting.

Your health is of great concern to all the world and you must, therefore, bow to the advice of your physicians.

With best wishes from your friend.

IKE

124 ¶ Exchange of Messages Between the President and Prime Minister Mohammed Ali of Pakistan Concerning the Wheat Grant.
June 29, 1953

His Excellency Mohammed Ali
Prime Minister of Pakistan
Karachi, Pakistan

I appreciate the warm expression of your gratitude for the action of our people in providing wheat for your stricken country. Our response to your call was made in the American tradition of giving help to the best of our ability where help is needed. It is also a true measure of the friendly feeling and admiration which Americans have for the people of Pakistan. We are proud to count your vigorous, young nation among our friends.

DWIGHT D. EISENHOWER

NOTE: The Prime Minister's message follows:

I have received with much pleasure the news that you signed, on the 25th June, 1953, the Bill providing one million tons of wheat grant to Pakistan. This news has been received here with a general sense of relief because we know now that with this generous aid we shall be able to meet the food shortage with which Pakistan was faced. This generous grant from the people of the United States of America and the promptness with which your Government has acted is a fine practical proof of friendliness and good will which the United States of America bears towards my country. I assure you that this timely help, which will relieve distress in the country, has earned the deep gratitude of the nation.

I also wish to convey my personal thanks to you and your Government for all that has been done to help Pakistan.

MOHAMMED ALI

125 ¶ Special Message to the Congress Requesting General Legislation Authorizing the Use of Agricultural Commodities for Foreign Emergency Relief. *June 30, 1953*

To the Congress of the United States:

Because of the great productivity of our farms, the people of the United States have been able, on several occasions in recent years, to come to the aid of friendly countries faced with famine. In 1951 agricultural supplies were provided to India, and only recently wheat has been made available to the people of Pakistan. In both instances, we were able to provide assistance in meeting famine or other urgent relief requirements by using stocks of commodities held by the Commodity Credit Corporation. On each of these occasions the Congress has been forced to add consideration of these emergency programs to its very heavy workload. This procedure not only adds to the Congressional burden but also slows the speed with which this government can come to the assistance of a nation urgently needing relief.

I therefore believe it advisable to have general legislation which, within appropriate limitations, would permit the President to meet these situations. The legislation I am requesting would give the President the authority to utilize agricultural commodities held by this government, but it would limit that authority to meet only the occasional needs arising from famine or other urgent relief requirements.

The objectives of such a program are not to be confused with the principal objective of our Mutual Security Program. The Mutual Security Program aims at promoting the long range security of the United States by assisting our friends to strengthen their long range economic and defensive capabilities. The program I am now proposing aims at mitigating the hard blows of unusual and urgent emergencies.

Since we cannot adequately foresee the specific needs to be met under the legislation I am requesting, we cannot now determine the most effective and equitable conditions under which such assistance may be rendered in a particular situation. Consequently, I am requesting authority to establish, when the need arises, the terms and conditions under which these agricultural commodities shall be made available.

In order that there may be a minimum of delay in assisting nations stricken with famine or having other urgent relief requirements, I am requesting that the Commodity Credit Corporation be given authority to make available from its stocks the necessary agricultural commodities to meet these emergency needs. To prevent impairment of the operations of the Commodity Credit Corporation, and to permit necessary budgetary adjustments, I am recommending an authorization to reimburse the Commodity Credit Corporation to the extent of its investment in commodities furnished by it, plus any other costs, including interest, which it may incur in carrying out programs authorized under this act. When the costs of any programs carried out under terms of this act can be ascertained, the Congress will be asked to appropriate the necessary funds to reimburse the Commodity Credit Corporation. I further propose that the authority to undertake programs of famine and other urgent relief assistance under this legislation expire on June 30, 1955.

DWIGHT D. EISENHOWER

NOTE: The act enabling the President to furnish emergency relief assistance, approved August 7, is Public Law 216, 83d Congress (67 Stat. 476).

126 ¶ The President's News Conference of *July* 1, 1953.

THE PRESIDENT. I have very little to volunteer to occupy your attention this morning.

One thing, if you are interested in my personal movements: I hope to be out of town for the weekend, up in Camp David, and to spend Saturday and Sunday there, as I did last week—very quietly, doing nothing.

The other thing—and of real importance—is this continued unrest in the satellite countries. I suppose most of you have read in detail Chancellor Adenauer's speeches on the subject. I must say that my own thinking goes a great deal along with his; that here we have a place advertised as the workers' paradise, and we have the repressions of tyranny finally resulting in spontaneous revolt that seem to spread like wildfire with no prior plan, almost—at least his speeches certainly indicate that.

It merely, I believe, reinforces the western contention that people who have known freedom still rate it as the highest of human values, and when it is taken away from them—and I mean freedom in the true and deep sense—that eventually man comes to the conviction that even life itself is worth spending for freedom. I think it is a most significant lesson to all of us.

Certainly the suffering of those people excites our pity just as it does our admiration, because it does seem unreasonable that people can't be allowed to live their own lives in this world. Certainly, it seems unreasonable to people who live in the Western World.

Now, I just make this one observation, ladies and gentlemen, because I have been following that movement. I have known some of those peoples very well, I admire them, and I visited some of the countries. I feel deeply moved by the things they are going through.

Other than that, I have nothing to volunteer, and so we will go right to the questions.

Q. Merriman Smith, United Press: Mr. President, is there anything you can tell us about the Korean situation? Particularly, are you hopeful or optimistic about the prospects of an armistice?

THE PRESIDENT. Of course, it is a confused situation, and there is not anything to tell you in detail that I think would make any real story.

There is this to remember: the enemy is still in North Korea— that is the principal enemy.

We are having an acute example of the difficulties that arise among allies that are really dedicated to the same principles and same basic ideas, but when we come to their application in a particular area or in a particular subject, a particular direction, we find that we get into difficulties. It is the history of coalitions; we shouldn't be too discouraged about it.

On the other hand, the differences are very real. People in emotional states are very apt to even overstate their cases, and it becomes extraordinarily difficult to get a reasonable solution.

However, I will say this: I still, in my own mind and in my very deepest convictions, believe that a satisfactory solution is coming out of it.

Q. David P. Sentner, Hearst Newspapers: Mr. President, can you tell us what the major objectives may be at the meeting of the Big Three foreign ministers on July 10th, and how it may affect the proposed Bermuda meeting?

THE PRESIDENT. If I repeat myself in front of this group, I hope you will know that I so frequently have to talk; so often I forget the body that I have explained something to. But in the very inception of the Bermuda meeting it was hoped that there would be as little formality about it as possible, as little writing out of rigid agenda that would say, "We will reach a solution on X, Y, and Z."

What we were hoping was to get together and discuss in a friendly fashion the whole world situation, picking up those points where we had common interests and discussing them in a friendly way, to see whether or not it wasn't possible to develop a really satisfactory common purpose, common effort, in these vital regions or problems.

That was unfortunately put off due to the illness of the Prime Minister. But the need for discussing these various problems

464

around the world—after all, there is Korea, there is NATO, there is Indochina, and Malaya; there is the Middle East; there are all sorts of problems to discuss; there is the business of trade— to meet and discuss these things in friendly fashion, in my opinion, should be done often.

This meeting that they are having, again, is in a more or less friendly and partially informal fashion of the first concept. They are going to have this talk. They are starting, I believe it is the 10th. Now, there is nothing that I can tell you that we hope as a definite and specific purpose to come out of it, except this increase of understanding among us.

Q. Raymond P. Brandt, St. Louis Post-Dispatch: Mr. President, have you talked to Secretary Dulles about the purging of the books in the overseas libraries?

THE PRESIDENT. Only to the extent to ask him what had happened. He did do this: he sent me back the law under which those libraries were established. Have you read that?

Q. Mr. Brandt: Yes.

THE PRESIDENT. I find that they were established with a very limited purpose. So I told him I wanted to talk further with him about it now, because obviously you can't violate the law, and he has sent me quite a memorandum. He and I are going to talk further about it.

Q. Mr. Brandt: Has he shown you a new directive yet?

THE PRESIDENT. No. As a matter of fact, he tells me that there is no directive he has issued that could possibly be responsible for some of the things we hear have happened.

Now, I think that I don't want at the moment to talk too much further about it, because that is as far as I have gotten in digging down to the bottom. I was unacquainted with the provision of the law.

Q. Mr. Brandt: Do you and he hope to get a clear directive eventually?

THE PRESIDENT. Certainly, I hope that.

Q. Mr. Brandt: Is it possible?

THE PRESIDENT. I think it should be, yes; I think it should be. I have never varied on this thing from the time that I first thought about books, as I think I referred to last time, to go back to the statements I made at Columbia; I still believe those things.

There is no question as to where I stand. Now, I think that we can make it clear so that any reasonable person can understand exactly what we mean.

Q. Mr. Brandt: If I may point out, I think there was some confusion between your Dartmouth speech and your press conference speech in which you said it was perfectly all right for the State Department to burn books or to do as they pleased with them.

THE PRESIDENT. I said burned books? You dig that out; I only believe I said that——

Q. Mr. Brandt: No, you said the State Department can do as it pleased.

THE PRESIDENT. I don't even know whether I said that. I said that that government would be foolish to promulgate and help to support the distribution of a book that openly advocated its own destruction by force.

I pointed out that in this Communist area one judge, at least one court, had found 11 men guilty because they were in this Communist conspiracy, guilty of trying to destroy the United States by force, as I read the verdict.

I said they would be foolish to help promulgate and disseminate such a book. I don't think I said anything else about it.

Q. Mr. Brandt: I think there was a phrase there——

THE PRESIDENT. What was that phrase?

Q. Mr. Brandt:——that they could do as they pleased about it. Someone asked if you approved of burning.

THE PRESIDENT. I don't think I said they could do as they pleased; if I have, then I would like to look at it. I would like to see it and in what connection, because I did say this: I get responsible people, and I expect them to carry out the policies of the Government.

Q. Mr. Brandt: One of the points was whether the books by Communists which are not on communism should be in the libraries.

THE PRESIDENT. I am not going to answer that strictly. You must read the law from which these particular libraries are established, and it says this: books about American life, about the American system of government, and the things that touch its own interests, in furthering its own interests. It is a very limited purpose in that law.

Q. Mr. Brandt: I am not standing up for any writer, but one of the writers was Dashiell Hammett who writes detective stories. So far as I know—and I have read several of them—I don't see anything communistic about them, but they were thrown out of the libraries.

THE PRESIDENT. Who were they thrown out by?

Q. Mr. Brandt: Well, the list was given out; it was—thrown out——

THE PRESIDENT. Here? In Washington?

Q. Mr. Brandt: Oh, no; by the libraries overseas.

THE PRESIDENT. I think someone got frightened. I don't know why they should. I wouldn't; I will tell you that, I wouldn't.

Q. Anthony H. Leviero, New York Times: Mr. President, is there anything you can tell us about the report by William H. Jackson?

THE PRESIDENT. Well, I would say this: he has made his report, but he made it in a form open to discussion. We had a long discussion about it either yesterday or the day before yesterday. It is coming back in final form and, as I recall—now, this is not a promise, but as I recall—it is planned to publish the summary and transmitting letter. So you will have it at first hand and we won't have to guess at its various details. I mean that is very soon, the summary of the report.[1]

---

[1] Released July 8; cited in footnote to Item 128.

Q. Mr. Leviero: Mr. President, were they unanimous in their findings?

THE PRESIDENT. So far as I know. I assume that on all such important subjects they had their fights, but as given to me there was no minority report given.

Q. Edward J. Milne, Providence Journal and Bulletin: Mr. President, are you going to oppose in the House the cuts by the Appropriations Committee in your defense budget?

THE PRESIDENT. Well, I wouldn't even comment on that until I see them all in detail. The only way you could oppose them would be to send word to the Senate on where you were badly hurt; I don't know what else you could do.

Q. Mr. Milne: As I understand it, the cuts were announced on Saturday. I wondered if you had taken any action since Saturday to ask the leadership up there to oppose the cuts?

THE PRESIDENT. Well, I don't say "to oppose them"; on specific items we told them what we need, we think, as a minimum. Of course there is always the opportunity if you get into a jam to go back to Congress and tell them what kind of a jam you are in. I am not going to comment in detail on those things at the moment, because it is all still in the hands of Congress; and it is a good time to keep still and let them work out their problems, I think.

Q. Roscoe Drummond, Christian Science Monitor: Mr. President, may I return to the matter of the revolt behind the Iron Curtain?

THE PRESIDENT. Yes.

Q. Mr. Drummond: I would like to ask whether you feel that the events which are now taking place create an opportunity for the administration to take any tangible action to support liberation in line with its stated objectives?

THE PRESIDENT. We have always said we are for free elections in those countries. I do not believe that there is any thought of taking any physical action of any kind that could be classed as intervention.

I do think that in all of the normal activities of a people, of a government—the Government here—the statements, the speeches, the talks of members of Government should be directed towards showing what is the meaning of this kind of thing under these situations, and to try to show people that are suffering like that that they do have friends in the world and people that are standing by to help so far as is possible.

Q. Alan S. Emory, Watertown (N.Y.) Times: Mr. President, I wondered if you could tell us whether or not you were satisfied with the cooperation and treatment afforded to your legislative program to date by the Republican majority in Congress.

THE PRESIDENT. Well, I don't think that is much of a question; I must say I think that is pretty general. But I do think this: I think that the whole Republican Party is gradually showing that it has taken over responsibility and is getting itself organized steadily to carry that responsibility, discharge it. Whether or not they always agree with me is not so important as that we get a progressive, needed program out before the people for their guidance and observance.

Q. W. L. Beale, Jr., Associated Press: Mr. President, I wonder if you would like to clarify your position on the Bricker constitutional amendment in the light of what Senator Knowland said yesterday indicating that you may have changed your mind about the necessity or the need for such amendment.

THE PRESIDENT. I have never changed my mind in this respect: I have always stated that I don't believe that any treaty can circumvent or supersede our Constitution.

Now, I don't believe it can now, but if there is any amendment necessary to make that simple statement, then such an amendment, if it would quiet fears anywhere in this whole country, would have my support.

I will never agree to anything that interferes with the constitutional and traditional separation of powers between the departments, and the necessary coordination as specified by our Constitution. So you get into a matter of words and semantics.

What I am getting down to is this: the Attorney General is working with the people on the Hill to see whether there is any possible language that satisfies their viewpoint or the particular viewpoint as represented by Senator Bricker and, at the same time, acceptable to the administration. But never would I agree with a disturbance of the constitutional powers between departments.

Q. Sarah McClendon, El Paso Times: Sir, I believe it was around April 29 that Secretary McKay recommended to you that Marvin Nichols be appointed Bureau of Reclamation Commissioner. Are you going to approve that recommendation and appoint Mr. Nichols?

THE PRESIDENT. I don't remember; I can say nothing about it.

Q. Mrs. McClendon: There was a United Press story, sir, to the effect that Mr. C. D. Jackson of your staff was opposing it.

THE PRESIDENT. Well, I can say this: I don't think C. D. Jackson ever came to me and said anything about an appointment. I don't know anything about these stories, but I do say this: when we have appointments to announce, why, we always get them out as fast as possible. [*Laughter*]

I really am not trying to be facetious, but the whole thing has slipped my memory, whatever you are talking about. So there is no use in trying to talk about it at the moment.

Merriman Smith, United Press: Thank you, Mr. President.

NOTE: President Eisenhower's twelfth news conference was held in the Executive Office Building from 10:30 to 10:46 o'clock on Wednesday morning, July 1, 1953.

127 ¶ Memorandum on Community Chest and United Defense Fund-USO Campaign in the National Capital Area. *July 1, 1953*

To the Heads of Executive Departments and Agencies:

For the fall Red Feather Campaign for the Community Chest Federation and the United Defense Fund-USO in the National

Capital Area I have approved the appointment of the Honorable Douglas McKay, Secretary of the Interior, as Chairman for the Government Unit.

I ask that you give him your fullest measure of support and assistance. All persons in authority in the Federal and District Government, I am sure, will extend their complete cooperation to this important charitable appeal. Such cooperation would logically include the assumption of equitable unit goals, the effective solicitation of all employees, and the setting up of an adequate collection method for the convenience of those who wish to make contributions on an installment basis.

In the National Capital Area the Community Chest Federation unites six Community Chests and more than one hundred Red Feather Agencies in one federated campaign to provide local health, welfare and recreational programs which are so vital to the building of a healthy, strong and safer community in which to live, work and play.

Included in the Red Feather Campaign this year will be the appeal of the United Defense Fund which includes, among others, the USO–USO Camp Shows and United Community Defense Services. These programs are essential to the morale and happiness of our men and women of the Armed Forces both at home and overseas.

It is my hope that all officials and employees will be given the opportunity to contribute and that they will do so generously, mindful of the fact that this is one appeal for the yearly support of over one hundred Red Feather agency programs and the UDF–USO. When you give—give your fair share to support these worthwhile services for a full year.

DWIGHT D. EISENHOWER

128   ¶ The President's News Conference of
July 8, 1953.

THE PRESIDENT. One or two items, ladies and gentlemen, of possible general interest. We have had a committee, as you know, called the Jackson Committee, studying the whole field that has been called by many names, but popularly known by the name of psychological warfare. Its report, of course, is largely confidential, but at my direction they have made a summary of the report which will be handed out by Mr. Hagerty around noon today, probably around 12 o'clock.

It is very interesting; and, of course, it is trying to draw together into one place in the Federal Government responsibility for all this kind of action.[1]

In Korea, as you know, the Communists have accepted our suggestion that the talks be resumed looking toward the consummation of a truce.

Now, I just want to make it clear again: everybody in the United States, I believe, understands the aspirations of President Rhee and has a very warm spot in their hearts for what South Korea has done in this whole business. We must never lose sight of the fact that this is an incident in a great ideological struggle, as well as a struggle just by arms.

We look forward to a reunification of Korea by peaceful means and intend to work for it.

The question, though, of carrying on hostilities and trying to accomplish objectives by warfare in this world of today is something, of course, that you have to weigh against the future and

---

[1] The summary of the report by the President's Committee on International Information Activities, headed by William H. Jackson, is published in the Department of State Bulletin (vol. 29, p. 124). The Committee recommended, among other things, recruitment of the ablest personnel obtainable for service overseas, a more effective overseas information program, and the establishment within the National Security Council of an Operations Coordinating Board. Such a board was established on September 3, 1953, by Executive Order 10483 (3 CFR, 1949–1953 Comp., p. 968).

the success of the United Nations, for which we all hope that there will be a great success.

As a matter of fact, that is about all there is to say about the Korean thing at the moment; there is no new development of which I am aware.

On Germany, I received a telegram signed by the president of the AFL and the president of the CIO. They are over there as members—in Stockholm, they are actually meeting—they are over there as American representatives of a great union of labor organizations, free labor organizations from the free countries. They made certain recommendations with respect to Germany.

The significant thing to me was that the workers of the world protest at the situation of the workers in Eastern Germany and in the satellite—well, in Eastern Germany specifically at the moment. That, to me, is certainly a very significant factor in the world opinion and in the psychology; the workers believe that the workers in Germany, supposed to be the workers' paradise, are really treated in a way that is unjustifiable.

Now, I think with those brief observations, we will go directly to the questions.

Q. Charles T. Lucey, Scripps-Howard Newspapers: Did you discuss the Pennsylvania governorship with Senator Duff, and have you urged him to run for the governorship next year?

THE PRESIDENT. I don't participate in the kind of detail which you intimate in local political questions.

I have talked of many things, including listening very carefully to Senator Duff, but I have urged him to do nothing. I merely talked on this basis, that we, locally and federally, as a party, are trying to establish a record that gains the admiration and respect of the American people. That is what I am talking about. They will have to decide their local questions themselves.

Q. D. Harold Oliver, Associated Press: Does that go for Virginia, too?

THE PRESIDENT. Virginia?

Q. Mr. Oliver: Yes, the governorship race. I was asked to have you go on record about that.

THE PRESIDENT. Actually, yes, the same observation applies. I don't consider it my function to interfere in the local and State elections. After all, there are certain responsibilities placed upon the President of the United States. There are certain attitudes I think that he is expected normally to observe. I hope to do that.

Now, my own contention is this: the only worthwhile political program, particularly for the party in power, is to present at each new election, to the people of the United States, an accomplishment, a worthwhile progress that earns approbation. I can see no other way of approaching this thing, and I don't see how the President could interfere or attempt to interfere appropriately in the local political struggles—city, county, State, or anything of that kind.

Q. Sarah McClendon, Lubbock Avalanche-Journal: We in the Southwest, Mr. President, as my editors tell me, appreciate very much what you and Mr. Benson have done to alleviate the drought conditions, but they say that there is going to be need for more aid and a long-range program. I wonder if you think there is anything the Government can do to prevent the effects of such a drought in the future?

THE PRESIDENT. I don't think you can prevent the effect, because drought is a meteorological condition that even the most powerful governments seem to be helpless in front of.

Now what they can do is this: plan for help, alleviation of distress, and so on—in other words, the old theory of prevention of disaster to great bodies of our citizens, particularly when that disaster could not be foreseen. Actually, I believe that the Governors of that whole region are to meet soon, again, to discuss these things. From them, I would expect worthwhile suggestions. We have moved only a little bit at a time, but certainly we hope to do what an enlightened and humanitarian America would expect us to do with respect to a whole area like that, that is so stricken.

Q. Marvin L. Arrowsmith, Associated Press: Mr. President, on the Korean situation, have you had any indication from your representative there that Syngman Rhee would be willing to go along with the proposed truce?

THE PRESIDENT. Well, I really feel this, Mr. Arrowsmith: there is little more to be said about the Korean situation than has already appeared in the papers.

As I said last week, or at a recent press conference, there is a difficult question of misunderstanding, and I think it is unfortunate when we know so clearly that our hearts are in the same places; but those things do occur. We have to proceed step by step in the hope that methods and procedures adopted will constantly lead us further toward the realization of those hopes.

That does not mean that there are no troubles. There are; and exactly how it is going to come out, no man can foretell exactly.

Q. Elmer Davis, American Broadcasting Company: Isn't this so-called acceptance of the truce terms just about what the Communists said before? They still say they accept if we will bring Syngman Rhee in line and if we will round up all the prisoners. Is that anything new?

THE PRESIDENT. Where do you get all this information? I haven't got it.

Q. Mr. Davis: I saw it on the wires about a half hour ago.

THE PRESIDENT. No. I think you are starting with a premise that just defies answer; because there is no such thing contemplated.

Q. Edwin Dayton Moore, United Press: Dr. J. Robert Oppenheimer and Gordon Dean have expressed a belief that the U.S. Government should make available to its allies and the American people more information on atomic weapons, both ours and our estimates of the Russians'. Do you agree?

THE PRESIDENT. Well, you are asking a question in very specific terms.

First of all, I assume that you are meaning, should the law be amended? There is a law, as you know, that strictly limits the kind of information to be given.

Personally, I think the time has arrived when the American people must have more information on this subject, if they are to act intelligently. I happen to be one of those people that believe that an informed American population makes good decisions.

I believe the time has come that the law, as written, is really outmoded. As you know, much of it was written in the hope, and possibly the expectation, that we could keep secret the manufacture of the bomb. Well, we know it has been manufactured elsewhere, so it would seem that certain parts, at least, of that law are outmoded. I think the time has come to be far more, let us say, frank with the American people than we have been in the past. That naturally has to include, then, your allies. Whatever you tell publicly, they are bound to know, and I think that the cooperative attitude here is important.

[*Confers with Mr. Hagerty*] Mr. Hagerty reminds me that this whole subject is discussed in some degree in that Jackson report. You can find further information on it there.

Q. Pat Munroe, Salt Lake City Deseret News: Mr. President, my question concerns one of those appointments in the Interior Department. There are reports that the morale among the Indian tribes is rather poor now, because of the fact that the Indian Commissioner has not been appointed as yet. I wonder if you had any idea when we might expect something on that?

THE PRESIDENT. The selection of the right people for these jobs, of course, is a difficult business. I promised, during the campaign, to the Indian tribes that they, themselves, would be consulted in the character and type of man they wanted as the head of the Indian Bureau.

Ever since, I think, he has taken office, Secretary McKay has really been looking for the right person. He hasn't given me a late report, but that is a difficult job possibly to find a man that we think capable of carrying on this work properly and finding one that they think is exactly the right man.

Now, since you have raised the question, I will look it up and make it a point for a future conference; but I don't have any better answer at the moment.

Q. Roscoe Drummond, Christian Science Monitor: Mr. President, twice recently an official spokesman of the State Department has refused to give out information on the directive which governs the selection of books in overseas libraries, and has refused to give either the names of the books that are being removed or being put back. Now, on one occasion the official spokesman explained that this was a part of the cold war strategy and had to be classified.

I would like to ask whether you feel that that kind of information should be withheld or made public, and whether you think that withholding it is in line with your new security directives.

THE PRESIDENT. Mr. Drummond, now, I hope that you are not going to try to demand that I keep in touch with every step-by-step development in all the manifold and multitudinous departments and agencies of this Government. What I did ask them and direct them to do is this: for the State Department to sit down with the information section and work out a program that would be in line with the views I have so often expressed on this. It is my opinion and my conviction that that program is soon to be published and made public. So, generally speaking, to answer your question—would its withholding from the public be in line with what I believe about information to the public? No, I don't think it would. Consequently, I think there is going to be something coming out soon that will satisfy you on this point. I think that probably their evading the question has been because they were busily engaged in a new look with everybody involved; and they are coming out with something that ought to be, I should think, satisfactory.[1]

---

[1] On July 15 the State Department issued a release consisting of a statement by the Administrator of the International Information Administration together with new instructions on selection of books for the International Information libraries (Department of State Bulletin, vol. 29, p. 121).

Q. Robert E. Clark, International News Service: Mr. President, there have been suggestions in Great Britain recently that the Big Three conference would be switched to London because of Churchill's illness. Would you be willing to go to London for a Big Three conference?

THE PRESIDENT. The question was whether I would be willing to go to London for a Big Three conference.

As far as personal convenience is concerned, once you get in an airplane and start out, it doesn't make any difference much whether you travel 6 hours or 3 hours. I hadn't thought about this. I did see where, in answer to a question, Mr. Butler said it would look logical if Mr. Churchill's health allowed a meeting in London but not elsewhere, that we might hold it there. I must say that I have no real personal feeling about it one way or the other. We were going to meet in Bermuda, which is on British territory, anyway; so I would not think there was any great significance. I should add, no proposal has been made to me of any kind, nor, so far as I know, to the State Department. I think it was merely a comment made in passing and has no great significance.

Q. Mrs. May Craig, Maine Newspapers: Mr. President, so much has been said about the protections thrown around enemy prisoners that we hold under the treaty, some American families are wondering about the protection for our men, and if we would have any access to them at all, particularly if the Reds should say that some of them do not want to come home.

THE PRESIDENT. Mrs. Craig, you raised one of the questions, of course, that makes this whole business of negotiation a really heavy one. It weighs on the heart and not merely on, let us say, the logical processes of the brain.

Now, under the terms of the armistice, that is clearly guaranteed; each side has the right to go to the other where they claim there is anybody that doesn't want to return, and go through exactly the same processes in each side. So, as far as the armistice terms, as I have seen them—this is not revealing any of the new terms because it has always been there—there is equal opportunity on both sides.

Q. Nat S. Finney, Buffalo Evening News: Mr. President, action on the Dondero-Miller bill, which will control whether there be private or New York State redevelopment of Niagara Falls, has been held up pending Governor Dewey's visit. Governor Dewey opposes the Miller bill. Do you have any position on that which you could describe at this time?

THE PRESIDENT. Well, here is a point. In 1950—I believe it was 1950—when the treaty was made with Canada, Congress made a definite reservation that in this one case it reserved to itself the right and the authority to say exactly how that power should be developed. In the ordinary or normal case, the process would be to refer this to the Federal Power Commission. So, here we have a case where Congress has decided that it should take unto itself this authority.

Now, I don't question their right to do so in the first place, nor their right now to decide. For myself, I have always announced that I believe that maximum local authority should be exercised in the handling of all of these problems, and I would say my own philosophy largely would be, when you don't have interstate problems, that the State itself decides who and how these things should be done. But in this case, I say, it is a very special one. I can take no action nor even express a specific opinion, I should think, until the bill as drawn, and if passed, is presented to me. Then, of course, with all my advisers, there would be an analysis of it and action taken.

Q. Oscar W. Reschke, German Press Agency: Mr. President, it has been suggested in connection with the East German uprisings that EDC should be put aside for the time being or considered of secondary importance and everything should be done in first priority achieving German unity. What are your views, Mr. President?

THE PRESIDENT. First may I ask your identity?

Q. Mr. Reschke: Reschke, German Press Agency.

THE PRESIDENT. No, I don't think they should be put aside. I do believe strongly in the unification of Germany. As a matter of fact, I happen to be one of those who believed in it in 1945. I went into Germany with the same hatreds and prejudices about the Hitler group that had caused this war; and unquestionably I included a certain sense of guilt in my own mind that applied to the whole German people for allowing this thing to occur. But it didn't take long reflection after the shooting stopped—it didn't take long reflection to see that Germany was bound to be always a great and influential part of that Central European complex, and therefore was going to affect the fortunes and lives of all of us. I believe it should be allowed a decent opportunity to unite itself; I worked for it when I was a member of—the—what did we call it? The Berlin Council? I forget the exact name—but you know, when all four of us used to meet there.

Now, I believe today that it is a proper aspiration for Germany—the reunification of Germany. I have always believed also that the EDC, the whole NATO concept, just like the United Nations concept under which it is authorized, is a peaceful one. I believe that free elections as of now can be held whether Germany belongs to the EDC or whether it does not. So I am personally in favor of pushing right ahead on the theory that we have done nothing wicked and nothing wrong, and intend nothing wicked or wrong; to go ahead with it at the same time that we support the German aspiration to be united.

Q. John Madigan, Hearst Newspapers: Mr. President, have you seen and read the *Democratic Digest,* which comes out in the first edition tomorrow?

THE PRESIDENT. No, I have not.

Q. Chalmers M. Roberts, Washington Post: Do I take it from your comments on Germany, sir, that you don't believe that there is anything incompatible between German unification and German participation in EDC?

THE PRESIDENT. Certainly from my viewpoint there is not. I should like to make it clear, I have done nothing that I know of since 1945 that any just man in the world could interpret as aggressive, aggressive in intent, or would be compatible with what you might call forceful imperialism. I believe that this world has got to have peace or it is going to be "or else" for our civilization. Everything that I have been a party to or tried to support has been with that purpose.

Now, I don't deny for a second that I can be badly mistaken. I can make my errors just as quickly and possibly even more seriously than most people. But I do believe that. So therefore, I don't believe that EDC has one single danger for anybody else in the world except in the single case if they attack. That is all that it is meant for.

Q. Joseph R. Slevin, New York Journal of Commerce: There has been talk that an armistice in Korea would bring on a decline in United States business activity. Would you give us your views on the present strength of the economy and its prospects for the balance of the year?

THE PRESIDENT. Frankly, you ask a question on which I have two specific conferences a week, and it comes up time and time again. I just don't believe that it would be wise for me to describe or balance for you hopeful signs on one side, unhopeful on the other, because it takes a real study of the thing. I would refer you rather to people like the Secretary of Commerce or Dr. Burns, the head of the Economic Advisers, or someone like that, where you could have a long talk.

Personally my own conviction out of all these things is merely this: we can have a peaceful economy that is a prosperous economy and keeps employment at a very high level. That is the conclusion that I have formed. It does not mean that there might not have to be certain different changes and arrangements, but I know we can do it in my own heart.

Q. Barnet Nover, Denver Post: Mr. President, is there any reason why the job of Reclamation Commissioner has been held up for 6 months? The office has not been filled for 6 months.

THE PRESIDENT. As far as I know—again, you can't expect

me to know all the details of the trouble that is going on—as far as I know, any office that has not been filled has merely been because the people responsible for the selection have not found exactly the fellow they are looking for. As you well know, there are many, many qualifications that have to be met.

Edwin Dayton Moore, United Press: Thank you, Mr. President.

NOTE: President Eisenhower's thirteenth news conference was held in the Executive Office Building from 10:30 to 10:55 o'clock on Wednesday morning, July 8, 1953.

129 ¶ Exchange of Messages Between the President and Prime Minister Mossadegh on the Oil Situation and the Problem of Aid to Iran.
July 9, 1953

[Released July 9, 1953. Dated June 29, 1953]

Dear Mr. Prime Minister:

I have received your letter of May 28 in which you described the present difficult situation in Iran and expressed the hope that the United States might be able to assist Iran in overcoming some of its difficulties. In writing my reply which has been delayed until I could have an opportunity to consult with Mr. Dulles and Ambassador Henderson, I am motivated by the same spirit of friendly frankness as that which I find reflected in your letter.

The Government and people of the United States historically have cherished and still have deep feelings of friendliness for Iran and the Iranian people. They sincerely hope that Iran will be able to maintain its independence and that the Iranian people will be successful in realizing their national aspirations and in developing a contented and free nation which will contribute to world prosperity and peace.

It was primarily because of that hope that the United States Government during the last two years has made earnest efforts to assist in eliminating certain differences between Iran and the United Kingdom which have arisen as a result of the nationalization of the Iranian oil industry. It has been the belief of the United States that the reaching of an agreement in the matter of compensation would strengthen confidence throughout the world in the determination of Iran fully to adhere to the principles which render possible a harmonious community of free nations; that it would contribute to the strengthening of the international credit standing of Iran; and that it would lead to the solution of some of the financial and economic problems at present facing Iran.

The failure of Iran and of the United Kingdom to reach an agreement with regard to compensation has handicapped the Government of the United States in its efforts to help Iran. There is a strong feeling in the United States, even among American citizens most sympathetic to Iran and friendly to the Iranian people, that it would not be fair to the American taxpayers for the United States Government to extend any considerable amount of economic aid to Iran so long as Iran could have access to funds derived from the sale of its oil and oil products if a reasonable agreement were reached with regard to compensation whereby the large-scale marketing of Iranian oil would be resumed. Similarly, many American citizens would be deeply opposed to the purchase by the United States Government of Iranian oil in the absence of an oil settlement.

There is also considerable sentiment in the United States to the effect that a settlement based on the payment of compensation merely for losses of the physical assets of a firm which has been nationalized would not be what might be called a reasonable settlement and that an agreement to such a settlement might tend to weaken mutual trust between free nations engaged in friendly economic intercourse. Furthermore, many of my countrymen who have kept themselves informed regarding developments in this unfortunate dispute believe that, in view of the emotions which have been aroused both in Iran and the United Kingdom, efforts to determine by direct negotiation the amount of compensation due are more likely to increase friction than to promote understanding. They continue to adhere to the opinion that the most practicable and the fairest means of settling the question of compensation would be for that question to be referred to some neutral international body which could consider on the basis of merit all claims and counter-claims.

I fully understand that the Government of Iran must determine for itself which foreign and domestic policies are likely to be most advantageous to Iran and to the Iranian people. In what I have written, I am not trying to advise the Iranian Government on its best interests. I am merely trying to explain why, in the circumstances, the Government of the United States is not presently in a position to extend more aid to Iran or to purchase Iranian oil.

In case Iran should so desire, the United States Government hopes to be able to continue to extend technical assistance and military aid on a basis comparable to that given during the past year.

I note the concern reflected in your letter at the present dangerous situation in Iran and sincerely hope that before it is too late, the Government of Iran will take such steps as are in its power to prevent a further deterioration of that situation.

Please accept, Mr. Prime Minister, the renewed assurances of my highest consideration.

DWIGHT D. EISENHOWER

NOTE: The Prime Minister's message follows:

Dear Mr. President:

In the kind reply which you sent to my message of last January you suggested that I might inform you direct or through diplomatic channels of any views that may be of mutual interest.

In that message I had briefly referred to the hardships and privations which the Iranian people had undergone during the last two years in their efforts to attain their aspirations and also to the difficulties which the British Government has created for Iran in its support of the illogical claims of an imperialistic company.

During the few months that have elapsed since the date of that message the Iranian people have been suffering financial hardships and struggling with political intrigues carried on by the former Oil Company and the British Government. For instance, the purchasers of Iranian oil have been dragged from one court to another, and all means of propaganda and diplomacy have been employed in order to place illegal obstacles in the way of the sale of Iranian oil. Although the Italian and Japanese courts have declared Iranian oil to be free and unencumbered, the British have not as yet abandoned their unjust and unprincipled activities.

Although it was hoped that during Your Excellency's administration attention of a more sympathetic character would be devoted to the Iranian situation, unfortunately no change seems thus far to have taken place in the position of the American Government.

In the message which the Secretary of State sent me from Karachi, he expressed regret that the efforts of the United States to contribute to the solution of the problem of compensation had thus far been unsuccessful. It should be recalled that the Iranian Government was prepared to pay the value of the former Company's properties in Iran in such amount as might be determined by the International Court of Justice. It was also prepared to accept the jurisdiction of the said court with regard to the amount of compensation provided the British Government would state the amount of its claim in advance and that claim would be within the bounds of reason. Obviously the Iranian Government also had certain claims against the former Oil Company and the British Government which would have been presented at the time of the hearing of the case.

The British Government, hoping to regain its old position, has in effect ignored all of these proposals.

As a result of actions taken by the former Company and the British Government, the Iranian nation is now facing great economic and political difficulties. There can be serious consequences, from an international viewpoint as well, if this situation is permitted to continue. If prompt and effective aid is not given this country now, any steps that might be taken tomorrow to compensate for the negligence of today might well be too late.

We are of course grateful for the aid heretofore granted Iran by the Government of the United States. This aid has not, however, been sufficient to solve the problems of Iran and to ensure world peace which is the aim and ideal of the noble people and of the Government of the United States.

The standard of living of the Iranian people has been very low as a result of century-old imperialistic policies, and it will be impossible to raise it without extensive programs of development and rehabilitation. Unfortunately the aid heretofore granted has been in principle primarily of a technical nature, and even in this respect the assistance needed has not at times been accorded. For example, the Export-Import Bank which was to have advanced Iran twenty-five million dollars for use in the sphere of agriculture did not do so because of unwarranted outside interference.

The Iranian nation hopes that with the help and assistance of the American Government the obstacles placed in the way of sale of Iranian oil can be removed, and that if the American Government is not able to effect a removal of such obstacles, it can render effective economic assistance

to enable Iran to utilize her other resources. This country has natural resources other than oil. The exploitation of these resources would solve the present difficulties of the country. This, however, is impossible without economic aid.

In conclusion, I invite Your Excellency's sympathetic and responsive attention to the present dangerous situation of Iran, and I trust that you will ascribe to all the points contained in this message the importance due them.

Please accept, Mr. President, the assurance of my highest consideration.

DR. M. MOSSADEGH

The earlier correspondence referred to by the Prime Minister was dated prior to the inauguration. This exchange of messages was released on July 11 and is published in the Department of State Bulletin (vol. 29, p. 76).

130   ¶ Message to the President, AFL, and the President, CIO, at the International Confederation of Free Trade Unions Meeting in Stockholm.
July 9, 1953

[Released July 9, 1953. Dated July 8, 1953]

YOUR MESSAGE on behalf of the American Trade Union movement sent from the Third World Congress of the International Confederation of Trade Unions is a splendid example of the contributions that free trade unionism is making to the cause of freedom and justice all over the world. The Government of the U.S. shares wholeheartedly with you and your associates your feelings about the workers of East Berlin who by their heroism have demonstrated that totalitarianism has not extinguished the desire for freedom in the enslaved countries of Eastern Europe. I can assure you that this government will study carefully the proposals you have outlined in your message with a view to employing every peaceful means to lift the burdens of occupation from the German people.

DWIGHT D. EISENHOWER

NOTE: The message from George Meany, President of the American Federation of Labor, and Walter Reuther, President of the Congress of Industrial Organizations, dated July 6, was released with the President's reply. The message proposed that the United States press for immediate negotiations for free elections in a united Germany, for the establishment of free political parties and trade unions, and for the liberation of German workers imprisoned by the Soviet authorities. It also called for submission of a complaint to the United Nations against violations of human rights and freedom of association in Soviet occupied Germany.

The President's message was transmitted through the American Ambassador in Stockholm.

131 ¶ Letter to the Secretary of Agriculture Requesting a Study of the Problems of the Domestic Wool Industry. *July 9, 1953*

Dear Mr. Secretary:

Today I have acted on the recommendation contained in your letter of June 30, 1953, by requesting the United States Tariff Commission to investigate the effects of wool imports on the domestic wool price support program, as authorized under Section 22 of the Agricultural Adjustment Act of 1933, as amended.

You know my concern and reluctance with respect to any

measure which tends to hinder foreign trade. I profoundly believe that the security of our country and the cause of world peace demand that we move toward freer and wider trade with friendly foreign countries. I also believe that a real and permanent solution of the long-term wool problem can be found that is consistent with the expansion of our foreign trade. Any such solution must, in the interests of the United States, depend upon progressive action on the domestic front leading toward a better product, lower costs, and broader markets.

As a step in this direction, I believe it is desirable that this investigation by the Tariff Commission be supplemented by a broader study of the domestic factors which have contributed to the decline in sheep numbers and wool production in the United States. In this way we may be able, not only to alleviate an immediate situation, but also contribute materially to the solution of the more basic problems of the domestic wool industry. Therefore, I request that the Department of Agriculture immediately take appropriate steps to implement a comprehensive study of this type. It is important that this project not only analyze the retarding factors now at work with respect to United States wool production, but also set forth constructive suggestions which will promote the development of a sound and prosperous domestic wool industry and at the same time permit an expanding foreign trade.

In order that this study may be of value with respect to the present situation, I request that the findings be available at least in preliminary draft by the time the Tariff Commission makes its report under Section 22. When completed, the study would be submitted to the proposed Commission on Foreign Economic Policy for its consideration.

A copy of my letter to the Chairman of the Tariff Commission requesting an investigation of the wool situation under Section 22 is attached.

Sincerely,

Dwight D. Eisenhower

NOTE: The President's letter to the Chairman of the Tariff Commission was also released. It directed the Commission to institute an investigation and to report its findings and recommendations as promptly as practicable, in order to permit a de-cision to be made as early as possible during the 1953 wool marketing season.

The Secretary of Agriculture's letter of June 30 was not made public by the White House.

132 ¶ Message to the National Co-Chairmen, Commission on Religious Organizations, National Conference of Christians and Jews. *July* 9, 1953

Monsignor John A. O'Brien
Rabbi Maurice N. Eisendrath
Dr. John Sutherland Bonnell
National Co-Chairmen, The Commission on Religious
*   Organizations*
National Conference of Christians and Jews
New York, New York

I have received your telegram of today's date. I want you to know at once that I fully share the convictions you state. The issues here are clear. Generalized and irresponsible attacks that sweepingly condemn the whole of any group of citizens are alien to America. Such attacks betray contempt for the principles of freedom and decency. And when these attacks—whatever their professed purpose be—condemn such a vast portion of the churches or clergy as to create doubt in the loyalty of all, the damage to our nation is multiplied.

If there be found any American among us, whatever his calling, guilty of treasonous action against the state, let him legally and properly be convicted and punished. This applies to every person, lay or clergy.

The churches of America are citadels of our faith in individual freedom and human dignity. This faith is the living source of all our spiritual strength. And this strength is our matchless armor in our world-wide struggle against the forces of godless tyranny and oppression.

DWIGHT D. EISENHOWER

NOTE: The message from the National Co-Chairmen stated that the sweeping attack on the loyalty of Protestant clergymen and the charge that they were the largest single group supporting the communist apparatus was unjustified and deplorable. It further stated that the President was to be congratulated on his recent warning against casting doubt on the loyalty of the churches and synagogues. The message concluded as follows: "We fully recognize the right of Congress to investigate the loyalty of any citizen regardless of the office he may occupy, ecclesiastical or otherwise. But destroying trust in the leaders of Protestantism, Catholicism or Judaism by wholesale condemnation is to weaken the greatest American bulwark against atheistic materialism and communism."

133 ¶ Statement by the President Upon Signing Bill Concerning the Display of the Flag of the United States. *July* 10, 1953

[Released July 10, 1953. Dated July 9, 1953]

I HAVE TODAY approved S. 694, "To prohibit the display of flags of international organizations or other nations in equal or superior prominence or honor to the flag of the United States except under specified circumstances, and for other purposes."

This measure is intended to prescribe rules of guidance for the display of the flag of the United States when flown with the flag of the United Nations or with any other national or international flag.

Unfortunately, the wording of the bill is so arranged that it is susceptible of interpretations which are not intended and which would breach international usage. Only after reading the debate upon this bill does it become clear that the intent of the Congress is simply and correctly to assure that within the United States and its possessions the American flag is to be given its traditional place of honor and prominence when flown with other flags.

Legislative history cannot be incorporated in the statute books. Even if it could be, the other nations of the world could well question why the language of these rules of guidance for the display of the flag is not direct, distinct, and free of ambiguity.

At this time, I can do no more than to assure the people of the United States and the governments of other nations that this bill is not intended to conflict with international usage or with the flag codes of any nation or international organization, particularly as they affect display of the flag of the United Nations. I am requesting that the Department of State take whatever steps are necessary to convey this assurance to other governments and to international organizations.

At the same time, I want to express the hope that the Congress will clarify the language of this bill. I believe that such action is essential in the interest of international goodwill and comity. I believe that it is also essential in the interest of maintaining the clearest possible understanding of the importance which the people of the United States attach to the American flag as their national emblem.

DWIGHT D. EISENHOWER

NOTE: As enacted, S. 694 is Public Law 107, 83d Congress (67 Stat. 142).

134 ¶ Statement by the President Regarding Aid for the People of the Soviet Zone of Germany. *July* 10, 1953

CHANCELLOR ADENAUER has addressed to me a letter asking that the United States Government participate in aiding the people of Eastern Germany whose food supply has been steadily deteriorating.

I have been distressed to learn of the plight of the people of

Eastern Germany. I have, therefore, replied to Chancellor Adenauer informing him that this Government would join him in making food available to the people of Eastern Germany. Simultaneously, I have instructed the American Chargé d'Affaires in Moscow to make an offer of food to be distributed in Eastern Germany. I have directed the Secretary of State and the Mutual Security Administrator to take steps to see that this food is made available in Germany without delay. I have indicated to the Soviet Government my confidence that practical ways for immediate distribution can be developed so that the food shortages afflicting the East German population may be alleviated quickly.

I invite the other nations of the free world to join us in this action of aiding the people of Eastern Germany in this emergency.

NOTE: The letter from Chancellor Adenauer appears in the note to Item 135.

The text of a U.S. note to the U.S.S.R., in the form of instructions to the Chargé d'Affaires in Moscow, was also released. The note, together with the Soviet reply refusing the offer of food, is published in the Department of State Bulletin (vol. 29, p. 68).

135 ¶ Exchange of Letters Between the President and Chancellor Adenauer of Germany Concerning Aid for the People of the Soviet Zone. *July* 10, 1953

My dear Mr. Chancellor:

The receipt of your letter of July 4, 1953, in which you outlined the serious situation existing in the Soviet Zone of Germany concerning the supply of food for the population, has confirmed reports which I have received from High Commissioner Conant and which have been of considerable concern to me over the past few weeks.

I am, therefore, anxious to respond affirmatively to your appeal that this Government join you in aiding the people of East Germany in this hour when many of those demonstrating are demanding more food.

I have, therefore, today instructed the American Chargé d'Affaires in Moscow to offer the Soviet Government shipments of food for distribution to the population of East Germany. I have suggested that arrangements for the distribution be made between the staffs of the United States and Soviet High Commissioners in Germany and that consideration be given to distribution through German religious institutions.

I sincerely hope that this effort on our part to relieve the plight of the people in East Germany will be welcomed by the Soviet Government.

Sincerely yours,

DWIGHT D. EISENHOWER

NOTE: Chancellor Adenauer's letter follows:

My dear Mr. President:

During recent months, I have discussed with Dr. Conant, the United States High Commissioner for Germany, on repeated occasions the position of the population in the Soviet-occupied zone. The Federal Government watches with serious apprehension the steadily increasing political pressure to which the Germans living there are subjected. Apart from that, the steadily deteriorating food supply in the Soviet-occupied zone fills the Federal Government with growing anxiety. It is true that the events of 17 June 1953 have prompted the rulers of the Soviet Zone to announce, in this particular field, certain relaxations, but according to information received by us, it is extremely doubtful whether the Communist rulers are actually willing, or able, to fulfill these promises. Therefore, the food supply of the Soviet Zone must continue to be regarded as definitely endangered.

As it is, the Federal Government is, unfortunately, unable to remove the political pressure weighing upon the people in the Soviet Zone. However, it feels itself under an obligation to do everything in its power to at least protect the population from hunger as far as this will be possible.

The Bundestag, too, dealt with this question, during the last few days and requested the Federal Government on 1 July by a resolution to take all possible measures to ensure as speedily as possible an adequate supply of food for the distressed Soviet Zone and East Berlin.

The Federal Government, therefore, intends to make available funds on a large scale for food supplies to be sent to the Soviet-occupied zone. The churches and charitable organizations will be entrusted with the implementation of this action so as to ensure that these food supplies are used for the intended purpose.

I should much appreciate it if the United States Government, too, were prepared to participate in this aid action which is in the interest of the entire Western world.

Sincerely yours,

ADENAUER

See also Item 134 and note.

136 ¶ Letter to the Speaker of the House of Representatives Transmitting a Proposed Supplemental Appropriation for the Department of Agriculture. *July* 15, 1953

Sir:

I have the honor to transmit herewith for the consideration of the Congress a proposed supplemental appropriation for the fiscal year 1954 in the amount of $150,000,000 for the Department of Agriculture.

The Congress is already aware of the urgent necessity for immediate consideration of an appropriation of funds to implement the administration bill which I have signed, providing additional authority for emergency assistance to farmers and stockmen. The cumulative effect of continued drought in the Southwest during the past four years has created an unprecedented need for emergency credit and feed, in order to prevent serious damage to a major part of our agricultural economy.

I have been kept currently informed by the Secretary of Agriculture and through personal conferences with congressional leaders and representatives of the livestock industry. As you know, I have also made a personal inspection of the area and have met with the Governors of the six States designated as drought-disaster areas. This firsthand knowledge of the problems involved and the terrible consequences of the drought have impressed me with the courage and self-reliance of the people in these areas and their determination to work out their own salvation as fully as they can. I am no less impressed with their desperate need for help.

I wish to assure the Congress that the executive branch will continue to employ fully the resources available in assisting in the emergency. The States, local governments, and individuals involved, however, should strive to do everything possible within their power to overcome the situation and minimize the necessity for Federal aid.

Details of the proposed supplemental appropriation are set forth in the attached letter from the Director of the Bureau of the Budget, with whose comments and observations thereon I concur.

Respectfully yours,

DWIGHT D. EISENHOWER

NOTE: The letter was addressed to the Honorable Joseph W. Martin, Jr., Speaker of the House of Representatives. The attachment, also released, is published in House Document 208 (83d Cong., 1st sess.).

A supplemental appropriation was approved July 31, 1953 (67 Stat. 297).

137 ¶ Message Recorded for the Third National Boy Scout Jamboree. *July* 17, 1953

I AM VERY HAPPY to send greetings to all of you participating in the Third National Boy Scout Jamboree. I should very much like to be with you, for I recall, with real pleasure, my visit three years ago, to Valley Forge, Pennsylvania, where many of you attended the Second National Jamboree on the Fourth of July. It was a memorable experience. I shall never forget the enthusiasm and the spirit of dedication that seemed to fill the camp.

I learned there a genuine lesson, in the meaning of brotherhood and the spirit of united helpfulness.

Of course, the Boy Scout Movement continues to make progress. It yearly enriches our nation, and contributes generously to the economic, physical and spiritual resources of the country. So I am particularly glad to send congratulations to all of you responsible for this great achievement.

Among you, at this Jamboree there are, I am told, Boy Scouts, Explorers and Scout Leaders from every State in the Union, as well as from Hawaii, Alaska and Puerto Rico, in addition to some sixteen other countries. Each of you will make new friends, acquire new skills, appreciate new values.

And, in all likelihood, you will gain a new sense of the vastness and complexities of this nation and of the world. But I am confident that, in meeting and talking with your fellow scouts, you will gain a renewed awareness of the need for cooperating—working together—in our country and in the world. Bonds of common purpose and common ideals can unite people, even when they come from the most distant and diverse places.

This is an important lesson, and even if you learn no other, you will leave Irvine Ranch with a new wisdom.

I know that this will be a week filled with great memories for all of you. Good luck to each of you and best wishes for every success!

NOTE: The message was delivered by transcription to the Jamboree held at the Irvine Ranch, Newport Harbor, Orange County, Calif.

138 ¶ Exchange of Letters Between the President and Chancellor Adenauer Concerning the Soviet Government's Refusal To Admit Food for the People of East Germany. *July* 20, 1953

My dear Mr. Chancellor:

I share the regret expressed in your letter of July 13, 1953, at the refusal of the Soviet Government to admit the food which the United States Government offered the East German population in response to your appeal of July 4.

Immediately after the receipt of Mr. Molotov's rejection of my offer, I made it clear that the offer continues to stand and that the food continues to be available. Since it is our joint purpose to aid the people of Eastern Germany in spite of the obstacles which the occupation authorities of that area have created, I have directed the Secretary of State and the Director for Mutual Security to place quantities of these foodstuffs at your disposal for use in relieving the suffering of the people of Eastern Germany in the best available manner.

At the same time, we shall continue to make clear to the Soviet Government that the offer which was made on July 10, 1953, was motivated solely by humanitarian impulses and that the food is available if that Government wishes to permit its entrance into the Soviet Zone of occupation.

Sincerely,

DWIGHT D. EISENHOWER

NOTE: The text of Chancellor Adenauer's letter follows:

Dear Mr. President:

Your letter of July 10th has been conveyed to me through Ambassador Conant. Your generous offer to relieve the want of the population of the Soviet Zone through immediate and extensive deliveries of foodstuffs has touched me deeply. This spontaneous demonstration of humane readiness to help, which is in the best traditions of the American people, has caused great joy in all of Germany and especially has given new hope and new courage to the people in the Soviet-occupied zone of Germany. I should, therefore, like to express to you, in the name not only of the Federal Government but also in the name of the entire German people, my heartiest thanks.

It is with regret that I have learned that the Soviet Government has refused its cooperation in the relief action which you had planned. I would like to request that the delivery of foodstuffs should not as a result be withheld. On the contrary, I wish to express the hope that the foodstuffs may be placed at the disposal of the Federal Government, which for its part will do everything to make the food available in the most effective way possible for relief of the suffering of the population who have fallen into need as a result of the situation in the Soviet Zone.

ADENAUER

139   ¶ Veto of Bill for the Relief of Fred P. Hines. *July* 20, 1953

To the United States Senate:

I return herewith, without my approval, S. 152, "An Act For the relief of Fred P. Hines."

The bill directs the Administrator of Veterans' Affairs to pay to Mr. Fred P. Hines, the sum of $778.78, representing the amount claimed as the cost of private hospital and medical expenses incurred in 1948 in treating a disability not connected with his active military service.

Mr. Hines served in the United States Army during the Spanish-American War and was honorably discharged on November 18, 1898. He did not incur a disability while in the military service and he has not suffered any service-incurred disability since then.

This veteran is eligible for medical care and hospitalization in a Veterans' Administration hospital for conditions not of service origin, provided facilities are available and he is unable to pay for such care elsewhere. He has availed himself of Veterans' Administration treatment on numerous occasions. On the occasion in question he chose not to do so.

The record, I believe, reasonably supports the conclusion that this veteran had personal knowledge of the limiting rules and policy governing his case. He was aware that they precluded the Federal Government from assuming responsibility for the costs of private care. In 1947, he requested the Veterans' Administration to pay a private hospital bill which he incurred for a non-service-connected condition. By letter dated February 21, 1947, Mr. Hines was advised by the Veterans' Administration of the denial of his claim for the reason that the expenses were incurred for treatment of non-service-connected conditions.

Despite the legislative finding in the bill, the record establishes that a medical emergency did not exist when Mr. Hines first began to incur the private medical and hospital expenses involved in his claim. In my judgment, no question of professional or administrative malfeasance is involved.

The extenuating factors advanced in the Committee reports for special legislation do not, I believe, present acceptable grounds for equitable relief for Mr. Hines or the basis for exceptional and preferred treatment.

The plight of this elderly veteran provokes a spontaneous desire to lighten his burden. Were this an insolated case, I would have no hesitancy in approving this bill. But it is not. We have twenty million veterans who are eligible for hospital care in Federal hospitals under varying restrictive conditions. The precedent that would be established by approval of this bill cannot be dismissed. Many, many other cases have been denied similar relief. The Veterans' Administration annually, by administrative action, disallows more than 500 similar claims of Spanish-American War veterans alone for reimbursement of medical and hospital expenses based on equally justifiable reasons. The Veterans' Administration estimates that the same kind of claims filed annually by veterans of other wars aggregate several thousand annually.

I believe that in a Federal program as large as the veterans' hospital program it is particularly important to administer the

499

laws and regulations uniformly and with special favor for none. Yielding to compassion or special pleas would eventually destroy the effectiveness of the program. The end result would be to set aside the sound and desirable distinction between service-connected and non-service-connected disability cases. From every standpoint the choice presented by this bill is the same. If the bill were to be approved, it would mean acceptance of the premise that any veteran should be given the right to determine when and where and under what circumstances he may commit the Federal Government to the payment of private medical and hospital expenses for non-service-connected disabilities. I believe that the establishment of such a policy would be unsound and indefensible.

DWIGHT D. EISENHOWER

140   ¶ Telegram Congratulating Ben Hogan. *July 21, 1953*

Ben Hogan
City Hall
New York, N.Y.

Millions of Americans would like to participate with the New Yorkers today who are extending their traditional welcome upon your return from your magnificent victory. We are proud of you not only as a great competitor and a master of your craft, but also as an envoy extraordinary in the business of building friendship for America. With best wishes to you and Mrs. Hogan.

DWIGHT D. EISENHOWER

NOTE: The President's message was sent on the occasion of Ben Hogan's return to the United States after winning the British Open Golf Championship at Carnoustie, Scotland.

141 ¶ The President's News Conference of
July 22, 1953.

THE PRESIDENT. Good morning. If I am late, I apologize.

The two items that I should say are of the most general interest this morning come out of the Korean situation and out of East Germany. There is very little that I can add to the discussions we have had before, so far as Korea is concerned. There remain, of course, certain points of misunderstandings that create some doubt, but I can only say that I am still hopeful and reasonably confident that a reasonable armistice is to be signed soon. I don't know exactly when; I wouldn't predict that.

On Germany, we saw the dispatches this morning that locally the Soviet High Commissioner was resentful of our putting food into Berlin.

I think it was on July 10th that I said we would instantly put $15 million worth of food there to help out. We asked no remuneration, no return, no exchange of goods. We just put it there for humanitarian purposes; and, of course, it is difficult for us to understand why they should object to that, where they have any ground for objection to feeding hungry people.

I believe two shipments have actually gone, and I believe one is to go about tomorrow, completing the first portion of what we thought would be necessary for the relief of immediate hunger. I regret that there is difficulty arising. But as you know, we put it in the hands of Chancellor Adenauer himself, who was interested to get it over there and to deliver it, and it will still remain available in West Berlin. There is food there and people come to get it; so long as they are not prevented from coming to get it they will continue to get it.

Now, those are the only two items that I thought of that I had something to say about, so we will go right to the questions.

Q. Edward T. Folliard, Washington Post: Others have reviewed and appraised your first 6 months in office. I wondered if you would have a go at it, and give us an estimate of the situation?

THE PRESIDENT. Well, I will tell you: certainly I wouldn't want, in answer to a question, to take advantage of that to use up the next 25 minutes in a long talk.

Q. Roscoe Drummond, Christian Science Monitor: We wouldn't mind if you did.

THE PRESIDENT. I would be completely deceitful if I tried to pretend that everything that I thought we could have done in this 6 months has been done. But after this turnover of authority of last January—it makes no difference on which side of the political philosophy you yourself may believe, may exist, and may belong—you can see that there was a very, very great, almost revolutionary activity necessary to pick up where others had left off and to begin again. There were opposing policies and ideas coming in after 20 years of another type of philosophy. Not always, though—and here I want to make this very clear—not always must we say that everything that has been done before is wrong. I have never said that, and no reasonable man would; but there are certain areas in which disagreement was obvious.

Now, you get new people, you get new ideas working, and you find that frictions develop. In such a thing as the governmental organization, we have two and a half million civilians. How can you change people's thinking even when they may be only in an important operational position? You have got to get policy worked out so that two and a half million people can implement it. It is a long, laborious process.

Then, of course, the party: either party that is in power is not in itself a completely homogeneous whole; it is divided up into different kinds of thinking on particular subjects, whether it be foreign trade or taxes or revenues or whatever you are doing in the proper functioning of a Federal government. You have these differences; so trouble develops.

I personally believe that we must always think of government as persons. You get a group of persons who are in the legislature and who are in the executive branch; and they try to work out, hammer out on the anvil of logic and fact and statistics, certain programs that they believe best for 157 million people and their relationships with others in this world.

That is laborious, and it is slow. I personally believe this: if it were accomplished too quickly—even if every change were for the better—if it were accomplished too quickly, it would be wrong.

You cannot take a railroad and have a right angle turn in it, a sharp right angle turn; you have to build a curve. Now, you have to do that with such things as involve two and a half million people. Great policies, great types of problems, fall upon that government.

So all I am trying to say is that the change is gradual; it is not so rapid as to be completely satisfying even to a person who, I think, is as patient as I am; certainly I try to be patient.

But there has been progress made. I personally believe that every day the people in this Government—and I am not referring now merely to one party—the people in the Government, the executive and the legislative, are coming to see a little bit closer eye to eye on the great important problems that affect the United States of America.

That, to my mind, is progress. Because my job here, as I see it, is not to create friction, not to accentuate differences, but to bring people together so we can actually achieve progress, not to be particularly dramatic or just to do something to get another headline, but to get progress for the United States of America.

Now, in that sense—and that is a theory of gradualism, there is no question about it—we are making progress, but we have not gone as fast as I should like. That is the sum total of it.

Q. Elizabeth Carpenter, Southwestern Newspapers: The Little Rock, Arkansas, *Gazette* asked me if I would ask you to comment on the extent, if any, that politics figured in the declaration of drought disaster counties.

I think their question stems from the fact that the unsuccessful

Republican candidate down there made a public statement saying that if the people had had the foresight to elect him, some of the Arkansas counties which were passed over for drought aid would have been not passed over.

THE PRESIDENT. Well [*laughing*], I am not going to get righteously indignant, but this is the first time I have heard the word "politics" brought up in connection with that drought program. Certainly I didn't go down there to talk to the Governors—I didn't ask them their politics, I didn't ask them who they favored or anything else.

This is a question of people being in a plight, and we are trying to help them out. Anyone who raises the question of politics is raising a question which I had not even heard of before, and which I will not entertain now.

Q. Neal A. Stanford, Christian Science Monitor: Mr. President, you spoke of certain points of misunderstanding on the Korean truce. Are those points of misunderstanding with the South Koreans or the North Koreans, and can you pinpoint the differences?

THE PRESIDENT. No, I can't pinpoint them for this reason: the whole arrangements to be made in the truce itself are still in executive session. They are confidential and secret, and I will not talk about anything that could be remotely interpreted as my violating that particular thing.

Now, some of the misunderstandings with the south have been put in the papers. There is no use reviewing those. There has been a different approach springing, possibly, out of the different locations of these people. But as far as the differences with the north are concerned, they are on the secret basis, as I understand it.

Q. Harry W. Frantz, South American Service, United Press: I don't know if you have received enough reports yet from your brother's mission that you wish to comment on. I have in mind the fact that many countries gave a very elaborate and generous reception to your brother, and I thought you might make some mention of it.

THE PRESIDENT. Only this: every country where he has visited has then sent to me a file of clippings, pictures, official reports, and so on. So far as I can see, the trip is accomplishing everything for which I hoped.

I am trying to pay a call, to pay my respects, and I am doing it through the person of my brother, to all of these heads of the South American states; to assure them in this fashion of our interest in them, our recognition that we have in certain respects a common fate, and we had better work it out together.

The reception accorded him makes me feel that they are looking at it in the same way. I have had very little in the way of detailed report from him, almost nothing.

Q. Felix Cotten, International News Service: Mr. President, I have been asked to ask you certain questions about the Korean matter. Not that I want to labor the thing, but there were reports that a new message has been delivered to Mr. Rhee by Mr. Briggs, and the Foreign Minister is quoted as saying that "the South Korean Government considers the Robertson-Rhee agreement broken, and we will not observe any implementation of the armistice."

I just wondered if you cared to comment on that particular phase of the matter?

THE PRESIDENT. No, I have no further comment that I think of that I can make on Korea. I don't think it would be helpful. I'm sorry.

Q. Richard L. Wilson, Cowles Publications: Something you said in response to Mr. Folliard's question brought this question into my mind. A number of people have urged that you bring some discipline into the Republican Party by cracking down on McCarthy. In here you have previously said that your objective was not to create friction but to bring people together.

I wonder if that remark could be made to apply to your philosophy regarding Senator McCarthy?

THE PRESIDENT. I must remind you again that I never deal in my statements, to you or to anyone else, in terms of personalities, and I don't now.

I merely say that if a democracy, with all of its different viewpoints and approaches to our various problems, is going to make progress, someone has to take on the onerous job of trying to search out, analyze, and bring together the majority of view, or what you might call the bulk of public opinion, and get it translated into law where necessary, into regulation, or into policy.

You cannot get ahead merely by indulging extremist views and listening to them. What do they bring? They don't bring majority action.

What I am trying to do is to get what I believe to be the commonsense approach of America to its various problems, to get them implemented and to get ahead.

Now, where I have to go into opposition to any person, I try to do it on the basis of principles, on the basis of utter convictions, on the basis of my own conscience. I am not going to take time, either in public or private, to question the motives of anybody else; that is between him and someone else, not between him and me.

I am going to stand for what I believe to be right. If that is found to be in opposition to what someone else says, publicly or privately, then that is too bad; but that is what I am going to stand for. So, I am not going to do it through terms of personalities.

Q. Sarah McClendon, El Paso Times: Mr. Sam Rayburn, the House Democratic leader, told the House yesterday that he hoped before they had to pass on the bill limiting oil imports, on a bill establishing a quota for oil imports, that they would get the advantage of your views. Would you like to say what you think about limiting oil imports?

THE PRESIDENT. Well, you know, by and large, I believe we have got to have freer trade in the world. I believe we are particularly anxious that all of our Western Hemisphere friends prosper.

When we begin to apply these types of beliefs to this question of limiting oil imports, why, I may have in the long run to change my opinions a little bit. I think that I wouldn't want to do it, certainly, from the Western Hemisphere.

Now, that is just shooting from the hip, and without the advantage of talking to my advisers on it; but I certainly—in the Western Hemisphere—don't think we should indulge in it yet.

Q. Glenn M. Green, Jr., McGraw-Hill Publications: Mr. President, I believe that question related to the so-called second Simpson bill, which is about to be brought up in the House. Do you believe, Mr. President, that that bill in any way conflicts with your previously expressed position on trade and trade policy?

THE PRESIDENT. I personally don't want to change the laws under which we are operating until we have had this opportunity under the year's extension of the Reciprocal Trade Act to study it absolutely.

With respect to this question and the previous one, I would be foolish to pretend to a profound knowledge of all of these things. Someone comes in and presents one viewpoint, someone else another; it takes a long time to get these varied viewpoints and arguments analyzed, put together, and reach what you can call a stated policy. So on neither question do I have an irrevocable policy.

I do just believe, in general, we should be given now the chance to continue the existing arrangements until we can study it through the finest body of people we can put together.

Q. Marvin L. Arrowsmith, Associated Press: The House Appropriations Committee has voted to cut the foreign-aid funds by a billion dollars. Do you believe that the program can operate successfully under those circumstances?

THE PRESIDENT. Well, Mr. Arrowsmith, of course, I have never tried to fix an exact dollar level as indicative of the worthwhileness or the destruction of a policy.

Now, I want to make this clear: I have been around the fringes, at least, of this problem for a long time. I have never looked upon what we now call MSA as giveaway programs. Everything I do in my present office, and what I did before, was approached basically from this viewpoint: where lies the enlightened self-interest of the United States? And when I find that that leads me inevitably into the conclusion that we must have strong worthwhile alliances with other people in the world, then I look to see how we can establish those alliances and maintain what I call collective security.

To my mind—and this is the way I approached the determination of the amount of money in that MSA appropriation—I put it right square alongside our own security program, because I think that is exactly where it belongs.

We are looking at the position of the United States in the free world, its ability to establish collective security, which means its own security; and those two should be viewed together.

So, at least I want to say this: when we go at that program, I don't think merely of how much are we cutting here and there; how are we affecting the security and the position of the United States of America, that is the way I look at it.

Now, I think, and I have been doing a lot of studying on it, I think that cut is too heavy.

Q. Frederic W. Collins, Providence Journal: Mr. President, this goes back to some of the questions on foreign-trade legislation. Could you tell us whether you yourself favor the innovation of a partisan majority on the Tariff Commission?

THE PRESIDENT. Well, I don't think you mean to load your question, but no one ever before put it to me in terms of partisan majority.

The only time it was put up to me was that people in the Government, including Congress, had gotten impatient by the fact that stalemates took place over there, which kept a subject so long that you could not really force it out of that Commission. I accepted the solution of adding an individual, from one side or the other.

Now, I never thought of it as a partisan thing. I was perfectly ready to take one fewer. It is something, all right, that raised more sound and fury than I had anticipated, because I looked at it probably not as deeply as I should have. That may be so; but at the time it was proposed, it looked to me like merely a way of putting some decisiveness in a board in which I had heard there had been indecision.

Q. Ray L. Scherer, National Broadcasting Company: Sir, may we have permission to quote you directly on your reply to Mr. Folliard's question on the 6 months' review?

THE PRESIDENT. Oh, no, I think not. You might take a sentence or two, and take it to Mr. Hagerty; but I think if we start that, then I would have to come over to see you with written documents, and I don't think any of you would want me to do that.

Q. [*Speaker unidentified*]: Mr. President——

THE PRESIDENT. I just feel—excuse me one second; and I appreciate your due consideration, because I am warm, too—but I just feel that we had better keep these on the informal basis on which we started, or we are likely to suffer in the long run.

Edwin Dayton Moore, United Press: Thank you, Mr. President.

NOTE: President Eisenhower's fourteenth news conference was held in the Executive Office Building from 10:32 to 10:53 o'clock on Wednesday morning, July 22, 1953. In attendance: 141.

142   ¶ Statement by the President on a Proposed Amendment to the Constitution Relating to Treaties.   *July* 22, 1953

SENATOR KNOWLAND has today introduced a resolution to amend the Constitution of the United States. Its purpose is to assure that treaties entered into by the President and consented to by at least two-thirds of the Senate in behalf of the United States shall not override the Constitution. It provides that treaties and executive agreements shall not violate the Constitution, and that the courts may so declare; that in the future the Senate shall vote on treaties by recorded yeas and nays as is the case now with a vote on overriding a veto; and that the Senate may in each instance, when considering the ratification of a treaty, if it so determines, provide that it shall not be effective as internal law save by congressional action.

This resolution has my unqualified support.

Under our form of Government, the President has the duty to conduct foreign affairs. Every American knows this to be our traditional policy which has functioned so well during the lifetime of our Republic.

While I have opposed other amendments which would have had the effect of depriving the President of the capacity necessary to carry on negotiations with foreign governments, I am glad to support the Knowland Amendment for it confirms that this Presidential power cannot be used contrary to the Constitution.

All action of the President, either domestically or in foreign relations, must be within and pursuant to constitutional authority. Consequently I am unalterably opposed to any amendment which would change our traditional treaty making power or which would hamper the President in his constitutional authority to conduct foreign affairs. Today, probably as never before in our history it is essential that our country be able effectively to enter into agreements with other nations.

As President I have taken an oath to defend the Constitution. I therefore oppose any change which will impair the President's traditional authority to conduct foreign affairs. Senator Wiley and others who have joined in the defense of these constitutional powers so important to the integrity and safety of our nation, are entitled to commendation and support for their efforts.

It is my belief that the reassurances contained in the Knowland

Amendment meet all legitimate demands that have been made in this field of foreign relations.

143 ¶ Letter to the Chairman, Senate Appropriations Committee, on the Mutual Security Program. *July 23, 1953*

[Released July 23, 1953. Dated July 22, 1953]

Dear Mr. Chairman:

I wish to bring to your urgent attention my deep concern with the Mutual Security Appropriations now before you for consideration.

This program and these appropriations directly involve the security of our own Nation. The program is specifically directed toward strengthening the collective security of the free nations—in which the safety of our Nation is inescapably involved. The sums requested were carefully worked out in connection with, and as an inseparable part of, our entire security program comprising the United States military forces and the Atomic Energy Commission. By strict rescreening, they were reduced one-third from those requested in the budget of the outgoing Administration.

Our country must exercise constructive and courageous leadership, for its own sake as well as for the sake of the other free nations. Invariably, if leadership falters in the face of grave danger in a complex situation, the result is disastrous. The amounts now in the Mutual Security Program have already been reduced and vigorously rescreened; deep cuts will certainly be received, on both sides of the Iron Curtain, as evidence of faltering.

As you know, I have never taken the attitude that an exact dollar in this program marks the difference between success or failure. But it is my conviction that grave consequences would follow from a major cut below the requested amounts carefully scrutinized and unanimously approved by my key advisers, including the Secretary of State, the Secretary of the Treasury, and the Secretary of Defense, as well as the Director for Mutual Security.

The funds requested for military assistance are indeed large. They are large because that is the size of the threat before us. They are large because the implements of military strength are not cheap.

It must be remembered, however, that our funds are exceeded by much larger funds expended by our NATO and other allies themselves. Our tanks, planes, ships, and ammunition are essential if we are to take advantage of the readiness of other nations throughout the world to join together with us in a firm posture of strength. Across the world—from the impressive buildup of military strength in NATO, to the bitter fighting against Communist forces in Indo-China—we have allies who rely on us to provide certain missing ingredients in their military strength. We must not slow down the momentum of strength and growing unity.

I realize that these military assistance appropriations involve a substantial question of judgment as to the necessary amount of "lead time" that must be allowed to permit delivery of equipment on schedule in the future, and that this lead time allowance has an important effect in the amount to be appropriated in any one year. I know from first-hand observation that the lead time required in almost every case—the building up of a division in Turkey, or a jet squadron in Norway, or an armored unit in France—has been a very long one. The emphasis in our program on major items of equipment, such as aircraft and ships, and the volume of our very important offshore procurement require a relatively large amount of lead-time financing. This necessary equipment-pipeline accounts for the large amounts of carry-over funds in this program, as reflected in my request.

I have requested these funds only to meet demonstrated military requirements, including only essentials for forces that our allies are now in process of raising, training, and maintaining to receive this military equipment. The responsible members of this Administration have proven their alertness in identifying possible savings; we have reported these savings to the Congress, and we have made full allowance for them in our request. This Administration will continue to exercise that same care in the management of funds, and will take every advantage of opportunity to economize in the use of funds with which they are entrusted.

I wish also to emphasize the importance of economic and technical assistance for the Near East, for India and Pakistan, for Latin America, and for the Far East, where it is vital that the people see evidence of improved conditions of living flowing from freedom and independent sovereignty as contrasted to totalitarian methods. And I place great value on the work of the United Nations International Children's Emergency Fund, with its cooperative approach by many nations in the interest of children of many areas of the world, and on the related United Nations Technical Assistance Program, which brings to the people of the underdeveloped areas concrete evidence that the United Nations is actively assisting their quest for economic progress. These programs, many of which require only modest amounts of money, are an integral part of our program for America's security.

This is a program for building strength. Evidence is beginning to appear in many parts of the world of the success that comes from a firm foreign policy backed by growing strength and unity on the part of the free nations. This, of all times, is not a moment to hesitate. It is, above all, a time to make more strong and effective our relationships with all other free peoples, a moment to help speed the momentum of their growing strength.

Sincerely,

Dwight D. Eisenhower

NOTE: The letter was addressed to the Honorable Styles Bridges, Chairman of the Senate Committee on Appropriations. The appropriation act was approved August 7, 1953 (67 Stat. 478).

144　¶ Statement by the President on the National Security Training Commission and on Military Manpower Policies.　*July* 23, 1953

I HAVE NOMINATED to the United States Senate Julius Ochs Adler, Warren Atherton and Dr. Karl T. Compton to fill the vacancies now existing on the National Security Training Commission.

The National Security Training Commission was created by Public Law 51, 82nd Congress, to study and submit National Security Training plans and exercise civilian control over such a program. The three gentlemen whose names I have submitted to the Senate, serving with the two military members, Lieutenant General Raymond S. McLain (ret.) and Admiral Thomas C. Kinkaid (ret.), will complete the membership of this Commission. Upon his confirmation by the Senate, I shall designate Mr. Adler to be Chairman.

I am requesting the Commission to submit to me not later than December 1, 1953, a report which shall include, but not be limited to, (1) an examination of inequities in the present method of securing men for our Armed Forces' reserves and the burdens imposed, with suggestions to remedy these inequities; (2) the feasibility and desirability of operating a military training program to supply trained non-veteran reserves while at the same time continuing induction for service; and (3) the relationship of such a program to the building of a strong and equitable citizen reserve sufficiently advanced in training to permit regular forces to expand rapidly from peace strength to war strength. I am also requesting the Office of Defense Mobilization to submit to me by December 1, 1953, a definitive report on the availability of manpower to operate simultaneously a military training program and supply our active duty military personnel, including an analysis of the impact of such a program on our requirements for agricultural, scientific, professional, technical and skilled personnel.

I am confident that it is the will of this nation that the responsibilities for its defense should be shared as equally as possible by all of its citizens.

And yet, as our veterans of Korea return home they find themselves under legal compulsion to shoulder a six-year reserve obligation. Our only effective military reserve under this present system is—and apparently will remain—composed almost wholly of men who have already served the nation in the Korean War, World War II, or both.

I also find that under the present system thousands of our young men have not yet assumed any military obligation to our country. Men who have not been inducted for Korea not only escape the ordeals of that conflict. They also undertake no reserve obligation.

Thus our system requires our soldier of today also to carry the future national defense burden ahead of the man who has received no training, has done no service, and has assumed no reserve obligation.

These inequities appear to me to directly contravene some of the most basic principles of our society.

I have had doubts, and have voiced them publicly, that sufficient manpower would be available to supply our active-duty military personnel requirements and a military training program at the same time. I have, however, reviewed our manpower data in the light of the recent reduction in the size of the standing forces, and I am hopeful that the studies I have requested of this matter can produce suggested remedies for the inequities which have long characterized our military manpower policies.

NOTE: The Commission's report is entitled "20th Century Minutemen, a Report to the President on a Reserve Forces Training Program" (Government Printing Office, 1954). See also Item 7 in the 1954 volume, this series.

145 ¶ Statement by the President Upon Appointing Members of the Second Hoover Commission. *July* 24, 1953

THE FORMER PRESIDENT of the United States has once again placed his great talents at the disposal of the government, and I am sure that I speak for the people of the nation as I take this occasion to thank him publicly for responding to this call to duty.

The government is fortunate that Mr. Farley has likewise agreed to help the Commission in its work. His knowledge of government and its functions will be of inestimable value to the tremendous task confronting the Commission.

NOTE: The act establishing the Commission on Organization of the Executive Branch of the Government (Second Hoover Commission) was approved by the President on July 10, 1953 (67 Stat. 142). On July 24 the White House announced that the President had appointed Herbert Hoover and James A. Farley as public representatives, and had designated the Attorney General, Herbert Brownell, and the Director of the Office of Defense Mobilization, Arthur S. Flemming, as representatives of the executive branch. Additional members were appointed by the President of the Senate and the Speaker of the House of Representatives.

146 ¶ Letter to Chancellor Adenauer of Germany Concerning the Uprisings in East Berlin and East Germany. *July* 25, 1953

[Released July 25, 1953. Dated July 23, 1953]

My dear Mr. Chancellor:

During the development of the conversations between the U.S. Secretary of State and the Foreign Ministers of Great Britain and France, it occurred to me that it might be helpful if I were to write you a letter in amplification of the thoughts so tightly compressed in the final communique.

It seems to me that certain definite patterns are emerging from the situation in East Germany and the Eastern European satellite countries—patterns which will unquestionably have a profound effect upon the future, including the proposed meeting of the Foreign Ministers of the Four Powers.

I think, therefore, that it will be useful for me to share my thoughts with you in some detail at this time.

Great historical developments, such as the recent Berlin and East German anti-Communist demonstrations, rarely have single roots. Nevertheless, I am quite certain that future historians, in their analysis of the causes which will have brought about the disintegration of the Communist Empire, will single out those brave East Germans who dared to rise against the cannons of tyranny with nothing but their bare hands and their stout hearts, as a root cause. I think also that those same historians will record your own extraordinary steadfastness in the cause of European peace and freedom over many, many years.

In analyzing these recent developments, there appear to be five points of greatest significance.

First, this eruption against Communist oppression was spontaneous. I know that I need not go into any elaborate denial with you of the fantastic explanation put out by Moscow that the uprising was caused by American provocateurs. No provocateur of any nationality can persuade human beings to stand up in front of rumbling tanks with sticks and stones. Such action comes from the heart and not from any foreign purse.

Second, this uprising was not just a momentary flash of desperation. The continuing news of disorders in Eastern Germany indicates a fundamental and lasting determination to be fully and finally free, despite long years of stern Sovietization.

Third, nowhere were the rioters "bourgeois reactionaries" or "capitalist warmongers." They were workers. Therefore, the martyrs who fell before Russian Communist guns were the very same workers in whose name the Kremlin has falsely and cynically built their empire of oppression, their far-flung "workers' paradise."

Fourth, the fact of the uprising, the conduct of the German Communist leaders during the event and their actions since the event, all indicate the complete political bankruptcy of the SED.

Fifth, and to me of utmost significance, when the riots developed in the Russian sector of Berlin, the workers' chant was, "We want free elections." In this phrase, the people clearly and simply summed up their yearning for the alleviation of their grievances and sufferings.

The combination of these five facts actually forms the background for that portion of the July 15 Foreign Ministers' communique dealing with German unification and free elections. And the communique itself, as you know, is actually the diplomatic confirmation of your own earlier statements, of my June 26 cable to you, and most important, of the Resolution of the German Bundestag of June 10.

For the past many months there have been endless arguments and debates on both sides of the Atlantic over the respective priorities of such words and phrases as "unification," "peace treaty," "free elections," "withdrawal of occupation troops," etc.

It has always seemed to me—and these recent events, to me at least, clearly confirm the thought—that there can be no solution without free elections and the formation of a free all-German government, leading to unification. From that point on can flow a logical, orderly sequence of events, culminating in an honorable peace treaty and the re-emergence of a new united German Republic, dedicated to the welfare of its own people, as a friendly and peaceful member of the European family of nations.

To this first step of free elections, the Government of the United States will continue to lend the full force of its political, diplomatic, and moral support.

There are sincere people in Germany, in the nations of Western Europe, and even in my own country, who have come to believe that free elections, and therefore the unification of Germany, contradict and possibly exclude the concept of the European Defense Community which has been ratified by both your Houses of Parliament and is now before your Constitutional Court. I do not and have never accepted this theory that the EDC and unification of Germany are mutually exclusive. Quite the contrary.

As the three Foreign Ministers stated at the conclusion of their recent meeting in Washington, since the European community corresponds to the lasting needs of its members and their people for peace, security and welfare, it is looked upon as necessary in itself and not linked up with existing international tensions.

It has long been my conviction that the strengthening of the Federal Republic, through adoption of the EDC, the contractual agreements and further progress in the integration of Western Europe, can only enhance the prospects for the peaceful unification of Germany, by increasing the attractive power of this prosperous Western Germany vis-a-vis the Soviet Zone, an attractive power which has already been demonstrated by the steady stream of refugees in recent months, as well as the demonstrations which began on June 17. This increasing contrast between Western and Eastern Germany, the latter with its bankrupt regime and impoverished economy, will in the long run produce conditions which should make possible the liquidation of the present Communist dictatorship and of the Soviet occupation.

While a future all-German Government must obviously be free to choose the degree to which it wishes to enter into defensive and other arrangements compatible with the principles of the United Nations, I can hardly imagine that it would seek the path of complete and premature disarmament in the presence of other nations still heavily armed. I believe this is a matter worthy of serious attention. Those who in Germany believe they can suggest an easy, safe solution through defenseless neutralization should carefully ponder the true wisdom and safety of such a course.

Speaking for America, and I believe the rest of the free world share this view, I can say that there has been enough bloodshed and enough misery and enough destruction in the past fifty years, to deter any people or any Government of the West from any ideas of military aggression.   But the peace we all so dearly seek cannot be maintained through weakness.   EDC will be the simplest, most unequivocal, and most self-evident demonstration of strength for peace.

No one can foretell what the unfolding months will bring, but it can certainly be said that the workers of Berlin's Soviet Sector and the workers of East Germany, with the workers of Czechoslovakia, have started something that will have an important place on the pages of history.   May the concluding chapter of that history record the reemergence of freedom, of peace, and of happiness.

With kindest personal regard,

Sincerely,

DWIGHT D. EISENHOWER

NOTE: The final communique of the conversations of the Secretary of State with the Foreign Ministers of Great Britain and France is published in the Department of State Bulletin (vol. 29, p. 104).

147 ¶ Radio and Television Address to the American People Announcing the Signing of the Korean Armistice.   *July* 26, 1953

[Broadcast from the White House at 10 p.m.]

My fellow citizens:

Tonight we greet, with prayers of thanksgiving, the official news that an armistice was signed almost an hour ago in Korea. It will quickly bring to an end the fighting between the United Nations forces and the Communist armies.   For this Nation the cost of repelling aggression has been high.   In thousands of homes it has been incalculable.   It has been paid in terms of tragedy.

With special feelings of sorrow—and of solemn gratitude—we

think of those who were called upon to lay down their lives in that far-off land to prove once again that only courage and sacrifice can keep freedom alive upon the earth. To the widows and orphans of this war, and to those veterans who bear disabling wounds, America renews tonight her pledge of lasting devotion and care.

Our thoughts turn also to those other Americans wearied by many months of imprisonment behind the enemy lines. The swift return of all of them will bring joy to thousands of families. It will be evidence of good faith on the part of those with whom we have signed this armistice.

Soldiers, sailors, and airmen of 16 different countries have stood as partners beside us throughout these long and bitter months. America's thanks go to each. In this struggle we have seen the United Nations meet the challenge of aggression—not with pathetic words of protest, but with deeds of decisive purpose. It is proper that we salute particularly the valorous armies of the Republic of Korea, for they have done even more than prove their right to freedom. Inspired by President Syngman Rhee, they have given an example of courage and patriotism which again demonstrates that men of the West and men of the East can fight and work and live together side by side in pursuit of a just and noble cause.

And so at long last the carnage of war is to cease and the negotiations of the conference table is to begin. On this Sabbath evening each of us devoutly prays that all nations may come to see the wisdom of composing differences in this fashion before, rather than after, there is resort to brutal and futile battle.

Now as we strive to bring about that wisdom, there is, in this moment of sober satisfaction, one thought that must discipline our emotions and steady our resolution. It is this: we have won an armistice on a single battleground—not peace in the world. We may not now relax our guard nor cease our quest.

Throughout the coming months, during the period of prisoner screening and exchange, and during the possibly longer period of the political conference which looks toward the unification of Korea, we and our United Nations Allies must be vigilant against the possibility of untoward developments.

And as we do so, we shall fervently strive to insure that this armistice will, in fact, bring free peoples one step nearer to their goal of a world at peace.

My friends, almost 90 years ago, Abraham Lincoln at the end of a war delivered his second Inaugural Address.   At the end of that speech he spoke some words that I think more nearly express the true feelings of America tonight than would any other words ever spoken or written.   You will recall them:

"With malice toward none; with charity for all; with firmness in the right as God gives us to see the right, let us strive on to finish the work we are in . . . to do all which may achieve and cherish a just and a lasting peace, among ourselves, and with all nations."

This is our resolve and our dedication.

148   ¶ Special Message to the Congress Concerning Increased Aid for the Republic of Korea.   *July* 27, 1953

To the Congress of the United States:

The signing of the truce in Korea makes it imperative that the United States immediately initiate a program of expanded aid to the Republic of Korea to assist in its rehabilitation and economic support.   Such a program, affecting the whole future of the Republic of Korea, must extend over several years, and I shall make further recommendations concerning that program to the Congress at its next session.

At this time I urge upon the Congress the passage of interim legislation which will authorize the President to use, for the rehabilitation and economic support of the Republic of Korea, a sum up to 200 million dollars from the savings in expenditures in the Department of Defense that result from the cessation of hostilities.

The need for this action can quickly and accurately be measured in two ways. One is the critical need of Korea at the end of three years of tragic and devastating warfare. The second is the opportunity which this occasion presents the free world to prove its will and capacity to do constructive good in the cause of freedom and peace.

The extent of devastation suffered by the people and the economy of Korea is staggering. Since the outbreak of war in 1950, 1 million South Koreans have been killed. More than 2½ millions have become homeless refugees. Five million depend in whole or in part upon relief to stay alive. Property destruction exceeds 1 billion dollars. This colossal economic disaster has made all the more remarkable the courage and magnitude of the Republic of Korea's military effort.

This government has been constantly aware that all that has been won by this valiant struggle could be imperilled and lost by an economic collapse. Poverty and despair could inflict wounds beyond the power of enemy guns. Knowing this, we and our allies, throughout the period of hostilities, took necessary measures to keep the Korean economy from buckling under the strain. We were able, through Defense appropriations, to meet minimum relief needs and to contain the threats of disease and unrest. We contributed important support to the program of the United Nations Korean Reconstruction Agency. We provided important incidental benefits to the Korean economy through payments to the Republic of Korea for the local currency requirements of our military forces.

But these measures cannot suffice. They were necessarily designed to meet the immediate exigencies of fighting a war. They cannot be expected either to meet the huge total cost of this effort or to set the foundation for a healthy peacetime economy.

The facing of these needs has been the subject of the most careful study. I directed that a first-hand survey of them be undertaken in Korea more than three months ago. The completed survey has been reviewed by the National Security Council. On the basis of its analysis and recommendation, I am convinced that the security interests of the United States clearly indicate the need to act promptly not only to meet immediate relief needs but also to begin the long-range work of restoring the Korean economy to health and strength.

While this program is geared to meeting simply indispensable needs, its precise shape in the future must to some extent be governed by future events. It must take account of the fact that our objectives in Korea are not completely attained so long as Korea remains divided; and the assistance now proposed is carefully designed to avoid projects which would prove value-less in a united country. The implementation of the program will depend upon the continued cooperation of the Government of the Republic of Korea with the United States and the United Nations Command.

There is, as I have said, a second fact beyond the desperate need of Korea which, I believe, must govern our action at this time. It is the chance—and the need—for the free peoples to give clear and tangible testimony to their awareness that true peace means more than the simple absence of war. It means moral and material health. It means political order and eco-nomic progress. It means the living hope, in the hearts of all peoples, that tomorrow can bring a more just, a more free, a more productive life than today.

No people on earth has proved more valiantly than the people of Korea their right to hold and cherish this hope. Ours is the task to help and nourish this hope—for the sake of one brave people, and for the sake of all peoples who wait and watch to see if free men can be as wise in the ways of peace as they have proved courageous in the ways of war.

DWIGHT D. EISENHOWER

NOTE: The interim legislation re-quested by the President was author-ized by the act approved August 7, 1953 (67 Stat. 425).

149   ¶ Veto of Bill Pertaining to Improvements to
Two Business Properties in the District of Columbia.
July 29, 1953

To the House of Representatives:

I return herewith, without my approval, H.R. 3087, "To
authorize the Board of Commissioners of the District of Columbia
to permit certain improvements to two business properties situated
in the District of Columbia."

The two properties involved, owned by private corporations,
are occupied as gasoline filling stations, in a residential use district.
Under the zoning regulations promulgated pursuant to the Act
of March 1, 1920, as amended by the Act of June 20, 1938, the
two stations may be continued as such in the category of nonconforming uses because they were in existence prior to the enactment of the zoning statute. However, except under certain
conditions, these nonconforming uses cannot be physically extended, enlarged, or improved. At present there are approximately five thousand nonconforming uses in the District of
Columbia. We should not single out two of these and provide
benefits for them which cannot be enjoyed by any of the other
many nonconforming uses.

In addition to its discriminatory nature, the bill would adversely
alter the basis of comprehensive planning in the District. The
city of Washington was planned with great care. However, before control of land use under a comprehensive plan was adopted
in 1920, many uses grew up that did not harmonize with any
orderly plan for the Nation's Capital. Although the zoning act
permitted continuation of these nonconforming uses under uniform regulations, it was plainly intended to prevent changes
which might perpetuate or magnify the adverse effects of these
uses.

The bill would subvert both the purposes of the zoning act
and the objectives of the comprehensive plan for the Nation's

Capital by sanctioning the practice of "spot zoning." It constitutes an invitation for further exceptions which, if enacted into law, would frustrate comprehensive planning and make impossible the orderly development of the Federal city.

DWIGHT D. EISENHOWER

150 ¶ Message Recorded for Use in Connection With the Observance of National Vegetable Week. *July 30, 1953*

I AM HAPPY to have been asked to participate in this observance of National Vegetable Week.

Nowhere else in the world are people fed so well—or in such great variety as here in the United States.

The number of different vegetables available to the average housewife insures this variety. And the huge amounts of food produced by our vegetable farmers assure people in great portions of the world that they will not go hungry.

On the personal side, it happens that I was once a small operator in the business of raising and selling vegetables.

The first money I ever earned was the result of a venture of this kind—55 years ago. From that day to this, I've felt that the production of vegetables is filled with challenge and interest. I've tried it in such widely separated places as Fort Myer, Virginia, in Europe, and in the State of Washington.

I am particularly happy, therefore, to salute the great army of American vegetable growers during this special week in their honor. My best wishes go to all of them.

151   ¶ Statement by the President on the
Responsibility of the United States Information
Agency.   *July* 30, 1953

OUR OVERSEAS information service never carried a heavier
responsibility than it does now.   The service must clearly and
factually present to the world the policies and objectives of the
United States.   It is not enough for us to have sound policies,
dedicated to goals of universal peace, freedom, and progress.
These policies must be made known to and understood by all
peoples throughout the world.   That is the responsibility of the
new United States Information Agency.

NOTE: The President's statement was   tion of Theodore C. Streibert as the
made on the occasion of the nomina-   Agency's first Director.

152   ¶ Special Message to the Congress
Requesting Legislation Raising the Debt Limit.
July 30, 1953

To the Congress of the United States:

   The Administration in cooperation with the Congress has
moved promptly and vigorously to reduce earlier recommendations for appropriations for the fiscal year 1953–54 by about $13
billion and to reduce the prospective deficit by about one-half.

   However, operations for the fiscal year just ended have produced a deficit of $9.4 billion.   In addition, the Government on
June 30th was faced with $81 billion of appropriations authoriz-
ing expenditures for which the money must be provided as the
bills are presented from time to time.

   Despite our joint vigorous efforts to reduce expenditures, it
is inevitable that the public debt will undergo some further
increase.

On June 30th last the public debt was $266 billion. To meet the Government's cash requirements for this current quarter it was necessary to borrow over $6 billion in July, bringing the national debt now to over $272 billion. To meet necessary expenditures and to maintain a safe working balance of funds it will be necessary to borrow more money before the next session of the Congress. This will carry the debt above the present legal limit of $275 billion.

Under present circumstances, the existing statutory debt limit is so restrictive that it does not allow the financial operating leeway necessary to conduct the government's fiscal affairs effectively. This is specific with respect to the seasonal variations of federal receipts and disbursements and also in view of the uncertainty as to the future income and expenditure levels.

I must, therefore, request of the Congress legislation raising the statutory debt limit. It is my recommendation that the limit should be increased to $290 billion.

DWIGHT D. EISENHOWER

153   ¶ Special Message to the Congress on the Nation's Natural Resources.   *July* 31, 1953

To the Congress of the United States:

In the stress of dealing with urgent problems of peace and security and budget appropriations and tax revenues, we sometimes overlook the fundamental importance to our national well-being of constructive, forward-looking policies designed to conserve and improve the Nation's natural renewable resources.

Before the Congress adjourns, therefore, I believe it will be useful to focus attention on some of our basic land and water resource problems and to point the way for constructive efforts to improve the management and use of these resources.

In my State of the Union Message, I called attention to the

vast importance to this Nation now and in the future of our soil and water, our forests and minerals, and our wildlife resources. I indicated the need for a strong Federal program in the field of resource development. At the same time I pointed to the necessity for a cooperative partnership of the States and local communities, private citizens, and the Federal Government in carrying out a sound natural resources program.

In addition to the immediate danger of waste resulting from inadequate conservation measures, we must bear in mind the needs of a growing population and an expanding economy. At present we are faced with excess reserves of some agricultural commodities and the need for production adjustments to gear our agricultural economy to current demands. But in the long-run, we shall need to give increased attention to the improvement and reclamation of land in its broadest aspects, including soil productivity, irrigation, drainage, and the replenishing of ground water reserves, if we are adequately to feed and clothe our people, to provide gainful employment, and to continue to improve our standard of living.

Our basic problem is to carry forward the tradition of conservation, improvement, and wise use and development of our land and water resources—a policy initiated 50 years ago under the leadership of President Theodore Roosevelt. To do this within the framework of a sound fiscal policy and in the light of defense needs will require the maximum cooperation among the States and local communities, farmers, businessmen and other private citizens, and the Federal Government. It will require the development of clear guidelines to be established by the Congress as to the proper functions of the Federal Government. It will require the revitalization of renewable resources by users who should be entitled to reasonable assurances in connection with authorized uses. It will require adherence to sound principles for the financing and the sharing of the cost of multiple-purpose land and water resource development. It will require improved Federal organization to accomplish a more logical division of responsibilities among the various Federal agencies in order that resource development programs may be carried on with the greatest efficiency and the least duplication.   And it will require comprehensive river basin planning with the cooperation of State and local interests.

This administration is moving ahead in the formulation of sound organization and improved policies for the use of our soil, our public lands, and our water resources.   I have requested, and the Congress has granted through Reorganization Plan No. 2, increased authority for the Secretary of Agriculture to improve the organization of the Department of Agriculture.   I have recently established by Executive Order a National Agricultural Advisory Commission.   A review is being made of the basic power policies of the Federal Government in connection with multiple-purpose river basin development as it relates to private economic development.   The Corps of Engineers is making a study of the basis for State and local financial participation in local flood protection works.   There are under detailed study various proposals for dealing with the complicated problems of overlapping and duplicative authority among the several resource development agencies.   And the Bureau of the Budget and the resource agencies are reviewing the present standards and procedures for evaluation and cost allocation of water resource development projects.

It is fortunate that today there is a growing recognition on the part of land users and the public generally of the need to strengthen conservation in our upstream watersheds and to minimize flood damage.   Inadequate conservation measures and unsound land use patterns vastly increase the danger of loss of valuable topsoil from wind erosion in time of subnormal rainfall and from water erosion in time of floods.

This should be done as an integral part of our total flood control and water use program.   In our past efforts to better utilize our water resources, to control floods and to prevent loss of life and property, we have made large investments on the major waterways of the Nation. Yet we have tended to neglect the serious waste involved in the loss of topsoil from the Nation's farms and the clogging of our streams and channels which results from erosion on the upper reaches of the small streams and tributaries of the Nation's rivers.

It is important, too, for groups of farmers banded together in local organizations, such as soil conservation districts and watershed associations, to take the initiative, with the technical advice and guidance of the appropriate federal and state agencies in developing adequate plans for proper land use and resource improvement in watersheds throughout the Nation. As these plans are prepared and local agreement and cooperation are assured, I believe that we should move ahead in the construction of works of improvement and the installation of land treatment measures as rapidly as possible consistent with a sound overall fiscal program.

As we move forward in a cooperative and coordinated soil and water conservation program, we must not overlook the essential role played by the Federal Government in the management of public lands. Approximately 50 per cent of the land area of the Western States is owned and managed by a number of Federal agencies. The National Park Service administers parks and monuments having national significance. The Forest Service administers the national forests, with their valuable timber lands and grazing resources, and in cooperation with State and local interests protects critical watersheds. The Bureau of Reclamation and the Corps of Engineers manage lands in connection with water resource projects built by these agencies. Fish and wildlife are protected by the Fish and Wildlife Service. The Bureau of Indian Affairs administers Indian lands, and the great public domain remaining is administered by the Bureau of Land Management.

The Federal Government has a responsibility to manage wisely those public lands and forests under its jurisdiction necessary in the interest of the public as a whole. Important values exist in these lands for forest and mineral products, grazing, fish and wild-life, and for recreation.   Moreover, it is imperative to the welfare of thousands of communities and millions of acres of irrigated land that such lands be managed to protect the water supply and water quality which come from them.   In the utilization of these lands, the people are entitled to expect that their timber, min-erals, streams and water supply, wildlife and recreational values should be safeguarded, improved and made available not only for this but for future generations.   At the same time, public lands should be made available for their best use under condi-tions that promote stability for communities and individuals and encourage full development of the resources involved.

While, as I have indicated, our major problem is to carry for-ward a tradition of improvement and conservation of our natural resources, the best means of achieving this objective depends on keeping up with changing conditions.   For example, the prob-lems of water resource development in the West are undergoing considerable change.   The pattern of Western growth has broad-ened substantially in recent years.   Industrial expansion has been extensive and varied.   Increased activities in mineral and fuel processing have occurred.   Urban expansion has been well above the national average in many communities.   These developments have brought about strong competition for existing water supplies and have stimulated the need for a broader approach in planning new water resource developments.   As a consequence, the Federal role in the cooperative development of these resources should now be re-examined in the interest of achieving a better balanced pro-gram for Western growth.

Conserving and improving our land and water resources is high priority business for all of us.   It is the purpose of this Ad-ministration to present to the next session of the Congress suitable recommendations for achieving the objectives set forth in this Message.   I am confident that the studies of governmental organi-zation and functions authorized by this Congress can also make an important contribution to the solution of these problems.   As the Congress moves ahead on a constructive legislative program in the resource field, it will have my full support and cooperation. We must build a balanced program for the use and development of all our natural resources. Such a program is indispensable to maintaining and improving our standard of living as we make the future secure for a growing America.

DWIGHT D. EISENHOWER

154 ¶ Statement by the President on the Death of Senator Robert A. Taft. *July* 31, 1953

THE PASSING of Robert A. Taft is a tragic loss to America.

The brilliant son of our twenty-seventh President, Senator Taft served the people of Ohio and the nation with distinction and integrity. He will be greatly missed on Capitol Hill where his unimpeachable character and his vast knowledge of the business of good government played such an important part in Congressional decisions over many years.

The Senate has lost one of its leading members of all times, the American people have lost a truly great citizen and I have lost a wise counsellor and a valued friend. Mrs. Eisenhower and I extend to Mrs. Taft and the family our heartfelt sympathies in the personal loss that they have sustained.

NOTE: In addition to the foregoing statement, the President issued Executive Order 10474 (3 CFR, 1949–1953 Comp., p. 954) which provided that, as a mark of respect to the memory of Senator Taft, the flag of the United States should be flown at half-staff on the White House and Federal Government buildings in the District of Columbia and the State of Ohio until interment.

155   ¶ Special Message to the Congress
Transmitting Proposed Changes in the Social
Security Program.   *August* 1, 1953

To the Congress of the United States:

In my message to the Congress on the State of the Union, I
pointed out that there is urgent need for making our social security
programs more effective.

I stated that the provisions of the Old Age and Survivor's Insurance law should cover millions of our citizens who thus far have
been excluded from participation in the social security program.

Retirement systems, by which individuals contribute to their
own security according to their own respective abilities, have become an essential part of our economic and social life.   These
systems are but a reflection of the American heritage of sturdy
self-reliance which has made our country strong and kept it free;
the self-reliance without which we would have had no Pilgrim
Fathers, no hardship-defying pioneers, and no eagerness today to
push to ever widening horizons in every aspect of our national
life.

The Social Security program furnishes, on a national scale, the
opportunity for our citizens, through that same self-reliance, to
build the foundation for their security.   We are resolved to extend that opportunity to millions of our citizens who heretofore
have been unable to avail themselves of it.

The Department of Health, Education, and Welfare, with the
counsel and assistance of twelve outstanding consultants, has been
carefully studying the difficult technical and administrative aspects of this effort.

The Secretary of that Department has now recommended the
specific additional groups which, in the judgment of the Department and its consultants, should be covered under this program.
The Secretary has also recommended the means by which these
additional groups can be brought into the system most equitably,

with full consideration for the new groups as well as those who have heretofore contributed to the insurance system. The Secretary's recommendations would effectively carry out the objectives that I expressed in my Message to the Congress on the State of the Union and I am pleased to transmit them to the Congress for its consideration.

Under the attached plan, approximately 10½ million individuals would be offered social security protection for the first time. About 6½ million of these would be brought into the system; the remaining 4 million would be eligible for coverage under voluntary group arrangements. New groups to be covered would include self-employed farmers; many more farm workers and domestic workers than are now covered; doctors, dentists, lawyers, architects, accountants and other professional people; members of many state and local retirement systems on a voluntary group basis; clergymen on a voluntary group basis and several other smaller groups.

As the Committee on Ways and Means of the House of Representatives proceeds with its studies to improve the Social Security Act, I strongly commend to it this plan for the extension of coverage to most of the major groups not now covered by any social insurance or public retirement system. This is a specific plan for a specific purpose—the extension of coverage. Other important improvements in the Social Security Act are now under study and will be the subject of further recommendations.

There are two points about these proposals which I cannot stress too strongly. One is my belief that they would add immeasurably to the peace of mind and security of the individual citizens who would be covered for the first time under this plan; the second is my belief that they would add greatly to the national sense of domestic security. The systematic practice of setting aside funds during the productive years to build the assurance of basic retirement benefits when the productive years are over— or to one's survivors in the event of death—is important to the strength of our traditions and our economy. We must not only preserve this systematic practice, but extend it at every desirable opportunity. We now have both such an opportunity and a definite plan. I commend it to the Congress for its consideration.

DWIGHT D. EISENHOWER

NOTE: Secretary Hobby's recommen-   published in House Document 225
dations, in the form of a letter to the   (83d Cong., 1st sess.).
President dated July 24, 1953, are

156 ¶ Remarks at the Governors' Conference, Seattle, Washington. *August 4, 1953*

Governor Shivers, Governor Langlie, my friends:

It is a little bit of a misnomer to call this an address. I am here for a number of purposes, but among them is not that of making a long and so-called important speech for the record.

The first thought that strikes me, as I stand up, is that Governors' conferences have changed their type a bit. They used to have a table something like this, all right, but they did not have so much pulchritude in the rear. I did not know that there was an audience of this kind. Nevertheless, while I had on my mind to talk of things that I thought would be of interest to the Governors, I hope that the remainder of the audience won't find these things too boring.

Now, first of all, I am here for a very simple purpose, because of my indestructible conviction that unless we preserve, in this country, the place of the State government, its traditional place—with the power, the authority, the responsibilities and the revenues necessary to discharge those responsibilities, then we are not going to have an America as we have known it; we will have some other form of government. And my thought was that if I could come here to pay my tribute of respect to the great responsibilities that you men as executive heads of your States must carry, on behalf of all our people, then that alone would justify my trip.

Now, within this concept, of course, is that of the need for the executive heads of each of these States to perform services for their people, the people for whom they serve as chief executives, that are almost without scope and without limit. By this I mean that merely because a chief executive signs the bills that are presented to him, presents to his legislature a program that he believes to be conceived in the best interests of his State, that is not enough. In this modern and complex time, the problems that affect each of our lives very intimately and very definitely, are very difficult to understand. A chief executive in no matter what echelon, be it city, State, or Federal, has many sources of information, accurate information, that are often denied to the people in general. Or if they are not denied, they come to the people through certain reports that are difficult to relate one to the other, and therefore to see their significance.

I believe that a chief executive has, among other things, the responsibility of informing his own commonwealth—his own State—about these major problems all the time, be it Korea, Indochina, taxes, the debt limit—no matter what. He has the chore of using the facilities open to him—including that of making talks. He has the chore of trying to inform the people in that State, so that they will in turn support reasonable programs, nationally as well as statewide. And indeed, I think at this point, national and statewide, it is again very, very difficult to establish a clear dividing line.

We know this: unless the United States is prosperous, unless it is strong, unless it is secure, there is no strength, there is no prosperity, there is no security for any State. Consequently, we instantly conclude there is no true division in the scope of our concern for the people we are attempting to serve. The dividing line we seek is really how we coordinate our several functions so that we are not doing exactly the same thing but so that the efforts of each complement the other.

That is the reason that one of the first acts of mine when I went to Washington—and supported by a Cabinet, and indeed by advisers that are now sitting around this table and occupy Governors' chairs—I asked for a Commission that would study this proper division between State responsibilities and Federal responsibilities—not for one instant meaning that we divide our concern about these major problems of the world, in which we have the responsibility of helping to inform our people. And I do not mean at all that that is an exclusive job—there are many other agencies that have to help to do this. But we have that responsibility. I do mean that unless we find a way of dividing up these responsibilities, we are bound to blur too indefinitely the line that divides our several functions, and eventually, as I say again, it will not be the American system as we have known it.

Now, this goes into every field of activity of which I can think. Long years ago, you know, they attempted to establish security establishments; that was the combination of regular and professional groups, supported by what we call national reserves, and then the State National Guard which we later federalized. All of that was done in an effort to bring together the best capabilities of the State and of the national Government to provide security for us at all times, and with the least possible cost. And indeed, in spite of the criticism that has been directed at it, I believe this: I believe if every citizen, every State, and the national Government would do its proper job under that concept, it would still be a good one for the United States. The trouble of it is jealousies develop, inefficiencies, then recriminations start, and we have more fun criticising than we do working constructively.

It is odd—of course it's no new discovery of the human mind—but it is odd, isn't it, that we have so much more fun calling the other fellow a so-and-so, than getting out and doing something to correct either the error that he has committed, or that we may have committed. It is probably one of the things, though, that no executive is ever allowed to forget, even for a minute.

If we go into the field of agriculture, if we go into the field of Federal power, and the conservation of all the resources of the United States, we find this same community of purpose, with the necessity for division of responsibilities obtaining it.

As I understand it, this morning you are going to try, in a round-table conference, to sort out in your own minds, and possibly sort out in our minds, what these divisions should be. Certainly I know of no one in the Federal Government today, no matter what his job, who thinks he knows all the answers. He cannot fail to benefit from discussion on those subjects. In certain instances, I think, there are obvious truths that prevail. Unless we are partners in some of these things, they cannot be done. But if partnership is going to consist only in talking about local rights and central responsibilities—responsibility particularly when it is financial—if that is going to be the pattern, there is no hope.

When we share responsibility, we share responsibility all the way through, financial as well as for seeing that a thing is effectively operated. If we obey this principle the closer we keep government and every kind of governmental responsibility and authority close to the people, calling in the Federal Government where there is a clear service for it to perform, which could not be performed adequately without its cooperation and its partnership; then, I think, we will be headed in the right direction.

This thing applies to this great problem—I don't know whether you have yet talked about it, but I am sure it is one of the subjects of your conference: civil defense. Civil defense is absolutely impossible without the complete and enthusiastic cooperation, not merely of Governors, not merely of mayors, but of every man, woman, and child in the United States. Here is one thing that can't be handled except by people themselves. It is perfectly clear that the first thing that is needed, if you are going to have an effective civil defense against a possible attack in this country, is an ordered or disciplined movement and action on the part of the people in the face of emergency. Just as you train young children to go in orderly fashion toward the nearest exit in school in case there is fire or emergency, that is the way people must be trained or instructed.

If they are unwilling to accept that, there is no hope of digging shelters. You could dig all the shelters in the world and kill all the people trying to get into them, if they were in panic. They wouldn't even know where they were. Some of you people, possibly a good many of you here, have been present in a heavy bombing raid. You have seen the panic that overtakes people. The indispensable ingredient of any civil defense is some self-control. And that is all that discipline is. On top of it, then, is an ordered plan that takes people to a position and place of safety. On top of that, you can build a number of artificial and organized defenses, even to include your warning services and things that the Federal Government takes over in the field of actual active defense. But without this orderly action on the part of the civilian population, all civil defense measures will fall flat to the ground.

As it is today, suppose we had a drill out in front of the biggest department store in Seattle. Any American would feel self-conscious if you gave him the job, let us say, of going out and helping to drag in the fire hose, or getting out the medical supplies that were stored in one of the corners, or standing out on the sidewalk with a bucketful of sand. He sees the population going by. He feels self-conscious and embarrassed.

Now, there's the job that leadership has to overcome. How are we going to get America to do these things, seriously and soberly and knowing they are necessary?

The Federal Government has a very wide, definite, fixed responsibility in this whole program. But they can never do it unless localities down to the last individual will cooperate.

I could go on enumerating every kind of problem that comes before us daily. Let us take, though, for example, one simple problem in the foreign field. You have seen the war in Indochina described variously as an outgrowth of French colonialism, and its French refusal to treat indigenous populations decently. You find it again described as a war between the communists and the other elements in southeast Asia. But you have a confused idea of where it is located—Laos, or Cambodia, or Siam, or any of the other countries that are involved. You don't know, really, why we are so concerned with the far-off southeast corner of Asia.

Why is it? Now, first of all, the last great population remaining in Asia that has not become dominated by the Kremlin, of course, is the sub-continent of India, including the Pakistan government. Here are 350 million people still free. Now let us assume that we lose Indochina. If Indochina goes, several things happen right away. The Malayan peninsula, the last little bit of the end hanging on down there, would be scarcely defensible—and tin and tungsten that we so greatly value from that area would cease coming. But all India would be outflanked. Burma would certainly, in its weakened condition, be no defense. Now, India is surrounded on that side by the Communist empire. Iran on its left is in a weakened condition. I believe I read in the paper this morning that Mossadegh's move toward getting rid of his parliament has been supported and of course he was in that move supported by the Tudeh, which is the Communist Party of Iran. All of that weakening position around there is very ominous for the United States, because finally if we lost all that, how would the free world hold the rich empire of Indonesia? So you see, somewhere along the line, this must be blocked. It must be blocked now. That is what the French are doing.

So, when the United States votes $400 million to help that war, we are not voting for a giveaway program. We are voting for the cheapest way that we can to prevent the occurrence of something that would be of the most terrible significance for the United States of America—our security, our power and ability to get certain things we need from the riches of the Indonesian territory, and from southeast Asia.

Now that is the kind of thing that it is not good enough that someone just shouts in Washington. All of us must understand it, because out of that kind of thing grows the need for taxes. The security of the United States is not just the business of the Secretary of Defense and the Congress and the President and the

Secretaries of the Services. It is the business of every man, woman and child. And if it is their business, then it is the business of all of us. We need help. I don't care what the problem is.

I think I have done all this talking, my friends, just to get back to this one truism. Unless the Governors of the States—and you notice I am talking to you regardless of partisanship; I don't give a "hoot" whether you are a Democrat or a Republican, in this kind of job you are Americans. In the Federal Government we are Americans. Unless we can cooperate on the basis of understanding of the facts, and progress steadily, surely, and confidently in carrying out a program that we believe will establish the security of the United States, not only from a gun, from a bomb, from some kind of destructive act of an enemy, but in its economy to make sure that its surpluses are carried abroad and in return for those surpluses we get back the raw materials and other articles that will allow these people to buy these surpluses; unless we have that kind of economic strength, we are going to have to live a very different kind of life than we do.

This can all be done only through cooperation. This is not partisan policy. No one has a monopoly on truth and on the facts that affect this country. We must work together.

Now, I have said things, probably, that you have heard every time someone has gotten up. All of us protest our readiness to cooperate. As I see it, one of the basic purposes of such conferences as these ought to be to pinpoint the ways we will get together and to work together. Because of my utter conviction in this direction, I invited you, as you know, to come to Washington. I have come out here. I will probably accept every invitation you ever extend to me and I will send you more.

I want to describe something to you, for just a moment. I probably long ago used up my time; but you know, there is one thing about being the President, it is hard to tell him to sit down. I have heard a lot of speakers get up and paint for us two brilliant crossroads—the United States is at the crossroads, follow this road to security and salvation, this one to destruction and death. I don't believe any such thing. And I don't believe it ever has been true. If these roads were so clearly marked out, and we could convince ourselves that here was the road to salvation, and there to destruction, we would have sense enough to follow this road. The facts are not those at all. The facts are that out here on the extremes of these problems are paths that will lead us to destruction, one in one way, one in another. What we have got is a great hinterland in between these two roads, and through them is some kind of practicable route for all of us to walk together to decency and to progress. Not to immediate salvation and the rainbow's end, not at all—but to progress to doing something for 160 million people, and in doing so, to do something also for all the world. Because we are all interlocked, just as the State and the National Government is, at home.

Now, what our problem is—the very difficult problem—is to find these trails, these trails through these great extremes—difficult to climb, difficult to discern, difficult to mark out, sometimes, because it is done by the process of trial and error. But that is our job. And we should measure up to that, with all the work, all the disappointments, the frustrations, such as when the Senate won't extend the debt limit when you know you need it—you had that explained to you last night. Of course, there are frustrations, and there are disappointments and setbacks, but unless we continue intelligently and assiduously, together, to search out that proper route in this maze of broken hills and rough country, then we are not doing our duty. We are not carrying out our oaths that each of us take.

Now, I have heard the Federal administration criticised much in the last 6 months because they say, "Where is the program?" "What are you going to do in farm policy?" Well, it's pretty difficult to do anything, and to give you one little farm policy in nice choice words, when one group wants grain prices as high as they can, and the cattle and poultry raiser or the dairy producer says, "If you don't get these grain prices down, there's going to be no agriculture." So these aren't simple little things.

The program is this: to work with all those of like mind who are devoted to the United States of America and find ways in which progress, in which work, in which thought and intelligent action will help us all. Not just the farmer, not just the laborer, not just the capitalist, not just the banker—all of us. Help us move forward a little bit to a better life, a better spiritual life, intellectual opportunity and material well-being.

Now, I have gone a long ways around the "cabbage patch" this morning to tell you why I am here. But I hope that out of these rather wandering thoughts and statements you have discovered something of why a number of my Cabinet and I—and other assistants in Washington—came out here to meet with you. We regard it as a rich opportunity, and that is why we are here.

Thank you.

NOTE: The President spoke at the Olympic Hotel in Seattle, Wash. In his opening words he referred to Governor Allan Shivers of Texas, Chairman of the Governors' Conference, and to Governor Arthur B. Langlie of Washington.

157 ¶ Memorandum of Disapproval of Bill Repealing the Admissions Tax on Motion Picture Performances.   *August 6, 1953*

I AM WITHHOLDING my approval of H.R. 157, entitled, "To provide that the tax on admissions shall not apply to moving picture admissions."

My reasons for taking this position are that we cannot afford the loss of revenue involved and that it is unfair to single out one industry for relief at this time.

In my message to the Congress on May twentieth, I said: "Tax receipts will apparently fall considerably short of our necessary expenditures during the next fiscal year. In view of this fact, I have come to the conclusion that no reductions in tax rates should become effective during this calendar year." In accordance with this policy, the Treasury Department advised the Chairmen of the House Committee on Ways and Means and the Senate Committee on Finance of its opposition to this bill.

Because of the need for revenue I recommended an extension of the excess profits tax for six months and the extension has now been made. Tax relief for one industry now would be inconsistent with that action.

It is estimated that the repeal of the admissions tax on motion picture performances, which has been on the books at the present rate since April 1, 1944, would result in a gross loss of revenue of $200 million. After allowing for a resulting increase in corporation income taxes, the net loss is estimated to be between $100 million and $120 million a year.

It is not contended by the industry that the present scale of admission prices which reflects the 20 percent tax is responsible for the existing distress situation in the industry. Indeed, the industry apparently expects in many cases to maintain the present price to consumers even though the tax is repealed.

There is distress in large but not all segments of the industry. The basic causes of the industry's distress, however, arise from new forms of competition.

A strong case can also be made for tax relief in other industries which are subject to high excise taxes, including other forms of entertainment subject to the admission tax. If relief is to be given to motion picture theaters at this time it would not be fair to refuse relief to these other industries. If widespread relief were given, however, the loss in revenue would be very large.

As I said in my message of May twentieth, "the wide variety of existing excise rates makes little economic sense and leads to improper discrimination between industries and among consumers. Specific proposals for a modified system of excise taxation will be included in the recommendations for tax revision that will be submitted to the Congress next January."

The Treasury analysis has already progressed to the point where

I can say that I will include a recommendation for a reduction in the admissions tax in my proposals for a modified system of excise taxation. Action could be taken by the Congress early in 1954 and relief could be given at that time.

It is for these reasons that I cannot give my approval to the repeal of the tax on admissions to motion-picture performances. The country cannot afford a loss of revenue at this time. Furthermore, it would not be fair and would be discriminatory to give relief under a single excise tax and then only to one of the industries subject to that tax.

DWIGHT D. EISENHOWER

158 ¶ Statement by the President Upon Signing the Farm Credit Act of 1953. *August 6, 1953*

IT GIVES ME great pleasure to approve the Farm Credit Act of 1953, H.R. 4353.

On September 18, 1952, in a speech at Omaha, Nebraska, I said in part:

"We will remove the Federal domination now imposed on the farm credit system. Employees of these farmer-owned self-supporting institutions should not be Federal appointees. A Federal Farm Credit Board, elected by farmer members, should be established to form credit policies, select executive officers, and to see that sound credit operations will not be endangered by partisan political influence."

The Farm Credit Act of 1953 meets many of the objectives which I announced at Omaha. It provides for a Federal Farm Credit Board. The President is required to consider nominations of the farmer and cooperative members of the Federal Farm Credit System in choosing that Board. It authorizes the Board to select its principal executive officers. It vests in the Board the power to adopt policies to guide the operations of the Farm Credit System within the framework of the law.

The Farm Credit System has a splendid record of service to the American farmer. A part of the credit for that service goes to the farmer participation in the membership of the district boards. The extent of that participation on the district boards is also increased by the Farm Credit Act of 1953.

With the changes made by this law, I visualize increased progress in the amount of farmer ownership in the Farm Credit System, a more commendable record of service to farmers in the future, and more assurance that the farmers of this country will have a sound, nonpolitical Farm Credit Administration.

The signing of the Farm Credit Bill marks another milestone in our march toward an agriculture which is productive, profitable, responsible, and free from excessive regulation.

NOTE: The Farm Credit Act of 1953 is Public Law 202, 83d Congress (67 Stat. 390).

159   ¶ Radio Report to the American People on the Achievements of the Administration and the 83d Congress. *August 6, 1953*

[Broadcast from the White House at 9:30 p.m.]

My fellow Americans:

A mark of free citizens, proud and wise enough to govern themselves, is the searching scrutiny they turn upon the purposes and the performance of their own government.

It is the historic habit of a free people—it is *our* habit—to ask our Government at frequent times: Where are we going? How far have we come?

These questions arise logically in these very days. The first session of the 83d Congress has adjourned. The laborious work of the committees has ended. The debates have closed. The roll calls have been taken. A record has been written.

In the few moments we have this evening, let us take a look at that record.

The array of legislative actions, at first glance, seems bewildering in variety and complexity. It includes:

A revised defense program for a reorganized Defense Department working on a reduced defense budget;

Reorganization of whole Government departments;

Revised plans to help arm our allies in freedom;

Short-term extension of onerous but needed taxes;

Indefinite lifting of futile economic controls;

Emergency aid to drought-stricken areas of our own land;

Extension of legislation to aid and increase our commerce with the peoples of all lands;

Wheat to feed Pakistan;

Programs to rebuild Korea;

Simplification of customs regulations;

Admission of refugees;

Enactment of a multitude of normal appropriation bills.

With such an array of new legislation, it is little wonder that the intelligent citizen asks: what do all these things mean? *Where are we going?*

The first part of the answer is this:

Such actions as these are not the chance results of some wildly spinning wheels of governmental machinery.

These acts reflect thoughtful planning. They have demanded work—the earnest, exhausting work of hundreds of conscientious legislators. They denote purpose—clearly defined purpose.

When I first appeared before the 83d Congress 6 months ago to deliver the administration's message on the State of the Union, I tried to define what I referred to as "the grand labors" confronting this Government. They were these:

"Application of our influence in world affairs with such fortitude and foresight that it will deter aggression and eventually secure peace;

"Establishment of a national administration of such integrity and efficiency that its honor at home will ensure respect abroad;

"Encouragement of those incentives that inspire creative initiative in our economy, and

"Dedication to the well-being of all our citizens and to the attainment of equality of opportunity for all."

These purposes give meaning and sense to all that has occurred in these last 6 months.

We have adhered firmly to these purposes.

Let us begin with the first: the exercise of our influence in world affairs in the quest of lasting peace.

And here let us begin with that tragic land of war: Korea.

We made plain from the outset our determination, shared by our allies in the United Nations, to find—to fight for however long to win—an honorable armistice in Korea. We speeded the equipment and training of Republic of Korea troops, inspiringly led by President Syngman Rhee. We firmly—and successfully— upheld the right of prisoners of war to choose their own future.

We have now gained a truce in Korea.

We do not greet it with wild rejoicing. We know how dear its cost has been in life and treasure. We know how grave are the problems to be met before the people of Korea enjoy real unity and security.

Yet we also soberly know that we have won two precious victories.

We have shown, in the winning of this truce, that the collective resolve of the free world can and will meet aggression in Asia—or anywhere in the world.

And we have won the opportunity to show that free people can *build* in *peace* as boldly as they *fight* in *war*.

We have already given signs of our power and will to do just that. The Congress has authorized the spending of 200 million additional dollars for the reconstruction and rehabilitation of South Korea. This action springs directly from the heart of America, which has contributed so generously to private relief organizations like the American-Korean Foundation working to heal and help our stricken ally. I have now invited all the skilled specialists of the United States forces in Korea—engineers, signal corps, technicians of all kinds—to offer their knowledge to help rebuild the land whose freedom they have helped so bravely to save.

There is no finer task that could be entrusted to these men.   I know that under the leadership of General Clark, General Weyland, Admiral Briscoe, and General Taylor, the results will bring pride to every American.   Our purpose is sane and simple: to make secure and productive the freedom that has been saved—and to make it inspiring for the *people* for *whom* it has been saved.

For we know this: no military victory, no diplomatic triumph, no precision-perfect foreign policy of our own can mean very much for very long—if it does not bring hope to hundreds of millions of people who live today in fear or need or hunger.   As surely as we seek lasting peace, we shall find it only as these people come to have faith in their own future in freedom.

This, then, is, in one area, the wise and purposeful *use* of our strength of which I spoke 6 months ago.

We have pursued the same objective on the other side of the world.   In Western Europe, we have seen—and constantly aided—the slow, steady growth of unity, of economic health, and of military defense.

With the nations of Western Europe now producing even more than they did before World War II, it has become possible to devote most of our foreign operations to the needs of military defense.   This means, for us as Americans, that these billions of dollars directly serve our *own* national security.   They have thereby made possible part of the great savings effected in our own Department of Defense.

The Senate vote of 69-to-10 on this issue was the largest such vote ever united in support of this kind of program.   This reflects something more important than money.   It signifies an unprecedented unity that crosses party lines and promises steady purpose in the conduct of our foreign affairs.

All these developments—from the still smouldering East to the strengthening West—could not fail to have impressed the peoples of the Soviet world. Neither purges nor police nor prisons have been able to stifle the growing cries for food—and for freedom. Cold oppression has been repaid with cold hate.

In Germany, we have urged the Soviet Union to join with the Western nations in speeding that nation's unity. Even as we have acted, the people of Germany have delivered an eloquent message of their own to Soviet occupation authorities. It has been a message of defiance—delivered by the thousands of Berlin workers who stormed through their streets in the memorable June uprising; and the tens of thousands who have defiantly come to West Berlin for the needed food sent by this Government for their relief.

Our action in Berlin—this reaching out to people to help, to feed, to strengthen their faith in freedom—partakes of the same spirit directing our course in Korea.

There is a significant connection between these distant spots on the great globe.

Berlin and Korea have been two of the scenes chosen by the Communist world for flagrant acts of aggression since World War II.

Today precisely these *same two* places present dramatic evidence of the will of free men to stay free and to make freedom work.

No clearer proof is needed of the power of the free world not only to defeat what is evil but also to *create* what is good.

We intend to keep the knowledge of that power before all men.

The essential force behind this power is the unity of the free world; and one essential basis for that unity, in turn, is economic health nourished by mutually beneficial trade. The 83d Congress has shown clear understanding of this truth. This is the significance of the Congress's actions in simplifying our customs regulations and extending the Reciprocal Trade Act. These actions again testify to that growing unity of opinion which rises above party lines to see clearly the need for profitable trade throughout the free world. These actions—while consistent with concern for our own industries—recognize also our own dependence upon vital foreign markets and foreign sources of raw materials.

Again and again, as we have faced these problems of international trade and world diplomacy, we have stressed the central fact that we are concerned with the plain needs and hopes of the ordinary peoples of the earth. So we have undertaken the shipping of a million tons of wheat to help meet the famine in Pakistan. So the Congress has authorized this Government to make available excess reserves of crops to friendly nations in need. And so we have authorized the entry into the United States of some 214,000 refugees. These are men and women of the same character and integrity as their and our ancestors who, generation upon generation, have come to America to find peace and work, to build for themselves new homes in freedom.

In all these ways, then—in every deed and decision—we have sought to apply our strength in the world so as to deter aggression and to secure peace. We have accepted the burdens of world leadership with clear mind and confident heart—for we know that to strengthen other free men is to serve our own freedom and safety.

I come now to the *second* great objective of which I spoke 6 months ago—the building of an honest, efficient administration, honored at home and respected abroad.

The repair and reorganization of so huge a piece of political machinery as the United States Government is a colossal undertaking.

We have made a good start.

We begin with certain negative tasks.

There were some security risks still in the Government. They have been swiftly expelled.

There were some incompetents. They are lingering no longer than it takes to discover them.

There were simply too *many* people on the payrolls. We have reduced that number by stringent hiring policies that have cut the total by many tens of thousands.

The positive task of bettering government has produced less dramatic but even more profound results.

We submitted to the 83d Congress 10 major reorganization proposals. All 10 were approved. This is an unprecedented record.

Reorganization itself bears upon plans and practices of even wider scope. The whole area of Federal-State relations is being put under review by a Commission to bring order and sense into a field full of confusion and conflict. And within the Federal Government itself, both the executive and the legislative branches have worked with patience and good will to ensure that this Government not be divided against itself.

This mutual consideration between Congress and the President is less tangible but more vital than any reorganization bill ever passed or contemplated.

Vital to coherent and consistent policy, mutual confidence can never be legislated into existence. It is no easy thing to achieve. It certainly is not easy to perfect at a time when one great party, after 20 years of political life in the opposition, ousts another from office. Such an event casts both parties in new, strange roles. The strangeness for the party newly come to power, in this case, is dramatized by the fact that there is in the Senate not a single Republican who had ever held Senatorial office when a Republican President was in the White House.

I mention this to underscore the significance of the good will which, I believe, has been built, fast and firmly, between the executive and legislative branches. The two have differed many times. They have debated long and candidly. But the final results testify to a prevailing common purpose which is a credit to the high sense of duty of this 83d Congress.

That common purpose—I must add—found one of its most effective supporters in the late Senator Robert A. Taft. Its great advance was among the last and most important of his many important public achievements. Today, I know of no greater inspiration to all men seeking good, just government than the memory of his courage, his integrity, and the spirit of selfless cooperation that so brilliantly marked the last months of his life.

The building of this kind of government has proceeded simultaneously with our seeking of the third great objective I cited 6 months ago—the encouragement of creative initiative in our economy.

This serious, long-range purpose cannot record headline-making results in a few weeks or months. But—again—I believe the bright beginnings are clear for all to see.

We have, first of all, faced the tough facts of the Government debt. The last 23 years have seen this debt climb by 258 billions—at the relentless average rate of more than 11 billions a year. This, of course, includes a part of the inescapable cost of war. Yet the terrible momentum of that increasing debt could not be allowed to continue. Neither could it instantly be arrested. The weight of obligations made 2 and 3 years ago has forced upon us, as you know, the possibility of our having to raise the debt limit later this year. For one thing is a certainty: bills already contracted by the Government must be paid the day they become due.

In so critical a time of transition, we have done what sense and honesty dictate. We delayed lowering or removing taxes which, however harsh, provide essential revenue if the tide of debt is to be turned. We did not delay in cutting deep into governmental expenditures. The Executive and the Congress reduced the previous administration's budget request for the current year by almost 13 billion dollars—an amount representing some 80 dollars for every American.

This striving to bring the budget under control—as I have said before—is no mere academic, technical exercise challenging Government accountants. It profoundly influences the buying power of your dollar. It vitally affects every family in our land.

Our over-riding concern is not with elaborate theories of economics, but the plain well-being of all the people. And the balancing of the Government's budget is critical simply because it can help every family in our land to balance its own budget.

Moreover, in pursuit of this great objective of encouraging individual initiative, we have taken a series of major economic decisions. To free our economy from bonds that denatured healthy and necessary competition, we abolished a labyrinth of needless controls. To reform a tax structure that threatens to smother free initiative, the Treasury and the appropriate committees of the Congress have begun a total review of our tax system. Their recommendations will be ready for action by the next session of Congress.

I repeat: all these actions, governed by a single purpose, are not mere gestures in honor of preconceived economic dogmas. They reflect our awareness of the mighty productive power of individual enterprise to which America itself is history's greatest testimony.

Upon the productive might of the individual American depend the wages, the diet, the health, the homes of millions of families. Upon this productive might depends even more—the preservation of freedom itself in this, its age of greatest peril.

Now, what of the fourth and last great objective which I set forth last February: dedication to the well-being and the equal opportunity of all our citizens?

This objective affects, directly or indirectly, every action of this Government. For every deed of this Government is tested, judged, and inspired by this resolve—to serve the well-being of 160 million Americans.

In this spirit, there has been created a new Cabinet division— a Department of Health, Education, and Welfare—to carry steadily forward all the labor of care that we associate with schools, pensions, clinics, hospitals.

In this same spirit, the Congress authorized prompt emergency farm loans to our drought-stricken areas of the Southwest; and representatives of every farm area and organization have been brought together to help shape laws making our farm population more productive and more secure than ever. Today I signed a piece of legislation which farm organizations have been seeking for many years. This new legislation provides for increased participation by farmers in the farm credit system.

Serving this same purpose, we have been preparing specific recommendations on labor legislation to submit to the next session of Congress—to make sure and clear the rights of workers and unions, to promote increased industrial output and lasting industrial peace.

Through the cooperative action of many citizens and organizations, we have prepared recommendations for the extension of Old Age and Survivors Insurance coverage to 10½ million Americans, that they too may be encouraged to look forward to an old age of health and independence.

We have used the power of the Federal Government, wherever it clearly extends, to combat and erase racial discrimination and segregation—so that no man of any color or creed will *ever* be able to cry, "This is not a free land."

These, then, are some of the things we have been doing—and the reasons why.

They all total—I repeat—only a little more than a beginning.

I know of no official of this administration so foolish as to believe that we, who in January came to Washington, have seen and conquered all the problems of our Nation.

The future, both immediate and distant, remains full of trial and hazard.

The end of our staggering economic burden is not yet in sight.

The end of the peril to peace is not clearly in view.

There is only this in sight: a firm and binding purpose that guides *all* our objectives—our every deed.

This purpose is to serve and to strengthen our people, all our people, in their faith in freedom and in their quest of peace; and to strengthen all other peoples who share with us that faith and that quest.

In this short summary of the record, you can see how this single, supreme purpose rules and relates foreign relations; world trade; defense appropriations; reorganization of Government departments; domestic programs affecting agriculture, labor, and industry; taxes; debts; tariffs.

This ruling purpose inspires all the men who are your servants in Government—men from the professions, the trades, from business, from farm and factory—each representing a part of America in such a way as to make a united America.

The men and women in the Congress, the men and women in the executive departments, in both appointive and civil service offices—all are working together to serve you with this common purpose.

I know no other purpose, no other toil, worthy of America.

160 ¶ Statement by the President Upon Signing the Refugee Relief Act of 1953. *August 7, 1953*

THIS EMERGENCY immigration legislation is, at once, a significant humanitarian act and an important contribution toward greater understanding and cooperation among the free nations of the world.

In enacting this legislation, we are giving a new chance in life to 214,000 fellow humans. This action demonstrates again America's traditional concern for the homeless, the persecuted and the less fortunate of other lands. It is a dramatic contrast to the tragic events taking place in East Germany and in other captive nations.

This legislation also offers encouragement to the other friendly nations which are today affording asylum to refugees and escapees. It is my hope that, in our action, by our direct participation with them in this great humanitarian work, we are giving them cause to continue their efforts with renewed enthusiasm.

The enactment of this legislation provides abundant proof of the progress that teamwork between the legislative and executive branches of the Government can achieve. It is also a stirring example of bipartisan statesmanship.

The leaders of the great religious faiths who are here today to witness the signing of this bill have, in years past, made notable contributions to similar programs. I am sure that their continued activity and enthusiasm will be major factors in ensuring the success of this program.

I am delighted to sign this bill and, in so doing, to welcome the 214,000 refugees who will soon come to our shores. They—as I said in last night's Report to the Nation—are men and women of the same character and integrity as our ancestors who, generation upon generation, have come to America to find peace and work, to build for themselves new homes in freedom.

NOTE: The Refugee Relief Act of 1953 is Public Law 203, 83d Congress (67 Stat. 400).

161   ¶ Statement by the President Upon Signing the Trade Agreements Extension Act of 1953.

August 7, 1953

I HAVE TODAY signed the Trade Agreements Extension Act of 1953 extending our trade-agreements legislation for an additional period of one year and providing for the creation of a Joint Executive-Legislative Commission on Foreign Economic Policy.

This action by the Congress, coupled with the excellent progress made in the field of customs simplification, reaffirms the will and purpose of the United States to cooperate with other friendly countries in the development of a large and growing volume of world trade on a mutually profitable basis. In addition, through the establishment of a Foreign Economic Policy Commission, this legislation will enable the executive and legislative branches of our Government to undertake a careful and thorough review of our foreign economic policy in order to make it more responsive to the needs of our time.

Our present trade-agreements program, although helpful in the past, is inadequate in many ways and does not fully meet the requirements of our international relations today.

Its renewal, however, provides us with a breathing space, during which the United States will have the opportunity to develop a policy based upon a full understanding of our national interests, domestic and foreign, and an appreciation of the fact that those interests are inseparable from the interests of the free world as a whole.

I am confident that the Commission created by this law will approach its task in this spirit and that its work will provide the foundations on which a new and constructive foreign economic policy can be erected.

NOTE: The Trade Agreements Extension Act of 1953 is Public Law 215, 83d Congress (67 Stat. 472).

162 ¶ Memorandum of Disapproval of Bill for the Relief of Ethel Hudson Morrison.

August 7, 1953

I AM WITHHOLDING approval from S. 754, "For the relief of Ethel Hudson Morrison."

This measure was enacted to overcome, for the benefit of the claimant, the provisions of the general law governing entitlement to the remaining proceeds of a National Service Life Insurance policy which matured in July 1943. It does this by resorting to legislative directive requiring the Administrator of Veterans' Affairs to assume, in the administration of the National Service Life Insurance Act of 1940, as amended, that the claimant "stood in loco parentis" to the insured and that she was the "designated sole contingent beneficiary" of his insurance policy.

The facts in this case are not disputed. The policy of the deceased designated his mother as principal beneficiary and the claimant, Ethel Hudson Morrison and William McKee Morrison, Jr., aunt and cousin, respectively, as contingent beneficiaries. The mother died in 1948. The aunt alone seeks to recover the remaining unpaid installments under the policy.

Prior to August 1, 1946, the law governing National Service Life Insurance policies did not permit either an aunt or a cousin to be named as a beneficiary. The law did recognize, as proper beneficiaries persons who, under certain circumstances, stood in loco parentis to the insured. Mrs. Morrison attempted, unsuccessfully, to establish such a relationship. The original application was administratively denied, and the affirming decision of the Board of Veterans' Appeals was not appealed to the courts, as was the claimant's right.

I consider this measure unacceptable for a number of reasons:

First, it is desirable, generally, in accordance with the right granted by the National Service Life Insurance Act of 1940, as amended, that disagreements with rulings of the Veterans' Administration be reviewed by the courts, thus exhausting all the remedies provided by the terms of general legislation.

Second, the directives of the bill, in providing for this claimant alone, seemingly defeat the intent of the insured that the cousin also should share. I find nothing in the record of the case to justify or explain setting aside the wishes of the insured in this respect.

Third, the National Service Life Insurance trust fund would become obligated for the liability were the bill approved. In view of the contract rights of existing policyholders, I share the doubt of the Veterans' Administration as to the legality of the proposed action.

Fourth, this legislative overruling of the decision of the Board of Veterans' Appeals seems to be based only on the less dominant considerations of the in loco parentis proceedings. Nowhere in the legislative history is any reason advanced for dismissing the considerations which the administrative decision found dominant and controlling. Even though Mrs. Morrison did care for the insured after his father's death, the fact remains that he was at no time actually living apart from his mother.

Far more fundamental is the objection I have heretofore expressed to setting aside the principles and rules of administration prescribed in the general laws governing veterans' benefit programs. Uniformity and equality of treatment to all who are similarly situated must be the rule if the Federal programs for veterans and their beneficiaries are to be operated successfully. Otherwise, inequity is added to inequity, as is fully revealed by statistics reported by the Veterans' Administration. More than 3,200 claims of designated beneficiaries for the proceeds of National Service Life Insurance have been denied because they were not within the permitted classes of beneficiaries. There may be cases in which the circumstances are unique and justify waiver of the law. In my judgment, this is not such a case.

DWIGHT D. EISENHOWER

163 ¶ Memorandum of Disapproval of Bill for the Relief of Mary Thaila Womack Webb.
August 7, 1953

I AM WITHHOLDING my approval from S. 953, "An Act for the relief of Mary Thaila Womack Webb."

This measure, in providing a special exception from the general laws administered by the Veterans' Administration, would render this claimant potentially eligible to receive a pension for the non-service-connected death of a veteran of World War I. It does this by resorting to a legislative directive that she shall "be deemed to be the widow" of the deceased veteran.

Under existing law the establishment of legal widowhood is prerequisite to death benefits administered by the Veterans' Administration. The claimant cannot meet this prescription because a prior marriage of the veteran was never legally dissolved. Both the veteran and the beneficiary had a contrary belief, and they married in good faith. The Congress has accepted the good faith of the claimant in entering into the marriage and the belief that she was the legal wife of the veteran during the eighteen years of their association.

I understand fully the motivation of the action taken by the Congress in this case but I cannot agree that the principles and rules of administration prescribed in the general law should be set aside except in unique and most compelling circumstances of equity. The Federal programs for veterans and their beneficiaries, if they are to be successful, require unswerving uniformity of rule and equality of treatment to all who are similarly situated. If the law is to be changed, it should be changed for all.

We must not, in this benefits field, heed the special plea or the emotional appeal of the hardship case. Legal requirements of fact should not be supplanted by fiat or legislative fiction applying to an individual. To do so would result only in the compounding of inequities, as is apparent from statistics reported by the Veterans' Administration. More than 2,700 claims for death benefits were disallowed by the Veterans' Administration during the last fiscal year for the reason that relationship to the deceased veteran could not be established. I am informed that at least a majority were cases similar to that of the present claimant.

In the light of these facts I could take no other action than to withhold approval of this bill.

Dwight D. Eisenhower

164 ¶ Statement by the President Upon Signing the Customs Simplification Act of 1953.
August 8, 1953

I HAVE TODAY approved H.R. 5877, the Customs Simplification Act of 1953. This statute will authorize the Treasury Department to make much needed changes in the regulations governing the procedures of the Bureau of Customs. The new law will permit the elimination of many obsolete but time-consuming requirements, contribute to a more efficient utilization of available personnel, and eliminate a number of inequities in the former law.

In my first message to the Congress, I indicated that one of the important measures which should be undertaken was legislation to modernize customs procedures. By the enactment of H.R. 5877, the Congress has completed a major portion of the legislation needed for this purpose. It is gratifying that the few provisions suggested by the Treasury and passed by the House but deferred for further study by the Senate and thus not contained in this Act have been included in a new bill (H.R. 6584) introduced by Mr. Jenkins of Ohio which has passed the House of Representatives and which will receive the consideration of the Senate at the beginning of the second session of the 83rd Congress.

NOTE: The Customs Simplification Act of 1953 is Public Law 243, 83d Congress (67 Stat. 507).

165   ¶ Letter to Heads of Departments and Agencies Concerning Further Economies in Government.   *August 11, 1953*

[Released August 11, 1953. Dated August 6, 1953]

Dear ——————:

Ever since the date of Inauguration, every member of this Administration has been dedicated to the purposes of efficiency and economy in government. Now that Congress is adjourned, it is time to attack the problem with renewed vigor. It is absolutely essential that you begin immediately to take every possible step progressively to reduce the expenditures of your department during the fiscal year 1954. In addition to this action, you will be expected to make substantial reductions in your requests for new appropriations and in the level of your expenditures for the fiscal year 1955, beyond those already indicated for the fiscal year 1954.

It is imperative that you emphasize a critical review and maximum feasible reductions of expenditures in areas which have attracted the attention and concern of the Congress and of the public as possible sources of waste, inefficiency, duplication, and excessive or nonessential costs.

Every level of the staff of your Department should be made aware of the necessity for doing this and of the importance of their cooperation as a vital part of its accomplishment.

Sincerely,

DWIGHT D. EISENHOWER

NOTE: This is the text of identical letters sent to the heads of all departments and of the principal agencies of the Federal Government. The letter was released at Lowry Air Force Base, Denver, Colo.

166 ¶ Statement by the President Upon Signing Bill Relating to State Jurisdiction Over Cases Arising on Indian Reservations. *August* 15, 1953

ALTHOUGH I HAVE grave doubts as to the wisdom of certain provisions contained in H.R. 1063, I have today signed it because its basic purpose represents still another step in granting complete political equality to all Indians in our nation.

The bill confers jurisdiction on the States of California, Minnesota, Nebraska, Oregon and Wisconsin, with respect to criminal offenses and civil causes of action committed or arising on Indian reservations within such states. The bill has resulted from a process of exhaustive study of the innumerable laws and regulations applying to our several Indian groupments and was arrived at in the states affected after long negotiation in full consultation with the Indians themselves. The Indian tribes regard this as a long step forward in removing them from the status of "second class" citizens.

Indeed, in the five states where state jurisdiction will soon be paramount, the Indians have enthusiastically endorsed this bill. The bill preserves the basic safeguards against loss of property rights accorded the Indians by Federal treaties, agreements and statutes, and further safeguards the tribal customs and ordinances of the tribes affected when not inconsistent with the general laws of the respective states.

Three Indian tribes that have effective law and order organizations of their own, asked to be excluded from the purview of the bill. These tribes are the Red Lake band of Chippewa, in Minnesota; the Warm Springs tribe in Oregon; and the Menominee tribe in Wisconsin. Because of their effective organizations, they are, in response to their wishes, excepted from this bill.

My objection to the bill arises because of the inclusion in it of Sections 6 and 7. These Sections permit other states to impose on Indian tribes within their borders, the criminal and civil jurisdiction of the state, removing the Indians from Federal jurisdiction, and, in some instances, effective self-government. The failure to include in these provisions a requirement of full consultation in order to ascertain the wishes and desires of the Indians and of final Federal approval, was unfortunate. I recommend, therefore, that at the earliest possible time in the next session of the Congress, the Act be amended to require such consultation with the tribes prior to the enactment of legislation subjecting them to state jurisdiction, as well as approval by the Federal government before such legislation becomes effective.

I am requesting the Secretary of the Interior to press forward vigorously with the program of cooperative study that he has already so successfully undertaken with the Indians. I also wish to express my earnest hope that the Governors of the several states will fully cooperate with the Secretary of the Interior in this program, and will ascertain the views of the Indians of their states in connection with any action proposed to be taken under Sections 6 and 7 of the bill.

Much progress has been made and much greater progress will result through full consideration being accorded our Indian citizens.

NOTE: As enacted, H.R. 1063 is Public Law 280, 83d Congress (67 Stat. 588). The statement was released at Lowry Air Force Base, Denver, Colo.

167 ¶ Memorandum of Disapproval of Bill for the Relief of Harold Joe Davis.   *August* 15, 1953

I AM WITHHOLDING my approval from H.R. 1460, "For the relief of Harold Joe Davis."

This measure would pay the sum of $10,000 to Harold Joe Davis, of Tulsa, Oklahoma, as compensation for alleged permanent disability growing out of injuries sustained in a Japanese bombing attack at Dutch Harbor, Alaska, in 1942.

There is conflicting evidence regarding the facts in this case. It is undisputed, however, that the claimant was fire chief at the Navy's installation at Dutch Harbor, when it was bombed by the Japanese in 1942 and that, as a result of this bombing, he was injured while in the performance of his duties. It is not entirely clear whether the claimant was an employee of a government contractor at the time of his injury or whether he may not have been a de facto employee of the United States. Nor is it clear just what the nature and extent of his injuries were nor to what extent they were responsible for his present condition.

Either as an overseas employee of a Government contractor or as an employee of the United States, the claimant was entitled to periodic disability compensation under laws administered by the Bureau of Employees' Compensation if he sustained a compensable disability in the course of his employment. However, for reasons unknown, he did not file a claim with that Bureau until some seven years after the bombing injuries were incurred, a time interval well beyond the statutory period within which such claims had to be filed. His claim was subsequently rejected not only for failure to file timely but also because, on the basis of hearings on the merits, it was determined that no present disability existed as a result of the 1942 injuries.

I find no justification for this proposed award. In amount, it bears no relation to any indicated measure of damages. It constitutes a method of payment which is at variance with the periodic compensation benefits provided by existing law. Its sole justification seems to be that the claimant is unable to meet the substantive and procedural requirements of compensation statutes of general applicability.

In view of the conflicting evidence in the case, however, I believe that the claimant should be afforded the opportunity to advance any additional evidence he may have in support of his claim. I would, therefore, be willing to approve a bill which would permit a determination of the claimant's employment status at the time of his injuries and which would then permit him, notwithstanding any statute of limitations, to file a claim under the law applicable to that status. In this way the claim will be processed under accepted procedures, fair to both the individual and the Government. In my opinion, such a bill gives the fullest possible recognition to the equities in favor of the claimant and should be productive of a result in keeping with the degree of disability he so unfortunately sustained as a result of his war injuries.

DWIGHT D. EISENHOWER

NOTE: The memorandum was released at Lowry Air Force Base, Denver, Colo.

168   ¶ Memorandum of Disapproval of Bill for
the Relief of Colonel Harry F. Cunningham.
August 15, 1953

I AM WITHHOLDING my approval from H.R. 2158, "For the relief of Colonel Harry F. Cunningham."

This measure directs the payment out of seized German assets now under the control of the United States of the sum of $12,500 to Colonel Harry F. Cunningham, of Lincoln, Nebraska, as compensation for architectural services rendered the former German Government prior to World War II.

In the late 1930's the claimant was retained by the former German Government as the architect for an embassy which it was proposing to build in Washington. After rendering fairly extensive services, the claimant disassociated himself from the project when he found himself at odds with the military policies Germany was then following. The outbreak of hostilities a short time later resulted in the complete abandonment of the project and the embassy has never been built.

Subsequently, the claimant filed alternative claims with the Department of Justice under the Trading with the Enemy Act, the statute which governs the distribution to various claimants of the assets of the German Government and of German nationals which were seized at the beginning of World War II. He desired relief in the alternative, either on the basis of a lien against specific real property owned by the German Government in the District of Columbia or on the basis of an ordinary debt owing for services rendered. The lien basis for the claim was rejected because a lien could not legally be asserted against governmental property and because the claimant's services never resulted in specific improvements to the property in question, ordinarily a condition precedent to the assertion of a valid lien. However, a claim based on the existence of a debt for personal services rendered is now pending before the Department of Justice, and although no final determination can be made until processing of related claims under the Trading with the Enemy Act has been accomplished, it appears that the claimant will ultimately have his debt claim approved in such amount as is found to be owing to him.

This case has one major issue, revolving around the question of whether the facts and circumstances warrant the special treatment proposed for this claimant. In my opinion they do not. The claimant has an acknowledged claim under the Trading with the Enemy Act. The provisions of that Act were designed to provide orderly and equitable procedures for the distribution of vested enemy property. I do not believe these procedures should be ignored merely because it can be shown that proceeds in excess of the amount of the present claim have been realized from the sale of a portion of the land formerly owned by the German Government on which the embassy was to have been built. There are thousands of other debt claims equal or higher in priority to Colonel Cunningham's. At present there can be no assurance that the ultimate realization on vested German property will permit these to be paid at full value. It would clearly be discriminatory to place this claim in a preferred position.

Furthermore, I cannot subscribe to the view that the bill should be approved because such action will provide for prompt settlement of an acknowledged claim. All claimants would like to have prompt settlements. No valid reason is given for preferring this claimant ahead of all others. To set aside the procedures prescribed by general law would lead other claimants to seek special legislation to speed the settlement of their claims. To my mind this is one of the exact contingencies that the Trading with the Enemy Act was designed for.

DWIGHT D. EISENHOWER

NOTE: The memorandum was released at Lowry Air Force Base, Denver, Colo.

169 ¶ Memorandum of Disapproval of Bill for
the Relief of the City and County of Denver,
Colorado.   *August* 15, 1953

I HAVE WITHHELD my approval from H.R. 2750, "For the
relief of the city and county of Denver, Colorado."

This bill would authorize a payment of $4,741.72 to the city
and county of Denver, on account of street improvements in front
of property of the United States adjoining Lowry Air Force Base.
This represents the amount that would have been assessable
against the property if it were privately owned.

Considered simply in terms of the specific facts, the claim for
payment seems equitable.   The Department of the Air Force
has stated that the improvements "are definitely beneficial and
desirable to the community and to the adjacent Federal property."   Since there is no legal authority under which the Department can make payment, special private legislation is the only
avenue of relief presently available.

But the claim covered in this bill is not unique, nor are the
facts so peculiar and local that approval would set no precedent.
On the contrary, there are indications that if the bill is approved
other communities may be expected to press similar—and perhaps
equally meritorious—claims to payment for local improvements
adjacent to Federal real property.

A long established principle of law and policy in our Federal
system of government is the constitutional immunity of the Federal Government from State and local taxation, including special
assessments, and the reciprocal constitutional immunity of State
and local governments from Federal taxation.   A breach of one
immunity could weaken the other.

In the past, the Congress has never consented to the general
application of special assessments to property of the Federal Government.   Legislation has been enacted from time to time grant-

ing limited consent to State or local taxes designated Federal properties or activities, or providing for payments in lieu of taxes under specified conditions. A few of these laws have permitted special assessments on certain Federal properties. On the other hand, the Congress has had before it bills proposing to grant general consent for the levy of special assessments for local improvements beneficial to Federal Government property, but such legislation has not been enacted.

The present Congress recently approved my recommendation that a Commission on Intergovernmental Relations be established to study the means of achieving a sounder relationship between Federal, State, and local governments. I believe that the exercise of taxing powers is within the scope of the Commission's assignment, and I shall request that its report include recommendations as to how to solve the many difficult problems which arise in the field of intergovernmental tax immunities.

The basic question underlying the enrolled bill, H.R. 2750, is whether the Federal Government should adhere to its constitutional tax immunity or should forego it in this particular instance and possibly in other cases. Since this involves the question of modifying a long established policy, I believe that it should be decided broadly and deliberately, rather than through a succession of piece-meal decisions on individual requests. Moreover, I believe such a decision can best be reached in the light of the general suggestions which will be derived from the work of the Commission on Intergovernmental Relations.

DWIGHT D. EISENHOWER

NOTE: The memorandum was released at Lowry Air Force Base, Denver, Colo.

170   ¶ Citation Accompanying Medal of Honor
Awarded to Second Lieutenant George H. O'Brien,
Jr.   *August* 17, 1953

THE PRESIDENT of the United States in the name of The Congress takes pleasure in presenting the Medal of Honor to

SECOND LIEUTENANT GEORGE H. O'BRIEN, JR.,
UNITED STATES MARINE CORPS RESERVE,

for service as set forth in the following

CITATION:

For conspicuous gallantry and intrepidity at the risk of his life above and beyond the call of duty as a Rifle Platoon Commander of Company H, Third Battalion, Seventh Marines, First Marine Division (Reinforced), in action against enemy aggressor forces in Korea on 27 October 1952. With his platoon subjected to an intense mortar and artillery bombardment while preparing to assault a vitally important hill position on the main line of resistance which had been overrun by a numerically superior enemy force on the preceding night, Second Lieutenant O'Brien leaped from his trench when the attack signal was given and, shouting for his men to follow, raced across an exposed saddle and up the enemy-held hill through a virtual hail of deadly small-arms, artillery and mortar fire. Although shot through the arm and thrown to the ground by hostile automatic-weapons fire as he neared the well-entrenched enemy position, he bravely regained his feet, waved his men onward and continued to spearhead the assault, pausing only long enough to go to the aid of a wounded Marine. Encountering the enemy at close range, he proceeded to hurl hand grenades into the bunkers and, utilizing his carbine to best advantage in savage hand-to-hand combat, succeeded in killing at least three of the enemy. Struck down by the concussion of grenades on three occasions during the subsequent action, he steadfastly refused to be evacuated for medical treatment and continued to lead his platoon in the assault for a period of nearly four hours, repeatedly encouraging his men and maintaining superb direction of the unit. With the attack halted, he set up a defense with his remaining forces to prepare for a counterattack, personally checking each position, attending to the wounded and expediting their evacuation. When a relief of the position was effected by another unit, he remained to cover the withdrawal and to assure that no wounded were left behind. By his exceptionally daring and forceful leadership in the face of overwhelming odds, Second Lieutenant O'Brien served as a constant source of inspiration to all who observed him and was greatly instrumental in the recapture of a strategic position on the main line of resistance. His indomitable determination and valiant fighting spirit reflect the highest credit upon himself and enhance the finest traditions of the United States Naval Service.

DWIGHT D. EISENHOWER

NOTE: The citation was released at Lowry Air Force Base, Denver, Colo. See also Item 229.

171 ¶ Statement by the President Approving a Statement of Policy on Electric Power by the Secretary of the Interior. *August* 18, 1953

THE SECRETARY OF THE INTERIOR is today announcing a policy governing the planning, generation, distribution, and disposal of electric power for which the Department of the Interior is the responsible agent under the law.

This policy is in accord with the principle that the states and local communities, private citizens and the Federal Government itself should cooperate in an effort actively to encourage the development of the natural resources of the country.

I fully approve of this policy, and the various Cabinet officers and agency heads who are directly concerned have expressed, after careful review of the problem, their full agreement. It is my hope and my considered belief that, translated into action, this policy will serve the best interests of all the people of the United States.

NOTE: The President's statement was released at Lowry Air Force Base, Denver, Colo.

The Department of the Interior Power Policy, dated July 31, 1953 (11 pp.), was released by the Department together with a 3-page statement relating to the policy and a 1-page summary noting comparisons of the new policy with past practices.

172 ¶ Exchange of Messages Between the President and King Paul of Greece Concerning an Earthquake Disaster. *August* 18, 1953

[Released August 18, 1953. Dated August 14, 1953]

TOGETHER with the people and Government of the United States I express my profound sympathy to the suffering people of Greece whose families have been killed or injured and homes destroyed in the recent earthquake. Rest assured the American Red Cross and United States Government agencies already assisting will continue to see you through this disaster.

DWIGHT D. EISENHOWER

NOTE: King Paul's message follows:

I was greatly touched by your kind message, and together with my people am indeed grateful to you personally and to the government and the people of the United States for your sympathy and prompt assistance in our disaster. I would also like to express to you our warmest thanks for the valuable aid given to us by the American Red Cross and the United States Government agency as well as for the courageous and efficient help of the United States Navy and Air Force to our distressed areas.

PAUL R.

The messages were released at Lowry Air Force Base, Denver, Colo.

173 ¶ Statement by the President Concerning Aid by the Red Cross to Victims of the Earthquake Disaster in Greece. *August* 18, 1953

I AM pleased to learn that the American Red Cross is responding to the appeal of the Greek Red Cross to assist in relieving the distressed victims of the tragic earthquake in Greece.

As Honorary President of the American Red Cross I am confident that the people of the United States will respond generously in helping to alleviate the suffering of the people of Greece who have contributed so much to our common cause of freedom.

NOTE: The statement was released at Lowry Air Force Base, Denver, Colo.

174 ¶ Citation Accompanying Medal of Honor Awarded to Private First Class Alford L. McLaughlin. *August* 18, 1953

THE PRESIDENT of the United States in the name of The Congress takes pleasure in presenting the Medal of Honor to

PRIVATE FIRST CLASS ALFORD L. MC LAUGHLIN,
UNITED STATES MARINE CORPS,

for service as set forth in the following

CITATION:

For conspicuous gallantry and intrepidity at the risk of his life above and beyond the call of duty while serving as a Machine Gunner of Company I, Third Battalion, Fifth Marines, First Marine Division (Reinforced), in action against enemy aggressor forces in Korea on the night of 4–5 September 1952. Volunteering for his second continuous tour of duty on a strategic combat outpost far in advance of the main line of resistance, Private

575

First Class McLaughlin, although operating under a barrage of enemy artillery and mortar fire, set up plans for the defense of his position which proved decisive in the successful defense of the outpost. When hostile forces attacked in battalion strength during the night, he maintained a constant flow of devastating fire upon the enemy, alternately employing two machine guns, a carbine and hand grenades. Although painfully wounded, he bravely fired the machine guns from the hip until his hands became blistered by the extreme heat from the weapons and, placing the guns on the ground to allow them to cool, continued to defend the position with his carbine and grenades. Standing up in full view, he shouted words of encouragement to his comrades above the din of battle and, throughout a series of fanatical enemy attacks, sprayed the surrounding area with deadly fire, accounting for an estimated one hundred and fifty enemy dead and fifty wounded. By his indomitable courage, superb leadership and valiant fighting spirit in the face of overwhelming odds, Private First Class McLaughlin served to inspire his fellow Marines in their gallant stand against the enemy and was directly instrumental in preventing the vital outpost from falling into the hands of a determined and numerically superior hostile force. His outstanding heroism and unwavering devotion to duty reflect the highest credit upon himself and enhance the finest traditions of the United States Naval Service.

Dwight D. Eisenhower

NOTE: The citation was released at Lowry Air Force Base, Denver, Colo. See also Item 229.

175 ¶ Citation Accompanying Medal of Honor Awarded to Private First Class Robert E. Simanek. *August* 20, 1953

THE PRESIDENT of the United States in the name of The Congress takes pleasure in presenting the Medal of Honor to

PRIVATE FIRST CLASS ROBERT E. SIMANEK,
UNITED STATES MARINE CORPS,

for service as set forth in the following

CITATION:

For conspicuous gallantry and intrepidity at the risk of his life above and beyond the call of duty while serving with Company F, Second Battalion, Fifth Marines, First Marine Division (Reinforced), in action against enemy aggressor forces in Korea on 17 August 1952. While accompanying a patrol en route to occupy a combat outpost forward of friendly lines, Private First Class Simanek exhibited a high degree of courage and a resolute spirit of self-sacrifice in protecting the lives of his fellow Marines. With his unit ambushed by an intense concentration of enemy mortar and small-arms fire, and suffering heavy casualties, he was forced to seek cover with the remaining members of the patrol in a near-by trench line. Determined to save his comrades when a hostile grenade was hurled into their midst, he unhesitatingly threw himself on the deadly missile, absorbing the shattering violence of the exploding charge in his own body and shielding his fellow Marines from serious injury or death. Gravely wounded as a result of his heroic action, Private First Class Simanek, by his daring initiative and great personal valor in the face of almost certain death, served to inspire all who observed him and upheld the highest traditions of the United States Naval Service.

DWIGHT D. EISENHOWER

56616—60——40

NOTE: The citation was released at Lowry Air Force Base, Denver, Colo. See also Item 229.

176 ¶ Letter to Lewis W. Douglas Concerning Report on His Financial and Economic Mission to the United Kingdom.   *August 24, 1953*

[Released August 24, 1953. Dated July 21, 1953]

Dear Lew:

The report of your mission following up the financial and economic discussions held in Washington last March between representatives of the United Kingdom and the United States is here and I have now had a chance to read it carefully.   It is clearly the product of your own studious attitude and your great understanding of dollar-sterling relationships.

Your study strikes me as a most valuable contribution toward illuminating the still dark corners of this highly significant matter. It has in it a vein of candor, both with respect to the United Kingdom's position and our own, which is, I think, refreshing and very useful.   I plan to transmit for study a copy of this report to the head of each department and agency of the Executive Branch concerned with foreign economic policy.   It is my intention to release the report when I forward it to the Chairman of the Commission on Foreign Economic Policy upon its formation in the near future.   I regard your study as an important document for the consideration of that Commission.

In accepting this report and releasing you from the assignment you undertook in my name and as the Secretary of State's deputy, I want you to know of my genuine gratitude for this new chapter in your long record of dedicated public service.   Please convey my thanks also to those who assisted you in this useful contribution to one of the perplexing problems of our time.

With warm regard,

Sincerely,

DWIGHT D. EISENHOWER

NOTE: The report is in the form of a letter to the President dated July 14. Together with the President's letter to Mr. Douglas, and a letter transmitting the report to the Chairman of the Commission on Foreign Economic Policy (see Item 177), the report was released at Lowry Air Force Base, Denver, Colo. It is published in the Department of State Bulletin (vol. 29, p. 275).

177 ¶ Letter to Clarence Randall, Chairman, Commission on Foreign Economic Policy, Transmitting the Douglas Report. *August 24, 1953*

Dear Mr. Randall:

I am transmitting herewith the report of the Lewis Douglas mission following up the financial and economic conversations held between representatives of the United Kingdom and of our Government in Washington last March.

The analysis and findings of the Douglas report represent, in my opinion, a real contribution to thinking in the field of dollar-sterling relationships. I commend the report to the earnest attention of you and your associates as you undertake your canvass of the whole broad field of foreign economic policy.

Sincerely,

DWIGHT D. EISENHOWER

NOTE: See Item 176 and note.

178 ¶ Exchange of Letters Between the President and Prime Minister Zahedi Concerning the Need for Increased Aid to Iran. *September 1, 1953*

Dear Mr. Prime Minister:

I have received your letter of August 26 regarding the problems which you face in Iran. The American people continue to be deeply interested in the independence of Iran and the well-being of the Iranian people. We have followed policies in Iran, as in other countries of the free world, designed to assist peoples of those countries to bring about economic development which will lead to higher standards of living and wider horizons in knowledge and opportunity. I am gratified that the aid which we have extended has contributed to the security of Iran and to the raising of the technical efficiency of the Iranian people. I am also pleased to have your assurance that your Government desires to maintain friendly relations with other members of the family of nations and that it will pursue a policy of eliminating such differences as may exist or which may develop with other countries in a spirit of friendliness and in accordance with accepted principles of international intercourse.

In an effort to assist you in dealing with your immediate problems, I have authorized my Ambassador to Iran to consult with you regarding the development of our aid programs there. I recognize that your needs are pressing. Your request will receive our sympathetic consideration and I can assure you that we stand ready to assist you in achieving the aspirations for your country which you have outlined.

Please accept, Mr. Prime Minister, the assurances of my highest consideration.

DWIGHT D. EISENHOWER

NOTE: Prime Minister Zahedi's letter follows:

Dear Mr. President:

I wish to express to you and through you to the American people the appreciation of the Iranian Government and people for the aid which the United States has extended to Iran during recent years. This aid has contributed much to the security of the country and to the raising of its technical efficiency. The assistance which the United States is already rendering Iran, helpful as it is, is unfortunately not sufficient in amount and character to tide Iran over the financial and economic crisis which I find it to be facing. The treasury is empty; foreign exchange resources are exhausted; the national economy is deteriorated. Iran needs immediate financial aid to enable it to emerge from a state of economic and financial chaos.

Iran also requires aid of an economic character to enable it to carry out programs which the government is preparing for developing its agriculture and industry, for exploiting its rich mineral resources, for improving its transport and communications, for strengthening its internal and foreign trade, and for raising the health, education and technical levels of the Iranian people.

The people of Iran are anxious to have a prosperous, orderly country in which they can enjoy higher standards of living and make greater use of their talents and resources. They are willing, if given an opportunity, to work hard in order to obtain these objectives, but the realization of their aspirations may be delayed for some time unless they receive technical, financial, and economic aid from abroad. I hope that the United States will find it possible at this critical moment in Iranian history to come to my country's assistance as it has done on occasions in the past.

In conclusion, I would like to emphasize that it is the intention of the new Government of Iran not only to strengthen the country internally but also to improve its international position. The government desires to maintain friendly relations with the other members of the family of nations on a basis of mutual respect. It will pursue a policy of eliminating such differences as may exist or which may develop between other countries and itself in a spirit of friendliness and in accordance with accepted principles of international intercourse. I am sure that I voice the feelings of the great majority of the people of Iran when I state that Iran desires to contribute its share to the maintenance of peace and to the promotion of international goodwill.

Please accept, Mr. President, the assurance of my highest consideration.

GENERAL F. ZAHEDI

The letters were released at Lowry Air Force Base, Denver, Colo.

On September 5 the White House announced that the President had made available on an emergency basis $45 million to be used for the immediate economic assistance of Iran under the Mutual Security Act. The release pointed out that the amount was in addition to existing U.S. technical assistance and military programs in Iran.

179 ¶ Memorandum on the Community Chest and United Fund Campaigns. *September* 4, 1953

To the Heads of Executive Departments and Agencies:

Under date of June 22, 1953 I addressed a communication to you regarding cooperation of the Federal government in the fall campaigns of Community Chests and United Funds to be held all over the country.

In order that we may reinforce our assurance of cooperation I have approved the appointment of George M. Humphrey, Secretary of the Treasury, as Vice-Chairman for the Federal government of United Community Campaigns. Through Mr. Humphrey you will receive further word of detailed arrangements so that all employes of the Federal government in communities throughout the United States and its territories and possessions may have the opportunity to subscribe and to pay their subscriptions over an extended period.

I am confident that you will be glad to join with Mr. Humphrey in this program which involves support of voluntary health and welfare services in more than 1700 local communities and which also includes support of the United Defense Fund. The service of the USO to the armed forces, help to communities overwhelmed by defense activities and relief to Korea are all provided, as you know, through the United Defense Fund.

DWIGHT D. EISENHOWER

NOTE: The memorandum was released at Lowry Air Force Base, Denver, Colo.

180 ¶ Letter to the Commissioner of Indian
Affairs Concerning His Meetings With the Major
Tribal Groups.   *September* 5, 1953

[Released September 5, 1953. Dated September 2, 1953]

Dear Commissioner Emmons:

This Administration, as you know, has pledged itself to consult with the Indian people of this country and to give them every opportunity for a full expression of their desires, suggestions, hopes and aspirations. In order to fulfill this pledge, I am asking you, as my personal representative, to go into the home territory of the Indians during the next several months and meet with each of the major tribal groups of the country.

Please emphasize to the Indian people our sincere desire for the benefit of their views. While we cannot anticipate that there will always be perfect agreement between the Indians and their Government as a result of these conferences, it is essential for us to learn firsthand their thoughts, needs, and aspirations. Only with such knowledge can we move forward with a warm and realistic understanding in shaping policies and programs for the future administration of Indian affairs.

I realize that the task I am assigning you will be arduous and that it will make heavy demands on your time and energies during the next few months. I am confident, however, that our Indian citizens will appreciate the effort you are making and the spirit directing it.

Please express to each of the Indian groups you meet my warm personal greetings and my heartfelt personal assurance that our ruling aim in Indian affairs is to meet and to deal with them justly and progressively on all matters at all times.

Sincerely,

DWIGHT D. EISENHOWER

NOTE: The letter was released at Lowry Air Force Base, Denver, Colo.

181   ¶ Statement by the President: Labor Day.
September 7, 1953

IN THIS year of continuing international tension, we commemorate with an unusual measure of gratitude in our hearts,
the day set aside as a salute to American labor, and we contemplate with renewed appreciation the principles that make and
keep us a free people.

The workers of America are witnesses, before the world, of the
strength, the pride and the prosperity that alone can be won by
free labor. They are strong in their independent unions. They
are proud beyond the temptations of political subservience. They
are an indestructible bulwark of free government.

These witnesses to freedom's blessings give the lie to the sly
evil of the promises of totalitarianism. They mock the false insinuation that economic well-being can be purchased only at the
cost of political freedom. They are the final answer to those who
prate freedom and practice slavery, who excuse terror and aggression in the name of concern for the very workers whose lives
they stifle.

Free American labor has won for itself the enjoyment of a
standard of living unmatched in history. The contemporary
world knows no comparison with it. There is only brutal contrast
to it. To this, there is no more pitiful and dramatic testimony
than the food which this free people has been able to send to feed
hundreds of thousands suffering the peculiar torments of the
proletarian paradise of Eastern Germany.

This is a day sincerely to salute American labor: its freedom,
its dignity, its matchless productive genius—and the lesson it
records for all men to read, for all time to come.

NOTE: The statement was released at Lowry Air Force Base, Denver, Colo.

182 ¶ Statement by the President on the Death of Chief Justice Vinson. *September* 8, 1953

I SHARE the nation's shock and grief over Chief Justice Vinson's untimely death. He was my close personal friend for many years and a statesman and jurist whom I admired deeply.

A man of exemplary character, he possessed great human understanding, appreciation of our national heritage and a keen mind. He has filled positions of great responsibility in all three branches of Government—legislative, administrative and judicial. In all of them he served with efficiency, dignity and integrity. He was an outstanding citizen whose death is a loss to America.

NOTE: In addition to the foregoing statement, the President issued Proclamation 3031 (3 CFR, 1949–1953 Comp., p. 205) which provided that, as a mark of respect to the memory of Chief Justice Vinson, the flag of the United States should be flown at half-staff for 30 days on all Government buildings in the United States and in foreign countries, and that appropriate civil, military, and naval honors be rendered. The statement and the proclamation were released at Lowry Air Force Base, Denver, Colo.

183 ¶ Statement by the President on the Occasion of the Jewish New Year. *September* 10, 1953

I AM happy to extend my warmest greetings to all Americans of Jewish faith on the occasion of the Jewish New Year.

Among the greatest lessons your history can teach, as the world struggles to find its way toward peace, are the patience and good will that have so frequently seen expression in the thousands of years of Jewish life. May this New Year bring to peoples of good faith everywhere the reassurance that more tranquil days are indeed near, and that the citizens of all nations will learn to live together with the understanding and harmony that God-loving people so fervently desire.

DWIGHT D. EISENHOWER

NOTE: The statement was released at Lowry Air Force Base, Denver, Colo.

184 ¶ Letter Accepting Resignation of Martin P. Durkin as Secretary of Labor.
September 10, 1953

Dear Martin:

As I told you this morning, I deeply regret the necessity expressed in your letter of August thirty-first compelling you to return to private life. I have no course, however, but to respect your wishes, and to accept your resignation as of this date.

You will be both missed and remembered. I say this not only with the warmth of a friend, but also as one deeply concerned with all the problems that are the special charge of the Department of Labor.

Your patient skill and rich experience have been of unique value. They have enabled you, in a remarkably short time, to summon talent and to initiate policies that can inspire a truly effective Department of Labor in the future. You know, I believe, beyond the need of reiteration, my personal conviction that the principal key to the strength of our working democracy is the assurance of both industrial peace and the vitality of our free labor unions. The extent to which these purposes can be served by the Federal Government in large measure depends upon the vigor and capacity of our Department of Labor. You can be sure that these simple convictions—which, I know, you fully share and which have governed our decisions to this date—will prevail with equal force in the future.

I sincerely extend to you my warm wishes for a career of renewed distinction in whatever you undertake, and my lasting

appreciation for the spirit of unselfish service that has characterized your work in this Administration.

Sincerely,

DWIGHT D. EISENHOWER

NOTE: Mr. Durkin was appointed   the President's reply were released at
Secretary of Labor on January 21,   Lowry Air Force Base, Denver, Colo.
1953. His letter of resignation and

185 ¶ Exchange of Letters Between the President and Mayor Ernst Reuter Concerning Conditions in Berlin. *September* 18, 1953

[Released September 18, 1953. Dated August 22, 1953]

My dear Mayor Reuter:

Thank you very much for your kind letter of August 10. I
also am most gratified by the success which the cooperation of
the Berlin authorities, the Federal Republic and the United States
Government has achieved in bringing urgently needed food as
tangible evidence of our friendship to the unfortunate people of
Soviet occupied Germany. I am impressed with the overwhelming response and with the courage displayed in the face of the
many obstacles which the communist authorities have put in the
way of these people. It is clear to me that the people of Soviet
occupied Germany understand that their welfare deeply concerns
the free world which, as you point out, is determined to help them
in every way possible.

The American people have not lost sight of the serious difficulties with which the people of West Berlin must cope so long as
they are separated from their fellow Germans in the East and
West, and cannot enjoy free communication and unimpeded
access to supplies of raw materials and markets for their production. While great progress has been made in raising the level
of economic activity and employment in West Berlin we all realize

587

that much remains to be done. The present investment and work relief programs in Berlin were, I am informed, carefully developed in the light of the needs of Berlin and the ability of the Berlin authorities, business and labor, to assist in the creation of additional jobs in existing or new enterprises.

I have no doubt that the Berlin authorities can improve present programs in consultation with the Bonn authorities and the Office of the United States High Commissioner. If proposals can be devised which would give promise of a further substantial increase in employment in Berlin, the United States Government would be prepared to explore with the Federal Republic what further steps the two governments might find it possible to take to achieve this objective.

Sincerely,

DWIGHT D. EISENHOWER

NOTE: Mayor Reuter's letter of August 10 follows:

Mr. President:

Mr. Leo Cherne forwarded to me the picture taken in Washington in March 1953 when you were kind enough to receive me. It was very kind of you to write on this photograph a personal dedication in remembrance of my visit to you. Thanking you for your kindness I should like to avail myself of the opportunity to express my warmest thanks for the food gift which we are at present distributing to the people of the Soviet Zone and East Berlin.

As a matter of fact, this gift is the most effective way of assisting these really destitute people. Everybody attending the distribution of the food is deeply touched by the patience, with which these people wait for hours, by their poor clothing and also by their joy upon receiving their share. We shall do all we can in order to organize the distribution of the gift so that as many of these distressed people as possible are given an opportunity to participate in this relief program. There is no doubt that the distribution of food contributes much to demonstrate to these people that they have not been forgotten by the free world and that the free world backs them and is determined to help them wherever possible. Every food parcel so distributed strengthens the natural and unalterable ties between these people living under unbelievably difficult economic and political conditions and the free world.

In order to cope with the unexpectedly great rush numerous West-Berliners have volunteered their help for the distribution. This attitude of the people of West Berlin is all the more remarkable as a considerable part of the people of West Berlin are also living in needy circumstances. In spite of every effort made by us, there are still 225,000 unemployed who have to live on unemployment insurance and unemployment benefit. You know that in spite of all difficulties, the people of Berlin have never been diverted from their determination to maintain and defend the freedom and independence of Berlin. Without the unparalleled attitude of the Berliners during the last years, the revolts of June 16 and 17 which attracted the attention of the whole world would have never happened. Therefore, I should like to express my conviction and hope that, the stronger and healthier Berlin is as a whole, the greater will also be the power radiating from the city into the surrounding Soviet Zone. Therefore, the reduction of the number of

unemployed in Berlin is an urgent political and moral concern of the entire free world. If we succeed in creating before long another 50 to 100 thousand places of work, we shall be in a position to add another decisive victory to the moral and political success achieved by the events of June 16 and 17 and the distribution of food which is still being carried through.

If, besides expressing my thanks for the kind dedication you wrote on the photograph, I spoke of the sorrows and needs of Berlin, I have done so, Mr. President, because I am well aware of the understanding and sympathy you have always shown for the needs of this city and its people.

With the renewed assurance of my highest esteem, I remain, Mr. President,

Yours sincerely,

ERNST REUTER

The letters were released at Lowry Air Force Base, Denver, Colo.

186 ¶ Statement by the President Concerning the New Commission on Intergovernmental Relations. *September 18, 1953*

COMPLETION TODAY of the membership of the Commission on Intergovernmental Relations marks the commencement of an historic undertaking: the elimination of frictions, duplications and waste from Federal-State relations; the clear definition of lines of governmental authority in our nation; the increase in efficiency in a multitude of governmental programs vital to the welfare of all Americans.

The members of the new commission are distinguished, able, wisely informed in the area of study, and broadly representative in the problem area.

They have my deep appreciation and, I am sure, the appreciation of all Americans for their willing dedication of their valuable time and talent to this great national purpose.

NOTE: A list of the 25 members of the Commission, of which Clarence E. Manion served as Chairman, was released with the President's statement at Lowry Air Force Base in Denver, Colo. See also Items 16, 39, above.

187 ¶ Address at the New England "Forward to '54" Dinner, Boston, Massachusetts. *September 21, 1953*

My fellow Americans:

After the embarrassing generosity of the compliments that have been paid me this evening from this platform, you can well understand that I am in some danger of thinking a little too well of myself. Thank goodness, many years ago, I had a preceptor, for whom my admiration has never died, and he had a favorite saying, one that I trust I try to live by. It was: always take your job seriously, never yourself.

Now, in spite of this embarrassment, I would like on this occasion and in front of this audience, to say just a word of my obligation to some of the political leaders that have appeared here this evening, and who do us so much honor by their presence.

I have just been introduced by Senator Saltonstall, the Chairman of the great National Defense Senate Committee, and as such a crucial and key figure in that great body. Very naturally, I am happy to be with my colleague and old friend, Chris Herter, your Governor, whom I expect again to be Governor.   And then John Lodge, Governor of Connecticut, and Governor Cross of Maine—and I shall not forget it is the northeastern of our States. And Senator George Aiken, Chairman of that great Agricultural Committee; and Secretary of Commerce, my colleague in Washington, Sinclair Weeks.   And of course, every day each of us has many reasons for feeling indebted to Ambassador Henry Cabot Lodge for his work in the United Nations.

Of course, I cannot possibly list all of the great individuals who are here this evening, but certainly I must mention my friend Governor Gregg of New Hampshire, and Lieutenant Governor Johnson, Senator Flanders; and finally I think there must be something unique that we can have here on the platform this evening both the present and the future Speaker of the House of Representatives in Washington, and the present and the next President Pro Tem of the Senate.

I suggest that a list of names such as I have just recited gives some idea of the brilliance of the political leadership that this great section of our country—the thumb of our country, if you please—has produced.   I pay here my tribute to them.

Now, ladies and gentlemen, the Republican Party is nearing the 100th Anniversary of its founding.

Now, we would be wise, I think, to recall briefly the circumstances of that event, just a few months short of 100 years ago. It came with the meeting of a small group of rebellious Whigs and disenchanted Democrats in the little town of Ripon, Wisconsin.   Other towns, understandably coveting the honors of history, dispute the particular claim of this Wisconsin community.   And indeed political dissent and disillusion were seething in those years far across town limits and state borders.   Everywhere the tremors of a divided nation were felt.   To many, the drift toward civil war seemed fatefully sure.   But there is no dispute as to the purpose inspiring the many groups who reached for a new hope and a new party which they called Republican.   That purpose, everywhere plainly defined and passionately proclaimed, was to halt the extension of the institution of slavery.

We, who shall shortly be celebrating the 100th Anniversary of that party that came so to birth, find ourselves, too, living in a time dark with the shadow of dreaded war. It is a time, too, which has seen an institution of slavery—now elevated to the awful dignity of a political philosophy and inspired with the terrible ambition of world conquest—divide not a nation, but the world, against itself. And at this precise time again there has come the summons of the American people calling upon the Republican Party to redeem the hopes of the past and to save the promise of the future.

The circumstances of this anniversary, then, call for much more than the oratory of self-congratulation. They call for more than any display—however justified—of partisan pride. For even as we meet as Republicans, our minds are troubled by problems and stirred by sentiments far transcending the self-interest of a political party. Our hearts are filled with concern for the welfare and the safety of our country. Such concern instantly and inevitably involves attention to the strength and security of the whole free world. We therefore see our Party not as an end in itself but as a magnificent means—a means through which countless thousands of devoted citizens can cooperate in the conquering of problems that beset free men everywhere. I believe, therefore, you will agree that my duty as President is to address you, not as partisans, but first, and above all, as patriots of America and citizens of the world.

In this spirit, I suggest that there is one particular and indispensable way in which each one of us can take part in this Republican Centennial. This way has none of the color of a fireworks display, none of the thrill of a political convention. It is a simple matter of faith and purpose: to define clearly and honestly, in our own minds the kind of political party in which we believe and which we propose to maintain.

To do this is, of course, not simple at all. It is to define the political institution to which our energies are dedicated—and upon which can depend even the future of freedom itself.

What I presume to suggest to you, I cannot, of course, myself evade. As your guest this evening, I have accorded myself the privilege, therefore, of addressing aloud to you some of my own thoughts on the Party in which I believe.

It is logical to look for the clearest marks of a Party in its record in office. The record of the present Administration is too short to be anything like definitive. But the facts that are plain are also indicative of deeply held ideas of the widest meaning.

There are, already in this record, these facts:

We have observed and practiced true bi-partisanship in international affairs, believing that no matter what domestic differences can create and animate parties at home we must present a substantially solid American front to all with whom we deal abroad.

We have seen a cessation of fighting in the Korean War, giving us relief from the pain of casualty lists and allowing us to work more effectively for the nation's security against threats originating anywhere in the world.

We have given to the world the clearest testimony to our firm allegiance to the common cause and needs of free peoples everywhere. We have sent shipments of wheat to Pakistan, medical and reconstruction supplies to Korea, food to Berlin. We have promised that our country will welcome tens of thousands of refugees from the terror of enslavement in lands of darkness. Recognizing that neither freedom nor safety can be found by any one nation alone, we have continued to build coalitions to promote, on a cooperative basis, the security of all.

We have lifted stifling artificial controls from our economy, counting upon the American genius for creative initiative to advance the frontiers of our prosperity beyond the hopes of past generations.

We have simplified customs regulations. Knowing that materials from abroad are as vital to our economy as foreign markets to receive our goods, we have initiated a review of our entire

593

tariff policy. This looks toward the encouragement of greater and more equitable trade among all free nations. To permit time for this, the Congress extended the Reciprocal Trade Act.

We have used the legitimate and necessary authority of the Federal Government to steady farm prices, meanwhile blueprinting the extension of social security coverage to more than 10 million unprotected citizens.

Dedicated to the fullest use of the nation's resources for the welfare of all, we have redefined policy on public power to assure the maximum of local participation and decision in projects that require the partnership of national, state and local governments.

We are continuing to study and will submit to the next session of the Congress, recommendations for making more secure our industrial peace and productivity, more clear and explicit the rights of labor, its unions and its employers.

We have undertaken with determination the work of cleaning up governmental operations, and have made extraordinary progress with this job that so badly needed doing. We have reorganized more than half a dozen major departments and agencies of the Federal Government. The introduction of top business management methods into governmental activity—while it may be painful to some—is proving its worth daily in greater efficiency and lowered costs.

We have reduced government expenditures by billions of dollars—making a balanced budget something a bit nearer to realization than an accountant's dream. The many billions of dollars cut from the requests of the prior Administration have been referred to by Senator Bridges. In addition, 6½ billions have been taken from the former estimate of the current expenditures.

We have, in our respect for priceless civil and human rights, used the Federal authority, wherever it clearly extends, to erase the stain of racial discrimination and segregation. We are making certain that every government employee is a loyal American. But we have opposed the confusing of loyalty with conformity, and all misguided attempts to convert freedom into a privilege licensed by censors.

These are some of the deeds of this Administration which serve as witnesses to some of the truths we hold. They are eloquent enough, perhaps, in certain areas. But many are little more than fragments. They suggest rather than define the character and purpose of those who support or who belong to the Republican Party.

If we turn from the legislative record of one Congressional session to the Party history of a hundred years, we learn more that is indicative—and yet little that is conclusively clear and binding upon us today.

The fact is not surprising. A century of history records the changes in institutions: it does not fix their mold. And this was a century of shattering change: from before Bismarck to after Hitler, from the Third French Empire to the Fourth French Republic, from Disraeli to Churchill, from Tsar Nicolas I to Malenkov.

Over such a span of time, the only perfectly consistent institution was a dead institution. And the Republican Party was—and is—very much alive. A fact easily forgotten is that through all those years—from the first year of War Between the States in 1861 to the first year of the New Deal in 1933—the Republican Party was in office three-fourths of the time. It helped mold each age and was itself molded by each age—the extremist Party in one day, the champion of something called "normalcy" in another. With America and with the times, it restlessly changed; sometimes growing, sometimes faltering, sometimes partially divided—in short, behaving like a normal, healthy political party in a vital, thriving Republic.

The ascendancy of the Party through the great part of this great century is the clearest answer to the feeble but persistent myth that the Republican Party is simply a conspiracy against change. The century abounds with such answers. They begin with the Emancipation Proclamation. And they continue:

In the 1860's and '70's: the Thirteenth, Fourteenth and Fif-

595

teenth Amendments; the purchase of Alaska and the Midway Islands; the First Homestead Act;

In the 1880's and '90's: creation of the Civil Service Commission; the Sherman Anti-Trust Act; the declaration of the Open Door Policy in China; the first Inter-American Conferences; the beginning of a national conservation program with the establishment of the first national forests;

And from 1900 to the 1930's: establishment of a Department of Labor and a Department of Commerce; the Pure Food and Drug Act; the strengthening of the Interstate Commerce Commission; the breaking of the great trusts; the first Bureau of Housing in the Federal Government; the first gigantic multiple-purpose dam; the model Railway Labor Act; the Kellogg-Briand Pact; the creation of a Federal Power Commission.

These deeds are the record of a Party that has grown as America has grown—seeing and meeting its needs, its responsibilities, and its aspirations.   It fears change no more than it fears life.   It knows that the two are one and the same.

Now, my friends, from all this we learn one truth: the living definition of this Party, at this moment in our history, is not to be found in the fine print of a legislative record, nor beneath the dust of our historic archives.   It can only be found in our own hearts and minds.   Born of change—born to change—this Party is and it will be what we make it.

In this sense, let us speak of the Party in which we believe.

We can—I think—define this Party first by its spirit and secondly by its principles.

Its spirit has distinctive marks.   It is young.   It is sober.   It is confident.   And it is free.

Each of these marks means something quite specific.

This Party is—and must be—young in spirit and in thought. It must be young for the simplest of reasons: because it has been charged with the hopes of the youth of America.   A new generation of Americans is looking toward us with a gaze—both hopeful and watchful—that can be neither ignored nor evaded.   For this generation's hopes for peace, for jobs, for just wages and decent homes, depend upon our foresight, our candor, our courage. And to be worthy of this trust, we must, in the deepest sense, care more for their hopes than for their votes.

This Party is sober in spirit, for its sense of responsibility makes it so. We know of no great problem before us that can be solved by the invention of a slogan. We aspire to proving ourselves more gifted in civics than in theatrics. We are more concerned with today's cares than tomorrow's headlines. We believe that there is no cleverness of phrase that can cover shallowness of thought. We confess that if America—its government and its people—is bravely to meet the trials of this age of peril, we know of no substitutes for hard work, intensive thought, constructive criticism, and a readiness to sacrifice.

This Party is, at the same time and in the same degree, confident of the future. We believe that our thinking and our emotions are unclouded by various brands of cynicism that bear the label of political sophistication. We do not think that America is decadent—nor that free nations are incapable of achieving unity—nor that free peoples are too witless to govern themselves prudently. We are confident of the strength of our physical resources—the fullness of our harvests, the speed of our assembly lines, the skills of our scientists and the stamina of our soldiers. And we are no less confident of the resources in the hearts and minds of our people.

And this Party of ours is free. We are the political captives of no section or interest of our country—and we are the prisoners of no static political or economic dogmas ruling our decisions. As a result, it is inconceivable to us to address a single group or element as a political province or dependency. And we face and make decisions not in the light of some rigidly preconceived political axiom, but in the only light in which we can clearly discern what is just—the peace and the well-being of our whole people.

And so, if I have described, however inadequately, the spirit of this Party, this brings us logically and inevitably to the stating of its principles. These—however many they may seem to be upon analysis—I venture to summarize in this one statement of belief:

We are one nation, gifted by God with the reason and the will to govern ourselves, and returning our thanks to Him by respecting His supreme creation—the free individual.

Here we stand. Here, also—if you will—are the plain moral precepts, which define our cause and govern our conduct.

We are one nation and one people.

We—this American society—are not the product of some tentative, calculating, self-interested social contract or alliance between conflicting classes and sections. We are not some perilously balanced equation of political convenience in which labor plus farm plus capital plus management equals America.

In the American design—as we perceive it—each group in our nation has special problems. None has special rights. Each has peculiar needs. None has peculiar privileges.

We believe in people, in all the people: laborer and banker, preacher and teacher, doctor, lawyer, farmer, machinist, white collar worker, housewife, miner, artist, merchant, rancher, farm hand, switchman, clerk—all of them.

The supreme belief of our society is in the dignity and freedom of the individual. To the respect of that dignity, to the defense of that freedom, all effort is pledged.

This is no mere academic assertion. This sovereign ideal uncompromisingly decrees that, in this age of peril, the security of our whole nation—the preservation of our free system—must direct every thought and every decision. We know the enemies of freedom to be equipped with the most terrible weapons of destruction. We know, then, that we can meet them with only one answer: there is no sacrifice—no labor, no tax, no service—too hard for us to bear to support a logical and necessary defense of our freedom.

I repeat: this sovereign faith of ours in the freedom and dignity of the individual is infinitely more than a dry and lifeless philosophic doctrine. It is the nerve and the fiber of our very laws.

This supreme ideal—not merely the votes of so many Congressmen or Senators—is what sends aid to drought-stricken areas, guarantees an income to farmers, banishes needless restrictions on individual enterprise, guards the free union of workers, extends the protection of social insurance to the aged and to the needy.

This sovereign ideal we believe to be the very source of the greatness and the genius of America.

In this, we proclaim nothing very new. It was seen clearly by a wise French visitor who came to America considerably more than a century ago. He patiently and persistently sought the greatness and genius of America in our fields and in our forests, in our mines and in our commerce, in our Congress and in our Constitution, and he found them not. But he sought still further and then he said:

"Not until I went into the churches of America and heard her pulpits flame with righteousness did I understand the secret of her genius and power.

"America is great because America is good—and if America ever ceases to be good—America will cease to be great."

I read those words to such an audience as this once before. It was here in Boston, 11 months ago, in this hall. The utter truth they held for me then, they hold today.

But these words contain not only a promise but a warning. And as they apply to America, so they must apply no less to the political party which is America's chosen servant in these days.

No more as a party than as a nation can we expect to find our greatness in anything but dedication to the good of America.

We can destroy our cause—even with decent intent—in a number of ways. There are as many roads to disaster.

We must shun them all.

We must, even in our patriotism, guard against that prideful nationalism which impatiently breaks the bonds binding all free peoples. For, in our age, both just principle and selfish interest conspire to impress upon us one single truth: the cause of free men is one everywhere—and the whole suffers from a wound anywhere.

We must, even in our honest political fervor, fear neither partisan criticism nor self-criticism. For the pretense of perfection is not one of the marks of good public servants.

And we must, even in our zeal to defeat the enemies of freedom, never betray ourselves into seizing their weapons to make our own defense. A people or a party that is young and sober and confident and free has no need of censors to purify its thought or stiffen its will. For the kind of America in which we believe is too strong ever to acknowledge fear—and too wise ever to fear knowledge.

This is the kind of America—and the kind of Republican Party—in which I believe.

I do not know how to define it with political labels. Such labels are, in our age, cheap and abundant. But they mean as little as they cost.

We are many things.

We are liberal—for we do believe that, in judging his own daily welfare, each citizen, however humble, has greater wisdom than any government, however great.

We are progressive—for we are less impressed with the difficulties we observed yesterday than the opportunities we envision tomorrow.

And we are conservative—for we can conceive of no higher commission that history could have conferred upon us than that which we humbly bear—the preservation, in this time of tempest and of peril, of the spiritual values that alone give dignity and meaning to man's pilgrimage on this earth.

So, in spirit, we go back through this century of wild and wondrous change, to find that, after all, certain truths have changed not at all. For the first Republican President asked himself: "What constitutes the bulwark of our own liberty and independence?" And Lincoln answered his own question.

"It is not our frowning battlements," he said, "our bristling seacoasts. Our reliance is in the love of liberty which God has planted in us. Our defense is in the spirit which prizes liberty as the heritage of all men, in all lands, everywhere."

This truth the whole last century could not change.

It is our prayer and our task that, one hundred years from now, the same can be said by this people—thankful and free and at peace.

For the great honor you have done me, ladies and gentlemen, in coming here and listening so courteously to me, I thank you humbly from the bottom of my heart.

NOTE: The President spoke at 9:30 p.m. at the Boston Garden.

The dinner was sponsored by Republican Committees and by members of the Republican National Committees in the six New England States.

188 ¶ Exchange of Messages Between the President and Chancellor Adenauer on Aid for the People of East Germany and East Berlin. *September 22, 1953*

[Released September 22, 1953. Dated September 21, 1953]

Dear Mr. Chancellor:

Thank you for your letter of August 30, 1953, in which you expressed the gratitude of the people of East Berlin and the Soviet occupied zone for the help given by the United States in the food relief program. I am glad that this program has helped to alleviate the great need of these unfortunate people whose courage in the face of oppression has been admired the world over.

At the same time you call my attention to the need for warm clothing and footwear for these same people—need which might become acute during the coming winter. I can assure you that this Government is aware of this need. It is my belief that the American people will gladly and liberally respond to your plea as many of them have done in similar situations in the past through various voluntary agencies. I shall therefore bring your letter to the attention of the American people knowing that they will contribute generously to the organizations which will undertake to provide such clothing and other required and related items.

Accept, Mr. Chancellor, the renewed assurance of my highest esteem.

Sincerely,

DWIGHT D. EISENHOWER

NOTE: Chancellor Adenauer's message follows:

My dear Mr. President:

It is with deep gratitude that the people of East Berlin and of the Soviet occupied zone receive the food relief granted them, thanks to speedy action of the United States administration. I on my part should like to express again my sincere gratitude for this relief. Your generous readiness to help these people in distress encourages me to submit to you another wish:

Winter will come within a few months, and we must reckon with the fact that the population of the East Sector and of the Soviet occupied zone will be in great need of warm clothing and footwear. The Federal Government will do everything in its power to alleviate distress in that respect as well. However, I should be particularly grateful if the United States administration would see its way of promoting that relief program by making warm clothing, underwear, stockings and shoes available to the men, women and children in the distressed areas.

Accept, Mr. President, the renewed assurance of my highest esteem.

ADENAUER

189 ¶ Remarks at the American Bankers Association Convention. *September* 22, 1953

Mr. Chairman, ladies and gentlemen:

My brief appearance before this great convention is for me a very happy opportunity. It is my pleasurable duty to invite you, on behalf of my associates in Government and of myself, to this city, and to wish for you a very successful and a very enjoyable convention.

But being here gives me opportunity to express to you something more than the ritualistic words of welcome, no matter how sincere they may be—which they are. It gives me an opportunity, for example, to thank you for your splendid work in helping sell and distribute the Government's savings bonds to all our people. With more than 40 million of them owning more than $50 billion worth of the Government's obligations, we know that there is still in our country the incentive and the determination to save—an incentive and a determination that have been responsible for so many of the good things this Nation enjoys.

Beyond this, your coming here brings to the Government a very great opportunity for cooperative work in this whole field of finances, the soundness of money, its circulation and its use.

I realize that our Secretary of the Treasury, and other members of the administration will appear before you to give you their latest thinking on certain of the important subjects that interest you. But I want to assure you, first of all, that this is not an administration that thinks it has all the answers. It is not an administration that sits up in an ivory tower of lonely isolation and gives words of wisdom that all of you must obey—or be wrong. We are here not only to do our duty in government, but to learn. And through such meetings as this, we learn a lot.

You people, with your fingers on the pulse-beat of the American economy, come here, and by your presence and by your exchange of thoughts among yourselves, and with our people, will leave us, we hope, wiser than when you came. And so for this kind of thing I come before you to thank you for your help, for your patriotic interest in the whole American scene, and what we are doing, and where we are going.

These are the things that interest America today. And they are going to be solved only as all segments of our economy and our political life meet with each other, consult with each other, and therefore reach answers that are truly American—all American, not representative of any particular class or group alone, but for all of us.

And so, for all these reasons, so haltingly expressed, I assure you that this administration and I are delighted that you are here. We consider it a great honor and a privilege to meet you, to extend greetings, and to exchange ideas.

And now my very sincere and best wishes, again, for a most enjoyable convention, and hoping that you will come back again.

Thank you very much.

NOTE: The President spoke at 10:02 a.m. in Constitution Hall. His opening words "Mr. Chairman" referred to W. Harold Brenton, President of the American Bankers Association.

190 ¶ Remarks at the First Meeting of the Commission on Foreign Economic Policy. *September 22, 1953*

NO GROUP of citizens has been called to a higher mission than the one on which you are setting forth today.

The economic health of our own country and that of other friendly nations depends in good measure on the success of your work. Your task is to find acceptable ways and means of widening and deepening the channels of economic intercourse between ourselves and our partners of the free world. It is essential that we help develop new markets for our great productive power and at the same time assist other nations to earn their own living in the world.

Because your inquiry is so basic, you will encounter difficulties— some old and some new. In dealing with them, I commend to you an attitude both realistic and bold. Above all, I urge you to follow one guiding principle: what is best in the national interest.

NOTE: The Commission on Foreign Economic Policy, consisting of 7 members appointed by the President, 5 members from the Senate appointed by the Vice President, and 5 members from the House of Representatives appointed by the Speaker, was established by title III of the Trade Agreements Extension Act of 1953 (67 Stat. 473). Clarence B. Randall served as Chairman. See also Item 161.

191 ¶ Remarks to the Members of the United States Committee for United Nations Day.
September 23, 1953

Mr. Watson, ladies and gentlemen:

There is obviously one deep and abiding bond that joins us together—those of us here this morning. You have faith and belief in the United Nations, and so do I. Mr. Watson has thanked me for my efforts on its behalf. Rather, I think, it is up to me, as the political head of this Government, to thank each of you for your voluntary efforts in support of that great institution.

With all its defects, with all the failures that we can check up against it, it still represents man's best organized hope to substitute the conference table for the battlefield. It has had its failures, but it has had its successes. Who knows what could have happened in these past years of strain and struggle if we hadn't had the United Nations? I think it is far more than merely a desirable organization in these days. Where every new invention of the scientist seems to make it more nearly possible for man to insure his own elimination from this globe, I think the United Nations has become sheer necessity.

So when I thank each of you, I am thanking you not only as an official act from a government that is committed irrevocably to the support of this United Nations, but I am thanking you for having the wisdom to see what the alternatives are facing humanity and civilization in the world today and, moreover, for your initiative, your readiness to go forward and support something so necessary to decency, to justice, and to peace in the world.

And that is my word of thanks. Goodbye.

NOTE: Immediately before the President spoke, Thomas J. Watson, Chairman of the U.S. Committee for United Nations Day, presented him with a bound volume containing testimonials of member organizations reaffirming their support of and belief in the United Nations. The President spoke at 9:30 a.m. in the Rose Garden at the White House.

192   ¶ Remarks to the Fall Meeting of the President's Committee on Employment of the Physically Handicapped.   *September* 23, 1953

Admiral McIntire, and ladies and gentlemen:

There are many commissions and committees that carry with them the title of President's committee or commission. There is none that engages the interests of my heart, or of which I am prouder, than this one.

I should like to explain a little bit of the very intimate interest I have in your work. I was one of those individuals that was designated in World War II to bear heavy field responsibility for the execution of America's purposes abroad, and that inevitably resulted in sorrow, in disaster, coming to many American homes.

Every man who had to bear such responsibilities, whether he were a corporal or a five-star general, if he were concerned at all with America as such and with the people he led, could not escape the prayerful hope, almost the fear, concerning the possibility that he might cause one unnecessary death, or one unnecessary disablement of an individual. He lived with it all the time—how to attain these purposes with the least distress to America's citizenry, and to the allied citizenry.

So, out of that grew the hope that those people could do something to help alleviate the results of that kind of action. I see General Eaker here this morning, my old comrade-in-arms, who went with me throughout the entire war. I have no doubt that the feelings I am so haltingly trying to express are shared fully by him—whatever he could do by way of interest, in the way of helpfulness, to let people know who had to suffer, who had to pay part of America's cost for achieving its purposes, are not irrevocably condemned to a life of inactivity or uselessness.

So this Committee, in doing the work that you are doing for the gainful, profitable employment of people who otherwise might be considered completely unfit—I must assure you, that you have the heartfelt support of every man who has had to bear the kind of responsibility that I have referred to.

I will tell you a little story. In about the early part of 1944, I had a corps that was not performing quite in the way I thought it should, and of course the trouble was the commander. I sent to Washington and gave them the name of the man I wanted. I got a telegram back from General Marshall, which said: "I agree with you, he is a very fine leader, but he is in the hospital; he has arthritis in the knees and the doctors won't give him a clear bill of health. I am afraid we can't send him."

And I sent back a message which said: "Please send this man right away quickly. It's his head and his heart I want. I will carry him to battle on a litter, for a man simply because he has arthritis in the knees is still fitted to do the job I want."

I am trying to show you that we can, after all, even in war, over-emphasize this question of complete physical normalcy.

Incidentally, you will be glad to know the sequel was that that man led his corps brilliantly throughout the rest of the war, and fully met every expectation I had of him.

Now, in the work you do, if there comes a time when you think a word of mine, an act of mine, can help along in this grand thing your are doing, you have only to command me. Certainly, in that respect, I am your servant. I am forever obligated to you for what you are doing.

Thank you very much.

NOTE: The President spoke at 10:40 a.m. in the Departmental Auditorium. In his opening words he referred to Vice Admiral Ross T. McIntire, Chairman of the President's Committee on Employment of the Physically Handicapped. Later in his remarks he referred to Lt. Gen. Ira C. Eaker (Ret.) and General of the Army George C. Marshall.

193   ¶ Message to the 72d Annual Convention of the American Federation of Labor in St. Louis.

September 23, 1953

[Text read by the Vice President]

TO THE 72d Annual Convention of the American Federation of Labor, I send my sincere good wishes.   In this expression, I am certain that all Americans heartfully join.

We Americans are proud of our trade unions.   Their history of honorable achievement, spanning more than a half century, testifies to the wisdom and strength of free labor.   The reward of that history for labor—in partnership with resourceful capital, enlightened management and inventive genius—has been the attainment of the highest standard of living man has ever achieved.

This triumph has meant much more than the amassing of worldly goods and their generous distribution through our whole society.   It has meant proof that free men can know the blessings of both abundance and justice—beyond all boasts or dreams of slave economies.   And it has meant, in time of desperate peril to our nation, the strength enabling free men everywhere to beat back the assaults of totalitarian aggression.

From the ranks of labor have come other contributions to the nation.   These have been things of the spirit: the selfless devotion of working men and women and their leaders to the whole public welfare—reasoned respect for the rights and needs of others—deep love of country, inspiring a patriotism no less meaningful in mine and factory than on the battlefield.

I state these facts not as sentimental tributes but as the basic and unshakable convictions of this Administration.   They are neither lightly spoken nor loosely held.   They are principles governing our understanding of labor and the making of every decision concerning labor.

I had the honor of appearing before your convention last year before my election as President.   I said then that I believed that all slanted, partisan appeals to the men and women of labor—any design to make of them a kind of political bloc—was an affront to the dignity of labor and a disservice to the unity of America. I believe that still.

I also gave you a pledge. It was in these words: "To the limit my judgment can discern, you will always get both justice and fairness from me . . . I will always try to be a true friend of labor." And *that* is no less true today.

There is nothing remarkable about this. It is the sense and sentiment of every thoughtful American. So, while judgments on labor problems may frankly and forcefully differ on specific ways and means at specific times, they are honest judgments held by men of good will as to what will best serve labor's interests. Such differences are healthy and constructive so long as the final goals are always kept in view—a vigorous and free trade union movement, a healthy and thriving industry, and the betterment of all the people.

I know that your convention will, in this spirit, deliberate on many critical issues before you.

Of this deliberation, a great part will focus on changes in the Labor-Management Relations Act, 1947, generally known as the Taft-Hartley Act.

This legislation affects virtually every sector of our economic life. Its discussion is too serious to be governed by passion and invective, rather than cool reason and common sense. Epithets of "anti-labor" or "anti-industry" and the like are worse than empty. They are utterly obsolete in a climate of opinion and understanding that realizes the folly of class hostility.

The issues at stake are not the possessions of a class or group. They are not the partisan property of any political party. They belong to the whole of America—and so must the hearts and minds resolving them.

I frankly repeat the estimate of the Taft-Hartley Act which I have stated often in the past. And even though the past six years have revealed a number of defects which should be corrected, I believe that its enactment was a substantial contribution to the quest for sounder labor-management relations. I believe that the experience under the Act has confirmed its essential soundness.

These defects have been under critical study by this Administration. The objectives of this study have been and continue to be these:

(1) to remedy defects which cause concern on the part of working men and women over possible results or uses of the Act to their detriment;

(2) to insure administration of the Act in the manner that is efficient, speedy, and impartial;

(3) to allow freedom for the healthy growth of trade unions, while respecting the legitimate rights of individual workers, their employers, and the general public;

(4) to work to the end that there be less rather than more Government interference in labor-management affairs.

These are distinct, clearly defined purposes. I believe them worthy of the confident support of all thoughtful Americans.

These purposes have governed our actions from the outset. Shortly after the new Administration took office, and after a series of preliminary conferences, you will recall that I entrusted this study of the Taft-Hartley Act to an informal committee, consisting of Executive officials and Legislative leaders who had an intimate knowledge of the Act and its operation. This committee immediately went to work—holding the most detailed discussions week after week.

In the work of this committee, the wealth of knowledge and experience of the Honorable Martin Durkin, then Secretary of Labor, was an asset of great value. Losing the benefit of that knowledge and experience was considered unfortunate by me and by every member of the committee. We all regretted the necessity he felt of returning to private life.

While this committee has not as yet completed its task and submitted its recommendations to me, it has, since the start of its deliberations, considered many specific proposals for amendment of the Act, and is in substantial accord on a heartening number of these. Its deliberations are continuing, and you can be assured that its members from time to time will seek the counsel of your leaders. It will make its recommendations to me before the end of the year. These recommendations—together with such others as I may receive—will have my most careful study. I shall send my own suggestions to the Congress at the opening of its session in January.

I think I fully appreciate the importance of all of this deliberation to American labor—and to America itself. The progress already made has been great and looks toward the fulfillment, at the coming session of Congress, of the pledges we made last year.

I venture one further thought. Serious as is the particular piece of legislation dominating the thoughts of your convention, it manifestly is but a part of the great problems facing American labor today.

These problems reach from the humblest home and smallest workshop in our land to the most distant areas of this troubled earth. The nourishing of the spirit of freedom in our land—its churches, its universities, its unions, its every public forum; the arming of our defenses; the stimulation of healthy world trade; the vigilant guarding of civil rights; the firm development of a government of integrity and clear purpose—all these are the vital concerns of our free unions who themselves can only live in freedom, or die with it.

I know that this awareness is within you all.

I know that American labor, now as in the past, will grasp these great issues as essentially its own, and with greatness of heart and strength of mind, meet them with the wisdom which has already put free men everywhere forever in its debt.

DWIGHT D. EISENHOWER

194　¶　Letter to the Chairman, Air Coordinating Committee, Requesting a Review of Aviation Policy.　*September 23, 1953*

Dear Mr. Murray:

The increasing importance of aviation as an instrument of national policy and to our national welfare makes it desirable that there be available to the government agencies, the aviation industry, and the public, a clear and comprehensive statement of the aviation policies of this Administration.

In a field so dynamic as aviation, our policies and programs must be flexible and capable of growth. It has been over five years since a broad review of U.S. aviation policy was completed; many events of major significance have occurred in the interim.

I therefore request that you, as Chairman of the Air Coordinating Committee, direct it to undertake a comprehensive review of our aviation policy, and to prepare a statement of present United States policies in the primary areas of aviation interest, for my consideration and approval. This should be done in consultation with appropriate industry, local government and private aviation groups.

Sincerely,

Dwight D. Eisenhower

NOTE: The statement requested by the President was submitted by Chairman Robert B. Murray, Jr., in the form of a report dated May 1, 1954, and entitled "Civil Air Policy" (Government Printing Office, 1954, 71 pp.).

195 ¶ Memorandum Directing Federal Agencies To Participate in a Civil Defense Exercise.
September 25, 1953

To the Heads of Executive Departments and Agencies:

The need for effective civil defense planning is still vital to our national welfare. But national plans and preparations are of little value without active participation at local community levels. The Director of the Office of Civil Defense for the District of Columbia, through the Deputy Director of Federal Buildings Services, has again scheduled a Civil Defense Exercise to be held on November 5, 1953. I recognize that such tests are essential to the proper training of Federal employees in their local civil defense duties and I continue to urge all Departments and Agencies to prepare for these exercises to the fullest extent possible.

Accordingly, it is directed that each Department and Agency of the Executive Branch of the Federal Government in the Metropolitan Area of Washington participate in the Civil Defense Exercise which will be held on November 5, 1953.

DWIGHT D. EISENHOWER

196 ¶ Message Recorded for the United Community Fund Campaigns.
September 27, 1953

[Broadcast over all television and radio networks]

My fellow Americans:

I have spoken to you in recent months about some very big and serious problems—problems that have to do with our very life as a nation, and with the future peace and security of all free people. These have been grim problems, involving clashing wills and conflicting purposes. Many of them have seemed to present a picture of man's inhumanity to man.

Tonight I am glad to talk to you informally about the other side of that picture—about man's humanity to man. Let us never forget that side of the picture. For it is part of the great religious and spiritual heritage that all men share as children of God. Our task is to release it and to put it to work in the world.

But first, let's put it to work in our hometown communities.

That is what we shall be doing next week when, in some 1700 cities and towns throughout the United States and Canada, the United Community Campaigns will get under way.

These campaigns will be called by different names—the Community Chest, the United Fund, the Good Neighbor Crusade—but they will have one common purpose. That purpose will be to raise, through one united campaign instead of many scattered appeals, the funds needed by the voluntary health, welfare, and recreation agencies of each community.

In every community of our land there are children who need help, adults who are sick in body and troubled in mind, handicapped people who want the chance to live normal, useful lives, lonely old folks who need comfort and kindness. These are the people who, in each town and city, are helped by the community compaigns.

National organizations also, fighting disease and misfortune, benefit from these campaigns. The United Defense Fund, with its USO and its Camp Shows, is another of the vitally important organizations which gain every time one of us contributes to a community fund.

But no cause gains more dramatically from these contributions than the cause of democracy itself. For every united campaign is an inspiring symbol of that great characteristic of democracy— the volunteer spirit. The true slogan of a true democracy is not "Let the government do it." The true slogan is, "Let's do it ourselves." In this spirit, citizens from all walks of life, of all religious faiths and racial backgrounds, unite annually to work and to give together. This is the spirit of a people dedicated to helping themselves—and to each other.

The united community campaigns hope to realize a total of 280 million dollars. This is a big undertaking—but it is not too big for this great nation. I am confident that you will give generously to the volunteer worker who visits you in your home or your place of business.

He will be speaking for man's humanity to man.

He will be speaking for America.

197 ¶ Statement by the President on the Death of Mayor Ernst Reuter of West Berlin. *September 29, 1953*

THE SUDDEN DEATH of Mayor Ernst Reuter of West Berlin is a great loss not only to the citizens of his city and country but also to the peoples of the free world. Mayor Reuter was a born leader. His was a rare combination of talents, including courage, intelligence, energy, and dedication to the cause of freedom. Liberty-loving people everywhere will mourn his passing and salute his memory.

198 ¶ The President's News Conference of *September 30, 1953.*

THE PRESIDENT. Of course, I don't suppose that there is any more important news than that world series—if a fellow just had any advance information about it.

I could start off, I think, by confirming something that is certainly by no means news any more—that is, that I intend to designate Governor Earl Warren as Chief Justice of the United States.

615

There has been an item in the press that I should like to make an observation about: it is this forced retirement of Cardinal Wyszynski in Poland.

I think that the heart of America resents this kind of thing very deeply. I believe we understand that without freedom of religion and freedom of thought, without some evidence that the other side is ready to honor it, observe it, at least in some measurable degree, that it makes very discouraging the effort to reach real understanding in the world.

I have no doubt the State Department may have some formal statement on the incident. For myself, I must say I consider it a discouraging development.

As you know, just before Congress adjourned, the administration asked that the debt limit be raised so as to provide the certainty that all bills could be met on time when presented.

The savings in expenditures that we have been able to make, the study of the September 15 tax receipts, make it appear that no special session will be necessary and that we will get through to January and still have something left.

I don't announce that with complete certainty, but that certainly is what the probabilities are at the moment. So we don't anticipate any special session unless, of course, there is some radical change, some unexpected thing. I would assume you would understand that such a caution as that is implicit in anything I should say in the way of prediction.

I notice that there continues to be speculation about a retail sales tax in this country by the Federal Government.

For many years, I think, I personally have put my adverse conclusions on such a tax so far as the Federal Government is concerned, and made them public long before I ever thought that I would be in a place I had any responsibility about it.

The Treasury Department has made a study, however, and they find that all of the logic in the situation is that this is a field that belongs to local municipalities and States, and not to the

Federal Government. Certainly, therefore, they have no intention of trying to do otherwise.

Now, those are a few of the subjects that struck me as having some immediate interest for you as I came over. So, as usual, we will take the rest of the period for questioning.

Q. Merriman Smith, United Press: Mr. President, since we last saw you there has been an announcement that the Russians have at least the knowledge and possibly the ability to make a thermonuclear bomb. Does this knowledge or will this knowledge have any effect on your planning for defense spending next year?

THE PRESIDENT. Quite naturally, this is a material or physical fact of the utmost importance to the world. Particularly, it makes us more interested than ever in determining just what are the intentions of the U.S.S.R. and their associated countries in honestly attempting to reach some kind of negotiated situation in which all of us can have confidence.

Now, the knowledge that they have this bomb is, of course, an acute one for the Defense Department. I should say that it is a fact that is probably causing each of us more earnest study—you might say almost prayerful study—than any other thing that has occurred lately. I might say, in connection with that, that I do hope when I can get sorted out in my own mind and with my advisers exactly how we should approach this whole subject of the international situation, the relief of tension in the world, and this growing destructiveness of the world's armaments, when I can get that all straightened out, I expect to go before the United States and tell them—be very frank in telling them—the facts on which my studies have been based and the conclusions that the administration and I have reached. Just when this can be done I am not prepared to say; because it is very, very intricate, and any attempt to do this is very apt to react in a number of ways.

But we have friends abroad; we must be very careful that they understand always we have one intention in the world—peace. We don't want any war, and anyone who has had certainly the kind of experience with war that I have had can say this with such a passion, almost, as to put war at the very last of any possible solutions to the world's difficulties.

I believe we have gone far enough in this so you could say that the only possible tragedy greater than winning a war would be losing it. Just war should be out from the calculations of all of us, and we should proceed from there.

Now we want all of our friends to understand this thoroughly; but because we have to talk from positions of strength, and because we have to take rudimentary precautions for our own security, we will not quail from any sacrifice necessary to provide that security.

If you don't look out, these intentions are misunderstood, and badly misunderstood. They say we are pugnacious or we are impulsive or we have lost all faith in the conference table. Now those things are far from the truth; they are to the contrary of the truth, and so we must be very careful.

Another thing is, you don't want to frighten anyone to death in this world. As I have said to you before, frightened people cannot make good decisions. So, therefore, you have to understand our own strength—the strength of the free world, the strength of America—at the very same time that you are weighing also our dangers and our risks.

So, after this rather roundabout way of answering your question, Mr. Smith, the fact is that anyone would be foolish to try to shut their eyes to the significance of the event of which you speak.

Q. Raymond P. Brandt, St. Louis Post-Dispatch: Mr. President, the chief justiceship is probably the second most important position in Government. Can you tell us the process by which you reached the selection of Governor Warren, whom you consulted, and what qualifications you sought?

THE PRESIDENT. I saw in the paper a statement that very aptly summarized my own viewpoint.

From the very beginning, from the moment of the unfortunate death of my great friend, Mr. Vinson, I have been thinking over this whole thing. I certainly wanted a man whose reputation for integrity, honesty, middle-of-the-road philosophy, experience in Government, experience in the law, were all such as to convince the United States that here was a man who had no ends to serve except the United States, and nothing else. Naturally, I wanted a man who was healthy, strong, who had not had any serious illnesses, and who was relatively young—if you can call a man of approximately my age relatively young—relatively young with respect to some others that I was thinking of.

On balance, to my mind he is a man who will make a great Chief Justice; and so I selected him.

Q. Mr. Brandt: May I ask another question as a newspaperman? Is it going to be the policy of this administration to leak such important news to friendly newspapers?

THE PRESIDENT. I don't know whether I could stand here in front of this group and give a quick answer to that. I think that I have trusted subordinates who may occasionally leak news for purposes they consider proper. If they do, I don't think I would interfere with them.

Q. Mr. Brandt: I mean, we would like to understand the ground rules because we are under a handicap, and if the others get it a whole——

THE PRESIDENT. Let me tell you on that—if there are any complaints, I wish you would put them down in complete detail in front of Mr. Hagerty, who will bring them to me. I didn't know there were any complaints, and I would not want to take in front of such a body as this and give an answer to you when I am not acquainted with details, and don't want to give snap answers that could lead us all into trouble.

If there is anyone here that has ever found me in a position that he thought I was not trying to be fair, I would like to hear that also.

I have been meeting with the press now for a good long 12 years, I think, and I certainly try to play fair with all of them.

Q. Francis M. Stephenson, New York Daily News: Mr. President, if your subordinates are going to leak news, I would appreciate it if you would include us in on it! [*Laughter*]

Q. Robert L. Riggs, Louisville Courier-Journal: Mr. President, you used the words "retail sales tax." Do you include in that the general manufacturers excise tax?

THE PRESIDENT. Well, you have excise taxes, and always have had, in our country. You will understand that we are now working really night and day on a tax program to present to the Congress when it meets again, and you could not expect me to go into details of exactly what we are going to do and exactly what we are not going to do. We are certainly going to try to be equitable and we certainly are going to try to make an efficient tax.

Q. Joseph A. Loftus, New York Times: What qualifications are you looking for in the Secretary of Labor, and when do you expect to appoint one?

THE PRESIDENT. On that one, I will give you an answer that I think I have never given anyone yet in this thing, and that is "No comment."

Q. Mr. Loftus: One more question, sir: can you say whether you suggested that Martin Durkin take another position in the administration?

THE PRESIDENT. No, I have made no suggestion.

Q. William H. Lawrence, New York Times: Mr. President, in your reply just a moment ago on the tax question, can you tell us the general policy that you are looking for in this tax study? Do you expect higher taxes, lower taxes, about the same general revenues?

THE PRESIDENT. Very obviously, the whole take from the United States, that is, the whole take in this Federal budget, has to be gauged against what you have to spend.

Now, the Security Council has been studying these problems all summer long. After each one the executive has come to see me; we have gone over this whole thing. It is a question of expenditures, and, therefore, the kind of a tax program that will give the necessary revenue.

In connection with that, you will know that we have this commission on the relationship between States and localities and the Federal Government now studying, and unquestionably they will have something to say about it. We are trying to produce tax programs that are fair and just and will produce the necessary revenue. What the exact amounts are going to be, I can't possibly tell you.

Q. Jay G. Hayden, Detroit News: Sir, not to be repetitious, but to avoid misunderstanding, you seem to have definitely eliminated the retail sales tax, but in answer to Mr. Riggs' question, I gather you do not so definitely eliminate the possibility of a manufacturers tax?

THE PRESIDENT. I didn't eliminate anything. I said that there have always been excise taxes in this country of some kind. Now, just exactly how those will be reassorted, I don't know. That is part of the Treasury's planning at this moment.

Q. Mr. Hayden: But it is still in study?

THE PRESIDENT. I am saying I am making no further statement outside of the fact that this retail tax—which seemed to bother everyone so much—I state that we are not going into that.

Q. J. Newman Wright, Passaic Herald-News: Do you intend, sir, to take any part in the gubernatorial campaign in New Jersey, that is, make speeches?

THE PRESIDENT. Me?

Q. Mr. Wright: Yes, sir.

THE PRESIDENT [*laughing*]. I don't want to be too facetious, but sometimes I think that words just fall on the desert air.

I have constantly stated I will not participate in local campaigns. They are not my business. So what I am trying to do is, here, with an administration of trusted associates, in cooperation with the Congress, to set a record that people who want to support that administration have a good foundation on which to stand. That is my job, not to go into these local contests.

Q. Carroll H. Kenworthy, United Press: I want to ask about the bases agreement signed with Spain last Saturday; are you pleased with that agreement and what is the significance of it?

THE PRESIDENT. What is what?

Q. Mr. Kenworthy: What is the significance of the agreement?

THE PRESIDENT. Well, the significance of the agreement is that it is a *quid pro quo;* they had certain things that we need and are valuable to us, and we made certain arrangements in order to get those things.

I might say that this thing has been in the mill for a long time, has been thoroughly discussed with congressional leaders, and we believe it is something that will work to the benefit of the United States.

Q. Robert E. Clark, International News Service: Do you intend to use your Taft-Hartley injunction powers to halt the scheduled midnight dock strike?

THE PRESIDENT. Actually, a communication on this subject just reached the White House—just within a matter of hours, I think. It has been referred to the Labor Department, and I will be advised on it sometime during the day. Just what will happen I don't know.

Q. William P. Flythe, Jr., Hearst Newspapers: Mr. President, may I ask you about these international conferences, have you anything to say, sir—these proposed international conferences?

THE PRESIDENT. Well, the State Department, of course, keeps me constantly advised of what has been proposed. They are studying as to how we can take full advantage of any opportunity to discuss in friendly and understanding fashion with the U.S.S.R. and others the problems facing the world.

Certainly we want to release and lower tensions, but exactly how and when to do these things is a difficult matter. We don't want to do things in such a way as to make things worse instead of better.

So we have not had the final word on that.

Q. G. Gould Lincoln, Washington Star: Do you expect the

Chief Justice to be here when Court opens?

THE PRESIDENT. Yes, I do. Actually, of course, it was one reason that I felt we must not tarry too long with it, because there is a full job to do.

Q. Carlton Kent, Chicago Sun-Times: Mr. President, do you expect to reschedule the Bermuda conference with the British and French Prime Ministers that was postponed this summer?

THE PRESIDENT. Well, it has not come up as yet. As a matter of fact, I don't know anything about the Prime Minister's health. It has not been suggested to me at all.

Q. Mr. Marin, International News Service: Mr. President, the visit of your brother, Dr. Milton Eisenhower, to Latin America has aroused great hopes of an improvement in relations between the United States and Latin American countries. Twenty Latin American countries now are anxious to know when Dr. Milton Eisenhower will present officially his report to you.

THE PRESIDENT. As a matter of fact, I think it will be very soon. He came down to see me on Sunday. There have been some personal things happened, including some very serious illness, and so on, that prevented him from doing some of the things that he would otherwise have done. But it will come along, I think, very soon. That is what he told me—he expected to deal with it very soon.

Q. Mr. Marin: And that will be a basis for a new study of the policies, would you say, between——

THE PRESIDENT. Of course. I will tell you, my brother is too smart a man to think he learned all about our Latin American friends in one 6-week trip through their countries, but he certainly came back with a tremendous admiration and a hopefulness about the situation. He will, therefore, make suggestions to our State Department, and I am certain of this, they will not ignore them; they will study them sympathetically. [*Laughter*] I meant that, my friends, in the kindliest of ways because—[*laughter*]—I want to assure you they are the ones that asked my brother to go. So I assume that they are serious.

When that is done, I imagine that they may even publish parts or all of his report; I don't know.[1]

Q. Mr. Marin: May I state on behalf of the South American press that he was a wonderful Ambassador, your brother.

THE PRESIDENT. Thank you very much; thank you.

Q. Marvin L. Arrowsmith, Associated Press: I do not know whether your earlier remark on the labor situation applies to this or not, but I have been requested to ask you. As you know, former Secretary of Labor Durkin said that you broke an agreement on the proposed Taft-Hartley changes; Vice President Nixon said you didn't, and it was all apparently a misunderstanding. Could we have your version on that conflict?

THE PRESIDENT. I will not give you a version on that conflict because, as you people know, I have consistently refused ever to speak of a personality publicly. It is not my business as President.

I will say this: to my knowledge, I have never broken an agreement with any associate of mine in my life. If I have ever broken an agreement, it was something that I did not understand was made. Now, I have never broken one that I know of. And if there is anyone here who has contrary evidence, he can have the floor and make his speech.

Q. Milton B. Freudenheim, Akron Beacon Journal: Mr. President, can you tell us when you will announce permission to sell the synthetic rubber industry?

THE PRESIDENT. No, I can't because it has not come up to me yet, and I can't do it. I will have them look it up and see if there is something on it.

Q. Alice A. Dunnigan, Associated Negro Press: Recent statements from the Department of Defense indicate that integration in schools on military posts may be delayed until 1955. I understand that Senator Humphrey has brought this matter to your attention by letter stating that such delays were unnecessary.

---

[1] Dr. Milton Eisenhower's report, entitled "United States-Latin American Relations," was released by the White House on November 22, 1953. The report is published in the Department of State Bulletin (vol. 29, p. 695).

THE PRESIDENT. Who brought it to me?

Q. Mrs. Dunnigan: Senator Humphrey of Minnesota.

THE PRESIDENT. I have not seen it.

Q. Mrs. Dunnigan: You have not seen it?

THE PRESIDENT. I have not seen the letter.

Q. Mrs. Dunnigan: I was going to ask was there any reply yet?

THE PRESIDENT. No. I will have Mr. Hagerty look it up and let you know; I haven't seen it.

Q. Mrs. Dunnigan: Have you any comment on this issue?

THE PRESIDENT. No; this is the first time that it has come up this fall.

Q. Edward T. Folliard, Washington Post: I see some of our colleagues are straining at the barrier here, but I have a request to make of you, sir, and that is that you alternate these news conferences, holding some in the forenoon, some in the afternoon.

As it is, the afternoon papers invariably get the break on the news. By the time the story gets to the morning papers much of the life has gone out of it, and it would make a lot of us happier if you would.

THE PRESIDENT. Mr. Folliard, I am willing to take a look at it. Remember this, though, that there is also a President of the United States involved in these things, and the burden of adjusting these things into a schedule that, in spite of some adverse comment, is really a busy one and a burdensome one. [*Laughter*] It is pretty tough; and to come down into the afternoon where you ordinarily try to get some hours to devote to your study, to going after papers rather than to meeting people, and conferences, it could raise some difficulties with me.

I am perfectly ready to look at it as sympathetically as I know how, because certainly I have no reason for favoring one group over the other. I would be glad to talk it over with Mr. Hagerty.

Merriman Smith, United Press: Thank you, Mr. President.

NOTE: President Eisenhower's fifteenth news conference was held in the Executive Office Building from 11:30 to 11:54 o'clock on Wednesday morning, September 30, 1953. In attendance: 239.

199   ¶ Statement by the President: National Newspaper Week.   *September 30, 1953*

To the Newspapers of the Nation:

National Newspaper Week prompts us all to renew our awareness of the remarkable national service rendered daily by the newspapers of America.

Our free press does more than tell our people the history of our times. It explains that history, interprets it, and, so doing, often actually helps to create that history.

A free press and a free society are essentially one. As the press can know freedom only in a democratic state, so democracy itself is fortified by a free press.

This strengthening of our society is, of course, the antithesis of the ignoble service performed by the press of totalitarian countries. The effectiveness of a free press is virtually to be measured by the integrity, candor and responsibility of its criticism.

On this occasion I am happy to send warm greetings to the reporters, editors and publishers of our Nation's newspapers. I know—as they must themselves—that they are custodians of a majestic trust, a solemn responsibility: to help arm our people with the knowledge and understanding without which free choice, free government, free men could not be.

DWIGHT D. EISENHOWER

200   ¶ Joint Statement by the President and President Remón Cantera of Panama.   *October 1, 1953*

IN THE SPIRIT of the close friendship that unites the peoples and Governments of Panama and the United States, we have considered the main aspects of the unique relations existing between the two countries prompted by an earnest desire to make such relations as satisfactory as possible.

In our conversations we have dealt mainly with that part of our relations which springs directly from the fact that the canal which connects the waters of the two oceans and the zone adjacent thereto run through the heart of the territory of Panama and, therefore, certain questions have arisen, the solution of which is of great importance.

In considering these relationships, we have deemed it opportune in the first place to reiterate the basic principles set forth by our governments in 1933 and 1936.

We have agreed that these basic principles applicable to the relations between the two countries should have as a consequence the adoption of measures tending to make them more effective to the end that there should be an equitable benefiting of the two nations which made possible the construction of a canal as well as an enabling of the commerce and industry of Panama to take advantage of the market offered by the Canal Zone and by the ships transiting the Canal.

We have equally agreed that inasmuch as the two countries have a mutual and vital interest in the work of the Panama Canal, the principle of equality of opportunity and treatment must have full effect in regard to the citizens of Panama and the United States employed in the Canal Zone as set forth in the exchange of notes of March 2, 1936 on this subject and that wherever circumstances should be found which in any manner interfere with the observance of that principle, appropriate measures will be taken by the United States.

In conformity with the first of the two principles, above stated, we have recognized the advisability of giving due consideration, in the cases of lands granted in the past for Canal purposes which are no longer needed for such purposes in order that arrangements may be agreed upon for the transfer of those lands to the Republic of Panama.

It is extremely gratifying that the commissions set up by the two governments to review our relations and the operation of our treaties are already at work with a view to entering into any arrangements that may be found necessary to insure for the future a mutually advantageous and satisfactory relationship.

The President of the Republic of Panama has expressed during the course of these conversations his deep appreciation for the cordial and friendly attitude of the President of the United States and has reiterated the expressions of sincere friendship which animate the people and Government of Panama in respect of the people and Government of the United States of America, and also has expressed his full solidarity with the United States in the defense of democracy and Panama's unflinching will to cooperate with it, as the Republic has already done in the two world wars, in the maintenance of peace and security within a free world.

The President of the United States on his part has expressed the interest of the people and Government of the United States in the welfare of the people and Government of Panama. He has assured the President of the Republic of Panama that all of the points which the representatives of Panama desire to raise would receive the most sympathetic consideration in the light of the especially close relations existing between the two countries. In view of the nature of the special bonds between the two countries he has expressed the desire of the United States to continue to cooperate in the development of Panama's national economy.

It is felt that this meeting has achieved a high measure of mutual understanding and confidence which in the common interest of the two nations and of the free world must characterize the ties between them.

201 ¶ Remarks at Dedication of Red Cross
Chapter House for the District of Columbia.
October 1, 1953

Mr. Folger, ladies and gentlemen:

This morning, as the time drew near for me to come over to
this dedicatory ceremony, a very efficient staff officer undertook
to give me the accustomed briefing. I have been plied with facts
about this building, the number of activities that will take place
within it, about the character of the blood donor campaign in
Washington, your great and admirable degree of participation in
Red Cross work.

Obviously, he thought I should talk about these things. But
I have the prerogative of disregarding advice, which I seem often
to do, and I decided that each of you workers knew more about
such things and these statistics than did I, and it would add very
little to your education, and certainly nothing to your entertainment for me to repeat them.

Rather, I decided, in the minute or two that I should like to
impose on you this morning, to resume the effort that I have
been making now for 11 years. For me it is a frustrating effort.
It has been an effort to try to explain to the Red Cross, whenever
I have met with any body of its representatives, what it means
to me, and how deep is the sense of appreciation during those 11
years I have felt toward it.

I once participated in another dedication of a Red Cross building. It was in early June in London, England, 1942, and it was
my first real war contact of that war with the Red Cross. It was
a building far different from this one—partly bomb-riddled. But
there, as I saw those people mobilizing to do their part in the war,
to care for the wounded in the hospitals, to look after the sick, to
look after the correspondence of those who couldn't do it, to run
clubs of entertainment, to adhere to the slogan they had, "A home
away from home," and the service of the Red Cross employees,

including being a companion to some lonely soldiers as they went to the early movies of those days, or things as menial as scrubbing floors—from that time on as I have followed them, and they have gone along with the armies in the field, I have been trying to tell the Red Cross what they mean to me. As I say, I have never succeeded. I doubt that I ever shall.

But this morning, one idea I would like to express is a simple one. We have many examples nowadays of man's selfishness, man's brutality and inhumanity to man, man's readiness to forget the golden rule and to live by some standard that he thinks will immediately advantage him at the expense of his fellows. We have this in the international field; we have it far too often and discouragingly among groups or classes at home. The Red Cross, the nature of its slogan, of its purposes, the work that has been done through it, and the people that belong to it, bring to us, as we tend to greater discouragement about such things, realization that man is also made of nobler qualities than these of selfishness and greed and personal advantage. He is made up also of sacrifice, of neighborliness, of love for fellow humans.

It seems to me that the Red Cross personifies, as nearly as any organization of which I can think, those great and noble virtues of man that are the richest heritage from the Almighty.

I thank you very much for the honor of being invited to participate in the dedication of this building to that kind of purpose.

NOTE: The President spoke at 12:10 p.m. His opening words referred to John C. Folger, Chairman of the District of Columbia Chapter of the American National Red Cross.

202 ¶ Remarks to State Directors of Civil Defense. *October* 1, 1953

I SUGGESTED that I get the opportunity to say a word to you. Not that I can add anything to your own realization of your work, but I can assure you of something about the attitude of the Federal Government toward you. We are quite well aware of its importance, and we are certainly determined to support you.

Please don't get discouraged when you feel no visible progress. It is awfully hard to awaken people to a sense of responsibility without trying to create hysteria—which we certainly don't want to do. It is awfully hard to awaken people to a sense of responsibility that produces a steady and periodic work or effort.

We must be real leaders. We must never be discouraged. So no matter what happens, no matter what things look like at the moment, please keep going. As far as I can see, it is only through persistence, through continuing to achieve those things in which we believe, that we can finally continue to, one, give ourselves that confidence that comes from the maximum preparation on our own part; and second, have a finer influence, if we are confident, for bringing about a basis for the solution of the world's problems, because we can talk calmly from a position of strength, a feeling of safety and not of hysteria. That is what we are trying to get into our hearts and minds—a sense of the realization not only of the dangers, but our own strength to balance it, and our ability to meet it.

Now I feel I am the last one ever to minimize your difficulties, but also I feel the last one to admit you are not Americans. I don't believe Americans give up in the face of difficulties. That is my story today. Thank you very much.

NOTE: The President spoke in the Rose Garden at the White House.

203 ¶ Letter to the Attorney General Directing Him To Petition for an Injunction in the Maritime Strike. *October 5, 1953*

Dear Mr. Attorney General:

On October 1, 1953, by virtue of the authority vested in me by Section 206 of the Labor Management Relations Act, 1947 (Public Law 101, 80th Congress), I issued Executive Order 10490, creating a Board of Inquiry to inquire into the issues involved in labor disputes between employers (or associations by which such employers are represented in collective bargaining conferences) who are (1) steamship companies or who are engaged as operators or agents for ships engaged in service from or to North Atlantic ports from Hampton Roads, Virginia, to Portland, Maine, or from or to other ports of the United States or its Territories or possessions, (2) contracting stevedores, (3) contracting marine carpenters, or (4) other employers engaged in related or associated pier activities, and certain of their employees represented by the International Longshoremen's Association.

On October 5, 1953, I received the Board's written report in the matter. A copy of that report is attached hereto.

In my opinion these unresolved labor disputes have resulted in a strike affecting an entire industry or a substantial part thereof engaged in trade, commerce, transportation, transmission or communication among the several States and with foreign nations, which strike, if permitted to continue, will imperil the national health and safety.

I therefore direct you, pursuant to the provisions of Section 208 of the Labor Management Relations Act, 1947, to petition in the name of the United States any District Court of the United States having jurisdiction of the parties to enjoin the continuance of such strike where such action is necessary to secure a resumption of trade, commerce, transportation, transmission or communication among the several States and the foreign nations, and for such other relief as may in your judgment be necessary or appropriate.

Very sincerely yours,

Dwight D. Eisenhower

NOTE: An injunction was granted on October 5 by the District Court for the Southern District of New York.

The Board's report of October 5, and its final report of December 4, were made available through the Federal Mediation and Conciliation Service. Final negotiations for settlement of the dispute were concluded on April 2, 1954.

204 ¶ Message Recorded for the Dedication at Indiana University of a Tablet Honoring Ernie Pyle. *October* 5, 1953

TO ALL of you participating in the ceremony honoring Ernie Pyle, I am delighted to send my warmest greetings.

I met Ernie Pyle in the midst of war and counted him my good friend. I remember him as a man of small stature, of high courage, of great understanding and love for his fellows. I remember him as a reporter who won the devotion of millions merely by writing the familiar everyday facts of life as he saw them.

Both in war and in peace, Ernie Pyle conceived it his duty to write the truth with the vigor of simplicity. His name is a symbol of integrity in his profession, and—for all citizens—a living testimony to patriotism. I am proud to join in this testimonial to him by so many of his colleagues.

NOTE: The ceremony at Indiana University, where a bronze tablet was dedicated to the memory of Ernie Pyle by the Sigma Delta Chi fraternity, was held in conjunction with the observance of National Newspaper Week.

205 ¶ Address at the Sixth National Assembly of the United Church Women, Atlantic City, New Jersey. *October* 6, 1953

Mrs. Wyker, Governor Driscoll, distinguished guests, and representatives of America's church women:

For the cordiality of your welcome, I am deeply grateful, and I would hope that through this group I could thank each of the citizens of this city who stood along the road as the cavalcade came in from the airport and who were so gracious in their greetings. For every smile I saw, I am truly grateful—if it was meant for me.

At the outset of my talk, I should like to express, first, my appreciation of the honor I feel in speaking before this assemblage. An invitation to occupy this platform would confer distinction upon any man—perhaps I should say any mere man; for you are gathered here in high purpose, inspired by an unshakeable faith in yourselves, in your country and in your God.

I can hardly hope that my words can further your purpose or deepen your three-fold faith.

That faith, immeasurable and imponderable, daily exemplified in millions of American families, is the prime strength of our great Nation. It is the very basis of our society. And it is the most heartening support for those whose obligation is to represent you in the conduct of national affairs, and community affairs.

Though I cannot enhance the spiritual wealth that is yours, perhaps I can, by identifying some of the circumstances of today that emphasize the value of this faith, encourage you to spread its influence into every human activity in every community across our land.

Now, of course, the cynic—the Marxist, or the worshipper of machines and numbers—will scoff that faith is no armor against artillery, that the spirit weakens fast before the blast of the bomb. But your husbands and brothers and fathers can testify that in the terrifying nakedness of the battlefield, the faith and the spirit of men are the keys to survival and victory.

Now, faith is evidently too simple a thing for some to recognize its paramount worth. Yet the present and the future demand men and women who are firm in their faith in our country and unswerving in their service to her. This is true in every basic unit of our political and social life—in the family, the community, the State, and the Nation.

This audience peculiarly symbolizes the smallest and the most important of these units—the American family. We of America have always recognized that the soundness of our Nation depends primarily upon the quality of our home and family life.

Now, while our homes have witnessed scarcely any of the horrors of the battlefield that are so familiar to citizens of Western Europe, we know that our former unique physical security has almost totally disappeared before the long-range bomber and the destructive power of a single bomb.

Today we are face to face with the most extraordinary physical development of all time—the application of nuclear fission and nuclear fusion to the world's armaments.

These discoveries in the field of science present in themselves no threat to man. Like other scientific developments, they are susceptible to good or evil use, depending upon the intent of the individual or group possessing them.

The mysteries of the atom are known to Russia. Russia's hostility to free government—and to the religious faith on which free government is built—is too well known to require recital here. It is enough for us to know that even before Russia had this awesome knowledge, she by force gained domination over 600 million peoples of the earth. She surrounded them with an Iron Curtain that is an effective obstacle to all intellectual, economic, and spiritual intercourse between the free world and the enslaved world. Now, of these two worlds, the one is compelled by its purpose of world domination, the other by its unbreakable will to preserve its freedom and security to devote these latest discoveries of science to increasing its stockpiles of destructive armaments.

Man's greatest scientific achievement, therefore, cannot yet be made exclusively to serve the advancement of man's welfare and happiness. Instead we are forced to concentrate on building such stores of armaments as can deter any attack against those who want to be free.

Men of faith everywhere must gain a broader understanding of these potentials, both destructive and constructive.

We must certainly make sure that all the world comprehends,

in simplest terms, the paramount alternatives of our day. The first of these alternatives is a wasteful and devastating contest in the production of weapons of inconceivable power. The other alternative is a world ever advancing in peace and prosperity through the cooperative effort of its nations and peoples.

The choice that spells terror and death is symbolized by a mushroom cloud floating upward from the release of the mightiest natural power yet uncovered by those who search the physical universe. The energy that it typifies is, at this stage of human knowledge, the unharnessed blast. In its wake we see only sudden and mass destruction, erasure of cities, the possible doom of every nation and society.

This horror must not be.

This titanic force must be reduced to the fruitful service of mankind.

This can come to pass only as one of the results of shaping a firm and just and durable peace.

Such a peace cannot be achieved suddenly by force, by edict, or by treaty. It can come only slowly and tortuously. It will not be won by dark threats or glittering slogans. It will be born only of courage, knowledge, patience, leadership.

To strive faithfully for this peace—even as our science constantly develops new methods of mass destruction—imposes upon us a host of intricate labors. We and our friends in the free world must build, maintain and pay for a military might assuring us reasonable safety from attack. From this position of secure confidence, we must seek to know and respond to the legitimate aspirations and hopes of all peoples. We must arrange trade systems that will provide each with the necessaries of life and opportunity for self-advancement. We must seek to understand and resolve age-old prejudices, ambitions and hatreds that still scar great parts of the whole world. And they must be removed, or at least ameliorated. We must provide machinery and techniques to encourage that peaceful communication and mutual confidence which alone can finally lift the burden of arms from the backs of men.

Now, these are some of the grand labors before us—the tasks and tests and problems that span the world.

For the spirit that will resolve them, however, we need not seek the source in distant places.

I deeply believe that one of the supreme hopes for the world's destiny lies in the American community: in its moral values, in its sense of order and decency, in its cooperative spirit.

We know—and all the world constantly reminds us—that the future well-being of humanity depends directly upon America's leadership.

I say emphatically that this leadership depends no less directly upon the faith, the courage, the love of freedom and the capacity for sacrifice of every American citizen, every American home, every American community.

I wish there were words of mine that could bring this truth home more certainly to each of us. I do not mean merely or only that our government and our leadership is the product of the qualities of each of us multiplied by 160 million. I mean more this: the example we give the world when we talk about noble virtues that are necessary if civilization is to attain that future for which it was designed, and for which obviously the Almighty intended.

We speak of sacrifice. If each of us would search our own memories; how often have we, as we urged economy upon government, local, city or state, urged that something not be given to us? "Don't build us a new post office; we don't need it; ours is good enough. Build it for the other city. Don't give me free postage, make me pay for what it costs to carry the letter."

What I am trying to get at is that America's policies abroad, to have any force, must be the reflection of the attitudes and qualities displayed by our people. No individual—no group of individuals, however brilliant, however eloquent, can possibly do any effective work in leading the world toward peace unless back of them is the mightiest force yet developed on God's footstool, and that is the force of a united America—an America determined to do a real and constructive job.

This means then, that there is a clear and compelling answer to the question in the hearts of all of us: how can we better fit ourselves to be worthy of freedom, to guard its virtues, to enjoy its bounty?

That answer is: by making each life, each home, each community more worthy of the trust it bears for all mankind.

This worthiness will come in the measure that we show ourselves truly convinced that the central facts of human life are human freedom, human rights, human obligations—all expressing that human dignity which is a reflection of man's divine origin and destiny.

Our purpose is to grow even beyond the golden dreams of our forebears—in material wealth, in intellectual stature, in spiritual strength. But to do so, each citizen and every community must match the founders of this Nation in fiery independence, confident optimism, sturdy self-reliance, and we must sustain that capacity for conquering difficulties that has always been a quality of America.

With this spirit, each of you, each of us—like, indeed, every American citizen—can arouse your own community to renewed awareness of the promise of freedom.

With your neighbors, you can join in work that even as it remakes your own town or hamlet helps remake the world.

For it is within your power to reach for, and to attain, that day when you and all your neighbors can proudly say:

"These things—here—in this community—we are faithful to freedom.

"Here in this town, our public schools are staffed and equipped to train our children splendidly, to be free and responsible citizens."

Ladies, not so long ago, I met with a small group of people, and

their purpose was to complain to me about certain things in our
public school system. And they directed some criticism at school
teachers, and what these teachers thought—their policies, the
philosophy they were teaching.

And I asked this group one question only. I said: "You recognize a teacher's great opportunity for influencing your children's
future, for the planting of good thoughts or bad thoughts, for the
teaching of a sound philosophy, or one that is based on falsity.
Have you had that teacher in your home? Have you had her, or
him, to dinner? Have you taken the trouble to find out for yourself what is the philosophy of these people to whom you are en-
trusting the most priceless possession you have, your children?"

"Now," I said, "many people have not been hesitant to join the
ranks of the critics and say these teachers are not doing a good
job. Then why haven't you done your part of the job—brought
them in, talked to them, to see whether you could straighten them
out, or get ones of which you approved?"

What I am trying to bring home, my friends, is that as we see
difficulties and defects in the body politic, in the social order, we
must never attempt, before our own consciences, to dodge our own
responsibilities.

And so we can say that, "Our teachers, loyal citizens to their
free country, enjoy true freedom of thought, untrammelled by
political fashion or expediency."

And we should go on and be able to say, "Here in this city our
libraries contain everything that can add to man's enlightenment
and understanding—respecting common decency but disdaining
any other censorship.

"Here our ministers and Sunday school teachers command the
respect that they so justly earn in teaching our sons and our
daughters the love of the Almighty.

"Here our hospitals and our clinics give faithful care to all who
are sick and cannot help themselves.

"Here in this community, our people—all our people—have the
chance to enjoy the arts, to learn, to become intimate friends with
the heritage of freedom.

"Here we rely not primarily upon government grant or political panacea but upon our own wisdom and industry to bring us the good and comforting things of life.

"Here we know not the sight or smell of slums that choke the spirit of men.

"Here all of us work to make our processes of government the best, the most honest and the most just, known to any men.

"Here we have welcomed with our hearts new citizens from distant lands, and here we thank them for the strength they have added to our own.

"Here there is true equality of opportunity for work, for education, for enjoyment of all freedom's blessings—for we know that whatever we have and hold is the work and the treasure of men of all races and color and creeds.

"Here, in this community, in short, any free man can be proud to live."

My friends, all that I have tried to express to you rests upon one truth in which I firmly believe. I tried to speak it on the day last January when I took the oath of office as President of the United States. That truth is:

"Whatever America hopes to bring to pass in the world, must first come to pass in the heart of America."

I know no more plain or pure ideal to which we can pledge our lives.

I know of no other way we can prove worthy of freedom.

For the very great honor of your invitation, my friends, I thank you once more.

NOTE: The President spoke in the Auditorium in Atlantic City at 11:55 a.m. In his opening words he referred to Mrs. James D. Wyker, President of the United Church Women, National Council of Churches, and to Governor Alfred E. Driscoll of New Jersey.

206   ¶ Memorandum Directing That
Agricultural Commodities Be Made Available To
Meet Relief Requirements in Bolivia.
October 6, 1953

[Released October 6, 1953. Dated October 5, 1953]

Memorandum for: The Secretary of State, the Secretary of Agriculture, the Director of the Bureau of the Budget, and the Director of the Foreign Operations Administration

In accordance with the recommendation contained in the memorandum of October 5, 1953, submitted by the Director of the Foreign Operations Administration, and pursuant to the authority vested in me by Public Law 216, 83d Congress, 1st Session, I hereby determine that up to $5,000,000 worth of agricultural commodities shall be made available out of the stocks of the Commodity Credit Corporation and transferred to meet the urgent relief requirements of Bolivia. This amount shall cover the Corporation's investment in the commodities and costs of delivery on board vessels in United States ports.

Arrangements for the operations of this relief program, including the specification of the commodities, shall be the responsibility of the Director of the Foreign Operations Administration, and the transfer of the commodities shall be upon such terms and conditions as the Director determines to be appropriate, after consultation with the Secretary of State. In connection with the furnishing of such assistance, the Secretary of State, after consultation with the Director, shall conclude a bilateral agreement with the Government of Bolivia.

Dwight D. Eisenhower

NOTE: See also Item 213.

207 ¶ Remarks at the Annual Meeting of the American Council on Education. *October* 8, 1953

Dr. Sterns, ladies and gentlemen:

One of the more pleasant duties devolving upon the Chief Executive is that of welcoming from time to time different groups and bodies here to the Nation's Capital. Of all these groups I can think of none in which I could possibly take greater satisfaction in serving as spokesman for the administration in these words of welcome than for this one.

You know, for a very brief period in my life, the educational group allowed me to be one of their members. They couldn't stand me very long, but I had a very wonderful experience while I was there. I learned many things about our educational group. One of them that impressed me more than any other was their dedication to ideals and to high purposes.

This morning I am not foolish enough to try to talk to you about your functions. You people, representatives of the great educational fabric of this whole Nation, know so much more about each of your problems than I do that it would be unpardonable for me to consume your time. But I can tell you about one of the effects that all of us hope will result from certain phases of your work.

I am talking about the understandings that must come about in the world, if we are to achieve, in this day and time, that sort of machinery—the kind of techniques—that will allow people to live together without intermittent blazing into conflict.

It is not enough that we merely know where another nation lies. It is not enough that we know something of their institutions, their history, their traditions. We must gain some understanding of those people as such. I have never forgotten my shock, once, when I saw a very modern-looking village deserted in a far corner of Africa. It had been deserted because the builders put running water into all the houses. The women rebelled, because there was now taken away from them their only excuse for social contact with their own kind at the village well. I suddenly understood that I didn't understand others. I had been guilty of the very great error of putting into their minds and hearts the same aspirations, the same kind of desires that I had. And it simply isn't so.

If we, therefore, are going to progress along the lines of these understandings, we can talk about all the diplomacy that it is possible to bring to bear upon it, we can talk about all the security we may achieve by arms, and by any other arrangements. But we are never going to make real progress unless the educational people, and groups, and institutions of all countries see this problem and get into it to help.

I personally believe that in your programs of interchange of students and professors and others in schools, is one of the great ways—one of the principal ways—that this can come about. Indeed, I believe so much in this, that I would like to see some exchange programs worked out between associations of manufacturers, and labor unions and everything else—not stopping when a man is 21 or 26 or 27 and we say his formal education is over, or at least he is going to end his educational processes. I believe in every phase of leadership. In all our countries, we have to seek and support these exchanges, because I believe through them we will have one method, one road to follow, in leading to that happy time when we can live in peace as well as security.

So, haltingly as I have expressed my simple thoughts, I hope that they help convince you that I am delighted to see you here, to see people trained in the processes of education, people of great minds meeting here to exchange ideas of how best may we achieve progress among all men—our own people, and those with whom we must necessarily live in this shrinking world.

For the honor of appearing before you, thanks to each one of you.

NOTE: The President spoke at 10:00 a.m. at the Statler Hotel in Washington. In his opening words he referred to Dr. Robert L. Sterns, Chairman of the American Council on Education.

208 ¶ The President's News Conference of *October* 8, 1953.

THE PRESIDENT. Please be seated. I did make it in the afternoon.

Q. Edward T. Folliard: Thank you, Mr. President. [*Laughter*] Everybody hopes that is a precedent.[1]

THE PRESIDENT. I have a few items here that I hope you will consider news.

A few days ago Mr. Lloyd Mashburn, Under Secretary of Labor, was tendered a very important position in one of the unions, and asked whether he could resign. His resignation was accepted, but he kindly agreed to wait, occupying his post until a successor to the Secretary could be appointed.

I have designated, and there will be sworn in, Mr. James P. Mitchell, now Assistant Secretary for Manpower and Reserve Affairs in the Army, a man with long experience in the labor field, and a man who, in my opinion, will be a very great success in that office.

Q. Edward Dayton Moore, United Press: Secretary or Under Secretary?

THE PRESIDENT. He is to be Secretary—Secretary of Labor.

I have accepted an invitation from the Government of Canada to visit Ottawa between November 13th and 15th. There is no specific purpose other than social and a courtesy call in making this visit. As you will recall, the Prime Minister of Canada visited here last May, and stayed for a day or two. I will stay 2 days.

By the way, these things that I am now giving to you from these papers, there will be documents when you go out so that you can get the exact titles and words and experience, and all that, as to these individuals and so on.

I will read you a draft statement. Again, there will be a copy of this. I want to read it, because I want to say exactly what I mean, if you don't mind.

---

[1] See closing discussion in news conference of September 30, Item 198 above.

[*Reading*] There have recently been a number of statements concerning the threat posed by Soviet progress in the development of atomic weapons. The facts, as we know them, are these: [*Interrupts reading*] Again, I tell you that you will have this verbatim.

[*Continues reading*] You will recall that our Government announced that the Soviet produced an atomic explosion in 1949 and two subsequent explosions in 1951. In August of this year we learned through intelligence channels of a Soviet test of an atomic device in which some part of the explosive force was derived from a thermonuclear reaction, that is to say, what is popularly known as the H-bomb. The Atomic Energy Commission announced this August 12th detonation as soon as sufficient evidence was in hand, and later announced that it appeared to be part of a test series.

The development did not come as a surprise. We had always estimated that it was within the scientific and technical capabilities of the Soviets to reach this point, and we have been on notice for some years that their own ingenuity has had the material assistance of what they learned of our program through espionage.

The Soviets now possess a stockpile of atomic weapons of conventional types and we must furthermore conclude that the powerful explosion of August 12th last was produced by a weapon, or the forerunner of a weapon, of power far in excess of the conventional types.

We therefore conclude that the Soviets have the capability of atomic attack on us, and such capability will increase with the passage of time.

Now, a word as to our own situation. We do not intend to disclose the details of our strength in atomic weapons of any sort, but it is large and increasing steadily. We have in our atomic arsenals a number of kinds of weapons suited to the special needs of the Army, Navy, and Air Force for the specific tasks assigned to each service.

It is my hope, my earnest prayer, that this country will never again be engaged in war. As I said in Atlantic City this week, with reference to atomic energy, "This titanic force must be reduced to the fruitful service of mankind." Real advances made by our Government in developing peacetime atomic power and other benign uses of atomic energy is evidence of the constructive goals that we have set for ourselves.

I have asked all members of this administration to refrain from comment on Soviet nuclear capabilities unless they first check their statements with the Chairman of the Atomic Energy Commission. [*Ends reading*]

As I said before, you will get an exact copy of that. Now, we will take questions.

Q. Frank van der Linden, Nashville Banner: You had a conference today with Governor Clement of Tennessee about and regarding TVA. Will you tell us what your reaction was regarding his pleading for TVA money?

THE PRESIDENT. Well, Mr. Clement is a very charming and a very persuasive gentleman, and I like him. He has a particular philosophy about the place of TVA in the American scene, and he has a very persuasive manner of presenting it.

I listened very carefully and was delighted to have his views, which is not to say that I agree in detail with him; but I was delighted to have them.

Q. Merriman Smith, United Press: Mr. President, I wonder if you could give us your version on why there have been such divergent statements about the Russian H-bomb program from various members of your Government?

THE PRESIDENT. No, I really have no explanation. We know this, ladies and gentlemen: when things of great moment happen, people reach conclusions, sometimes they just have reactions, and if they state them, they sometimes forget that their words are taken very seriously.

Now, I have no comment to make on anything that anyone has said from one end to the other. I gave you the facts as I think they should be given at this moment.

Q. David P. Sentner, Hearst Newspapers: Mr. President, in the face of this Soviet H-bomb threat, do you anticipate requesting a larger appropriation for defense in the next Congress?

THE PRESIDENT. When you say "defense," of course, you are covering a very large field.

What you are constantly trying to do in your studies, in your technical and professional examinations and in the Security Council, is to find out the best way to adjust our defenses and our own capabilities in the military field to this kind of a possible threat, which doesn't mean always that you necessarily have to go up in the gross amount of money requested, but you do certainly have to use a very definite scale of priority in meeting the threat that you find opposing you.

I am not prepared at this moment because our studies are not complete, as you know—they are going forward—I am not prepared to say what will be the degree of up or down that we will ask for.

Q. Mr. Sentner: Is it likely to affect your hope in balancing the budget?

THE PRESIDENT. Balancing the budget will always remain a goal of any administration that believes as much as we do that the soundness of our money must be assured, and that the unbalanced budget has a very bad effect on it.

That does not mean to say that you can pick any specific date and say, "Here, all things must give way before a balanced budget." It is a question of where the importance of a balanced budget comes in; but it must be an aim of any sound money program. But I do not say that the budget is going to be balanced on July 1, 1955.

Q. Robert W. Richards, Copley Press: Here your statement on the Russian hydrogen bomb potential seems to disagree with the Defense Secretary's estimate that it would be 3 years before Russia could start an atomic war, hydrogen-bomb war, and his caution to the country not to get panicky. Does this concur with that?

THE PRESIDENT. I would say that you shouldn't look for evil where there is none.

Now, anyone can have his own guess as to what is going to happen in the future. I think no one has tried to fool you; we have tried to give you facts. Certainly, I have tried to give you facts today, and I will not stand up here and tell you—certainly I had no intention—that this threat is right on your doorstep at this minute. I am trying to say the facts as we know them; I am going no further.

Q. William H. Lawrence, New York Times: Mr. President, could you tell us anything about your conference last week with Governor Stevenson and his suggestion to you of the possibilities of a nonaggression pact that would guarantee the boundaries——

THE PRESIDENT. The Governor—I think he said this; I am certain I am betraying no confidence—suggested several ways in which he thought approaches could be made where some of these tensions could be relieved in the world; among them was assuring all nations that we were ready to enter nonaggression pacts under acceptable conditions. I merely explained to him that everything of that kind was being studied in the State Department, and I was sure they would like a greater explanation of his particular ideas. And I am sure that he is giving them.

Q. Milton Friedman, Jewish Telegraphic Agency: Mr. President, now that the administration has successfully achieved the passage of your emergency refugee bill, can you tell us if the correction of what you described in your State of the Union Message as discriminations of the McCarran-Walter Act is part of the program for the second session of the 83d Congress?

THE PRESIDENT. I think I lost you a little bit. But if I understand your question, it is do we still have the hope of correcting what we believe to be imperfections in the bill? Is that right?

Q. Mr. Friedman: Yes, sir; that is right.

THE PRESIDENT. Well, while I have not gone back to the study of that question for some time, and I am not, therefore, ready to state positively that on my priority program there is certain "must" legislation in that regard, I will say this: if the people administering that bill, the people responsible for it, still believe there are imperfections, we shall certainly do our best to correct them.

Q. Fred W. Perkins, Scripps-Howard Newspaper Alliance: Mr. President, in view of the difficulty of getting the floor, I have three questions, and I will ask them all at once. [*Laughter*]

One, do you have a successor to Mr. Mashburn; and, two are you looking for a labor leader; three, did Mr. Mashburn in his letter of resignation intimate the same reason that was ascribed by Mr. Durkin for his resignation?

THE PRESIDENT. As to the first one, the Under Secretary has not yet been chosen. Secondly, there is no particular field to which I would confine my examination. I will look for the best man that I think we can find and, of course, the new Secretary will have a very large measure of responsibility and authority there. Finally, Mr. Mashburn's letter and my answer to it will be given to you outside as you go out.

Q. Richard L. Wilson, Cowles Publications: Mr. President, would you say that there is a greater or lesser prospect of balancing the budget now than there appeared to be 2 or 3 months ago?

THE PRESIDENT. Well, I don't believe I can answer the question with great accuracy, because at various times estimates of income and estimates of outgo vary.

I can only say, as I repeated a little while ago, this remains one of the firm objectives of the administration, as a means of saving life insurance policies, savings bonds, and all of the other things that the little investor of this country puts his money into.

Now, some day that must be reached; we just don't believe that you can continue to go on an inflationary spiral and have a sound country.

Q. Edward J. Milne, Providence Journal-Bulletin: I would like to get at the same thing in a different way, if I may.

Will you ask Congress for sufficient taxes to balance the budget at whatever level the expenditures for national defense require?

THE PRESIDENT. As I explained last week—something of that kind—outside of the one statement I made about the retail sales tax, this whole tax program is being worked out by the Treasury Department, with the Budget, with conferences with the people down at the Capitol. We are going to find out what we believe will be the best tax program, and I am not in position to comment on it in detail beyond that at this time.

Q. Chalmers M. Roberts, Washington Post: Mr. President, it has been suggested that Governor Stevenson brought you a personal message from Winston Churchill. I wonder if that is true, and if so, if it had anything to do with his request for a top-level meeting with the Russians?

THE PRESIDENT. He brought me warm greetings from my old friend; that is the only thing I recall—nothing at all about a meeting.

Q. Charles L. Bartlett, Chattanooga Times: Mr. President, would it be accurate to say that your conversation this morning with the Governor of Tennessee did not alter your view of the TVA as an example of "creeping socialism"?

THE PRESIDENT. Did not what?

Q. Mr. Bartlett: Did not alter your view of TVA as an example of "creeping socialism."

THE PRESIDENT. I think he brought to me certain facts that I was not completely aware of. I don't think that he probably convinced me completely to his point of view, let us put it that way.

Now, I never said that all of the TVA was—and you based your question a bit on a false premise. I said there were certain features of that development that were alarming from the viewpoint of my political philosophy, but I never said that the whole thing was such a terrible example of socialism.

Q. Merriman Smith, United Press: Mr. President, you told us last week that you were planning a report to the people based on studies of the international situation.

THE PRESIDENT. Yes.

Q. Mr. Smith: Can you give us any more information about when that might come along?

THE PRESIDENT. No, except that I am working awfully hard, that is all.

Q. Paul Scott Rankine, Reuters News Agency: Mr. President, it has been suggested in the press that Sir Winston Churchill might personally go to Moscow to see Malenkov by himself, in order to see whether there is a fruitfulness in a Big Four meeting. Have you any views on that proposal?

THE PRESIDENT. Well, I had not heard of any such suggestion. Therefore, I haven't studied it one way or the other.

Q. Paul Martin, Gannett News Service: Mr. President, when the Prime Minister of Canada came here you had discussions about the St. Lawrence Seaway. I wonder if your visit to Ottawa contemplates discussions on the Seaway and the Niagara power project?

THE PRESIDENT. I assure you again that I told you the exact truth.

I am going up there to pay a courtesy call, make a social visit. I will probably make one short address, because I believe I am asked to do it. I have no specific subject of any kind in mind.

Q. Marshall McNeil, Scripps-Howard Newspaper Alliance: May I ask you again about TVA, sir? Some of us understood the Governor to say that he had suggested to you the formation of some commission to gather facts about TVA, its power requirements and how they should be met. Is that true, sir?

THE PRESIDENT. That is right; he did.

Q. Mr. McNeil: Are you favorable to that suggestion?

THE PRESIDENT. Well, I don't know; I haven't looked at it yet. It has been just one of the things that has been fired at me today, like your question is fired at me now, and I just haven't had time to go further into it.

But I do like to get the facts on things, and I will certainly do my best to get them, so far as my own time will permit.

Q. Mr. McNeil: Can it be said that his suggestion is being considered by you?

THE PRESIDENT. It certainly is being considered by me.

Q. Joseph Chiang, Chinese News Service: Mr. President, do you have anything to say about Chinese General Chiang Ching-kuo's call on you last week?

THE PRESIDENT. I enjoyed it very much. He brought me a greeting from the Generalissimo, and brought me a copy of a book in Chinese. It was my own, and so he was doing it as a compliment. We just talked, really, about affairs in general, nothing specific with respect to China.

Q. Martin S. Hayden, Detroit News: Mr. President, I ask this because many of us are not well acquainted with Mr. Mitchell. Could I ask you the same question, sir, in reference to him that was asked about Chief Justice Warren last week, that is, what are the qualifications that attracted Mr. Mitchell to you, as Secretary of Labor?

THE PRESIDENT. A man, so far as I can find, of great character, whose interest is in people and not merely in, you might say, the economic processes of our country, a man who has had great experience in the whole labor field. He was, among other things, for a long time the labor relations man for, I believe, Macy's and then Bloomingdale's, and since then in the Army. I find that all of his associates, his superiors, and everybody else thinks that he is a man of extraordinary ability.

Merriman Smith, United Press: Thank you, Mr. President.

NOTE: President Eisenhower's sixteenth news conference was held in the Executive Office Building from 3:30 to 3:49 o'clock on Thursday afternoon, October 8, 1953. In attendance: 198.

209 ¶ Greetings to the Delegates to the 42d Conference of the Inter-Parliamentary Union. *October 9, 1953*

Mr. Chairman, Mr. Speaker, ladies and gentlemen:

On behalf of the Administration, it is my very great privilege, and my most pleasant duty, to welcome here the delegations from the Member nations of the Inter-Parliamentary Union, as well as all of their guests from other countries and representatives from the United Nations.

Believing as we do that there is no future for progress and civilization unless the conference table supplants the battleground as the arbiter of disputes, you can well understand the satisfaction of my associates and of myself that this meeting takes place in this Capitol of the United States of America.

Moreover, as we see it, there is a particular significance attaching to this particular kind of meeting. Most conferences are made up of appointed delegations representing the governments by which appointed, but only hopefully, and often only sketchily representing the peoples of the nation that that government controls.

Representative government is an expression of faith that free people can govern themselves. Consequently, since public opinion in a free country is the power and the force that gives validity to every proposal, the nearer we can come to bringing together the public opinions of nations, rather than merely their governmental representatives, the greater significance, and the greater importance should apply to such a meeting.

Parliaments, first instituted among men, long, long ago, are the symbol of public opinion. They are not only the symbol of that public opinion. They are the nearest approach we may make to bringing public opinion into one spot, crystallizing it and giving it expression—expression that we ourselves may understand, and that others may understand. Consequently, when the actual members of such parliaments meet together, it is not only a renewed expression of faith that free men can govern themselves, but that they understand that this system of government must necessarily be one whole throughout the world where people practice it. It cannot be separate, distinct, in any one nation.

To put it another way, it seems quite clear that free government could not possibly exist in any one nation alone. If any country, no matter how powerful, were an island of representative or free or democratic government, surrounded by dictators, it would soon wither and die away. It would, itself, have to become a dictatorship.

Consequently, I repeat, the stronger we can make this union among nations that choose to govern themselves, the more certainly will it exist in each of our nations, now and forever more.

For one who has had the task of helping to promote understanding among allies as they approached a military campaign and the battlefield I have often wondered why it is so difficult for nations to reach the kind of accord in peace that they are forced to reach in war.

Now, the cynic says it is because you use the word "forced," forced by a great fear to get together—in the words of an old sage of ours, "Hang together or hang separately." I refuse to admit that men cannot operate—free men—cannot operate as effectively on a constructive basis as they can when their sole purpose is the negative one of saving themselves from destruction.

And so, to each individual gathered here, I express, first, my satisfaction that you are here; secondly, my great faith that you can contribute something to this concept and this ideal of free government that is so dear to all of us; and thirdly, that in doing so you will have the satisfaction of knowing you are moving along the constructive road of progress, and not merely banding yourselves together to achieve only the defensive or negative concept of mere physical security. It is a great faith that must march forward. It cannot stand still.

And now, ladies and gentlemen, permit me to express to you the very great sense of distinction I feel personally—the great honor that I appreciate so deeply—in the invitation you have extended me to come here this morning.

Thank you.

NOTE: The President spoke in the chamber of the House of Representatives. Viscount Stansgate, President of the Council of the Inter-Parliamentary Union, presided at the opening session of the conference.

210 ¶ Statement Following Conference With Madame Pandit, President of the United Nations General Assembly.   *October* 12, 1953

MADAME PANDIT called upon the President and the Secretary of State in her capacity of President of the United Nations General Assembly.   Among other things she explained the tasks still before the General Assembly in relation to peace in Korea and the performance of the Armistice Agreement relative to prisoners of war.

The President expressed his great appreciation of the fact that the Government of India had been willing in the interest of peace to assume the difficult role of Chairman of the Neutral Nations Commission, a role inherently subject to criticism from both sides. The President and the Secretary of State told Madame Pandit that they would do everything possible to facilitate the work of the United Nations Command and the Neutral Nations Commission. The President particularly mentioned the reports he had received of the exemplary conduct of the Indian troops in the discharge of their duties as custodians of the prisoners of war who have elected not to be repatriated.

The President reaffirmed his faith in the United Nations and his determination that the United States should cooperate fully with it in all matters conducive to peace and justice in the world.

211 ¶ Remarks in Response to Birthday Greetings at Hershey, Pennsylvania. *October* 13, 1953

GOOD EVENING, my friends—and thank you a lot for the cordiality of your welcome.

Mrs. Eisenhower and I have many reasons to be thankful that we were able to make this trip today.   There may have been several thousand, or maybe many tens of thousands of reasons for the smiles we have encountered on the road, and here. And I must say to you, never in my life have I heard so many people sing "Happy Birthday."

I don't mean to be too partisan, but I am glad that there are this many Republicans in this region.

Thank you a lot.

NOTE: The President spoke in the Stadium at 6:20 p.m. He went to Hershey to participate in a rally of Pennsylvania Republicans on the eve of his birthday. See also Item 212.

212 ¶ Remarks at the Pennsylvania Republican Rally on the Occasion of the President's Birthday. *October* 13, 1953

Mr. Sharples, Fred, friends:

When the heart is full, the tongue is likely to stumble. But if you will bear with me a little while, I should like to try to tell you something of what this birthday means to me.

In the first place, please don't think there is any regret in my heart that I have reached the age of 63. Considering when I was born, had I not reached it, I know where I would be. And so I consider it something for which to be thankful, and not to regret.

Never, I think, has anyone had such a birthday. I have had that one who has been my life's companion by my side when I came here to meet this countryside filled with cordiality and hospitality. To each one here I say, could I only grasp your hand and try to say to you what I really feel, for your great kindness in coming out.

There have been a number of different emotions gone through my heart as I have seen some of the scenes. Those drilled, picturesque bands over in the stadium, I thought they were wonderful. To each of them I would like to give my thanks—to every waiter at the table, to every person that had anything to do with the decorations or the arranging of this whole party, the Sharples, of course, and Mr. and Mrs. Williams and all the others that I have met that have worked so hard to make this a great gathering of American folk.

Finally, we come down to this present just given to me. I have known about it for a long time. A thing such as this is far too important to risk any chance that it might be misunderstood. I believe here this evening, by this great group of patriots that have established these exchange fellowships, there has been initiated something that could well be the most meaningful thing that has happened in our time. Because, overshadowing everything with which we deal today, my friends, is the question of international relationships—international relationships of friendship and not enmity, not prejudice, not a preconceived notion that the other fellow is a skunk while we are pretty good fellows.

Knowledge itself is not enough. What we need is understanding, and this understanding will come from these young men and women as they go back and forth between our country and others, who have already achieved some place in life, who are marked as leaders, and who will carry back with them not only the skills and techniques of our country, or will bring their skills and techniques to ours, but they will carry understanding, an understanding of America's heart: that she wants peace—nothing else.

Such a birthday! I think I know possibly almost every man and woman whose name is signed at the bottom of this scroll. I tell you now, I could not be prouder than to have my name associated with theirs. Which means, also, because you are guests here this evening along with me and the hosts—I suppose you have a dual capacity—I am honored by the presence here of each of you.

And now, with your forbearance, could I speak a word to all the young folks down at the choir end of this great hall, who really mean the future of the United States.

This is, of course, a Republican gathering, but it is not a partisan gathering. And I should like to tell them, in a simple word, what the Republican Party is trying to do.

The Republican Party is trying to use all of its brains, all of the ability it has, all of its understanding of this world as it now exists, merely to establish the foundations from which you—you people down there, soon to take over—will carry this United States forward to greater blessings of liberty and freedom, under God, than it has ever known before.

Thank you very much, my very good friends.

NOTE: The President spoke in the Arena in Hershey at 9:36 p.m. In his opening words he referred to Philip T. Sharples, who served as host at the President's Birthday Party, and to orchestra leader Fred Waring. He later referred to Mr. and Mrs. Nathan B. Williams, Jr. Mr. Williams served as chairman of the rally.

Before the President spoke, Mr. Sharples presented him with the plans for the establishment of the first of the Eisenhower Exchange Fellowships.

213 ¶ Exchange of Letters Between the President and President Paz Estenssoro of Bolivia Concerning the Need for Economic Assistance. *October* 14, 1953

My dear Mr. President:

I have received your letter of October 1, 1953, in which you describe the very grave economic emergency now threatening Bolivia and in which you request financial and technical assistance from the United States.

The people of the United States feel deep concern for the welfare of the people of the sister Republic of Bolivia. The friendly spirit of cooperation between our two nations has in the past motivated the programs of technical assistance and the Export-Import Bank loans for economic diversification to which your letter refers. Our concern for the welfare of the Bolivian people motivated the recent decision to make a further purchase of

Bolivian tin at a time when this country had no immediate need for additional tin. This concern is founded today not alone on the traditional friendship between our two peoples but also on the realization that the security of the entire Free World is threatened wherever free men suffer hunger or other severe misfortunes.

We appreciate fully the fact that the present emergency in Bolivia is one which the Government and the people of Bolivia are unable to meet without the assistance of friends. The Government of Bolivia is already taking wise and courageous measures of self-help looking toward the diversification and stabilization of the Bolivian economy, but unfortunately these measures cannot produce their full effect in time to prevent severe suffering by the people of Bolivia in the immediate future.

To assist Bolivia in this emergency, and to help accelerate the economic diversification of your country, the Government of the United States will provide the following emergency aid in response to your request:

(a) As announced on October 6, I have determined that up to $5 million of Commodity Credit Corporation stocks of agricultural products shall be made available to meet the urgent relief requirements of Bolivia;

(b) In addition, the Director of the Foreign Operations Administration is allocating up to $4 million of Mutual Security Act funds to be used in providing additional essential commodities and services required by the people of Bolivia;

(c) In accordance with your request, most of the Bolivian currency funds accruing from the sale of these commodities to Bolivian consumers are to be used by your Government for projects which will contribute to the economic development of Bolivia;

(d) The United States contribution to the cooperative technical assistance program in Bolivia has been more than doubled, and the additional funds, together with the matching contribution of your Government, are to be used for a program of emergency food production.

In closing I wish to express my deep personal appreciation for the kind reference in your letter to the visit to Bolivia of my brother, Dr. Milton Eisenhower. He has given me a first-hand account of the situation in Bolivia, and he has been among the strongest advocates of assistance to your country.

Sincerely yours,

DWIGHT D. EISENHOWER

NOTE: President Paz Estenssoro's letter follows:

Your Excellency:

On August 13, 1953, the Government of Bolivia delivered to the Department of State and to other agencies of the Government of the United States of America a copy of a "Plan for the Diversification of Production."

That plan was formulated after the visit to this country of your brother, Dr. Milton Eisenhower, and his advisors, Messrs. Cabot, Overby, and Anderson of the Departments of State, the Treasury, and Commerce, respectively.

The qualities of an educator which Dr. Eisenhower possesses, his extraordinary comprehension, and his sympathetic grasp of the problems of my country made it possible for the conversations held with him and his advisors to be carried out with complete frankness and on the level of the broadest cordiality and mutual understanding. I therefore wish to express again to Your Excellency my appreciation for your vision in having asked Dr. Eisenhower to visit Bolivia as your representative.

The plan presented after those conversations for the study and consideration of the high officials of the Government of the United States of America deals with the technical and economic assistance which my country needs in order to diversify its economy, which is now dependent almost completely on tin, as well as to overcome the economic crisis caused by the low price of that mineral.

Since that moment the Bolivian financial situation has deteriorated dangerously. Our availabilities in foreign currency have diminished so considerably through the fall in the price of tin and other minerals that we find ourselves in the insurmountable difficulty of not being able to provide food and other essential articles for the people, since in order to import them we need foreign currency.

This circumstance impels me to address Your Excellency to ask you that those parts of the above-mentioned plan which refer to providing food and other essential articles for the people of Bolivia and to additional technical assistance indispensable for developing a program of emergency food production be considered and resolved urgently.

Such assistance, granted in time, will serve on the one hand to spare the people of Bolivia from the menace of hunger which hangs over them, and on the other hand will permit the alleviation of the present disequilibrium in our balance of payments.

Such measures as Your Excellency may take in this matter will constitute yet another step in the program of technical and economic collaboration which Bolivia has been receiving from the United States of America and which has made possible the construction of the important Cochabamba-Santa Cruz highway and of certain works in our petroleum and agricultural industries.

The Bolivian currency which would be obtained from the sale to the public of the food and other essential articles furnished us could be utilized to put into effect that part of the plan of diversification of the

Bolivian economy which might be carried out through the use of local currency.

I believe that Your Excellency will receive this letter with sympathy and good will, since it concerns the furnishing of aid to a people who, as is the case in Bolivia, are sincerely pledged to improve the democratic institutions inherent in the free world, to which they firmly adhere, and who furthermore are solidly with the principles of mutual security which govern the nations of the Western Hemisphere.

In thanking Your Excellency in advance in the name of the people of the Government of Bolivia for the measures which you may be good enough to take so that this assistance may reach us opportunely, I express sincere wishes for the happiness of the great American people, whose destiny Your Excellency guides so wisely, as well as for your personal well-being.

V. PAZ ESTENSSORO

214 ¶ Remarks at Willard, Ohio.
October 15, 1953

My friends:

You know I was raised in a place where you had to shout out loud in order to be heard a long ways, but I am not sure I can shout loud enough to reach way down there where those youngsters are and whom I would very much like to see.

When I was invited to come to Defiance College, one reason I wanted to do it was because I learned that this was the 150th year since Ohio's birth as a State. So I am here today, in this crowd, to pay my tribute, through you, to this great Commonwealth, and to tell you that everything that your Government can do to bring peace and decency in this world is being done.

Now, there are many kinds of problems that beset us in this world today, but every one of them is overshadowed by this: can we have a world of decency, justice, and peace, or must we always be fearful that war is just around the corner?

I believe that America can bring about a situation in which we can have peace. That is what we are working for.

So, as I bring you greetings today, I ask you one thing: to study this whole problem yourselves, to stand behind reasonable, decent proposals in the maintaining of strength, in the keeping of our peaceful relations with others, but retaining above all things our position of self-respect and decency in the world.

Now I am sorry that I can't shout any louder, but I do want to say to every one of you: I am so honored that you came down to let me say "Good morning, how are you," that I want to thank you here and now for the very great privilege you have given me.

Thank you.

NOTE: The President spoke at 9:55 a.m. when the train made a stop on the way to Defiance.

215 ¶ Remarks at the Cornerstone-Laying Ceremony for the Anthony Wayne Library of American Study, Defiance College, Defiance, Ohio. *October 15, 1953*

President and Mrs. McCann, Senator Bricker, Governor Lausche, other distinguished guests, and my fellow Americans:

I suppose it is not too important to anyone to have an explanation of my reasons for being here this morning. But, in a way, they are important to me, and I would like taking a moment of your time to express them. Some of them are distinctly personal.

For example, I am returning a call—I am returning a courtesy.
This choir that we see here came to Washington last January 20th
and did me the signal honor of being there at the time of the
Inauguration.   I am delighted to have this opportunity to return
such a neighborly call.

I am here because of my admiration and affection for two
people—Kevin and Ruth McCann.   Kevin McCann was with
me in the services, at Columbia.   They typify for me an American couple at its best.   Recognizing their obligations to the
society of which they are a part, they have never once hesitated,
in the years I have known them, to take the hard and difficult way
to discharge that obligation, instead of the easy way of enjoying
things that they thought were given to them by that society.

I am here because of my ultimate faith in education as the hope
of the world—Christian religious education, man's free access to
knowledge, his right to use it.   I believe that unless all negotiations between nations are based upon a growing understanding
among the peoples of those nations, there is no validity and no
permanence to whatever arrangements may be made.

And so I think that the function of the school commands the
presence of anyone in the United States, when there is a significant occasion in any one of our important schools, and that person
can find it proper to attend.

I am here because I want to pay tribute to one of the greatest
States in its 150th year.   I deem it a signal honor that I may be
here in order to say "Long live Ohio," not merely for 150 years
but on down through the ages—one of the brightest jewels of
that great crown they call America.

And long may this library here stand and serve the needs of
Defiance College.   May it help assure to all her students free
access to knowledge, just as the teachers of this institution will
help them make intelligent use of that knowledge.

Now, for me, today's ceremony means more than physical participation in the laying of a cornerstone.   This community and
this College have a deeper significance than anything done or

any words that can be spoken here this noon. On this spot we are close to landmarks in American history, and with us on this campus are thousands of young people who are tomorrow's builders of a greater and better America. So we see the past and the future joining with the present in this ritual of dedication.

At one spot in this town, I have been told, a stone marks the site of the first French mission on the Maumee River, established more than 300 years ago. At another, the earthworks of Fort Defiance remind us that 160 years ago the forward command post of the American Nation was here. Other landmarks are canal locks and monuments and buildings that recall the mighty expansion of the American economy from an agricultural society to the first place among the world's industrial powers.

Consequently, in Defiance, whose roots are deep in the American past, it is fitting that I humbly salute the generations of men and women, the builders of Ohio, in this, the sesquicentennial year of their State. They were explorers and trappers and missionaries, traders, and farmers, and teachers, diggers of waterways and skilled operators of an industrial empire. Above all else, however, in the story of their achievements, they helped construct a way of life—the American way of life, of which the cornerstone is an indestructible faith in man's dignity as a child of God.

We today live in communities across this land enjoying justice, opportunity, and freedom, because from the beginning of our history until this very day those generations labored and fought and sacrificed so that justice and opportunity and freedom might be every American's birthright.

In their foremost ranks stood one whose name will live in reverent memory so long as the Republic lives. Senator Robert Taft dedicated his life to the service of his State and his country. To every task he brought an informed mind, an insatiable hunger for the full truth, a zeal in the cause of justice and opportunity and freedom for all his fellow citizens. He stands out in his age as one of the great builders of the American way that is our heritage.

This heritage is our most precious possession. What we do individually to conserve it, to strengthen it, to enrich it, is the only true measure of our devotion to it. More than this, it is the only true measure of the claims we can possibly have on posterity's memory. The wealth we may accumulate, the public prestige we may enjoy, the social position we may obtain, are all meaningless in the long vista of time, unless all are made to serve the cause of human dignity and freedom. What value dollars, or acclaim, or position in a world where justice and opportunity and freedom are lost to us by force, by subversion, or by our own neglect?

A chief bulwark of our heritage against any such decay of the law has been and is and will be the American school system— from the one-room red brick building at a country crossroads to the largest of our universities.

In the days of the Constitutional Convention in Philadelphia, Thomas Jefferson wrote to a friend these words: "No surer foundation," he said of education, "can be devised for the preservation of liberty and happiness." Then, with the fervor of a lifetime devoted to the increase of liberty and happiness among men, he added, "Preach a crusade against ignorance."

The crusade was preached and was waged successfully. Impelled by it, our forebears added the school—the community school to the home that was the center of man's life as a family being, and to the church that was the fountain of his faith as a religious being. They were intent on providing an armory of knowledge where Americans might gird themselves for the obligations and the challenges that those Founding Fathers knew would be inescapable in a system of representative government.

The results are written across the history of our country. By every step taken to banish ignorance, we have increased our hold on liberty. By every measure taken to enlarge our comprehension of the world in which we live, we have amplified the possibilities for human happiness. We possess in our land a largeness of justice and freedom beyond our forefathers' dreams, because the education of our youth has been a primary goal of this Nation.

Our school system is more important than ever before, because the job of being an American citizen is more complex than ever before in our history. Knowledge and understanding and vision beyond the demands of yesterday are required of tomorrow's citizens. Our schools—all our schools—in consequence, must have a continuing priority in our concern for community and national welfare.

In our school system an important place is filled by the small, often church-related, liberal arts colleges. These institutions, for generations in the van of higher education, have covered our land. They have brought the advantages of college training to thousands upon thousands who, except for the existence of these institutions, could never have enjoyed this privilege.

Now, they are caught in a squeeze between temporary decreased enrollments and high costs. But the great traditions they bring to today's students of their own intellectual leaders and fervent patriots of the past must not be lost. The importance of the place they occupy in American life needs not fewer but more of them.

Indeed, I firmly believe that more extensive education than that obtainable in high schools must be brought to every community and every locality in such a way that every young person regardless of his means or his lack of means can go to school for a minimum of 2 additional years.

Now, today, each of these small, almost neighborhood colleges is striving to fit itself better to serve its students, its community, and its country. Each of them shares—as does every typical American home and every church—in the American inspiration, the American purpose, and American goals.

On this campus, typical of the small liberal arts college, I deem it a privilege, indeed I consider it a duty, to pay my tribute to these schools. Already they have contributed much to the American way. Their potential contributions to the country's future are beyond calculation.

So we participating in the dedication of this library are expressing our support of this kind of education, of this kind of school. Thus we are performing one of the duties of citizenship in a free nation. Thus we symbolize our continuing faith in man's ability, under God, to govern himself intelligently. Thus we hope to assure the future strength and the eternal freedom of America.

My friends, to each of you who has come out this morning and has done me the courtesy of listening to the thoughts I have expressed, my warm thanks. I am grateful to you.

NOTE: The President spoke at 11:45 a.m.

216 ¶ Address at the Annual Convention of the Future Farmers of America, Kansas City, Missouri. *October 15, 1953*

Mr. President, Governor Donnelly, other distinguished guests, my young friends:

There has just been conferred upon me, as I came up here, an honorary degree of Farmer of America. I hope you will allow me to say that not only am I very proud of this distinction, but I shall expect to profit from it. Now I believe it is my privilege to call upon the county agent, and even for some Department of Agriculture pamphlets. And with my farm in Pennsylvania, I need them.

Now, my young friends, I want to visit with you tonight about our country, and also about an important part of it—agriculture—to which you are devoting your lives.

But first, I want to extend my warm congratulations on the Silver Anniversary of your organization.

I wish we could have had similar organizations when I worked on the farm during my boyhood in Abilene, some 160 miles west of here.

Mastery of good farming is, of course, your immediate concern as Future Farmers of America. But for his well-being today, the farmer must look not merely to his own skills and his own fertile acres; he must look to the far corners of this broad land and on beyond to such far-off regions as Malaya and the Belgian Congo.

The interests of you young men and women cannot be limited, isolated, or described by any single term such as "agriculture." Your study in the coming years must range beyond your immediate problems and your home communities. Your vision must encompass the entire globe. Certainly, for you and your parents, the activities of the Secretary of State and the Secretary of Defense are as important as those of the Secretary of Agriculture. Your fortunes are and will be as directly and intimately affected by the foreign policies of the United States as they will be by any farm policy of the government.

By the same token, our agriculture has a far deeper meaning for the entire American people than is represented only in the abundant products of the soil. Our great cities, our mighty industries, our business and professional accomplishments, our educational institutions, our high living standards—are possible because of the efficiency and productivity of the American farm.

In some countries, roughly nine-tenths of the population must work on the land, in order to provide a living for themselves and to release one man for other types of duty. In our country that ratio is more than reversed. So that we have a great preponderant portion of our population free to go into other forms of activity that redound to the comfort and improved standards of living of all of us. In the same fashion your own agricultural interests and income are inseparably tied up with the health and prosperity of working men and women and the industries in our towns and cities. One element of our Nation can scarcely exist— and certainly cannot prosper—independently of the others.

This truth is applicable within agriculture itself. There is, for instance, the problem created by the desire of the cattle raiser for cheap feed, while the producer of that feed seeks a good market and high prices. The simple fact is that we must seek methods of increasing stability and prosperity in all elements of agriculture. Such an agriculture is imperative to the well-being of all Americans.

668

Because our national interest is so deeply involved, I think it will be well for us to take stock of where we are today and where we are headed for in agriculture. I am going to talk about this, my young friends, without apology, because I think you have as much interest in the matter as do your parents. I know you have a far greater understanding of the factors at work than did young people during my own youth.

Let us talk first about some disagreeable facts. There are difficult problems today in our agriculture—problems deeply rooted in our recent past. By last January, farm prices, farm income, and our agricultural exports had all gone into full retreat, while the cost of the things farmers bought were on the increase.

This economic grinding machine hurt many of our farm people, but especially young farmers just starting out—including many thousands of GI's who had turned to farming or returned to their farms, after the war. I understand and am deeply concerned with their problems.

Now, this developing cost-price squeeze found the Nation's cattlemen in especial difficulty early this year. It even forced many of them to liquidate all or part of their herds.

One of the first official acts of this Administration dealt with this problem. Price controls were promptly removed, as was the compulsory grading that had been obstructing the market. Secretary of Agriculture Benson then vigorously attacked the problem from the merchandising standpoint. He obtained the whole-hearted cooperation of cattlemen's associations—meat packers—wholesale and retail outlets. These efforts helped increase beef sales by 26 percent during the first 8 months of 1953 as compared to one year before.

Trying and difficult as was this situation, a disaster of nature's making came to aggravate the trouble. A drought of devastating intensity blistered the great Southwest. Economic misfortune confronted hundreds of thousands of Americans on ranches and farms. The cattle forced upon the market from the stricken areas further depressed prices.

669

Clearly, here was a case for action by a government that was concerned with the welfare of all our people.

Emergency government programs were quickly set up to provide low cost feed in the disaster areas. Emergency credit, reduced freight rates, increased government purchases of beef were swiftly arranged. Incidentally, I was just informed today by the Secretary that the reduced freight rates are to be continued by the railways. In this crisis, the Congress, responding to the national interest, provided 150 million dollars for emergency loans and low-cost feed and seed.

Now, that was during June and July. Since then the drought has grown more serious, especially here in Missouri. I assure you young people, your families, and Americans generally, that the Federal government is continuing, and will continue as long as necessary, to assist in meeting the misfortunes of our people in the drought areas. Only a few days ago, an additional ten million dollars were allocated from emergency funds to help pay the cost of transporting midwestern hay to drought-stricken livestock farmers.

Today, to develop additional plans to meet this situation, Secretary Benson and Director Peterson of the Federal Civil Defense Administration met here in Kansas City with the Governors of the States most seriously affected by the widening drought. Tomorrow morning, I shall meet with the Governors to receive their suggestions on the cooperation of their States with the Federal government in this important effort.

My own conviction is that the principle of partnership between the Federal government and the State governments should govern our approach to such emergency problems. Only in this way can we gain the dual advantages of local knowledge, efficiency and incentive on the one hand, and of the wider Federal resources on the other.

And yet there are many problems relating to agriculture that are predominantly Federal in character. There is evidence of this fact in the many constructive legislative steps taken thus far by the 83rd Congress—such legislation as raising the minimum quota limitations on the 1954 wheat crop—authorizing wheat for Pakistan—providing one hundred million dollars of farm commodities for relief to friendly nations—authorizing two hundred and fifty million dollars for foreign currencies to expend for farm commodities—inaugurating a new upstream conservation-type flood control program—authorizing reorganization of the Department of Agriculture—extending the Reciprocal Trade Agreements Act and creating a commission to study foreign economic policy. These and other actions by the Congress have been a significant contribution both to the present and to the future welfare of American farmers.

Now, before plans can be laid for the future of American agriculture, it is important for us to understand the major problem today.

This trouble, aside from the drought, is simply stated: our war-expanded agriculture produces more than enough, in some lines to meet market demands and reserve requirements at present prices.

Why, then, you may ask, hasn't this problem become more insistently troublesome before now?

I think, again, the reason is plain.

It was World War II inflation; then huge American agricultural exports, financed by American billions; then still another burst of inflation caused by the Korean War: it was these emergencies, these calamities, this rampant inflation, that provided the critical margin for high agricultural prices during the past decade. It was this series of events that blurred the basic problem and deferred its solution to later years.

I grew up among farmers. I know they do not want their future prosperity contingent upon crises of one sort or another. No one can hate war, inflation and crisis more than does the farmer. Instead the farmer wants farm programs that affect him to be orderly, long-lived, soundly-based and carefully devised by the best brains and experience in agriculture. This, I am sure, is especially the conviction of you young people. You have long lives still before you, and must think in terms of sound and lasting farm programs fitted to your future.

It is for such reasons as these that we have established an 18-member commission to help devise programs for the farmers' future—a commission—and please note this well—a commission with 12 active, practical farmers as members, to insure that practical men help form a sound national agricultural policy.

To secure this kind of practical help is why the Department of Agriculture has been working closely with the national farm organizations and through them, directly with active farmers to develop its own recommendations for a farm program that will solidly advance the whole Nation's interest.

That is why special commodity committees and the agricultural colleges are hard at work with the Department of Agriculture on the more technical problems.

It is why the Senate Committee on Agriculture has commenced studies of conservation and development of our land and water resources.

This is also why the House of Representatives Committee on Agriculture is now holding hearings right at the grass roots, taking testimony directly from active farmers and their leaders, to find out what the experienced farmer believes is necessary for a sound farm program.

Now, these are the most thorough probings into the fundamentals of American agriculture in many years. They have been actively under way for some time. While they have not yet been completed, I want to say now these three things about these broad efforts:

First, I intend to weigh carefully the many recommendations developed by these groups of men experienced in all these phases of agriculture. Based on those views, I will submit my recommendations to the Congress early next year on the kind of program I believe to be in the Nation's best interest.

And may I say, in connection with that, I look upon the formulation of a sound farm policy as a bi-partisan undertaking. The welfare of our farm families knows no politics and I assure you there shall be none in the approach to that problem by this Administration.

Second, just a word about price supports.

Now, these price support laws expire in December 1954. This means that in the next session of Congress, the one meeting this coming January, various plans will necessarily be considered and weighed and resolved. These alternatives are: first to extend present laws exactly as now written; second, to extend them with certain improvements; and third, to revise them radically in favor of an entirely new program. As all people in agriculture know, there is great diversity of opinion as to what should be done about these expiring laws.

We must—and we will—continue faithfully to administer present price support laws now on the statute books. Further, all of us know that the price support principle must be a part of any future farm program.

All of us likewise know that these are extremely complex issues. They are now being analyzed and worked at as hard as thoughtful people can do, with expert judgment being brought to bear from practical farmers themselves. I have kept in close personal touch with the progress of these studies. The goal is a solidly-based, comprehensive farm program that will remedy present difficulties in existing laws—a program that will build markets, safeguard farm income, and protect consumers.

The farmers need such a program in their own interest. Consumers need one in their own interest. But keep this clearly in mind: no program is going to be proposed by this Administration, nor, I am sure, would a program be passed by the Congress, that fails to provide solidly for the national interest by continuing prosperity in American agriculture.

Third, I think we are now ready to start hammering out this solidly-based program for the future.

Within ten days, on October 24th to be exact, I am calling together, to meet with me in the Cabinet Room at the White House,

673

the National Agricultural Advisory Commission. That commission will give to us the conclusions it has arrived at in its months of study.

Later, as your farm organizations and the Committees of Congress complete their essential studies, the Secretary and I will confer with the ranking members of these Committees and with your farm leaders to obtain the results of their grassroots studies now nearing completion.

Thus, in this fashion, we will firm up the needed program and we will have that program ready for the consideration of the Congress early next year. After that, of course, begin the exhaustive Committee hearings and debate in the Congress. The end result will be as sound and as carefully thought out a farm program as practical experience, expert knowledge, and good judgment can devise.

Now, my friends, I trust that this sketchy outline of the developing farm program has some interest for you because of your immediate economic and professional concerns. But, for just a moment, let us look at your wider interests as Americans and as citizens of the world—and at the kind of world in which you may spend your years. And let us not forget that the demands of those wider interests must always be met satisfactorily before specific programs affecting any profession or calling can have validity.

In the past half century our Nation's population has almost doubled. In the next six years our population will grow by the equivalent of the total present population of our great neighbor Canada. The promise that this rapid growth of our country holds out to all our people, and especially our farmers, is tremendous. It represents 7,000 more breakfasts, 7,000 more dinners, 7,000 more suppers each day than on the day before.

Combined with this rapidly growing market is the amazing progress in science and invention which daily opens startling new vistas for all of our people.

There is no foretelling what American ingenuity will offer the

Nation in the next few decades. In my lifetime have come the automobile, television, electronics, home freezers, widespread use of the telephone and electricity on our farms, good roads, power machinery, vastly improved fertilizer and insecticides—and not the least, civilian and military aircraft some flying beyond the speed of sound, some with a range of 10,000 miles.

With such startling developments in our recent past, who can foretell the promise of the future ahead of you young people?

In this developing society in which you are speedily to take a leading part, you must never permit your government to indulge in the fanciful notion that work for the individual is a thing of the past. My friends, this is true because if ever this should become a fact, if work were a thing of the past, all fun and joy in living would be gone. Your own property, your own security, your own opportunity, your own liberties, they must be earned— they cannot be bestowed upon you. It is government's function to preserve your possession of these rights and opportunities and privileges, and to protect you against every disaster which is of such a kind that the individual alone cannot conquer it. But in the necessity of constantly adjusting the processes of government so as always to provide for needed protection to its citizens, while at the same time insuring perpetuation of their economic, political and intellectual freedoms, here is where we find the great challenge of America.

So, what is promised you is opportunity to get ahead, to make of yourselves what you can. What is promised you, too, is a chance to keep a free government free—a government carrying forward in keeping with the Nation's ideals—a government of limited powers, preserving your freedom, responding to your will, and insuring that the Nation is secure.

I foresee no limits to your future. It is truly boundless. Anyone my age who truly believes in America sincerely congratulates you as you start the exciting and challenging journey through life, even though he cannot see and experience what you are going to see and experience. But he does know that the whole adventure will be more fascinating, more spectacular, more stimulating and more rewarding than were the events my generation has witnessed.

As I say good night to you, I deeply wish that I could be given the words to express the boundless confidence I have in the ability and character and the stamina of America's young people. I have lived with them and gained inspiration from them in peace and in war in many corners of the earth. To them, America is indebted for every military victory she has won, for wars are always fought and won by the young people.

Now, we know as you know, that keeping our Nation secure and the world at peace will remain the predominant, overshadowing problem until an equitable method of easing the world's tensions has been found, until we have devised a way to turn man's major effort from his own destruction to his own betterment and salvation. Beyond all doubt the aspiration of America is peace; to achieve it your government in all its branches is laboring earnestly and persistently, and in doing so seeks the understanding support of every single one of our citizens in this quest for peace.

In this question, as in all others of major import, the fortunes of you young people are more definitely at stake than are those of older groups. This world is yours to live in; you must help shape it to your desires and aspirations. I believe—and I deeply believe—that the energy, the courage, the imagination, the readiness to sacrifice, of American youth when united behind this purpose, will constitute such a force that obstacles will fall and victory finally emerge.

As you till your farms, go to school, plan your futures, raise your families, remember that only he can deserve America who stands forever ready to give America all he has.

To live for America as devotedly, as nobly as so many thousands have died for her is the greatest ambition any of her children can have. Fortified and strengthened by this one truth, there is no problem you will not solve. May God truly bless you all.

Good night.

NOTE: The President spoke at 8 p.m. in the Municipal Auditorium in Kansas City. In his opening words he referred to James Dillon, National President of the Future Farmers of America.

217 ¶ Statement by the President on Eric Johnston's Mission to the Near East. *October* 16, 1953

THE GOVERNMENT of the United States believes that the interests of world peace call for every possible effort to create conditions of greater calm and stability in the Near East.

The Administration has continuously undertaken to relieve tensions in this sensitive and important area of the Free World.

Last spring, the Secretary of State, John Foster Dulles, made a first-hand survey of the area.

In furtherance of this policy, I am now sending Mr. Eric Johnston to the Near East as my personal representative with the rank of Ambassador to explore with the governments of the countries of that region certain steps which might be expected to contribute to an improvement of the general situation in the region. In so doing, I have assured Mr. Johnston that he will have my full support and enjoy the widest possible latitude in dealing with all questions relevant to his mission.

One of the major causes of disquiet in the Near East is the fact that some hundreds of thousands of Arab refugees are living without adequate means of support in the Arab states. The material wants of these people have been cared for through the United Nations Relief and Works Agency. The Congress of the United States, over a period of four years, has appropriated a total of $153,513,000 to aid these refugees. It has been evident from the start, however, that every effort must be made by the countries concerned, with the help of the international community, to find a means of giving these unfortunate people an opportunity to regain personal self-sufficiency.

One of the major purposes of Mr. Johnston's mission will be to undertake discussions with certain of the Arab states and Israel, looking to the mutual development of the water resources of the Jordan River Valley on a regional basis for the benefit of all the people of the area.

In his conversations in the region, Mr. Johnston will make known the concern felt by the Government of the United States over the continuation of Near Eastern tensions and express our willingness to assist in every practicable way in reducing the areas of controversy. He will indicate the importance which the United States Government attaches to a regional approach to the development of natural resources. Such an approach holds a promise of extensive economic improvement in the countries concerned through the development of much needed irrigation and hydroelectric power and through the creation of an economic base on the land for a substantial proportion of the Arab refugees.

It is my conviction that acceptance of a comprehensive plan for the development of the Jordan Valley would contribute greatly to stability in the Near East and to general economic progress of the region. I have asked Mr. Johnston to explain this position to the states concerned, seek their cooperation and help them through whatever means he finds advisable.

Mr. Johnston left the United States on October 14th, following conversations with me, the Secretary of State, the Director of the Foreign Operations Administration and other officials.

NOTE: On November 17, the White House announced that Mr. Johnston had that day reported to the President on his mission, and that the attitude he had encountered gave him reason to believe that the Jordan Valley project would commend itself to the states concerned as a sound and constructive approach to some of the critical issues that contributed to tensions in the area. It was further announced that Mr. Johnston would proceed to the Near East for further discussions in the near future.

218 ¶ Remarks at the Dedication of the American Hereford Building, Kansas City, Missouri. *October* 16, 1953

Mr. President, Senator Darby, many distinguished guests, and my friends:

I think I scarcely need use up your time to try to tell you how honored I feel at being in this company. In the first place, this is my section of the world. At least, it is that section that I feel I have the greatest right to claim. Whenever I get again the ground of these great plains beneath my feet, I feel differently than I do anywhere else. And so, with you, although there may not be a face in the throng that I recognize, I feel at home—and I hope you will allow me to do so.

Now, when I had the distinction of receiving an invitation to participate in the dedication of this building, I thought that your president, your association, was really making a mistake. Had they been dedicating a building to the old mossy horn that still roamed the plains when I was still on the farm, I would have seen some aptness to the invitation. But there were many things about this particular one that puzzled me. You know when the old scrub cattle of the prairie began to disappear, when I was a very young boy, there were all sorts of new breeds appearing—Shorthorns, Angus, this white face, and the Galloway. Whatever has happened to the Galloway? He was a big black cow, you know, bigger than that Angus, and sort of woolly-haired. And the people who advocated him said he was going to give a lot of milk and a lot of beef, too, and was going to be a better cow than any of the rest.

But the white face seems, at least, in this section, to have taken over very greatly. I went to central Kansas today, and I noticed, in all the time I was on the ground, I saw only one herd that was not of the white faced breed. There was still someone who believed that the Black Angus was the best.

Now, one of the puzzling things about this white face when it appeared, none of us knew exactly how to pronounce the name; and I confess that all these years it never occurred to me to look it up exactly. But just before I came out here, I got a very cultivated gentleman, and I said, "How do you pronounce this word now, correctly?" And I carefully drove myself to say "Hairford." And that's what I came over here to say, but I have learned from your president that it's "Herford"; and now I feel natural and it's "Herford" from now on.

And there is another thing. Those of us, in those days when I was undoubtedly reflecting the opinion of my elders, because I certainly didn't have any opinion myself about the matter, confidently talked about the fact that the old scrub range cow would always hold its own, that these new-fangled, fancy animals coming in from abroad and elsewhere just didn't have what it took to make a living in the short-grass country.

Well, it shows you how wrong people can be, when they prophesy against progress. Those few herds that were scattered all through this country, down through Oklahoma and all of the other regions around here, have multiplied until if they were not all white face, they are all blooded cows. They are a heavy beef cow. They are producing this country's food on far less than that old scrub did. As a matter of fact too much of that cow went to horns and legs—that's about all there was to it, just enough body to connect the two. And when one of them took after you, you knew how fast they could go, too!

Now, this has grown into a tremendous industry. I saw today a statistic that every day the United States eats 33 million pounds of beef. When we begin to talk about statistics, we talk about something that is of the utmost importance to the United States. This great and wonderful living that we have has featuring among other things the finest diet in the world—and the Hereford produces most of it.

In any event, that industry has now reached the proportions that everything that affects it is of interest to the entire United

States. If cattlemen are in trouble, and certainly in the drought areas and all over they are, it is not merely the cattlemen that Government and all the rest of us must think about, we must think about the welfare of all the United States. We must approach all our problems in that way.

And so, regardless of my ignorance about all of these different breeds, from "Old Anxiety" and "Domino 99th," and all the rest of them, right down to the present, in spite of the fact that I don't know where the Galloway went or why the Shorthorn seemed to disappear or anything else, I do think there is one factor that makes it fitting that I should have the honor to read the words on this tablet and to cut the ribbon: that is, in the Office that has been entrusted to me for these years, I do represent the feeling, the convictions, of the United States. And those feelings and convictions are that this great Hereford industry is of transcendental importance to all of us.

And now, let me just read the words that are on this plaque:

"This monument erected as a tribute to the faith of the Pioneers, and the determination of the men who have carried on, to establish the Hereford Breed as leader in the beef cattle world.

"Dedicated October 16, 1953."

And before I cut this, wouldn't it be interesting to know what some of those old cattlemen—that drove their cattle from the south of Texas up that Chisholm Trail to Abilene—what they would think, if today they could see the great building erected to the honor of cattle—the successors to the ones that they drove up here.

And so I have the honor to dedicate this building to the usefulness, to the welfare of the Hereford Association of America.

NOTE: The President spoke at 7:50 p.m. In his opening words he referred to Herbert A. Chandler, President of the American Hereford Association, and Harry Darby, former Senator from Kansas. Following the ceremonies the President attended the American Royal Livestock and Horse Show in Kansas City.

219 ¶ Address in New Orleans at the Ceremony Marking the 150th Anniversary of the Louisiana Purchase. *October 17, 1953*

Mr. Chairman, Your Excellency the Ambassador of France, Your Excellencies the Ambassadors from other countries here represented, Governor Kennon, Mayor Morrison, Your Excellency the Archbishop, other distinguished guests—and my fellow Americans:

Before I shall try to expose to you the thoughts that I believe appropriate to this occasion, might I have a moment to express a personal word of thanks, not only on my behalf, but I am sure they would want me to speak for them—the other guests of your city today—on behalf of all of us, our thanks for the cordiality, the hospitality this city has displayed to us. We have been privileged to take part not only in an historically significant occasion, but in a most colorful one, and for my part, I owe a special debt of gratitude to Your Majesties King Rex and King Comus, for graciously allowing a part of this parade—your traditional parade—to take part in this ceremony this morning. It is the first time I have had the honor of seeing it, and I thoroughly appreciate it. Thank you.

My friends, we are today observing the anniversary of an event which ranks with the most important in our history.

The Louisiana Purchase effectively doubled the area of our young nation, brought this country unimagined wealth, and gave us strength and international influence beyond the dreams of our nation's founders just 25 years earlier.

We are observing the anniversary of an act which, though born of other nations' conflicts, involved the death of not a single American soldier. It was, for the United States, an act of peace.

It was also an act of vision and of daring.

It was daring for a new-born nation, lacking all modern communications making for unity, to venture into a huge, unexplored area of unknown natural hazards and little-known inhabitants. It was daring for such a nation to accept so heavy a debt as this unique purchase imposed upon it. It was daring for our two negotiators in Paris—Livingston and Monroe—to decide to accept Napoleon's surprising offer without fear of repudiation by their national leaders separated from them by the breadth of an ocean. It was daring for our President, Thomas Jefferson, to support their decision instantly and to face squarely the opposition not only of foreign powers but of political critics of great passion and small vision.

That daring, typically American, has been justified in rare measure. It has been justified to an extent which staggers the mind; to an extent which, mathematically, is almost incalculable.

What once was the Louisiana Territory, today embraces six of our forty-eight states and large parts of seven others. It was 900-thousand square miles. It is bordered by a river almost unmatched in length and unsurpassed in majesty.

The bounty of this area has been even more phenomenal than its size. Its total cost, after all other increments were added to the 15 million dollars, was 23 million dollars—the cost today of a single Navy cargo ship. For this outlay, what did America get?

Let me give you one interesting example:

One single state—of the thirteen originally involved in the Purchase—recently reported the value of one single crop in one single year.

The state was Iowa. The crop was corn. The value was over 700 million dollars. This sum is thirty times as much as was paid for the entire Louisiana Territory.

Only one other example shall I give you. It concerns this city of New Orleans, and, specifically, one part of this city—the Port of New Orleans. During the first four months of this year, there passed from the fields and cities of America, through the port of this city, exports valued at more than 250 million dollars. And this is a sum eleven times greater than the cost of the whole Territory.

Now I find this last example singularly meaningful—not to New Orleans alone but to all America. For here we see dramatically highlighted one of the critical facts of our national life—our dependence on foreign trade.

We all know that New Orleans has always been a vital American port. As you well remember, it was closure of this port that sharpened our nation's anxiety to buy from France the area around this city—to insure our frontiersmen this essential gateway to the open sea.

The passage of a century and a half has decisively underscored the need of that day. For today our whole economy turns and depends upon the commerce of the world through such ports as this.

Through such ports as this on this Gulf, on two oceans, on the Great Lakes, come almost all the tungsten used in our tool steel, almost all the nickel and practically all the chromite used in stainless steel.

The tin used in canning our food, the columbite and the cobalt that are needed in the manufacture of high alloys, the manganese that goes into our American steel, the hemp for our ropes and hawsers, all of these come, almost exclusively, from foreign markets.

This dependence of our industry is certain to increase as the tempo of our industry increases. It highlights the most compelling practical reason why we must have friends in the world. We know that nations of hostile intent would not trade with us except as it suited their own convenience. And this means that hostile rule of areas supplying us essential imports would place the American production line at the mercy of those who hope for its destruction.

But foreign trade means much more than the obtaining of vital raw materials from other nations. It means effectively strengthening our friends in the world at large—strengthening them not only to fortify their own economies—not only to be independent of direct financial aid from wealthier nations—but also to buy from us what we must sell to the world.

By making it possible for our friends to sell their products to us, we thus at once help them to be strong and enable them to earn the dollars by which they can, in turn, help our economy to be healthy and progressive.

Clearly, we need these friends abroad, just as they need us.

Consider some of our agricultural products which demand foreign markets—many of those products coming from the land originally involved in the Louisiana Purchase and much of them flowing through this port.

In the crop year 1951–52:

Of all the barley produced in this year, more than 12 percent was paid for outside our borders.

Almost 50 percent of all our wheat was paid for in foreign markets.

Almost 60 percent of our entire rice crop was bought by other nations.

With non-agricultural products, the facts are much the same. Half a million of our refrigerators and home-type freezers, more than 30 million dollars' worth of our sulphur, more than 250 million dollars' worth of our machine tools and our agricultural machinery, more than a quarter of all the lubricating oil, and almost half of all our copper sulphate—all these were paid for in foreign countries.

Now, these facts and figures affect every American, no matter who he is: all who work on our farms, all who labor in our industries. They can signify for our whole economy the difference between productive profit and paralyzing loss.

This is a partial measure of the material meaning of foreign trade to America.

And this dramatizes, with sharp clarity, the role that New Orleans has played in helping this country form and sustain the international friendships which we need and cherish. Through

685

such gateways as New Orleans, we have been able to trade with these friends on a fair and mutually profitable basis. We have been able to cooperate with them in projects developing their physical resources. There has been for a century and a half a stream of visitors flowing in both directions—from other countries to this, and from this to other countries. Through the knowledge and mutual understanding gained and spread by these people, there have been built friendships based upon mutual respect, mutual liking, and mutual need. Such friendships are many.

But there must be more. They must be stronger. They must be deeper. I think that almost any American traveling abroad these days experiences occasionally a sense of shock when he recalls an opinion about Americans in general held abroad, that seems to that American visitor to be so far from the truth. He finds himself considered immature diplomatically—impulsive—too proud of their strength—ready to fight—wanting war. He is shocked. He is considered rude. Even his deportment is not admired, because of unfortunate incidents on the part of individuals.

These friendships of which I speak, my friends, are so vital to us, that no American, no matter how exalted or how lowly may be his station, can afford to ignore them.

Each of us, whether bearing a commission from his Government or traveling by himself for pleasure or for business is a representative of the United States of America, and he must try to portray America as he believes it in his heart to be: a peace-loving nation, living in the fear of God, but in the fear of God only, and trying to be partners with our friends—and we accept for a friend anyone who genuinely holds out the hand of friendship to us, as we do to them.

And now this great port must meet the challenge of the coming decades. It offers foreign shippers 40 miles of river front. It is enhanced by a foreign trade zone. Its modern facilities are daily being enlarged and improved. It is manned by workers celebrated for their skill, their enthusiasm, and their vigor. It is an inspiring symbol not only of the vastly prosperous area whose anniversary we are this year celebrating, but of the nation it has served for the past 150 years. And with every item of commerce that comes in, with every one that goes out, let us strive to see that it is packaged in understanding, and handled in friendship.

Here, in the Port of New Orleans, we see reflected America's strength, her vitality, her confidence, her irrepressible desire for improvement, her magnificent ability to meet resourcefully the demands of changing times.

It has been thus—in New Orleans, in the Louisiana Territory, throughout the United States—during the past century-and-a-half.

With God's help, with our friends in the world, and with unity among ourselves, it will continue to be so, throughout all the years that lie ahead.

Thank you, my friends.

NOTE: The President spoke at 11:52 a.m. in Jackson Square. In his opening words he referred to Ernest V. Richards, Jr., Chairman of the Louisiana Sesquicentennial Commission; Ambassador Henri Bonnet; Governor Robert F. Kennon of Louisiana; Mayor De Lesseps S. Morrison of New Orleans; and The Most Reverend Joseph F. Rummel, Archbishop of New Orleans.

220 ¶ Remarks to a Group of Republican Workers in New Orleans. *October* 17, 1953

THANK YOU very much—thank you very much. This reminds me a little bit of last year, ladies and gentlemen. If you remember, I was nominated over in Chicago, and immediately all the party strategists came to give me advice. And most of it, I suppose, was good.

One thing they told me was to stay out of the South. That may have been good political advice, of course. I didn't know. Everybody knew I wasn't a politician—and I'm not yet. But one thing I did know: that I had promised a lot of people that if ever I got in politics, I was going to come to the South.   And so—come what may—I was going to keep that promise.

And so, the first crowd I ever met in the South was, I think, in Atlanta.   I don't know how many people were there, but they filled that whole square and down the side streets, all along the way—and the same in Jacksonville, Miami, and down that way. And finally, somewhere along in October—I think the day before my birthday—I got to New Orleans, and I don't think I ever saw so big a jam in one place.   Finally, I decided to do something. When I got over to Texas, I called up one of these party strategists, and I said "Just how big is a corporal's guard?"   As you know, when I was a lieutenant in the Army, a corporal's guard was about eight men.

Now, they say you can't have a two-party system in the South. Well, it looks to me like there is one here.   If you could take just the people in this room—this minute—and place them absolutely strategically all over the State of Louisiana—put them exactly where you want them—there is no question about the influence you would immediately swing.

You are people that respond to the requirements of leadership. You have got brains enough to know that it is the South that needs a two-party system, not a bunch of politicians—not a bunch of Democrats, or anybody else.   It's the South that needs a two-party system, if it is to be truly emancipated.

It has got to have such influence in all national affairs that, regardless of which party has come into power, the brains and the talent of the Southern States are as willing and as well organized, and as immediately available to the central government as if they came from some other region.

But let me give you some bitter experience—this much on a personal basis.   If the Republicans win today, they have to come down and find someone they trust and say here is a good man that can represent the viewpoint of this region.   Because almost everybody that has been in a political organization, that has been in political life, for years and years in the South has been Democratic.

Now you have the brains to know that, and that is the first requirement of leadership. Next, you have got enthusiasm. I know that, because John Wisdom tells me you have been here since 9 o'clock this morning. You couldn't possibly have gone to all the trouble of getting off today and be here to give me the opportunity to meet with you for these few moments, unless you had enthusiasm.

You have faith—or you wouldn't have done the work in the Southland that a Republican must do to hold up his head. Republicans haven't been too popular here for a good many decades, and you had to have faith to do what you could to restore the party to a position of complete respectability—and you have done it.

By the way, John Wisdom told me on the way out here that there was a Mayor and three councilmen of a little town somewhere elected in Louisiana. Is that Mayor here? I would like to see his hand. Good to see you! Congratulations!

I should like to say, gentlemen, that some very, very great oaks have grown from small acorns—and he looks like a pretty good-sized acorn to me.

But it does mean intelligence. It does mean enthusiasm. It does mean faith. Readiness to go to work—and work for what you want, and what you believe in.

What we must believe in is: honest government. The Republican Party is not of any particular use because it has a nice-sounding name. It is of use only if it can give the United States of America better government at home, and better understanding abroad. That is your dedication.

And I want to make one thing clear, my friends. We don't have to claim credit for all the deeds, all the talents, all the dedication, all the patriotism, in the Republican Party. Not at all. But we do know that unless there is competition in things like that, that free government can perish. That it is only intelligent, dedicated opposition that keeps people in power right up on their toes.

There is surely one way to keep both parties decent. That is for both parties to be strong, and composed of people who have one thought: the United States of America, and her standing in the world and at home.

Now that, my very good friends, I realize, is not a very profound message. Every one of you knows it—and knows the truth of every fact I have stated, just as well as I know it.

The only thing I do see worth while in this meeting, then, is that I may stand before you and, as the President of all the United States—not just of the Republican Party, but of the United States of America—give you my dedication to remain as true to that kind of undertaking and that kind of philosophy as I know how to do.

That kind of pledge will help you set about the task which at times must look hopeless. Well then, I assure you, that kind of help, as much as I can give, will always be there.

And one other word: don't ever let anyone get you hopeless in the long fight. I had an old general that I thought the world of as my teacher, years ago. And one day I was working on something pretty hard—down in Panama it was—something pretty hard. I didn't see any way out of it. And he said to me, "Well, I will tell you, Eisenhower"—he was from Mississippi, talked like that—"there is one thing sure: the harder a problem, the more necessary it is to smile. A tough one is never won by a long face. Don't forget that."

So among other things, keep a grin on your face.

Goodbye.

NOTE: The President spoke at 12:40 p.m. at Moisant Airport, New Orleans, La.

221 ¶ Toast to President Ruiz Cortines of Mexico at a Luncheon Before the Dedication of the Falcon Dam on the Rio Grande. *October* 19, 1953

Mr. President and friends from both sides of this international boundary:

I speak for all the citizens of my own country here present when I express to you, Mr. President, our tremendous satisfaction that you have honored us with this personal visit.

For your country, this country has only sentiments of friendship, of pride, and esteem. And those sentiments we express to you because you are the embodiment of your country: its official, its social, its political leader.

So, speaking not only for those here present, but I assure you, Mr. President, for all of that great body of our citizens who would like to be here but who cannot be here today, as we go to engage in this joint ceremony on the River, for all of them I say to you: may long life, health, and happiness be yours, and may the relationships between your country and mine be those only of friendship.

And for myself I say: I am proud that today I have been able to form a new personal, valuable friendship with you.

And now, ladies and gentlemen, may I ask all of you to rise and with me drink a Toast to the President of Mexico.

Your good health!

NOTE: The President proposed this toast at 2:08 p.m. at a luncheon held near the site of the dam. See also Items 222 and 223.

222   ¶ Address at the Dedication of Falcon Dam. *October* 19, 1953

Mr. President, Mr. Commissioners, and all those present from both sides of this international border, whom I am bold enough and certainly proud to call my friends:

To you, President Ruiz Cortines, permit me to address my first thought, as we meet to dedicate this great structure to the use of our two peoples. I prize the opportunity of meeting you personally. Moreover, I should like for you to accept my pledge that, as the political head of the United States of America, I shall ever deem it a privilege—and a useful service to my own country—to work with you cooperatively and in friendship. The citizens of the United States of America here gathered with the citizens of your people, are honored by your presence, as all, throughout our entire country, prize the friendship implicit in this meeting.

And President Ruiz Cortines, and all others present from south of this River, let me say that when I speak of friendship today—friendship between our two countries—I am by no means talking of that pale sentiment by which we often describe a chance meeting with an acquaintance on the street, nor do I mean for it to be used as a mere salute or as used, sometimes, in formal diplomatic language.

I mean, Mr. President, the kind of friendship that seeks—seeks earnestly and persistently to understand the viewpoint of the other, and then labors with sympathy and with all that is in the heart to meet the viewpoint of his friend.

To be here today, at this moment in the history of our two nations, fills me with pride and with hope. Pride is for the past—for this latest achievement of the united labor of our two peoples. Hope is for the future—for the kind of future that two such peoples, in such proven unity, can surely build.

More than a mute monument to the ingenuity of engineers, this Falcon Dam is living testimony to the understanding and the cooperation binding our two peoples.   More than any volume of words, the sound of its rushing waters and spinning generators speaks of this understanding.   And more meaningful and powerful than all the energy it shall generate is the force for common good which we can found in this cooperation.

This work is one of the most dramatic achievements of the International Boundary and Water Commission which conceived and executed its construction.   Founded almost sixty-five years ago, this Commission has repeatedly, throughout its history, resolved such problems as elsewhere in the world have flared into bitterness and into hostility.   It has done more.   It has provided the means for the peoples of two free, sovereign nations to work constructively for their common welfare.   And it has done yet more.   It has given the world a lesson in the way neighbor nations can and should live: in peace, in mutual respect, in common prosperity.

Behind the work of this historic commission—beyond even all the efforts of the governments of these two nations—is the spirit of two neighbor peoples.   This dam and all works like it can, in the deepest sense, be appraised or understood not simply as the achievements of officials and technicians, nor as the grand purchases bought by appropriations of vast sums of money.   Such works as this are created in the hearts of the citizens of two nations, citizens who respect and believe in one another.   They are bought with the most precious coin in the world—the goodwill among peoples.

I pay my tribute, then, to the men who really created this work: the citizen of the United States of Mexico, and the citizen of the United States of America.

Each of these men proudly proclaims himself a patriot of his own country.

But, what else is he?

First, he respects all that belongs to his neighbor—his culture, his history, his just possessions, and his honest aspirations.   He honors his neighbor's rich heritage as heartfully as he honors his

own. He respects the dignity of the other—and expects no less
from his neighbor.

He is, in yet deeper ways, a lover of freedom.   He is profoundly
aware of the ugly menace of totalitarianism, of its gaudy promise
and its grim practice.   He is particularly alert to that kind of
aggressive totalitarianism today propagating the deadliest divisions—class against class, nation against nation, people against
people.   In his heart and in his mind and in his conscience, this
man despises all the qualities and trappings of this totalitarianism:
its pretense, its slander, its self-seeking—its contempt of man
himself.

And, finally, this man knows his own true source of strength:
his own free, creative initiative—all the strength and dignity
which are his because God so endowed him.   This man—this
man on both sides of this border—he looks to no government—
neither his own nor someone else's—to chart his life.   He knows
that his own happiness and the healthy progress of his whole
nation alike are to be won essentially by his own hands and his
own brains.

In all this, the man we salute today is the same—on whichever
side of this border he lives.   Citizen of Mexico or citizen of the
United States, he is also citizen of the free world.

This—this I deeply believe, is the spirit that not only rules our
hearts here today but also unites this entire Hemisphere.

Extending southward from this spot is a continent of magnificent resources and infinite promise.

I need not emphasize the weight of the responsibilities that
fall upon the United States of America in our dealings with the
whole free world.   Understandably, I think, these have often in
the past conspired to center our attention on points of the globe
remote from this continent.   These responsibilities persist—indeed, they grow greater and increase.   But something else has
likewise increased: our awareness of the vital problems and the
exciting opportunities here in the lands of all the Americas.

To these lands, our attention is turned in warm friendship and constructive concern for the well-being of all our neighbors.

We hope to understand their needs and their problems.

We know of the longings of so many for a life enriched not only by greater material blessings, but also by the educational and cultural opportunities due all free men.

We know the scarcity of capital to provide vital stimulus to industry and agriculture—to all production enterprise.

We know the urgent demand for technical assistance in many areas.

We know the grave issues of international trade that must be resolved to allow productive prosperity for all.

We know these matters to be the common concern of all other nations and peoples—for whatever touches one of us touches all of us.

And above all we know this: the conquest of these problems is within the power of our united energy, skill, and determination.

Now, on this day, and on this border, there meet not only the heads of the governments of neighbor nations and fraternal peoples. Here meet the past and the future: the lesson of one, the promise of the second.

Out of this past—out of its trials, its not infrequent shows of national selfishness, its occasional sharp anxieties and differences—out of all this there has come and prevailed a kind of continental concert of spirit and will and purpose.

Ours is the imperishable spirit of free men, unswayed by the cheap promises of totalitarianism, undismayed by its blustering threats.

Our common purpose is the pursuit of a peace that is productive and lasting.

We seek, indeed, that age whose grandest monuments are not built to honor military or physical accomplishments, but rather those very different monuments: schools to teach our young, hospitals to heal our sick, roads to bear our commerce, power to give warmth and light, religious institutions to rouse the spirit, and the structure of abiding peace in which men may faithfully seek all that is good, all that is noble in life.

We confidently believe that such purposes continue to grow throughout this Hemisphere. Especially most important, we believe that your nation, under your leadership, is growing in that thought and in that purpose.

We humbly believe these purposes to be worthy enough to ask the blessing of the Almighty upon our peoples as we seek, with prayer and patience, their full attainment.

My friends, thank you very much.

NOTE: The President spoke at 3:45 p.m. In his opening words he referred to President Ruiz Cortines of Mexico, and to Commissioner David Herrera Jordán, Mexican Section, and Commissioner Lawrence M. Lawson, United States Section, of the International Boundary and Water Commission, United States and Mexico.

223 ¶ Remarks Following the Dedication of Falcon Dam. *October* 19, 1953

My friends:

May I first say that I deeply regret that there was not room out on that Dam to accommodate all the visitors who attended this historic event. But, by your coming, by your patience, even though you could not go out on the Dam, you demonstrated your understanding of what was really taking place today: the forging of another indestructible link in the friendship of two countries.

I do not intend, my friends, to keep you long today, but I would like to give you some idea of how firmly I believe in the necessity of international friendship.

If friendship does not replace the hostilities of the world, if the conference table does not displace the battlefield as the place where we shall settle our disputes, then civilization as we know it indeed has a meager future.

But if we build friendships—friendships that mean an attempt to understand the other fellow, to approach his problem sympathetically, and with the determination that he shall be helped just as much as we can in the solution of that problem, then we are going to make progress toward a future brighter than any civilization has known.

You young people—you young people still own, let us say, 60 years of our country—far more than I do.   If I am lucky I still own about 15—and I have to be lucky.   But you own America, you young people, and don't let anyone tell you that people have to be enemies.

Now, here today, if you can establish one new link of friendship with our nearest neighbors, you have made progress toward a future that you can turn over to your children with pride and confidence.

And so I say again, I am proud of you for coming out today in spite of the heat and the inconvenience, and the impossibility of getting out there to visit with the President of Mexico, and to hear the bands.   You came—showing that you understood what this means.   I am so proud of you, that if I don't go, I am going to get maudlin.

Thank you a lot.

NOTE: The President spoke at 4:06 p.m. near the Falcon Dam, shortly after making his formal address there (Item 222).

224   ¶ Statement by the President on the Death of William L. Hutcheson.   *October* 20, 1953

THE COUNTRY has lost an outstanding citizen and labor one of its most universally respected leaders in the passing of William L. Hutcheson.   Through his thirty-six years as President of the Carpenters' Union, he had the esteem of both the rank and file and management.   His long and vigorous service on behalf of the many thousands of workers in his organization was matched by his devotion to his country.   He was a true American.

225 ¶ The President's News Conference of *October* 21, 1953.

THE PRESIDENT. Please be seated. Good morning, how are you.

For my part, the most important thing that has happened to me is a swing around through Ohio, Kansas, Missouri, Louisiana, and Texas.

There were two real points to the trip—to meet with the Future Farmers and with the Governors' Conference out in Kansas City, and to meet with President Ruiz Cortines of Mexico.

Both stops seemed to have been well reported in some detail, and so I do not think that you people have any particular interest in any incident that I would know of, because I think you already know about them.

I would like to say this: I was very deeply gratified to see the Governors meet in Kansas City, and meet with the intention of working out a program by which individual States afflicted by the current disaster, the drought, can work with the Federal Government in a cooperative effort to relieve distress.

Moreover, they voluntarily extended that objective to the attempt to work out a long-range program, so that in the event of any kind of natural disaster States and the Federal Government can work together for instant relief on a logical basis of cooperation, and so that we would know exactly how we go about relieving distress without the delay of looking around for new authorizations, new legislation, new understandings between us.

I think that the great interest shown by these Governors in the responsibility of the local area as well as the help they expect from the Federal Government is very encouraging.

In line with that, immediately after that meeting Governor Donnelly of Missouri went home and called a special session; I believe his legislature is now meeting in Jefferson City to carry on this cooperative effort.

I have a number of details of the things that have been done

by the Federal Government and by the States in the past months
to relieve this drought situation.

We would be foolish to try to minimize its effects; it is very,
very serious. Rather than try to recite them to you now, about
what we have done in the way of credit and reduced freight rates,
supplementing the appropriations of emergency funds, about
cutting down the price of feed and of meal and so on, helping
to get in hay, I think that if you want those facts it would be
better for you to stop and get them from Mr. Hagerty. They
make an impressive array altogether. But, naturally, there is still
a lot of distress, a lot of things yet to be done.[1]

By the way, I want to say one thing about one officer this morning. I had General Dean for breakfast. I have long been an
admirer of General Dean, although he happened to be commanding one division in my command in World War II that I never got
to see in its entirety and, therefore, had never met him.

He had a most unusual experience. One thing that interested
me was that he was always fed well. He said never once in the
whole time he was captive was he fed less well than his own guards
and captors around him, which was an interesting thing.

He told about methods of indoctrination, treatment, and also
some of the conclusions he formed as a result of his experience on
both sides of that line in Korea. They were very interesting.

I can't, of course, take time now to tell you about them, but he
is a man, I think, who is well worth talking to. He's got a very
rich and unique experience behind him.

With that remark, I think we will go to questions.

---

[1] The President referred to a White House release summarizing the administration's
activities in relieving hardships caused by the drought. The following were enumer-
ated: the designation of drought disaster areas in 13 States, the making available at
greatly reduced rates of feeds owned by the Commodity Credit Corporation, an agreement by the railroads to reduce freight rates for the movement of Government-owned
feeds to drought areas, increased purchases of hamburger and canned beef to support declining prices, approval of more than $10 million in special livestock loans
under emergency credit legislation, and allocation of $10 million from emergency
funds to underwrite Federal participation in the distribution of hay in the drought
areas.

Q. Merriman Smith, United Press: Mr. President, can you tell us what General Dean's next assignment will be? Do you know, sir?

THE PRESIDENT. I think he is not certain. They have discussed one or two with him. He has not yet talked with the Chief of Staff.

I am personally anxious that he get into some place where the benefit of his unusual experiences will redound to the benefit of all of us, all of the Army; and if he has got anything that the rest of us can profit from, I would like to see it utilized.

Q. Richard L. Wilson, Cowles Publications: Mr. President, do you attach any general political importance to the election of a Democrat in a traditionally Republican district in Wisconsin?

THE PRESIDENT. Well, of course I realize that is a natural question for you to ask.

I will be frank with you, ladies and gentlemen, I think you are probably better analysts of local political situations than I, and I am going to leave the determination of what happened and why it happened, to you. I really don't know, and no one has given me a long or any detailed analysis of it.

Q. Ray L. Scherer, National Broadcasting Company: One of your Cabinet officers told us, Mr. President, that he thought the politicians were more stirred up about the farm situation than the farmers were. I was wondering what your impressions might be on that point, after seeing a number of them last week?

THE PRESIDENT. Frankly, there were several times when I should very much have liked to have collected up all of the press and picturemen that went with me on that trip and asked them what they were gathering, what their impressions were.

I would say that I thought the cattlemen and farmers were taking this more in their stride. After all, in my little home town of Abilene I had lunch with 40 people, most of whom, if they are not farmers themselves, own farms. And certainly, in view of my background with them, there was no reason for them holding back anything they wanted to say. My impression was they were not as concerned as some of the people that visit my office.

However, they don't minimize the seriousness of this thing, and they do hope that a long-range program can be worked out that will insure them against the calamity when they have no control over it.

Q. Robert J. Donovan, New York Herald Tribune: Mr. President, I had a question on congressional elections generally. You have told us, I think, on two occasions that it would be your policy not to interfere in local elections of any kind. I think the questions that have been asked before, though, have applied to gubernatorial elections or some local elections. Will you take part in the congressional election campaign next year?

THE PRESIDENT. Of course you know, Mr. Donovan, that I am deeply interested in what happens to the complexion of the Senate and of the House of Representatives, but I do not intend to make of the Presidency an agency to use in partisan elections.

I have the conception that although elected by only part of the population, as is evident, anybody occupying this office is President of all the people. He has got the responsibility of attempting to develop a program that is enlightened and progressive and for the benefit of all people. And if the success he has in getting assistance and associates around him in his working with the Congress in an effective way—not just in an apparent, you might say, out-in-front way, but in an effective way—so as to secure the enactment of such programs, then those people that are supporting him, people of his own party, people that are supporting that kind of a program, have a real umbrella under which to operate. That is the best thing I think he can do, both for, you might say—for his party, because he is working for his country.

I have no intention of going out and getting into partisan struggles in any district or in any State, because I know that I, for one, in such a State would resent that kind of intrusion from the President of the United States.

Q. Robert C. Albright, Washington Post: Mr. President, I was going to ask you if that statement applied to the Virginia gubernatorial——

THE PRESIDENT. To the what?

Q. Mr. Albright: To the Virginia governorship contest in the light of your statement in favor of the two-party system.

THE PRESIDENT. Well, of course, I believe in the two-party system. I believe in any area where there isn't a legitimate two-party system working, that that area itself suffers. I believe it is not really enjoying the full benefits that it could under our form of government. But I am not, I repeat *not,* going out and get into these things that are strictly local where, believing as I do in representative and free government, they have a right to choose as they please.

What I am trying to do with the party of which I am a part, is to establish a record that so nearly as possible a great overwhelming majority of Americans approve of it; and then we will get somewhere.

Q. Sarah McClendon, El Paso Times: Sir, I have two questions on these commissions. Some of the studies in the departments which you inaugurated and which the Cabinet officers started on Federal-State relationships were under way before the Manion Commission was set up. Will those studies, when they are finished, have to go to the Manion Commission before they are made public?

THE PRESIDENT. Well, I couldn't answer it because I am not certain as to the status of these.

Q. Mrs. McClendon: I found this week in the departments that some of the people say it will be your decision as to whether they have to go to the Manion Commission or the Hoover Commission.

THE PRESIDENT. They have not brought me those questions for decision yet.

Now, what I do believe is this: there have been often in this great and complex Government studies made one place, buried in the shelves, go into the dusty archives, and no one ever hears about them; and then someone gets an idea—say I get an idea and I want a study, and so I start a completely new one.

What I am anxious and have directed the proper members of

my staff is to make certain that all of these works of commissions are brought together so that we don't go over the same ground and repeat and just make it more expensive and nothing ever gets done. That is the general rule. The specific case of which you speak has not been brought to me.

Q. Mrs. McClendon: I see.

Now, sir, the other question is, will the reports of the Manion Commission have to go to the Hoover Commission before they can be considered final? Which commission would have precedence over the other? That question has already come up.

THE PRESIDENT. Well, I think, of course, there is naturally and obviously a relationship between them. I think they are each working independently of the other, except they exchange views as they go along on their work. I don't think the usefulness of one report becomes dependent upon the publication of the other. I don't believe so.

Q. Alan S. Emory, Watertown (N.Y.) Times: I wonder if I could return to the farm question for just a moment? In your swing through the West did you find that the farmers were satisfied or dissatisfied with the progress of farm policy in the Agriculture Department so far?

THE PRESIDENT. It is very difficult for anyone who is in a position that the President is ordinarily in on such a trip to give you a categorical answer. He gets impressions from particular people, but they often have preconceived notions, too.

Again I should say, if we could, I would like to have rise up here and take a vote among all of the people that went along on that trip, because they have a variety of opinion.

This is what I do believe: farmers are very happy that practical farmers, operating farmers, are going to constitute the great majority of the bipartisan commission that has been organized under the law as an advisory commission to the Secretary of Agriculture in all those things.

They have always been, and expressed themselves as being, very wary of academic answers to their problems. They are quite pleased that there has been a readiness to meet their problems on a broad scale.

They also understand that there is no special and specific answer for one farm problem to the exclusion of another. They are quite happy that the organisms for research, for looking into all these problems, are trying to approach it on a comprehensive basis.

Now, very naturally, when a cattleman comes up, and particularly if he is a feeder and paid 33 cents a pound or 34 cents for a calf, and now when it gets fat he can get 22 cents or something of that kind, he is very unhappy and he hopes that something will be worked out. But he does realize always—I think every farmer I talked to said, "Well, there are just too many cattle in the United States." And I had many suggestions as to how we could reduce the cattle population, but they really believed that is the first answer on it.

But I must say I couldn't give you just a categorical answer and say they are happy or they are unhappy. They realize they have got a problem, and they realize it is not easy to solve. They do hope that the answers and conclusions reached are not merely on an emergency basis but they can have some confidence in their semipermanence, let's say.

Q. Peter Heidenberger, Bavarian Broadcasting System: I have a question in regard to Germany. The German Chancellor, Dr. Adenauer, said yesterday that a delay in EDC should not penalize Germany. Do you have any comment on the European situation at this time and possible changes in the relation between EDC and Germany and this country?

THE PRESIDENT. No, I couldn't comment on that. I say this: I have a tremendous confidence in Chancellor Adenauer, I think he is a statesman, I think he is a real leader. And I would certainly study with the utmost interest anything he has to say, either publicly or privately, about the European situation. But on his specific comment, I could not say anything at this time.

Q. L. G. Laycook, Nashville Tennessean: Mr. President, have you reached any decision yet on Governor Clement's proposal that a special commission be set up to study TVA?

THE PRESIDENT. No, I haven't, for the simple reason that at the time he came here, I was about ready to depart. I think this is the first time the word TVA has come to me since then.

Q. Mr. Laycook: One other question, Mr. President: Dr. Manion on a nationwide television show on Monday night said he thought TVA ought to be sold to private business. Do you agree with him on that?

THE PRESIDENT. Well, I would certainly be a bold person if I thought that the interests of either those people or the United States would be served by just shooting from the hip and saying any such thing. As you know, I have always believed in the maximum of free enterprise. I don't emphasize merely the word "free," I mean also "enterprise."

I have urged the maximum of local and State participation in everything we do in a governmental fashion, but I have always stated that the TVA is an historical fact. I don't even know that it could be sold to private industry without doing something to wreck the whole system. After all, the Government uses a great portion of the power developed down there in the eastern part of the State. I have no comment on such a thing, because that would be a pretty drastic step, wouldn't it?

Q. Darwin R. Olofson, Omaha World-Herald: Mr. President, Secretary Benson yesterday announced a decision to support the prices of certain feed grains at the same level at which they had been supported previously. Can you tell me whether that specific decision was discussed with you prior to the announcement?

THE PRESIDENT. Support certain feed grains?

Q. Mr. Olofson: Yes; oats, rye, barley——

THE PRESIDENT. The generality has been discussed with me, and I have approved it thoroughly, in spite of the fact that we are providing cheap grain in the drought areas. I don't know what the specific decision yesterday was; I didn't see it. But I do know that Secretary Benson has moved, in all of these things, with my approval of the things he is trying to do.

56616—60——48

Q. Robert E. Clark, International News Service: Do you have any comment on the first American soldier to change his mind and come home after first choosing to stay with the Communists?

THE PRESIDENT. Well, except this, that I am glad that he took a second look and was not permanently influenced by the kind of indoctrination that was undoubtedly given him.

By the way, here is an interesting thing. Let me go back for just a minute, with your indulgence, to General Dean.

General Dean sat in a room 7 by 7 during all of his captivity; but during the early part of his captivity, this was occupied by from six to seven soldiers of the Communist army. Every day they went through 4 hours of indoctrination, those soldiers. They had to take books on communism. They laboriously copied page after page out of them. Then they had to outline them. Then they had to discuss among themselves the doctrines of communism.

Now, when you take the meager education that we give to our people, sometimes, as to what their obligation is to a free form of government, what it means to support it, what it means to keep it and to pass it on, you sometimes wonder that there weren't more of our people that succumbed, at least temporarily. I am sure that this lad that is coming back will never regret that decision.

Q. Milton Friedman, Jewish Telegraphic Agency: Mr. President, yesterday Secretary of State Dulles announced that economic aid for Israel was being cut off. Did the Secretary consult with you on this question, sir?

THE PRESIDENT. Yes.

Q. Paul Scott Rankine, Reuters News Agency: Mr. President, would you comment upon the achievements of the London conference of foreign ministers?

THE PRESIDENT. No, I think not. Secretary Dulles, I think, has had a press conference, and he has been very frank in his discussion of those things they are doing. I think it was valuable, and I certainly approve of that kind of thing. But I think he should talk about details himself.

Q. Edward J. Milne, Providence Journal-Bulletin: Mr. President, we have had a good deal of talk about the farm problem. I wonder if you have any comment on the problem which is worrying some of our city friends, of the increase in the cost of living, the continuing increase?

THE PRESIDENT. Well, I would tell you one thing about the increase in the cost of living. You have seen the statement made that the cost of living has reached an alltime high, but let me show you what the actual fact is. You go and look at the percentage of increase over the cost of living for recent years and then see how it has flattened out this year. It has gone up about 1.7 percent, and in none of the recent years, I think, has it failed to go up from 3½ or more—one year, I believe, 7 percent. The actual fact about the cost-of-living curve is that it is flattening out, which is far more important.

I certainly sympathize with particularly the white-collar workers of the cities that are caught between these squeezes all the time. The best we can do, as I see it, is strive for that middle-of-the-road—the conflict between the desire of people for more wages and the desire of other people to get more for their products, and try to keep a reasonable balance between these things so that everybody can profit. It is not easy, as everybody knows, because we do have conflicting interests. There has got to be some forbearance, some wider view, on the part of all of us than mere immediate selfishness or, as the Communists claim, finally free government won't be free government. They claim, as you know, that capitalism contains its own contradictions and its own elements of self-destruction. I don't believe it. I think we can solve it.

Q. Sarah McClendon, El Paso Times: Mr. President, there are some wide areas of industry that are not represented on this agricultural advisory body. Are you going to complete those gaps—are you going to name some more members of that body this week?

THE PRESIDENT. You mean, the one body?

Q. Mrs. McClendon: Yes, sir.

THE PRESIDENT. There is one of 18?

Q. Mrs. McClendon: Yes, sir.

THE PRESIDENT. As a matter of fact, you are asking me now out of my memory to remember exactly how many we have appointed.

Q. Mrs. McClendon: I believe there are several that you have not named yet.

THE PRESIDENT. Mr. Hagerty tells me we expect the designation to be made shortly.

Q. Nat S. Finney, Buffalo News: Mr. President, during this week, the Commodity Credit Corporation offered to the commercial banks of the country $360 million worth of what they call certificates in trust, which I understand will not show up on the balance sheet that comes under the statutory debt limit. I am curious as to whether you were familiar with that operation and whether you anticipated any further operation of that sort.

THE PRESIDENT. The United States, unless I am mistaken, has very, very many billions of contingent liabilities that don't appear in the national debt. The insurance you put back of deposits and mortgages and a great many other things are contingent liabilities of the Federal Government. They don't show up in the public debt because there are no bonds issued against them to make them valid.

Now, the specific thing you talk about, I remember that they came in and talked to me about these things, but just exactly what the implication of the item you bring up is, I am not sure. I wouldn't know.

Q. Else Ström, Aftontidningen (Stockholm, Sweden): Considering the difficulties of the neutral commission in Korea, do you have any comment to make on the O'Konski letter to Syngman Rhee on freeing the prisoners of war?

THE PRESIDENT. I have just heard, and not read, this letter. The Secretary of State has said he is going to study it before he makes any comment. Now, I can't possibly, because I have only an indirect report about it.

I would say this: no one can be more anxious than is the American Government to do a fair, decent thing by everybody in Korea so peace there can rest on something more permanent than just a quick little agreement of the moment. I am sure that anyone who goes along in that hope will have a friend in the American Government. That is all; I can't comment further.

Q. Joseph A. Fox, Washington Evening Star: Getting back to this farm situation a minute, sir, Senator Young said that he thought that Secretary Benson should resign. Is there any comment that you would care to make on that, sir?

THE PRESIDENT [*laughing*]. As a matter of fact, while I didn't see that statement, I believe it is the President's responsibility to decide who should be his principal associates and advisers. I have seen no one more dedicated to America than is Mr. Benson. I have seen no man who is more anxious to get the welfare of every American—the consumer in the city, the user of grain, the producer of grain, the user of beef, the producer of beef—to get all of them in a fair position with respect to each other, than is Secretary Benson. Now, because he can't produce a miraculous, one-line cure for all the evils, I, for one, am not going to be critical, because I have studied it myself.

I say that is my responsibility. Let us put it that way.

Q. Robert W. Richards, Copley Press: Mr. President, the Secretary has been administering a law passed by the last Congress which supports six basic crops at 90 percent of parity. During the campaign in Minnesota, you said that you couldn't understand why the farmers shouldn't have full parity rather than 90 percent of parity.

THE PRESIDENT. That is right.

Q. Mr. Richards: In other words, 100 percent of parity. Do you still feel that way?

THE PRESIDENT. I didn't say "price supports of 100 percent." I said the objective in any decent farm program in and out of Government should be to get them on the actual equality, which means that their prices that they get for things should be comparable to the prices they pay for things. But I never said that there should be rigid price-support laws at 100 percent of parity, never.

Merriman Smith, United Press: Thank you, Mr. President.

NOTE: President Eisenhower's seventeenth news conference was held in the Executive Office Building from 10:30 to 10:56 o'clock on Wednesday morning, October 21, 1953. In attendance: 162.

226 ¶ Citation Accompanying Medal of Honor Presented to Second Lieutenant Raymond G. Murphy. *October 22, 1953*

THE PRESIDENT of the United States in the name of The Congress takes pleasure in presenting the Medal of Honor to

SECOND LIEUTENANT RAYMOND G. MURPHY,

UNITED STATES MARINE CORPS RESERVE,

for service as set forth in the following

CITATION:

For conspicuous gallantry and intrepidity at the risk of his life above and beyond the call of duty as a Platoon Commander of Company A, First Battalion, Fifth Marines, First Marine Division (Reinforced), in action against enemy aggressor forces in Korea on 3 February 1953. Although painfully wounded by fragments from an enemy mortar shell while leading his evacuation platoon in support of assault units attacking a cleverly concealed and well-entrenched hostile force occupying commanding ground, Second Lieutenant Murphy steadfastly refused medical aid and continued to lead his men up a hill through a withering barrage of hostile mortar and small-arms fire, skillfully maneuvering his force from one position to the next and shouting words of encouragement. Undeterred by the increasing intense enemy fire, he immediately located casualties as they fell and made several trips up and down the fire-swept hill to direct evacuation teams to the wounded, personally carrying many of the stricken Marines to safety. When reinforcements were needed by the assaulting elements, Second Lieutenant Murphy employed part of his unit as support and, during the ensuing battle, personally killed two of the enemy with his pistol. With all the wounded evacuated and the assaulting units beginning to disengage, he remained behind with a carbine to cover the movement of friendly forces off the hill and, though suffering intense pain from his previous wounds, seized an automatic rifle to provide more firepower when the enemy reappeared in the trenches. After reaching the base of the hill, he organized a search party and again ascended the slope for a final check on missing Marines, locating and carrying the bodies of a machine-gun crew back down the hill. Wounded a second time while conducting the entire force to the line of departure through a continuing barrage of enemy small-arms, artillery and mortar fire, he again refused medical assistance until assured that every one of his men, including all casualties, had preceded him to the main lines. His resolute and inspiring leadership, exceptional fortitude and great personal valor reflect the highest credit upon Second Lieutenant Murphy and enhance the finest traditions of the United States Naval Service.

DWIGHT D. EISENHOWER

NOTE: See also Item 229.

227 ¶ Statement by the President on the Work of the National Agricultural Advisory Commission. *October 24, 1953*

I AM DEEPLY OBLIGATED to the members of the National Agricultural Advisory Commission for the important work they have done and are doing in behalf of America's farming community.

As a body of representative farmers, agriculturists, representatives of farming organizations and of agricultural educational institutions, they are engaged in helping the Administration to develop a federal farm program that will best meet differing and sometimes diverse interests of the entire farming population and of consumers as well.

They are properly proceeding on the assumption that only a well-thought out program, designed to meet the basic requirements of all elements of our population, can bring about that stability and general prosperity in American agriculture that we are all striving to achieve.

The preliminary discussion I have had today with the Commission convinces me that it will outline with the help of many other agricultural groups, developments in the present programs that will help farmers secure their fair share of the national income and work for the good of all.

I was heartened to find the view prevailing that market price adjustments in agriculture, which have been substantial over the past two years, now seem pretty well behind us. I sensed, too, a conviction among the members of the Commission that the outlook for business activity throughout the economy in the year ahead—a factor so essential to good markets for farm products—is generally reassuring.

Our discussions of the immediately pressing problems of the drought and the cattle price situation as well as other subjects produced valuable suggestions, which are now receiving intensive consideration by Secretary of Agriculture Benson. I was gratified to have the Commission's view that existing programs in these two critical areas are becoming increasingly effective.

NOTE: A statement to the President from the Commission members, outlining the Commission's activities and recommendations, was released with the President's statement.

228   ¶   Letter to Secretary of the Interior McKay
Establishing a Cabinet Committee on Minerals
Policy.   *October* 26, 1953

My dear Mr. Secretary:

One of the essential problems before our country is the establishment of a national policy relating to the production and utilization of minerals and metals.   The prudent use and development of domestic mineral resources, as well as assured access to necessary sources abroad, are indispensable to the operation of an active economy and a sound defense.

We must make sure, as Americans, that we have available mineral raw materials adequate to meet any contingency during the uncertain years ahead.   Chronic shortages of many minerals and metals have plagued us during every emergency, and the strength to meet any new crisis in large measure will depend on our ability to obtain these materials in sufficient amounts.   The problem is compounded, of course, by the ever growing requirements of an expanding economy.

As we look forward to the resolution of this problem, we now face depressed conditions within numerous metal mining districts, conditions that are a matter of grave national concern.   The mining industry has contributed in large measure to our present state of preparedness through vigorous expansion of its facilities. Every effort should be made to preserve this newly added economic strength through policies that would be consistent with our other national and international policies.

To point the way to the solution of this wide range of problems, I am establishing a Cabinet Committee, whose task will be the preparation of recommendations for consideration by myself and the Cabinet.   I am requesting you to serve as Chairman of the Committee.   By copy of this letter, I am designating the Secretary of State, the Secretary of Commerce and the Director of the Office of Defense Mobilization to serve as the other members.   I suggest that this Committee work in close cooperation with the Bureau of the Budget, the Department of the Treasury and such other departments and agencies of the Executive Branch, as well as private individuals and organizations, as are concerned with these matters.

A good deal of work has been done in recent years, both in and out of government, with respect to the minerals and metals field, including the inquiry by the President's Materials Policy Commission. I know that your Committee, in the course of its studies, will want to draw on this work.

As you know, the United States Tariff Commission was requested by resolutions of the Senate Finance Committee and the Committee on Ways and Means of the House of Representatives to make an investigation of the lead and zinc industries and to set forth the facts relevant to the production, trade, consumption and importation into the United States of these commodities. The Committee requested that the Commission submit the results of its investigation on or before March thirty-first next. It would be extremely helpful if your study could be completed for consideration well before that date.

Sincerely,

DWIGHT D. EISENHOWER

229 ¶ Remarks at the Presentation of Seven Congressional Medals of Honor.
October 27, 1953

My friends:

We have gathered here to symbolize the gratitude of America to seven young men who have won her Medal of Honor. As we assemble on such an occasion, I think there are a number of thoughts that must cross our minds. One of the first and natural ones is that if you ever have to get in a fight, you would like to have these seven on your side. Certainly we view with almost incredulity the tales that we hear told in these citations. It seems impossible that human beings could stand up to the kind of punishment they received and deliver the kind of service they have.

But I think the most predominating thought would be: could we be so fortunate that this would be the last time such a group ever gathered together at the White House to receive the Medal of Honor, a battlefield decoration?

Now of course, it is obvious that the future belongs to youth. In very special measure it belongs to these young men, because they have done so much. They must do more. Any man who wins the Nation's highest decoration is marked for leadership. And he must exert it.

And now, instead of leading in battle, they must lead toward peace. They must make certain that no other young men follow them up to these steps to receive the Medal of Honor. That is the service that the United States would like finally to give to all seven of you as their decoration.

So, along with our gratitude, with our salute to great soldiers, our affection to you and to your families, goes also our hope that you will be instrumental in bringing about a situation where there will be no more Medals of Honor.

Thank you very much.

NOTE: The President spoke on the North Portico of the White House at 12:20 p.m. He presented medals to 1st Lt. Raymond G. Murphy, USMCR, 1st Lt. James L. Stone, USA, 2d Lt. George H. O'Brien, Jr., USMCR, Sgt. David B. Bleak, USA, Sgt. Hiroshi H. Miyamura, USA, Pfc. Alford L. McLaughlin, USMCR, and Pfc. Robert E. Simanek, USMCR. The citations were read by Comdr. Edward L. Beach, Naval Aide to the President.

230 ¶ The President's News Conference of *October 28, 1953.*

THE PRESIDENT. I think you know, ladies and gentlemen, that the King and Queen of Greece are to be here this afternoon. They will spend the night with Mrs. Eisenhower and me. It gives us a certain personal pleasure in this case—as we ourselves were guests of the King and Queen at dinner some months ago, when I occupied a different status, of course, when I was head of NATO.

Quite naturally, it will be a pleasure to be the representative of the American people in giving a welcome to the heads of a state to which we owe so much in our civilization and our culture.

I was in conference this morning with the Secretary of State, and was delighted to learn that the State of Israel has accepted the approval that was given by the Security Council to the findings of the United Nations supervisory—I forget the exact name of the commission, but you will know it—over in Israel—that has been dealing with this water question.

As the result of that, we can proceed with our arrangements for the economic help of Israel, and I think the Secretary of State is to bring forward a specific recommendation, plans, very quickly, possibly today.

What was the third subject? Oh, yes, there is a mimeograph waiting for you when this conference is over. It deals with the United States Information Service, what we are trying to do in clarifying our purposes and objectives in this whole program of information. The mimeograph itself will contain a letter from Mr. Streibert, which is quite detailed, listing exactly what we expect to do.

The main thing is that in these factual programs that we intend to put out, we are trying to make the great objective the legitimate aspirations, the culture, of the people with whom we are dealing, and not trying to leave the imprint of our own pattern on them or to force any such imprint.

We are trying to cooperate with people in giving out factual information that will tend to show what we are striving for and what they are legitimately striving for are one and the same.

I think I won't go into that one any further because the mimeograph stands by itself.

I think those are the only three items I had in my mind when I came over here, so we will go right to questions.

Q. Merriman Smith, United Press: Mr. President, is it fair to say regarding Israel we have agreed to resume economic assistance for Israel?

THE PRESIDENT. Made a decision to resume, yes.

Here, Mr. Smith, from the beginning it was merely this: that we do these things under the, you might say, policies laid down by the United Nations. We attempt to support the United Nations. We don't attempt to prejudge anything, but we do believe that the United Nations must be supported in all of these activities, and the thing will be carried out exactly as originally programed.

Q. Roscoe Drummond, New York Herald Tribune: Mr. President, would you give us your reaction to the statement which Winston Churchill made in the Commons yesterday saying that there are few things that he would like more than the occasion to have some quiet informal talks with you?

THE PRESIDENT. Well, Mr. Drummond, of course, we are very old friends; Winston Churchill and I have been warm friends for years. I have certainly the admiration and respect for him that the ordinary American does; in addition, I have very great affection for him; I like to talk to him.

We have kept up a correspondence, kept in touch with each other through messengers, through occasional notes or telegrams.

We are constantly, you might say, looking for a chance where we might have informal friendly chats.

There is no plan though—I should make very clear—there is no plan now in being or that is under study for arranging such a meeting.

Put it this way: It is an expression, I think, of hope on both sides.

Q. David P. Sentner, Hearst Newspapers: Mr. President, in view of the drop in farm prices, would you care to comment upon the general economic outlook, at least, for the next 6 months?

THE PRESIDENT. Well, the whole general economic outlook is something on which I don't believe I would comment without almost the latest prepared and distinct suggestions, recommendations, studies of the Council of Economic Advisers, the Treasury, and Labor and Commerce and the other departments concerned.

The drop in cattle prices and farm prices, as you know, is something that has been going on for a long time, and something that has engaged the attention of a great many people during these late months.

We have moved into this, particularly in the cattle area, and particularly in the drought area, in every possible way that was open to us with the resources at hand: you know, with cheap feed, reduction of freight rates, the extension of credit and guaranteeing of credit, and lately, recently, even in making available certain amounts for helping in hay importations into the States where this is necessary.

Actually, out in Missouri, $1 million was made available as quickly as the program of cooperation between the State and the Federal Government was worked out.

Now, there has been, of course, some effect. The prices have been apparently, in the cattle market, largely stabilized; and the last few days have seen a steady rise, but they are far from satisfactory yet.

Last week and this week our intensified purchase program is just almost at its peak, 20 million pounds a week.

So, with the Government in to purchase, looking ahead to purchase supplies and stocking up for all of its lunch programs, its needs and requirements in other lines, we are hopeful that this cattle market is going to, and we believe that the cattle market has reached its peak, and is on the way up.

The cattle population next January 1st will certainly be no larger than it was on last January 1st, which is a great change. Consumption of beef is 30 percent, almost, above the comparable period of last year.

Now, the whole farm program has all sorts of difficulties and all sorts of complications. That is why we have had these studies going on.

I met only Saturday noon, as you know, I think, with the Agricultural Advisory Commission, and had a long talk with them. They are studying, and there will be a program ready to submit to the Congress when it comes in. It will try to be a comprehensive one that takes into consideration the needs not only in all areas, but in the various commodity groups, which is the thing that is so difficult. How do you balance off meat against grain, and still have respect for the consumer?

It is a pretty tough problem, but we will have a program.

Q. Mrs. May Craig, New England Press: Mr. President, in relation to the low prices that farmers are getting, I would like to ask you about the high cost of living to the consumers, and I would like to speak to you as consumer to consumer. Has Mrs. Eisenhower told you anything about your high cost of living in the White House?

THE PRESIDENT. I am not going to take up the time of this group by telling what I have heard about it—plenty. [*Laughter*]

Q. Mrs. Craig: Sir, I believe that you do have to pay individually the cost of meals for your staff; you do get rent free, but that is still your high cost of living, and I believe you said the other day that you expected to lose money on your term in the White House.

THE PRESIDENT. You know, Mrs. Craig, let's not bring that up. Anyone that goes into such position as this, I think if there is a sacrifice there that is the least of the troubles.

Q. Mrs. Craig: Well, sir, aren't you going to pay any attention to the consumer's side of it?

THE PRESIDENT. Why do you suppose we are working so hard? If you wanted to just take the easy way, guarantee everybody that comes in and wants anything, guarantee them everything. I am trying to work for 160 million people, I assure you. And I assure you that everybody around me is doing it, and the consumer is very, very important.

But let us remember this: farmers are also consumers, and you can't take this problem—I have emphasized time and again—and isolate it and deal with it in a vacuum.   There are 160 million people, and when Government does intervene, finds it necessary to intervene, that is the reason you must go so cautiously, you must have so much help from every possible sector of this economy; because otherwise you are going to get out of balance, and you create trouble instead of curing trouble.   So what we are trying to do is to make certain that the level of employment, the distribution of productivity of this country all works out so that it is fair to everybody.   And that means, of course, everybody is a consumer.

Q. Chalmers M. Roberts, Washington Post: Mr. President, there have been a number of stories lately that as changes in atomic weapons come along and our arsenal increases, this would make it possible for us to decrease the manpower in our Army and at some future date cut down on the number of our troops overseas, including those in NATO.

Could you tell us how far along—if this is true—how far along the thinking is, and whether there is any time element that you could speak of?

THE PRESIDENT. There exists no plan for reduction of any combat forces of the United States anywhere.

Now, we all know that the need for economy is very great. We all know that these new weapons have entered into the arsenals of the great powers, and they have a tremendous effect.   To say that they would have no effect on the composition of your military forces would be shutting your eyes to all history and to the logic of a situation of which certain factors are rather apparent.

Now, there is no plan of any kind at this time for reduction of combat forces anywhere.   On the contrary, as far as the Air Forces are concerned, as you know, they are occupying their bases, I believe our forces abroad are probably on the increase.

I assume you were talking about the conventional divisional type of military force.   There is no plan now existing, I repeat, for their reduction.

Q. Andrew F. Tully, Jr., Scripps-Howard Newspapers: Andrei Vishinsky made a speech in New York yesterday in which he said he saw no need for the Soviet Government to give any evidences of good faith before a Big Three meeting. Would you still insist upon such evidences before you attended such a meeting?

THE PRESIDENT. Well, I haven't studied in detail any remarks he made. I think that what I have said in the past on this subject is perfectly reasonable and logical.

We have had many examples of different meetings in the past being used merely for propaganda purposes.

Now, I should like to call attention to a peculiar situation of the President of the United States vis-a-vis, let's say, a Prime Minister of one of these other countries. He is the ceremonial head of the state; he leads the hospitality brigade, in other words, he has to be the leader in the entertainment—[*laughter*]—he is the ex officio head of a political party; and, finally, he has exactly the same work that all these other people do in trying to make political decisions that work for the good of his country.

Now, it is not so easy for him to talk lightly about these meetings as it might be for someone else.

So when we say "evidence of good faith," first of all, Mr. Dulles—I am sure I am right in this—has offered time and again to meet with anybody, and has been meeting, to discuss any problems.

The only thing I would say is this: if there is anything in the situation that can give us conviction that people are meeting in good faith, I will, in spite of any kind of handicap, I will do anything in the world that I think will be productive of advancing the cause of peace. I don't care what it would mean in inconvenience, what it would mean in anything else; I shall do it. But it is perfectly hopeless to do this thing until we know that there is honest purpose behind it.

Now, I don't define what we have to have in order to convince us on this purpose. It might be any one of a hundred things, I should think, but that we have got to know.

Q. Sarah McClendon, El Paso Times: Sir, there were approximately 350 cattlemen here this week from over 26 States, and they said they had asked to see you, and you would not see them. Will you say why?

THE PRESIDENT. That is not true. I offered to see these people if there was time or if there was any real reason for my seeing them, and no one suggested to me that I should see them.

This is the first I have heard of it, and when I say it is not true, I mean they may have asked somebody; certainly no request came to me, because I have informed my people that if they thought it was necessary or highly desirable for me to see these people, I would do it.

Q. Kenneth M. Scheibel, Gannett Newspapers: Mr. President, there have been suggestions that you call a special session of Congress to deal with the farm program. Have you given that any consideration?

THE PRESIDENT. Well, of course, we have watched all this developing farm situation, and especially the drought that is developing; and if the emergency character of that problem goes far enough, I assume you would have to call a special session.

As far as the general farm program, no, because we have several groups working as hard as they know how. If they have their program ready for submission to Congress on January 1st, from my viewpoint they are doing a magnificent job. So I would see no reason for dealing with the general farm program by special session.

Q. Bernard Mullady, Labor Press: Mr. President, we understand that Secretary Durkin had decided to advise the recommendation that the minimum wage be raised to $1 in place of the present 75 cents, that Acting Secretary Mashburn submitted that to the Bureau of the Budget. Will you tell us how you feel about that?

THE PRESIDENT. No such recommendation has ever been made to me. I have frequently talked about minimum wages to various people, but no recommendation has ever reached me of that kind, no suggestion has yet been made to me of raising the minimum wage or the amount by which it should be done, if done.

What has been suggested to me several times is the extension of minimum wage laws, and I was promised that this thing would be thoroughly studied in its probable effects upon our economy. Now, that is as far as we have gone.

Q. Frank van der Linden, Nashville Banner: Mr. President, you had a conference Monday with the Chancellor of Vanderbilt University. Will you tell us the outcome of that conference?

THE PRESIDENT. I don't remember whether I promised to keep that confidential or not. [*Laughter*]

The only thing is, I don't remember whether we promised to keep this confidential. He brought to me an invitation. Now, I won't discuss the time and place and all of that sort of thing, but he brought me an invitation to go somewhere.

Q. Mr. van der Linden: Mr. President, you didn't say whether or not you accepted it.

THE PRESIDENT. Well, the timing was such I could not possibly accept it now.

Q. Robert J. Donovan, New York Herald Tribune: Sir, in view of certain published accounts which seem to have caused some concern in the country, I wonder if I could presume to ask how you are feeling these days.

THE PRESIDENT. Well, I will tell you: as you people know, or some of you know, I have had sort of a sore elbow which has prevented me from getting my exercise to which I am accustomed, which I think I need, and which I love.

Aside from that, if I am not in good condition, the doctors have fooled me badly, because I feel fine. As a matter of fact, I underwent quite a series of tests just before we came back from Denver, and the reports given to me were cheering to a man of my age.

Q. Fletcher Knebel, Cowles Publications: Mr. President, yesterday you saw the Republican candidate from Virginia. Do you feel that that is in any way a departure from your policy of not interfering in local elections?

THE PRESIDENT [*laughing*]. I found out that Mr. Dalton is, of course, the Republican candidate for Governor. He came to see me about a drought in Virginia that you probably heard about.

There was not one word of politics that I recall mentioned. If there was, it was something inadvertently and in passing. The subject was the drought.

Now, at the risk of being just a bit verbose, let me recall to you people what I did say about this business of Presidential participation in local elections.

I doubt whether there is anyone here that would think it humanly or physically possible for me to go into 435 districts and electioneer. So, I should think, first of all, there is a physical limitation on what can be done that should be quite clear to all of us.

But secondly, if the President, as such, would have to acquaint himself with the local conditions under which people are running locally, I would think there would be a suspicion arising that he is not paying much attention to his main job, which is trying to be President for 160 million people.

Now, having said that, let me get this clear, quite clear: I said in my other statement, of course I am interested in the Republican organization and seeing Republican majorities come back. And I pointed out, I thought quite clearly, that I conceive it to be my job with the leaders and the members of my party in Congress, and all those we can get to go along with us, to produce a program that is so dynamic, so forward-looking, and so adapted to the needs of the United States, that everybody running under the umbrella of that program will have a great big bulge on anybody else. That is what I mean, and to say that I have no interest in these things is like saying I have no interest in drawing the next breath. Of course, I have.

I am trying to do it in a way that I believe is not only logical and necessary but in the only way that is meeting American needs and requirements.

Q. Robert L. Riggs, Louisville Courier-Journal: Mr. President, do you feel it would be improper for you to issue a request for the election of Republican Congressmen? You are the head of the Republican Party in the country, and the election of a Congress is a national event.

THE PRESIDENT. Well, I can't say in what form any statement of mine might take, and I doubt whether just a request that wasn't based on more logic than just a personal request would be effective.

What I do hope to do is with these people, these leaders and the members of this party, to produce a record that can stand on itself, and we can show what it is in all its details.

Q. Mr. Riggs: What I mean, you wouldn't feel debarred, would you, from taking issue with such requests?

THE PRESIDENT. Well, I don't believe I will shoot from the hip on that one.

Q. William H. Lawrence, New York Times: Following up Mr. Riggs' question, you have made the point to us here today, sir, that it would be physically and mentally unwise to try to absorb the problems of all 435 districts. This doesn't bar you, however, in the course of the next year, if you happen to be in somebody's congressional district, from giving him a pat on the back, does it?

THE PRESIDENT. As a matter of fact, I don't object; I am always complimented when somebody comes up and wants to have their picture taken with me. [*Laughter*] It sort of means they think I am not going to damage them.

So I think, I think that is sort of a compliment.

Look, I don't see why I have to take an extremist view on this thing. I repeat—I have got certain conceptions of what the President of the United States can logically and properly do.

Those things I shall do, but behind it all, I believe in party responsibility. I believe in it, and when we talk and give merely lip service to a two-party system in the United States, and then say there is no party responsibility, we are just guilty of self-contradiction.

Of course I believe in it, and I shall do my part from my place and within the bounds that I think should limit the President of the United States.

Q. Joseph A. Fox, Washington Evening Star: That would not prevent you, sir, then from going out and putting in a good word for the Republican Party, so to speak, citing the accomplishments of the administration?

THE PRESIDENT. The question is that this limitation I have placed upon myself would not prevent me from any proper platform of reciting the accomplishments of the Republican administration.

I think it would be more proper to say the accomplishments of Congress and the executive departments under the leadership of the Republican Party, because we are now, by the elections of last year, charged with the leadership; and I see no reason on earth that we shouldn't constantly try to lay out this record in front of the American people, because eventually they can make wise decisions only if they are properly and fully informed. That is what I try to do.

Q. Mr. Fox: If I might pursue this same subject a little further, sir: there was a story out of New York yesterday that Governor Dewey might be stepping out of Albany after he finished his term. Is there a possibility that he might be brought into the administration after that?

THE PRESIDENT. This question involves Governor Dewey. There was a story in the paper to the effect that he was going to step out of the governorship, and does this mean any possible connection with the national administration.

I should say this: my news of Governor Dewey's decision came from the newspapers. I haven't the slightest idea of his plans or his personal plans, of his availability for any kind of duty.

Of course, I think that in the great qualities of Governor Dewey—they are well known, and we don't have to take time here to eulogize him; but I have nothing at all of information that could give me any other kind of an answer to your question.

Q. Arthur Sylvester, Newark News: Mr. President, when you entered New Jersey a couple of weeks ago and had your picture taken with the Republican candidate for Governor, did you realize that he was under fire for having written Governor Dewey to pardon the labor racketeer, Mr. Fay?

THE PRESIDENT. I think at that moment I had never even heard of Mr. Fay, and so I knew nothing about it.

Actually, I went up to address a group of churchmen, and I was asked by the Senators, I think it was—yes, the Senators—whether I would meet a group in the building there, which I did.

Now, just as I said before, someone wanted a picture taken. I quite agreed; I was quite, as I say, complimented. That is all I know about it.

Q. Roscoe Drummond, New York Herald Tribune: Mr. President, might I ask whether your discussion with Senator Knowland this morning bore in part upon the problem and the ways of strengthening party responsibility in developing a legislative program?

THE PRESIDENT. Well, we talked about the methods for bringing promptly before the Congress the views of the administration, coordinated with the leaders, and so on, as to timing, their needs, their priority, and so on.

In other words, I suppose Senator Knowland and I talked about the general subjects applying to the future problems of the Congress and the Executive, exactly as you would expect. Now, that is as far as I know; there was nothing outside of that.

Merriman Smith, United Press: Thank you, Mr. President.

NOTE: President Eisenhower's eighteenth news conference was held in the Executive Office Building from 10:30 to 10:56 o'clock on Wednesday morning, October 28, 1953. In attendance: 152.

231   ¶ Directive Approved by the President for
the Guidance of the United States Information
Agency.   *October 28, 1953*

IN CARRYING OUT its responsibilities in accordance with
pertinent statutes and Presidential directives, the United States
Information Agency shall be guided by the following:

1. The purpose of the United States Information Agency shall
be to submit evidence to peoples of other nations by means of
communication techniques that the objectives and policies of the
United States are in harmony with and will advance their legitimate aspirations for freedom, progress and peace.

2. The purpose in paragraph 1 above is to be carried out
primarily:

a. By explaining and interpreting to foreign peoples the objectives and policies of the United States Government.

b. By depicting imaginatively the correlation between United
States policies and the legitimate aspirations of other peoples of
the world.

c. By unmasking and countering hostile attempts to distort or
to frustrate the objectives and policies of the United States.

d. By delineating those important aspects of the life and culture
of the people of the United States which facilitate understanding
of the policies and objectives of the Government of the United
States.

NOTE: The release of which this directive was a part also contained a
letter dated October 27 from the Director of the United States Information Agency. The letter stated that
the directive reflected the recommendations of the Senate's Special
Subcommittee on Overseas Information Programs and the concepts of
the President's Committee on International Information Activities.

232 ¶ Remarks of Welcome to King Paul and Queen Frederika of Greece. *October* 28, 1953

Your Majesties:

I count it an opportunity and a rare distinction to welcome the two of you here as the guests of our Nation in this Capital.

For Mrs. Eisenhower and myself it is a particularly happy opportunity that we may repay something of the hospitality you so graciously extended to us two years ago in Athens.

May your stay here be an enjoyable one, and may you find as much pleasure in our house as we did in yours.

NOTE: The President greeted King Paul and Queen Frederika on their arrival at the North Portico of the White House.

233 ¶ Toasts of the President and King Paul of Greece. *October* 28, 1953

Your Majesty the King, and Your Majesty the Queen, distinguished guests of two nations:

This house is honored this evening in the privilege of entertaining the heads of a state to which all Western civilization will be forever indebted.

Now this evening I shall not weary you with reciting those things which every schoolboy and every schoolgirl knows about the great achievements of Greece in science and art and philosophy. In all those things they have helped to make our Nation's and other Western Nations' civilization what it is.

Rather, I should like to talk for just a second about modern Greece. In this time, when all the world is divided by virtue of a struggle between those who believe in the essential dignity of man as a creature created in the image of his God, and those who contend that man is nothing but a pawn, a creature of the state, and has no reason for existence except as he can glorify that temporal power of the state, Greece ranks high as a champion on the side of human dignity and freedom.

As World War II started, Greece asked no favor except the opportunity to stand for those rights in which it believed, and it gave to the world an example of battle—although temporarily a losing one—a battle that thrilled the hearts of all free men and free women everywhere.

Because of that example, because of the privilege that has been mine and Mrs. Eisenhower's in knowing these two, the heads of the Greek state, the Government of the United States this evening is requesting a privilege of His Majesty the King, to accept from us an honor—the highest decoration that in time of peace our Government can confer upon a citizen of another country.

And with your indulgence, I shall read the Citation:

"The President of the United States of America, authorized by Act of Congress July 20, 1942 has awarded the Legion of Merit, Degree of Chief Commander to Paul I, the King of the Hellenes, for exceptionally meritorious conduct in the performance of outstanding services.

"Paul I, King of the Hellenes, has made a personal contribution of the greatest importance to the warm friendship between his people and the people of the United States. His devotion to the ideals which are shared by Greece and the United States has been reflected in the resolute manner in which he has led his people in the defense of those ideals against great physical odds. His interest in and support of unity of the free nations have been a magnificent example to his people who have willingly assumed the burdens of those who must guard freedom." Signed by the President.

Your Majesty, as I hand this to you, I am going to ask the company to rise and with me drink a Toast to Your Majesty the King and Your Majesty the Queen of Greece.

NOTE: The President proposed this toast at 9:55 p.m. at a state dinner at the White House. King Paul responded as follows:

Mr. President, your warm and gracious words and the great honor you have just bestowed on me, have deeply moved me, and I am sure that the Queen shares my feeling.

Your invitation to us to visit your great country has not only given us the greatest pleasure, but has also been a source of deep satisfaction to my people. For your gesture clearly demonstrates to all that the people of America are mindful of the sacrifices and efforts which the people of Greece have made in the cause of freedom and democracy.

From Greece, the land in which democracy was born, I bring you the salute of my people, to whom, allow me to say, Mr. President, you have long been a familiar and loved figure. But today we salute, in you, the head of the nation which leads the democratic world in the struggle against totalitarian aggression. In this effort, which requires patience and determination, we are completely and wholeheartedly at your side.

You know, Mr. President, that my people fought a 10 years' war against the forces of destruction. They defeated the Fascists in Albania. It was the first allied victory against the Axis. They resisted the Nazis to the bitter end. Their spirit was not broken by 4 years of devastating occupation. And then when other countries were beginning to enjoy the benefits of peace, a new and more horrible form of invasion came to ravage my desolated country. We stood up to resist this too, and America gave us the material equipment to do so, but the Greeks gave their

hearts and their strength and their lives to fight the invader. Greece is the first democratic country which completely defeated full-scale aggression by militant communism. We shall never forget that America came to our aid so generously in that hour of desperate crisis.

The reason why the Greek people have been able to go on fighting for so many years against such odds, and in the face of such overwhelming disaster, is that we believe, with all the faith of which we are capable, in the principles of freedom and democracy which are our ancient heritage.

That is why, when this menace appeared thousands of miles from our shores, the young men of Greece volunteered to fight in Korea, where I believe you will agree they have acquitted themselves well.

Your invitation to the Queen and to me to visit this wonderful country was enthusiastically welcomed by my people as an opportunity for us to express the gratitude of all of us to all the citizens of America for their understanding and assistance.

May I add, Mr. President, with some pride, that in the civil as well as the military field American aid is yielding fruit that cannot but be highly gratifying to the American taxpayer who has made considerable sacrifices on our behalf.

Not only have we defeated aggressors in war, but we are now building Greece into one of the bulwarks of democracy, strong politically, and a progressive and constructive administration, strong economically and strong militarily, presenting a firm barrier against further aggression in an area vital to the West.

In defending freedom and democracy with all our strength, we believe in my country—as you do in yours—that material power while very necessary is not in itself sufficient, that the true strength of our civilization lies in its spiritual and moral values.

It is a comfort and an inspiration to all of us to realize that this belief is fully shared and earnestly expressed by all the leaders of the American Nation. It is in this spirit that we place our trust in the vitality and excellence of our common institutions and traditions in the ultimate prevalence of good. And above all, we place our trust in God.

Mr. President, may I thank you once more for the honor you have bestowed on me, and through me to my country. And may I drink to your health, and my best wishes to you and to Mrs. Eisenhower.

234　¶ Remarks at the Fourth American Forest Congress.　*October* 29, 1953

Mr. Chairman, ladies and gentlemen:

It is my very happy, a very distinguished, privilege this morning to extend to each of you a welcome on behalf of the administration to your Nation's Capital.

The very character of your organization confers distinction upon anyone who may be invited before it. But you will realize that due to the number of conventions that meet in this city, there are at times staff discussions over in the White House as to whether or not they should send the President forth this morning to attend a little meeting of this kind.

Now, in this particular case, entirely aside from my own desires and determinations, I assure you there was no question. It happens that my principal staff officer is a forester. And there are two subjects of which I hear most, I think, when I am with him: New Hampshire and forestry.

I, of course, am not going to trespass upon your time to attempt a discussion of those professional and technical elements of your calling, of which you know so much more than I that it would be sheer presumption for me even to mention them.

I should like, though, to speak of just one or two points in which I think our interests are so clearly identical. The interest of this administration is to create a balanced but advancing economy and prosperity in this country.

Now, for any group of people who are engaged in the conservation of our resources, all of them, on the one hand, and at the same time in the production of a product which may range anywhere from 15 to 80 or 90 years, certainly you are concerned directly and by reason of your profession with a steady rather than an intermittent and hysterical-like action in the advancing forces—the advancing trends—of our economy. You deal more directly than most, I think, in futures—not merely a future of the day after tomorrow or who are we going to have in such an office, or what kind of activity will be going on in that place. You deal in decades, decades in the growth of your product, of the forests and the trees, and in the conservation of all those elements of our continent that make that possible.

Then again, when I think of the basic resource that is used so widely—you think of it—in clothespins and matchsticks, in shipbuilding and in construction, in the dissemination of news through the pulp industry—your interests again are not those that are confined merely to the forest. But when you go into the uses of your product, you are concerned with everything that touches the United States.

So is your Government. Its purpose is to understand, if possible, the problems of every special group in this country, but never to use the resources of this country to favor any group at the expense of others—to attempt to get that kind of balanced progress that can be sustained, that will not create upsets in our economy.

So you can understand, of course, the kind of interest we have in soil and water conservation.

When I first led an invading force onto another continent during the war, we went into northern Africa. It was difficult to believe that that area had once been the granary of the ancient world, that it provided the timber and almost all of the agricultural resources that were used in Italy and Greece and Sicily and through those more heavily populated countries.

Today, in such vast areas, there is just a stretch of sand and desert. The civilization that it supported, the cities that flourished, are gone—Timgad, probably one of the most famous destroyed cities on the earth, not far from the great city of Constantine.

That is the kind of thing that must never happen here. It is through the wisdom, the efforts, the dedication, and the devotion of such people as yourselves, that it will not happen. Too many of us are blind, or indifferent, or just completely ignorant of the facts that make that work so important.

So I think I can conclude with just this one word: I cannot tell you how much satisfaction it gives to me to know that intelligent Americans are meeting together, whose interests are as broad as this land, whose vision must be projected forward not merely till tomorrow—or possibly an election—but for a century.

What is going to be the character of this country? Is it going to favor the individual as it favored us? Is it going to give him an opportunity? Is it going to have the resources to give him that opportunity or would we have to degenerate into some kind of controlled economy, some kind of regimentation of all of the heritage? Of all the phases of our heritage that we have received—all of these God-given resources and privileges we enjoy—the one that I believe every true American wants to pass on, without any destruction, is that right of the individual to his own determination of what he shall think, of how he shall worship, of what he shall earn, of how he can save, and what he can do with his savings—subject to taxes [*laughter*]. I should remark here that even in such a crown of roses as we know has always been the portion and the share of our beloved America, there still are some thorns—taxes is one of them.

So again, as I bid you welcome, I also express this tremendous gratification that you are here for your Congress, this assembly.

I wish you the greatest of success, and to each individual—God bless you.

NOTE: The President spoke at the Statler Hotel in Washington. His opening words "Mr. Chairman" referred to Don P. Johnston, President of the American Forestry Association and Chairman of the Congress.

235 ¶ Letter to Representative Clement J. Zablocki on the Arrest of Cardinal Wyszynski of Poland. *October* 30, 1953

[Released October 30, 1953. Dated October 29, 1953]

Dear Mr. Zablocki:

I have your letter of October fourteenth regarding the action taken recently against a courageous leader of his Church, Stefan Cardinal Wyszynski, Primate of Poland. The arrest and internment of Cardinal Wyszynski is profoundly discouraging to those of us who look for signs of Communist willingness to respect basic human rights of freedom of thought and conscience. Without evidence of such willingness, it is difficult to believe that the Communist Governments intend to honor agreements which might be reached to reduce world tensions. You may recall that I spoke of this in connection with the arrest of Cardinal Wyszynski at my news conference of September thirtieth.

The calculated repression of all religious organization in the Communist States makes it apparent that wherever Communists are in position to use force and violence, they will do so in an effort to win domination not only over the body and mind of man, but over his soul as well. I share very strongly the conviction which was expressed in the condemnation of the action against Cardinal Wyszynski issued by the Department of State on September thirtieth, that the religious spirit of man will never be subdued or extinguished, and that it will remain a sustaining force in Poland during the present tragic suffering of the Polish people. It is my intention that this Government continue to take all ap propriate steps to see to it that Communist violations of the inalienable rights of man under God do not go unopposed, and that they are effectively exposed in every forum.

Sincerely,

Dwight D. Eisenhower

236 ¶ Statement by the President Recorded for the Program of the Committee on Religion in American Life.   *October 31, 1953*

EACH YEAR the Committee on Religion in American Life reminds us of the importance of faithful church attendance. It urges full support of religious institutions to the end that we may add strength and meaning to the religious virtues—charity, mercy, brother love, and faith in Almighty God. These spiritual concepts are the inspiration of the American way. It was once said, "America is great because America is good—and if America ever ceases to be good, America will cease to be great."

By strengthening religious institutions, the Committee on Religion in American Life is helping to keep America good. Thus it helps each of us to keep America great.

I earnestly hope that during November, and throughout this and every year, each American citizen will actively support the religious institution of his own choice.

NOTE: The President's statement was broadcast nationally over radio and television.

237 ¶ Statement by the President: American Education Week.   *November 3, 1953*

To the Patrons, Students and Teachers of American Schools:

The celebration of American Education Week summons the thoughtful attention of every American citizen.

The youth of our Nation—who are the future of our Nation— are the hope and the test of freedom itself. In homes, farms and factories—in the schools, senates, and churches of the next generation—the youth of today will tell by their deeds the fate of those values which, cherished by the free through centuries, have given life and dignity and purpose to our own America.

This—nothing less—is the measure of the task served by the teachers of our Nation today. Such a responsibility demands not only essential and elaborate material paraphernalia: buildings, endowments, salaries, laboratories. It demands, above all else, strength and perception of heart and of mind.

Our teachers are summoned to be patriots in the highest sense of the word: to teach the principles that bring freedom and justice to life; to make clear that enjoyment of liberties means acceptance of duties; and to impart the priceless knowledge that duty, in an age of peril, means sacrifice.

Our whole citizenry is summoned to help the teachers in their great work: not only to provide them with the resources they need, but also to guard with devoted vigilance the freedom of thought and discussion which inspire free men to teach all men how to be free.

DWIGHT D. EISENHOWER

238 ¶ The President's News Conference of *November* 4, 1953.

THE PRESIDENT. I imagine that today there are a lot of political questions tucked away all ready to spring, and I will give you my answers in advance.

Quite naturally, I am not completely pleased and happy with some results in some places, but I tell you, as I told you before, I believe the job of the administration in Washington is to provide a dynamic and forward-looking program for the United States. We are going to continue to do it, and believe that in the long run it will win.

56616—60——50

One other point, I have lost skirmishes before. [*Laughter*]

Q. Merriman Smith, United Press: Mr. President, may we quote that line, "I have lost skirmishes before"?

THE PRESIDENT [*laughing*]. All right, says Hagerty; I guess it is all right. I just don't want to start some precedents.

Now, I sincerely believe that the programs that are developing are for the welfare of 160 million people.

I believe the farm programs, the tax programs, the foreign aid programs, the expenditure programs, the programs of cleaning up Government, getting honesty, decency, efficiency, and good management, I believe all of them are going forward. They are slow, of course, but they are coming forward; and when they are exposed in their full performance to the American people, I have every confidence that they will approve of them.

Now, dropping that subject, I will read you one little statement on an important subject, and you can get this copy after you leave, so you don't have to copy this down. I believe they will be mimeographed. This is about the Soviet note.

[*Reading*] We are now studying the Soviet note received yesterday.[1]

It is negative and rejects the proposal which the United States, the United Kingdom, and France made for an early conference on Germany and Austria.

It seems further to seek to prevent such a conference by injecting impossible conditions regarding the European Defense Community, the NATO system of collective security, and the position of Communist China. The Soviet note manifests no intention to get together but an intention to create as many difficulties as possible.

Everywhere we have been trying to get to grips with the Soviet regarding the serious problems which exist between the free world and the Communist world.

---

[1] The Soviet note of November 3 is published in the Department of State Bulletin (vol. 29, p. 745).

We have tried time after time to get a meeting about Germany that will bring unification.

We have been trying to get a meeting about Austria which would liberate that country.

We are trying in Korea to get a meeting to deal with the problem of unification of Korea and withdrawal of our own as well as other foreign troops.

In the United Nations Armament Commission we have been trying to bring the Soviets to deal realistically with the problem of limitation of armament and restriction on the use of methods of mass destruction.

Peace for the world is the primary goal of the American people and the administration. As a people, we shall continue to be ready to discuss any issue with the Soviet under conditions which provide a clear and dependable basis for agreement. [*Ends reading*]

That is the only formal statement of my own I have to make today, so we will go to questions.

Q. Mr. Smith: Mr. President, getting back to the subject of the voting yesterday, Representative Clarence Brown, a Republican of Ohio, said just a little while ago, "The people voted for a change"—this is a direct quote—"and they don't feel that they got it." I wonder what your reaction to that is, sir?

THE PRESIDENT. Well, as you know, I never comment on what someone else has to say. Everyone is entitled to his own opinion and, I should think, to express it.

My own opinion is that the kind of change the people wanted is an orderly and progressive change, not just any other kind, that they are going to get it, and are getting it.

Q. Anthony Leviero, New York Times: Mr. President, I think you gave us an unfinished statement. I think you said you had lost skirmishes before. Does that mean you expect to win the war?

THE PRESIDENT. I never went into one to lose one. [*Laughter*]

Q. William H. Lawrence, New York Times: Mr. President,

Mr. Hagerty on Friday told us, in supplementing your own press conference remarks of last week, that you favored the election of every Republican in every election for any office anywhere.

I wondered, does that carry through into 1954, and without regard to the record of a Republican, let's say, in supporting your program?

THE PRESIDENT. No, I'll tell you: there, the statement, after all, had to be based necessarily on a certain assumption which takes into consideration the statement that I have made time and again, which I sincerely believe—a man standing for public office must have a clean record for honesty, integrity, before the public, and you must have confidence in his character.

Now, it is conceivable, of course, that those conditions will not always be met. Under such conditions I should think that it would be improper to go out to support any such person. But I want to bring this out: I have never said I was going in and endorse anybody by name anyway. I said I am going up here to say that I am working for the kind of support and teamwork the Republican Party can give me, and I am going to work for the production of a program of accomplishment that they can support; but I never by any manner of means said I was going out and name each man and say I support them. Let's don't have any mistake about this, because I saw myself misquoted last week.

I have said I believe in party responsibility, and I want to see Republicans come back here with a good comfortable majority so that parties can be held responsible by the American people for what we do.

But when you intimate that in advance I am going to take up every single individual and say "That person I believe in," that is another thing.

Q. Mr. Lawrence: Well, I wanted to, if I may, just carry this a bit further, sir. I was not getting so much at a dishonest candidate or one of bad character; I was trying to draw the line as to whether you would support Republicans who do not support you.

THE PRESIDENT. You bring that question up sometime when

you have got a little—I don't want to try to answer it now. I just don't think I can give you a good one.

Q. Robert W. Ruth, Baltimore Sun: About a year or so ago, Senator Jenner called General Marshall a front man for traitors, and the other day he said that he was standing by that statement. Do you have any comment on that?

THE PRESIDENT. I am sure that you people get weary of me repeating and repeating that I don't comment on what other people say.

I have time and again gone on record as to my admiration for General Marshall. To my mind, he is one of the great patriots I have encountered. He is one of the ablest men I have encountered; certainly one of the most dedicated men I have encountered. So, that is my answer to anyone who wants to talk about General Marshall in derogatory terms. I do not mean to say by any manner of means that I have forever agreed with him. I have sometimes disagreed with him, undoubtedly as you do with anybody, but I consider him one of the real public servants of our times.

Q. David P. Sentner, Hearst Newspapers: Mr. President, in view of the election results, do you contemplate any reappraisal of certain portions of your program, as it were, a new look on the program you will present to the next session of Congress?

THE PRESIDENT. No. My problem is to devise a program that meets the composite convictions of the group that is associated with me, that it is for the welfare of the United States; and some vicissitudes of politics here and there would have no effect on it whatever.

I don't mean to say we are not going to try to put it up forcefully and in good packaging. Of course, we will, but we are going to try to make it, mold it, on the same principles that I have talked ever since I was tempted to say I would enter the political field.

Q. Marvin L. Arrowsmith, Associated Press: Mr. President, do you believe that yesterday's results reflect any dissatisfaction with administration policy?

THE PRESIDENT. That is one I will let you answer yourself, Mr. Arrowsmith; you make those comments, I don't.

Q. Ray L. Scherer, National Broadcasting Company: Back to your program, sir: you said that this program, you hoped would be an umbrella under which your candidates could stand. I am wondering if you think it is at all possible or conceivable that a Democrat might sneak in under that umbrella? [*Laughter*]

THE PRESIDENT. As a matter of fact, I am told that several of them said they were under that umbrella. Actually, there are certain areas in the United States, as you well know, where a man could believe in the general political field exactly as I do, and be under another political label. So, that is the answer there: he would run on such a program.

Q. Robert E. Clark, International News Service: Mr. President, some of those areas presumably would be Texas and Louisiana. What if a Republican were running against a Democrat who you consider was under your umbrella; would you then support that Republican against that Democrat?

THE PRESIDENT. Now, you people are always trying to take me either into Texas, Kansas, or Maine or somewhere, and put me in a specific campaign fight.

I just don't think it is wise for me to comment about such things in advance other than to say my job is here, and I am very, very busy, I assure you, right here. Normally, I think those things will have to be left to the localities to battle out themselves.

Q. Merriman Smith, United Press: Mr. President, after we have gone over State to State here in a rather superficial manner, I wonder if you could tell us your ideas for correcting the situation that led to the result of the voting yesterday—from a party viewpoint?

THE PRESIDENT. Well, I will tell you, as you people know, I am a novice in politics; I have never claimed to be a politician.

I must pin my faith to this: I believe in the commonsense of the American people when they are informed. I believe we not only have to inform them as to the basic facts—some of them are rather stark and disagreeable facts in all these several problems— but we have to devise and put forward and enact a program that the mass of the American people will say is a good one.

Now, I don't know of any other way—not only to win votes; I don't know of any other way that deserves votes.

I don't believe you deserve votes unless there is a record of progress, a record of real accomplishment that can attract them.

Q. Richard L. Wilson, Cowles Publications: Mr. President, do you think that the policies of the Eisenhower administration were involved in any of these elections yesterday?

THE PRESIDENT. Again, I should say you have to answer that question; I don't know, I really don't know.

Q. Mr. Wilson: The reason I was asking was because of your original statement in which you said that you lost skirmishes before, and I wonder if that implied——

THE PRESIDENT. They asked me from the sense of the party; and as the titular head of the party, that was the answer I gave.

Q. Mr. Wilson: But you are not making a reference as to whether this was a test of your policy?

THE PRESIDENT. No, no, I wouldn't, no.

Q. Charles T. Lucey, Scripps-Howard Newspapers: Do you think, Mr. President, that failure of Republicans to get enough jobs and patronage so as to cause dissatisfaction in local organizations might weaken the party at election?

THE PRESIDENT. Well, I will say this, I have been told so. [*Laughter*]

That is the only thing; further than that I really have no opinion on it. I have no opinion on it.

Q. Mr. Lucey: Are you going to do anything about it?

THE PRESIDENT. This is what I believe very thoroughly: I believe that any administration coming in has to move as rapidly as is feasible and practicable to get policy-making positions and the very highest administrative positions properly filled by people who believe in the general policies pursued by that administration; but I also believe that unless we observe the sanctity of the civil service that our country will be in a very, very bad spot.

Now, the job is to steer your way through these two sometimes conflicting considerations.

Consequently, what is going on in these localities is a rather difficult, a rather tortuous, job of getting in between and protecting the civil service and getting rid of people that are trying to use civil service jobs for politics, which is prohibited by law, and also to get policy-making positions filled by people who believe as the administration does.

Q. Mr. Lucey: May I ask one more question?

THE PRESIDENT. Yes.

Q. Mr. Lucey: Are you planning legislation to take care of that situation—to free more jobs, that is?

THE PRESIDENT. Well, there has been none submitted to me, and I don't know whether any is necessary or not; I couldn't say for sure.

Q. Ruth S. Montgomery, New York Daily News: Do you think the prospects are very bright for a peace conference in Korea?

THE PRESIDENT. I can't guess that; that is too filled with imponderables, unknown factors.

I would say this: I can't see any reason for what we have done there recently, except as it does lead toward a political conference. That is what you are talking about, the political conference. So I am hopeful, and I would say in my mind the chances favor it; but there are so many possible obstacles, so many things that could upset the thing, that I would hesitate to put it as a flat prediction.

Q. Doris Fleeson, Bell Syndicate: You have given about 7 dinners at the White House for 115 people that have been described as dinners for the leaders of America; none of those 115 guests have been women. How do you square that with your antidiscrimination policy?

THE PRESIDENT. Well, I will tell you, Miss Fleeson, I tried to get two or three for dinner, and they told me I would have to be very careful because the women couldn't decide who should come. [*Laughter*]

Q. Miss Fleeson: Did women tell you that or did men tell you that?

THE PRESIDENT. Yes, exactly, women. I wouldn't take a man's advice in such a thing. [*Laughter*]

Q. Miss Fleeson: Were they women leaders of the Republican Party?

THE PRESIDENT. I don't think I will identify them.

Q. Anthony H. Leviero, New York Times: Mr. President, will you personally take the lead in submitting the farm program to Congress when Congress convenes?

THE PRESIDENT. I won't take the lead in submitting the details of the program. Unquestionably by the time that the State of the Union Message is ready that will be sufficiently outlined so that its purport and its general scope will be ready; but, of course, the exact program itself which is worked out by all of these groups, including this bipartisan advisory commission which I have met with already, that program will be presented by others.

Q. Mr. Leviero: Well, presumably, you would send that up though in a separate message, though later on?

THE PRESIDENT. Yes.

Q. Richard L. Wilson, Cowles Publications: Mr. President, were you consulted with respect to the reorganization of the Soil Conservation Service?

THE PRESIDENT. Why, of course, they couldn't do that without consulting me.

Q. Mr. Wilson: And did you approve it?

THE PRESIDENT. Yes; and I might say that my advisory commission, which I just spoke of, unanimously approved it. And there were, I think, 23 out of 24 major farm organizations approved it.

Q. Nat S. Finney, Buffalo Evening News: Mr. President, the question has arisen as to what degree the congressional Agriculture committees are a part of this consultation process on a farm program. I have specifically in mind, could a situation arise in which there would be two farm programs, the executive department's farm program and the program of the committees in Congress?

THE PRESIDENT. Well, I can say this only: over those people who I have any influence, I shall do my best to devise a program that will work for the long-term benefit of everybody that is touched by that program—the farmer—the farmer of all kinds; because, remember, there are conflicts among farmers themselves. One wants high-priced feed, one wants low-priced feed; and this conflict goes on in many areas. Of course, there are conflicts between consumers' interests and farm interests. My own idea is that we must develop a program that can be depended on to stand a long time, because it tries in a very definite and clear way to meet the best interests of all. There are unquestionably going to be conflicts and differences of opinion, and some of them will probably be hotly debated, as they should be; but that is going to be our purpose.

Q. Alan S. Emory, Watertown (N.Y.) Times: Mr. President, one of the major Republican campaign promises last year, one, I think, which was borne out in the election results was that the Republicans had pledged to clean up the mess in Washington.

I wondered if it is your understanding that any of the election results of yesterday might have applied to local messes?

THE PRESIDENT. Again, I think I will stay in Washington, if you don't mind. [*Laughter*]

I think I see the connotation of your question. I will say this: I believe that the American people do want, and properly want, honesty and integrity in every single dealing of their Government and all the people that have to do with it.

Q. Marvin L. Arrowsmith, Associated Press: Mr. President, the Republican Chairman, Leonard Hall, in commenting on yesterday's election results, said that there was no question about it, "That as of today we are in trouble politically." Do you agree with Mr. Hall?

THE PRESIDENT. Well, again, I give my own opinion, I don't refer to his: the Republican Party has for many years been a minority party in the United States. The only way they can possibly win elections is to win support from people who class themselves as independents or, let us say, like-minded people within the Democratic Party.

That means you don't do it merely on a basis of going out and a party machinery turning out the vote or anything of that kind. There has got to be something solid, progressive, and real on which to base your argument.

Now, I am not going to talk about whether we are in trouble or not. I never have gotten any great satisfaction out of looking backward, except to find out where I made my own mistakes. I do believe we are on the right line in attempting to produce a program, and that I am going to stick to.

Q. Anthony H. Leviero, New York Times: Mr. President, one more question: Columbia University is planning a bicentennial celebration, and has adopted the theme of man's right to knowledge and the free use thereof. I wonder if you have anything timely to say about that?

THE PRESIDENT. Well, I had a committee meeting, I think that came down yesterday morning, and gave me a book that they have published about New York City, a picture book, a very marvelous sort of thing.

The program was adopted before I left Columbia. Instead of just putting on the usual, you know, celebrations up there, we decided to conduct a campaign during 1954 among the universities of the world, all the world that we could reach, to support that theme—man's right to knowledge and the free use thereof. That is what is going on. For myself, when I left last fall, last winter, when I left New York, and one date I now have on my books, I promised to go back and participate in one of the ceremonies trying to advance this idea, this concept. So I will be back there sometime next June, the Lord willing and letting me live that long.

Q. Martin S. Hayden, Detroit News: Carrying out your thought again on the Republican Party needing the vote of independents, do you attach any significance, sir, to the fact that both in the Wisconsin and in the New Jersey congressional elections, the seats were vacated by very liberal Republicans, and more conservative Republicans were unable to hold them?

THE PRESIDENT. Well, you give a certain basis for your question that I didn't know to be the fact, because I didn't know either of the gentlemen running for office, and I never had a chance to talk to them.

I do believe this: I don't believe that the United States wants to return to 1892, I believe the United States wants to take a look at us where we are and see what to do now for the benefit of this whole and great Nation, its, as I might call it, equilibrium among its different parts at home and its standing abroad, to include certainly its safety and its security and its growing prosperity. Now, what these reasons were, again, I must leave to you for your own decision.

Q. Peter Edson, Newspaper Enterprise Association: Mr. President, on these political questions, I wonder if they could be stated another way. Do you think the results of the election were entirely the results of local conditions, and that national politics did not play an important part in them?

THE PRESIDENT. No, I can't give you an honest answer to that because I am just not familiar enough with it. I tell you again, I just don't have time to study these things in the detail that you would have to, to have a worthwhile opinion on such a subject. I don't know.

Now, I am advised here and there by individuals who come in, but you have the same access to them as I do. You are asking for my opinion, and I don't have it.

Q. Merriman Smith, United Press: Mr. President, do you feel that in the statements that you made about wanting the election of Republicans everywhere, the statements made by Mr. Hagerty, do you feel that these added up to an endorsement of Mr. Troast who was running for Governor of New Jersey?

THE PRESIDENT. I would say this: in the absence of any knowledge to the contrary of the fitness of such a person—and I was assured he was a fit man—I would think that my general statement that, by and large, I wanted to see the party made responsible in a definite way, I would consider that was that much of an endorsement, at least.

Now, that doesn't mean you go out and make speeches for an individual or get down into the local issues involved.

Q. Arthur Sylvester, Newark News: Mr. President, you said a moment ago that you had confidence in the good sense of the American people. Do you think they exercised it yesterday?

THE PRESIDENT. Of course, I do. I think that any district that goes and gives a majority, they know what they are doing. Now, they might be poorly informed and, possibly, one side's advertising or publicity, or whatever you want to call it, is better than the other, and they may get their case presented in better fashion.

I believe in the jury system, and I believe, by and large, there is no jury in the world as accurate as the entire American people, even if they can make errors occasionally. By and large, they were exercising good sense because they went to the polls and voted.

Merriman Smith, United Press: Thank you, Mr. President.

NOTE: President Eisenhower's nineteenth news conference was held in the Executive Office Building from   3:00 to 3:26 o'clock on Wednesday afternoon, November 4, 1953. In attendance: 162.

239 ¶ Letter to Myron M. Cowen Concerning the Philippine Elections. *November 6, 1953*

Dear Mr. Cowen:

Your letter of October twenty-seventh has been read with great interest, and I wish to inform you that I too regard the forthcoming Philippine elections as a vital test of democracy for the

Philippine Republic. However, I am confident that the people of the Philippines will meet this test, as they have met others, in a manner which will fully justify the esteem in which they are held throughout the free world.

I know that I speak for the American people when I say that all of us are indeed interested in what is happening in the Philippines. We rejoice in the upright manner in which the Republic of the Philippines is meeting the problems of a sovereign nation, for it is with some pride that Americans remember that Philippine independence is something that we long worked for and are pledged to respect and help guard.

The Philippine people, whom I know well, are a proud people. This justifiable pride derives in great part from their independence and their democratic political processes. I know that they will wish to stand before the world on their election day as having made full use of their political freedom and enlightened laws to elect a representative government of their own free choosing and dedicated to their service.

Sincerely,

Dwight D. Eisenhower

NOTE: Mr. Cowen was formerly U.S. Ambassador to the Philippines. His letter was released with the President's reply.

240 ¶ Remarks at the Annual Convention of the United Daughters of the Confederacy.
November 10, 1953

Mrs. Long, and ladies:

In the task that I have now, there are certain parts of it that are most enjoyable. One of them is the privilege that comes to me occasionally to welcome to the Capital City a body of people in which all present are animated by desire to serve our country.

That is the kind of thing that gives a lift to the day. And so, as I come over here, I want to assure you that what you are doing for me is sending me back to work with a better feeling than when I came. And for that, I thank you.

Someone said to me this morning, there are many reasons for associating together in the United States—but why a group perpetuating memories of the Confederacy? We refer to it often, you know, in our books, as "the lost cause." Well, I think it is because you have very peculiar and personal values to offer in the United States scene for the rest of us to study, and to be inspired.

Two persons that I want to talk about today are your possessions more than they are of the whole country, I suppose, although we claim them: Lee and Jackson.

As a life-long soldier, it was my duty to read about these two great men who were leaders in that profession. But for me it soon became much more than a duty. It became a great pleasure. It became an inspiration.

When we think of Lee, the qualities for which he stood, the things for which his name stands today, it seems almost redundant—superfluous—for anyone to try to describe them, even to himself.

For me, let me give you my opinion, in a simple way.

In my office I have obtained and put up etchings, or pictures, of a few great Americans: Washington, Franklin, Lincoln, and Lee. Lee was one man who early showed to all of us that a man could be a soldier who could fight with all that was in him—and fight brilliantly—for ideals in which he firmly and honestly believed, but still, at the same time, could be a great and noble character. He himself did not fall prey to the passions of the battlefield and to its contaminating filth and dirt. He remained always a pure soul that today makes us better people.

And he had the perfect lieutenant in Jackson—a man of great purity of spirit, great strength of mind of his own—who could nevertheless grasp the plan of his commander and then go off and execute it perfectly.

Possibly one of the most extraordinary battles of that whole

period of the mid-nineteenth century was that at Chancellors-
ville, where Jackson lost his life. And I will never forget, as I
used to look at the pictures in the books, that it never occurred
to me to look up his age. I thought any man with a beard that
long must be rather venerable. It was almost a shock to discover
that he was dead at 39. Today, when we think of a 39-year-old
general, we think of somebody who must have had a lot of favoritism to get there that quickly. He had behind him the great
accomplishments of those many dreary months of war. A strict
disciplinarian, who yet had one great support outside of his faith
in Lee—his unshakeable faith in his God.

These two people today are probably more influential than in
the days when they led the Confederate armies to so many victories up until 1865—Jackson till 1863.

They hold before us a veneration for ideals, a conviction that
to rise high in your profession you do not have to surrender principle. You can stand for what you believe.

I didn't come over here to make a speech, ladies. I do merely
want to say this with all the strength that I have: if you had no
other reason for existence except to hold before America the
memory, the accomplishments, the characters, the qualities, of
these two men, I still think your association would be well worth
while.

And I think in providing for a memorial to Robert E. Lee, you
have done something in which every single American, from one
end to the other, even if his own ancestors were bitter opponents
of these men in the middle of the nineteenth century, would be
proud to join in that effort.

Thank you very much for inviting me over. I hope you have
a good time while you are here.

NOTE: The President spoke at 10:25 a.m. at the Shoreham Hotel in Washington. In his opening words he re- ferred to Mrs. Glenn Long, President-General of the United Daughters of the Confederacy.

241 ¶ Remarks to the Staff of the United States Information Agency. *November* 10, 1953

Mr. Streibert, ladies and gentlemen:

I can't think of any really good reason to give you for absorbing this much of your time this afternoon. The only excuse I have is that I wanted to see you, in an effort to give some expression— no matter how faint—to my convictions as to the importance of your job.

This conviction is a very old one with me. Someone reminded me today that it was more than 11 years ago that I went across the Atlantic to assume heavy duties in connection with World War II. From that time on I have often been abroad and spent a great deal of time there. It has been almost frustrating to realize how little people in so many areas—and many of them classed as normally well-educated people—knew about the United States. And this had very grave consequences from time to time.

I became one of those who believe that this Government could not conduct satisfactory foreign relationships unless it did something very positive in the way of letting the world know: (a) what is deep in the American heart; (b) what is the general psychological reaction of Americans to a given set of human problems; and (c) what are the qualities or the motives that characterize the things—inspire the things, America is trying to do in the world.

We in our Fourth of July speeches say America seeks no dominion over others, she believes in the dignity of man. We say all the real things. And we believe them. They are true. But when you hear some of these things said to a foreigner, and he just replies "Propaganda," and walks off, you realize that something is wrong.

Now this organization, it seems to me, has so many qualifications to meet that you are almost a group—you are almost individuals set apart from all others. First you must know what Americanism really is. You have got to know that here a government, of, by, and for free men, is based solidly on some religious concept, for the simple reason that otherwise we cannot prove equality among men.

You have got to know something of the history of your country, how we came to what we are. You have got to believe with all your soul that it is this kind or this type of government and system that will allow people to reach the greatest degree of temporal happiness, at least, of which we are capable. That we can seek to express ourselves, to realize all that is within us, not only for ourselves but for those we love, our families, our friends, and that we realize also this can be done only in a world that has an equal right to its own government of its own choice.

If others should happen to take governments—forms of government—in which we do not believe, that is all right. But how are they going to be won from that? By learning, through absorption, and from seeing and from hearing how our system works.

Put it this way: we are now conducting a cold war. That cold war must have some objective, otherwise it would be senseless. It is conducted in the belief that if there is no war, if two systems of government are allowed to live side by side, that ours because of its greater appeal to men everywhere—to mankind—in the long run will win out; that it will defeat all forms of dictatorial government because of its greater appeal to the human soul, the human heart, the human mind.

So you have got to understand all these things in all their ramifications. Certainly I am not here trying to give you a lecture on the American dream and the American system. Most of you have to think about it each day. But I am saying, first you have got to understand it, then you have got to believe it, and then you have to live it.

Now, as I see it, you, therefore, have as your governmental job the thing that every American ought to be. But you have got to symbolize it. Every American standing before the world can scarcely consider that he is doing his full duty to his country unless he shows this belief in Americanism, and realizes that he is showing himself to others as the product of that system. He is one of those that this system has produced.

Now you, members of the United States Information Agency, have the job of making certain that all Americans will want to do this, and that it will be done so well, not in a dictatorial, not in an overbearing, not in a condescending way, but in the simple matter of living, and talking. It will be done so that others will understand the honesty of our purposes, the integrity of our position, and will in the long run, in this cold war, come to believe more and more in this form of government.

And then finally we can, I think, describe the objective of the cold war as to maintain some kind of arrangement for getting along in this world until enough of all the world's people come to believe with you, with us, that the things for which the Americans stand are those things which enrich human life, which ennoble man because he is an individual created in the image of his God and trying to do his best on this earth.

Now certainly I would not prescribe my own effort as a model for any of you. What you are here for is so important, what you are going to do and what you are doing is of such significance not only to us but to the world, to peace, that the last word I should like to say is this—my pledge of support: no one who serves in this organization with what his chiefs or his associates say is decency and to the best of his ability is ever going to suffer if I can help it. On the contrary, I shall try to do my best to pin the accolade of a "well done" to every such person. And it is because I believe from all the descriptions that Mr. Streibert and others responsible here have told me, because I believe you not only can achieve it but that you are on the road to doing it, that I come here to say good luck to each of you, and this administration is with you. Go ahead and do your chores, and you will earn everything the Government could possibly give you.

Good luck, and goodbye.

NOTE: The President spoke at 2:58 p.m. in the Department of the Interior Auditorium. In his opening words he referred to Theodore C. Streibert, Director of the United States Information Agency.

242 ¶ Message Recorded for a Testimonial Dinner Honoring Secretary of the Treasury George M. Humphrey. *November 10, 1953*

My fellow Americans:

It is a distinct privilege to join with you in tribute to my good friend and valued associate in the national Government, George Humphrey.

In the past three decades I have come to know many leaders in public and private affairs in our country and abroad.

Of these leaders of our time, I have found none to be abler—more dedicated—more courageous—more selfless and persevering in pursuit of the public good—than the Secretary of the Treasury, George M. Humphrey.

You and I are fortunate to have such a man in our Nation's service. In the Cabinet, in meetings of the important National Security Council, in personal conferences in my office, I can always count on George Humphrey to be a strong, able, and assertive counsellor—a man from whom sound and objective judgment is certain to be obtained, no matter what the issue involved.

I would deem it an honor to be personally present at this testimonial dinner, so as to share even more intimately in the tribute that the assembled group is paying to its guest of honor. But, denied that opportunity, I extend warm greetings to each of you present, along with my best wishes for a most successful evening. I am sure that it will live long in the memory of our great friend, the Secretary of the Treasury.

NOTE: The message was recorded on film for a dinner given at Saginaw, Mich., on November 10.

243   ¶ The President's News Conference of
November 11, 1953.

THE PRESIDENT. I have a few items that may be of interest.

I, of course, think we should all note that it is Armistice Day,
I suppose a national holiday for you people as well as for me. But
it seems to be about the only time this week we could have this
conference if we were going to, because, as I told you before, I
am leaving for Canada tomorrow night for a short visit.

However, Armistice Day has always meant a lot to all of us,
and if I could ask you people a favor, it would be that each of you
make some mention in your stories that it is Armistice Day, and
what Armistice Day really meant to us at one time. That would
be my speech on that subject.

The Canadian trip, as I told you, is really a courtesy call, but I
have been invited—I believe I told you this before, but if I did,
you will forgive me—I have been invited to address the Parliament up there. I intend to make the subject of my talk just a
general discussion of some of the problems that are common to
both countries and, of course, through the medium of that speech,
to pay my respects to the Canadian people to whom we feel so
close.

In this problem of segregation that has been always in the hands
of some of our people since last January, going ahead on different
fronts, the Navy has just made a very detailed report in the form
both of a letter to me and in a statistical report. You will find
it among the papers in the ordinary place when you leave here.
It is a very encouraging report, I must say.

The Philippine election seems, so far as we can see from reports—and I have only the newspaper reports—seems to be progressing in the way that we should like to see elections progress
in any free country. It looks like they are going without duress,
like there is no effort to rig it. They are going ahead as free elections, which is very encouraging.

This week we did have another election in this country. Last week, I believe, the question was asked whether I was pleased, and I had to qualify my answer very materially. This week I could say I am pleased. [*Laughter*]

With that remark we will go to questions.

Q. Merriman Smith, United Press: I wonder if you could tell us your reaction, your opinion, of ex-President Truman having been subpoenaed by the House Un-American Affairs Committee?

THE PRESIDENT. Well, no, I can't say a great deal about this. I will give you my connection and my feeling about this thing.

Some days back Mr. Brownell, the Attorney General, reported to me that there were certain facts that had been coming to light in his Department that he felt should be made available to the public, and that he felt moreover it was his duty to do so. He told me that they involved a man named White, a man whom I had never met, didn't know anything about.

I told him that he had, as a responsible head of Government, to make the decision, if he felt it was his duty to make these things public to do it on a purely factual basis.

He did tell me that the information had gotten to the White House, and that was all. So that was my last connection with it until this incident occurred of which you speak.

Now, I think once before, before this group, I tried to make quite clear that I am not going to be in the position of criticizing the Congress of the United States for carrying out what it conceives to be its duty. It has the right, of course, to conduct such investigations as it finds necessary; but if you asked me, as I understood it, my personal reaction, I would not issue such a subpoena.

Q. Edward Jamieson Milne, Providence Journal-Bulletin: Mr. President, do you yourself feel that former President Truman knowingly appointed a Communist spy to high office?

THE PRESIDENT. You are asking me for opinions, of course, based on nothing else except what I have told you and what I have read in the papers.

No, it is inconceivable; I don't believe that—put it in this way—a man in that position knowingly damaged the United States. I think it would be inconceivable.

Q. Raymond P. Brandt, St. Louis Post-Dispatch: Mr. President, my office asked me to ask this whole series of questions.

THE PRESIDENT. Just a minute. I am not sure of the custom here; you may have one question, but there are a lot of other people here.

Q. Mr. Brandt: I think they are pertinent to all of them.

THE PRESIDENT. Well, I will have to decide.

Q. Mr. Brandt: You answered the first one, did you know in advance of the Chicago speech.

The next question was were you consulted while plans were being laid to bring the White story out? You apparently offered——

THE PRESIDENT. No, the report was made to me that there was certain information that the Attorney General considered it his duty to make public, and he did mention the word "White," although as I say, I didn't know who White was.

Q. Mr. Brandt: Then the next question: did you know in advance of the plan to subpoena Truman, and did you approve? You've answered that.

Do you think Supreme Court Justices should be subpoenaed by Congress?

THE PRESIDENT. I am not a constitutional lawyer, and I would again say you are asking there my personal opinion, personal convictions. I probably in that position would not do it. I'd think there would be other means of handling it rather than issuing a subpoena.

Q. Mr. Brandt: Do you think the FBI report is justified in calling White a spy when a grand jury refused to believe it on the basis of FBI evidence, that was the grand jury investigation in 1947?

THE PRESIDENT. I know nothing about it; you will have to go to the record and the facts.

Q. Mr. Brandt: Do you think the administration's action in

virtually putting a label of traitor on a former President is likely to damage our foreign relations?

THE PRESIDENT. I reject the premise. I would not answer such a question.

Q. Mr. Brandt: What effect do you think such an action by the administration will have on the Russians, good or bad?

THE PRESIDENT. Let me say something: anyone who doesn't recognize that the great struggle of our time is an ideological one, that is, a system of regimentation and of virtual slavery as against the concept of freedom on which our Government is founded, then they are not looking this question squarely in the face.

Now, the attack against freedom is on many fronts. It is conducted by force, by the use of force and the threat of force, by subversion and bribery and boring from within, and it makes it necessary to practice more than ever that old saying, "The price of liberty is eternal vigilance."

I thoroughly agree with those who say we must be very careful how we apply our own activities, our own powers, our own authority in defending against this thing. We must not destroy what we are attempting to defend. So, just as earnestly as I believe we must all fight communism to the utmost, I believe that we must also fight any truly unjust, un-American way of uprooting them, because in the long run I think we will destroy ourselves if we use that kind of defense.

This is, however, something that is subject to the judgment of humans. They are fallible; and when they see all of the efforts we have made over these last years rejected—I mean our measures to make some peaceful arrangement, to see them rejected, the offers we made in 1946 about making available to all the world the entire atomic project that had been developed, every secret, make it available for peaceful use under any system that would give us confidence that all others were doing the same, and all the way down the line we have seen secrets stolen, we have seen all kinds of spywork go ahead—it is sometimes difficult to say there will never be an injustice.

But that, I say, must be the true path for every real American: to oppose these ideologies, these doctrines that we believe will destroy our form of government, and at the same time, to do it under methods where we don't destroy it. I can't define it any better than that.

Q. Robert G. Spivack, New York Post: Mr. President, taking up your answer to one of the previous questions, since Mr. Brownell has impugned the loyalty of a former President, and a grand jury said that it couldn't find a basis for indicting White, don't you think there is a moral obligation to make these reports, FBI reports, public?

THE PRESIDENT. No.

Q. Mr. Spivack: And we have no way of knowing——

THE PRESIDENT. I don't believe that you can make FBI reports available, as such. I believe you can extract a great deal of material from them, but there are too many things in them that must be protected.

As a matter of fact, the original FBI reports I will not allow to be shown to me except when I have to see them, because I just believe if we don't protect their sources of information we will someday destroy them.

Now, you also make a premise I don't accept. You said Mr. Brownell impugned the loyalty of a President. I don't know— certainly he never told me—that he said that the President of the United States ever saw the papers. He said they went to the White House. Now, that is all he ever told me, and I think you have made a mistake.

Q. Roscoe Drummond, New York Herald Tribune: Mr. President, without making any premise at all, could I ask you whether you feel that a charge should be publicly made against anybody, an accusation, without the evidence being publicly made so that the public can assess the basis of the accusation, regardless of the FBI?

THE PRESIDENT. I think the essentials of the evidence probably have to be made available, yes, I would agree with that.

I don't think—look, this goes back to what I said: I believe it is reckless, to say nothing of un-American, action to make from any kind of a favored position accusations where you are not prepared to show what has happened and to make available the essentials of that evidence.

Here, you have got a case where there are certain particular documents I don't think can be shown, but the essentials of the evidence certainly must be, so far as I know; and I don't know of any disposition to conceal it.

Q. Mr. Drummond: It has not come out yet, Mr. President.

Q. Mrs. May Craig, New England papers: Mr. President, I have been around for 25 years here, and I find myself befuddled by failure to get the truth.

Isn't the question here whether the charge is true, made by Mr. Brownell? Isn't that the basic thing? Should not former officials who know, come and tell the truth to the people as they knew it?

THE PRESIDENT. I think that is proper. I think you have asked a question that sort of answers itself.

What we want is the truth. So far as I know, the Attorney General has no intention of concealing anything except the particular form of a document, and I assume that other people, in giving their testimony, will do it in any way they see fit.

Q. Mrs. Craig: Do you think former officials should be protected in not coming forward and telling their share in public happenings?

THE PRESIDENT. I didn't say they should be protected. I was asked this question, how would I have done it; and I certainly would not, I said, issue the subpoena in the circumstances.

Q. S. Douglass Cater, Jr., The Reporter: Mr. President, what did you understand was the purpose of bringing information from the files of the FBI before a luncheon group instead of some official body, such as a grand jury, or another body of Congress, or something of that sort, by the Attorney General?

THE PRESIDENT. You can get direct evidence on that. I didn't even consider it. I was told that there was going to be certain information made available. It was. You can go to the Attorney General himself.

Q. Anthony H. Leviero, New York Times: Mr. President, I think this case is at best a pretty squalid one. But if a grand jury, under our system, has found a man—has, in effect, cleared the man or at least has decided it was insufficient evidence to convict him or prosecute him, then is it proper for the Attorney General to characterize that accused man, who is now dead, as a spy and, in effect, accuse a former President of harboring that man? That was quite plain in the statement of the Attorney General.

THE PRESIDENT. Look, all you are trying to get now is my personal opinion about certain things. I am not either a judge nor am I an accomplished lawyer. I have my own ideas of what is right and wrong, but I would assume this: you are asking me to answer questions where, with all of this in the public mind, the Attorney General is here to answer it himself. Let him answer it.

Q. Mr. Leviero: He has refused to answer the questions, you see. [*Laughter*]

Q. Andrew F. Tully, Jr., Scripps-Howard Newspapers: It is true that Mr. Brownell is here, but he won't see reporters. I wonder if we can ask you to exert your influence to get him to see us? [*Laughter*]

THE PRESIDENT. Well, of course, after all, I think that you are probably getting a little bit more impatient than he thinks you should be. I don't know exactly what he has in mind; I am certainly ready to talk to Mr. Brownell more about this when he returns to town, but I am not going to give him orders as to methods in which he handles responsibilities of his own office.

Now, this is what I want to say: I have found Mr. Brownell interested in justice and decency in cleaning up what he has got to clean up. We have gone ahead in many lower echelons; I believe there was a report published we had gotten some 1400 people that we thought were security risks. He publishes now a particular case, and it has aroused tremendous interest. Now we will see how he handles it, and I am not going to color his case or to prejudice his case in advance in what I say about it.

Q. Mr. Tully: Mr. President, could I ask one more question?

THE PRESIDENT. Yes.

Q. Mr. Tully: Can you give us any indication of when the proof of these charges is going to be offered by Mr. Brownell?

THE PRESIDENT. Of course I can't. I just told you that he has got to handle this case in his own way. I just say that I am not supposed, and I do not intend, to be one that is a party to what looks like rank injustice to anybody. That is all I can say on this.

Q. Anthony H. Leviero, New York Times: One more question. Insofar as we have been allowed to know the facts, the case rests on the testimony of two confessed traitors, Whittaker Chambers and Elizabeth Bentley. I wonder if the FBI independently has developed any evidence to sustain the charge of espionage?

THE PRESIDENT. Again you will have to ask Mr. Brownell; I don't know.

Q. Robert L. Riggs, Louisville Courier-Journal: There has been some question as to whether the FBI report said Mr. White was a spy or whether it says he associated with Communists. Did Mr. Brownell say to you that the FBI report called him a spy?

THE PRESIDENT. Ladies and gentlemen, I am going to answer my last question right now on this subject for this morning, at least.

I told you exactly, Mr. Brownell came in and reported to me that there was evidence that there had been subversive action in which high Government officials were aware of it; he gave me the name as Mr. White, and he said the evidence was so clear that he considered it his duty to lay it out because, he said, "Certainly, I am not going to be a party to concealing this," is the way he explained it to me. I said, "You have to follow your own conscience as to your duty." Now that is exactly what I knew about it.

Q. Paul Scott Rankine, Reuters News Agency: Mr. President, could you tell us anything about the subjects you expect to discuss at the Bermuda conference?

THE PRESIDENT. There is no agenda. The invitation and all the conversations and the communications on the subject are that we are to meet on an around-the-table basis to discuss problems of interest to the three governments, that is all, and on a very informal basis.

Q. Oscar W. Reschke, German Press Agency: Mr. President, is it being considered to ask the Government of the Federal Republic to send an observer to Bermuda to be at hand for the conversations?

THE PRESIDENT. Not that I know of.

Merriman Smith, United Press: Thank you, Mr. President.

NOTE: President Eisenhower's twentieth news conference was held in the Executive Office Building from 10:15 to 10:34 o'clock on Wednesday morning, November 11, 1953. In attendance: 175.

244 ¶ Statement by the President on the Elimination of Segregation in Civilian Facilities at Naval Installations.   *November 11, 1953*

THE SECRETARY OF THE NAVY has just submitted to me a full report on facilities used by civilian employees at naval installations in the southern States.

I agree wholeheartedly with him that the report is most encouraging for it proves conclusively that the Navy's policy of nonsegregation is completely effective.

There are, in all, 60 Naval activities on Federal-owned property in the South. Here are the facts:

1. Twenty installations reported, as of August 1st, that no segregation practices existed.

2. Seventeen additional installations, not initially covered in the August survey, also reported no segregation. One establishment—at Newport News—reported washrooms and toilets were segregated in a building located on non-Federal property.

3. Twenty-one further installations, which reported segregation practices in August, revealed segregation had been eliminated by November 1st. One installation—Charleston Shipyard—still reported partial segregation. At Charleston, segregation at drinking fountains and in cafeterias was eliminated, but washrooms are still separated. The Shipyard Commander stated that in these latter facilities restrictions would be eliminated late in December or early in January.

In summation, of 60 southern installations on Federal-owned property only one reported partial segregation. That is a record of accomplishment of which we all can be proud and I congratulate the Secretary of the Navy and his Department on a job very well done indeed.

NOTE: The Secretary of the Navy's report was made public with the President's statement.

245   ¶ Message on the Death of King Ibn Saud of Saudi Arabia.   *November* 11, 1953

His Majesty
Saud ibn Abd al-Aziz al-Saud
King of Saudi Arabia

It is with a profound sense of loss that I express my deepest sympathy to the Royal Family and people of Saudi Arabia upon the death of their illustrious father and ruler, King Abdul Aziz al Saud. His Majesty's statesmanship and sagacity as a ruler endeared him to the hearts of his people and won him universal renown. The American people were proud to count him and his nation among their most trusted and valued friends.

On this solemn occasion I wish to extend to Your Majesty, as your father's worthy successor, my good wishes upon your accession to the throne. I am confident that the warm bonds of friendship and mutual interest, which have bound our two countries so closely in the past, will remain firm and enduring under your able guidance. The people of Saudi Arabia are indeed fortunate to have their destiny served by a ruler so progressive and devoted to their welfare as yourself.

DWIGHT D. EISENHOWER

246 ¶ Address Before a Joint Session of the Parliament of Canada. *November* 14, 1953

Mr. Speaker of the Senate, Mr. Speaker of the House, Mr. Prime Minister, Members of the Canadian Houses of Parliament, distinguished guests and friends:

Mes salutations s'adressent également à mes amis canadiens qui parlent le français. Je sais que je fais preuve de grande témérité en essayant de m'exprimer, si peu soit-il, dans cette langue; aussi fais-je appel à votre indulgence pour les erreurs d'expression et de prononciation que je peux commettre en vous faisant part personnellement et directement de mes sentiments d'amitié et de haute estime. Je vous salue également pour la part importante que vous avez prise, de concert avec vos frères de langue anglaise, au développement de ce grand pays.[1]

Mr. Prime Minister, for the very great generosity of the personal sentiments expressed towards me, I am humbly grateful. For the reception Mrs. Eisenhower and I experienced here

---

[1] The following translation appears in the White House release of this address:

I include in my salutation my Canadian friends who speak the French language. Although I am more than bold to attempt even this slight venture into the speaking of that tongue, I ask your forgiveness for errors both in expression and in pronunciation as I take this means of conveying to you personally and directly my sentiments of friendship and high esteem. Likewise, I salute you for the great contribution you, together with your English-speaking brethren, have made to the growth of this great country.

throughout this city, we should like to extend to all your citizens—all your people—our very deep appreciation, especially for the honor of being received before this Body. I assure you you have given us distinction that we shall never forget.

Since World War II, I have now been privileged, three times, to visit this great country and this beautiful city.

On my first visit, more than seven years ago, I came to express to the Canadian people a field commander's appreciation of their memorable contribution in the liberation of the Mediterranean and the European lands. On my second, I came to discuss with your governmental leaders your country's role in the building of Atlantic security. Both visits, in the warmth and spirit of a great people's welcome, were days that I shall remember all my life.

This day, I again salute the men and women of Canada.

As I stand before you, my thoughts go back to the days of global war. In that conflict, and then through the more recent savage and grievous Korean battles, the Canadian people have been valorous champions of freedom for mankind. Within the framework of NATO, in the construction of new patterns for international security, in the lengthy and often toilsome exploration of a regional alliance, they have been patient and wise devisers of a stout defense for the Western world. Canada, rich in natural gifts, far richer in human character and genius, has earned the gratitude and the affectionate respect of all who cherish freedom and seek peace.

I am highly honored by the invitation of the Parliament that I address it. For your invitation is rooted in the friendship—the sense of partnership—that for generations has been the hallmark of the relations between Canada and the United States. Your country, my country—each is a better and stronger and more influential nation because each can rely upon every resource of the other in days of crisis. Beyond this, each can work and grow and prosper with the other through years of quiet peace.

We, of our country, have long respected and admired Canada

as a bulwark of the British Commonwealth and a leader among nations. As no Soviet wile or lure can divide the Commonwealth, nothing will corrupt the Canadian-American partnership.

We have a dramatic symbol of that partnership in the favored topic of every speaker addressing an audience made up of both our peoples—our unfortified frontier. But though this subject has become shopworn and well nigh exhausted as a feature of after dinner oratory, it is still a fact that our common frontier grows stronger every year, defended only by friendship. Its strength wells from indestructible and enduring sources—identical ideals of family and school and church, and traditions which come to us from the common past.

Out of this partnership has evolved a progressive prosperity and a general well-being, mutually beneficial, that is without parallel on earth. In the years ahead, the pace of our mutual growth will surely be no less.

To strive, even dimly, to foresee the wonders of Canada's next generation, is to summon the utmost powers of the imagination. This land is a mighty reservoir of resources. Across it, at this moment, there moves an extraordinary drama of enterprise and endeavor—Canadians, rapidly building basic industries, converting waters into hydro-electric energy, scrutinizing your soil for new wealth, pushing into the barrens of the North for minerals and for oil. You, of Canada, are building a magnificent record of achievement. My country rejoices in it.

More than friendship and partnership is signified in the relations between our countries. These relations that today enrich our peoples justify the faith of our fathers that men, given self-government, can dwell at peace among themselves, progressive in the development of their material wealth, quick to join in the defense of their spiritual community, ready to arbitrate differences that may rise to divide them. This Parliament is an illustrious symbol of a human craving, a human search, a human right to self-government.

All the free legislatures of the world speak for the free peoples of the world. In their deliberations and enactments, they mirror the ideas, the traditions, the fundamental philosophies of their respective nations.

On the other hand, every free nation, secure in its own economic and political stability, reflects the responsible leadership and the wise comprehension which its legislature has brought to the management of public affairs.

Now, this continent uniquely has been a laboratory of self-government, in which free legislatures have been an indispensable force. What is the result? It is a mighty unity built of values essentially spiritual.

This continent, of course, is a single physical and geographical entity. But physical unity, however, broken by territorial lines, fortress chains and trade barriers, is a characteristic of every continent. Here, however, independent and sovereign peoples have built a stage on which all the world can see:

First—Each country's patriotic dedication to its own enlightened self-interest, but free from vicious nationalistic exploitation of grudge or ancient wrong.

Second—A joined recognition that neighbors, among nations as among individuals, prosper best in neighborly cooperation, factually exemplified in daily life.

Third—An international will to cast out the bomb and the gun as arbiters and to exalt the joint search for truth and justice.

Here, on this continent, we present an example that other nations some day surely will recognize and apply in their relationships among themselves. My friends, may that day be close, because the only alternative—the bankruptcy of armament races and the suicide of nuclear war—cannot for long, must not for long, be tolerated by the human race.

Great has been our mutual progress. It foreshadows what we together can accomplish for our mutual good.

Before us of Canada and the United States lies an immense panorama of opportunity in every field of human endeavor. A host of jobs to be done together confront us. Many of them cry for immediate attention. As we examine them together in the work days ahead, we must never allow the practical difficulties that impede progress to blind our eyes to the objectives established by principle and by logic.

With respect to some aspects of our future development, I hope I may, without presumption, make three observations.

The first is: The free world must come to recognize that trade barriers, although intended to protect a country's economy, often in fact shackle its prosperity. In the United States, there is a growing recognition that free nations cannot expand their productivity and economic strength without a high level of international trade.

Now, in our case—yours and ours—our two economies are enmeshed intricately with the world economy. We cannot risk sudden dislocation in industry and agriculture and widespread unemployment and distress, by hasty decisions to accomplish suddenly what inevitably will come in an orderly economic evolution. "Make haste slowly" is a homely maxim with international validity.

Moreover, every common undertaking, however worthwhile it may be, must be understood in its origins, its application, its effects by the peoples of our two countries. Without this understanding, it will have negligible chance of success. Canadians and citizens of the United States do not accept government by edict or decree. Informed and intelligent cooperation is, for us, the only source of enduring accomplishment.

To study further the whole subject of United States foreign economic policy, we have at home appointed a special commission with wide representation including members of the Congress as well as spokesmen for the general public. From the commission's studies will come, we hope, a policy which can command the support of the American people and which will be in the best interest of the United States and the free world.

Toward the strengthening of commercial ties between Canada and the United States, officials of our two governments have for some months been considering the establishment of a Joint Economic and Trade Committee. This Committee, now approved, will consist of Cabinet officers of both countries. They will meet periodically to discuss in broad terms economic and trade problems and the means for their equitable solution. I confidently believe that out of this process, the best interests of both our countries will be more easily harmonized and advanced.

The second observation is this: Joint development and use of the St. Lawrence-Great Lakes Waterway is inevitable. It is sure and certain. With you, I consider this measure a vital addition to our economic and national security. Of course, no proposal yet made is entirely free from faults of some sort. But every one of them can be corrected—given patience and cooperation.

In the United States, my principal security advisers, comprising the National Security Council, favor the undertaking for national defense reasons. The Cabinet favors it on both security and economic grounds. A Committee of the United States Senate has approved a measure authorizing it.

This measure provides for United States participation in a joint development by both countries. The proposal now awaits action by the United States Senate which, I am confident, will act favorably on it or some similar measure. The ways and means for assuring American cooperation in this great project will, I hope, be authorized and approved during the coming session of the Congress.

I have noted with satisfaction the New York Power Authority's acceptance of the Federal Power Commission's license. With this act the stage is set for a start on the St. Lawrence Power Project which will add materially to the economic strength of both countries.

My third observation is this: You of Canada and we of the United States can and will devise ways to protect our North America from any surprise attack by air. And we shall achieve the defense of our continent without whittling our pledges to Western Europe or forgetting our friends in the Pacific.

The basic threat of communist purpose still exists. Indeed the latest Soviet communication to the Western world is truculent, if not arrogant, in tone. In any event, our security plans must now take into account Soviet ability to employ atomic attack on North America, as well as on countries, friendly to us, lying closer to the borders of the U.S.S.R. Their atomic stockpile will, of course, increase in size, and means of delivery will increase as time goes on.

Now, each of our two nations seeks a secure home for realization of its destiny. Defense of our soil presents a challenge to both our peoples. It is a common task. Defensively, as well as geographically, we are joined beyond any possibility of separation. This element in our security problem is an accepted guide of the service leaders, government officials and legislatures on both sides of the border. In our approach to the problem, we both realize that purest patriotism demands and promotes effective partnership. Thus we evolve joint agreements on all those measures we must jointly undertake to improve the effectiveness of our defenses, but every arrangement rests squarely on the sovereign nature of each of our two peoples.

Canada and the United States are equal partners and neither dares to waste time. There is a time to be alert and a time to rest. These days demand ceaseless vigilance. We must be ready and prepared. The threat is present. The measures of defense have been thoroughly studied by official bodies of both countries. The Permanent Joint Board on Defense has worked assiduously and effectively on mutual problems. Now is the time for action on all agreed measures.

Steps to defend our continent are of course but one part of the world-wide security program. The North Atlantic Treaty Organization, for example, is an essential defense of Ottawa, and of Washington, and of our neighbors to the South, as well as of communities thousands of miles to the eastward. Implicit in the consultations and detailed studies which must continue and in the defenses which we have already mounted is the need for world-wide vigilance and strength. But the purpose is defense. We have no other aim.

In common with others of the free world, the United States does not rely on military strength alone to win the peace. Our primary reliance is a unity among us forged of common adherence to moral principles. This reliance binds together in fellowship all those who believe in the spiritual nature of man, as the Child of God.

Moreover, our country assuredly claims no monopoly on wisdom. We are willing—nay, anxious—to discuss with friends and with any others all possible paths to peace. We will use every means—from the normal diplomatic exchange to the forum of the United Nations—to further this search. We welcome ideas, expressions of honest difference, new proposals and new interpretations of old ones—anything and everything honestly offered for the advancement of man's oldest aspiration.

There are no insoluble problems. Differences can be resolved; tensions can be relieved. The free world, I deeply believe, holds firmly to this faith, striving earnestly towards what is just and equitable.

My friends, allow me to interpolate here merely an expression of my own personal faith. I call upon all of those who are in responsible position, either in civil government or in the military world—in the dark days of 1940 and 1941 and 1942, there seemed no place from which to start to conquer the enemy that bid fair to enslave us all. Already he had put most of Europe under his heel.

When I stop to think of the bewilderment of our people—the fears of our people in those days, and then how in a few short years we were coming home to celebrate that great victory that we thought could at last mark the end of all wars, we see how fast human affairs, human outlooks can change, from one of despondency—almost of despair, in many quarters—to one of exultation.

Now today, as we fail to understand the intransigence that we feel marks others, as we try to color every proposal we make with what we believe to be reason, understanding—even sympathy, as we are nonplussed as to why these offers are never taken up, let us never despair that faith will win through.

The world that God has given us is, of course, material in its values, intellectual and spiritual. We have got to hand on to those who come after us this balance—this balance of values, and particularly the certainty that they can enjoy the same kind of opportunity in this spiritual, intellectual and material world that we, who will then be their ancestors, enjoyed before them.

That, it seems to me, is the real problem that Canada and the United States today have to meet. And it is the one reason I get such a thrill every time I come to this country, because here I sense in the very atmosphere your determination to work in that direction, not acknowledging defeat, certain that we can win because there are values that man treasures above all things else in the world that are now at stake.

The free world believes that practical problems can be solved practically; that they should be solved by orderly procedure, step by step, so that the foundation for peace, which we are building in concert with other nations, will be solid and unshakable. I deem it a high privilege to salute, through this their Parliament, the Canadian people for the strength they have added to this faith—and for the contribution they are making toward its realization.

Beyond the shadow of the atomic cloud, the horizon is bright with promise. No shadow can halt our advance together. For we, Canada and the United States, shall use carefully and wisely the God-given graces of faith and reason as we march together toward it—toward the horizon of a world where each man, each family, each nation lives at peace in a climate of freedom.

NOTE: The President spoke in the House of Commons in Ottawa at 11:13 a.m. His opening words referred to the Honorable Wishart Robertson, Speaker of the Senate, the Honorable Louis Beaudoin, Speaker of the House of Commons, and Prime Minister Louis St. Laurent.

247 ¶ Joint Statement Following Discussions With Prime Minister St. Laurent of Canada. *November* 14, 1953

THE FOLLOWING joint communique was issued by President Eisenhower and Prime Minister St. Laurent at the conclusion of the meeting of the Canadian Cabinet.

1. During the course of President Eisenhower's state visit to Canada, the Prime Minister of Canada and members of the Canadian Cabinet had an opportunity of having informal discussions with him on matters of mutual interest to the United States and Canada. The President and the Prime Minister last reviewed some of these questions when the Prime Minister visited Washington last May.

2. Views were exchanged on recent developments in the world situation and on measures which might bring about a relaxation of current international tensions. It was agreed that all efforts for peace and improved world conditions being made by the United Nations or elsewhere should be supported and the necessity of maintaining the strength, unity and determination of the free world to resist aggression was fully recognized.

3. The President and the Prime Minister agreed on the importance to the free world of healthy national economies and of the expansion of world trade on a multilateral basis. Satisfaction was expressed at the recent establishment of a joint United States-Canadian Committee on Trade and Economic Affairs. The importance of the St. Lawrence Seaway and Power Project was emphasized, and there was full agreement on the urgency of initiating the first phase—construction of the Power Project in accordance with arrangements which already have been made between the two governments.

4. In discussing the means of strengthening the security of the free world, the importance of collective arrangements under the North Atlantic Treaty Organization was emphasized, including

the special responsibility of the United States and Canada for building up the defenses of this continent. There was complete agreement on the vital importance of effective methods for joint defense, especially in the light of evidence of increasing technical capability of direct attack on both countries by weapons of great destructive power. Cooperation on joint defense matters had its origin in the Ogdensburg Agreement of 1940 which established the Permanent Joint Board on Defense. In 1947 the two countries issued a joint statement which set forth the principles and methods by which cooperation would be continued and strengthened. The full respect of each country for the sovereignty of the other is inherent in these principles. These principles are equally valid today when Canada and the United States, recognizing that the defense of North America must be considered as a whole, are undertaking further efforts for their joint security. The arrangements for collaboration which have proved satisfactory over the years provide a firm basis on which to carry forward the close relationship between Canada and the United States in matters of common defense.

248 ¶ Letter to Walter P. Reuther Extending Greetings to the 15th Constitutional Convention of the Congress of Industrial Organizations. *November* 16, 1953

[Released November 16, 1953. Dated November 12, 1953]

Dear Mr. Reuther:

To the Fifteenth Constitutional Convention of the Congress of Industrial Organizations, I extend greetings and good wishes.

When I last addressed a CIO Convention, I came to thank you for your magnificent performance in World War II in supplying the planes and tanks and ships and arms. You did your job, and you did it well.

Unfortunately, peace and freedom did not come to the world when the guns fell silent. America is still dedicated to achieving them. I know that American labor holds to that dedication. Proof is abundant that those of you who are today employed in plants supplying our Army, Navy, and Air Force and the armed forces of our Allies, have lost none of the spirit which in wartime was so magnificent. The maintenance of peace in the world depends directly upon America's ability to produce the materiel to give an aggressor pause. The productive might of America is the greatest bulwark of world peace. I know that leaders and members of American labor will never forget that fact. Your future and the future of your unions, in common with all free American institutions, will be determined by our ability further to strengthen our country in the uncertain period ahead.

I am glad the Secretary of Labor of the United States, the Honorable James P. Mitchell, can be with you for the Convention. I have selected him to be a member of my Cabinet because of his ability, his integrity, and his unreserved dedication to the public good. Already, in the few weeks he has served, he has impressed his colleagues in the Cabinet with his thorough understanding of the problems of labor, and with his determination to see that the aspirations and needs of working men and women are fully and forcefully represented at the highest level of government. Before he left for your Convention, I asked him to report back to me your ideas on matters of legislation and public policy.

I know you have a vital interest in the Taft-Hartley Act. I have previously stated my conviction that this law, while fundamentally sound, should be changed in some respects.

For months, members of the Administration have been engaged in a searching study of the Act. Our objective is to recommend improvement in order to make possible a more free and vigorous collective bargaining process, to reduce government intervention in labor-management relations, and to promote sound and peaceful industrial relationships so essential to the economic well-being of American working men and women and to the welfare of all elements of our nation.

I shall submit the resulting suggestions to the Congress when it convenes in January. In formulating these suggestions, our guide will be the fundamental principle that the law must be absolutely fair to the laboring men and women of this nation, to management, and to the public at large.

Our nation's goal is world peace. We are endowed by the Creator with a bounty envied by all the earth. Our greatest resources are in the spirit and the ideals of our people. Counted in these is our tradition for composing group differences in the broad public interest. I commend that tradition to you and to those with whom you deal as you pursue your deliberations in this period which, with God's help, future historians will be able to mark as a time of triumph for the values of free men everywhere.

Sincerely,

DWIGHT D. EISENHOWER

249 ¶ The President's News Conference of *November* 18, 1953.

THE PRESIDENT. First, I have a little statement on drought conditions and measures for meeting it. There is a statistical piece of paper that I won't even bother to read. Both of them will be available to you afterward so you don't need to take notes on it.

[*Reading*] Drought conditions in many parts of the country have continued to increase in severity. Portions of our livestock industry are facing virtual liquidation. Damage to the whole agricultural economy in these areas has been great. Hardship among thousands of farm families has been intense.

The Federal Government has been active for many months in devising and carrying out emergency programs to deal with the consequences of this drought. The administration is determined to continue these efforts vigorously. Every step that can legitimately be taken to alleviate these conditions will be taken.

In order to make possible—and this is the new part of it—in

order to make possible the continued flow of feed into these disaster drought areas at reduced prices until Congress reconvenes, I have today directed that the supplies of feed heretofore and hereafter furnished by the Commodity Credit Corporation under this program shall be without reimbursement to the Corporation from presently authorized funds. This direction, in conjunction with the $40 million appropriated by Congress and the funds allocated by me from the President's disaster emergency fund, will insure that the drought relief program shall go forward until Congress can review the program in January. [*Ends reading*]

The "without reimbursement" finding is the thing that adds a very great deal to the current possibility for dealing with it. As I say, there is an additional document of statistics that may be of some interest to you.[1]

As you know, during a recess of Congress there is a constant stream of congressional leaders meeting with the executive departments in an effort to produce legislative programs to be entered into the succeeding session of the Congress.

This has been going on, and the staffs of the executive departments have been working to produce such a program. On the 17th, 18th, and 19th of December we are asking all of the party leaders in both Houses to come in to sort of firm up and examine the various subjects that have been under study for the past many weeks, and to go into the program that will be submitted when Congress convenes.

It has to do, of course, with the State of the Union Message and all the supporting documents that will go along with it.

Now, in the course of the 17th, 18th, and 19th, we hope to get in a majority of the committee chairmen who have important

---

[1] The President referred to a White House release outlining other steps taken by the administration in aid of agriculture. The release covered such matters as drought relief (Federal aid extended to 15 States and Hawaii, including $110 million for farm credits and $50 million for emergency feed, grain, and hay), and the cattle price program (purchases equivalent to 750,000 head of cattle, sales promotion in cooperation with the beef industry resulting in increased prices on the farm for both feeder and slaughter cattle, and the reduction by half of rail rates for feed and cattle).

parts to play in the carrying out or effecting of the program so that everybody can be in accord.

There will probably be other meetings, as usual, after that date, but that will be sort of a full-dress get-together to make sure that we are all coordinated.

There has been some query directed to Mr. Hagerty about my personal plans for Thanksgiving, and he asked me if I would say I am going to Augusta—I hope. My children and grandchildren are in Georgia, and I hope to have the Thanksgiving holiday with them. If that is of any interest, that is the news; I hope to leave here something like the 24th and come back, then, on Sunday night.

Now, I think that is about all that I had of my own, and we are ready to take questions.

Q. Merriman Smith, United Press: Mr. President, I wonder if, from the disclosures that came out of the current aspects of the Harry Dexter White case, do you see any need for legislative recommendations to deal with this situation or similar situations?

THE PRESIDENT. I should like to make clear, ladies and gentlemen, that so far as this case itself is concerned, I haven't another single word to say about it, certainly not at this time, and don't intend to open my mouth about it.

Now, you raise another question, Mr. Smith, one that is of great significance; and I would hate to answer it, you might say, off the cuff because I haven't discussed the particular thing. I would, if that is of real interest to you, try to talk to some of my people and see if there is anything in the wind of that kind.

Q. Alan S. Emory, Watertown (N.Y.) Times: Mr. President, last Sunday on television, Mr. Leonard Hall, the Chairman of the Republican National Committee, left some of us with the impression that the No. 1 issue for the Republicans in next year's congressional campaign would be exposures of Communist infiltration in the Government under previous administrations.

I wondered what relative position in the campaign you thought this should take in relationship to the dynamic forward-looking program which you have mentioned to us?

THE PRESIDENT. I think I would express myself this way: issues in political campaigns are not made by any individual, and that includes the President of the United States. Issues are made, as I see it, by the needs of the country; and the needs of the country, I think, in many lines loom up as obvious and self-evident. We don't have to go into them in great detail here this morning.

Obviously, certain phases of our agriculture are in bad shape. We know that we have certain tax revisions and reforms and changes that are coming up, some of them already prescribed by law. We know that expenditures of the Federal Government is a thing on which we have been working. We know that the cleaning out in Government, of course, is important; but I believe it was in my state of the Union speech last January where I cheerfully acknowledged that the cleaning up of Government, the executive branches of Government, is an Executive responsibility.

I am proceeding with my associates as strongly and as earnestly and as thoroughly as I can in that direction, and I am certainly earnestly trying to do it without doing injustice to any individual, because I don't believe that we can afford to destroy inside what we think we are protecting from the outside.

Now, I hope that this whole thing will be a matter of history and of memory by the time the next election comes around. I don't believe we can live in fear of each other forever, and I really hope and believe that this administration is proceeding decently and justly to get this thing straightened out.

I hope that answers your question.

Q. Mrs. May Craig, Maine papers: Mr. President, does your reply to Mr. Smith cover the statement of Mr. Brownell yesterday that he would seek legislation to give immunity to certain witnesses who seek the protection of the fifth amendment? Did he discuss that with you?

THE PRESIDENT. That particular point has not been discussed with me.

Q. Mrs. Craig: That has not?

THE PRESIDENT. But that would be unquestionably his recommendation, and I will then discuss it. As I say, when I have made up my own mind about that, I wouldn't object to discussing it with this body. I don't want to now in the absence of a formed judgment of my own.

Q. Richard L. Wilson, Cowles Publications: Mr. President, when you referred to the meeting of September 18th and 19th——

THE PRESIDENT. December.

Q. Mr. Wilson: I mean December 17th, 18th, and 19th, I believe you said that you were asking all the party leaders. I wondered if you meant by that only the Republican leaders or also the Democratic leaders?

THE PRESIDENT. Well, of course, first we would get the Republican leaders and such Republican chairmen as need to come. But before, and well before the measures have to be acted on, well, I will certainly take adequate and effective measures to make certain, in these things that we regard as bipartisan in character, that the other side will be thoroughly consulted.

Q. Mr. Wilson: There has been some comment in the past of a critical nature that, perhaps, because of the newness of the administration there was a lack of team play in the last session of Congress. I wonder if this is an effort to—this meeting has any relation to that or whether there is any foundation to that?

THE PRESIDENT. Well, not necessarily to the criticism, Mr. Wilson; but I think that those of us who have had any experience in the job of putting people, humans, together, great numbers of humans, in support of any kind of a program or positive activity or project, it takes a lot of conference in composing of views. I don't intend to shirk my share of it, and to take my full responsibility for doing it. Now, that is really what I am trying to do.

Q. Edward T. Folliard, Washington Post: Mr. President, I understood you to say that you hoped that this whole Communist-in-Government issue will be a matter of history by the next election. Does that mean, sir, that you hope these committees of Congress that are investigating Communists in Government will have finished up their work?

THE PRESIDENT. Mr. Folliard, there have been many ways brought here in forms of questions to get me to comment on Congress.

I acknowledge that Congress has their rights, they have their constitutional duties and privileges; and while I can have personal opinion about these things, I see no reason really for publicizing or explaining them except when something that I believe is necessary, you might say, to the welfare of this country, where I have to speak out in a way that was unmistakable.

So I don't want to comment. We must acknowledge that right to investigate, I would say. I do sincerely trust that the need for any investigation, the need for it, will be so eliminated that all will see it.

Q. Nat S. Finney, Buffalo News: Mr. President, some time ago you spoke of being at work on a public statement regarding the country's problems, I believe it was fair to say, about continental defense and atomic energy and some other matters. Can you tell us what the state of that is now?

THE PRESIDENT. I can say it is the most difficult problem to deal with fairly and justly, when you consider the complicated nature of alliances, of our own situation, and it is one that I am still working on. I am still hopeful that before too long I can lay this more clearly than it has yet been placed before the American people and before the world.

But I simply must feel that the timing is correct and the information that I have is not needlessly alarming, so that I cannot be accused of falsely raising hysteria and, at the same time, being as frank as I know how. It is extremely difficult.

Q. J. A. Livingston, Philadelphia Bulletin: Mr. President, are you developing plans to counteract the decline in business which seems to be indicated by the drop in steel and auto output and employment?

THE PRESIDENT. Well, I don't know whether all of your statements are quite correct.   I believe that unemployment in October was the lowest it has been since 1943.

Q. Mr. Livingston: I said the drop in employment, Mr. President.

THE PRESIDENT. What's that?

Q. Mr. Livingston: I said the drop in employment.

THE PRESIDENT. Well, that is right; I think there have been some people who have moved out of what is called the employable class, older people, women, and some children.   I believe that is correct, in total employment.

Every week the subject of my conference with Dr. Arthur Burns, whom I consider one of the ablest men in this whole field, one of the subjects is to keep me informed as to what is going on there with his plans when dealing with the other parts of Government, as to what we can do, when we should do it, and how.

As you know, you get favorable and unfavorable indices about the future always at the same time, and it becomes a delicate matter of judgment.   I will say this to you again: when it becomes clear that the Government has to step in, as far as I am concerned, the full power of Government, of Government credit, and of everything the Government has will move in to see that there is no widespread unemployment and we never again have a repetition of conditions that so many of you here remember when we had unemployment.

Q. Frederick Kuh, Chicago Sun-Times: Mr. President, what are the main topics or ideas that you intend to discuss with the British and French Prime Ministers at Bermuda?

THE PRESIDENT. Most of them, I should think, would be obvious to you.   The United States, France, and Britain have in common a lot of problems.   We have NATO, we have many included problems in NATO; we are together in Korea; our attitude in Asia; we have Indochina.   We have numbers of problems around the world in which all of us have a very great stake, and where it is necessary that we have informal talks to see that we are proceeding toward solutions or in the formulation of policy on common ground; and if conversation can eliminate causes for friction, that is all to the good.

Actually, there is no formal agenda to be proposed by anyone that I know of at this conference. It is to be an informal talk among the individuals present.

Q. Chalmers M. Roberts, Washington Post: Mr. President, some time ago you saw the Prime Minister of Pakistan, and since that time there have been stories indicating that Pakistan would be interested in U.S. military aid, and might possibly grant us bases in that country. Would you comment on that as to whether you discussed it, and what you think?

THE PRESIDENT. Well, everybody knows that there are difficulties in that region, and I should say that America's policy is always in developing friendships with others, to try to get people to be friends with their own neighbors.

I should think we would be most cautious about doing anything that would create unrest and distress or fear or hysteria in the neighboring nation, say, in India. While the matter was not discussed in detail when the Prime Minister came to see me, the fact is our effort would be to produce a friendship with that entire subcontinent and not with just one group.

Q. Sarah McClendon, El Paso Times: Mr. President, I understand Senator Monroney spoke to you the other day about the small proportion of the price which the Government is paying for its processed beef. He said a small proportion was going to the cattlemen, and very small, compared to what went to the packers. Would you say what you think about that?

THE PRESIDENT. As you know, the Secretary of Agriculture did start an investigation some weeks ago to determine whether that price spread was justified.

Now, apparently—it is a bit technical and I hope I have it correctly—apparently the price spread between what the Government is paying for its lunch program and the prices paid actually at the central or big markets is not so out of line. But the unfortunate part about this is that many of these people liquidating small numbers of cattle come in and, at what are known as the small-town markets, will sell to a buyer at roughly sometimes not much over half of what they get at the big market. So there is a spread. He was coming in to suggest certain measures for closing that spread somewhat, and getting more money right down to the distressed farmer who has to get rid of his cattle. That plan has been sent over to Secretary Benson and, I believe, arrangements made for Senator Monroney to talk to Secretary Benson directly.

Q. Roscoe Drummond, New York Herald Tribune: Mr. President, may I return just a moment to the December 17 legislative meeting?

THE PRESIDENT. Yes.

Q. Mr. Drummond: And without assuming that many things may be discussed at this meeting, I just wondered if you could indicate some of the subjects which you think would be especially important to be a part of the legislative program in which you would be most interested.

THE PRESIDENT. There are so many things that I really don't know where to start.

But, after all, you have the security program, and the expenditure program of the whole budget. You have taxes. You have efforts, of course, to balance the budget. Those subjects are all related.

You will have a farm program that must be ready to go in; you must have certain amendments to the labor law and a report on the conclusions of the executive branch on this matter.

You will have the policy on public housing, slum clearance, on extension of social security to where it must go, and as pledged in the platform. There will be then, of course, the matter of foreign aid, particularly the security portion—military aid.

Well, there are numerous others that have to come up, Mr. Drummond, and I certainly don't want the list I have given you to be considered as exclusive. But it will be, I hope, as complete a program right at the beginning as we can possibly make it.

Now, there are one or two subjects where we will have to be still a bit general because commissions appointed, with the approval of Congress, will not yet have completely reported.

So, let us say in foreign trade, while I will unquestionably repeat my complete conviction that there has got to be an increase in foreign trade, a freer flow of trade throughout the world if we are going to have a free world really hang together, still I can't talk in detail of what that Commission says.

So, one or two subjects will have to be dealt with—possibly—generally; but, all in all, I hope it will cover the whole field.

Q. Daniel Schorr, CBS—Radio: You said you hoped the issue of communism in Government would be over by the next election, and you added later that you would not interfere with the legislative branch in that connection.

Can your words be taken, however, as meaning that you would not encourage persons in the executive branch or in the party of which you are the titular leader to keep that issue alive?

THE PRESIDENT. To keep what?

Q. Mr. Schorr: The issue of communism in Government alive; that you would not encourage people, the executive branch——

THE PRESIDENT. No. Look, let me make myself clear. I hope that there is no more active opponent of communism as an ideology in the world than I am.

I believe that our whole future prosperity and happiness in this country depend upon the earnestness of our support of free institutions.

Now, wherever that presses in on us, I expect to be there as well as I know how, opposing it. But I do say that with the measures we now take and the care we take to appointing people to Government, and with the care that we have taken to look over these people—as I gave you a report the other day, 1,456 people had left the service either by resignation or because of some difficulty in that regard—certainly I still believe that vigilance, eternal vigilance, is the price of liberty, and I expect to exercise it.

What I mean is that I hope that the suspicion on the part of the American people that their Government services are, after all, weak in this regard, that that will have disappeared through the accomplishments of the executive branch.

Q. Anthony H. Leviero, New York Times: Mr. President, have you had any recent discussion concerning the International Labor Organization, and if so, have you any comment to make on our relationships to it?

THE PRESIDENT. As a matter of fact, you caught me at an unfortunate time.

I had a long conversation yesterday with Dr. Shotwell, and I have looked into it; but I have laid aside certain subjects there for further study and examination, and I am really not prepared to talk on it intelligently.

Q. Marvin L. Arrowsmith, Associated Press: Mr. President, does it look to you now as though you may have to ask Congress to increase the national debt limit?

THE PRESIDENT. Well, I would say this, without now giving my personal judgment, because I haven't conferred with the Treasury in the last 3 or 4 weeks on this particular matter: I would say it is a decision that probably won't be finally reached until late December. As you know, if the bills coming in are of a certain size, then it is just a must, we must act; but you can always hope.

Q. Joseph A. Fox, Washington Evening Star: Mr. President, I want to get one thing cleared up. These bipartisan congressional conferences of which you spoke awhile ago, were those intended to be after Congress gets back rather than the preliminary sessions?

THE PRESIDENT. I can't give you the exact details because I haven't discussed the exact, what you might call, sequence of events. Certainly I want to conduct bipartisanship, particularly in foreign relations, on the basis where every view of the opposing party is consulted and, as in the past, accommodated just as much as we do our own. Now just how it will be done, Mr. Fox, I can't say.

Q. Mr. Fox: That is foreign affairs; you are not speaking of domestic affairs?

THE PRESIDENT. I am speaking of foreign affairs at the moment or, you might say, that domestic questions are always bound to come into any discussion of foreign affairs, as you know. So I don't mean to say if you mention domestic subjects they have to be thrown out of the room. I mean foreign affairs in all its aspects will be discussed with them.

Q. Fletcher Knebel, Cowles Publications: In light of Mr. Humphrey's speech in Detroit several weeks ago envisioning a possible deficit next year of eight or nine billion dollars, do you still have any substantial hope of balancing the budget?

THE PRESIDENT. For '55?

Q. Mr. Knebel: Yes.

THE PRESIDENT. No, I don't believe it can be done yet in '55. There are certain places, you know, where we believe that taxes we have had are unjust and probably stifle business more than they produce revenue, and that will create some gap.

There have been unusual expenditures, particularly in the farm program.

You see, for this past year, there was $800 million estimated for payments in farm products—don't quote me exactly, but as I remember, it was $1,880 million—so there have been some unusual expenses that caused a little trouble.

No, I don't believe we can do it in '55, as I see it now.

Q. Robert E. Clark, International News Service: President Truman has charged that your administration has now embraced McCarthyism. Do you have any comment on that?

THE PRESIDENT. I am ready to take the verdict of this body on that.

Q. Several voices: We didn't hear the question.

THE PRESIDENT. The question was whether this administration has embraced something called McCarthyism. To start with, it is a term that I don't particularly understand, but I said I am ready to take the judgment of this body whether there is any truth in such a statement.

Q. Frank van der Linden, Nashville Banner: Mr. Brownell has some other duties. He is supposed to present a brief to the Supreme Court in about 2 weeks regarding the Justice Department's position on the question of racial segregation in the public schools.

Do you plan to confer with him before he puts that brief in the Court?

THE PRESIDENT. Indeed I do. We confer regularly, and this subject comes up along with others, constantly.

Q. Francis M. Stephenson, New York Daily News: Mr. President, speaking of Mr. Brownell, the office of Solicitor General, I think, has been vacant since last February, and I was wondering has he ever made any recommendation to you on that, to fill that?

THE PRESIDENT. We have talked over people that we wanted to put there, but for one reason or another they either went to other tasks or something turned up that we couldn't get them.

We have been very, very interested in getting the finest man that we can in the United States for the job.

Merriman Smith, United Press: Thank you, Mr. President.

NOTE: President Eisenhower's twenty-first news conference was held in the Executive Office Building from 10:30 to 10:57 o'clock on Wednesday morning, November 18, 1953. In attendance: 179.

250 ¶ Remarks at a Luncheon Meeting of the General Board of the National Council of Churches. *November* 18, 1953

Mr. Chairman, ladies and gentlemen:

Among the more pleasant duties that devolve upon the Chief Executive is that of greeting here in the Capital bodies of American citizens that meet to devote themselves, and rededicate themselves to the service of America and to humanity.

When I think of this body as a religious body, I do feel, you might say, a bit of unfitness for being here. For though I am deeply religious in my convictions, I am certainly probably more fully aware than anyone else of my shortcomings as a religious being in the sense that we should like people to be.

Now I feel a very definite reason for being here. I happen to be the Chief Executive of a nation of which the Government is merely a translation in the political field of a deeply-felt religious faith. The Magna Charta, our Declaration of Independence, and the French Declaration of the Rights of Man were certainly nothing else than the attempt on the part of men to state that in their government there would be recognized the principle of the equality of man, the dignity of man. That is a completely false premise unless we recognize the Supreme Being, in front of whom we are all equal.

So the fact that our Government rests and is founded on a deeply-felt religious faith gives to my appearance, even before such a body, a certain validity—say, a certain fitness.

Moreover, a great deal of my life has been led in a profession that is supposed to be almost the antithesis of the profession of you men of the cloth. I used to uphold with very great ve-hemence the theory that we were identical in our purposes, in our dedication to free government which means in some form or another a dedication to the dignity of man and, therefore, to the glory of God.

I believe that every soldier—every American soldier, at least—seeking to find within his own soul some reason for being on the battlefield, for enduring the things he has to endure there, has in the long run got to fix this relationship in his own mind if he is to be really a soldier who can carry forward the terrible load that devolves upon him in those circumstances. And so I think, therefore, it is fitting that I should be allowed to come over and to greet this body.

I have one further reason for saying this: I believe that if there is one single word that could define free government, it is cooperation. Free government is based, among other things, on the theory that problems which the individual man cannot solve for himself will be solved by cooperation, not by regimentation.

As I understand it, this body is met to devise ways and means to cooperate in the great religious life of America, so that differences in dogma, or ritual—as a matter of fact, I am not sure just exactly how you describe it—will be minimized and cooperation will center around those things that are at the bottom of the life of this country: that is, the readiness to cooperate, the recognition that man is a person and an entity of dignity in front of his God, regardless of his religion or his race, or any other such things of inconsequential character. You are cooperating in order that this great recognition that man is after all basically a spiritual being and not merely an animal, or physical thing, you are cooperating to bring that understanding home with more force to each of us.

In doing so, I thoroughly believe that not only will it operate better and more effectively to the advancement of religion in the United States, it will advance all of us in the practice of democracy as it should be practiced in this country.

And so again I say, I still believe that unworthy as I am, it is fitting from the official standpoint at least, to say nothing of my personal convictions, that I bid you welcome to the Capital and hope you have a successful meeting.

Now, I might say I am going to address a group for a moment, before I hope to get in an afternoon of golf, that possibly will be more fitting to a soldier—I am going to talk to a bunch of icemen. And before I went to West Point that is what I was.

NOTE: The President spoke at 12:43 p.m. at the Statler Hotel in Washington. His opening words "Mr. Chairman" referred to Bishop William C. Martin, President of the National Council of Churches of Christ in the United States of America.

251 ¶ Remarks Upon Receiving an Honorary Degree From Catholic University.
November 19, 1953

Your Eminences, Your Excellencies, Right Reverend and Reverend Fathers, members and friends of the great family of Catholic University:

First, I should like to make of record the deep sense of distinction I feel in the honor conferred upon me by the trustees of this great university. I personally hold that the greatest honor that can come to an individual under the various aspects of our Western civilization is to be awarded an honorary doctorate by one of our great educational institutions.

I should like also to address a word to your new Rector. Now, my own sojourn as a President of a university was not long enough to entitle me to speak to him in words of advice. Moreover, sir, I should say that fairness and frankness compel me to say that I heard no great clamor or outcry or protest or incidents of any kind when I left the exalted ranks of college presidents and again donned the uniform of my country.

But I was privileged to stay long enough in such a position to confirm my belief—my faith—that in the institutions of higher learning, in the secondary and primary schools of this country, there is, almost, our greatest opportunity to help satisfy man's oldest yearning; to live in peace with his fellows.

I believe that in the university resides a great opportunity and a great responsibility to bring about a peace that is based upon the only durable values.

Those who seek peace in terms of military strength alone, I am certain, are doomed to end up in the agony of the battlefield. There is no peace only in tanks and in guns and in planes and in bombs—even with the most terrifying instruments of destruction that science has produced. I am convinced there is no peace alone in edicts and treaties, no matter how solemnly signed.

There is none in economic arrangements, no matter how favorable they will be. Not in these things alone. There must be knowledge, and there must be understanding to use knowledge. And the understanding cannot be only of ourselves and of our aspirations and of our hopes, and the knowledge that our purposes are pure. We must have understanding of others, and realize among other things that people the world over have, after all, many things in common.

It is my unshakeable conviction that no people, as such, wants war. On the contrary, I believe that the longing for peace among those people that we now must class as hostile to us is as great as it is among us. Else, why would their leaders have constantly to urge upon them an argument that we know to be false, that the free world wants war?

In this understanding, that I believe must undergird and substantiate the validity of any kind of peace treaty among the nations, is an understanding of the essential spiritual character of man. Here in such a university as this, it seems to me there is sort of a happy marriage between the determination to instruct in the spiritual and moral values of life, as well as to develop the intellectual capacity of the students. Only as they grasp these truths and learn to understand, to appreciate and to sympathize with these longings of mankind, are we going to build a true peace.

And so let us by no means neglect the strength that we must have, the military strength, the economic strength. Let us by no means neglect anything that we can do through the normal channels of diplomacy and by agreements among ourselves. But let us remember that we must achieve, first, among those who think somewhat as we do, a unity—a unity based upon an understanding of these basic aspirations and values. And then in that strength of unity, seek tirelessly to convince others that a world of peace will be a world of prosperity and happiness, the kind of world in which men can satisfy their natural longing—their material, their spiritual, and intellectual aspirations.

In all of these things, it seems to me, the university has a special responsibility—a special opportunity. And in that sense, I address myself to the new Rector in terms of envy. Unworthy as I am, I should like to have that task.

Thank you very much.

NOTE: The degree of Doctor of Laws was presented to the President by the Most Reverend Patrick A. O'Boyle, Archbishop of Washington. During his remarks the President referred to the Most Reverend Bryan J. McEntegart, Rector of the University.

252 ¶ Remarks Upon Receiving the America's Democratic Legacy Award at a B'nai B'rith Dinner in Honor of the 40th Anniversary of the Anti-Defamation League. *November 23, 1953*

Mr. Chairman, Mr. Schultz, ladies and gentlemen:

For such an award, from such a group, I shall ever be grateful. No matter how unworthy any individual may be, no matter how much he may appreciate his own shortcomings in attaining the ideals in which he himself believes, it is still a moment of the most intense satisfaction when some organization standing as it does— as this one does—for the great human rights, chooses to present its annual emblem to that individual. So I thank you.

Ladies and gentlemen, for many years I have been served by able staffs, in war and in peace. I have a staff now of which I am intensely proud. It is composed of individuals who are capable, efficient, and they are dedicated to my welfare and to my success. They are always anxious that I do well, no matter where I appear. And tonight was no exception. I have been briefed and briefed and briefed. I have heard more lectures on civil liberties, the people who have stood for them, the dangers to them; and what I should say than you can imagine.

Now, from the beginning I was aware of one thing—possibly

two, I should say. First: any man who has been served by staffs, no matter how dedicated, must learn when to say no. And secondly: I knew that I was appearing before a body of experts, and I was not going to talk about something of which they knew a lot more than I do.

And so, with your indulgence, I want to tell you about an idea that came to me as I was sitting here this evening. When I saw an array of artists appearing on the stage, there suddenly came back to me an old Fourth of July statement—all the speeches that men used to make on the Fourth of July. Now I am not going to take up your time with the two hours that they used to spend in getting to the only punch line that they had: "I am proud to be an American!"

As you looked at that array of artists, weren't you proud that a man's ability, or a lady's ability, entitled them to appear before such a body as this?

Now, why are we proud? Are we proud because we have the richest acres in the world? I have heard that the Nile Valley is one of the richest places in the world; now it has a great nation, but do you want to give up your citizenship for that of a nation that has merely the richest ground, the richest minerals underneath its soil? I have heard that the European annual production on its acres is about double that of ours, by reason of their devoted work—hand work on their farms. But we don't want to be citizens of Europe. We don't want to go any place, even if their buildings are older than ours, or their culture is older, or they are more sophisticated. We love America.

Why are we proud? We are proud, first of all, because from the beginning of this Nation, a man can walk upright, no matter who he is, or who she is. He can walk upright and meet his friend—or his enemy; and he does not fear that because that enemy may be in a position of great power that he can be suddenly thrown in jail to rot there without charges and with no recourse to justice. We have the habeas corpus act, and we respect it.

I was raised in a little town of which most of you have never heard. But in the West it is a famous place. It is called Abilene, Kansas. We had as our marshal for a long time a man named Wild Bill Hickok. If you don't know anything about him, read your Westerns more. Now that town had a code, and I was raised as a boy to prize that code.

It was: meet anyone face to face with whom you disagree. You could not sneak up on him from behind, or do any damage to him, without suffering the penalty of an outraged citizenry. If you met him face to face and took the same risks he did, you could get away with almost anything, as long as the bullet was in the front.

And today, although none of you has the great fortune, I think, of being from Abilene, Kansas, you live after all by that same code in your ideals and in the respect you give to certain qualities. In this country, if someone dislikes you, or accuses you, he must come up in front. He cannot hide behind the shadow. He cannot assassinate you or your character from behind, without suffering the penalties an outraged citizenry will impose.

Now, you know, I must go back for a moment to what I said awhile ago. I picked up my own subject as I came here. The only responsibility I have is to watch some individual in front of me, who has cards after I have used up all my time. I just notice he says go ahead, it's all right.

I would not want to sit down this evening without urging one thing: if we are going to continue to be proud that we are Americans, there must be no weakening of the code by which we have lived; by the right to meet your accuser face to face, if you have one; by your right to go to the church or the synagogue or even the mosque of your own choosing; by your right to speak your mind and be protected in it.

Ladies and gentlemen, the things that make us proud to be Americans are of the soul and of the spirit. They are not the jewels we wear, or the furs we buy, the houses we live in, the standard of living, even, that we have. All these things are wonderful to the esthetic and to the physical senses.

But let us never forget that the deep things that are American are the soul and the spirit. The Statue of Liberty is not tired, and not because it is made of bronze. It is because no matter what happens, here the individual is dignified because he is created in the image of his God. Let us not forget it.

I am not going to try to be spectacular and ask you all to rise in imitation of the Allegiance to the Flag, and repeat the old Fourth of July statements, as I once did when I was 6 years old in the McKinley campaign. A good Republican won that year. We all said, after the speaker, "I am proud to be an American."

But if I could leave with you one thought, you not only will repeat it every day of your life, but you will say, "I will do my part to make it always true for my children and my grandchildren."

Thank you.

NOTE: The President spoke at 7:54 p.m. at the Mayflower Hotel in Washington. In his opening words he referred to Philip M. Klutznick, National President of B'nai B'rith, and Henry Edward Schultz, National Chairman of the Anti-Defamation League.

253 ¶ Remarks of the President on Thanksgiving Day in Augusta, Georgia. *November* 26, 1953

AMERICA, of course, has countless things for which to be thankful on this November 26th. But I think the most important is this: for the first Thanksgiving in the last four, we sit down to our traditional Thanksgiving feast without the fear of the casualty list hanging over us. We don't, longer, have to worry about the killing in Korea.

Now, my wife and I are just exactly like many thousands of other families in America tonight. We have home our son. But what is far more important than that is that our grandchildren have home their daddy; our Barbie has her husband home.

We are very, very thankful, and I am certain that I speak for thousands and thousands of other families in America, when I say: may we never again have to have our loved ones go off to war.

254 ¶ The President's News Conference of *December* 2, 1953.

THE PRESIDENT. Two or three subjects this morning, ladies and gentlemen, I will volunteer.

First, about the United States delegation going to Bermuda, the list has been mimeographed, and it is outside.[1] You may pick it up as you go out.

My plane, with most of the party aboard, at least, will leave at 8 o'clock on Friday morning.

The occasion promises to be a very busy one from all I can see, but there is really no formal agenda as usually characterizes such meetings. In other words, while I can't say that any subjects will not be discussed, I have no list of subjects that will be discussed.

Some of you may have been following the reports that have come from the countries that Vice President Nixon has visited. The reports coming to me both through the news channels and through official reports are most encouraging.

He will be back on December 14 and, of course, all of us are looking forward to getting his personal report. His visit, I am

[1] Members of the U.S. group as announced by the White House follow: the President; the Secretary of State; Thomas E. Stephens, Secretary to the President; James C. Hagerty, Press Secretary to the President; C. D. Jackson, Special Assistant to the President; Douglas MacArthur II, Counselor of the Department of State; Livingston T. Merchant, Assistant Secretary of State for European Affairs; Robert R. Bowie, Director, Policy Planning Staff, Department of State; Frank Nash, Assistant Secretary of Defense; Comdr. Edward L. Beach, Naval Aide to the President; and Maj. Gen. Howard McC. Snyder, Physician to the President.

certain, has done much to bring the feeling between our own Government and the Governments of these Asian countries which he has visited into a closer concert, and for both of us to realize how many of our interests are parallel and, therefore, create an atmosphere for cooperation.

Now, there—of course, some of you may have noticed in the papers, there have been a number of subjects that have been attracting a lot of interest, and getting a lot of headlines.

Now, I have prepared a written statement, and the reason I have written it is for two reasons really: one, is because it is going to be the only words I have to say on these different subjects; but, secondly, so that you may have personal quotes, if you want to use them. You will get this paper outside, and you can use it for any purpose that you see fit.

[*Reading*] I am in full accord with the statements made yesterday by Secretary Dulles in his press conference.[2] I would like to add this comment to what he said: the easiest thing to do with great power is to abuse it—to use it to excess. This most powerful of the free nations must not permit itself to grow weary of the processes of negotiation and adjustment that are fundamental to freedom. If it should turn impatiently to coercion of other free nations, our brand of coercion, so far as our friends are concerned, would be a mark of the imperialist rather than of the leader.

What America is doing abroad in the way of military and economic assistance is as much a part of our own security program as our military efforts at home. We hope to be able to maintain these overseas elements of our security program as long as our enlightened self-interest requires, even though we may, and probably we always will, have various differences of opinion with the nations receiving our aid.

We do this because unity among free nations is our only hope for survival in the face of the worldwide Soviet conspiracy backed

---

[2] Secretary Dulles' statement is published in the Department of State Bulletin (vol. 29, p. 811).

by the weight of Soviet military power. This struggle dominates all other considerations of our times. The issue—freedom versus communism—is a life and death matter. To my mind it is the struggle of the ages.

This fact arouses justifiable concern about communism in our own Government. I repeat my previously expressed conviction that fear of Communists actively undermining our Government will not be an issue in the 1954 elections. Long before then this administration will have made such progress in rooting them out under the security program developed by Attorney General Brownell that this can no longer be considered a serious menace. As you already know, about 1500 persons who were security risks have already been removed. Fair, thorough, and decent investigations, followed by unhesitating corrective action, are the most effective—and the only efficient—way to get this necessary job done.

By next fall I hope that the public, no longer fearful that Communists are destructively at work within the Government, will wish to commend the efficiency of this administration in eliminating this menace to the Nation's security. The people must have the facts on this important subject in order to reach sound conclusions. As provided for in the liberalized regulations of this administration, established facts, so far as the national security permits, will continue to be made available.

The best way to keep subversives out of the Government is not to employ them in the first place. The administration will continue to hunt for any that are present and, of course, any subversives located by a congressional committee will be removed promptly just as will any others.

In all that we do to combat subversion, it is imperative that we protect the basic rights of loyal American citizens. I am determined to protect those rights to the limit of the powers of the office with which I have been entrusted by the American people.

In my judgment, the efficiency and vision with which the Government is administered by this Republican administration, and whether or not the Congress enacts a progressive, dynamic program enhancing the welfare of all the people of our country, will determine the future political complexion of the Congress and the future of the administration. I am convinced that those who fight for the program that I shall soon submit to the Congress will deserve and will receive the respect and support of the American people.

In any event, unless the Republican Party can develop and enact such a program for the American people, it does not deserve to remain in power. But, I know that these sentiments are shared by the vast majority of the Republicans in this country, particularly by my close associates both in the Senate and in the House of Representatives. Because of this unity of feeling such a program will be enacted. [*Ends reading*]

Now, that is what I am going to say about these late headlines, and on that and any closely related subjects, there is not another word to say. With that one proviso, I will mount the usual weekly cross and let you drive the nails.

Q. Marvin L. Arrowsmith, Associated Press: Mr. President, on the basis of the latest Russian note, what do you feel are the prospects for a meeting of the Western powers with representatives of the Soviet Union?

THE PRESIDENT. Well, I think, Mr. Arrowsmith, there has to be a lot of study given to this matter.

I wouldn't want to make a real guess at this moment because while I have conferred with the Secretary of State about it several times, we have decided that this is, of course, one subject that must be studied very thoroughly before we express an official opinion about it.

Q. Anthony H. Leviero, New York Times: Mr. President, I have a question which you may consider related to that statement; if so, I would respectfully withdraw it, and that is, have you considered the creation of a national commission to study this whole problem of Communists and spies in Government?

THE PRESIDENT. Just before I came over here, one of the staff brought in to me a notice—it is something that had escaped my attention so far—that this had been suggested. I simply haven't studied it. There have been, of course, a number of outsiders called in to see whether this has been a real menace—to take a look. I would say this: I will approach such a proposition with an open mind, take a look at it. I just haven't formed a real conclusion as yet.

Q. David P. Sentner, Hearst Newspapers: Mr. President, would you care to state whether the present position of the United States on the entry of Communist China into the U.N. will be a subject for negotiation at Bermuda, I mean negotiation, not discussion?

THE PRESIDENT. I should say—and I think this view is shared by all my associates—that under present circumstances that question is not open to negotiation with anybody, under present circumstances.

Q. Walter T. Ridder, St. Paul Pioneer Press and Dispatch: Mr. President, could you tell us what your own personal and specific hopes will be as to what comes out of the Bermuda conference?

THE PRESIDENT. You will pardon me if I reminisce just a little bit. In war, when you go and launch a battle, you know there are certain things you can do; you know there are a few other things that will come along if you have reasonably good luck, and then you have some very big hopes; so it applies here in a way. I couldn't possibly describe all the hopes that might eventually grow out of such a meeting. There are certain things that we know will happen.

In conversations with my very old and very good friend, Sir Winston, and with Mr. Laniel, whom I know and admire, but I have not known him like I know Sir Winston, there should come about a better understanding among us of each other's problems—of the situation, for example, of France in Indochina, of Britain in Iran and Egypt, and all those places, and ourselves in certain areas of the globe.

We can get a better understanding of what each is trying to do, and see whether we can't coordinate all of our actions so as to be fair to everybody in this world that we want and are trying to gain as our friends, and still not get into clashes, one with the other.

All of this business of international negotiation—and I have been aware of this for a long time—is very intricate, very delicate; and it seems even more easy for international associates to develop quick and sometimes violent misunderstandings of the other fellow's motives than it is right here in Washington among some of the different groups. [*Laughter*]

Now, it is an effort to keep these from occurring or to cure such as have occurred, that such a meeting basically takes place. But in doing so you take up a whole series of specific problems. Frankly, you practically move around the world discussing this, discussing that, what do we do, what is the best thing to do, and try to reach a composite and cooperative decision on the thing.

Now, that is, I think, the best that I can say on the whole subject as of this moment.

I have, of course, a number of things that I know I am going to bring up, just as little details of these points that I am now speaking. Mr. Dulles may have others. I don't know whether he mentioned them yesterday or not; but in any event, as I said before, there is no formal agenda for the meeting.

Q. Chalmers M. Roberts, Washington Post: Mr. President, Secretary Dulles did say yesterday that in his view the real basic issue between the West and the Soviet Union was the question of whether the Russians would ever admit what he called "a fresh breath of freedom behind the Iron Curtain." Would you agree with that view?

THE PRESIDENT. Well, I should say there are many, many ways of expressing the hope that the aspirations and actions of these two great categories of nations in the world can be brought into a common realization that only through peaceful solutions to our problems is there any happiness or any prosperity for anybody.

There are many ways of stating it, but I certainly believe that we are going to be adamant on one thing: the right of ourselves to have the government of our own choosing; and, certainly, in principle the right of every other nation to have a government of its own choosing—certainly anybody that is classed as our friend.

Now, if you carry that principle on into action, I think then nobody that believes as we do could possibly have any kick. Foster must have meant something like that when he said "a breath of freedom," which must have meant giving to all satellite countries the right to determine their own form of government. I believe that that defines it about as well as I would know how.

Q. Joseph C. Harsch, Christian Science Monitor: Mr. President, if this also borders on the forbidden zone, I will also respectfully withdraw it.

Sir, last week you referred in a speech you made to the right of Americans to face their accuser. Since you made that statement some question has been raised as to the extent to which that right is actually recognized or can be in the security operations of the Government.

My question is, have you taken any steps to determine the proper relationship between the right and the security of investigations of the Federal Government?

THE PRESIDENT. Do you mean security investigation within the Federal Government?

Q. Mr. Harsch: Within the Federal Government, sir, yes.

THE PRESIDENT. The one point I must make clear: employment in the Federal Government is not a right of citizenship, it is a privilege; and if there is real justifiable belief and conviction that a person is a risk, you certainly cannot keep them in a delicate position, and in certain instances probably couldn't keep them at all.

In other words, when you are looking into the fitness of an individual to work for the Federal Government, it is not the same as assassinating a man's character or charging him openly with being a spy.

So, for one thing that I have insisted upon, that there be no effort in this security program to assassinate anybody's character, and to damn him forever as a spy or anything of that kind.

But I do believe that there is some difference between determining whether or not a man should work for the Federal Government and charging any one of us here with a heinous crime of any kind.

Q. Daniel Schorr, CBS—Radio: Mr. President, you made a rather cautious statement about the latest Russian note, as did Secretary Dulles yesterday, saying that it needed further study.

In view of that, do you know what was the basis for Foreign Secretary Eden's statement in Commons the day before yesterday, that he had every reason to believe the United States would endorse the idea of a meeting with the Russian Foreign Minister?

THE PRESIDENT. Well, we have time and again issued invitations. Now, the thing that needs study is, are the conditions that we consider indispensable reasonably met; that is what requires very serious study. Moreover, following the policy in which I most sincerely believe, of treating our allies as partners, there comes the problem of discussing with governmental leaders in the world just what are their attitudes and beliefs and convictions.

No one individual or no one country possesses all the wisdom in the world, so there is a lot of investigation to be done before serious moves of this kind are undertaken; that is all I meant.

Q. Mr. Schorr: Does that mean, sir, that this Government is willing to have such a meeting on suitable conditions?

THE PRESIDENT. We always have said that under conditions in which we could be assured of the good faith of the meeting, we were always, and as a matter of fact, we have joined in issuing invitations.

Q. Mr. Schorr: Since we have asked for a meeting on Germany and Austria ourselves, if assured that the meeting will discuss Germany and Austria, at least first, would that be considered a suitable condition?

THE PRESIDENT. Well, I am not going—look, you are putting

down conditions that I don't know are going to exist, and I think I will just stop speculating on this point at this moment.

Q. Laurence H. Burd, Chicago Tribune: Mr. President, do you expect to have specific recommendations for tax revision ready for Congress in January or soon after?

THE PRESIDENT. Yes, I think so; yes. As you know, in Washington time seems to have a habit of collapsing on you; right at the moment that you get into the very busy work of preparing budgets and programs, people have to leave and go off to NATO meetings, and I am suddenly going to Bermuda, and everything happens. I don't say there might not be a few days' delay here or there, but in general, yes.

Q. Mr. Burd: Well, in view of your previous statement that you don't expect to balance—don't think you can balance the budget——

THE PRESIDENT. Yes.

Q. Mr. Burd: ——in the next—will these recommendations be directed at more total revenue than we are now getting or——

THE PRESIDENT. No, I doubt if we can get more total revenue or should try to get more total revenue.

Q. Mr. Burd: Then it is a more long-term objective to bring expenditures down?

THE PRESIDENT. Indeed, yes.

Q. Mr. Burd: To our present or somewhat lower tax level?

THE PRESIDENT. Yes, through constant improvement in management methods and in those improvements we even take credit in advance. We are certain that these people can produce savings through management improvement, elimination of all kinds of duplication, so that the budget will reflect that belief and conviction.

On top of that, constantly under study is every phase of the defensive program, which, all in all, takes 70 percent of the budget. There, it becomes a very serious question because you certainly don't want, and I think no one wants, to damage the security prospects of this country. That is clear. So the question becomes, how do you cut expenses in that great——

Q. Mr. Burd: Is it still your view that the business tax, the corporate tax, should be held at its present level rather than drop back next spring?

THE PRESIDENT. Well now, I am not going to talk about the details of this, because I have promised the Secretary of the Treasury, among other things, that I would not talk about its details. I don't know what this means and what corporations might do.

I think, if you will excuse me, I will wait until that program comes up.

Q. Anthony H. Leviero, New York Times: Mr. President, have you any views now on the proposed cut of 10 percent in the Army? Secretary Wilson mentioned that.

THE PRESIDENT. Oh, I don't know that I could specify a percentage. I do know that the Korean war is now in, let's say, at least in a quiescent state; it's gone to a cold war status. We don't have casualty lists.

Therefore, the supplies that are going out are no longer great quantities of ammunition and all that sort of thing. Supporting units don't need to be as strong, do they? You don't have to have all the way the pipeline constantly crowded with people to take care of casualties. There are savings all the way along the line.

Moreover, let us remember that without the fault of anybody, the Korean partial mobilization was made under conditions of hurry, of "get the thing done," and it would be only miraculous if there were no mistakes made on the side of, let's say, overmobilization. So the problem is to find the people in this whole Military Establishment that are not necessary and that, I think, is what Secretary Wilson is referring to. Certainly units that are closest to the hostile position are not going to be reduced in strength, by no manner of means, until the time comes that political considerations make such movement possible.

Q. Mrs. May Craig, Maine papers: Mr. President, during the last campaign much was said about corruption in the Department of Justice under the Democrats. Are you aware of the Democratic charges now being made against your Department of Justice?

THE PRESIDENT. Well, I have seen a lot of headlines about one individual, at least, but that is all. Oh, yes, you mean in these outlying cities?

I had a conference with the Attorney General, and he tells me he is going to release, I suppose today, a complete factual statement on all of these things. I don't mind telling you, ladies and gentlemen, as far as I am concerned, I will help go after corruption wherever it can be found in Government.

As far as my confidence in the Attorney General is concerned, it is exactly what it is in all other members of my Cabinet. I would not know how to change any one of them for the better; and that does not mean that any of us, particularly including me, will not and has not made mistakes.

I am not going to say that there is any human on this earth that is perfect. I have got a little too much sense for that; but I do say that the motives, the actions of these people, are inspired by one thing, the good of this country, and we will publish every fact the national security will allow in order that people can judge of this conviction for themselves.

Edwin Dayton Moore, United Press: Thank you, Mr. President.

NOTE: President Eisenhower's twenty-second news conference was held in the Executive Office Building from 10:33 to 10:58 o'clock on Wednesday morning, December 2, 1953. In attendance: 189.

255 ¶ Joint Statement by the President, the
Prime Minister of the United Kingdom, and the
President of the Council of Ministers of France
Following the Bermuda Conference.
December 7, 1953

THE PRESIDENT of the United States, the Prime Minister of
the United Kingdom and the President of the Council of Ministers of the French Republic, accompanied by the Foreign Ministers of the three countries, met in Bermuda from the 4th to 7th of
December, 1953. At their meeting they discussed their policies
regarding many parts of the world where their countries have
obligations. On the conclusion of the Conference they issued the
following statement:

I.

Our meetings symbolized and confirmed the unity of purpose
of our three countries. We found ourselves in accord on our
analysis of the problems confronting us and have agreed on various measures essential for their solution.

Confident that our united strength is the best guarantee of
peace and security we are resolved to maintain our joint efforts
to perfect it. If the danger of aggression now appears less imminent, we attribute this to the mounting strength of the free
world and the firmness of its policies.

We shall remain resolute in maintaining our solidarity and
vigilant against efforts to divide us.

With their material and moral resources we are confident that
the free peoples can provide both for their security and for their
well being. We dedicate ourselves to work together towards
these ends.

II.

The North Atlantic Treaty is and will remain the foundation
of our common policy. We discussed means of developing the de-

fensive capacity of our Alliance. Lord Ismay, the Secretary-General of the North Atlantic Treaty Organisation, was present at the conversations on this subject.

In the continuing development of a united Europe, including Germany, we seek the best means of achieving greater prosperity, security and stability for its free peoples. We reaffirmed that the European Defence Community is needed to assure the defensive capacity of the Atlantic Community of which it will be an integral part. Within this framework it will ensure intimate and durable cooperation between the United Kingdom and United States forces and the forces of the European Defence Community on the Continent of Europe. The French Minister of Foreign Affairs explained the problems facing his Government in regard to the European Defence Community.

We cannot accept as justified or permanent the present division of Europe. Our hope is that in due course peaceful means will be found to enable the countries of Eastern Europe again to play their part as free nations in a free Europe.

III.

Our three Governments will lose no opportunity for easing the tensions that beset the world and for reassuring all nations that they have no cause to fear that the strength of the West will be invoked in any cause of wrongful violence. On the contrary it is the fundamental principle of the United Nations Organisation, which we serve, that the guarantees against aggression shall be universal in their application.

We are confident that if we remain strong, united and steadfast it will become possible gradually to solve the stubborn problems which have too long been unsettled.

In this spirit we have examined the latest note from the Soviet Government. We approved the text of our replies, which should lead to an early meeting of the four Foreign Ministers. Our hope is that this meeting will make progress towards the reunification of Germany in freedom and the conclusion of an Austrian State

Treaty and thus towards the solution of other major international problems.

IV.

We reviewed the situation in the Far East. The immediate object to our policy continues to be the convening of the political conference provided for in the Korean Armistice agreement. This would provide the means for reaching a peaceful settlement of the Korean question and for making progress in restoring more normal conditions in the Far East and South East Asia.

In Indo-China we salute the valiant forces of France and of the three Associated States of Indo-China fighting within the French Union to protect the independence of Cambodia, Laos and Viet Nam. We recognise the vital importance of their contribution to the defence of the free world. We will continue to work together to restore peace and stability in this area.

V.

Our meetings have reinforced our solidarity, strengthened our resolve, and fortified our hopes. Confident in our common purposes and united in our views we shall persevere in our policies, whose sole aim is to foster and assure peace.

256 ¶ Address Before the General Assembly of the United Nations on Peaceful Uses of Atomic Energy, New York City. *December* 8, 1953

Madame President, Members of the General Assembly:

When Secretary General Hammarskjold's invitation to address this General Assembly reached me in Bermuda, I was just beginning a series of conferences with the Prime Ministers and Foreign Ministers of Great Britain and of France. Our subject was some of the problems that beset our world.

During the remainder of the Bermuda Conference, I had constantly in mind that ahead of me lay a great honor.   That honor is mine today as I stand here, privileged to address the General Assembly of the United Nations.

At the same time that I appreciate the distinction of addressing you, I have a sense of exhilaration as I look upon this Assembly.

Never before in history has so much hope for so many people been gathered together in a single organization.   Your deliberations and decisions during these somber years have already realized part of those hopes.

But the great tests and the great accomplishments still lie ahead.   And in the confident expectation of those accomplishments, I would use the office which, for the time being, I hold, to assure you that the Government of the United States will remain steadfast in its support of this body.   This we shall do in the conviction that you will provide a great share of the wisdom, the courage, and the faith which can bring to this world lasting peace for all nations, and happiness and well-being for all men.

Clearly, it would not be fitting for me to take this occasion to present to you a unilateral American report on Bermuda.   Nevertheless, I assure you that in our deliberations on that lovely island we sought to invoke those same great concepts of universal peace and human dignity which are so clearly etched in your Charter.

Neither would it be a measure of this great opportunity merely to recite, however hopefully, pious platitudes.

I therefore decided that this occasion warranted my saying to you some of the things that have been on the minds and hearts of my legislative and executive associates and on mine for a great many months—thoughts I had originally planned to say primarily to the American people.

I know that the American people share my deep belief that if a danger exists in the world, it is a danger shared by all—and equally, that if hope exists in the mind of one nation, that hope should be shared by all.

Finally, if there is to be advanced any proposal designed to ease even by the smallest measure the tensions of today's world, what more appropriate audience could there be than the members of the General Assembly of the United Nations?

I feel impelled to speak today in a language that in a sense is new—one which I, who have spent so much of my life in the military profession, would have preferred never to use.

That new language is the language of atomic warfare.

The atomic age has moved forward at such a pace that every citizen of the world should have some comprehension, at least in comparative terms, of the extent of this development of the utmost significance to every one of us. Clearly, if the peoples of the world are to conduct an intelligent search for peace, they must be armed with the significant facts of today's existence.

My recital of atomic danger and power is necessarily stated in United States terms, for these are the only incontrovertible facts that I know. I need hardly point out to this Assembly, however, that this subject is global, not merely national in character.

On July 16, 1945, the United States set off the world's first atomic explosion. Since that date in 1945, the United States of America has conducted 42 test explosions.

Atomic bombs today are more than 25 times as powerful as the weapons with which the atomic age dawned, while hydrogen weapons are in the ranges of millions of tons of TNT equivalent.

Today, the United States' stockpile of atomic weapons, which, of course, increases daily, exceeds by many times the explosive equivalent of the total of all bombs and all shells that came from every plane and every gun in every theatre of war in all of the years of World War II.

A single air group, whether afloat or land-based, can now deliver to any reachable target a destructive cargo exceeding in power all the bombs that fell on Britain in all of World War II.

In size and variety, the development of atomic weapons has been no less remarkable. The development has been such that atomic weapons have virtually achieved conventional status within our armed services. In the United States, the Army, the Navy, the Air Force, and the Marine Corps are all capable of putting this weapon to military use.

But the dread secret, and the fearful engines of atomic might, are not ours alone.

In the first place, the secret is possessed by our friends and allies, Great Britain and Canada, whose scientific genius made a tremendous contribution to our original discoveries, and the designs of atomic bombs.

The secret is also known by the Soviet Union.

The Soviet Union has informed us that, over recent years, it has devoted extensive resources to atomic weapons. During this period, the Soviet Union has exploded a series of atomic devices, including at least one involving thermo-nuclear reactions.

If at one time the United States possessed what might have been called a monopoly of atomic power, that monopoly ceased to exist several years ago. Therefore, although our earlier start has permitted us to accumulate what is today a great quantitative advantage, the atomic realities of today comprehend two facts of even greater significance.

First, the knowledge now possessed by several nations will eventually be shared by others—possibly all others.

Second, even a vast superiority in numbers of weapons, and a consequent capability of devastating retaliation, is no preventive, of itself, against the fearful material damage and toll of human lives that would be inflicted by surprise aggression.

The free world, at least dimly aware of these facts, has naturally embarked on a large program of warning and defense systems. That program will be accelerated and expanded.

But let no one think that the expenditure of vast sums for weapons and systems of defense can guarantee absolute safety for the cities and citizens of any nation. The awful arithmetic of the atomic bomb does not permit of any such easy solution. Even against the most powerful defense, an aggressor in possession of the effective minimum number of atomic bombs for a surprise attack could probably place a sufficient number of his bombs on the chosen targets to cause hideous damage.

Should such an atomic attack be launched against the United

States, our reactions would be swift and resolute. But for me to say that the defense capabilities of the United States are such that they could inflict terrible losses upon an aggressor—for me to say that the retaliation capabilities of the United States are so great that such an aggressor's land would be laid waste—all this, while fact, is not the true expression of the purpose and the hope of the United States.

To pause there would be to confirm the hopeless finality of a belief that two atomic colossi are doomed malevolently to eye each other indefinitely across a trembling world. To stop there would be to accept helplessly the probability of civilization destroyed—the annihilation of the irreplaceable heritage of mankind handed down to us generation from generation—and the condemnation of mankind to begin all over again the age-old struggle upward from savagery toward decency, and right, and justice.

Surely no sane member of the human race could discover victory in such desolation. Could anyone wish his name to be coupled by history with such human degradation and destruction.

Occasional pages of history do record the faces of the "Great Destroyers" but the whole book of history reveals mankind's never-ending quest for peace, and mankind's God-given capacity to build.

It is with the book of history, and not with isolated pages, that the United States will ever wish to be identified. My country wants to be constructive, not destructive. It wants agreements, not wars, among nations. It wants itself to live in freedom, and in the confidence that the people of every other nation enjoy equally the right of choosing their own way of life.

So my country's purpose is to help us move out of the dark chamber of horrors into the light, to find a way by which the minds of men, the hopes of men, the souls of men everywhere, can move forward toward peace and happiness and well being.

In this quest, I know that we must not lack patience.

817

I know that in a world divided, such as ours today, salvation cannot be attained by one dramatic act.

I know that many steps will have to be taken over many months before the world can look at itself one day and truly realize that a new climate of mutually peaceful confidence is abroad in the world.

But I know, above all else, that we must start to take these steps—*now*.

The United States and its allies, Great Britain and France, have over the past months tried to take some of these steps. Let no one say that we shun the conference table.

On the record has long stood the request of the United States, Great Britain, and France to negotiate with the Soviet Union the problems of a divided Germany.

On that record has long stood the request of the same three nations to negotiate an Austrian Peace Treaty.

On the same record still stands the request of the United Nations to negotiate the problems of Korea.

Most recently, we have received from the Soviet Union what is in effect an expression of willingness to hold a Four Power Meeting. Along with our allies, Great Britain and France, we were pleased to see that this note did not contain the unacceptable preconditions previously put forward.

As you already know from our joint Bermuda communique, the United States, Great Britain, and France have agreed promptly to meet with the Soviet Union.

The Government of the United States approaches this conference with hopeful sincerity. We will bend every effort of our minds to the single purpose of emerging from that conference with tangible results toward peace—the only true way of lessening international tension.

We never have, we never will, propose or suggest that the Soviet Union surrender what is rightfully theirs.

We will never say that the peoples of Russia are an enemy with whom we have no desire ever to deal or mingle in friendly and fruitful relationship.

On the contrary, we hope that this coming Conference may initiate a relationship with the Soviet Union which will eventually bring about a free intermingling of the peoples of the East and of the West—the one sure, human way of developing the understanding required for confident and peaceful relations.

Instead of the discontent which is now settling upon Eastern Germany, occupied Austria, and the countries of Eastern Europe, we seek a harmonious family of free European nations, with none a threat to the other, and least of all a threat to the peoples of Russia.

Beyond the turmoil and strife and misery of Asia, we seek peaceful opportunity for these peoples to develop their natural resources and to elevate their lives.

These are not idle words or shallow visions. Behind them lies a story of nations lately come to independence, not as a result of war, but through free grant or peaceful negotiation. There is a record, already written, of assistance gladly given by nations of the West to needy peoples, and to those suffering the temporary effects of famine, drought, and natural disaster.

These are deeds of peace. They speak more loudly than promises or protestations of peaceful intent.

But I do not wish to rest either upon the reiteration of past proposals or the restatement of past deeds. The gravity of the time is such that every new avenue of peace, no matter how dimly discernible, should be explored.

There is at least one new avenue of peace which has not yet been well explored—an avenue now laid out by the General Assembly of the United Nations.

In its resolution of November 18th, 1953, this General Assembly suggested—and I quote—"that the Disarmament Commission study the desirability of establishing a sub-committee consisting of representatives of the Powers principally involved, which should seek in private an acceptable solution . . . and report on such a solution to the General Assembly and to the Security Council not later than 1 September 1954."

The United States, heeding the suggestion of the General Assembly of the United Nations, is instantly prepared to meet privately with such other countries as may be "principally involved," to seek "an acceptable solution" to the atomic armaments race which overshadows not only the peace, but the very life, of the world.

We shall carry into these private or diplomatic talks a new conception.

The United States would seek more than the mere reduction or elimination of atomic materials for military purposes.

It is not enough to take this weapon out of the hands of the soldiers. It must be put into the hands of those who will know how to strip its military casing and adapt it to the arts of peace.

The United States knows that if the fearful trend of atomic military buildup can be reversed, this greatest of destructive forces can be developed into a great boon, for the benefit of all mankind.

The United States knows that peaceful power from atomic energy is no dream of the future. That capability, already proved, is here—now—today. Who can doubt, if the entire body of the world's scientists and engineers had adequate amounts of fissionable material with which to test and develop their ideas, that this capability would rapidly be transformed into universal, efficient, and economic usage.

To hasten the day when fear of the atom will begin to disappear from the minds of people, and the governments of the East and West, there are certain steps that can be taken now.

I therefore make the following proposals:

The Governments principally involved, to the extent permitted by elementary prudence, to begin now and continue to make joint contributions from their stockpiles of normal uranium and fissionable materials to an International Atomic Energy Agency. We would expect that such an agency would be set up under the aegis of the United Nations.

The ratios of contributions, the procedures and other details would properly be within the scope of the "private conversations" I have referred to earlier.

The United States is prepared to undertake these explorations in good faith. Any partner of the United States acting in the same good faith will find the United States a not unreasonable or ungenerous associate.

Undoubtedly initial and early contributions to this plan would be small in quantity. However, the proposal has the great virtue that it can be undertaken without the irritations and mutual suspicions incident to any attempt to set up a completely acceptable system of world-wide inspection and control.

The Atomic Energy Agency could be made responsible for the impounding, storage, and protection of the contributed fissionable and other materials. The ingenuity of our scientists will provide special safe conditions under which such a bank of fissionable material can be made essentially immune to surprise seizure.

The more important responsibility of this Atomic Energy Agency would be to devise methods whereby this fissionable material would be allocated to serve the peaceful pursuits of mankind. Experts would be mobilized to apply atomic energy to the needs of agriculture, medicine, and other peaceful activities. A special purpose would be to provide abundant electrical energy in the power-starved areas of the world. Thus the contributing powers would be dedicating some of their strength to serve the needs rather than the fears of mankind.

The United States would be more than willing—it would be proud to take up with others "principally involved" the development of plans whereby such peaceful use of atomic energy would be expedited.

Of those "principally involved" the Soviet Union must, of course, be one.

I would be prepared to submit to the Congress of the United States, and with every expectation of approval, any such plan that would:

First—encourage world-wide investigation into the most effective peacetime uses of fissionable material, and with the certainty that they had all the material needed for the conduct of all experiments that were appropriate;

Second—begin to diminish the potential destructive power of the world's atomic stockpiles;

Third—allow all peoples of all nations to see that, in this enlightened age, the great powers of the earth, both of the East and of the West, are interested in human aspirations first, rather than in building up the armaments of war;

Fourth—open up a new channel for peaceful discussion, and initiate at least a new approach to the many difficult problems that must be solved in both private and public conversations, if the world is to shake off the inertia imposed by fear, and is to make positive progress toward peace.

Against the dark background of the atomic bomb, the United States does not wish merely to present strength, but also the desire and the hope for peace.

The coming months will be fraught with fateful decisions. In this Assembly; in the capitals and military headquarters of the world; in the hearts of men everywhere, be they governors or governed, may they be the decisions which will lead this world out of fear and into peace.

To the making of these fateful decisions, the United States pledges before you—and therefore before the world—its determination to help solve the fearful atomic dilemma—to devote its entire heart and mind to find the way by which the miraculous inventiveness of man shall not be dedicated to his death, but consecrated to his life.

I again thank the delegates for the great honor they have done me, in inviting me to appear before them, and in listening to me so courteously.   Thank you.

NOTE: The President's opening words referred to Mme. Vijaya Pandit, President of the United Nations General Assembly.

257   ¶ Statement by the President Concerning the United States Program for Assisting Escapees and Refugees.   *December 8, 1953*

I BELIEVE that the task of caring for the escapees should have the highest emphasis in the minds of all the free world, and I am happy that the United States has already done so much of this work. It is the unswerving aim of the United States that the burden of arms, the fear of oppression, and the need of flight shall, some day, be lifted from mankind in order that there may no longer be refugees or escapees, and that all may live in peace and freedom.

NOTE: The release of which this statement was a part announced that the program for escapees, begun in the spring of 1952, would continue under a $9 million authorization by the President from mutual security funds. The release added that the program was under the direction of the Foreign Operations Administration, that more than 6,000 escapees had already been resettled, primarily in Canada, Australia, South America, and the United States, and that the program operated in the Far East, as well as in Western Europe, aiding refugees from Communist China.

258   ¶ Statement by the President Calling for Aid to the Victims of the Fire in Pusan, Korea. *December 11, 1953*

ADDING TO the already overwhelming misery in Korea, the refugee-packed city of Pusan recently suffered the greatest fire in its history. More than five thousand homes were destroyed, leaving thousands of sparsely clad and malnourished refugees without shelter. In addition to the very great amount of voluntary work they are doing to help the people of the brave Republic of Korea, American and other United Nations troops are now doing everything possible within their resources to provide the emergency aid so desperately needed as a result of this disaster.

Today, as we approach the Christmas season, I call upon all Americans to give generously to support the work of such groups as The American-Korean Foundation, American Relief for Korea, C.A.R.E., Church World Service, war relief services of various religious welfare organizations, and the other of our fine voluntary groups who now face this additional challenge and responsibility. Such aid is particularly fitting during this Christmas period.

259 ¶ Remarks to the Officers of the Pan American Medical Association.
December 12, 1953

THE LETTER that I am delivering to you is an official endorsement of your work. I can't tell you how delighted I am that you have taken such a professional interest in the great problems of health in the Western Hemisphere. Whatever can properly be done to help out the efforts of your Association, you can be sure that, while I have so stated in my letter, I will surely do.

I am sure that every step that produces better solidarity in the Western Hemisphere is to the good of the United States of America. I am sure also that every representative here of other American countries would feel the same way about that solidarity with respect to his country. So I am all for it.

I will see you out on the North Portico for a picture in a few minutes.

NOTE: See Item 260 for text of the letter referred to by the President.

260 ¶ Letter to Dr. Joseph J. Eller, Executive
Director, Pan American Medical Association.
December 12, 1953

Dear Dr. Eller:

It was indeed a pleasure for me today to meet with the distin-
guished physicians representing the Pan American Medical
Association, and I am happy to send my warm greetings to the
members who will participate in the forthcoming Ninth Inter-
American Medical Cruise Congress to be held this January aboard
the S.S. "Nieuw Amsterdam" and in Caracas, Venezuela; Ciudad
Trujillo, Dominican Republic; St. Thomas, Virgin Islands; San
Juan, Puerto Rico and Havana, Cuba.

I am profoundly interested in the expansion of the Association's
scholarship program, to the end that the level of professional skill
may be raised. Moreover, the program you have pursued during
the past twenty-six years of interchanging medical knowledge and
friendship among the doctors of this hemisphere and which carries
out your credo, "The practice of medicine has no national, racial
or religious boundaries," certainly promotes understanding and
cooperation among the American nations.

You and your colleagues in the Pan American Medical Association may be assured of my support in these endeavors.

Sincerely yours,

DWIGHT D. EISENHOWER

261 ¶ Letter to the Governors of the States
Calling for a Conference on Highway Safety.
December 14, 1953

[Released December 14, 1953. Dated December 11, 1953]

Dear —————:

The mounting toll of death and injury on our highways long
ago reached a point of deep concern to all of us. It stands before

America as a great challenge—humanitarian and economic—and must be met by urgent action.

I have examined the "Action Program for Highway Safety" which you and the other Governors have developed in cooperation with interested organizations and public officials having jurisdiction over highway safety.   It is a sound and workable program, but effective citizen leadership is needed to help you put this great crusade into organized action on a scale far bigger than ever before.

Accordingly, I have called a Conference on Highway Safety for Washington next February seventeenth, eighteenth and nineteenth.   The Conference will serve to focus more public attention on the problem and stimulate active leadership in every community.

I should appreciate your designating an appropriate group of your outstanding citizens as a delegation to represent your state. Since the Conference program will be built around seven basic groups—labor, agriculture, business, women, public officials, media of public information and other organizations (service, fraternal, religious, veterans, etc.), I would hope that your delegation will include representatives from each of these categories.

Will you please forward the names of your state's delegates to the Conference on Highway Safety, Room 1107, General Services Building, Washington 25, D.C.   Secretary of Commerce Weeks, General Chairman, will send you detailed background information on the Conference shortly.

Naturally, we would be happy to have present all Governors whose schedules and responsibilities would permit attendance. At any rate, I am depending on your active cooperation and support to make this Conference most effective.

Sincerely,

DWIGHT D. EISENHOWER

NOTE: This is the text of identical letters addressed to the Governors of the 48 States and to the President of the Board of Commissioners of the District of Columbia.

262   ¶ Remarks Opening the White House Conference of Mayors.   *December* 14, 1953

Mr. Peterson, and I suppose I may address the audience collectively as Your Honor the Mayor:

I assume this is an historic occasion. I have not looked up my history carefully, but I know of no other time when the President of the United States felt it necessary to invite to a conference the Mayors of our cities, in order that they might together discuss—and the staffs might discuss with you—national security.

In our Constitution there is an expression "To provide for the common security"—a responsibility that, of course, falls upon the national government. Our government is a Republic, and there is a division of power, not only functionally but geographically, with the hope that the maximum of power will be reserved at the local level. And with power goes responsibility.

But the real occasion for this particular type of conference is that for the first time in history, cities have become principal targets for any enemy seeking to conquer our Nation. The city has moved from a position of support in the rear. That position of the spiritual, the moral, the intellectual, the industrial and mobilization support for armies and navies and air forces—has moved out in a very distinct way into the front line.

And so that creates problems. They can be solved only if we consult together and act intelligently. I do not mean to say, of course, that the Federal Government is disabused of responsibility—has lost its responsibility merely because the target is a city. Far from it. But now we have got to a place where the matter can no longer be handled by professional or organized military forces, and where we must all act together in the operation of any plan necessary for our safety.

I think it is most easily described or explained by the simple truth that what would be necessary is the readiness of fire departments, hospital and health departments, police departments, sanitation departments with our water and our sewage and all the rest of it—all must be prepared to handle their jobs.

Now, if the Federal Government tried to come in to do that, in that preparatory period, it would certainly be unwarranted interference and justifiably resented. As a matter of fact, it would be impossible. So, of course, we all have jobs. In the carrying out of our job here, we intend to do everything that is reasonable, decent and proper in supporting the cities in meeting their own problems.

But again, I want to point out something about fighting—about war. Many of you here, of course, have been through the very worst parts of our past war. One great military leader said, "The moral is to the physical in war as three is to one," and I think every soldier who has come after him has believed that he understated the case.

The winning of war—the effectiveness in such things—is in the heart, in the determination, in the faith. It is in our beliefs in our country, in our God, everything that goes to make up America.

Now, first of all, then, this great problem lies in one that is really outside the realm of money and the material preparation. It is in conviction and belief, in readiness and discipline and all of the things that need to be done by the population to save itself. It isn't easy.

When a threat is not immediate with us, the ordinary American is not particularly anxious to get out and do a drill that he thinks has a little bit of the infantile about it. He possibly sees himself back in primary school, where we had drills on evacuating the schoolroom, in case of fire. But there was a very great principle there.

Ordered haste will save you, and panic will destroy you. So it is, first of all, against the incidence of panic that we must be prepared. In other words, there must be understanding produced by leadership, inspired leadership—leadership that is unafraid.

Now I probably could use no words that would exaggerate my concern that this thing is done, because I believe it is so feasible and possible to do it.   On the other hand, I would not have you think from any words of mine that I believe we haven't time to do this, that we must move in hysteria and in such tense concern that we get nothing intelligent done.   I don't believe that for an instant.   The United States is far too strong, its resources too great.   It is rich in its allies and it is rich in its own material, human, and spiritual resources.   We can do this job, and do it in such a way that we will very greatly add to the reluctance of anybody to attack us.

But, of course, they know that with every increase in the destructiveness of weapons, with every increase in the ability to place those weapons where they choose, that the value of surprise in war—always great—has gone up tremendously.

In other words, Pearl Harbor was a disaster because it was a surprise.   Had everybody been ready and waiting, the attack could not have been launched.

We have got, within reason, to be ready.   I think no one has ever described the defense needs of the United States better than did Washington, who said, "We must always retain a respectable posture of defense."   This means, if you are going to apply that term, that everybody has to use his judgment.   We can't be an armed camp.   We are not going to transfer ourselves into militarists.   We are not going to be in uniform, going around yelling "Heil" anything.   We are simply going to do our job, but do it intelligently.

And knowing a disaster can occur where we can visualize times when the fire department and police department are practically paralyzed and all the water mains are broken and no lights in town, now, what do we do?   How much warning have we had?   What can we do?   It is getting over reasonable preparation without being hysterical.   That is our job.

I never like to talk too somberly because I don't believe that the courage of America is such that you have to deal in dread terms too long.   All I am trying to do is appeal to the common sense of America to do what is necessary, not to lose our freedoms, not to

be a people that walk constantly in the shadow of fear.
   Thank you very much.

NOTE: The President spoke at the State Department auditorium. In his opening words he referred to Val Peterson, Administrator of the Federal Civil Defense Administration.

263   ¶ Statement by the President Requesting Reports to the FBI of Violations of the Atomic Energy Act.   *December* 15, 1953

ON SEPTEMBER 6, 1939, January 8, 1943, and July 24, 1950, Presidential Directives were issued requesting all enforcement officers, both Federal and state, to report promptly all information relating to espionage, sabotage, subversive activities and related matters to the nearest field representative of the Federal Bureau of Investigation.

The Federal Bureau of Investigation is charged with investigating all violations of the Atomic Energy Act, including the illegal export or import of fissionable material, the illegal possession or transportation of fissionable material and the illegal production, transfer, or possession of any equipment or device utilizing fissionable material or atomic energy as a military weapon. "Fissionable material" means plutonium, uranium-235 or other material which the Atomic Energy Commission has determined to be capable of releasing substantial quantities of energy through nuclear chain reaction. I am requesting that all enforcement officers, both Federal and state, report all information relating to violations of the Atomic Energy Act to the nearest field representative of the Federal Bureau of Investigation.

I suggest that all patriotic organizations and individuals likewise report all such information to the Federal Bureau of Investigation in the same manner.

264 ¶ Message to Stanislaw Mikolajczyk
Conveying Greetings to the International Peasant
Union Forum. *December* 16, 1953

[Released December 16, 1953. Dated December 15, 1953]

Mr. Stanislaw Mikolajczyk
President, International Peasant Union
Carnegie Endowment International Center
New York, New York

To all participating in the International Peasant Union Forum,
I am happy to send greetings.

I hope that your study of agriculture as practiced under communistic dictatorships receives wide attention. Few areas of
human endeavor are so fundamental to the political stability and
economy of nations as agriculture. The difficulties that communism's leaders are experiencing in forcing collectivization and
political regimentation upon the great peasant populations of
Eastern Europe are therefore especially significant.

In examining this situation you are performing an important
service to the free world. You have my best wishes for the success of your deliberations.

DWIGHT D. EISENHOWER

265 ¶ The President's News Conference of
December 16, 1953.

THE PRESIDENT. The items I have this morning, ladies and gentlemen, are, I think, fairly short, and possibly of not too great
importance.

I would like to make mention of the Vice President's return
and, particularly, of the very splendid reports that I got, both
from the press and official circles in each country that he visited.

He and Mrs. Nixon represented our country on such a visit, I think, in an admirable fashion.

I haven't asked him whether he intends—it just occurred to me this second—whether he intends to prepare a report on his trip in the fashion that my brother did after coming back from South America. If he does, I suppose that it will become available to you at an appropriate time.

As you know, starting tomorrow morning, we are having a series of conferences lasting over 3 days, having here the legislative leaders to go over with the executive officials the features of the program that will be submitted to the Congress very early in January.

Now, the purpose of such a program is to have an exchange of views on all important problems; to lay out in front of these people, who have been busy on other affairs, the essential results of the staff work that has been done in gathering information and making analyses, and so on; and to secure a general meeting of the minds with respect to such a program before it is presented to the Congress. In other words, it is merely, as we see it, a pursuance of the procedures that must be observed if our kind of government is to operate successfully.

As most of you know, we will have the traditional Christmas tree lighting on the afternoon of the 24th. I shall make a very short talk, part of it inside, and then go out to light the Christmas tree. The next day, I hope to take off for Georgia, where I hope to combine several things; but unfortunately this time I have to take more than the average amount of work with me because, as you know, January is going to be a very busy month. I have two or three messages to work on, and it will be a pretty tough time.

I am concerned that every time—and this is not off the record, but I would like to make a word of explanation—I am concerned with every time the President moves, a number of people whose jobs require them to go along, including a number of the people here present. I must say that it seems to me unfortunate, the

only days I can find to get away, and get away from some of the
pressures of the appointment card in order to work, that it dis-
commodes some of you during that period. For that I am sorry,
but I don't see any real answer to it.

Apparently it is your job to go along, some of you, and if I
discommode you, I apologize in advance. But I do tell you this:
I have no idea of conducting any political conferences or meeting
anybody or doing anything but go to a quiet place to do some
work with my own staff, my own people, to see my grandchildren,
and to get a bit of exercise which is now beginning to be 2 or 3
weeks behind me. So that is the story of my going away.

Now, I think that I have consumed enough of the time here,
and we will start the questions.

Q. Merriman Smith, United Press: Mr. President, are you
prepared to ask Congress next year for changes in the atomic
energy law which would permit sharing of our weapons and
atomic materials with the NATO forces?

THE PRESIDENT. There are certain changes in the law that
are necessary before America can realize the full value with its
allies out of the development that has been going on since the
World War in this weapons field.

Now, there are no changes contemplated by me or by the
Chairman of the Atomic Energy Commission that have anything to do with the scientific processes of nuclear fission or building of weapons or anything else. But where we are attempting
to assure the integrity of a line, where we feel that our interest
requires to hold it, it is simply foolish for us to think that we cannot or must not share some kind of information with our allies
who would be dependent upon the same kind of support of this
kind as we will.

In other words, it is a very limited field, but certain revisions of
the law are necessary before we can do anything. You must
remember that the law was passed under conditions that are not
even remotely resembling what they are now.

Q. Paul R. Leach, Chicago Daily News: Mr. President, as I

understand it—and, perhaps, I am wrong on this—but it would seem to me that what you proposed in your speech at the United Nations was not merely to share with our allies but with other friendly or even neutral nations; is that correct?

THE PRESIDENT. This is what I stated: that the United States would be prepared to donate a decent proportion of its products in this line with others, in which I said the Soviet Union would have to be one under that plan, and that the United Nations would assemble certain scientists—in which, of course, we would have a part—in order to evolve the best ways in which new developments could be made available to humanity.

A little slant on this idea, is this: today, every time you say the word "atomic," we think only in terms of weapons and destructiveness, and we think principally in terms of two nations. I think all countries, all peoples, ought to have their minds drawn to the fact that here in this development may be, and certainly will be, if we study it hard enough and work on it hard enough, a means of improving the lot of all humanity.

Now, frankly, that is what I am trying to get all people to understand.

Q. Alan S. Emory, Watertown (N.Y.) Times: Mr. President, Governor Dewey told us last Friday that he had laid out the facts of the State's case on Niagara power redevelopment in his conference with you. I wonder if you would tell us if he did a good selling job?

THE PRESIDENT. He merely laid out to me what he was going to go and place before the people that have the responsibility in this regard.

As you will recall, in the case of the Niagara River, Congress reserved to itself at that time the power to make the decision as to the method by which that power would be developed.

He merely described to me what New York's position was in the thing and what he was going to do.

He didn't apparently attempt to sell me anything; he just told me some facts he was going to tell someone else.

Q. Marietta Dake, Niagara Falls Gazette: Mr. President, if it were up to you, do you favor the development of the Niagara River by the Federal authority, the State authority, or private enterprise?

THE PRESIDENT. I just remarked that Congress reserved this to itself. I don't believe I will comment on it in detail except to say this: I have always believed that States have a very great power of decision in these cases as to what they want to do.

Now, in rivers and water lines and other things that involve all the United States, the Federal Government cannot dodge, and should not try to dodge, its share of the responsibility, its partnership in the case.

Here, where you have a river that I believe is wholly within New York State, I should say that New York State ought to have a very great influential part to say; but I am not going to be here and say Congress hasn't a right to do it exactly as it said it was going to do it.

Q. Chalmers M. Roberts, Washington Post: Mr. President, in answering Mr. Smith's question about sharing atomic matters with the NATO allies, I think you referred to the possibility of sharing information. However, some of the stories from Paris on Secretary Wilson's speech imply an actual sharing of weapons or our putting atomic weapons in the hands of our NATO allies. Is that a correct interpretation?

THE PRESIDENT. Well, I wouldn't stand here and just, with an offhand decision, tell you exactly what we would have to do in the long run.

I think it would depend entirely upon circumstances.

After war started, if you ever had that tragic eventuality, you would use atomic weapons through whatever means that would best advance the interests of the United States. Just like any other weapon, then, I should think that if someone else could in a particular place use it better, more advantageously, well, probably you would make it——

Q. Mr. Roberts: Is it correct, then, sir, to infer that there has been no decision by the administration as of today to have any such sharing plan?

THE PRESIDENT. There is going to be no decision until Congress passes on this. Every move that we make in talking and studying this, we take this up with the proper—you know, the Joint Committee on Atomic Energy in the Congress; and until Congress passes the law, I will assure you we are not going to violate the law.

Now, I will just tell you, there are many, many ways in which this can be done; but the principle for the United States is, what best advances the enlightened self-interest of the United States? That is what will be the principle that will guide me in any decision I have to make.

Q. Mr. Roberts: Sir, it is perhaps not clear. I meant to say decision by the executive branch to ask the Congress for a change which would allow a sharing of the actual weapons with the allies.

THE PRESIDENT. I don't believe that you could answer any question in that sweeping way. I would say it depends upon the circumstances and what will best meet the needs of the military situation at the moment and at the time.

Now, if that becomes necessary, why, I would see no reason why you shouldn't do it in whatever way would best advance the interests of the United States.

Q. Nat S. Finney, Buffalo Evening News: You will forgive a somewhat elaborate question. You said in your speech that atomic power is here now today?

THE PRESIDENT. That is right.

Q. Mr. Finney: I believe the Atomic Energy Act contains a section which requires in the event of such a development that a special report be made to you, and I think by you to the Congress on the political, social, economic, and international implications of this development. Do you plan to have such a report made?

THE PRESIDENT. Of course, such a report would be made first by the Atomic Energy Commission, who would certainly give it to me.

When I said here now today, as you know, we have produced an engine that is run by atomic power; I pointed out that is a capability and not yet a useful thing for all the world because it is too expensive to run it, just in terms of money.

If you want to get electric power from this kind of a thing, you have to get it within the range that it is an economic practicability.

Now, all of those things you talk about, I suppose, will come about. Frankly, you bring up a detail of responsibility on me I didn't know about; I will have to look them up.

Q. Frederick Kuh, Chicago Sun-Times: On the same subject, Mr. President, is it your intention or hope that whatever happens the proposals for a pool of fissionable materials should be worked out among the non-Communist countries?

THE PRESIDENT. Well, I made a proposal in good faith; I was very serious about it. It had been talked over really for many weeks with all of my chief advisers and with legislative people that have responsibility in this field.

Until we see where that proposal is leading, I don't believe I will speculate on what would be the next step.

As you know, or I hope you know, I never believed in admitting defeat, and even a rejection of this offer would not stop me from seeking every possible way we can to make the best possible use out of this scientific development.

Q. Robert G. Spivack, New York Post: Mr. President, aside from the point you raised in the U.N. speech, would you review for us what you think were the principal accomplishments at Bermuda?

THE PRESIDENT. That is an odd thing. I twice before this body said we were going to have a friendly talk. There was no agenda. Frankly, I didn't see any need for a—what do you call them?—final communique, because we met to have a friendly talk. But apparently there was some belief among—maybe among some of you people—that there was going to be something happening and, therefore, you wanted to know about it.

There were friendly talks took place to try to clarify our several positions on a number of problems. That was the accomplishment. From my viewpoint, it was worth while; although I must say I doubt that it was newsworthy.

Q. John C. O'Brien, Philadelphia Inquirer: Mr. President, I hesitate to interrupt this discussion of atomic energy, but I have been asked to ask you a question involving the mechanics of newspaper production. For the guidance of our headline writers, do you object to the use of your nickname in headlines? [*Laughter*]

THE PRESIDENT. Well, no, of course I don't. All my life I have answered to that nickname, and I realize that individuals have their own ideas of the customs that should be applied to an office such as that one I now hold. I would say that everybody's sense of the fitness of things and of good taste is the deciding factor.

So far as I am concerned, it makes not the slightest difference, not the slightest difference.

Q. G. Gould Lincoln, Washington Evening Star: Mr. President, has any part of the program that you are to discuss been written—I mean, with the legislators—and if not, will any part of the program be written at these conferences that you are to have at the White House?

THE PRESIDENT. I am not so certain that I understand your question, but here is the point: we have been working for quite a while on the State of the Union speech, which I am going to work harder on probably next week. That, in its broad outlines, will contain the objectives and the means of the program.

Now, at the same time in each department there has been going forward the most intensive study: in Treasury, on taxes; in Mrs. Hobby's department, on every kind of thing from old-age insurance; and in the Department of Labor, on unemployment insurance; in Cole's agency, on housing. So the thing has been going on; because this program can't be all in one short, nice, handy document of one page that I like.

It will be, first, a message; and then there will be supporting documents like the budget itself, and you know how thick that is. That will be a tremendous supporting document in this program.

So it is perfectly correct to say that much has been written, but nothing except in principle has been completely finalized; the principles by which we are going to act, you will find largely in the Republican platform.

This administration is one that believes in keeping its promises, and we are going to try to do it in every way we can.

Q. James B. Reston, New York Times: Sir, could you tell us anything about your instructions to Mr. Bohlen upon your atomic energy idea, and say anything about the reaction of Mr. Molotov to his visit?

THE PRESIDENT. The instructions to Mr. Bohlen went through the Secretary of State. I do not know whether the Secretary of State has talked about this or not—it never occurred to me—and I don't know this minute whether this would be sort of a privileged communication. But he was told to notify the Soviet Foreign Office in advance that such a talk was to be made, and to be made with the most serious purpose in the world.

Now, reactions, as you know, are slow, and they are coming along. We haven't had a final reaction, as far as I know.

Q. Sarah McClendon, El Paso Times: Mr. President, the El Paso Valley Cotton Association says that tomorrow, when you meet with Republican leaders, you will take up the question of increasing the minimum wage. Will you tell us if they have the correct information or if you plan to propose that?

THE PRESIDENT. I am going to talk about no details of the program that is coming up.

Q. Pat Munroe, Albuquerque Journal: Mr. President, my question concerns the embattled War Claims Commission. I noticed with interest that one of the two members that was ousted says that she regrets that the Commission is now falling into political hands. But I wondered if you had any specific changes in mind there other than the removal of the top personnel, any specific changes in mind with, for example, the paying of Korean POW's or whether you would extend the life of the Commission?

THE PRESIDENT. No, I have nothing to say on the thing at the moment. Actually, it is something that has been discussed over a period of months, and it was presented to me that certain changes were necessary. Finally, they came up with the recommendations for those changes, and they were made.

Now, I have no detailed study before me that I know of—or haven't had; I may be mistaken, and I don't want to be, because over the past many months things have happened I wouldn't recall on the spur of the moment. But so far as I can recall, there has been no specific recommendation for a complete change of direction or for termination of this Commission.

Q. Frederic W. Collins, Providence Journal: Mr. President, I wonder whether you would fill us in on the origin and development of the central ideas you did propose at the U.N., and how far back they go, where they started, and so forth.

THE PRESIDENT. You know, I would if I could. I have been interested ever since the war in reading many documents about the developments of that war, as to who first thought of such and such an attack or who first thought of this or that or the other.

So far as I know and as I can recall—and I am certainly not going to swear as to the truth of this—I think that I originated the idea of a joint contribution to a central bank in an effort to get all people started on thinking in different terms about this whole business of atomic energy, and under such a way that inspection was not automatically required and, therefore, gave the other side an automatic reason for rejecting it before you got started.

I hoped it would open up many lines of study, and I still hope so.

As far as I can recall now, from that first germ there have been many, many people contributing to this thing; we have had many serious discussions about it.

Q. Edward T. Folliard, Washington Post: Mr. President, you have told us that 1,456 persons have been separated from the Government service under the security program. I wonder if it would be possible, at least in the near future, to give us a breakdown on this figure; that is, tell us how many of these people were separated for heavy drinking, how many for morals, how many, if any, for outright spying, how many for Communist association or affiliation? Naturally, I wouldn't expect the names, only figures or percentages.

THE PRESIDENT. I would very much doubt it. While I have not talked in detail about this thing—and I don't mean to say that I am incapable of changing my mind; I, of course, could— but you see, numbers of these people that come up, they are not charged with just one idea.

We are talking about security risks: if a man has done certain things that you know make him, well, a security risk in delicate positions—and I don't care what they are—where he is subject to a bit of blackmail or weakness of, let's say, being *non compos mentis* for a little while, anything of that kind can enter into it; although you may be looking toward the fact that he possibly could become a subversive under those reasons.

I think it would be very difficult and, therefore, I would say my answer would be, generally speaking, no, I could not give a breakdown. But I would not, by any manner of means, hesitate to talk about it with my own people.

Q. Mr. Folliard: The reason I ask, Mr. President, is that there is a widespread opinion, I am told, that all 1,456 are spies or suspected spies. Now, I am sure you never meant to give that impression.

THE PRESIDENT. No. We made it very clear, if they will go back and look at the original directive, we said the word "loyalty" didn't really describe what you were trying to do.

In the Federal Government you are trying to get the finest people you can, and if they become security risks, you have to discharge them because they are not good security risks; but that doesn't always impugn their loyalty, not by any manner of means.

Q. Mr. Folliard: Without going into any figures, Mr. President, are you in a position to say that these people are not all suspected spies or potential spies or——

THE PRESIDENT. Well, the word "potential" covers so many

things, Mr. Folliard, that I wouldn't—I would say this: they are discharged for a number of reasons, and not all of them had the word "subversion" or "disloyal." They were poor security risks, and I think there is a very clear distinction.

Q. Alice A. Dunnigan, Associated Negro Press: Mr. President, I was wondering whether you could tell us whether the legislative conference will this week discuss any civil rights legislation?

THE PRESIDENT. Civil rights legislation?

Q. Miss Dunnigan: In the legislative conferences.

THE PRESIDENT. As I remarked, I am not going to talk about the details of this program. But civil rights legislation, identified as such, I doubt will come up.

There will be many things, I hope, will be affecting the people of the United States as a whole, but I am sure that there is nothing that could be identified just as civil rights legislation.

Q. Robert E. Clark, International News Service: Mr. President, the Secretary of State startled some of our NATO allies by his blunt warning that we may be forced to reappraise our troop commitments in Europe unless the European army comes into being. Do you fully support his statements in that regard?

THE PRESIDENT. Well, of course, I didn't read his statement; but, ladies and gentlemen, the law of our land—read the Richards amendment—what can the Secretary of State say? The law of our land says that 50 percent of this year's appropriation—I believe, starting January 1st, isn't it—50 percent of the appropriation must be given out through EDC. If EDC is not produced, what do we do?

I am a little bit astonished that anyone should take this as something new and, particularly, blunt; but it is just one of the things that the Richards amendment requires of us.

Now, I understand, of course, that he has repeated many things in which most of us believe, that a greater unification of Europe, politically, economically, militarily, will greatly add to the safety of the Western World. We are for it. I don't know exactly what words he used, but I must say that the facts I have just recited are plain for all to see; the facts of the case are there.[1]

Q. Anthony H. Leviero, New York Times: Mr. President, there have been reports recently that executive branch agencies are handing confidential personnel files to congressional committees. Is there any truth to that, do you know?

THE PRESIDENT. You mean FBI confidential files?

Q. Mr. Leviero: No, sir; personnel files having to do with security and loyalty.

THE PRESIDENT. You ask me a question I have never heard of before. If any such thing is being done—I believe it has been the practice for a long time to give certain summaries of information, but as far as I know, no confidential personnel files are going out of the proper repositories. I would have to ask, and you would have to go to the department where you believe it is being done, and just ask the Secretary because I haven't heard of it.

Q. Mr. Leviero: Well, sir, under the practice followed under the order of your predecessor, any department doing that would have to clear with the White House. I wonder if any of that has been done?

---

[1] On December 23 the White House released the following statement:

At today's meeting of the National Security Council, the President received with satisfaction the report on NATO made by Mr. Dulles, Mr. Humphrey, Mr. Wilson and Mr. Stassen, who attended the Ministerial Council Meeting in Paris. They reported that NATO is functioning efficiently, and is continuing to develop the strength and cohesion needed to provide security on a long-term collective basis.

The President was informed concerning the prospects of bringing into being the European Defense Community, a matter which has long been of deep concern to him. He considers this the only practical proposal for ending permanently the recurrent strife between France and Germany, provoked twice in our own generation by German militarism, and of creating a solid core at the center of the NATO structure. The President shares the view which had been expressed to the Council by Secretary Dulles, that failure soon to consummate the EDC would confront the United States with the necessity of reappraising its basic policies as regards Europe.

The President also was informed of the operations of the European Coal and Steel Community which has already brought together, in limited unity, the six nations which are prospective members of the European Defense and Political Communities. He was encouraged that the Coal and Steel Community is now in effective operation, and reaffirms his hope that ways might be found to enable the United States to assist, on a loan basis, in modernizing and developing the natural resources within the jurisdiction of this Community, in accordance with his letter of June 15 to the Senate Foreign Relations Committee and the House Foreign Affairs Committee.

THE PRESIDENT. I will say this, nothing has been cleared with me personally that I can recall. Look, ladies and gentlemen, let us have one thing straight. In a job such as this, all of you realize there has got to be a terrific amount of decentralization, and any man worthy to be a chief of a great organizational body must do two or three things: one of them, pick the people he trusts; two, delegate authority and responsibility to them; and three, back them up and, particularly, take responsibility for any failure or any blunder that occurs.

Now, some of these people can be doing things which I know they wouldn't bother me with; so I am not going to say nothing like this has been done. I merely say that something like this I don't know about.

I am perfectly ready to have Mr. Hagerty ask about it, see if he can find out. So far as I know, nothing has happened.

Q. Marvin L. Arrowsmith, Associated Press: Mr. President, you said awhile back that reaction to your U.N. speech had been slow in coming. Has there been any official reaction, any Soviet reaction at all, that has come to your attention, beyond what has been in the papers?

THE PRESIDENT. Nothing except what has been reported in the papers.

Now, I should have added, from all other countries that I know of, including from the Ambassadors who have come to dinner lately, reaction has been fervent, and I would say very favorable. I was talking, when I meant a reaction, I thought someone asked a question that implied Soviet reaction. That we are still waiting for.

Q. Charles L. Bartlett, Chattanooga Times: Mr. President, these legislative proposals, will they go to the congressional leaders as more or less firm and final recommendations or will they be subject to modification according to the discussions that follow during the next 3 days?

THE PRESIDENT. They will certainly be subject to modification in detail; that was one reason for having these things.

As far as principle is concerned, the purpose, the plan of carrying out a great program, that has been developed and it is my responsibility to present it to them. I know it, and I suppose everybody knows it in the United States.

But when it comes to details, let's say, of a particular tax or a particular expenditure or a particular operation in any field, why, of course, it is subject to modifications of that character. That is one of the reasons for having such a meeting.

Q. Mrs. May Craig, New England papers: Mr. President, General Dean has said that perhaps our young soldiers would be better able to withstand captivity by the enemy if they had had discipline all their lives early; that he was dismayed by some of the juvenile delinquency in this country. Now, you have been a general, you are a President and a father and a grandfather. Would you say something about this problem of juvenile delinquency?

THE PRESIDENT. I don't like to use the words "juvenile delinquency" because I have a very firm conviction that that term ought to be translated into parental failure; that is what I think.

Now, I think every single man that has had to bear responsibilities in war, responsibilities for employing America's youth to win a victory, has been appalled frequently at the lack of understanding on the part of America's youth as to what America is, what are the conditions that could make her fight, and therefore what are the great underlying reasons that could lead that boy finally to the battlefield to risk his life, not just for property, not just for even what you might call national rights, but for some fundamental values in life. When you are trying to get a division ready for battle, and when a commander finds the need to go out and to try to start from the beginning to give this boy a fundamental reason why he is in uniform, it is pretty discouraging.

I didn't read General Dean's statement, I don't know what he said; but I do say that, after all, the young are America; they are the America of today and, certainly, the America of the future. It is our responsibility to try to see that they are given the understanding we think we inherited from our forefathers, our traditions, given to them in a serious, understanding way that while they are having their fun and enjoyment in life that they should have, they really are getting an understanding of America. That is what I think.

Merriman Smith, United Press: Thank you, Mr. President.

NOTE: President Eisenhower's twenty-third news conference was held in the Executive Office Building from   10:31 to 11:05 o'clock on Wednesday morning, December 16, 1953. In attendance: 161.

266 ¶ Statements by the President on the First Day of the Republican Legislative Conference in the Cabinet Room.   *December* 17, 1953

[Remarks at the opening session at 8:30 a.m.]

I HAVE CALLED this meeting of the Republican leaders of the Senate and House of Representatives and the Chairmen of the various standing committees for the purpose of advising with me on the legislative program which I propose to set forth in the President's State of the Union and Budget Messages.

I am very happy to see you and have your cooperation at this time. With it we can all look forward to another successful, sound and productive session of Congress. I am convinced—as I know you are—that the people of this country are looking to the Republican Party to continue to enact a forward-looking, progressive program that will serve the welfare of 160 million people, and I know we shall succeed.

This will be in furtherance of the program we started last year which, among other things:

Stopped the shooting and casualty lists in Korea.

Reduced by thirteen billion dollars the previous Administration's requests for new appropriations.

Cleared the way for January tax reductions in personal income taxes and excess profits taxes.

Stabilized the purchasing power of the citizen's dollar and stopped inflation.

Removed stifling controls on our economy.

Extended emergency aid to agriculture and assisted those in drought-affected areas.

Removed security risks from Federal service on the simple premise that those disloyal to or unsuitable for Federal Government cannot work for it.

Strengthened our defenses and those of the free world against Communist aggression.

Enacted emergency legislation permitting additional immigration in urgent situations.

In accordance with our agreement, I expect to deliver my State of the Union Message to the Congress personally on January 7th, the day after the Congress convenes. The Budget Message and the Economic Report will be sent up soon thereafter. Under these circumstances, I know you realize that all of the matters that we will discuss will be confidential. In order, however, to give the public information and minimize speculation, I shall make a statement at the end of each day, in which I shall give a general report on how the meetings progressed as well as the names of those who attended each session.

The American people have vested in the Republican Party the responsibility of government. With that responsibility we have a great opportunity to advance the welfare of our country. Now let's go to work.

[Statement at the end of the first day]

THE CONFERENCE opened this morning at 8:30 a. m. with a general discussion on the legislative program I propose to submit to the Congress. Those attending this part of the meeting included: the Cabinet, the Congressional leaders, and members of the White House staff.

The opening statement that I made to the meeting has already been released and the discussion followed this general outline.

Representative John Taber, Chairman of the House Appropriations Committee, and Representative Dewey Short, Chairman of the House Armed Services Committee, joined the conference after this general discussion. During the remainder of the morning the conference dealt with matters affecting the defense program, foreign operations, absentee voting for overseas armed services personnel, and the Federal budget. Mr. Kyes, Mr. Stassen, Mr. Cutler, and Mr. Dodge presented detailed analyses of these respective subjects. The Defense, Foreign Operations, and Budget administrators reviewed what they found when this Administration took office; what had been accomplished this year and what goals the Administration is seeking to attain during the coming year.

The fiscal outlook was for a continuation of the substantial progress this Administration has already made in its revision of the Budget for fiscal 1954 that was prepared by the previous Administration. In fiscal 1955, we will continue this progress by further reduction of expenditures and further reduction of new spending authority.

At the afternoon session the Conference was joined by: Senator Homer E. Capehart, Chairman of the Senate Banking and Currency Committee; Senator H. Alexander Smith, Chairman of the Senate Committee on Labor and Public Welfare; Representative Jesse P. Wolcott, Chairman of the House Banking and Currency Committee; Representative Samuel K. McConnell, Jr., Chairman of the House Education and Labor Committee.

In the first part of the afternoon, Mr. Cole, the Administrator of the Housing and Home Finance Agency, presented for consideration a legislative program with especial emphasis on assisting low income families in obtaining good housing accommodations.

Next the Secretary of Labor discussed the plans of the Labor Department and outlined suggested amendments to the Taft-Hartley Act. Also, he discussed changes in the Unemployment Compensation program providing for extended coverage. The

Secretary of Commerce also attended this session.

The Secretary of Health, Education, and Welfare then started a discussion of the health plans of her Department. Mrs. Hobby will continue discussion of other topics tomorrow.

On the basis of our first day of conference, I am sure I speak for all at the conference when I say that the leaders of the Republican Party will continue to present a successful, sound, and productive program that will serve the welfare of 160 million Americans.

267 ¶ Remarks at a Dinner Commemorating the 50th Anniversary of Powered Flight. *December* 17, 1953

President Johnson, and ladies and gentlemen:

It is indeed a great honor to have the privilege of addressing the aristocracy of aviation. Moreover, it is a very and even greater honor to join with you in honoring two names, those of the Wright brothers, which names will glow brightly in America's history as long as this country may endure.

Before such an audience as this, I shall not be foolish enough to talk at length about the accomplishments and the history of aviation. By no means would I get up before a college of surgeons and discuss or instruct in an intricate operation, and I am not going to make that kind of mistake here.

But I do want to refer to one element—one development—in the history of aviation: speed.

Recently, in reading about the Wrights, I noted that in that early year of 1903, when 30 miles an hour was achieved that was a very good performance. Then I noted, almost in the same day's paper, that someone recently flew 1,650 miles an hour. In 50 years we multiplied the speed of travel by 50 times. And let's go ahead until 2003. My grandson will then be half a dozen years younger than I am now. But if we keep up this same rate, he will see airplanes traveling at 82,500 miles an hour, if my mental arithmetic is somewhat correct.

Now, beyond that you have only to double it and you are at the speed of light. Then we will have the physicists talk about what is going to happen when you pierce the radiant barrier. It will be an interesting problem for them: if you travel faster than light, will you go blind?

This speed has become characteristic not only of the vehicle the great aviation industry has produced, but of the people. I shall tell you a little incident about one of your speakers this evening. A little more than 11 years ago tonight, we landed in North Africa. My headquarters was at Gibraltar. I had an aviation chief, and a question came up about aviation involving, really, the flight of some P–38's from Britain on down to Gibraltar. We needed them badly. I knew nothing of what they could do. So I sent for my Chief, General Doolittle. Not to be found. And so on my own I had to decide that a P–38 could fly that far, so I sent a cable and said send them on down.

Now, when Jimmy Doolittle came in, I said, "Where have you been?" And with his eyes glowing, he said, "I was flying a fighter plane against some French ships."

"Well," I said, "Jimmy, that is very interesting." And I said, "We have got a number of second lieutenants over there flying the ships, and you can be one of two things, a second lieutenant on a fighter ship or you can be my chief of aviation and a major general." I assure you, never did a potential second lieutenant get promoted faster.

Now, there are other characteristics about their personnel that have brought aviation to the point that it is today. I think they are vision and imagination, courage and perseverance.

Now, as the airplane of today is so much more complicated than the ship that the Wright brothers flew at Kitty Hawk as almost to defy comparison, so is our world of today a far more complicated thing than it was in those simple early days of this century.

This world is traveling in the speed of the complexity and intricacy of its problems almost as fast as aviation has come ahead. Indeed, I think maybe aviation is symbolic of what has happened to us.

Now I subscribe to every word that has been said here this evening about air power. It is important to us. It is a deterrent to potential enemies. It is absolutely needed in this day and time to us, if we are to preserve this country inviolate to attack.

But my belief goes far beyond that. I do not believe that in any amount of armed force, of whatever nature, is there real safety over the long run for any nation. The power of the surprise attack grows too great, and with every further step in the perfection of the airplane, with the terrifying increase in the power of bombs, we get to the point that the side that denies the moral and spiritual values in life preserves over people who live as we do such a terrifying advantage that something must be done about it.

Now that something, I submit, my friends, is the same vision, the same imagination, the same courage and the same perseverance that brought the Wright brothers' ship today to the B–52 and the B–47, and this new 1,650-mile job.

You people, as you build this air force, as you maintain it, as you keep it on top in quality, and wherever necessary in quantity, you must turn your imaginations and these great talents that you have displayed to our country in the widest sense. You must think in the deepest of spiritual and moral values, and how we are going to protect them, because there finally will be the capstone, as I see it, of all the service that the aviation industry can possibly do to our beloved country.

Again my friends, my profound thanks to each of you for the warmth and cordiality of your welcome, and for listening to me so courteously.

Good night.

NOTE: The President spoke at 10:24 p.m. at the Statler Hotel in Washington. His opening words referred to Vernon A. Johnson, President of the Aero Club of Washington.

268 ¶ Statements by the President on the Second Day of the Republican Legislative Conference. *December* 18, 1953

[The agenda for the morning session]

THE CONFERENCE this morning will discuss four main topics, as follows:

The Secretary of the Treasury will discuss taxes and the debt limit with the Congressional leaders.

The Chairman of the Atomic Energy Commission will discuss proposed amendments to the Atomic Energy Act. Representative W. Sterling Cole and Senator Bourke Hickenlooper, Chairman and Vice Chairman of the Joint Congressional Committee on Atomic Energy, will participate in this discussion.

The Secretary of State and the Director of the Foreign Operations Administration will discuss foreign affairs. Senator Alexander Wiley, Chairman of the Senate Foreign Relations Committee; Representative Robert B. Chiperfield, Chairman of the House Foreign Affairs Committee; Senator Hickenlooper and Representative Cole will participate in this discussion.

The Secretary of Health, Education, and Welfare will discuss social security and aid to the physically handicapped and continue a discussion of the health plans of her Department. Representative Carl T. Curtis, Chairman of the Subcommittee on Social Security of the House Ways and Means Committee will participate in this discussion.

[The agenda for the afternoon session]

AT THE AFTERNOON session of the Conference the following subjects will come up for general discussion.

The Secretary of Commerce, the Chairman of the Joint Chiefs of Staff, the Counsel to the President, and Mr. Cutler, Special Assistant to the President, will discuss the St. Lawrence Seaway. Senator Alexander Wiley, Chairman of the Senate Foreign Relations Committee, and Representative George A. Dondero, Chairman of the House Public Works Committee, will participate in this discussion.

The Counsel to the President will next discuss Hawaiian statehood. Senator Hugh Butler, Chairman of the Senate Interior and Insular Affairs Committee, and Representative A. L. Miller, Chairman of the House Interior and Insular Affairs Committee, will attend this session.

The Secretary of Commerce and the Secretary of Agriculture will then bring up the question of public works, including highway, flood control, reclamation and water conservation problems. Senator Edward Martin, Chairman of the Senate Committee on Public Works, Senator Butler and Representatives Miller and Dondero will participate in these discussions.

The final subject to be discussed this afternoon will be the Administration's farm program. The Secretary of Agriculture will lead this discussion which will be participated in by Senator George D. Aiken, Chairman of the Senate Agriculture and Forestry Committee, and Representative Clifford R. Hope, Chairman of the House Agricultural Committee.

[Statement at the end of the second day]

ON THE SECOND DAY of conferences with Congressional leaders and Chairmen of Senate and House Committees, eight main subjects were discussed. They were:

Taxation. Because of reductions in expenditures already made and presently planned, it was agreed that the way was cleared for January tax reductions in personal income taxes and excess profits taxes.

Atomic Energy. Discussions were held on proposed amendments to the Atomic Energy Act. One phase of the discussions dealt with the prospects of peacetime, civilian development of uses of atomic energy.

Foreign Affairs. The Secretary of State reviewed the world situation for the Congressional leaders.

Social Security and Aid to the Physically Handicapped. Expanded coverage of old age and survivors' insurance, together with improvements in the Social Security system were discussed. Extension of health facilities as well as improved plans for the physically handicapped were likewise summarized.

St. Lawrence Seaway. The St. Lawrence Seaway project was discussed by the Secretary of Commerce and the Chairman of the Joint Chiefs of Staff from the standpoint of our national defense.

Hawaiian Statehood. The question of statehood for Hawaii was discussed and it was pointed out that the Republican Platform urges "immediate statehood" for that territory.

Public Works. A program for better roads was outlined by the Secretary of Commerce. Flood control and reclamation projects, as well as careful programs to conserve the water resources of our Nation were also discussed in detail.

Agriculture. The Secretary of Agriculture reviewed the agricultural accomplishments of the Administration in 1953 and made certain proposals for an agricultural program after the present law expires on December 31, 1954. Among this year's accomplishments were:

Removal of controls from livestock and meat.

Establishment of a drought emergency program with more than 1,000,000 tons of feed distributed in the drought areas; reduced rail rates placed in effect and 18 States and one Territory (700 counties) receiving the benefit of the program.

A stepped-up beef purchase program that resulted this year in Government buying of 249,000,000 pounds of beef.

Extension of supports, where necessary, even when no storage facilities were available.

Expansion of facilities for storage of grain.

Reorganization of the Department of Agriculture, the creation of an independent Farm Credit Administration, and the establishment of a bipartisan Agricultural Advisory Committee.

The conference will continue tomorrow with morning and afternoon sessions.

269   ¶ Statements by the President on the Last
Day of the Republican Legislative Conference.
December 19, 1953

[The agenda for the final sessions]

AT THE MORNING SESSION, the following subjects were
scheduled for discussion.

The Attorney General will discuss several proposals designed
to provide more effective investigation and prosecution, not only
of subversive elements in our society, but also of criminals who
presently take advantage of certain loopholes in the law.   Senator
Joseph R. McCarthy, Chairman of the Senate Government Operations Committee; Senator Alexander Wiley, Chairman of the
Senate Foreign Relations Committee; Representative Chauncey
W. Reed, Chairman of the House Judiciary Committee; and Representative Harold H. Velde, Chairman of the House Un-American Activities Committee, are to participate in these discussions.

The Under Secretary of Health, Education, and Welfare will
discuss reorganization plans for the Executive Branch of the Government.   Representative Clare Hoffman, Chairman of the
House Government Operations Committee, and Senator Mc-
Carthy will take part in this discussion.

A general discussion of interstate and foreign commerce is
then scheduled to be presented by the Secretary of Commerce and
Senator John Bricker, Chairman of the Senate Interstate and
Foreign Commerce Committee.

Representatives of the State and Justice Departments are
scheduled to discuss the Bricker Amendment with Senator
Bricker and Congressional leaders.

The final subject on the schedule for the morning is a discussion of home rule for the District of Columbia.   The President of
the Board of District Commissioners and the Chairmen of the
Senate and House District of Columbia Committees, Senator

Francis Case and Representative Sid Simpson, will participate in this discussion.

At the afternoon session, the subjects to be discussed are postal rates, Civil Service, and Veterans affairs.

The Postmaster General and the Chairman of the Civil Service Commission, together with Senator Frank Carlson and Representative Edward H. Rees, Chairmen of the Senate and House Post Office and Civil Service Committees, will discuss the first two subjects.

The Veterans Administrator and Representative Edith Nourse Rogers, Chairman of the House Veterans Affairs Committee, will participate in the discussion of Veterans affairs.

[Statement at the conclusion of the conference]

FOR THREE DAYS, I have discussed with the Congressional leaders and with the Chairmen of the standing committees of the Senate and the House the legislative program which I propose to submit to the Congress in January.

We have made much progress at these Conferences. The Executive Branch of the Government, the Congressional leaders and the Committee chairmen will cooperate fully in carrying out this program. As a result, I know that the people of this country will see the Republican Party continuing to enact progressive programs serving the welfare of all 160 million Americans.

During our discussions, representatives of the Executive Branch of the Government—Cabinet officers and Heads of important agencies—outlined certain phases of the program to be presented in January and reviewed the accomplishments of the Administration during this past year. We covered a wide range of topics— although not all-inclusive of the recommendations that I shall submit to the Congress. These topics were fully discussed. In virtually every instance it was agreed by all to press for their enactment by the Congress.

The fundamental principles that have guided the Administration in the development of the program can be stated simply:

The program will be based, in principle and in philosophy, on the 1952 Republican platform. In that platform, the Party pledged itself to carry out certain obligations to the American people and to the community of free nations. If we are to continue to deserve public support, we must live up to these declared pledges and bring to our people a sound, constructive and comprehensive program which will:

1. Use as a measure of every element of American foreign policy the one simple rule: does it advance the interests of America? In that vein, it is clear that we must continue to strengthen the unity of the free world to resist Communist aggression.

2. Present a domestic program that will give our people a guarantee that they can depend on this Administration to protect the security, the welfare, and the economic stability of each individual citizen.

The program will soon be ready for presentation to the Congress. I am confident that it will be supported by the great majority of our citizens.

270 ¶ Message to René Coty Congratulating Him on His Election as President of the French Republic. *December 23, 1953*

His Excellency René Coty
President of the French Republic
Paris, France

Please accept my congratulations upon your election to the Presidency of the French Republic. I am confident that, during your term in office, France, true to her tradition, will provide inspiration and leadership to our common efforts to advance the cause of peace, well-being and human dignity for the peoples of the world.

DWIGHT D. EISENHOWER

271   ¶ Remarks Upon Lighting the National
Community Christmas Tree.   *December* 24, 1953

[Broadcast over radio and television at 5:09 p.m.]

*My fellow Americans—here in Washington, in your homes across
the Nation and abroad—and in our country's service around the
world:*

This evening's ceremony, here at the White House, is one of
many thousands in America's traditional celebration of the birth,
almost 2,000 years ago, of the Prince of Peace.

For us, this Christmas is truly a season of good will—and our
first peaceful one since 1949. Our national and individual blessings are manifold. Our hopes are bright even though the world
still stands divided in two antagonistic parts.

More precisely than in any other way, prayer places freedom
and communism in opposition, one to the other. The Communist can find no reserve of strength in prayer because his doctrine
of materialism and statism denies the dignity of man and consequently the existence of God. But in America, George Washington long ago rejected exclusive dependence upon mere ma-
terialistic values. In the bitter and critical winter at Valley
Forge, when the cause of liberty was so near defeat, his recourse
was sincere and earnest prayer. From it he received new hope
and new strength of purpose out of which grew the freedom in
which we celebrate this Christmas season.

As religious faith is the foundation of free government, so is
prayer an indispensable part of that faith.

Tonight, richly endowed in the good things of the earth, in the
fellowship of our neighbors and the love of our families, would it
not be fitting for each of us to speak in prayer to the Father of all
men and women on this earth, of whatever nation, and of every
race and creed—to ask that He help us—and teach us—and
strengthen us—and receive our thanks.

Should we not pray that He help us? Help us to remember that the founders of this, our country, came first to these shores in search of freedom—freedom of man to walk in dignity; to live without fear; beyond the yoke of tyranny; ever to progress. Help us to cherish freedom, for each of us and for all nations.

Might we not pray that He teach us? Teach us to shun the counsel of defeat and of despair of self-pride and self-deceit. Teach us, and teach our leaders, to seek to understand the problems and the needs of all our people. Teach us how those problems may reach solution in wisdom and how best those needs may be met. But teach us, also, that where there may be special problems, there can be no special rights; and though there may be special needs, there can be no special privileges. Teach us to require of all those who seek to lead us, these things: integrity of purpose; the upright mind, selfless sacrifice, and the courage of the just. Teach us trust and hope and self-dependence. Teach us the security of faith.

And may we pray that He strengthen us. Strengthen us in understanding ourselves and others—in our homes, in our country, and in our world. Strengthen our concern for brotherhood. Strengthen our conviction that whatever we, as Americans, would bring to pass in the world must first come to pass in the heart of America. Strengthen our efforts to forge abroad those links of friendship which must one day encircle the world, if its people are to survive and live in peace.

Lastly, should we not pray that He receive our thanks? For certainly we are grateful for all the good we find about us; for the opportunity given us to use our strength and our faith to meet the problems of this hour. And on this Christmas Eve, all hearts in America are filled with special thanks to God that the blood of those we love no longer spills on battlefields abroad. May He receive the thanks of each of us for this, His greatest bounty—and our supplication that peace on earth may live with us, always.

272 ¶ Statement by the President on Reducing American Forces in Korea.   *December* 26, 1953

THE FIGHTING in Korea was ended by an armistice which has now been in effect for five months. We do not need as much ground strength there now as when there was fighting. That is the more true because of the capabilities of ROK forces which were substantially built up during the war. Also our growing national air power possesses greater mobility and greater striking force than ever before.

Accordingly, I have directed that the United States ground forces in Korea be progressively reduced as circumstances warrant. As an initial step, two Army Divisions will soon be withdrawn and returned to the United States.

While the United States is acting in good faith to preserve the armistice and accomplish its purposes, we remain alert to all possibilities. Therefore, I emphasize that the action being taken does not impair our readiness and capacity to react in a way which should deter aggression and, if aggression should nevertheless occur, to oppose it with even greater effect than heretofore.

Recently the United Nations members which had forces in Korea clearly stated that, together, we would be united and prompt to resist any renewal of armed attack. The same statement pointed out that "the consequences of such a breach of the armistice would be so grave, that, in all probability, it would not be possible to confine hostilities within the frontiers of Korea."

United States military forces in the Far East will be maintained at appropriate levels to take account of the foregoing and to fulfill the commitments which the United States has undertaken in that area, and which are vital to the security of the United States. These forces will feature highly mobile Naval, Air, and Amphibious units.

Thus, we move forward in pursuance of our broad policy to make evident to all the world that we ourselves have no aggressive intentions and that we are resourceful and vigilant to find ways to reduce the burdens of armament and to promote a climate of peace.

NOTE: In his statement, the President quoted from the Special Report of the Unified Command on the Armistice in Korea. This report was submitted to the Secretary General of the United Nations on August 7 and is published in the Department of State Bulletin (vol. 29, p. 246).

The President's statement was released at Augusta, Ga.

273 ¶ Memorandum Approving Defense Procurement Policies in Aid of Areas of Economic Distress. *December* 29, 1953

Memorandum for: The Secretary of Defense; the Chairman, Atomic Energy Commission; the Administrator, General Services Administration

The Director of the Office of Defense Mobilization recently issued a Manpower Policy designed to increase the number of defense contracts that are placed in areas where there has been a large amount of unemployment. At the same time he directed that new defense plants located in areas where unemployment has been high over a considerable period of time should be given a rapid tax write-off on a larger percentage of their capital investment than would otherwise be the case.

I am in complete agreement with both of these policies.

I would appreciate it if you would communicate my views on this matter to all procurement officials. I am asking the Director of Defense Mobilization to provide me with periodic reports on the results achieved under the two directives.

DWIGHT D. EISENHOWER

NOTE: The memorandum was released at Augusta, Ga.

Appendix A—White House Press Releases, 1953

NOTE: Includes releases covering matters with which the President was closely concerned, except announcements of Presidential personnel appointments and approvals of legislation with which there was no accompanying statement.

Releases relating to Proclamations and Executive Orders have not been included. These documents are separately listed in Appendix B.

For list of Press and Radio Conferences, see subject index under "News Conferences."

Subject

January

20 Inaugural Address

22 Statement by the Press Secretary announcing nomination of Charles E. Wilson as Secretary of Defense

24 White House statement concerning resignation of Adm. Alan G. Kirk, Director, Psychological Strategy Board

24 White House statement announcing nomination of Allen W. Dulles as Director and Lt. Gen. Charles P. Cabell as Deputy Director, Central Intelligence Agency

24 White House announcement listing members of the crew of the President's plane

26 Statement by the President on establishing the President's Committee on International Information Activities

28 White House announcement of appointment of Val Peterson as Administrative Assistant to the President

29 White House statement on appointment of James J. Wadsworth as Deputy Chief of Mission of the United States to the United Nations

29 Letter to the President of the American National Red Cross accepting the position of Honorary Chairman

29 Memorandum on the Red Cross Campaign

30 White House announcement of appointment of Bernard M. Shanley as Acting Special Counsel to the President

Subject

January

30 White House statement concerning the Consumers' Price Index

February

1 Remarks recorded for the American Legion "Back to God" Program

2 Annual message to the Congress on the State of the Union

2 Message to Queen Elizabeth II on the floods and hurricanes in the British Isles

2 Message to Queen Juliana on the storms and floods in the Netherlands

2 Message to King Baudouin I on the storms in Belgium

3 White House announcement of appointments of Homer H. Gruenther, Bryce N. Harlow, and Gerald D. Morgan as special assistants on the White House staff

3 White House statement on policies to be applied in arriving at recommendations for revision of the 1954 budget

4 White House announcement of nomination of Clarence A. Davis as Solicitor for the Department of the Interior

4 White House announcement of nominations of Ralph A. Tudor, Orme Lewis, and Fred G. Aandahl as Under Secretary and Assistant Secretaries of the Interior, and of Craig R. Sheaffer as Assistant Secretary of Commerce

863

Subject

February

4 Message from the Queen of England in response to the President's message on storms and floods in that country

5 Message from the Queen of the Netherlands in response to the President's message on storms and floods in that country

5 Remarks at the Dedicatory Prayer Breakfast of the International Christian Leadership

6 White House announcement of the appointment of a Cabinet Committee on flood relief in the British Isles and Western Europe

7 Message to the Boy Scouts of America on their 43d anniversary

7 White House announcement of the forthcoming nomination of Clare Boothe Luce as Ambassador to Italy

9 White House statement on the annual report of the Air Coordinating Committee

9 Joint statement by the Majority Leader of the Senate and the Speaker of the House of Representatives following White House conference on the legislative program

11 White House announcement of appointment of Paul F. Wagner as Special Assistant in the White House Office

11 Statement by the President after reviewing the case of Julius and Ethel Rosenberg

12 Interim report of the President's Cabinet Committee on Flood Relief in the British Isles and Western Europe

13 Letter from Mrs. Eisenhower to Paula Martin

14 Letter from the Apostolic Delegate to the Assistant to the President concerning Julius and Ethel Rosenberg

16 White House announcement of appointment of C. D. Jackson as Special Assistant to the President

Subject

February

16 Letter to Col. C. M. Boyer, Executive Director, Reserve Officers Association, concerning National Defense Week

16 White House announcement of reappointment of Lawrence M. Lawson as a United States Commissioner, International Boundary and Water Commission, United States and Mexico

17 Letter to James W. Cothran, Commander in Chief, Veterans of Foreign Wars

18 Letter to Chairman, Tariff Commission, concerning imports of brier wood pipes

18 Letter to Chairmen, Senate Finance and House Ways and Means Committees, concerning imports of brier wood pipes

18 White House announcement of nomination of Karl L. Rankin as Ambassador to the Republic of China

18 White House announcement of nomination of John Moors Cabot as Assistant Secretary of State for International Affairs

18 White House announcement of nomination of James Clement Dunn as Ambassador to Spain

18 White House announcement of appointment of David K. E. Bruce as observer to the Interim Committee of the European Defense Community and as representative to the European Coal and Steel Community

19 White House announcement of appointment of Delmont L. Chapman and Marvin McClain as members of the Agricultural Advisory Committee

19 White House announcement of appointment of Roger M. Kyes, Deputy Secretary of Defense, as a member of the President's Committee on International Information Activities

19 White House announcement of designation of Val Peterson as Acting Administrator, Federal Civil Defense Administration

Appendix A

56616—60——58

Appendix A

866

Appendix A

867

Appendix A

868

Appendix A

869

Appendix A

Appendix A

871

Appendix A

Appendix A

873

Appendix A

874

Appendix A

875

Appendix A

876

Appendix A

Appendix A

Appendix B—Presidential Documents Published in the Federal Register, 1953

PROCLAMATIONS

Appendix B

EXECUTIVE ORDERS

Appendix B

881

Appendix B

Appendix B

Appendix B

PRESIDENTIAL DOCUMENTS OTHER THAN PROCLAMATIONS AND EXECUTIVE ORDERS

Appendix C—Presidential Reports to the Congress, 1953

Subject	Published	Sent to the Congress	Date of White House release
Annual report of the Air Coordinating Committee for the year 1952	H. Doc. 82	Feb. 9 (H) Feb. 10 (S)	Feb. 9
Report of the Secretary of State on the Operations of the Department of State	H. Doc. 115	Mar. 30	. . . .
Report of the National Capital Housing Authority for the fiscal year ended June 30, 1952	. . . . .	Apr. 13	. . . .
Report on Inclusion of Escape Clauses in Existing Trade Agreements	H. Doc. 205	July 9	July 9
Report of the National Advisory Council on International Monetary and Financial Problems . . .	H. Doc. 214	July 27	. . . .
Report on United States Participation in the United Nations	H. Doc. 222	July 31	July 31
Report of the Office of Alien Property, Department of Justice, for the fiscal year ended June 30, 1952	. . . . .	Aug. 1	. . . .
Report on the Mutual Security Program covering operations ended June 30, 1953	H. Doc. 226	Aug. 17	Aug. 17
Thirty-fourth Report on Lend-Lease Operations for the year ending December 31, 1952	H. Doc. 233	Sept. 28	Sept. 28

Appendix D—Rules Governing This Publication

[Reprinted from the Federal Register, vol. 24, p. 2354, dated March 26, 1959]

TITLE 1—GENERAL PROVISIONS

Chapter I—Administrative Committee of the Federal Register

PART 32—PUBLIC PAPERS OF THE PRESIDENTS OF THE UNITED STATES

PUBLICATION AND FORMAT

Sec.

32.1 Publication required.
32.2 Coverage of prior years.
32.3 Format, indexes, ancillaries.

SCOPE

32.10 Basic criteria.
32.11 Sources.

FREE DISTRIBUTION

32.15 Members of Congress.
32.16 The Supreme Court.
32.17 Executive agencies.

PAID DISTRIBUTION

32.20 Agency requisitions.
32.21 Extra copies.
32.22 Sale to public.

AUTHORITY: §§ 32.1 to 32.22 issued under sec. 6, 49 Stat. 501, as amended; 44 U.S.C. 306.

PUBLICATION AND FORMAT

§ 32.1 *Publication required.* There shall be published forthwith at the end of each calendar year, beginning with the year 1957, a special edition of the FEDERAL REGISTER designated "Public Papers of the Presidents of the United States." Each volume shall cover one calendar year and shall be identified further by the name of the President and the year covered.

§ 32.2 *Coverage of prior years.* After conferring with the National Historical Publications Commission with respect to the need therefor, the Administrative Committee may from time to time authorize the publication of similar volumes covering specified calendar years prior to 1957.

§ 32.3 *Format, indexes, ancillaries.* Each annual volume, divided into books whenever appropriate, shall be separately published in the binding and style deemed by the Administrative Committee to be suitable to the dignity of the office of President of the United States. Each volume shall be appropriately indexed and shall contain appropriate ancillary information respecting significant Presidential documents not published in full text.

SCOPE

§ 32.10 *Basic criteria.* The basic text of the volumes shall consist of oral utterances by the President or of writings subscribed by him. All materials selected for inclusion under these criteria must also be in the public domain by virtue of White House press release or otherwise.

§ 32.11 *Sources.* (a) The basic text of the volumes shall be selected from the official text of: (1) Communications to the Congress, (2) public addresses, (3) transcripts of press conferences, (4) public letters, (5) messages to heads of state, (6) statements released on miscellaneous subjects, and (7) formal executive documents promulgated in accordance with law.

(b) Ancillary text, notes, and tables shall be derived from official sources only.

FREE DISTRIBUTION

§ 32.15 *Members of Congress.* Each Member of Congress shall be entitled to

886

one copy of each annual volume upon application therefor in writing to the Director.

§ 32.16 *The Supreme Court.* The Supreme Court of the United States shall be entitled to twelve copies of the annual volumes.

§ 32.17 *Executive agencies.* The head of each department and the head of each independent agency in the executive branch of the Government shall be entitled to one copy of each annual volume upon application therefor in writing to the Director.

PAID DISTRIBUTION

§ 32.20 *Agency requisitions.* Each Federal agency shall be entitled to obtain at cost copies of the annual volumes for official use upon the timely submission to the Government Printing Office of a printing and binding requisition (Standard Form No. 1).

§ 32.21 *Extra copies.* All requests for extra copies of the annual volumes shall be addressed to the Superintendent of Documents, Government Printing Office, Washington 25, D.C. Extra copies shall be paid for by the agency or official requesting them.

§ 32.22 *Sale to public.* The annual volumes shall be placed on sale to the public by the Superintendent of Documents at prices determined by him under the general direction of the Administrative Committee.

*   *   *   *   *

ADMINISTRATIVE COMMITTEE OF
THE FEDERAL REGISTER,
WAYNE C. GROVER,
Archivist of the United States,
Chairman.
RAYMOND BLATTENBERGER,
The Public Printer,
Member.
WILLIAM O. BURTNER,
Representative of the Attorney
General, Member.

Approved March 20, 1959.
WILLIAM P. ROGERS,
Attorney General.
FRANKLIN FLOETE,
Administrator of General Services.

[F.R. Doc. 59–2517; Filed, Mar. 25, 1959;
8:45 a.m.]

INDEX

Index

[References are to items except as otherwise noted]

Index

[References are to items except as otherwise noted]

Atomic Energy Act, 265
 Amendments proposed, 268
 Violations, 264
Atomic Energy Commission, 143, 263
 News conference remarks, 54, 208, 265
Atomic Energy Commission, Chairman
  (Lewis L. Strauss), 268
 Memorandum, 273
 News conference remarks on, 12, 265
Atomic Energy Commission, International,
  proposed, 256
Atomic energy for peaceful uses, 50, 268
 Address at United Nations, 256
  News conference remarks, 265
 International atomic pool, President's
  proposal, 265
 News conference remarks, 54, 208, 243,
  265
Atomic information exchange, question of,
  128, 265
Atomic weapons. *See* Nuclear weapons
Attlee, Clement R., 77
Attorney General, Acting, regulations re,
  51
Attorney General (Herbert Brownell, Jr.),
  269
 Broadcast with the President, 95
 Hoover Commission, representation on,
  145 n.
 Injunction in maritime strike, letter, 203
 News conference remarks on, 22, 109,
  126, 243, 249, 254
 President's Conference on Administra-
  tive Procedure, 59
 Public school integration, recommenda-
  tions re, 249
 Security information, new procedures,
  110
 Security program, 6, 254
 White (Harry Dexter) case, 243
 Witnesses, immunity from self-incrimi-
  nation, recommendation re, 249
Augusta, Ga., 249, 253
Australia
 Defense treaty with United States, 96
 Escapees settling in, 257 n.
 Wheat for Pakistan relief, 97

Austria
 Four-power conference on, proposed,
  238, 254
 News conference remarks, 238, 254
 Treaty with, proposed, 50, 255, 256
Aviation
 50th anniversary of powered flight, 267
 Speed, progress, 267
 U.K.-Soviet talks on air safety over
  Germany, 41
Aviation policy review, letter to Robert B.
  Murray, Jr., 194
Awards and citations
 America's Democratic Legacy Award,
  acceptance, 252
 Distinguished Service Medal, Gen. James
  A. Van Fleet, 19
 Legion of Merit, King Paul of Greece,
  233
 Medal of Honor
  Bleak, David B., 122, 229 n.
  Dewey, Duane E., 27
  McLaughlin, Alford L., 174, 229 n.
  Miyamura, Hiroshi H., 229 n.
  Murphy, Lt. Raymond G., 226, 229 n.
  O'Brien, Lt. George H., Jr., 170,
   229 n.
  Simanek, Robert E., 175, 229 n.
  Stone, Lt. James L., 229 n.

"Back to God" program of American
  Legion, remarks, 5
Bankers Association, American, remarks,
  189
Bartlett, Charles L., 208, 265
Baseball team, Washington, D.C., 41
Bases, U.S., in Spain, 198
Bastian, Judge Walter M., 59
Battle, Gov. John Stewart, 79
Baudouin I, message, 7
Bauer, Dr. Louis H., 29
Beach, Comdr. Edward L., 229 n., 254
  ftn. (p. 800)
Beale, W. L., Jr., 126
Beaudoin, Louis, 246 n.
Beebe, Brig. Gen. R. E., 71

892

Index

[References are to items except as otherwise noted]

Index

Index

[References are to items except as otherwise noted]

Index

Index

Coolidge, Calvin, 31
Copper prices, 22
Cornell, Douglas B., 22, 109
Corporate taxes, 84, 254
Corps of Engineers, 37
    Flood control study, 153
    Water resources projects, land management, 153
Cothran, James W., letter, 13
Cotten, Felix, 141
Cotton association, El Paso, Tex., 265
Coty, Rene, message, 270
Council of Economic Advisers, 230
    Reorganization Plan 9, message, 93
Council of Economic Advisers, Chairman (Arthur F. Burns), 128, 249
Court of Justice, International, 129 n.
Courts, Federal
    Circuit Court of Appeals, Tenth, 107
    District Courts
        Colorado, 107
        District of Columbia, 116
        Southern New York, 203 n.
    See also Supreme Court, U.S.
Cowen, Myron M., letter, 239
Cowles, Mrs. Gardner, 109 ftn. (p. 439)
Cowles, John, 33 n.
Cox, J. Earl, 59
Craig, May, 12, 15, 22, 31, 37, 41, 54, 62, 77, 88, 109, 128, 230, 243, 249, 254, 265
Creagh, Edward F., 88
Cross, Gov. Burton M., 187
Cuba, Havana, 260
Cunningham, Col. Harry F., relief of, disapproval, 168
Currencies, foreign, 6
Curtis, Repr. Carl T., 268
Custer State Park, S. Dak., 102 n.
Customs simplification, 6, 70, 187
    Approval of bill, 164
Cutler, Robert, 2 n., 33, 266
Czechoslovakia, anti-Communist demonstrations, 146

Dahl, Lt. Gov. C. P., 100 n.
Dairy products
    Butter, 12, 109
    Prices, 12
Dake, Marietta, 265
Dalton, John N., 79 n.
Dalton, Theodore R., 230
Dams
    Hydroelectric vs. multiple purpose, 77
    See also specific projects
Danaher, John A., 59
Daniel, Sen. Price, 54
Darby, Harry, 218
Dartmouth College
    Commencement exercises, remarks, 104
    News conference remarks, 109, 126
Daughters of the Confederacy, United, remarks, 240
Davidson, Jean, 54
Davis, Elmer, 128
Davis, Harold J., disability compensation claim, disapproval, 167
Dean, Gordon E., 128
Dean, Maj. Gen. William F., 225, 265
Deaths, statements, etc.
    Abdul Aziz Ibn al Saud, 245
    Freeman, Douglas S., 106
    Hutcheson, William L., 224
    Queen Mother Mary, 34
    Reuter, Ernst, 197
    Stalin, Joseph, 24
    Taft, Sen. Robert A., 154
    Vinson, Fred M., 182
Debt, national, 6, 159
    Limit on, 6, 159, 198, 249
    Statement, 152
    News conference remarks, 198, 249
Declaration of Independence, 8, 69, 78, 259
Dedicatory occasions. *See* Addresses, remarks, etc., on commemorative or dedicatory occasions
Defense, Department of, 40
    Committee on Department of Defense Organization, 61
    Defense Supply Management Agency, 61

Index

[References are to items except as otherwise noted]

901

Index

[References are to items except as otherwise noted]

Index

Index

[References are to items except as otherwise noted]

Index

[References are to items except as otherwise noted]

[References are to items except as otherwise noted]

Index

Index

[References are to items except as otherwise noted]

Index

[References are to items except as otherwise noted]

Index

[References are to items except as otherwise noted]

Index

[References are to items except as otherwise noted]

Index

Index

[References are to items except as otherwise noted]

Index

[References are to items except as otherwise noted]

Index

Index

Index

[References are to items except as otherwise noted]

Index

Index

Index

Index

Index

Index

[References are to items except as otherwise noted]

Index

Index

Index

[References are to items except as otherwise noted]

Index

[References are to items except as otherwise noted]

929

Index

Index

Index

[References are to items except as otherwise noted]

Index

O

933